The Mainstream of Civilization

Second Edition

Since 1789

The Mainstream

Second Edition

JOSEPH R. STRAYER
Princeton University

HANS W. GATZKE
Yale University

E. HARRIS HARBISON
Late of Princeton University

# of Civilization

Since 1789

Harcourt Brace Jovanovich, Inc.

New York / Chicago / San Francisco / Atlanta

The Mainstream of Civilization   Since 1789
Second Edition

Cover: courtesy of NASA, Houston, Texas

Maps by J. P. Tremblay

© 1969, 1974 by Harcourt Brace Jovanovich, Inc.

ISBN: 0-15-551560-8

Library of Congress Catalog Card Number: 73-19410

Printed in the United States of America

Preface

It requires a certain amount of courage to attempt to write a history of civilization in one volume. Once the task has been accomplished, however, it is easier to do it a second time. As before, we have deliberately omitted certain details so that we could discuss as fully as possible the basic characteristics of each civilization and of different periods in the history of each civilization. We have tried to emphasize connections and interrelations—the ways in which politics, economics, art, scholarship, and religion all influence one another. We have tried to capture the flavor of each age—the unique combination of beliefs, activities, and institutions that distinguishes one society from another. In choosing the illustrations and the inserts in the text we have tried to give some idea of the diverse and ever-changing ways in which men have looked at and lived in their world. Finally, we have tried to consider the most difficult of all historical questions—the nature of and the reasons for change in human communities. Why and how do new institutions, new activities, new ideas rise and flourish? Why do they fade away? There are no easy answers to these problems; all we can do is suggest lines of inquiry that the reader may wish to pursue.

Obviously, it is easier to assess the characteristics and achievements of an ancient civilization than those of the one in which we live. The story of the Roman empire is ended; the story of the United States continues. Obviously also, it is more important to know details about the nature and background of problems that are still with us than details about problems that were solved (at least partially) long ago. For these reasons the book broadens as it reaches the nineteenth century. More infomation is provided and more events are described in the hope that the reader will better understand the present state of the world.

We trust that no one will passively accept our interpretations or believe that our book is an adequate summary of human history. Our work is only an introduction, an attempt to persuade the reader to think deeply about history and to study it in detail. We are convinced that historical-mindedness is a necessity of human life. Consciously or unconsciously, we all base our estimates of the future on our knowledge of the past. It is important, then, that our knowledge of the past be as accurate and as deep as possible.

We lament the untimely death of one of the original members of the group, Professor E. Harris Harbison. His material has been revised to include the results of recent research, but we have built on the foundation that he gave us. We have also found the contribution of our former collaborator, Professor Edwin L. Dunbaugh, to be helpful in our revision.

The authors are greatly indebted to the following historians, who critically read *The Mainstream of Civilization* and made many valuable comments and suggestions: Jeremy Adams, Yale University; William Allen, University of Connecticut; John Eadie, University of Michigan; Erich S. Gruen, University of California at Berkeley; William W. Hallo, Yale University; Ramsay MacMullen, Yale University; Richard Marius, University of Tennessee; and Raphael Sealey, University of California at Berkeley.

J. R. S.
H. W. G.

Foreword *The Study of History*

Consciously or unconsciously, all of us are historians. We can plan for the future only because we remember the past. We can add to our knowledge only because we do not lose memory of former experiences. Everyone, from the peasant to the scholar, tries to meet new situations by discovering familiar elements that make it possible to evoke analogies with the past. An individual who has lost his memory, who has forgotten his own history, is helpless until he has recovered his past or has slowly built up a new past to which he can refer.

What is true of individuals is also true of societies. No community can survive and no institution can function without constant reference to past experience. We are ruled by precedents fully as much as by formal laws, which is to say that we are ruled by memories of the past. It is the memory of common experiences that unites individuals into communities, and it is the memory of his own experiences that makes a child into an adult. Some of the memories may not be happy ones, but in reacting against them we are still linked to the past that produced them.

If everyone is his own historian, if individuals and societies necessarily draw on their memories of the past in order to deal with the present, then what is the need for formal, scholarly history? Isn't it enough to remember only the history that serves our immediate needs?

It is not enough, for two reasons. Human memory is fallible; individuals and societies forget many things that might be useful in solving their problems. This is why we have written records (which are a kind of formal history); this is why illiterate peoples try to preserve their customs and traditions through repeated oral recitations by the elders of the tribe. Second, the more complicated a society becomes, the narrower the range of individual experience in proportion to the total of possible experiences. A peasant living in a medieval village shared most of the experiences of his neighbors, and village custom gave solutions of a sort even to rare and unusual problems. No one living in an urbanized society shares many of the experiences of his neighbors, let alone the experiences of the millions of people throughout the world with whom he is connected by political and economic ties. No one can sum up the past experiences of his society, and of the societies with which his own interacts, with a few customary formulas; and yet these past experiences place a heavy burden on the present. In facing any problem, we look for familiar elements; if these are lacking, we feel fearful and helpless. Knowledge of history increases the chance of finding something familiar in a new and difficult situation.

Certain card games show how this process works at an elementary level. There is almost no chance that one distribution of cards will be repeated in a subsequent deal in bridge. Yet a person who has played several thousand hands of bridge should be able to make intelligent decisions and predictions even though every deal presents a new situation. He should be able to use his high cards and long suits effectively; he should be able to make some shrewd guesses about the location of cards in other hands. Not every experienced player will develop these skills. Some people are unable to generalize from their past experiences, and others cannot see analogies between the present and the past. But, generally speaking, an experienced player will make better use of his cards than a person who has played only ten hands. There is such a thing as a sense of the realities and possibilities of social activity, which can be developed from a knowledge of history.

At the very least, the past has left us the problems that we are trying to solve and the patterns of living that we are seeking to modify. At the most, we may find in the past suggestions for understanding and coping with the present. It is the historian's task to study the behavior of man in the past, to uncover facts, sort them, mass and link them, and so provide connections between past and present.

At the same time the historian must avoid certain pitfalls along the way. Connections with the past cannot be broken, but they can be misrepresented or misunderstood. Primitive peoples have little sense of chronology; they are apt to stir all their memories into a timeless brew of legend. At a more sophisticated level, the past has been used as a means of justifying present values and power structures. Many writers, from ancient times down to the present, have found historical examples to prove that their people were specially favored by the gods, that their state was founded and strengthened by heroes of superhuman ability, that virtue and wisdom (as defined by the author) have always brought success while folly and vice have led to disaster. "History is philosophy teaching by example," said an ancient Greek (Dionysius of Halicarnassus), and it was more important for the examples to be edifying than for them to be true.

But it is not difficult to avoid deliberate distortions of the past. What *is* difficult is to avoid distortions caused by the incompleteness of our knowledge of the past. Many human activities have left few traces, especially in written records. For example, for thousands of years agriculture has been the chief occupation of the human race, but there are still serious gaps in our knowledge of the history of agriculture. "The short and simple annals of the poor" are short because information is scanty. If we had better information we would probably find that the life of a poor man in any period was anything but simple; it must have been filled with an unending series of nagging problems. In general, we know more about political history than social history, more about the privileged few than the unprivileged masses, more about the history of art than the history of technology, more about the ideas of philosophers and religious leaders than about the beliefs of the common people.

Historians have become more skillful in recent years in finding material that gives a better-balanced picture of the past. Archeology reveals not only the palaces of kings, but the homes of ordinary people with their tools, their toys, their cooking utensils, and even fragments of their food. Gods and heroes may dominate the great works of art, but the common folk going about their ordinary business are there too—on Greek vases, Roman tombs, and portals of Gothic cathedrals. Discoveries of hoards of coins reveal unexpected trade relations. Aerial photography can bring out traces of ancient methods of plowing land and dividing fields. Even the written records, which have been studied for centuries, contain hitherto unused facts about such things as family life, migrations, and changes in economic patterns. There are still many holes in the record, but there is no reason to complain about lack of material.

The historian's greatest difficulty is not in discovering facts, but in deciding what facts can be ignored, or merely sampled, or clumped together in a single generalization. No one could master all the facts in yesterday's issue of the *New York Times,* and there are files of newspapers that run back to the eighteenth century. No one could master all the facts brought out in a single session of the Supreme Court, and the records of American courts and of the English courts from which they were derived go back to the twelfth century. To deal with the overwhelming mass of facts, historians have to arrange them, link them together, establish meaningful sequences of causes and effects.

The massing and linking of facts is not only essential, if history is to rise above the level of a catalogue; it is also inevitable, since it is the way the human mind deals with past experience. We do not recall every word we have exchanged when we decide that a certain person is a good friend. We do not remember every paragraph we have read when we decide that we like a certain book. But, while the process of massing and linking is essential and inevitable, this operation is the point of greatest danger in any kind of historical thinking. Consciously or unconsciously, one can mass facts to produce a misleading impression, even though each individual fact is true. Any governmental system can be made to appear obnoxious by discussing only the cases in which there is clear evidence of corruption or oppression. Any society can be wreathed in a golden haze by dwelling only on its accomplishments in art, literature, and scholarship. Individuals and communities can become convinced that the whole world is conspiring against them if they remember only the occasions when they were treated unjustly. The nature of the sources themselves may cause distortion. For example, it is very easy to find material on political life in the city of Rome during the first century of the Roman Empire. It is difficult to collect evidence on provincial government or on social and economic development. The natural tendency is to overemphasize court intrigues and to pay little attention to such topics as economic growth or the spread of Latin culture throughout the West.

There is no easy way to overcome these problems, but an understanding of the principle of interconnectedness will help. No one is a purely political, or economic, or ideological being, and societies are composed of such varied human beings. Historians must look for the ways in which these (and other) forces interact. For example, the kind of food men eat can affect their whole social structure: a society dependent on olive oil for its fats will differ in many ways from one that depends on animal products such as lard, butter, and cheese. Religion can have an influence on trade: medieval churchmen aided the growth of Mediterranean commerce by importing silk for their vestments, incense for their ceremonies, and precious stones for their altar vessels and relic boxes. Trade in turn can influence the development of a religion: often it has been the merchant who prepared the way for the missionary. Ideas, technologies, institutions, social patterns, shifts in consumer preferences interact in complicated and bewildering ways. For example, increased use of easily washable cotton clothing in modern Europe improved personal hygiene and thus may have reduced death rates and contributed to growth of population. At the same time, increased demand for cotton encouraged the extension of slavery in the United States and thus was one of the causes of the Civil War.

Full realization of the connections among all human activities should lead to three conclusions. First, there are multiple causes for every event; single explanations for change are almost always wrong. Second, change in any one part of the social pattern may affect any other part of the pattern. Finally, the connections lead back into the past and therefore the past influences the present.

The relationship between continuity and change is an interaction that the historian must watch with special care. All societies change and yet all societies retain some connection with the past. The most "traditional" society is less traditional than it realizes; the most "modern" society is more influenced by tradition than it would like to believe. The Anglo-Saxons, theoretically bound by immemorial custom, invented the office of sheriff about the year 1000 A.D. The Americans, theoretically free to create an entirely new political structure, have preserved the office of sheriff with many of its original powers. Conquests and revolutions do not break all the connections with the past. Even where there has apparently been a complete break, the roots of a society may again grow down into its past. Roman law practically vanished from the West after the fifth century A.D.; it reappeared as a powerful force in the thirteenth century.

If there were no continuity, there would be no use in studying history, since nothing in the past would have any bearing on what is done today. If there were no change, there would be no history; a few years of practical experience would teach anyone all he needed to know about human behavior in society at any time and in any place. But, in the world as it is, the forces that make for change are modified and even distorted by habit and custom, the forces that make for continuity are weakened and limited by new desires and new ideas. It is of some importance to understand where, why, and to what degree the desire for change prevails.

It is easy to see multiple, interlocking activities and rapid rates of change in the modern world. It is less easy to get a sense of the complexity and capacity for change of premodern and non-European societies, which is why the history of such societies often seems flat and uninteresting. The European Middle Ages are summed up as an "Age of Faith"; the history of much of Asia is dismissed with talk of the "unchanging Orient." Yet the Middle Ages were also a period of state-building, economic growth, and technological invention—activities that have influenced the modern world fully as much as the Christian Church. The "unchanging Orient" produced all the great world religions, and each of these religions was a powerful force for change. Moreover, there are advantages in studying societies that are less complex and in which rates of change are less rapid than in our own. It is easier to observe and to draw conclusions about human behavior when the number of variables is small and changes do not come so fast that their effects are blurred.

A good historian, then, will try to give adequate attention to a wide variety of human activities, to discuss the interactions among these activities, and to trace the connections between past and present. But these principles cannot be applied mechanically. A writer who is careful to give an exactly equal amount of space to politics, economics, religion, the arts, and scholarship will probably not produce an adequate description of a society. The importance and even the identity of each of these activities varies with time and place. Religion had more influence on Indian than on Chinese society. Economics and politics merge in primitive societies, such as that of the early Germans. It is probably true that the vast majority of the world's scientists were born in the twentieth century; this could not be said of theologians. Thus the impact of scholarship on early societies is different from its impact on modern societies. To understand such variations and transformations, the historian must be more than a meticulous scholar. He must develop a feel for the period he is writing about, a sense of how people lived and worked and thought. It takes time and experience to acquire this feeling for the past, but once it has been acquired historians can give reasonably accurate, and occasionally penetrating, descriptions of earlier societies.

It is this understanding of the development of human society that gives history its chief value. History, even at its worst, gives us the comforting and necessary feeling that there are some familiar elements in a changing world and that there is some hope of understanding the changes that do occur. History at its best gives us a chance of reacting sensibly to problems as they arise. It does not guarantee the correctness of our responses, but it should improve the quality of our judgment. Good judgment about human behavior in society is badly needed today.

A Note on the Paperbound Edition

This volume is part of a variant printing, not a new or revised edition, of *The Mainstream of Civilization,* Second Edition. Many instructors have requested a three-volume version that would enable them to fit the text into the particular patterns of their teaching and scheduling. To meet that request, the publishers have prepared this printing, consisting of three separate volumes that exactly reproduce the text of the one-volume version of *The Mainstream of Civilization,* Second Edition. The first of these volumes starts with the beginnings of western civilization in the ancient Middle East and continues through the Middle Ages. The second volume begins with the late Middle Ages, repeating two chapters (Chapters 13 and 14), and ends with Napoleon. The third volume repeats the chapter on the French Revolution and Napoleon (Chapter 23) and carries the account forward to the present day. The variant printing, then, is intended as a convenience to those instructors and students who have occasion to use one of the three parts of *The Mainstream of Civilization.* Consequently, the pagination and index of the one-volume version, as well as its illustrations, maps (except for the color maps), and other related materials, are retained in this printing. The difference between the one-volume and the three-volume versions of the book is a difference only in form.

Contents

23

24

25

26

29

30

31

32

33

Introduction

This is a history of civilization, with emphasis on the civilization developed by the peoples of Europe. Like all histories, it must be selective. Incomplete as our record of the past is, it is still too full to permit discussion in a single book of all civilizations or even of all events in the history of one civilization. The principles that have guided our selection of topics may be indicated by a definition of our subject. We must answer two questions: What is civilization, and what has been the role of western civilization in creating the conditions that we find in the world today?

Civilization is derived from the Latin word for city, *civitas.* There is reason to emphasize this derivation, for every great civilization has had great cities, and the basic characteristics of civilization are easiest to observe in cities. Civilization is first of all *cooperation*—men working together to satisfy their material and spiritual needs. It requires *organization*—as soon as several people start working together there must be some sort of social, political, or economic pattern to regulate their activity. It encourages *specialization*—as soon as several people begin to cooperate in an organized way there are obvious advantages in dividing the work so that no one man has to do everything for himself. The character of a particular civilization is determined by the type and degree of the organization and specialization of that civilization. Ten thousand Greeks living in a small city-state could accomplish much more than ten thousand Indians scattered through the forests of North America. A few hundred men specializing in science have done more to change our civilization in the last few centuries than millions of artisans working through past ages. Intensive organization and specialization can produce spectacular results, and they can also create spectacular problems.

Civilization requires faith in certain ideals and values as well as skill in organization and techniques. The immediate and direct advantages of organization and specialization are not very apparent to most people. Organization sets limits on personal freedom, and specialization makes a man dependent on other men who may not be wholly trustworthy. In the long run the advantages are greater than the disadvantages, but farseeing, enlightened self-interest is a very rare human quality, probably rarer than altruism. And if men hesitate to give up present benefits for advantages in their own future, they will be even more hesitant if the advantages are to be gained only by their descendants. There is always resistance to increasing the scale and scope of organization; there is usually resistance to new types of specialization. This resistance can be overcome only by belief that there is something more important than the individual—a religion that emphasizes cooperation, a divinely appointed ruler or ruling class, a nation that has become almost a divinity, a theory of society that has taken on the aspects of a religion. There is a close connection between the dominant beliefs of a people and the kind of civilization it creates.

This history of civilization examines, more than anything else, how and why people have worked together. It is concerned with political history because the political record helps us to understand why people have been more successful at some times than at others in organizing on a large scale, and why some types of organization have proved more effective than others. It is concerned with economic and social history because economic and social organization has a direct effect on both political organization and the type and degree of specialization. It is concerned with the history of ideas and their manifestations in art and literature because organization and specialization are possible only within a framework of accepted beliefs. The interactions among political organizations, economic institutions, and dominant beliefs determine the character and development of a civilization.

Western civilization is only one, and by no means the oldest, of the civilizations that have left a historical record. The earliest civilizations touched Europe and the West only slightly; they centered in the river valleys of Egypt, the Near East, and China. Only with the appearance of the Greek city-states after 1000 B.C. can we see the beginnings of a civilization that belongs to the same family as our own. The Greeks drew heavily on the older civilizations of their neighbors, but they reorganized their borrowed materials and added significant elements to them. Ideas and forms of organization that have remained important in western civilization for over twenty-five hundred years first appear in ancient Greece. The Romans followed the Greeks as the dominant people in the Mediterranean basin. Like the Greeks, they borrowed from their predecessors, rearranged the old materials in new ways, and added ideas of their own, especially in government and law. Roman civilization is the direct ancestor of the civilization of modern European countries. There has never been a time, from the first conquests of the Roman Republic down to the present, when Roman law and Roman political ideas were not being dicussed in some parts of the Continent.

Yet, while there is unbroken continuity between the civilization of the Greeks and the Romans and that of the modern West, it is well to remember that continuity is not identity. Much has been added—for example, the ideas brought in by Christianity—and much has been changed. Greco-Roman civilization was neither western nor European; it was Mediterranean. It was most highly developed on the eastern shores of the Mediterranean, and it was greatly influenced by the Orient. France and Spain were colonial outposts that contributed little to Greco-Roman civilization; Germany, Scandinavia, and the Slavic countries were outside the limits of the civilized Mediterranean world.

This Mediterranean civilization ran into trouble in the fourth and fifth centuries A.D. The economic organization proved unsatisfactory, and loyalty to the political organization weakened. As the Roman Empire slowly crumbled, the unity of the Mediterranean basin was destroyed, never to be restored. The southern and eastern shores became part of an Arab empire, part of the non-European Moslem civilization. A remnant of the old Roman Empire, centering around Constantinople, became the Byzantine Empire. This empire developed its own civilization—Christian in belief, Greek in language, but strongly influenced by the East in organization. Byzantine civilization made a great impression on the Slavic peoples of Eastern Europe and had some influence on the Latin and Germanic peoples of the West. But it was never fully integrated with the civilization that grew up in western Europe. The western Europeans thought of the Byzantines as remote and somewhat untrustworthy relatives, who might hand out valuable gifts from time to time but who were too eccentric to live with. This attitude, in turn, has made it difficult to integrate eastern and western Europe, since the eastern countries borrowed much more from Byzantium than did those of the West.

With the Arab and Byzantine empires developing separate civilizations, the western European remnant of the old Mediterranean world was thrown back on its own resources. These were at first not very great. Western Europe saved only a fragment of its Roman inheritance, and this Roman inheritance was itself only a fragment of the old Mediterranean civilization. Moreover, the Germanic peoples of northern and central Europe, who had never been included in the Mediterranean world, were for a time dominant in western Europe. They brought in some new ideas and institutions, but they were backward in both political and economic organization. They were slow in assimilating the fragments of Roman civilization that remained, and even slower in developing effective types of organization. In the same way, the Christian religion, which eventually had great influence on European civilization, was only slowly absorbed by the half-barbarized Latins and the half-civilized Germans. For six centuries Europeans struggled with the problems of assimilating the Roman inheritance, integrating Latin and Germanic peoples, and implementing the basic ideas of Christianity. Only when this triple task was done did western Europe at last achieve an independent and consistent civilization. Only then could it profit from its contacts with the more highly developed civilizations of the Arab and Byzantine worlds.

Once it was established as a separate and viable entity, western European civilization developed rapidly. Many of our basic institutions and ideas, such as universities and representative assemblies, were worked out in the twelfth and thirteenth centuries. But this western European civilization was confined to a very small area. Its center was in the North, in a triangle bounded by Paris, Cologne, and London. The peripheral countries—Spain, Ireland, Norway, Sweden, Poland, Bohemia, and Italy—did not share in all the manifestations of this civilization, though they accepted its basic ideas. And beyond these countries the influence of western European civilization dropped off sharply. It had little effect on the Moslem world and none whatever on the peoples of Africa and Asia who lived beyond the limits of Moslem influence. It had some impact on Byzantium, but not enough to erase the differences that separated Byzantium from the West. There were some contacts with Russia, but the Russians were probably more influenced by the Byzantines. And the Mongol conquest of the thirteenth century weakened the ties that the Russians had with the West and forced them to face east for two centuries.

Meanwhile, another group of civilizations had developed in the Far East, in India, China, and Japan. Each had its own characteristic values—religious in India, secular and political in China, military in Japan. All three tended to become somewhat self-satisfied and isolated; neither India nor China, for example, was as interested in foreign voyages in the sixteenth century as it had been earlier. In all three the economic system was still based largely on village agriculture. Finally, in spite of promising beginnings, none of the Far Eastern civilizations had developed a strong scientific tradition. These characteristics put the Far Eastern countries at a disadvantage in dealing with Europeans, who were deeply interested in strange lands and peoples, were beginning to develop an economy based on machine production, and were just about to make their first important scientific discoveries.

The great voyages of exploration and the great mechanical inventions, both of which began in the fifteenth century, enabled western European civilization to emerge from its narrow corner and to spread throughout the world. Eastern Europe gradually accepted much of the civilization of the West, though the process was never complete. Three new continents—North America, South America, and Australia—were occupied by Europeans, and a fourth, Africa, was dominated by them. Asia, with its old civilizations and its dense population, was not so easily overrun, but even Asia was profoundly influenced by the European impact. Thus, for the first time, all the peoples of the world were brought into contact with a single civilization. The results of this great experiment are only beginning to be apparent.

There is some justification, then, for the conventional division of history into Ancient, Medieval, and Modern. Ancient history deals with the period in which some of the basic elements of western civilization were developed and passed on to later peoples. But Ancient history must be focused on the Near East and the Mediterranean, not on Europe. It must give greater weight to Greece, Asia Minor, Syria, Mesopotamia, and Egypt than to Gaul, Britain, or Germany. Medieval history deals with the period in which a distinct western European civilization appeared. But this civilization was confined to a small part of the European peninsula, and it had little influence outside that area. During the Middle Ages each great region of the world had its own civilization, and no one civilization was able greatly to modify another. Modern history deals not only with the rapid development of western European civilization in its old homeland but also with relations between that civilization and the rest of the world.

This growth and diffusion of western civilization has gone so far that we have perhaps entered a fourth period in its history. This period is marked by the appearance of distinct types of western civilization in the different areas occupied by Europeans, and, even more, by the revitalization of other civilizations following their contact with the West. Both the appearance of different types of western civilization and the revival of old civilizations are stimulating factors; they should help to prevent ossification and decay. Unfortunately, a stimulus can also be an irritant, and the reactions among competing civilizations may lead to efforts for mutual destruction rather than for mutual instruction.

The history of civilization begins in obscurity and ends with a question mark. Yet past experience is our only guide in solving present and future problems, and knowledge of our history may help us answer the great question with which we are faced today, that of the survival of civilization in any form.

The Mainstream of Civilization

Second Edition

Since 1789

23

The French Revolution and Napoleon

The French Revolution marked a turning point in European history. The events that began to unfold in 1787 and that terminated with the fall of Napoleon Bonaparte in 1815 unleashed forces that altered not only the political and social structure of states but the map of Europe. Many attempts were made, in France and in other European countries, to undo the work of the Revolution and to repress the ideas of liberty, equality, constitutionalism, democracy, and nationalism that the Revolution had inspired. But the Old Regime was dead, in France at least, and a Europe dominated by monarchy and aristocracy and by a hierarchical social order could never be fully restored. With the coming of the French Revolution, then, we enter into a more modern world—a world of class conflict, middle-class ascendancy, acute national consciousness, and popular democracy. Together with industrialization, the Revolution reshaped the institutions, the societies, and even the mentalities of European men.

THE ORIGINS OF THE FRENCH REVOLUTION

By the last half of the eighteenth century, France appeared to have overcome the dismal cycle of famine, plague, and high mortality that, in the preceding century, had inhibited both demographic and economic growth. The vast majority of Frenchmen who lived in the villages and tilled the fields were better off than their counterparts in most of Europe. French peasants, for example, owned some 40 percent of the country's farmlands. The mild inflationary trend that characterized much of the eighteenth century increased the wealth of large landowners, and surplus wealth in agriculture served to stimulate the expansion of the French economy as a whole. Modest advances in the textile and metallurgical industries, the construction of new roads and canals, and urban growth were other indications of economic development.

Yet, despite evident signs of prosperity, there was great discontent and restlessness in France in the 1780s. French institutions were obsolete, inefficient, and uncoordinated. They were controlled by the nobility and by self-perpetuating corporations of hereditary officeholders. To anyone touched by the ideas of the Enlightenment they seemed irrational and unjust. The middle classes, especially, were offended by the legal and social distinctions that kept them from attaining high office or exerting political influence. Every bishop in France was of noble birth; only nobles could receive commissions in the army; bourgeois plans for economic reform were constantly thwarted by the privileged classes. The economy, particularly in agriculture, remained unstable and subject to fluctuations that could drive the peasants and urban poor to starvation. An inefficient and inequitable tax system yielded too small an income to support the state, discouraged economic growth, and fell most heavily on the poor. On the eve of the Revolution, France faced a conjuncture of crises. Three of these crises—the agrarian distress, financial chaos, and the aristocratic reaction—were particularly acute.

Agrarian Distress

Wretched weather and poor harvests in 1787 and 1788 further weakened an agricultural economy that was already in difficulties. The poorer peasants lived at a subsistence level at best; with poor crops they starved. The purchasing power of well-to-do peasants declined. Grain shortages led to sharp price increases, particularly in the cost of bread. Moreover, from the late 1770s the long-term growth of the French economy had been interrupted in several important areas, such as the wine trade, and between 1776 and 1787, agricultural profits generally declined, though not to the low levels of the first part of the century. Nevertheless, noblemen and other large landowners, who had become accustomed to high profits, sought to save their own declining fortunes by demanding from their tenant farmers dues and obligations that had long been neglected. The countryside was ripe for revolution.

Financial Chaos

The finances of Louis XVI's government were a shambles. By 1787 one-half of the nation's tax revenues went to service the massive public debt that Louis XIV had left to his successors. France's involvement in the Seven Years' War and in the American War for Independence had driven the government further along the road to bankruptcy.

Napoleon astride his charger Tauris. By the sculptor E. Fremiet.

The French peasant supports the clergy and the nobility in this eighteenth-century cartoon. The rabbits and doves eating the peasant's grain were protected by law for the sport of the upper classes.

of this assembly, which met in February 1787, were drawn largely from the privileged orders and refused to support Calonne.

The king now dismissed Calonne and put in his place one of Calonne's chief opponents, Lomenie de Brienne, Archbishop of Toulouse. This prelate, though a member of both the higher nobility and the higher clergy, soon came to the same conclusions as Calonne. He tried to enact a similar reform program, but the *Parlement* of Paris, the most privileged of all the corporations of officeholders, refused to register the royal edicts. It declared that only the Estates General could approve such measures. When Brienne tried to break the opposition by exiling the magistrates of the *Parlement* and then by abolishing the high courts, he touched off furious protests by many members of the upper bourgeoisie and the nobility. In the face of attacks by the socially and politically powerful, the government backed away from its reform program. In July 1788, the king yielded to the opposition and ordered a meeting of the Estates General for May 1789.

The Aristocratic Reaction

During the 1780s, then, aristocratic demands on the peasantry were aggravating the distress of the countryside, and aristocratic resistance to tax reform was hampering the government in its attempts to revamp the nation's financial structure. These were two facets of the aristocratic reaction that was directly responsible for the coming of the French Revolution.

The tremendous strength of the French privileged classes had been built up steadily during the reigns of Louis XV and Louis XVI. At every turn the poor, the aspiring middle class, and enlightened reformers in government confronted the fact of privilege. Some men of the Enlightenment, in particular Voltaire, and such royal ministers as Turgot and Calonne encouraged the king to rationalize state finance and to bring a measure of justice to French society at the expense of the privileged groups. Louis XVI supported several of these plans for reform, but he always backed

Without a reform of the tax system the king could not meet his obligations. But such a reform would mean an attack on the privileges of the upper classes, and this Louis could never quite summon the courage to do.

Three ministers in succession struggled with the problem. The first, the Swiss banker Necker, was dismissed by the king in 1781 after he had proposed some modest reforms. Necker's successor, Calonne, thought he could carry on without much change. But as the deficit mounted he grew alarmed, and in 1786 he proposed a much more radical reform program than Necker's. The most striking provision of Calonne's program was a direct tax on all landowners—noble and commoner, lay and clerical. To oversee the assessment of the new tax, Calonne suggested that the king create local and provincial assemblies in which all men of property would be represented regardless of social status. In addition, older taxes, such as the *taille*, which weighed upon the lower orders, were to be reduced. Calonne's reforms struck at the very heart of the system of privilege and the social hierarchy of the Old Regime.

Calonne, aware that there would be bitter opposition to his plans, persuaded Louis XVI to call a conference of notables in the hope that they could be induced to back his program. But the members down when the privileged classes protested. By the 1780s it appeared that the French king was the prisoner of the nobility and that he would do nothing to displease them.

Moreover, the nobles were particularly skillful in confusing the issue. Certain privileges, such as those that protected the laws, institutions, and customs of the provinces from encroachments by the central government, limited the arbitrary power of the king. They could be called liberties rather than privileges. These liberties were compared to the restrictions on royal power in England, and the English were regarded as the freest people in Europe. Thus the nobles could resist royal attacks on any form of privilege by asserting that the king was going to attack all privileges and all liberties and that he was simply trying to get rid of all restrictions on his power. Through this device, the nobility and the *parlements* were able to gain wide support and considerable sympathy when they resisted the arbitrary orders of the king, even when those orders were directed toward desirable ends.

There were those, however, who were not deceived by the rhetoric of the privileged orders. The hesitations of the king and the intransigence of the aristocracy increased the bitterness of large sections of the population. They wanted to put an end to privilege, and they felt that the unreformed monarchy would not help them in this struggle. The attack on privilege and the demand for equality were the driving forces in the Revolution from beginning to end. Aristocratic stubbornness and royal weakness made it impossible to achieve equality by the peaceful road of reform. In the end, privilege could be destroyed only by an attack on aristocracy and monarchy.

THE FRENCH REVOLUTION AND THE KING

The Estates General, which had not met since 1614, was convened by the king at Versailles on May 5, 1789. The electoral process by which deputies were selected was a relatively generous one: All adult French males had the right to vote, in-

directly, for representatives to the Third Estate, which served the interests of the commoners. Moreover, following some recent examples in provincial assemblies, the Third Estate was given twice as many representatives as those of either the First or the Second Estate. The First (clerical) and Second (noble) Estates represented the privileged orders. The king had asked that all local electoral assemblies draw up *cahiers de doléances*—lists of grievances—to submit to the Estates General when it met. Thus in the months preceding the convening of the Estates General, a great political debate occurred. Almost all politically minded men agreed that the monarchy should yield some of its powers to an assembly and seek consent to taxation and legislation. By 1788 some noblemen were willing to go part way in abolishing privileges and in equalizing taxation. But the early debates in the Estates General revealed that the lawyers and bourgeois who represented the Third Estate were bent on a much more drastic reform.

The Estates General and the National Assembly

The mood of the Third Estate was best expressed by one of its deputies, the Abbé Sieyès. In a famous pamphlet, *What Is the Third Estate?*, Sieyès argued that the real French nation was made up of people who were neither clergymen nor noblemen, and that this majority should have the decisive voice in all political matters. This idea, which approached the doctrine of popular sovereignty, was translated into action during the opening debate on voting procedures in the Estates General. Since the Third Estate had as many representatives as the other two combined, it wanted the three Estates to meet and vote together. A few liberal nobles and a somewhat larger number of the lower clergy were sure to support the Third Estate, so joint meetings would give the Third Estate a clear majority. The king and the privileged orders, on the other hand, demanded that the Estates vote separately. This was traditional procedure in meetings of the Estates General, and it assured that the first two Estates would retain control.

Caricature of the Abbé Sieyès.

The Oath at the Jeu de Paume, painting by Jacques-Louis David. The deputies of the Third Estate, joined by some of the clergy and nobility, swear not to disband until they have drafted a constitution.

The Third Estate not only rejected the king's plan for separate meetings; on June 17 it declared itself the National Assembly of France and invited the other Estates to sit with it. The National As-sembly then assumed the right to approve all taxation as well as the right to withhold all taxation if its political demands were not met. In the face of this bold initiative, the king hesitated but finally resorted to a show of force. On June 20 Louis XVI had the Third Estate barred from its usual meeting place. The deputies then convened in a nearby indoor tennis court and took an oath not to disband until they had drafted a constitution. This Tennis Court Oath was the first great act of the bourgeois revolution in France.

In a dreary repetition of the political ineptitude he had shown in previous crises, Louis missed his chance to act as impartial mediator between the hostile Estates. On June 23 he went before the Estates General and offered a program of reform that only partly satisfied the demands of the Third Estate for tax reform and did nothing to abolish the privileges

The Tennis Court Oath   June 20, 1789

The National Assembly, considering that it has been summoned to establish the constitution of the kingdom, to effect the regeneration of public order, and to maintain the true principles of monarchy; that nothing can prevent it from continuing its deliberations in whatever place it may be forced to establish itself; and finally, that wheresoever its members are assembled, *there* is the National Assembly:

Decrees that all members of this Assembly shall immediately take a solemn oath not to separate, and to reassemble wherever circumstances require, until the constitution of the kingdom is established and consolidated upon firm foundations. . . .

From *A Documentary Survey of the French Revolution,* ed. by John Hall Stewart (New York: Macmillan, 1951), p. 88.

of the nobility. At about the same time, the king began to concentrate troops around Versailles and Paris. His aim was to put down any disturbances that might occur should he decide to dissolve the Assembly. By now, however, neither partial reform nor brute force was a sufficient answer to the political crisis. The revolution had already become a battle between those who desired a more equal and open society and those who wanted to preserve the privileges of the aristocracy.

The Popular Revolt

Most of the deputies in the Third Estate were lawyers, professional men, and lesser office-holders. Their aspirations were those of the French bourgeoisie. In the urban centers and the countryside resided yet another element of the Third Estate—the mass of artisans, shopkeepers, and peasants who lived in poverty or on the edge of it. Their aspirations and needs were not identical with those of the deputies at Versailles. But in the summer of 1789 a series of spontaneous popular disturbances and revolts broke out that linked, for the moment at least, the bourgeoisie and the common people in an uneasy alliance against the aristocracy.

Notable among these uprisings was an attack on July 14 on the Bastille, a royal fortress and prison in Paris. By the end of June the city of Paris had grown tense. The economic depression of the 1780s and the poor harvests of 1788 and 1789 had reduced the urban poor to misery, and to misery was now added the fear that the king and the aristocrats were conspiring to dissolve the Estates General. When the king's troops appeared on the outskirts of the city, the Parisians well understood why they were there. The immediate reaction of the citizens was to arm themselves. It was their search for arms that brought the leaders of the Parisian electoral assembly and a crowd of journeymen and workers from the faubourg Saint-Antoine to the Bastille on July 14. The commandant at first barred the gates and fired on the crowd. He then lost his nerve, opened the gates, and the crowd stormed in and slaugh-

tered the garrison. This was typical of the royal government's behavior during the first stages of the Revolution; it used just enough force to anger the people but never enough to subdue them.

The fall of the Bastille was an event of small consequence in itself—the crowd had destroyed little more than a building—but its implications were immense. The attack was regarded as a blow against royal despotism. It demonstrated that the Revolution was not simply a debate over a constitution. Of greatest importance, it brought the city of Paris and the political leaders of Paris to the forefront. A new, insurrectionary municipal government was formed; henceforth Paris would shape the direction of the Revolution. Finally, the events in Paris set off revolts in the provinces.

About the same time that the Parisian crowds were taking the Revolution into their own hands, the French peasants, also disappointed with the slow pace of reform, began to take action of their own. Like the poor of the cities, the peasants had been heartened by the political promise of the winter of 1788–89. They had patiently drawn up their *cahiers* and they had chosen their electoral committees; then they had waited confidently for relief to follow. The Estates General met in May. Spring passed and summer came, but the peasants were still poor; they were still not allowed to till the unused land of the nobles; and they still had to pay their customary dues.

Then, during July 1789, the month of the storming of the Bastille, rumors spread through rural France that there would be no reforms and that the aristocrats were coming with troops to impose reaction upon the countryside. The result was panic and rioting throughout the country. During the "Great Fear," as it is called, frightened peasants gathered to defend themselves against the unnamed and unseen enemy. Once assembled and armed, however, they turned against the enemy they knew—the local lord. Though the lords themselves were rarely in residence, peasants all over France burned their chateaux, often tossing the first brand into the countinghouse, where the hated records of their payments were kept.

Storming the Bastille, July 14, 1789. The revolutionary leader is accepting the surrender.

The Declaration of the Rights of Man

August 27, 1789

1. Men are born and remain free and equal in rights; social distinctions may be based only upon general usefulness.
2. The aim of every political association is the preservation of the natural and inalienable rights of man; these rights are liberty, property, security, and resistance to oppression.
3. The source of all sovereignty resides essentially in the nation; no group, no individual may exercise authority not emanating expressly therefrom.
6. Law is the expression of the general will; all citizens have the right to concur personally or through their representatives in its formation; it must be the same for all, whether it protects or punishes. All citizens, being equal before it, are equally admissible to all public offices, positions, and employments, according to their capacity, and without other distinction than that of virtues and talents.
10. No one is to be disquieted because of his opinions; even religious, provided their manifestation does not disturb the public order established by law.
11. Free communication of ideas and opinions is one of the most precious of the rights of man. Consequently every citizen may speak, write, and print freely, subject to responsibility for the abuse of such liberty in the cases determined by law. . . .

From *A Documentary Survey of the French Revolution*, ed. by John Hall Stewart (New York: Macmillan, 1951), p. 114.

The Destruction of Privilege

The popular revolts and riots had a profound impact on the king, the aristocracy, and the deputies of the Third Estate alike. Louis XVI recognized the National Assembly and ordered the clergy and the nobles to sit with the Third Estate. He also recognized the revolutionary government of Paris and authorized the formation of a national guard composed largely of members of the bourgeoisie. But the king received no credit for his concessions from the revolutionary leaders, who felt, quite rightly, that his sympathies were still with the nobles. At the same time, Louis' indecision had discouraged many of the strongest supporters of the Old Regime. The most reactionary noblemen, headed by the king's brother, the Count of Artois, began to leave the country. Other members of the aristocracy sought to preserve their property by making dramatic concessions to the call for reform.

On the night of August 4, one nobleman, the Viscount de Noailles, stood before the Assembly and proposed that all feudal levies and obligations be abolished. In a performance at once impressive and bizarre, nobles, clerics, and provincial notables arose to renounce noble privileges, clerical tithes, and provincial liberties. In effect, the Old Regime was dismantled in one night of heated oratory, and the way seemed clear for the Assembly's main business—to provide a constitution for France. The implementation of the concessions of August 4, however, was somewhat less tidy. The structure of aristocratic privilege was indeed abolished by decree, along with tax exemptions and hereditary office-holding, but peasants were to continue paying customary dues to their lords until they had redeemed them. Only when the Revolution reached a more radical stage was this obligation abolished.

The Declaration of the Rights of Man

On the whole, the National Assembly had succeeded in wiping out the privileges of the upper classes, the corporations of office-holders, and the provinces. Now it faced the task of creating new political, legal, and administrative structures for the country. The ideological framework for this task was set forth by the constitution-makers in the Declaration of the Rights of Man, which they adopted on August 27, 1789.

In this preamble to a constitution yet unformed, the members of the National Constituent Assembly (that is, the National Assembly acting in its constitution-making role) established a set of principles idealistic enough to sustain the enthusiasm of the mass of Frenchmen for the Revolution and sweeping enough to include all humanity. The basic ideas of this document were personal freedom, equality under the law, the sanctity of property rights, and national sovereignty. The first article declared that "men are born and remain free and equal in rights." There were to be no class privileges and no interference with freedom of thought and religion. Liberty, property, security, and resistance to oppression were declared inalienable and natural rights. Laws could be made and taxes levied only by the citizens or their representatives. The nation, not the king, was sovereign, and all power came from and was to be exercised in the name of the nation. Thus was established the framework for a system of liberty under law. The Declaration was a landmark in the fight against privilege and despotism, and it had a great appeal to revolutionary and democratic factions throughout Europe.

The October Days

The Declaration of the Rights of Man was not simply a page lifted from John Locke, the *philosophes*, and the Americans. It was a highly political document hammered out in an Assembly that was showing itself to be increasingly divided. There were those among the moderate leaders of the Assembly who found the Declaration too radical and sweeping. These men desired to reconcile Louis XVI with the Revolution and to construct a constitutional system on the English model with a monarch guided by an assembly controlled by the rich and the well-born. The issues that divided the crown and the country could not, however, be compromised. Louis simply refused to give formal approval to the decrees and the Declaration that followed the night of August 4.

The three Estates ''hammer out'' a new constitution in this contemporary engraving.

The king's recalcitrance, the divisions in the Assembly, and the food shortages combined to produce yet another popular explosion. On October 5, 1789, a crowd of some 20,000 armed Parisians marched on Versailles, demanding bread and insisting that the royal family return to Paris. The king considered flight, but he was persuaded by Necker, who had been recalled to the government, and by Lafayette, leader of the National Guard, to appease the crowd and leave Versailles. On October 6 the king, Queen Marie Antoinette, and the royal family drove into Paris in their carriage, surrounded by shouting crowds, and established themselves at their palace in the center of the city. A few days later, the National Constituent Assembly followed.

The Parisians seemed satisfied with the king's capitulation, and the Assembly, together with the king and his ministers, turned to the question of the constitution. Henceforth, however, the deliberations of the Assembly were to take place in the heated atmosphere of Parisian politics. Here in the capital many political clubs were formed to debate the issues. The most famous of these was the Jacobin Club, which included many of the radical members of the Assembly. Here too were political agitators, journalists of all opinions, and, above all, crowds that could be mobilized to bring pressure on the Assembly. From the autumn of 1789 on, the Revolution became more and more a Parisian affair.

The Achievements of the National Constituent Assembly, 1789–91

It took two years to make the constitution. By the end of that time the government had been reorganized, the Church had been dispossessed of its lands, and the rights of Frenchmen had been more clearly defined. Here are the main results of the Assembly's complex and lengthy deliberations:

The Monarchy. By acts passed in September 1789, Louis XVI was reduced from his position as a monarch by divine right to the role of a constitutional officer of the nation. He was given the right of suspensive veto over legislation, a right that allowed him to delay the passage of laws for two years. The monarchy remained a hereditary institution, and the king retained control of military and foreign affairs.

The Legislature. The Constitution of 1791 provided for a unicameral Legislative Assembly, elected for two years. The Assembly had the power to initiate and enact legislation and to control the budget. It also had the exclusive right to declare war. Members of the Constituent Assembly were forbidden to serve in the new legislature, an unfortunate decision that barred experienced men from a body that had few precedents to guide it.

The Electorate. The Constitution did not provide for universal manhood suffrage. It divided Frenchmen into active and passive citizens. Only the former, who met a property qualification, had the right to vote. The active category comprised some 4 million men in a total population of about 25 million. Active citizens voted for electors, who in turn elected the Legislative Assembly. These electors, as well as office-holders in the Assembly, were drawn from some 50,000 of the country's wealthiest men. Even with these restrictions, a far larger percentage of the population could vote and hold office than in England.

The Administration. The elimination of aristocratic privilege invalidated most of France's local administration, which had been controlled by the nobility or small oligarchies of office-holders and rich bourgeois. The Assembly completed the process of dismantling the administrative apparatus of the Old Regime by abolishing all former provinces, intendancies, and tax farms. On a clean administrative map they drew eighty-three departments, roughly equal in size, with uniform administrative and judicial systems. Administration was decentralized and put in the hands of some 40,000 local and departmental councils, elected by their constituents.

The Church. The reorganization of the French Church was decreed by the Civil Constitution of the Clergy promulgated in August 1790. The Assembly confiscated the lands of the Church and, to relieve the financial distress of the country, issued notes on the security of the confiscated lands. These notes, or *assignats,* circulated as money and temporarily relieved the financial crisis. In addition, clergymen became paid officials of the state, and priests and bishops were to be elected by property-owning citizens.

The Constitution of 1791, together with the Declaration of the Rights of Man, summed up the principles and politics of the men of 1789. In its emphasis on property rights, its restrictive franchise, and its fiscal policy, the Constitution had a distinctly bourgeois bias. To look upon the document simply as a product of selfish interest, however, would be to underestimate the achievement of the constituents. A new class of peasant proprietors had been created. The framework for a society open to talent had been established. Administrative decentralization, it was thought, had overcome the prevailing fear of despotism. Equality before the law, if not political equality, had been made a fact. These were impressive and revolutionary achievements. But to succeed and mature, the new order established by the Constituent Assembly needed peace, social stability, and the cooperation of the king. None of these was forthcoming. Within a year the Constitution of 1791 had become a dead letter, and the Revolution had entered a new phase.

The Failure of Constitutional Monarchy

The Constitution of 1791 was most certainly an imperfect instrument. The Civil Constitution of the Clergy, for example, offended the pope, who had not been consulted. His disapproval forced a crisis of conscience upon French Catholics. Many bishops and priests refused to accept the Civil Constitution, and they found broad support in the country. Schism in the Church became a major factor in the eventual failure of the Assembly to create a stable government for France. Moreover, the restrictive franchise opened the constitution-makers to the charge that they wanted to substitute a wealthy oligarchy for an aristocracy. Such obvious defects, however, were not

Portrait of Louis XVI during his imprisonment at the time of the revolution, by Joseph Ducreux.

model, began to denounce the radicalism and violence of the French. Edmund Burke, in particular, saw clearly the radical nature of the Revolution. In his *Reflections on the Revolution in France* he insisted on the importance of tradition in preserving an orderly society and declared that it was folly to abandon time-tested institutions in favor of new ones based on abstract ideas. And everywhere French refugees spread counterrevolutionary propaganda urging Europe's monarchs to intervene.

The Legislative Assembly, September 1791–September 1792

The Legislative Assembly met in an atmosphere of intrigue, fear, and factional strife. The Assembly, itself bitterly divided, was deprived of the hard-won political experience of the men who had drafted the Constitution.

There were two issues on which it was almost impossible to find a solid majority. The first was the position of the king. He could not be trusted, and he would not commit himself to the principle of equality, on which everyone did agree. Was it worth compromising with the king in order to preserve the constitution and the unity of the country? If not, how far should the Assembly go in restraining or in punishing the king?

The second problem, which caused even sharper divisions of opinion, was that of defining "equality." Was the emphasis to be on equality before the law, or on equality of opportunity, or on political equality, or on economic equality, or on a mixture of two or more of these ideals? Here there was not only no clear majority, but no consistency within groups and even within individuals.

There were no parties in the Assembly, but there were the "clubs," loosely organized associations with affiliates in the provinces. One of the largest and best-organized groups was the Jacobin Club, with 136 members out of the 745 representatives. The Jacobins were republicans and wanted to get rid of the king. But they were also well-to-do bourgeois; no poor man could afford to pay their membership dues. They were far from agreement on political and

alone responsible for the failure of constitutional monarchy. The principal culprit was the monarch himself.

At the head of the government stood a king who was thoroughly discredited. In June 1791, Louis XVI tried to escape from France in order to join the forces of counterrevolution outside the country. He very nearly succeeded but was caught at Varennes, near the eastern frontier, and was brought back to Paris. This humiliating episode destroyed what little authority Louis still possessed. In order to keep himself from being completely displaced, he swore to obey the new constitution; but he was now no more than a figurehead. From the very beginning, the constitutional monarchy was flawed.

At this point the situation was complicated by outside pressures. Louis' fellow monarchs were unhappy over the way in which their royal colleague was being treated. The privileged orders in other countries feared that the leveling principles of the Revolution would spread. The English, many of whom had sympathized with the Revolution so long as it seemed to be following an English economic equality, or on the pace at which change should take place. They were divided into at least two factions. One faction was led by Brissot de Warville, the ablest politician in the Assembly. The other, composed mainly of Parisians, eventually found a leader in Maximilien Robespierre.

As it turned out, the issue that temporarily united the Assembly was that of declaring war on Austria. Stupid diplomacy by European monarchs, even more stupid politics in the French royal court, and a very real threat of counterrevolution convinced millions of patriotic Frenchmen that the forces of reaction were about to destroy all that had been gained since 1789 and that war was the only way to save their country and their freedom. The Emperor of Austria and the King of Prussia in the Declaration of Pillnitz (August 1791) proclaimed that European monarchs must unite to restore order and monarchy in France. This was largely bluff, but it sounded ominous. Some conservative ministers thought that a victorious war against Austria would strengthen the king and allow him to end the Revolution. However, Louis XVI and his Austrian queen, Marie Antionette, apparently hoped for a French defeat that would lead to the restoration of royal authority.

External threats and court plots played into the hands of Brissot's republican faction. Brissot believed that a crusade to unseat the monarchs of Europe would rekindle the revolutionary fervor of the French people and rally them around his plan to establish a republic in France. He was opposed in the Jacobin Club by Robespierre, who feared that a war would strengthen the conservatives and lead to dictatorship. But Brissot proved the stronger, and the powerful Jacobin Club passed a resolution advocating a declaration of war. Brissot took the issue before the Assembly and in April 1792 all but seven deputies voted for war with Austria.

The First War of the Revolution

The declaration of war transformed the Revolution. With war came the end of the monarchy and the constitution. With it also came terror and dictatorship. France became not simply the home of the Revolution but the exporter of revolutionary ideals. Finally, under the stress and emotions of war, France became a modern, unified nation-state.

The war began badly. The French army lacked leadership and discipline. The government was short of money and hampered by factional disputes. The royal family and their supporters encouraged the enemy. It is not surprising that the Austrians and their allies, the Prussians, were soon able to advance along the road to Paris.

Two things saved the Revolution at this moment of crisis. The Austrian and Prussian generals, who were at least as incompetent as the French, delayed and divided their forces. And there was a genuine outburst of patriotic and revolutionary enthusiasm in France. It was during this crisis that the *Marseillaise* was composed, a stirring appeal to save the country from tyranny. The French kept on fighting, despite their failures, and their army did not melt away as the refugee nobles had predicted. As a result, when the Austro-Prussian army was checked at Valmy in September 1792, its cautious commander decided to call off the invasion. The allies had lost their best chance to crush the Revolution before it gathered strength.

THE FRENCH REPUBLIC

During these gloomy months, when everything seemed to be going wrong, the radical politicians of Paris gained a commanding position in the government. These Jacobins—Robespierre and Georges-Jacques Danton were the most important—based their power on national guards summoned to protect the capital, on the Parisian crowds, and, from August 9, 1792, on an insurrectionary Paris commune that replaced the legal municipal government. The poorer classes were suffering from an economic depression caused by war and political uncertainty, and they were terrified by the thought that the Old Regime might be revived. The bourgeois radicals in the

Playing cards of the French Revolution. Liberty and Equality have taken the place of kings and queens.

Assembly never fully sympathized with the desire of Paris artisans and workers for economic equality, but they could agree with them on the need for drastic political changes. In August the Jacobins touched off an uprising in Paris that forced the Legislative Assembly to suspend the king from office and to issue a call for a revision of the constitution. A National Convention, elected by universal manhood suffrage, was to determine the new form of the French government. The events of August triggered what is often called the Second French Revolution. This revolution began with the deposition of Louis XVI; it ended in a bloody terror that consumed its own leaders. In many ways it confirmed Edmund Burke's most hysterical prophecies. And yet the Second French Revolution did not follow inexorably upon the first. War created its own necessities, survival being the most pressing.

The Convention and the Jacobins

The National Convention met in Paris on September 21, 1792, in the wake of a fierce bloodletting earlier in the month—the so-called September massacres. These massacres, which took the lives of some 1,300 prisoners in Paris, were part of a pattern of fear, terror, and revolutionary justice that persisted throughout much of the Convention's three-year rule.

The delegates to the Convention were elected by a minority of Frenchmen, despite universal manhood suffrage. Many citizens were repelled by the deposition of the king and the violence of the summer of 1792. Others were intimidated. Some were excluded from the electorate by governmental decree. Thus the most radical elements of the French population had disproportionate strength in the elections. Not surprisingly, many of the delegates were Jacobins.

The Jacobins, however, were divided. The followers of Brissot, now called the Girondists, made up one faction. They dominated the Convention in its early months. In general, the Girondists represented the interests of provincial republicans, and they were bitterly opposed to

the Paris Commune. Their foreign policy was aggressive and expansionistic. It was they, for example, who issued a manifesto in November 1792 offering France's aid to all revolutionaries throughout Europe. In domestic affairs, the Girondists were relatively moderate—at least when compared to their Parisian enemies. On the prime issue of 1792, the fate of the king, the Girondists urged that Louis XVI be imprisoned for the duration of the war. There was little doubt then—and less now—that Louis was guilty of treason. But the resolution condemning him to death passed by only one vote. He was guillotined on January 21, 1793. This victory for the so-called Mountain—Robespierre's and Danton's faction—was followed by a purge of the Girondists in June 1793. The architects of France's war policy were among the first victims of that policy.

The Jacobins and the War

The Girondists fell before their Jacobin opponents in the wake of crushing French defeats by an overwhelming new coalition of European powers. The death of Louis XVI, France's designs on Holland, and its annexation of Savoy and Nice prompted England, Spain, Portugal, and several lesser states to join Austria and Prussia in the war against France. In the face of such a formidable combination, the French armies suffered a series of reversals. The victor of Valmy, General Dumouriez, was badly defeated in Belgium, and, in the spring of 1793, he defected to the enemy.

Now the government, under the direction of a Committee of General Defense (later the Committee of Public Safety), undertook to organize the entire nation for war. It applied conscription on a nationwide scale for the first time in modern European history. It raised huge armies, far larger than those of Louis XIV, far larger than those that could be called up by the old-fashioned monarchies against which France was fighting. And it supported those armies by means of confiscation and heavy taxes. The armies were organized by a military genius, Lazare Carnot, an engineer who made a science out of the service of supply. He also established the division as a tactical unit.

The monarchies of Europe, which were used to fighting limited wars with limited resources for limited gains, were overcome by a French nation organized for war. They could not afford to arm all their people; they still depended on the old officer corps for their leaders. And, much as they despised the Revolution, they were still not prepared to sacrifice all their resources to put it down. Other problems distracted the crowned heads of Europe: England was seeking colonial conquests, and the eastern powers were still concerned with the Polish problem. So the French recovered from the blows of 1793 and by the late spring of 1794 had broken through into the Low Countries. When the Convention ended its work in 1795, France was stronger and held more territory than it had under Louis XIV at the height of his power.

The Instruments
of Jacobin Rule

Military success was achieved only through the intensive and often brutal organization of the French people. The Constituent Assembly's program of administrative decentralization had left France without any effective chain of command linking the National Convention in Paris to the provinces. Moreover, the Convention was an ungainly body, incapable of swift action. Into this void moved the radical Jacobins. In the provinces, Jacobin clubs virtually replaced local governing bodies and through their committees of surveillance controlled public life. At the center, executive power was entrusted to two committees—the Committee of Public Safety and the Committee for General Security. The former wielded almost dictatorial power over France from July 1793 until July 1794. It had twelve members, of

whom Robespierre was the most important.

The genuine achievement of the twelve capable men who composed the Committee of Public Safety is often overlooked because of the "Reign of Terror" they imposed on France. The Terror, however, must be put into the context of the problems that confronted Robespierre, Carnot, and their colleagues. From early 1793 there had been a series of internal rebellions against the government. Conservative peasants of the Vendée, a region in the west of France, had revolted against the national conscription and in favor of their priests who opposed the Civil Constitution. Later in the year, the Girondists, who opposed what they thought was excessive centralization, stimulated local uprisings in some large provincial towns. In the heat of war, such rebellions appeared treasonable, and the Terror was used as a political weapon to impose order. Also, during much of the Committee's tenure, Parisian politicians, both to the left and to the right of Robespierre, maneuvered to secure power. Terror, against Danton among others, was a weapon in these internecine conflicts. There was an economic terror directed against war profiteers and hoarders. Finally, there were local terrors, uncontrolled from the center, in which Jacobins and undisciplined representatives of the government took revenge on their enemies. In the end, the Terror gained a certain momentum of its own, and the list of suspects grew. Among the factors in Robespierre's fall was the fear of the Convention that its remaining members would soon become victims of revolutionary justice.

In all, some 40,000 people were killed by the government and its agents. The largest number of victims were peasants; next came rebellious citizens of provincial towns and politicians. Some hundreds of thousands of suspects were imprisoned and proper judicial procedures, such as the right of the accused to counsel, were undermined. Even the Committee of Public Safety finally divided over the excesses of the Terror. When military successes restored a measure of stability to France, the National Convention reasserted its authority. Among its first acts was the arrest and execution of Robespierre in July 1794.

Jacobinism and French Society

The militant phase of Jacobinism was of relatively short duration. The Committee of Public Safety ruled for a year, and Robespierre had complete authority for only four months. Thus, beyond the brilliant organization of the national defense, the Jacobins made few permanent contributions to French institutions and society. Certain of their acts, however, have remained of symbolic significance to the French Left. Among these were the guarantees of the right to a public education for all and the right of public welfare for the poor; these guarantees were set forth in an abortive constitution drawn up in 1793. In addition, the Jacobins were responsible for decrees establishing price controls and providing for the division of confiscated property among the poor. These decrees, however, were not enforced with much zeal because they were not the product of a conscious social philosophy. They were political acts designed to win over the disaffected crowds in the cities and the landless peasants at a time of national crisis. The Jacobins were radical democrats who believed deeply in political equality; they were not socialists. With their fall in the summer of 1794, the Revolution fell back into the hands of the propertied bourgeoisie. It was this class that in the end gained most from the Revolution.

The Directory, 1795–99

In 1795 the Convention finally presented France with a constitution. It provided for a five-man executive board, called the Directory, and a two-house legislature. Even the republican-oriented Convention had been sufficiently sobered by the Terror to abandon its promise of universal suffrage, and the franchise was weighted in favor of the propertied classes. Once in office, the Directory proved both corrupt and incompetent. It maintained a militantly aggressive foreign policy and allowed the French economy to deteriorate disastrously. A more or less communistic movement led by "Gracchus" Babeuf received some support from the poor, but was easily suppressed. The French poor were still largely artisans and peasants—property owners and not wage-earners. More dangerous was a royalist revival. Elections in 1797 demonstrated such an upsurge in royalist sentiment

"Here lies all of France." An engraving of Robespierre guillotining the executioner after having guillotined everyone else in France.

that the results had to be cancelled. The Directory's single source of strength was the army. With the economy foundering and popular unrest increasing, the Directory was ripe for the *coup d'état* that in 1799 brought one of its most successful generals, Napoleon Bonaparte, to power.

NAPOLEON'S RISE TO POWER

Napoleon Bonaparte was born on the island of Corsica in 1769, shortly after the island had been annexed by France. The Bonapartes were members of the minor nobility of Corsica, and at the age of nine Napoleon was admitted to a military school in France. From that time on, he knew no other life than the army. When most of the aristocratic officer corps left France after the fall of the monarchy, Napoleon stayed on to serve the Republic. He rose to become a brigadier general in 1793 at the age of 24. He helped to reconquer Toulon—one of the towns that rebelled against the Convention in 1793—and he suppressed a riot against the Convention in 1795. By 1797, when the Directory felt its power slipping, Barras, one of the Directors, realized that Napoleon's support could be valuable. He sought Napoleon's friendship first by introducing the young general to one of his cast-off mistresses, Josephine Beauharnais (whom Napoleon married), and then by giving him command of an army that was preparing for an invasion of Lombardy, a province in northern Italy that was then under the control of Austria.

The Italian campaign of 1797 was a success. It removed Austria from the war, gave France control of northern Italy, and established Napoleon's reputation as an outstanding general. After the defeat of the Austrians only England was still at war with France. In 1798 Bonaparte took an army by sea to Egypt, where he hoped to sever England's lifeline to India. He easily defeated the Egyptians, but the English admiral Horatio Nelson sank the French fleet near the mouth of the Nile. Napoleon's army, trapped in Egypt, was soon decimated by disease and dysentery. In the midst of this crisis, Napoleon heard that the Directory was in danger of falling and that some of the Directors wanted to create a military dictatorship. Leaving his army in Egypt, he made his way secretly back to France to offer his services to the conspirators.

The most important Director was the Abbé Sieyès, and it was with this former leader of the First French Revolution that Napoleon conspired. On November 9, 1799, he used military force to compel the legislators to abolish the Directory and substitute a new government in which a board of three consuls would have almost absolute power. The conspirators asked Napoleon to serve as one of the consuls. Apparently they hoped he would provide the personal popularity and military power needed to support a regime that would be dominated, behind the scenes, by the other two consuls. But when the new constitution was written— at Napoleon's orders—the general emerged as First Consul and virtual dictator of France. When the French people were invited to endorse the constitution in a plebiscite, they voted overwhelmingly to accept it. To Frenchmen exhausted by years of revolution, terror, and economic instability, Napoleon seemed to be the guarantor both of the gains of the Revolution and of order.

NAPOLEON AND DOMESTIC REFORM

Bonaparte was, above all, a military man, and his fortunes always hinged on military success or failure. Yet his domestic reforms were profound and enduring. If the French Revolution gave the country an ideology that, henceforth, would both inspire and divide Frenchmen, Napoleon gave France many of its characteristic institutions. Better than any eighteenth-century monarch, Bonaparte fulfilled the *philosophes'* dream of an enlightened despot.

Between 1799 and 1801 Napoleon led a series of successful campaigns against the coalition that England, Austria, and Prussia had formed to defeat him. He wanted to win a favorable peace so that he could devote himself to consolidating his position in France. Hostilities ended

Gros' portrait of Josephine, Napoleon's wife. This portrait hung in Napoleon's bedchamber.

in 1801 and did not break out again on any major scale until 1805. Napoleon used those four years to restore domestic concord and economic stability and to establish a network of administrative institutions that gave coherence and uniformity to the work of his government.

Perhaps Napoleon's most characteristic contribution was the *Code Napoléon*. From the debris of the laws left by the several legal systems of the Old Regime and the succession of revolutionary governments, Napoleon's advisers compiled a uniform legal code that is still the basis of French law. The Code maintained in theory the revolutionary concept of the equality of all men before the law, but it was in fact far less egalitarian than the laws of the revolutionary era. It emphasized, for instance, the authority of the state over the people, of business corporations over their employees, and of male heads of families over their wives and children. Property rights received particularly strong protection under the Code.

Other Napoleonic reforms followed a similar pattern. They often upheld in principle the ideals of the Enlightenment and the Revolution but served in practice to strengthen France's new authoritarian state. Napoleon retained, for instance, the division of France into eighty-three uniformly administered departments. He used the departmental system, however, not to foster local responsibility, as had been intended, but to create a highly centralized administration controlled directly by the First Consul through field administrators called prefects. He also instituted a nationwide system of public schools that not only educated the young—an ideal of the *philosophes*—but imbued them with an exaggerated patriotism and devotion to their ruler.

In reforming France's finances Napoleon followed the British and American examples by chartering a privately owned national bank to provide both a depository for government funds and a source of credit for French businessmen. With government deposits as security, the bank issued paper money as legal tender. Increased currency, a stable franc, and improved credit helped to improve France's shaky economy. Napoleon also resolved that perennial problem of the Old Regime—taxation—by developing uniform taxes collected directly from each individual by paid officials.

Although Napoleon himself was far from religious, he understood better than his republican predecessors that domestic peace could not be achieved until the religious question had been settled. Accordingly, he concluded an agreement with Pope Pius VII, the Concordat of 1801, which regularized the situation created by the Revolution. Although the document recognized that the majority of Frenchmen were Roman Catholics, the Catholic Church was not to be the established church in France. Church properties confiscated during the Revolution were not to be restored. Moreover, the First Consul retained the right to appoint

Unfinished portrait of Napoleon by Jacques-Louis David, the imperial court painter.

Political Maxims of Napoleon

These extracts from communications to the Council of State (1801–1804) come from the period when Napoleon was First Consul and was trying to construct a civilian government.

We have finished the romantic period of the Revolution; we must now start to make it into history, to see only what is real and possible in applying its principles and not what was speculative and hypothetical. To follow any other policy today would be to philosophize and not to govern.

I shall respect public opinion when its judgments are legitimate, but it has whims that must be scorned. It is the duty of the government to enlighten public opinion, not to follow it in its errors.

One can lead a people only by promising it a future; a chief of state is a seller of hopes.

Constitutions should be short and obscure. . . . A constitution should be drafted in such a way that it will not hinder the actions of a government and not force the government to violate it. . . . If there are problems with a government that is too strong, there are many more with a government that is too weak. Things won't work unless you break the law every day.

My system is very simple. I believe that in the circumstances, it is necessary to centralize power and increase the authority of the government in order to build a nation. I am the constitution-making power.

Trans. from Edouard Driault, *Napoléon: Pensées pour l'Action* (Paris: Presses Universitaires de France, 1943), pp. 30–34.

bishops. Through the Concordat of 1801, Napoleon regained the loyalty of French Catholics to the official government and at the same time won the gratitude of those who owned former church properties.

Although Napoleon brought a form of enlightened despotism to France, he did so at the expense of much of the individual liberty that had been the first principle of the Enlightenment. The legislative institutions created by the Constitution of 1799 were a sham. Political opposition was punished by police action, and the press was strictly censored. Napoleon's training was military, and too often his solution to political and even social problems was force. Nevertheless, his government in its early years was popular. He preserved the property of those who had gained from the Revolution. He satisfied the social ideal of the Revolution by maintaining equality before the law, equality in taxation, and careers open to all men of talent. In his own administration, he incorporated royalists, constitutionalists, and Jacobins. With such accomplishments to his credit, he easily won popular approval when he declared himself First Consul for life in 1802. And two years later, on December 2, 1804, the nation rejoiced when, in the presence of the pope, he crowned himself Emperor of the French.

THE NAPOLEONIC EMPIRE

Napoleon did not create French imperialism; he inherited, indeed he had been an agent of, a policy of aggressive expansion undertaken by the Convention and the Directory. A satellite republic had already been established in Holland in 1795, and during the victorious campaigns against Austria toward the end of the decade French armies had brought revolutionary ideals and French power to Switzerland and parts of Italy. This burst of French expansion had come to an end when Napoleon signed separate peace treaties with Austria, in 1801, and England, in 1802. Large-scale hostilities were resumed only in 1805, but from that time until Napoleon's ultimate defeat ten years later, France was almost constantly at war.

If Napoleon could have avoided war he might have established his empire as the dominant state in Europe. But his own insatiable ambition and the continuing enmity of England made war almost inevitable. Napoleon could not resist the temptation to extend his sphere of influence by entering into intrigues in Germany and Italy. England was determined to keep France from becoming the dominant political and economic power in Europe. French control of the Low Countries violated a basic rule of English foreign policy—namely, to keep these invasion bases and commercial centers out of the hands of a strong power. Moreover, the British and their ablest statesman of the period, William Pitt the Younger, were convinced that Napoleon was using the peace to ready France for yet another war. Pitt soon was able to persuade other continental states that they must join England to restore the balance of power and resist the spread of French influence in central Europe.

Napoleon was just as ready for war as was England. He felt that his empire could never be secure and that his plans for Europe could never be achieved until England had been thoroughly defeated. The two states drifted into war in 1803, and other continental powers—Austria, Russia, and finally Prussia—joined England.

It was a difficult war for the two major contestants. Napoleon could not gain control of the sea, and without this control he could not subdue England. He made his greatest effort in 1805 when he concentrated his army at Boulogne and tried to pull the English fleet out of the

A cast of the imperial seal of Napoleon, "Emperor of the French, King of Italy, Protector of the Confederation of the Rhine."

Channel by an elaborate set of naval feints in the Atlantic. But the English were not deceived. While one fleet guarded England against invasion, another, under Nelson, caught the French and their allies off Cape Trafalgar and annihilated them (October 21, 1805). Napoleon was never again able to threaten England with invasion. The English, on the other hand, could not defeat the French on the Continent and were dependent upon the armies of their allies.

By the fall of 1805 the armies of the Russian and Austrian emperors assembled in central Europe for a combined assault on Napoleon. Instead of waiting for the attack, Napoleon marched an army deep into central Europe and took the Austrian and Russian generals by surprise. He defeated the Austrian and Russian forces first at Ulm, and then again in the most spectacular of all his victories, at Austerlitz, on December 2, 1805.

With Austria defeated and Russia in retreat, Napoleon followed up his victory with a complete reorganization of the German states. He abolished the Holy Roman Empire and eliminated many of the small German principalities. Out of these petty states he created a satellite system composed of fourteen larger states that were united in a Confederation of the Rhine; Napoleon served as president of this German Confederation.

Prussia, which had not at first joined the coalition against Napoleon, entered the fray in 1806 and was soundly defeated at Jena in October of that year. King Frederick William III was forced to accept a humiliating peace and to become an ally of France. The following spring, Emperor Alexander I of Russia again sent an army against Napoleon, only to have it defeated at Friedland in June 1807. In three campaigns in three successive years, Napoleon had defeated the three strongest powers on the Continent and established his position as master of Europe. Russia was too large to occupy, but Napoleon had taught Emperor Alexander the futility of opposition. A few weeks after Friedland, Napoleon and Alexander held a dramatic meeting near Tilsit. Alexander recog-

nized Napoleon's supremacy in the West, and Napoleon agreed not to intervene in Russia's internal affairs or to prevent Alexander from extending Russian influence into the Ottoman-controlled Balkans.

Napoleonic Europe and the Continental System

Napoleon was now at the summit of his power. All Europe, save England, was to some degree under his rule. France, Belgium, Germany west of the Rhine, and parts of Italy and Illyria constituted a French Empire ruled directly by Napoleon as emperor. Holland, Westphalia (a Napoleonic creation in Germany), and southern Italy were theoretically independent kingdoms, over which Napoleon placed three of his brothers as kings. Northern Italy was also a kingdom, with Napoleon himself as king. The Grand Duchy of Warsaw was carved out of Prussia's Polish territories and given to France's ally, the King of Saxony. In 1808, the Bourbon monarch of Spain was overthrown and replaced by Napoleon's brother Joseph.

England alone resisted the tide of French expansion. From 1806 on, Napoleon tried to weaken England by wrecking English trade with the Continent. This so-called Continental System imposed heavy penalties on anyone trading with England and forbade the importation of English goods. Since England produced the cheapest manufactures and was a good market for food and raw materials, this ban put a heavy strain on the economies of the continental countries. England made the strain worse by blockading all countries that subscribed to the French system. The English blockade was harsh enough to drive Denmark into a close alliance with France and to help cause the War of 1812 with the United States. But on the whole it caused less ill will than Napoleon's decrees. It was simply impossible for the European economy to function properly without English trade.

Napoleon himself had to allow exceptions and grant special licenses, a procedure that irritated everyone who did not receive such favors. Smuggling became a highly organized and profitable business, and attempts to enforce French regulations strengthened the opposition to Napoleon everywhere. Most important of all, it led to a quarrel between Napoleon and Alexander of Russia.

Emperor Alexander had not been entirely happy with the results of his alliance with Napoleon. France had gained vast territories; Russia had acquired only Finland and Bessarabia. Napoleon's creation of the Grand Duchy of Warsaw menaced Russia's control of the Polish lands it had seized in the 1790s. But the great and overwhelming grievance of the Russians was the Continental System. Russia needed English markets for its grain, and Alexander would not and could not enforce the rules against trade with England. Napoleon, bent on the destruction of England, could not tolerate this breach in his system, which was already being weakened by the ill will of other rulers. He requested Alexander to stop the trade; when Alexander refused, Napoleon prepared to invade Russia.

The Weaknesses
of the Napoleonic Empire

When Napoleon undertook his Russian campaign in June 1812, his hold on Europe and even on the French was weakening. Initially, French expansion had been greeted with some enthusiasm by parts of the conquered populations. Hatred of privilege and desire for equality were as strong in many parts of Europe as in France. The conquering French armies broke the archaic political and social structures of many states. Within the Empire, the *Code Napoléon* was established, the privileges of the Church and aristocracies were abolished, and fetters on local industry and commerce were removed. Napoleon saw himself, in other words, as the "revolution on horseback" and sought to impose a new order on Europe—a new order that was enlightened, rational, and French.

This vision of Napoleon's was, at best, only partially achieved, and even those who had most enthusiastically received the invading French armies soon perceived that imperialism was a more important component of the Napoleonic

system than was liberation. The Continental System contributed to a general economic crisis in Europe that alienated the commercial and industrial interests. High taxes and conscription were imposed on the tributary states. And the French system was enforced by tight police surveillance. Napoleonic tutelage, even at its most benevolent, appeared incompatible with the libertarian and nationalistic ideals of the French Revolution.

Increasingly, Napoleon was beset by the growth of nationalistic feelings and national resistance to his rule. In Germany, Italy, and Spain, national awakening was intimately linked to the opposition to French hegemony. This opposition took many forms. In Italy and Germany cultural movements arose that emphasized the common history, language, and literature shared by the fragmented parts of these countries. In Spain resistance was expressed in a more violent manner when rebellions broke out in 1808 against the regime of Joseph Bonaparte. It was in Spain that Napoleon first confronted guerrilla warfare and first encountered serious failure. A Spanish victory at Baylen in 1808 was the initial break in the emperor's record of invincibility. By 1812, the Spanish rebels, with the help of an English army under Wellington, had driven the French from Madrid and had organized a constitutional government that controlled more than half the country.

The appearance of a well-organized English army on the Continent was one indication that the balance of power in Europe was beginning to shift against Napoleon. There were other signs, the most important of which was the recovery of France's nominal ally and potential enemy, Prussia. After the humiliating defeat of the Prussians at Jena, the process of reconstructing the kingdom was begun. Under Generals Gneisenau and Scharnhorst, the Prussian army was modernized and a form of universal military training for young men was introduced. To revitalize the country, another reformer, the Baron vom Stein, persuaded the king to abolish serfdom and to grant a large measure of liberty to Prussian municipalities. Stein's social

Contemporary engravings of French soldiers of Napoleon's era. Top: A sharpshooter of the Imperial Guard; below: a cannonier.

legislation was limited in its effects, but the military reforms allowed Prussia to play a significant role in the final defeat of Napoleon.

At the same time that his enemies were strengthening themselves and challenging the French monopoly of force on the Continent, Napoleon began to lose his grip on the French people. French economic domination of Europe, which had been one of the goals of the Continental System, failed to materialize, and France, like the rest of the Continent, suffered from the economic crisis that marked the last years of Napoleon's reign. Internally, the regime grew more repressive, and Napoleon became increasingly intolerant of criticism and even of his ministers' advice. After his divorce from Josephine and his marriage to an Austrian princess, Maria Louisa, Napoleon more and more took on the airs of an Old Regime monarch. In the end, those Frenchmen who had provided him with his magnificent and spirited army were exhausted by the burdens of empire.

The Invasion of Russia and the Fall of Napoleon

In June 1812 Napoleon marched into Russia with 600,000 men, the largest army ever assembled up to that time. Only about a third were French. Most had been recruited in the German states or in other dependencies. Napoleon expected to deliver a fast and decisive blow, but the Russians, so greatly outnumbered, did not give battle. Instead they retreated, drawing Napoleon behind them. After one costly but inconclusive engagement at Borodino, Napoleon occupied Moscow in September and waited for Alexander to offer peace terms. But no message came.

After five weeks Napoleon realized that he could not keep so large a force in Russia through the winter, and on October 19 he began the long march westward. Almost immediately he encountered difficulties. Since the land through which he passed had already been burned by both armies, he lost thousands of men to disease and starvation. When the cold weather came, the weakened soldiers were no match for the elements. As the remnants of Napoleon's army stumbled closer to the frontier, Polish and German soldiers deserted and headed homeward. When Napoleon reached the German border in December, he could not muster 100,000 men. If Austria or Prussia had chosen to launch an attack at this time, the war could have been ended. But the allies as yet had no clue to the enormity of the disaster.

Once on German territory, Napoleon fled in disguise to Paris and organized a new army that he marched toward the Russian border in the spring of 1813. But defeat had deflated the Napoleonic image, and Napoleon was badly beaten at Leipzig in October by the combined armies of Austria, Prussia, and Russia. Napoleon lost about two-fifths of his men and retreated back across the Rhine. Meanwhile, the British general Wellington defeated another French army in Spain and crossed the border into southern France. On March 31, 1814, the combined armies entered Paris, and one week later Napoleon abdicated. After some debate, the allies restored the Bourbons to the throne of France and then called a peace conference in Vienna to settle the fate of the rest of Europe.

Napoleon was exiled to the island of Elba, off the Italian coast. But he still had

The Retreat from Moscow

The following is from a letter written by Napoleon to his Minister for Foreign Affairs, November 29, 1812.

The army is strong in numbers, but terribly disorganized. It would take a fortnight to reconstitute the regiments, and where is a fortnight to come from? The disorganization is due to cold and privations. We shall soon be at Vilna: shall we be able to hold out there? Yes, if we can do so for a week; but if we are attacked during the first week, it is doubtful whether we could stay there. Food, food, food! Without it, there is no limit to the horrors this undisciplined mass of men may bring upon the town. Perhaps the army will not rally until it is behind the Niemen. . . . I am particularly anxious that there should be no foreign agents at Vilna. The army is not for exhibition purposes at the moment.

As quoted in J. M. Thompson, *Napoleon Self-Revealed* (Boston: Houghton Mifflin, 1934), p. 319.

one battle to fight. In March 1815 he escaped and landed in the south of France. The army proved loyal to the deposed leader and Napoleon was soon in control of France once again. But the allies were prepared. Napoleon was conclusively defeated at Waterloo on June 18, 1815, and three days later he abdicated for the second time. The allies now exiled him to St. Helena, a small and remote island off the Atlantic coast of Africa. The era of the Revolution and Napoleon had ended.

The era had ended, but it could not be effaced. The allies could restore a Bourbon to the throne of France, but the new king, Louis XVIII, could not restore the Old Regime. He had to keep many of Napoleon's officials. He had to preserve the Napoleonic administrative system and the Concordat with the Church. He had to accept both the revolutionary principle of equality under the law and the revolutionary land settlement. He had to grant a constitution to his people. It was a conservative constitution with a very limited electorate, but it meant that

the king's rule was not absolute. And throughout Europe the great ideas of the Revolution—liberty, equality, and nationalism—lived on, and with them the new and dangerous concept of Revolution as a means of attaining social and political goals. These ideas were only partially recognized in some countries and totally suppressed in others, but they persisted everywhere—smoldering coals that were to burst into flame again and again during the nineteenth century.

The political balance of power in Europe had been permanently altered. No one could restore the petty states of Germany or the feeble republics of Italy. No one could ignore the claims of Russia to have, for the first time, a voice in the affairs of western Europe. No one could fail to recognize the tremendous strides that England had made in industry and commerce during the wars. Conversely, for the first time in two centuries, France was no longer the richest and strongest European state. These were some of the new political facts with which the diplomats at Vienna had to deal.

Retreat of Napoleon's army across the Beresina River, 1812, by an anonymous painter.

Suggestions for Further Reading

Note: Asterisk denotes a book available in paperback edition.

General The best general work on the French Revolution is the authoritative study by G. Lefebvre, *The French Revolution* (1962–64). A somewhat different interpretation may be found in F. Furet and D. Richet, *The French Revolution* (1970). C. Brinton, *A Decade of Revolution, 1789–1799** (1934), in the *Rise of Modern Europe* series, is a fine introductory summary. Valuable source material may be found in J. H. Stewart, *A Documentary Survey of the French Revolution* (1951). J. M. Thompson, *The French Revolution** (1943), is a solid standard work. R. R. Palmer, *The Age of the Democratic Revolutions*, 2 vols. (1959–64), places the French Revolution in its broad European perspective. He published a revised and shortened version as *The World of the French Revolution* (1971). The same is done more briefly in N. Hampson, *The First European Revolution: 1776–1815** (1969), and, with a neo-Marxian approach, in E. J. Hobsbawm, *The Age of Revolution** (1962).

The Social History of the Revolution An excellent introduction to the social history of the Revolution is N. Hampson, *Social History of the French Revolution* (1962). The essays in J. Kaplow, ed., *New Perspectives on the French Revolution** (1965), are indispensable for an understanding of the social movement. A. Cobban, *The Social Interpretation of the French Revolution* (1964), is an important revisionary statement. On the role of the masses, see G. Rudé, *The Crowd in the French Revolution** (1959), which breaks new ground. E. Barber, *The Bourgeoisie in XVIIth Century France** (1955), discusses the background of bourgeois discontent. Valuable material on the aristocracy may be found in F. L. Ford, *Robe and Sword: The Regrouping of the French Aristocracy after Louis XIV** (1953).

Major French Interpretations of the Revolution Alexis de Tocqueville's *The Old Regime and the French Revolution** (1956) presents the classic view of the Revolution as the continuation of the centralizing tendencies of the Old Regime. G. Lefebvre, *The Coming of the French Revolution* (1947), gives an excellent picture of France in the first year of the Revolution and states precisely and clearly the nature and problem of the French Revolution as a whole. For a treatment from the republican side, see F. V. A. Aulard, *The French Revolution*, 4 vols. (1901, 1910). A. Mathiez, *The French Revolution** (1928), is a sympathetic leftist interpretation of the Revolution.

Special Topics Perhaps the best introduction to the Convention and the Reign of Terror is the brief study by J. M. Thompson, *Robespierre and the French Revolution** (1953). R. R. Palmer, *Twelve Who Ruled** (1941), is a fascinating account of the Reign of Terror written from a biographical approach. D. M. Greer, *The Incidence of Terror During the French Revolution* (1935), is a grisly statistical account of who was actually executed and how. The role of Paris in the Revolution is the subject of A. Soboul, *The Parisian Sans-Culottes and the French Revolution* (1964). On party politics during the Legislative Assembly and the Convention, see M. J. Sydenham, *The Girondins* (1961). The fall of the Jacobins and the period of the Directory are dealt with authoritatively in G. Lefebvre's *The Thermidoriens** (1937) and in the same author's *The Directory** (1946).

Napoleon and the Napoleonic Empire G. Bruun, *Europe and the French Imperium** (1938), in the *Rise of Modern Europe* series, is a good general introduction. Recent biographies of Napoleon include J. M. Thompson, *Napoleon Bonaparte* (1952), and F. Markham, *Napoleon** (1966). The best guide to interpretations of the period and perhaps the best book on Napoleon in English is P. Geyl, *Napoleon: For and Against** (1949). The best treatment in any language are the two volumes by G. Lefebvre, *Napoléon* (Eng. translation, 1969). On Napoleon's domestic policy, see R. Holtman, *The Napoleonic Revolution** (1967). Both R. B. Mowat, *The Diplomacy of Napoleon* (1924), and H. C. Deutsch, *The Genesis of Napoleonic Imperialism, 1801–1805* (1938), remain standard works on foreign policy. The best recent treatment of Napoleon's military career is D. Chandler, *The Campaigns of Napoleon* (1966). O. Connelly, *Napoleon's Satellite Kingdoms* (1965), deals with the rule of Napoleon and his relatives over most of Europe. G. H. Lovett, *Napoleon and the Birth of Modern Spain*, 2 vols. (1965), tells a dramatic story. Napoleon's relations with the two peripheral powers of Europe are treated in C. Oman, *Britain Against Napoleon* (1944), and in A. Palmer, *Napoleon in Russia* (1967).

24 The Search for Stability, 1815–1850

Le ventre législatif, by Honoré Daumier (1809–79). The political ideal of the middle class in the early nineteenth century has been aptly characterized as "government of the wealthy, for the wealthy, by the wealthy." The result is shown with biting irony in this lithograph of the French legislature in 1834. The title means "the legislative belly."

The unrest that had prevailed in Europe since the French Revolution did not end with the defeat of Napoleon. Another half-century was to pass before the Continent once again gained a semblance of stability. Many of Europe's troubles, of course, stemmed from the long and costly series of recent wars. But there were other causes of unrest. Politically, Europe continued to feel the effects of the issues first raised by the French Revolution—notably liberalism and nationalism. Intellectually, the years after Napoleon saw the flowering of the Age of Romanticism, with its protest against the rationalism of the Enlightenment. Economically and socially, the Continent in the first half of the nineteenth century began to feel in earnest the effects of the "Industrial Revolution," which had already begun in England in the eighteenth century (see Chapter 25). This chapter concentrates mainly on political and intellectual developments. But we must keep in mind that political tension was often the manifestation of underlying economic and social unrest. The rapid increase of Europe's population alone—from 192 million in 1800 to 274 million in 1850—could not help but have unsettling economic and political results. And the fact that more and more people now lived in cities did much to change the everyday lives of many Europeans.

Europe's search for stability after 1815 was marked by a contest between the forces of the past and the forces of the future. For a while it seemed as though the traditional agencies of power—the monarchs, the aristocracy, and the Church—might once again resume full control. But potent new forces were ready to oppose this relapse into the past. With the quickening of industrialization, there was now not only a middle class of growing size and significance but a wholly new class, the urban proletariat. Each class had its own political and economic philosophy—liberalism and socialism, respectively—which stood opposed to each other as well as to the traditional conservatism of the old order. It was inevitable that these rival classes and ideologies should clash. The resulting revolutions did not end until 1850. By that time the forces of the past were

still not defeated, but they were everywhere on the defensive.

Economic growth and ideological unrest were not the only causes for revolution in the early nineteenth century. There was also the force of nationalism, which made itself increasingly felt among Europeans everywhere. Nationalism as an awareness of belonging to a particular nationality was nothing new. What was new was the intensity that this awareness now assumed. There were still some signs of eighteenth-century cosmopolitanism, especially among the aristocracy. But for the mass of the people, nationalism became their most ardent emotion, and national unification or independence their most cherished aim.

Generally speaking, the early nineteenth century was a major phase in the slow change from an essentially aristocratic and agrarian society into an increasingly democratic and industrial society. The problem before political leaders everywhere was to give political expression to the economic and social changes resulting from the industrial transformation of Europe. In trying to do this, they hoped to bring some degree of stability to their deeply unsettled world.

THE RESTORATION OF THE OLD ORDER

The first task facing the allies after defeating Napoleon was to bring order to a continent that had been disrupted by two decades of war. Europe's statesmen in the main tried to restore conditions as they had been before the French Revolution. In domestic affairs they adopted the principle of "legitimacy"—that is, they brought back the rulers who had been ousted by revolution or war. In international affairs they tried to reconstruct the balance of power that had been upset by France. In retrospect this preoccupation with the past may seem shortsighted. But experience shows that most peace settlements are made with a view to the past rather than a vision of the future.

The Congress of Vienna

Peace conferences are usually dominated by a few leading statesmen. In

Two contemporary views of the Congress of Vienna. The caricature portrays Talleyrand and Castlereagh (left) deliberating whether to join the merry dance of England's allies, Frederick William III, Metternich, and Alexander I. The king of Saxony fears the loss of his crown, while the Republic of Genoa (right) plays up to the powers in the hope of keeping its independence. The other view, a group portrait of the peacemakers by Isabey, dignifies the occasion.

1814–15 the decisive figures were Austria's chancellor Prince Metternich, Britain's foreign minister Lord Castlereagh, Tsar Alexander I of Russia, the Prussian King Frederick William III, and France's foreign minister Prince Talleyrand. The fact that the vanquished French were thus able to make their voice heard shows the moderation and common sense of the victors.

The final peace with France was concluded at Paris in November 1815. France was the first to experience the principle of legitimacy. The new French king, Louis XVIII, was the brother of Louis XVI and the uncle of the dauphin, Louis XVII, who had died. Considering the many hardships the French had inflicted upon Europe, the peace settlement was remarkably lenient. France was reduced to its frontiers of 1790; it had to pay an indemnity; and it had to submit to an allied army of occupation.

The settlement with France, however, was only part of the work of restoration. A far more difficult task was to reorder the affairs of the rest of Europe. This was done at a separate conference in Vienna. The Congress of Vienna aroused high hopes among those Europeans who desired a stronger voice in the government of their respective countries or who, like the Germans and the Italians, longed for national unification. Their hopes were to be disappointed. The statesmen at Vienna, notably Metternich, had been deeply disturbed by the excesses of revolution and war and thus were firmly opposed to the forces of liberalism and nationalism in whose name these excesses had been committed.

Considering the conflicting aims of the powers, it is surprising how much was actually achieved at Vienna. Following the principle of legitimacy, the Bourbons were restored in Spain and Naples, and other legitimate rulers were put back on their thrones in the smaller Italian states. Yet the idea of legitimacy was frequently ignored, especially in the case of republics like Genoa and Venice, neither of which regained its independence. To maintain the balance of power and to keep France from repeating its recent aggression, the countries along its eastern frontier were either enlarged or otherwise strengthened. In the north, the Republic of Holland was given a king and was joined with the former Austrian Netherlands (Belgium). In place of the defunct Holy Roman Empire, a loosely joined confederation of thirty-nine states was set up in Germany. This was a far cry from the united nation that many Germans had hoped for. To provide an effective barrier to French expansion in the southeast, Switzerland was reestablished as an independent confederation and was declared perpetually neutral. The protective belt against France was completed by strengthening the Kingdom of Piedmont in northern Italy. In compensation for relinquishing Belgium, Austria received the Italian provinces of Lombardy and Venetia as well as the Illyrian provinces and the Tyrol (some of which Austria had ruled before 1789). This made Austria the leading power in Italy and the leading opponent of Italian unification.

Most of these changes caused no major difficulties, chiefly because the great powers saw eye-to-eye on them. One issue, however, caused much disagreement and at one point threatened to plunge the powers into war. That issue was Poland. A favorite scheme of Tsar Alexander I at Vienna was to pose as the "liberator" of Poland by setting up a Polish kingdom under Russian tutelage. The other powers objected to this: Prussia and Austria because they expected the return of those parts of Poland they had held before Napoleon, and England because it had no desire to see Russia grow too powerful. To gain his end,

Alexander promised the Prussians compensations elsewhere if they would support his Polish scheme. The result was a deadlock at Vienna, with England and Austria facing Russia and Prussia. An armed conflict was narrowly avoided when Talleyrand threw the weight of France behind England and Austria. The compromise that was reached was more advantageous to Prussia than to Russia. Russia received part of Poland, though less than hoped for, while Prussia got compensations in northern and western Germany that made it a powerful contender for leadership within the newly formed German Confederation and the

EUROPE IN 1815

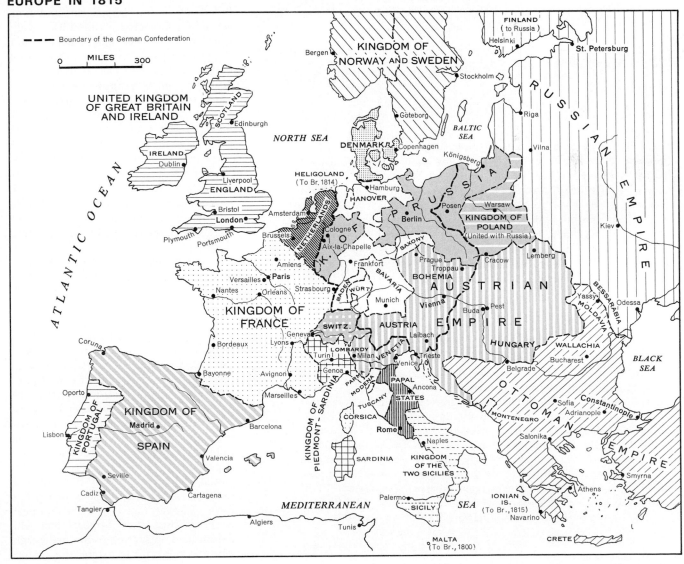

Prince Metternich
(1773–1859), by Sir Thomas
Lawrence.

guardian of Germany's interests along the Rhine.

Until we learned through first-hand experience the difficulty of setting the world in order after a major war, the Congress of Vienna used to come in for considerable criticism. It is true that the Vienna settlement ignored the stirrings of nationalism and the hopes for more popular government that the French Revolution had awakened. But more widespread than the middle-class dreams of nationalism and liberalism in 1815 was the hope for peace and order. It was in fulfilling this hope that the statesmen of Vienna scored their major success. There was no war among the great powers for forty years, and no war of worldwide dimensions for a whole century.

Metternich

PRO

He was a statesman of unusual proportions: the greatest foreign minister that Austria ever had, and one of the greatest masters of international politics in the history of the modern European states. . . . He lifted Austria from its deepest downfall to a proud height. . . . He had the greatest part in bringing it about that for thirty years Europe enjoyed comparative international peace, and that during this time, in the center of the continent, learning and art could have a period of the most salutary, quiet cultivation, capital and the spirit of enterprise could undergo a strong increase, and religion and religious communities could experience intensification and consolidation.

CON

The question has often been raised whether he was not rather a good diplomat than a statesman. The question appears to be thoroughly justified: he lacked virtually all the characteristics necessary to a real and great statesman—courage, resolution, strength, seriousness, the gift of breadth of vision, the correct evaluation of the fruitful forces of the future, in brief, everything creative. . . . All revolutions, he held, came not from economic misery or dissatisfaction with bad political conditions, but arose from the secret societies, visionaries and doctrinaires. The new, world-moving force, the idea of national self-determination, counted for nothing with him. Peoples, in his eyes, were "children or nervous women," "simpletons." Liberalism to him was a "spectre" which must be banished by forceful action, a mere fog, which would disappear of its own accord.

From Heinrich von Srbik, *Metternich, der Staatsmann und der Mensch* (Munich, 1925); and Viktor Bibl, *Metternich, der Dämon Oesterreichs* (Vienna, 1936), as quoted in Henry F. Schwarz, ed., *Metternich, the "Coachman of Europe"* (Boston: D. C. Heath, 1962), pp. 15–16, 22–23.

The "Holy Alliance" and the "Concert of Europe"

An indication of how sincerely the framers of the Vienna settlement sought peace may be seen in the arrangements they made to maintain it. The most famous of these, though the least important, was the "Holy Alliance" of Alexander I. The tsar had long shown signs that he thought of himself as a savior of the world. In this role he proposed to his fellow monarchs that they should conduct their relations with one another and with their subjects in a spirit of Christian love. To humor the tsar, most European rulers signed his "Holy Alliance"; but it never achieved any practical significance.

Of far greater importance than this "piece of sublime mysticism and nonsense" (as Castlereagh called it) was the Quadruple Alliance signed by England, Austria, Russia, and Prussia at the time of the final peace treaty with France in 1815. Its primary purpose was to prevent any future French violation of the peace settlement. But the powers also agreed to hold periodic conferences (ultimately to include France as well) to discuss matters of general European concern. This was an important innovation. For the first time statesmen seemed to realize that peace might be preserved by dealing with crises before they led to general war. The "Concert of Europe" was thus born.

As it turned out, however, this congress system was not a great success. At the very first meeting, at Aix-la-Chapelle in 1818, it became clear that the powers did not really see eye-to-eye on the fundamental purpose of their system of international government. To Castlereagh, the Quadruple Alliance was mainly an instrument for keeping France in its place and for maintaining international peace. To Alexander I, on the other hand, the Alliance seemed a convenient means of maintaining domestic peace as well. This difference was clearly revealed when Alexander proposed a new alliance that would guarantee not only the territorial *status quo* in Europe but also the existing form of government in every European country. This latter proposal met with determined opposition from Castlereagh, who did not want to extend the alliance "to include all objects, present and future."

The problem of whether to aid legitimate governments against revolution became acute shortly after Aix-la-Chapelle when a whole series of revolutions suddenly broke out over most of southern Europe. Here was a welcome opportunity for Alexander to repeat his plea for joint intervention. But Britain again voiced its opposition. And to underline his determination not to meddle in the affairs of other nations, Castlereagh refused to attend the Congress of Troppau (1820), at which such intervention was to be discussed.

With England absent, the other powers were able to adopt the "Troppau Protocol," which promised military aid to any government threatened by revolution at home. The effects of the Protocol became clear in 1821. In that year a third congress, at Laibach, commissioned Austria to send its forces into the Italian peninsula to put down the liberal insurrections there. Britain protested, but in vain. Similar action was taken at the next and last congress, which met at Verona in 1822. Again the continental powers, against England's objections, sanctioned the dispatch of a French force to put down a Spanish revolution in 1823.

Diplomacy by congress, so promising at first, had thus failed. It had failed because of a fundamental divergence among the victors over the issue of political change, with Britain opposing and the rest of the powers supporting intervention in the domestic affairs of other states to prevent liberal or national uprisings. There were other efforts to hold congresses, but England refused to attend.

A Wave of Reaction

The revolutions of the early 1820s, which are discussed below, were caused by the wave of reaction that followed the peace settlements of 1815. Wherever a legitimate monarch returned, he hastened to restore conditions exactly as they had been before he was ousted. In Spain and Naples the returning Bourbons abolished the liberal reforms that had been granted in 1812. In the Papal States, Pope Pius VII abolished French legal reforms, reestablished the Jesuits, revived the Inquisition, and put the Jews back into ghettos. In Piedmont, Victor Emmanuel I had the French botanical gardens torn up by the roots and the French furniture thrown out of the windows of his palace.

Elsewhere in Italy and over much of Europe the picture was the same. Both Frederick William III of Prussia and Francis I of Austria favored rigorous measures of repression in their respective countries. By tradition as well as actual power, Austria dominated the Diet of the new German Confederation at Frankfurt. Here it was Metternich who used his influence to suppress liberal or national stirrings wherever they appeared in Germany. As protests against this repressive "Metternich System" grew more vociferous, Austria and Prussia in 1819 pressured the Frankfurt Diet into adopting the so-called "Carlsbad Decrees," which strictly limited intellectual freedom, especially at the universities.

There were very few exceptions to this general rule of reaction. It was felt even in England, whose foreign policy at least was more enlightened than that of the continental powers. There was much unrest in postwar Britain, chiefly due to economic causes. Overproduction during the war caused prices to fall, which in turn led to lower wages and growing unemployment. To remedy Britain's ills,

Detail from a print showing British troops charging protesters at the Peterloo Massacre.

Johann Wolfgang von Goethe, from a medal by the French sculptor David d'Angers in 1829, three years before Goethe's death.

Illustration from Goethe's *The Sorrows of Young Werther,* by Daniel Chodowiecki (1726–1801).

a number of middle-class radicals advocated that the government be liberalized through parliamentary reform. But any agitation for reform was met by stern repression. In 1819, after the so-called Peterloo Massacre—when the constabulary of Manchester charged into a peaceful public meeting on parliamentary reform, causing many casualties—Parliament passed the repressive "Six Acts," which was England's version of the Carlsbad Decrees.

THE ROMANTIC PROTEST

Before considering the several waves of revolution that swept over Europe between 1820 and 1850, we must examine the intellectual climate in which these events took place. Much of the political turmoil of the generation after Napoleon had its counterpart and its cause in the spiritual ferment associated with the "Age of Romanticism."

The Main Characteristics of Romanticism

The term *Romanticism* defies clear definition. It differed not only from country to country but from Romanticist to Romanticist. It inspired reactionaries as well as revolutionaries. It made conservatives look longingly to the past and liberals look hopefully to the future. It meant escapism for some and a call to action for others. But with all these contradictions, there were certain characteristics that most Romanticists shared. Most prominent among these was their protest against the rationalism of the eighteenth century. The Enlightenment, with its emphasis on the rational nature of man and the rational order of the universe, had largely ignored irrational forces. It had been a brilliantly civilized but overly intellectual age. We have already seen some earlier reactions to this narrow rationalism. The French Revolution and the age of Napoleon had given further impetus to this protest. Reason, it seemed, was not the solution to man's problems that the *philosophes* had promised it to be. If reason had failed, what was there left to turn to but its opposite—faith? As the French writer Madame de Staël wrote in 1815: "I do not know exactly *what* we must believe, but I believe *that* we must believe! The eighteenth century did nothing but deny. The human spirit lives by its beliefs. Acquire faith through Christianity, or through German philosophy, or merely through enthusiasm, but believe in something!"

The desire "to believe in something" was characteristic of Romanticists everywhere. The typical Romantic followed his heart rather than his head. As the hero of Goethe's romantic novel *The Sorrows of Young Werther* exclaimed: "What I know, anyone can know—but my heart is my own, peculiar to myself." The Romantic was an individualist. The *philosophe* of the Enlightenment had spoken of Man, as though he were the same everywhere. The Romanticist stressed differences among men and felt that each should be a law unto himself. Much of Romantic writing was devoted to the strong personality, the hero, both in history and in fiction. One manifestation of Romanticism's interest in the individual was the growing vogue of autobiographies. One of the most revealing of these was Rousseau's famous *Confessions.* It was Rousseau also who regarded education as a means of realizing a person's individuality. The Enlightenment, with its belief in the essential sameness of human minds, had been interested in formal rather than individualized education. Rousseau held that the best education was practically no education at all. Each child should be left to develop his own abilities and potentialities.

While many Romanticists took a lively interest in the world about them, others used their imagination as a means of escape. To the eighteenth-century *philosophe* the world had appeared as a well-ordered mechanism. To the Romanticist, on the other hand, nature was a mysterious force whose moods expressed his innermost feelings: The Enlightenment had liked landscapes that showed the civilizing influence of man. Romanticism, by contrast, preferred its nature wild—waterfalls, the roaring sea, majestic mountains—or dreamlike—veiled in mist or bathed in mellow moonlight, the kind of landscape painted by Constable and Turner in England or Caspar David Friedrich in Germany.

"Cloister Graveyard in the Snow," Romantic painting by Caspar David Friedrich, 1810.

This Romantic love of the unusual or the unreal in nature was frankly escapist. As factories began to disfigure the landscape and cities began to encroach on their surrounding countryside, the Romanticist longed to return to an unspoiled and simple life. He abhorred the ugliness and artificiality of city life and extolled the virtues of country folk, whose customs, tales, and songs he hoped to preserve. The escapism of the Romanticist took other forms as well. Some Romantic writers let their imagination roam in faraway, exotic places; others preferred to dwell in the realm of ghosts and the supernatural. Still others escaped into the realm of religious emotion.

Romanticism and Religion

The close relationship between Romanticism and religion is obvious, since both stressed the emotional, irrational side of man. Catholicism in particular answered the Romanticist's need to "believe in something." The mystery of Catholic theology and the splendor of its ritual provided just the kind of emotional experience the Romanticist craved. As a result, many romanticists returned or were converted to Catholicism, and the Catholic Church, which had been on the defensive since the French Revolution, was able to reassert itself. In 1814, the Jesuit order was officially restored. In 1816, divorce, which had been permitted in France since the Revolution, was once again abolished. In Spain and parts of Italy, the Inquisition returned. And almost everywhere on the Continent, education once again became a monopoly of the clergy.

Veneration of the Past

The revival of religious interest was closely allied to the general veneration the Romanticists showed for the past. The Enlightenment had derived much of its inspiration from the ancient Greeks and Romans. To the eighteenth century their civilizations had appeared particularly reasonable and attractive. The intervening period, from about 400 to 1200 A.D., had been merely "Dark Ages" of ignorance and superstition. It was to these hitherto neglected centuries that the Romanticists now turned, attracted by the mystery, the glamor, and the grandeur that had survived in medieval castles and cathedrals.

The Romantic interest in the Middle Ages, by arousing an interest in the past, also awakened a general interest in the study of history. The eighteenth century

Cultural nationalism: Russian peasants dancing, nineteenth-century Russian print.

The Ingredients of Nationalism

1. A certain defined (often vaguely) unit of territory (whether possessed or coveted).

2. Some common cultural characteristics such as language (or widely understood languages), customs, manners, and literature (folk tales and lore are a beginning). If an individual believes he shares these, and wishes to continue sharing them, he is usually said to be a member of the nationality.

3. Some common dominant social (as Christian) and economic (as capitalistic or, recently, communistic) institutions.

4. A common independent or sovereign government (type does not matter) or the desire for one. The "principle" that each nationality should be separate and independent is involved here.

5. A belief in a common history (it can be invented) and in a common origin (often mistakenly conceived to be racial in nature).

6. A love or esteem for fellow nationals (not necessarily as individuals).

7. A devotion to the entity (however little comprehended) called the nation, which embodies the common territory, culture, social and economic institutions, government, and the fellow nationals, and which is at the same time (whether organism or not) more than their sum.

8. A common pride in the achievements (often the military more than the cultural) of this nation and a common sorrow in its tragedies (particularly its defeats).

9. A disregard for or hostility to other (not necessarily all) like groups, especially if these prevent or seem to threaten the separate national existence.

10. A hope that the nation will have a great and glorious future (usually in territorial expansion) and become supreme in some way (in world power if the nation is already large).

Boyd C. Shafer, *Nationalism: Myth and Reality* (New York: Harcourt Brace Jovanovich, 1955), pp. 7–8.

had viewed the world as a well-ordered, static mechanism that had been set in motion at some specific time in the past. To the Romanticist, on the other hand, the world was an organism that had grown slowly, changed constantly, and was still growing and changing. In an effort to retrace this gradual change, historians in the early nineteenth century developed a careful method of inquiry, using historical sources—documents and other remains—to gain a truer understanding of the past. Historical scholarship, as we know it today, originated in the Age of Romanticism.

Nationalism and Conservatism

One of the things a study of the past teaches us is that mankind has gradually come to be divided into separate groups, living in common geographic areas, usually speaking the same language, and sharing the same historic experiences. In time, all these elements together create a common feeling that may be called "national consciousness." Some such feeling had existed in countries like England, France, and even Germany since medieval or early modern times. To transform this national consciousness into nationalism, however, something more was needed—a sense not only of being different from, but of being superior to, other national groups. This pride in one's nationality is largely a state of mind. Its first modern manifestations may be seen in the French Revolution and the Napoleonic wars. With its appeal to the emotions, this new nationalism fitted quite naturally into the climate of Romanticism. To the Romanticist, nationalism, like religion, provided something in which he could believe. Unfortunately, however, with the memories of the recent wars still fresh in their minds, some Romanticists, notably in Germany, tended to express their nationalism in unpleasantly strident tones.

Nationalism in the early nineteenth century was a revolutionary creed. Since it aimed at the liberation of peoples from foreign domination or their unification into a common state, it posed a threat to the established order. In defense of that order, a new political philosophy had already appeared during the French Rev-

A German peasant girl in her native costume; painting by Ludwig Emil Grimm, 1828.

olution, the philosophy of conservatism. Its leading proponent was the Englishman Edmund Burke. We have seen how Burke, in his *Reflections on the Revolution in France,* had warned against the ultimate consequences of that upheaval. He had in particular attacked the revolutionaries for their eighteenth-century belief that man was innately good and endowed with certain natural rights. Far from having any natural rights, man, according to Burke, merely inherited the rights and duties that existed within his society. Since these rights and duties had developed through the ages, they constituted an inheritance that no single generation had the right to destroy. Burke also rebuked the eighteenth-century idea that government was the result of a contract among its citizens. Instead, he held that the state was an organism, a mystic community, to which the individual must submit.

Burke's conservatism, with its veneration for the past, its organic view of society, and its prediction of many of the dire consequences of the French Revolution, had great appeal to the generation after 1815. Like nationalism, conservatism greatly attracted the Romanticists, and Burke found ardent proponents and imitators on the Continent. Initially, conservatism and nationalism were often in conflict. Nationalism, to achieve its ends, was not averse to revolution, the very thing most conservatives abhorred. Conservatism, on the other hand, in its opposition to radical change, often became indistinguishable from outright reaction, which opposed change of any kind. Only gradually did it become clear that nationalism, once it had reached its goals, tended to become conservative in order to defend its gains.

There was one point, however, on which conservatives and nationalists agreed from the beginning, and that was their admiration of the state as the highest social organism. The leading advocate of the supreme importance of the state was the German philosopher Georg Wilhelm Friedrich Hegel. Like the conservatives, Hegel viewed the state as an organism that had evolved historically. Only in submission to a powerful state, Hegel held, could the individual achieve his true freedom. To be strong, a state must be unified, preferably under the authority of a monarch. Each state, according to Hegel, had its own particular spirit, and by developing that spirit it contributed to the World-Spirit. "The State," Hegel wrote, "is the Divine Idea as it exists on earth." As such it is not bound by the usual laws of morality; its only judge is history. The course of history had evolved in three stages: the Oriental, in which only a despot was free; the Greek and the Roman, in which a few were free; and finally the Germanic, in which all would be free. It was his stress on the unique position of Germany and of Prussia that endeared Hegel to German nationalists.

The Impact of Romanticism

Romanticism, as this brief analysis shows, was a bundle of contradictions. It helps us understand the conservatives, who made the Vienna settlement, as well as the liberals who tried to overthrow it. It was a movement affecting all provinces of human life and thought. It was particularly strong in the arts, not only in literature but in all forms of artistic expression, especially music. The influence of Romanticism was deep and widespread. All the nations of Europe contributed to it, and it also was a vital force in the United States. Politically, America during the nineteenth century continued its emancipation from Europe. But culturally there were not two worlds—the New World continued to be influenced by, and continued to influence, the Old.

The Romantic protest, or at least the Romantic attitude, did not, of course, end with the Romantic era. Its influence is felt to the present day. Romanticism has been criticized as a rebellion against reason, against measure, against discipline, and a surrender to the murky passions and emotions of the human heart. The old Goethe, himself a Romantic in his youth, looked back with nostalgia to the reasonableness and clarity of eighteenth-century classicism. "Classic," he said, "is that which is healthy; romantic that which is sick." Romanticism, it is true, did destroy the clear simplicity and unity of thought that had prevailed during the Enlightenment. There was no longer one dominant philosophy that

James Monroe by Gilbert Stuart.

expressed all the aims and ideals of western civilization as rationalism had done during the eighteenth century. But then rationalism had provided a narrow, one-sided view of the world, ignoring whole provinces of human experience. Romanticism did much to correct that unbalance. By insisting that the world was not the simple machine it had seemed since Newton and that man was not a mere cog in that machine, Romanticism provided a more complex but also a truer view of the world. With its emphasis on evolution throughout the universe, and its stress on the creativity and uniqueness of the individual, Romanticism came as a breath of fresh air after the rigid formalism of the Enlightenment. This was its major and lasting contribution.

THE FIRST WAVE OF REVOLUTIONS, 1820–29

The restoration of the old order saved Europe from major international wars, but it was also responsible for the almost unbroken series of domestic wars and revolutions that lasted for more than a generation. We have already noted the unrest in Germany and England shortly after 1815. In France, the assassination in 1820 of the Duke of Berri, who was in line to be Louis XVIII's successor, was the signal for abandoning the moderate course Louis had tried to steer. More serious, however, than these sporadic acts of violence was the whole wave of revolutions that swept through southern Europe in the 1820s.

Revolt in Southern Europe

The first of these revolutions broke out in Spain in 1820, where the army rebelled against being sent to South America to put down the revolutions in the Spanish colonies. From Spain revolution spread to Portugal and somewhat later to Italy. In every case it was the army that took the initiative, forcing reactionary monarchs to grant liberal constitutions. The situation in Italy was particularly complicated. The Italian peninsula was still divided into a number of sovereign states of varying size, the most important being the Kingdom of the Two Sicilies in the South, the Papal States in the center, and the Kingdom of Piedmont in the North. In addition, Austria ruled directly over the northern provinces of Lombardy and Venetia and exerted influence over the rest of Italy indirectly through Austrian or pro-Austrian rulers in many of the smaller Italian states. The revolutions in Italy, therefore, were directed not merely against the reactionary policy of the various local rulers but against the alien influence of Austria in Italian affairs; the motives of the Italian revolutionaries were national as well as liberal.

As a result of these upheavals, the old order in much of southern Europe seemed to be on the way out. But the initial success of the revolutions did not last. The revolutionaries everywhere constituted only a small minority, finding little support among the apathetic mass of illiterate peasants. In addition, there was much disagreement among the leaders when it came to establishing more liberal regimes. But more harmful than the lack of popular following and the

The Monroe Doctrine

In the wars of the European powers in matters relating to themselves we have never taken any part, nor does it comport with our policy so to do. It is only when our rights are invaded or seriously menaced that we resent injuries or make preparation for our defense. With the movements in this hemisphere we are of necessity more immediately connected, and by causes which must be obvious to all enlightened and impartial observers. The political system of the allied powers is essentially different in this respect from that of America. . . . We owe it, therefore, to candor and to the amicable relations existing between the United States and those powers to declare that we should consider any attempt on their part to extend their system to any portion of this hemisphere as dangerous to our peace and safety. With the existing colonies or dependencies of any European power we have not interfered and shall not interfere. But with the governments who have declared their independence and maintained it, and whose independence we have, on great consideration and on just principles, acknowledged, we could not view any interposition for the purpose of oppressing them, or controlling in any other manner their destiny, by any European power in any other light than as the manifestation of an unfriendly disposition toward the United States.

From President Monroe's Message to Congress, December 2, 1823.

inexperience of the revolutionaries was the intervention of outside forces. Austria, with the blessing of Prussia and Russia, intervened in Italy in 1821, and France intervened in Spain in 1823. Only in Portugal was a semblance of parliamentary government maintained, thanks to the support of Great Britain.

The Monroe Doctrine

With reaction triumphant, there was now a possibility that the powers might try to help Spain recover its colonies in Latin America. Largely under the impact of the French Revolution and the Napoleonic conquest of their mother country, the Spanish colonies, beginning in 1810, had followed the example of the United States and declared their independence. In this they had the sympathy of both the United States and Great Britain, whose commercial interests were eager to gain access to the South American market. In 1822, Britain's new foreign secretary, George Canning, proposed a joint declaration by England and the United States to oppose any European intervention against the Spanish colonies.

But the United States was concerned not only about South America but about the possible extension of Russian influence southward from Alaska and about England's designs on Cuba. President Monroe, therefore, decided to act on his own. In a message to Congress in December 1823, he warned that any attempt by the powers of Europe to extend their influence over the Western Hemisphere would be considered a "manifestation of an unfriendly disposition toward the United States." The immediate effectiveness of the Monroe Doctrine, of course, depended on the backing of the British navy rather than on the insignificant power of the United States. For that reason, Canning was justified in his famous boast that he "called the New World into existence to redress the balance of the Old."

The Greek War of Independence

The revolutions in the Iberian and Italian peninsulas, in their aims as well as their failures, had all been quite similar. But the most important revolution of the 1820s, the Greek War of Independence, was quite a different matter. That war was almost entirely motivated by nationalism. And while the other revolutions failed largely because of outside intervention, the Greek revolt succeeded because the powers helped rather than hindered it. The Greek revolt against the Ottoman Empire was merely the latest chapter in the slow disintegration of that sprawling state. The Serbs had already staged a successful revolt after 1815. Greek nationalism had been gathering force for some time, especially among the "Island" Greeks, whose far-flung commercial contacts had put them in touch with western ideas. The Island Greeks had founded a secret society, the *Hetàiria Philikĕ*, and it was this society that

Mahmoud II (1784–1839), Sultan of Turkey at the time of the Greek revolts.

inspired the uprising in early 1821 that started the war against Turkey.

The Greeks, however, were no match for the Turks, especially after the sultan called in his Egyptian vassal, Mehemet Ali, to help him. The great powers, though they watched events in Greece closely, at first were kept from intervention through mutual jealousies. But when the very existence of the Greeks seemed at stake they realized that something had to be done.

Public opinion in the West had favored the Greek cause all along, and the pressure of this "Philhellenism" was partly responsible for the intervention of the powers. In 1827, British, French, and Russian squadrons destroyed the combined Turkish and Egyptian navies in the battle of Navarino. The following year, Russia declared war on Turkey. After brief fighting, the Turks had to submit to the Treaty of Adrianople (1829). Its terms were moderate, except that Russia was given a protectorate over the Danubian principalities of Moldavia and Wallachia, which later became Rumania. After some further negotiations, Greece was set up as an independent kingdom.

The Decembrist Revolt in Russia

While the Greek uprising was still going on, there had been one other attempt at revolution, this time against the most powerful stronghold of reaction, the tsarist regime in Russia. Like the Spanish and Italian revolts, it failed. The enigmatic Alexander I, who liked to pose as a liberal while actually becoming more and more reactionary, left the direction of Russian affairs largely in the hands of his efficient but equally reactionary adviser, Alexis Arakcheiev, who used Alexander's fear of revolution to build a regime of ruthless political oppression.

This policy of oppression naturally aroused the opposition of the few liberal elements in Russia. Many members of the upper class had come in contact with western liberal ideas during the wars against Napoleon and the subsequent allied occupation of France. These officers founded several secret societies. An opportunity for the conspirators to act came in December 1825, when Alexander

suddenly died and there was some doubt about which of his brothers would succeed him. The revolt failed, however, because it was mostly confined to the army and its leaders were disunited and lacked popular following. Even so, this so-called Decembrist Revolt was significant. Earlier uprisings in Russia had been entirely spontaneous. Here, for the first time, was a revolt that had been planned by a small minority with a definite program. The Decembrist uprising served as an inspiration to all later revolutionary movements in Russia. Meanwhile, the December events inspired in Alexander's successor, Nicholas I, an almost pathological fear of revolution. For thirty years he remained the leading proponent of reaction abroad and repression at home.

THE SECOND WAVE OF REVOLUTIONS, 1830–33

The first wave of revolutions after 1815, far from upsetting the old order, merely seemed to have strengthened its hold. The uprisings had been too sporadic, the work of small army cliques with no following among the mass of the people. The second wave of revolutions was different. It started among the people of Paris, and from there it spread over most of Europe, leaving behind some important political changes.

The French Revolution of 1830

The first years of the restored Bourbon monarchy in France had been peaceful ones. Louis XVIII had tried sincerely to rally his deeply divided country. But he found it increasingly difficult to do so. To the liberals, led by Lafayette, the new constitution, the Charter, with its limited franchise did not go far enough. To the royalists, or "Ultras," led by the king's brother, the Count of Artois, the Charter was the source of all France's ills. Up to 1820, Louis had been able to maintain a moderate, middle-of-the-road course. But after the assassination of the Duke of Berri, the royalist faction gained the upper hand and moderation came to an end.

Louis XVIII died in 1824 and was succeeded by the Count of Artois, as

Nicholas I, Tsar of Russia, (1825–55); sketch by Sir Edwin Henry Landseer (1802–73).

Louis XVIII, painting by F. Gerard, 1823.

Charles X of France portrayed as a reactionary crab moving backward; anonymous caricature, 1830.

Charles X. Reaction now went into full force. While liberal opposition became more outspoken, the government's policy became more repressive. In 1829 Charles appointed as his first minister one of the most notorious reactionaries, the Prince de Polignac. In the past the king had always been careful to enlist parliamentary backing. This situation now changed. In the spring of 1830, when the Chamber turned against the government, Charles simply dismissed it. And when new elections brought in another liberal majority, Polignac had the king promulgate the Five Ordinances, which dissolved the Chamber, imposed strict censorship, and changed the electoral law so that the government in the future would be sure of a favorable majority.

Discontent with this arbitrary policy came to a head in the July revolution of 1830. The hope of the men who fought on the barricades—workers, students, some members of the middle class—was for a republic. But this was not what the more moderate liberals wanted. Much as they hated the high-handed government of Charles X, they were equally opposed to a republic, which recalled the violent phase of the earlier French Revolution. It was due to the careful machinations of these moderates that France emerged from its July revolution as a constitutional monarchy rather than a republic.

The new king was Louis Philippe, Duke of Orléans. Though a relative of the Bourbons, he had stayed clear of the royalists and had affected a thoroughly bourgeois mode of life. Events in France, of course, violated the *status quo* established in 1814 and 1815. But the other powers had been taken too much by surprise and were too little united to take any action. Their attention, furthermore, was soon caught by events elsewhere, as the French example set off a whole series of revolutions in other countries.

Revolution in Belgium

The first to follow the lead of France was Belgium. Its union with Holland at Vienna had not proved very successful. The only area in which the two countries got along was in economic matters, and even there the Belgians in time developed grievances. Still, there had been hardly any agitation for Belgian independence prior to 1830; seldom has nationalism arisen so suddenly and found such quick fulfillment. In August 1830, in part inspired by events in Paris, rioting broke out in Brussels. King William I tried to save the situation by granting a separate administration for Belgium, but he was too late. The Dutch troops sent to quell the uprising were quickly defeated; but the ultimate fate of Belgium depended on the attitude of the great powers. Although France and England looked favorably upon the new state, the three eastern powers were hostile. Since Austria and Russia were preoccupied with disturbances in Italy and Poland, however, any aid to Holland was out of the question. In December 1830 the five powers agreed to recognize the independence of Belgium. The new state was to remain perpetually neutral.

Europe in Revolt

France and Belgium were the only nations in which the revolutions of 1830 achieved any lasting success. But there was hardly a country that did not feel the tremors of revolution. Across the Rhine the events in Paris caused wild excitement among German intellectuals, though there was little echo among the people. Some of the smaller states rid themselves of rulers who were particularly corrupt and vicious, and others won moderately liberal constitutions.

Southern Europe, the scene of revolution a decade earlier, was also aroused by the news from Paris. Struggles among rival claimants to the thrones in Spain and Portugal, together with disturbances fostered by liberals, created widespread confusion. Both nations finally emerged, at least nominally, as constitutional monarchies. In Italy, where secret societies such as the *Carbonari*, or "charcoal burners," were flourishing, revolutions broke out in several states. The revolutionaries hoped to receive aid from France, and had they done so they might have won. But Louis Philippe could not afford to antagonize Austria, and Metternich had a free hand. Again Austrian troops restored the legitimate rulers, who then took revenge against the insurgents.

The Polish Insurrection of 1830

The bloodiest struggle of all in 1830 took place in Poland. The Kingdom of Poland already had been a source of constant trouble to Alexander I. Under Nicholas I tension mounted further. Like revolutionaries elsewhere, the Polish insurgents had founded a number of secret societies to propagate nationalism and to prepare for revolution. When rumors reached Poland in 1830 that Nicholas was planning to use Polish forces to help put down the revolutions in France and Belgium, the conspirators decided to act. Had the Polish people stood united, the revolt might have succeeded. But the revolutionaries were split into moderates and radicals, with neither faction having much following among the mass of the peasants. The hope, furthermore, that England and France would come to their aid proved vain. Even so, it took almost a year before Russia was able to subdue the rebellious Poles and impose a regime of severe repression. For two generations Russian Poland remained a sad and silent land.

Reform in Great Britain

There was one other country besides France and Belgium where unrest in 1830 and after led to major political changes. More than any other nation, Great Britain had been feeling the effects of rapid industrialization. The change from an agrarian to an industrial society could not help but have political repercussions. That England was able to make this adjustment without a revolution was due to its long parliamentary tradition and able political leadership. Britain did share in the initial wave of reaction after 1815. With George IV, the worst of George III's sons, succeeding his father in 1820, and with the Tories in control of Parliament, little relief was in sight.

Beginning in 1822, however, a new and more enlightened element within the Tory Party became aware of the political implications of economic change. The first sign that some relief from repression was imminent came with the reform of Britain's criminal code after 1822, which drastically reduced the number of capital crimes. In 1824 the Combination Acts, forbidding workers to organize, were repealed. In 1828 a new Corn Law modified the duties on foreign grain, thus lowering the price of bread. The most important reform of the 1820s, however, was the establishment of religious equality. In 1828 the Test and Corporations Acts, which barred Protestant dissenters from holding state offices, were repealed; and in 1829 the Emancipation Bill permitted Catholics to sit in Parliament.

In most of these reforms the liberal element among the Tories had the support of the Whigs. The leaders of the Whig Party differed little from their Tory rivals in social background and outlook. But while the main backing of the Tory Party continued to come from the landed gentry and the established church, the Whigs were supported by the rising merchant and manufacturing class. For that reason they became the main advocates of parliamentary reform. To the Whigs, parliamentary reform meant giving a fairer share of representation in Parliament to the well-to-do middle class. This they were finally able to achieve in 1832.

The Great Reform Bill of 1832 was passed only after domestic unrest had at

The Great Reform Bill of 1832 is the subject of this contemporary cartoon. Political corruption is put through the "reform mill" to emerge as a triumphant Britannia.

THE REFORM BILL.

times brought England to the verge of revolution. Under the new bill, the franchise was extended to about half again as many voters and proper representation was given to the new industrial towns. The workers and the poor were still left without a vote, but this was no different from the situation that prevailed elsewhere in Europe. Even though there was no change in Britain's form of government in 1832, the Reform Bill was every bit as much a revolution as the overthrow of Charles X had been in France. Both were significant stages in the rise to power of the middle, or upper middle, class.

East and West

Because the revolutions in the early 1830s were successful only in western Europe, they helped widen the already existing gap between the powers of the East and the West. France and England, constitutional monarchies both, had seen to it that the revolution in Belgium succeeded. Austria, Russia, and Prussia, still essentially autocratic, had suppressed the uprisings in Germany, Italy, and Poland. The main reason for the success of revolutions in the West had been their popular support. The middle class had taken the lead, but it had been aided by the urban lower class. East of the Rhine, revolutions had found little popular backing and had failed. Industrialization, which had bolstered the ranks of the middle and lower classes in the West, had as yet made little headway in the East. But while the revolutions in western Europe had been successful, they had chiefly benefited the middle class. The workers, who had done much of the rioting and fighting, were left with empty hands. In the West as in the East, therefore, the revolutions of 1830 left much unfinished. Here is the main cause for the third and largest wave of revolutions, which swept across Europe in 1848 and 1849.

THE THIRD WAVE OF REVOLUTIONS, 1848–49

The third wave of revolutions lasted for over a year and affected most of Europe.

Among the major powers, only England and Russia were spared, though England came close to revolt. There were, of course, countless differences among all these upheavals, but there were also some notable similarities. Generally speaking, the revolutions of 1848 were a further attempt to undo the settlement of 1815. In Italy, Germany, Austria, and Hungary the fundamental grievance was still the lack of national freedom and unity. There was also the desire for more liberal governments and for the abolition of the many vestiges of feudalism that still remained. But these were secondary aims. Nationalism was the dominant concern of the revolutionaries in central Europe. In western Europe, neither nationalism nor feudalism was any longer an issue. There the chief aim of revolution was the extension of political power beyond the upper middle class. The revolutionaries did not always agree on how far this liberalization should go. The middle class wanted merely to widen the franchise to include the more substantial citizens, whereas the working class wanted political democracy for everyone and some measure of social and economic democracy as well. With the revolutions of 1848, socialism for the first time became an issue in modern politics.

Aside from these political causes, there were also economic reasons for the outbreak of revolutions. Despite, or because of, the unprecedented economic growth of Europe since 1815, there had been several severe economic crises, the latest in 1846–47. These upsets particularly affected the lower classes. The small artisan was fighting against the competition of large-scale industry, which threatened to deprive him of his livelihood. At the same time, the industrial workers in the new factories were eking out a marginal existence on a minimum wage. There were also periodic crises in agriculture, primarily as a result of crop failures. Economic hardship, then, in many cases preceded and helped precipitate political action.

There were other common features among the revolutions of 1848. They were all essentially urban. The leaders came from the middle class, with lawyers, journalists, and professors especially prominent. Much of the actual

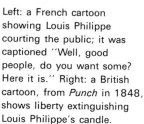

Left: a French cartoon showing Louis Philippe courting the public; it was captioned "Well, good people, do you want some? Here it is." Right: a British cartoon, from *Punch* in 1848, shows liberty extinguishing Louis Philippe's candle.

fighting was done by the urban lower classes, by artisans and workers. Students also played an important part. None of the revolutions had any agrarian program beyond the abolition of feudal dues and services. Once these had been abolished, the conservative peasants withdrew what little initial support they had provided the revolutions.

Europe, in the spring of 1848, was discontented and restless. The causes of discontent differed from middle class to workers to peasants. But so long as these three groups stood united, it was easy for them to overthrow the old order. When it came to building something new, however, all the differences among the revolutionaries asserted themselves. The history of revolution in 1848 is a frustrating tale of missed opportunities.

The "July Monarchy" in France

The key nation in the events of 1848 was again France. The reasons for the failure of Louis Philippe's government are not too obvious. France under the "July Monarchy" (so-called after the month of its birth in 1830) was prosperous and progressive, with a liberal constitution, a free press, and a competent king. Louis Philippe had all the bourgeois virtues—he was thrifty, kindly, and

industrious. He was served by capable ministers, and until about 1846 trade and industry flourished. France, which had fallen behind England economically as a result of the French Revolution, had started to regain some lost ground. Yet with all these advantages, the July Monarchy was far from popular. The French, it has been said, were bored. They were bored by a colorless king, bored by a dull domestic policy that favored the wealthy, and bored by a foreign policy of peace and compromise. Most Frenchmen still smarted from the defeat of Napoleon. Only a glorious foreign policy could wipe out that humiliation. But no sooner was there an opportunity for such a policy than the genuine pacifism of Louis Philippe spoiled it.

In time the opposition against Louis Philippe became crystallized in three groups: the Liberals, the Bonapartists, and the Republicans. The Liberals wanted a further extension of the franchise. The Bonapartists hoped to overthrow Louis Philippe in favor of Prince Louis Napoleon, the emperor's nephew, who promised to restore to France some of the glories associated with his uncle's name. As for Republicanism, it had its roots in the failure of the radicals to assert themselves in 1830. As the number of workers increased, Republican feeling became more widespread. And since the workers also began to make economic demands, Republicanism gradually became tinged with socialism.

Discontent in France mounted after 1846, primarily for economic reasons. In the fall of that year, Europe was hit by a serious depression. In France, as elsewhere, rising prices and growing unemployment particularly affected the workers. Yet the government made no effort to help them, and the lower classes became more and more restive. To ease the situation, Liberals and Republicans joined forces in the summer of 1847 to hold a series of political meetings to discuss parliamentary reform. In February 1848 the government's ban against such a meeting brought on a peaceful popular demonstration. As a precaution, the king called out the army, and in the ensuing confrontation several of the demonstrators were killed. Blood had been spilled and the revolution was on. Major bloodshed was avoided by Louis Philippe's decision to abdicate and go to England. On February 25 a republic was proclaimed.

The Second French Republic

In a very short time and with little loss of life, a tremendous change had been brought about. The people who had been cheated out of the fruits of revolution in 1830 now had reached their goal; the days of upper-middle-class predominance seemed to be over. But this radical phase of the revolution did not last. The new provisional government was faced with tremendous difficulties. Paris was in a constant state of turmoil, with several political factions jockeying for position. Some wanted to concentrate all efforts on domestic reforms; others were more concerned with carrying the revolution beyond the French borders. The socialists in the government proclaimed the right to work and introduced a system of "national workshops," which had been advocated by the socialist Louis Blanc (see p. 585).

In this period of confusion, the elections to the new National Assembly came as a severe shock to the radicals. Of some 900 delegates elected, fewer than 100 supported the radical Republi-

cans. The main reason for this sudden shift lay with the French peasantry, whose aims had been largely met by the first French Revolution and who had subsequently become staunchly conservative.

But the radical element did not intend to give up without a fight. There now followed a series of clashes between the radicals in the provisional government and the moderate National Assembly. Tension came to a head in the bloody "June Days," when the Assembly dissolved the workshops, which it considered breeding-grounds of discontent. The workers again took to the barricades, and the resulting street fighting was the most savage ever, causing thousands of casualties. By the end of June 1848 the back of lower-class resistance had been broken, and the middle class once again could make its wishes prevail. The Constitution of the Second French

The February Days in Paris

I spent the whole afternoon in walking about Paris. Two things in particular struck me: the first was, I will not say the mainly, but the uniquely and exclusively popular character of the revolution that had just taken place; the omnipotence it had given to the people properly so-called—that is to say, the classes who work with their hands—over all others. . . . Although the working classes had often played the leading part in the events of the First Revolution, they had never been the sole leaders and masters of the State. . . . The Revolution of July [1830] was effected by the people, but the middle class had stirred it up and led it, and secured the principal fruits of it. The Revolution of February, on the contrary, seemed to be made entirely outside the bourgeoisie and against it. . . .

Throughout this day, I did not see in Paris a single one of the former agents of the public authority; not a soldier, not a gendarme, not a policeman; the National Guard itself had disappeared. The people alone bore arms, guarded the public buildings, watched, gave orders, punished; it was an extraordinary and terrible thing to see in the sole hands of those who possessed nothing, all this immense town, so full of riches, or rather this great nation: for, thanks to centralization, he who reigns in Paris governs France. Hence the terror of all the other classes was extreme; I doubt whether at any period of the revolution it had been so great, and I should say that it was only to be compared to that which the civilized cities of the Roman Empire must have experienced when they suddenly found themselves in the power of the Goths and Vandals.

The Recollections of Alexis de Tocqueville, trans. by Alexander Teixeira de Mattos, ed. by J. P. Mayer (New York: Columbia University Press, 1949), pp. 72–75.

Republic set up a single legislative Chamber of Representatives, to be elected by universal male suffrage. Executive power was vested in a powerful president, to be elected by the people.

The first presidential election took place in December 1848. There were five candidates, among them Prince Louis Napoleon. The French middle class and the French peasants wanted a strong man as president, a man who would banish the "red peril" of socialism. Such a man, they felt, was Louis Napoleon. The first Napoleon had taken over the reins of government after a similar revolution fifty years ago, and he had brought order at home and glory abroad. Why should history not repeat itself? The victory of Louis Napoleon by an overwhelming majority was thus due chiefly to the glamor of his name. A sign that he was ready to live up to that name came four years later, in 1852, when he proclaimed himself Emperor Napoleon III. History seemed about to repeat itself.

The Italian Revolution of 1848

History seemed also to be repeating itself in Italy. Revolution had broken out in Sicily as early as January 1848. From there it had spread north. By the middle of March, most of the Italian states except Lombardy and Venetia had won liberal constitutions.

The origins of the Italian *Risorgimento* (meaning "resurrection") can be traced back to the eighteenth century. The agitation for national liberation and unification had gained momentum during the Napoleonic period. But the hopes of Italian patriots and reformers, as we have seen, had been dashed repeatedly since 1815. Despite the failure of the uprisings of 1830, however, Italian intellectuals had continued making plans for the future of their country. Out of the maze of their projects, three main schemes had emerged: Giuseppe Mazzini, a noted Liberal and an ardent Italian nationalist, advocated the formation of a free, united, and republican Italy. Vincenzo Gioberti, a moderate Liberal and a priest, objected to the republican and centralizing tendencies of Mazzini and instead proposed

a federated monarchy with a liberal constitution, headed by the pope. The election of a reputedly liberal pope, Pius IX, in 1846 gave special emphasis to Gioberti's proposals. A third scheme for the future of Italy looked forward to Italian unification under the leadership of the house of Piedmont-Sardinia. Here, then, were three different schemes for the liberation and unification of Italy. Each was tried, and each failed. The fact that there were several plans, rather than one, in part accounts for that failure.

With Austria the main obstacle to Italian unification, the outbreak of revolution in Vienna (see p. 563) naturally aided the Italian cause. As insurrections broke out in the Austrian provinces of Lombardy and Venetia, Charles Albert of Piedmont, in March 1848, gave way to popular pressure and declared war on Austria. Contingents from other Italian states joined the Piedmontese. Pius IX, however, could ill afford to support a war against Austria, the leading Catholic power of Europe. His neutrality and subsequent flight from Rome dashed the hopes of those who had looked to the pope as the leader of Italian liberation.

The war of Piedmont against Austria likewise ended in failure. The forces of Charles Albert were no match for the

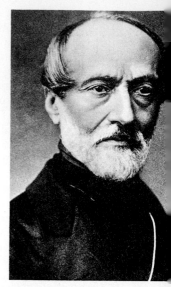

Giuseppe Mazzini (1805-72), Italian nationalist.

Dutch caricature of 1852 showing Pope Pius IX removing his "savior's" mask and revealing his true face when he resumed power in 1849.

seasoned troops of the Austrian general Radetzky, especially after the Austrian government had succeeded in putting down its revolution at home. The final defeat of Charles Albert at Novara in March 1849 ended, for the time being, the chance of uniting Italy under the leadership of Piedmont-Sardinia.

Mazzini's alternative for the unification of Italy, the creation of a republic, also was given a brief chance. With Pius IX away from Rome, radicalism had a free hand. In February 1849 a constituent assembly proclaimed the Roman Republic, under the leadership of Mazzini, and with an army led by another hero of Italian unification, Giuseppe Garibaldi. But as Austria regained its position in northern Italy and as the troops of Ferdinand II reconquered Sicily, the Roman Republic became a liberal island in a sea of reaction. To make matters worse, Louis Napoleon, newly elected president of France, tried to ingratiate himself with his Catholic subjects by sending an expeditionary force against Rome. It defeated the forces of Garibaldi and thus ended the dream of a republican Italy.

The revolution in Italy had failed. It had done so chiefly because the Austrians had once again proved too strong and because the Italians had proved too little united. Piedmont, having been the only state to put up any fight, earned the leadership in Italian affairs. To rally the rest of Italy behind the national cause, the people had to be promised not only unification but political liberty as well. This the government of Piedmont, now under Victor Emmanuel II, realized. Alone among Italian states, Piedmont kept the liberal constitution that had been adopted during the revolution. It thus became the hope of Italian nationalists and liberals alike.

Revolutions in the Habsburg Empire

In Italy, revolution had erupted before it did in France. But the outbreaks in Austria were directly touched off by the events in Paris. The Habsburg Empire had long been ripe for revolution. Its government was cumbersome and corrupt, and Metternich's efforts at reform had been of no avail. The main problem facing the Austrian Empire was its conglomeration of nationalities. Besides the Germans in Austria proper, there were the Magyars in Hungary, the Czechs and Slovaks in Bohemia and Moravia, the Poles in Galicia, and the Italians in Lombardy and Venetia. None of these regions, moreover, was entirely inhabited by one nationality; almost everywhere the peoples just mentioned, together with Slovenes, Croats, Serbs, Ruthenians, and Rumanians, created a situation of utmost ethnic confusion. With the advent of nationalism, this situation endangered the very existence of the Habsburg Empire.

In addition to the demands of these subject peoples for some measure of autonomy, there was also a growing demand for governmental reforms in Austria proper. Industrial progress had swelled the ranks of the middle class and had created an urban proletariat, both of which now added their voices to the liberal protests of university professors and other intellectuals.

The news of the revolution in Paris, however, caused much more excitement among the subject nationalities than it did in Austria. There were some student demonstrations and some violence in Vienna, and a deputation of citizens asked for the resignation of Metternich. But he resigned under pressure from the imperial family rather than from the populace. With Metternich gone, events moved swiftly and smoothly. The emperor removed himself to Innsbruck, and the citizens of Vienna elected a National Assembly to draft a constitution. One of the Assembly's first acts was to lift the last feudal burdens from Austria's peasants, completing a process begun by Joseph II two generations earlier.

From Vienna, revolution spread to other parts of the Empire. The uprisings in Lombardy and Venetia have already been discussed (see p. 562). In Bohemia, except for some local unrest, things remained quiet until early in June of 1848. At that time, disturbances broke out in connection with the first Pan-Slav Congress in Prague, which proclaimed the solidarity of the Slavic peoples against the Germans. Popular demonstrations

Prince Metternich, *ca.* 1858. This photograph of the Austrian statesman was taken shortly before his death.

NATIONALITIES OF THE HABSBURG EMPIRE

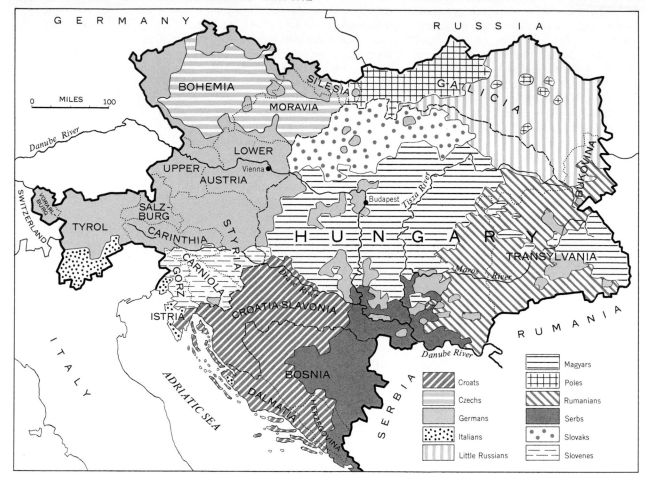

were quelled when Austria's military governor ordered the bombardment of Prague. This was a significant event, for it was the first major setback of revolution anywhere in Europe. In Hungary, meanwhile, the Austrian government had agreed to the March Laws, which guaranteed a large measure of self-government. Hungary also followed the Austrian example in abolishing the remains of feudalism. But while the Hungarians thus secured freedom for themselves, they refused to grant the same freedom to the Croats within their own borders. Austria could thus play one nationality against the other. In September 1848, Croatian forces with Austrian backing invaded Hungary.

With imperial armies scoring successes against the revolutionaries in Bohemia, Hungary, and Lombardy, the tide of revolution in the Austrian Empire was

definitely turning. A second, more radical outbreak in Vienna in October 1848 was soon put down. The Austrian government was now entrusted to Prince Felix Schwarzenberg, a strong-willed reactionary who urged the emperor, Ferdinand I, to resign in favor of his nephew, Francis Joseph. In March 1849 Schwarzenberg dissolved the National Assembly and imposed his own centralized constitution on the whole Empire.

By early spring of 1849 the Austrian government was again in control everywhere except in Hungary. At this point Francis Joseph accepted the offer of Nicholas I of Russia to help put down the Hungarians. The tsar was motivated by feelings of monarchical solidarity and by the fear that revolution might spread to the Danubian principalities and Poland. Hungarian resistance was finally crushed by the joint invasion of Russian and Austrian forces and by simultaneous uprisings among the Slavic peoples of southern Hungary. By mid-August of 1849 Austria was once again in control of its own house.

The "Germanies" in Revolt

The victory of reaction in Austria, as we have seen, affected the fate of revolution in Italy. It had a similar effect in Germany. There the chances for the success of revolution actually seemed most favorable. Unlike Austria, Germany did not suffer from ethnic disunity, nor was there any need to expel a foreign power, as there was in Italy. The failure of the revolution was due to many causes, most important among them the division of the country into many separate states and the general apathy of the population. The majority of Germans seemed content to lead a life of modest comfort and to pursue cultural rather than political interests.

Still, there was enough ferment among German intellectuals to keep alive the agitation for a united and liberal Germany. These aims also found support among the growing industrial middle class. The formation of a German customs union, or *Zollverein,* had eased the movement of goods throughout Germany and thus aided both commerce and industry. But industrialization had also brought many hardships, especially to the artisans. Another discontented group were the peasants in eastern Germany. Since their liberation from serfdom, they were often unable to make a living on their small holdings and instead had to become agricultural or industrial laborers. This economic discontent, which became especially strong during the 1840s, added a new dimension to the liberal and national aims of the German intellectuals. Had the revolutionary leaders understood and utilized this discontent, the results of the revolutions might have been different.

The first German uprising occurred in Bavaria before the events in France. But only with the news from Paris did the revolutions become general. Because Prussia, next to Austria, played the leading role in the German Confederation, events in Berlin were watched with par-

Carl Schurz's Recollections of 1848

One morning toward the end of February, 1848, I sat quietly in my attic chamber, working hard at the tragedy of "Ulrich von Hutten," when suddenly a friend rushed breathlessly into the room, exclaiming: "What, you sitting here! Do you not know what has happened?"

"No; what?"

"The French have driven away Louis Philippe and proclaimed the Republic."

I threw down my pen—and that was the end of "Ulrich von Hutten." I never touched the manuscript again. We tore down the stairs, into the street, to the market-square, the accustomed meeting-place for all the student societies after their midday dinner. Although it was still forenoon, the market was already crowded with young men talking excitedly. . . . In these conversations . . . certain ideas and catchwords worked themselves to the surface, which expressed more or less the feelings of the people. Now had arrived in Germany the day for the establishment of "German Unity" and the founding of a great, powerful national German Empire. First in line the convocation of a national parliament; then the demands for civil rights and liberties, free speech, free press, the right of free assembly, equality before the law, a freely elected representation of the people with legislative power, responsibility of ministers, self-government of the communes, the right of the people to carry arms, the formation of a civic guard with elective officers, and so on—in short, that which was called a "constitutional form of government on a broad democratic basis." Republican ideas were at first only sparingly expressed. But the word "democracy" was soon on all tongues, and many, too, thought it a matter of course that if the princes should try to withhold from the people the rights and liberties demanded, force would take the place of mere petition. . . . We were profoundly, solemnly in earnest.

From *The Reminiscences of Carl Schurz,* 3 vols. (New York: McClure, 1907–08), Vol. I, pp. 111–13. Quoted in Geoffrey Bruun, *Revolution and Reaction, 1848–1852* (New York: Van Nostrand, 1958), pp. 125–27.

ticular interest. Prussia, since 1840, had been ruled by the brilliant but unstable Frederick William IV. The new king started out with a series of liberal reforms, but his liberalism, like that of Alexander I, was largely a pose. When the revolution came to Berlin in March 1848, Frederick William was easily frightened into appointing a liberal ministry and agreeing to a constituent assembly. But the old regime in Prussia was not really beaten, especially since the Prussian army had remained intact. While middle-class delegates were drawing up a liberal constitution, the lower classes were agitating for more drastic changes—including universal suffrage, socialism, and even a republic. These radical demands drove the middle class, including the well-to-do peasants, back into the arms of reaction. When news reached Berlin in the fall of 1848 that the Austrian government was successfully moving against the revolution in Vienna, Frederick William dissolved the Constituent Assembly and later imposed his own constitution. By the end of 1848, the revolution in Prussia had been defeated.

But German liberals did not give up hope. Since spring, another assembly had been in session in Frankfurt to draft a constitution for all of Germany, rather than for Prussia alone. Its delegates had been elected by the people. The majority were professional people, including many professors. Deliberations dragged on for almost a year. The main argument developed over the question of whether or not the new German state should be under the leadership of and include Austria. The *grossdeutsch* (greater-German) faction, which favored this solution, was opposed by the *kleindeutsch* (small-German) group, which advocated the exclusion of Austria and the leadership of Prussia. The issue resolved itself when the victory of reaction in Vienna disqualified Austria in the eyes of German liberals.

The Frankfurt Constitution, which was finally adopted in March 1849, called for a constitutional monarchy with a parliament elected by universal suffrage. The Frankfurt Parliament elected Frederick William IV as "Emperor of the Germans." But the king of Prussia refused a crown that was offered him by the people. He would accept it only from his fellow princes. With reaction everywhere triumphant, Frederick William's refusal all but finished the revolution in Germany. There were some last flashes of violence in the smaller states, but Prussian troops soon restored order. The attempt of the German people to build a unified nation under a government of their own choosing had failed.

England in the Age of Reform

The one country in Europe where many people had expected revolution to strike first was Great Britain. And yet, except for a brief flare-up in Ireland, the British Isles proved the major exception to the rule of revolution in western Europe. The Reform Bill of 1832 had been merely the most prominent of a large series of reforms. Most important among these was the establishment of free trade. Britain's merchants and industrialists had long agitated against import duties, but tariffs had been defended on the grounds that the government needed the income. With the reintroduction of the income tax in 1842, however, that argument lost ground, and protective tariffs were gradually abolished. Only in agriculture did they survive. To fight for the abolition of agricultural tariffs, the Anti-Corn Law

The Chartist Petition of 1848

The Committee on Public Petitions [of the House of Commons] strongly feel the right of petition; consider the exercise of it as one of the most important privileges of the subjects of the realm; and feel the necessity of preserving the exercise of such privilege from abuse.

And, having also a due regard to the importance of the very numerously signed petition forming the subject of the present report, they feel bound to represent to the House, that in the matter of signatures there has been, in their opinion, a gross abuse of that privilege.

The honorable Member for Nottingham stated, on presenting the petition in question to the House, that 5,706,000 signatures were attached to it. Upon a most careful examination, . . . the number of signatures has been ascertained to be 1,975,496. It is further evident to your Committee, that on numerous consecutive sheets the signatures are in one and the same handwriting. Your Committee have also observed the names of distinguished individuals attached to the petition, who cannot be supposed to have concurred in its prayer, and as little to have subscribed it: amongst such occur the names of Her Majesty in one place, as Victoria Rex, April 1; the Duke of Wellington, K. G.; Sir Robert Peel, etc., etc., etc.

In addition to this species of abuse, your Committee have observed another equally in derogation of the just value of petitions—namely, the insertion of names which are obviously altogether fictitious, such as "No Cheese," "Pugnose," "Flatnose," etc. . . .

From *The Annual Register for 1848* (London, 1849), pp. 126-27. Quoted in Geoffrey Bruun, *Revolution and Reaction, 1848–1852* (New York: Van Nostrand, 1958), pp. 184–185.

League had been formed in 1839. In 1846 its relentless pressure succeeded and the Corn Laws were repealed.

Along with this agitation for economic freedom, there also arose during the 1830s a movement for greater political freedom. The Reform Bill of 1832 had been a disappointment to the lower classes, among whom the so-called Chartist Movement gained its major support. The movement took its name from the "People's Charter" of 1838, drawn up by a group of radical reformers and calling for a further democratization of Parliament. But this radical program met heavy opposition, and Parliament repeatedly turned down petitions based on the Charter. By 1848 discontent had mounted to such a pitch that there seemed to be a real threat of revolution. The Chartists prepared a "monster petition" with some six million signatures (many of them false) and started a demonstration to present it to Parliament. When it began to rain, however, the demonstrators let themselves be dispersed peacefully. The truth of the matter is that a good deal of the discontent in the Chartist Movement was economic, which had disappeared with the repeal of the Corn Laws and a general increase in prosperity. Henceforth workers were turning more and more to trade unionism as a means of improving their status. England thus remained a quiet haven of refuge in the upheavals of 1848, giving asylum to refugees from revolution and reaction alike, including Metternich as well as Marx. Many of the revolutionaries, however, preferred to leave Europe altogether; the United States received them with open arms.

Why Did the Revolutions of 1848 Fail?

The revolutions of 1848 thus had failed everywhere. They had done so because of weaknesses in the revolutionary camp, because of the continued strength of the forces of reaction, and because the economic conditions that helped bring on the revolutions did not last. The economic picture in many countries improved, despite the unsettling effect of revolution.

Barricade in Milan, from the *Leipziger Illustrierte Zeitung,* 1848.

The weakness of the revolutionaries was due partly to the lack of well-defined programs or else the existence of too many different programs and to the indecision of their leaders. This indecision led to waste of valuable time, which the reactionaries used to prepare for counterrevolution. But the primary weakness of the revolutionaries was lack of widespread popular support. The middle class, in most countries, did not really want a revolution. It preferred to achieve its aims through reform, as had been done in England. But once revolution came, sometimes by spontaneous combustion, the middle class tried to reap its benefits. Much of the actual fighting in the revolutions was done by the workers, and the workers wanted more than limited democracy for the well-to-do. They wanted complete democracy, political and, in some cases, economic as well. To the middle class, these demands, especially the socialist ones, not only threatened its political predominance but its very existence. This bourgeois fear of a "red peril" was exaggerated. Despite the incendiary language of the *Communist*

Manifesto (which appeared in 1848; see p. 587), the majority of the lower class were perfectly ready to follow the leadership of the middle class if that would improve their condition. But the middle class did not live up to these lower-class expectations; as a result the lower class more and more came to distrust the men it had helped gain power.

Not only was there disunity among the revolutionary forces within each country, there was no attempt to coordinate the revolutions in different countries. While the forces of reaction worked together, there was little collaboration among the revolutionaries. On the contrary, almost everywhere their programs showed traces of a selfish nationalism. There was nationalism behind France's talk of spreading the blessings of revolution. The Germans wanted to unite all German-speaking peoples, but they also wanted to lord it over the Poles and they actually carried on a brief war against the Danes. The Poles wanted to be liberated and united, but they did not want to see the Ukrainians win the same benefits. And the Hungarians behaved every bit as selfishly toward the Croats as the Austrians did toward the Hungarians.

Yet, though reaction won a full victory in 1849, the revolutions of 1848 had not been entirely in vain. Some changes for the better were preserved. In France, political power had been considerably broadened. In Italy some leaders had learned useful lessons of how to go about achieving unification. In Austria the abolition of serfdom during the revolution could not be undone, and Metternich did not return to power. Even in Germany, where the failure of revolution probably had more tragic long-range consequences than anywhere else, a few lasting gains were made.

The mid-century revolutions came at a turning point in European history. Up to this time, the economy of the Continent had still been largely agrarian. From now on, industrialization was really to take hold. Metternich, the dominant figure after 1815, had in many ways been a relic of the eighteenth century. The future was to belong to a different, more modern, type of politician. Two forces emerged from the revolutions that henceforth were to dominate the history of Europe—nationalism and socialism. Neither was new, but both had lost much of their earlier idealism and utopianism. Nationalism and socialism respectively became the main issues in the struggle of nation against nation and class against class.

Suggestions for Further Reading

Note: Asterisk denotes a book available in paperback edition.

General   The most stimulating introduction to the half-century following the French Revolution is E. J. Hobsbawm, *The Age of Revolution, 1789–1848** (1962). G. F. E. Rudé, *Debate on Europe, 1815–1850** (1972), is a critical discussion of the period's historiography. J. L. Talmon, *Romanticism and Revolt: Europe, 1815–1848** (1967), emphasizes ideas rather than social and economic forces. Good detailed treatments are F. A. Artz, *Reaction and Revolution, 1814–1832** (1934), and W. L. Langer, *Political and Social Upheaval, 1832–1852** (1969). The book by J. Droz, *Europe between Revolutions, 1815–1848* (1968), is a new appraisal by a noted French social historian. Among national histories, the following stand out: É. Halévy, *History of the English People in the Nineteenth Century,** Vols. II and III (1926); T. S. Hamerow, *Restoration, Revolution, Reaction: Economics and Politics in Germany, 1815–1871** (1958); A. J. P. Taylor, *The Hapsburg Monarchy, 1809–1918** (1948); A. Cobban, *A History of Modern France,** Vol. II (1957); A. J. Whyte, *The Evolution of Modern Italy, 1715–1920** (1944); and A. Lobanov-Rostovsky, *Russia and Europe, 1789–1825* (1947). The emergence of liberalism is traced in G. Ruggiero, *History of European Liberalism** (1927), and H. J. Laski, *The Rise of European Liberalism* (1936). Some standard works on nationalism are C. J. H. Hayes, *The Historical Evolution of Modern Nationalism* (1931), H. Kohn, *The Idea of Nationalism** (1944), and by the same author, *Prophets and Peoples: Studies in Nineteenth-Century Nationalism* (1946). More recent studies are B. C.

Shafer, *Nationalism: Myth and Reality** (1955), and A. Cobban, *The Nation State and National Self-Determination* (1969).

The Restoration of the Old Order	The standard works on the diplomatic settlements after Napoleon are C. K. Webster, *The Foreign Policy of Castlereagh, 1812–1822*, 2 Vols. (1931), and *The Congress of Vienna, 1814–1815** (1934). H. Nicolson, *The Congress of Vienna: A Study in Allied Unity, 1812–1822** (1946), is briefer and makes delightful reading. Good biographies of the leading figures at Vienna are: G. de Bertier de Sauvigny, *Metternich and His Times* (1962); C. Brinton, *The Lives of Talleyrand** (1936); L. I. Strakhovsky, *Alexander I of Russia* (1947); and J. C. Bartlett, *Castlereagh* (1967). See also P. K. Grimsted, *The Foreign Ministers of Alexander I (1969)*. On Castlereagh's successors, see H. W. V. Temperley, *The Foreign Policy of Canning, 1822–1827* (1925), and C. K. Webster, *The Foreign Policy of Palmerston, 1830–1841*, 2 vols. (1951). The diplomatic aftermath of the Congress of Vienna is discussed in H. G. Schenk, *The Aftermath of the Napoleonic Wars: The Concert of Europe* (1947); P. W. Schroeder, *Metternich's Diplomacy at its Zenith, 1820–1823* (1962); and H. A. Kissinger, *A World Restored** (1957). The situation arising from the revolutions in Latin America is summed up in D. Perkins, *Hands Off! A History of the Monroe Doctrine** (1941). See also B. Perkins, *Castlereagh and Adams: England and the United States, 1812–1823* (1964).

Romanticism	A good introduction to the complexities of Romanticism is J. B. Halsted, ed., *Romanticism** (1965). Another useful collection is H. E. Hugo, ed., *The Romantic Reader* (1957). I. Babbitt, *Rousseau and Romanticism** (1919), is a classic indictment. See also W. J. Bate, *From Classic to Romantic** (1946), and J. Barzun, *Classic, Romantic and Modern** (1961). The impact of Romanticism on political thought is treated in the works on nationalism cited above, as well as in H. S. Reiss, *The Political Thought of the German Romantics* (1955); C. Brinton, *The Political Ideas of the English Romanticists** (1926); and R. H. Soltau, *French Political Thought of the Nineteenth Century* (1931). On conservatism, see R. J. S. Hoffman and P. Levack, eds., *Burke's Politics* (1949); and E. L. Woodward, *Three Studies in European Conservatism* (1929).

Revolutions before 1848	Good accounts of the numerous upheavals in the 1820s and 1830s may be found in the general histories cited above. For events in France, see also J. Plamenatz, *The Revolutionary Movement in France, 1815–1871* (1952); N. E. Hudson, *Ultraroyalism and the French Restoration* (1936); and G. de Bertier de Sauvigny's pro-royalist *The Bourbon Restoration* (1966). Recent biographies of leading figures include D. W. Johnson's *Guizot* (1963), and T. E. B. Howarth's *Citizen King* (1961), on Louis Philippe. For the Greek revolution see C. M. Woodhouse, *The Greek War of Independence* (1952). Russia's Decembrist revolt is the subject of A. G. Mazour, *The First Russian Revolution, 1825** (1937). On events in Belgium and Poland see J. A. Betley, *Belgium and Poland in International Relations, 1830–1831* (1960). The general subject of the disintegrating Ottoman Empire is admirably summarized in M. S. Anderson, *The Eastern Question, 1774–1923** (1966). Much has been written on parliamentary and social reforms in Great Britain. Especially recommended are E. L. Woodward, *The Age of Reform, 1815–1870* (1938); N. Gash, *Politics in the Age of Peel* (1953); A. Briggs, ed., *Chartist Studies* (1960); M. Hovell, *The Chartist Movement* (1925); and D. Owen, *English Philanthropy, 1660–1960* (1964). On social unrest, see R. J. White, *Waterloo to Peterloo* (1957), and G. F. E. Rudé, *The Crowd in History, 1730–1848** (1964), which deals with both England and France.

The Revolutions of 1848	Among several attempts to present a comprehensive picture of these confusing events, the most successful is P. Robertson, *Revolutions of 1848: A Social History** (1952). G. Bruun, *Revolution and Reaction, 1848–1852** (1952), gives a brief introduction, supplemented by documents. R. Postgate, *Story of a Year: 1848** (1955), describes vividly the revolutions as seen from England. A. Whitridge, *Men in Crisis: The Revolutions of 1848* (1949), concentrates on a few leading figures in various countries. V. Valentin, *1848: Chapters in German History* (1940), is learned but fragmentary. D. Gwynn, *Young Ireland in 1848* (1949), tells a sad story. Among specialized works on various aspects of the revolutions, the following deserve mention: D. C. McKay, *The National Workshops: A Study in the French Revolution of 1848* (1933); J. Blum, *Noble Landowners and Agriculture in Austria, 1814–1848** (1948); A. J. P. Taylor, *The Italian Problem in European Diplomacy, 1847–1849* (1939); and L. B. Namier, *1848: The Revolution of the Intellectuals** (1947).

Coke-smelting on the coalfields of Upper Silesia in Germany, lithograph made in 1841.

25 The Coming of the Industrial Age

Much of the political tension in Europe during the first half of the nineteenth century was a manifestation of underlying economic unrest caused by the gradual transformation of Europe's economy from agriculture to industry. This change is usually dated from the middle of the eighteenth century, but it did not become pronounced until after 1815. From then on it gathered momentum, first in England and later on the Continent, until by the end of the nineteenth century most of western Europe had become industrialized.

This industrialization of society is often referred to as the "Industrial Revolution." But this term has come in for some criticism. The change from agriculture to industry, it seems, was a gradual process of evolution rather than the sudden change implied in the term *revolution*. When one considers the total effect of this transformation from agriculture to industry, however, the term *revolution* seems more than justified. By vastly improving the means of communication, industrialization has made the world seem much smaller; by enabling more people to make a living, it has made the world much more crowded; and by raising the standard of living, it has made life infinitely more comfortable. Industrialization has elevated some nations that heretofore were insignificant and has demoted others that did not have the manpower or the raw materials that industry requires. Industrialization has dissolved a rigid and hierarchical order of society and has substituted a fluid and egalitarian mass society.

Not all these changes have necessarily been for the better. While industry created wealth for some, it merely emphasized the poverty of others. While it made nations and individuals more dependent on each other, it also increased their rivalry for a share of the riches the world has to offer. The preoccupation of modern industrial society with material well-being has diverted mankind from more spiritual concerns. But while one may wonder how beneficial the change from agriculture to industry has been in some areas, about the magnitude of that change there can be no doubt.

THE ROOTS OF MODERN INDUSTRIALISM

Modern industrialism, quite simply, is the mass production of goods by means of machines driven by generated power and set up in factories. There had been few mechanical inventions before the eighteenth century. During the Middle Ages, consumer goods had been produced by hand and for local consumption. With the Age of Discovery and the "Commercial Revolution" in the sixteenth century, the rate of production had increased to provide goods for export. Since the small artisan did not have the capital to buy large quantities of raw materials, to produce a large stock, and

to sell it in a distant market, a class of wealthy capitalists and merchants began to inject themselves into the production process. They supplied the artisan with raw materials and sometimes with tools, and they took over the finished product to sell at a profit. This "domestic," or "putting-out," system had become quite common by the seventeenth century. There were even a few simple machines, but they still had to be operated by humans or animals, or by the natural power of wind or water. During the eighteenth century the trend toward large-scale production was accelerated by numerous mechanical inventions that increased the speed and thus the volume of production. The most important step came with the application of steam power to these new machines. This step brought the decline of the domestic system and the gradual shift of production from home to factory.

It was no accident that modern industrialism should have had its start in the eighteenth century. The intellectual climate of the Enlightenment, its interest in science, and its emphasis on the good life were particularly favorable to such a development. The beginnings of modern

---

The Age of Revolution, 1789–1848

Words are witnesses which often speak louder than documents. Let us consider a few English words which were invented, or gained their modern meanings, substantially in the period of sixty years with which this volume deals. They are such words as "industry," "industrialist," "factory," "middle class," "working class," "capitalism," and "socialism." They include "aristocracy" as well as "railway," "liberal" and "conservative" as political terms, "nationality," "scientist," and "engineer," "proletariat" and (economic) "crisis." "Utilitarian" and "statistics," "sociology," and several other names of modern sciences, "journalism" and "ideology," are all coinages or adaptations of this period. So are "strike" and "pauperism."

To imagine the modern world without these words (i.e., without the things and concepts for which they provide names) is to measure the profundity of the revolution which broke out between 1789 and 1848 and forms the greatest transformation in human history since the remote times when men invented agriculture and metallurgy, writing, the city and the state. This revolution has transformed, and continues to transform, the entire world.

From E. J. Hobsbawm, *The Age of Revolution, 1789–1848*, Mentor edition (New York: World Publishing Co., 1962), pp. 17–18.

industrialism fall into the period after 1760, and the acceleration of industrialism was most pronounced in England. England's parliamentary government gave some voice to the rising commercial and industrial classes; it had large colonial holdings and far-flung commercial interests; it had a sound financial system and sufficient surplus capital; and it had an ample supply of basic raw materials and manpower. The manpower had been made available in part by drastic changes in British agriculture—an "Agricultural Revolution"—which converted farmers into laborers and materially increased Britain's food supply.

THE AGRICULTURAL REVOLUTION

Most of the land in Britain before the eighteenth century was still worked under the open-field system, which meant that the holdings of individual owners were scattered about in many strips, separated from those of other landholders by a double furrow. In addition, each landholder shared in the common pastures and woodlands of his community. This arrangement was of particular advantage to the small farmers and cottagers, who participated in the grazing and fueling rights of the "commons." But the open-field system was both inefficient and wasteful. The prevailing method of cultivation was still the medieval system of three-field rotation, under which one-third of the land remained fallow each year. Any attempt to change this routine by experimenting with new crops was impossible, since all strips in a given field had to be cultivated at the same time and planted with the same crop.

The "Enclosure Movement"

Beginning at the time of the Tudors, an "enclosure movement" had started in England, under which the scattered strips of individual owners were consolidated into compact holdings surrounded by fences or hedges. Enclosure meant a gain of usable land because it did away with the double furrows, and it made cultiva-

tion much easier. But since enclosure also entailed a division of the commons, it worked to the detriment of the small farmer, who thereby lost part of his livelihood. As the population of England increased, agricultural production for the general market rather than for local consumption became more profitable. The trend toward more efficient large-scale farming, and especially sheep raising, through enclosures therefore gained momentum. It reached its climax in the eighteenth century. Between 1702 and 1797, Parliament passed some 1,776 enclosure acts affecting three million acres. In each case the larger landowner profited at the expense of the smaller farmer. Left with too little land of his own and deprived of his share in the commons, the small farmer had no choice but to become a tenant farmer or move to the cities. Many took the latter course, providing some of the manpower without which the rapid growth of Britain's industry could not have taken place.

The enclosure movement brought hardships to many people, but it brought a dramatic improvement in agriculture. Freed from the restrictions of collective cultivation, landowners were now able to try new methods and new crops. This enabled them to grow more food on the

A result of the "Agricultural Revolution": a German threshing machine of the 1850s.

same amount of land. The improvement was such as to give substance to the term "Agricultural Revolution." Like its industrial counterpart, the Agricultural Revolution at first was almost entirely restricted to Britain. Only with the advent of industrialization did the larger landholders on the Continent seriously begin to experiment with British methods. The small peasants, on the other hand, continued in their backward ways. As new industrial centers developed, new markets for agricultural produce opened up. Improvements in transportation, furthermore, facilitated marketing; and new scientific discoveries brought larger crop yields. These and other developments brought renewed hope for western Europe's farmers, who were gradually being pushed to the wall by the rising industries and were beginning to feel the competition of the fertile agrarian lands of eastern Europe and America.

THE BEGINNINGS OF INDUSTRIALIZATION

Inventions and the Rise of the Factory System

The early history of industrialization is related to the rise of mechanical inventions. There were few of these at first, but they multiplied as one discovery created the need for another. When John Kay invented his flying shuttle in 1733, enabling one weaver to do the work of two, the need arose for some new device that would speed up spinning. This demand was met in 1764 by James Hargreaves and his spinning jenny, which permitted the simultaneous spinning of eight or more threads. A few years later, Richard Arkwright devised the water frame, and in 1779 Samuel Crompton perfected the "mule," a hybrid that combined features of both Hargreaves' and Arkwright's inventions. These improvements in spinning in turn called for further improvements in weaving. In 1787 Edmund Cartwright patented a new power loom. After it was perfected, the demand for cotton increased. Cotton production received a boost when an

American, Eli Whitney, in 1793 developed the cotton "gin," which speeded up and cut the cost of removing the cotton fiber from its boll. Almost all the early inventions were made in the cotton industry: it was a new industry, it had a large overseas market, and cotton lent itself particularly well to mechanical treatment.

Since most of the earlier devices were small, relatively inexpensive, and hand-operated, they could be used as part of the domestic system in the workers' cottages. Arkwright's water frame, however, was large and expensive, and it needed water power to operate. Arkwright, therefore, moved into the heart of the English textile region of Nottingham, where he opened the first spinning mill in 1771. By 1779 he was employing some 300 workers who operated several thousand spindles. With this important innovation, the modern factory system had been born. Arkwright's example was soon followed by other manufacturers, especially as the steam engine became the major source of power for newer and larger machines.

The Steam Engine

Of all the inventions in the early years of industrialism, the steam engine was the most important. Until the advent of electricity it remained the chief source of power, and even in our atomic age its usefulness has not ended. The development of the steam engine is closely related to the two industries that ultimately proved basic to all modern economic progress—coal and iron. At the beginning of the eighteenth century the smelting of iron was still done by charcoal. The depletion of Britain's wood supply, however, and the discovery, shortly after 1700, of a process for smelting iron with coke, shifted the emphasis to coal. The mining of coal was made considerably easier by a primitive steam engine, developed by Thomas Newcomen, that was used to pump water from the coal mines. This early eighteenth-century engine was a long way from the kind of steam engine that could be used to run other machines. The credit for developing such an engine belongs to the Scotsman James

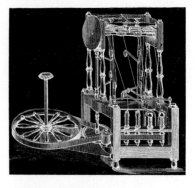

Arkwright's spinning-frame, patented in 1769. It was the first self-acting machine to spin threads fine and hard enough for a weaver to use as the cloth warp.

Watt, who patented his first steam engine in 1769. By 1800 some 300 steam engines were at work in England, mostly in the cotton industry. The use of steam engines, of course, further increased the need for coal and iron. Improvements in iron production, on the other hand, in turn led to improvements in the making of steam engines. The interaction of one discovery with another continued to be a major characteristic of industrial development.

Early Industry on the Continent

Prior to 1815 the "Industrial Revolution" was chiefly a British phenomenon. An economic revival in France after 1763, helping to make up for the loss of the French colonies to Britain, had been interrupted by the French Revolution. But the "continental system" of Napoleon, which excluded British goods from the Continent, had proved most beneficial to French industry.

In the rest of Europe there were not even the beginnings of modern industrialization. Economic development in Germany was retarded by political disunity. The rich coal fields of the Ruhr and Silesia were hardly worked before 1815, and what little industry there was, especially in textiles, still operated under the "putting-out" system. Russia, Italy, and Austria were almost wholly agrarian. Even after 1815, continental industries were slow to assert themselves against British competition. It was only after the advent of the railroad in the 1830s that the situation began to improve.

THE RAILWAY AGE

Transportation in the Eighteenth Century

Industrial development was closely related to the improvement of transportation. England again had a special advantage in being able to use coastal shipping for the movement of bulky goods. But like any other country it depended on roads and canals for inland transportation. As industrialization increased the need for transport and travel,

the construction of toll roads and canals became a profitable business. England added thousands of miles to its system of roads and canals during the eighteenth century, and France before the Revolution had the finest highway system in Europe. Napoleon improved the situation further by pushing highways far into Germany and the Netherlands. In eastern Europe, however, paved roads were rare. Prussia's kings constructed canals and improved riverways, but the movement of goods was hampered by innumerable tolls and tariffs. Farther east, dirt roads that regularly turned to mud and rivers that ran shallow during the summer and froze during the winter were the only arteries of communication.

The Advent of the Railroad

The railroad, which was to change all this, had its start in England. Well before 1800, horse-drawn carts, moving first on wooden and later on iron rails, had been used to haul coal and iron. During the 1820s there were several hundred miles of such "rail ways." The problem of providing a faster means of locomotion was solved by putting the steam engine on wheels. The first commercial steam railroad was opened between Stockton and Darlington in 1825. By 1840 Britain had some 800 miles of track, and by 1850 it had more than 6,000. On the Continent, the railroad was slower in taking hold. The first railroad in France was opened in 1837, and by the middle of the century there were 2,000 miles of track. Germany then had 3,000 miles, Austria 1,000 miles, and Italy and Russia had merely a few fragmentary lines.

The economic impact of the railroad, of course, was overwhelming. Here was an entirely new industry, answering a universal need, employing thousands of people, offering unprecedented opportunities for investment, and introducing greater speed into all industrial and commercial transactions. England, already far ahead of the Continent in economic development, took the Railway Age pretty much in stride. England had been the workshop of the world for some time, and there seemed to be no prospect that it would cease to be. Railroad construction vastly increased the demand for

"The Railway King," a Victorian caricature.

coal and iron, and England continued to lead the world in the production of both.

England also maintained its lead in shipping. The shipping industry was slow to feel the impact of steam. Even though Robert Fulton's steamboat had made its first successful trip on the Hudson River in 1807, it was not until 1840 that Samuel Cunard established the first transatlantic steamer line. Even then the inefficiency of marine engines and the large amounts of coal needed for long voyages retarded the development of steamship service. Well into the second half of the nineteenth century the fast clipper ship remained the chief means of ocean transport.

There were other important innovations and inventions in the early nineteenth century, with England again leading the way. The introduction of the penny post in 1840 helped business and private individuals alike. The telegraph, invented by the American Samuel Morse, was first used extensively by Julius Reuter's news agency, which was established in 1851, the same year in which the first submarine cable was laid under the English Channel. A reduction in the stamp tax in 1836 substantially lowered the price of newspapers, and by the middle of the century the circulation of the British press had risen more than threefold. The communication of news and ideas kept pace with the faster movements of goods and persons.

The Railway Age on the Continent

In May 1851 the "Great Exhibition of the Works of Industry of All Nations" opened in London. This first "world's fair" was dramatic proof of Britain's industrial world leadership, but it also showed that other nations were beginning to profit from its example. The country in which industrialization made the most rapid progress was little Belgium. An ample supply of coal and a skilled labor force were the chief reasons,

The opening of the Stockton-Darlington Railway on September 27, 1825; drawing by J. R. Brown.

Prince Albert's ticket to the Great Exhibition of 1851.

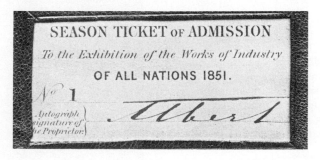

SEASON TICKET OF ADMISSION

To the Exhibition of the Works of Industry

OF ALL NATIONS 1851.

N° 1

Autograph signature of the Proprietor.

Albert

but technical aid by British engineers and investment of British capital also helped.

In France, economic development was much slower. The French had lost some of their best coal mines to Belgium in 1815; and while European populations were increasing, the French birth rate, by the middle of the century, had actually begun to decline. Still, with all the encouragement given to commerce and industry by the July Monarchy, the middle class could not help but prosper. Pig-iron production, generally considered an index of industrial development, increased fourfold in France during the thirty years after 1825; but it was still only one-quarter that of Great Britain. While England's population by the middle of the century was more than half urban, France remained predominantly rural. This made large imports of food unnecessary and accounted for a self-contained domestic market.

In both Italy and Germany political disunity slowed down economic growth. Industry in northern Italy remained insignificant until later in the century. In Germany, the *Zollverein* did much to aid industrial development. Machines, imported from England, were being used more and more in the textile industry. With the sinking of the first deep pit in the Ruhr in 1841, coal production began in earnest. Even so, France, despite much slimmer resources, still produced more coal than Germany. As for pig iron, the total German output in 1855 was only half that of France. Railroad construction in Germany made rapid progress during the 1840s. The absence of natural obstacles kept construction costs far below those of Great Britain. It was the progress in railroad building that gave some inkling of the tremendous economic vitality of the German people, which was merely awaiting political unification to assert itself.

Beyond western and central Europe, industrialization had made hardly any headway by 1850. Austria and Russia were still predominantly agrarian. Industrial development depended first and foremost on an abundant supply of free labor. This supply did not exist in Austria until after the last feudal restrictions were abolished in 1849, and in Russia it had to wait until the abolition of serfdom in 1861. Outside Europe only the United States was showing signs of industrialization. By 1850 New England had become largely industrialized, but the total output of American industry was still behind that of France and far behind that of Britain. Like Germany, America was to become a leading industrial power only toward the end of the century.

THE SOCIAL EFFECTS OF INDUSTRIALIZATION

The beginnings of modern industrialization in the eighteenth century appeared to bear out the belief of the Enlightenment that human reason and ingenuity had the power to perfect the world. The invention of labor-saving machines promised to transform man from a beast of burden into a creature of leisure. But that promise soon began to fade. The "Industrial Revolution," in the beginning at least, benefited only a minority, the middle class, while it brought utmost misery and destitution to the growing proletariat. It was only after industrialization had outgrown its infancy that its blessings came to be shared by more and more people.

London Slums (1872), by Gustave Doré.

Population Growth

Many of the early difficulties of industrialization were due to the unsettling effects that the tremendous population growth had on European society. Between 1815 and 1914, the population of Europe increased more than twofold, from 200 million to 460 million. Another 40 million Europeans during this time emigrated to other parts of the world, especially the United States. The rate of growth differed from country to country. It was largest in Russia, less in England and Germany, and least in France. Population growth was probably due less to an increase in the birth rate than to a decrease in the death rate. This decrease had many causes: improvements in medicine and public sanitation, absence of major wars, greater efficiency in government and administration, the revolution in agriculture leading to better diets and more ample food supplies, and, most important, the acceleration of industrial development. Industry provided the means whereby more people could live, and the increase of population, in turn, supplied the necessary industrial labor force and swelled the ranks of consumers. The growth of population and the increasing industrialization of society thus acted upon and served to stimulate each other.

Working-Class Misery

With the increase in population and the growth of industry there came a further important change in European society—the movement of people from the country to the city. Large-scale urbanization had been virtually unknown before the early nineteenth century. But as workers began to flock to the mills, small villages grew into crowded towns and quiet towns into noisy cities. This sudden influx of people brought on wretched housing conditions. Teeming slums lacking in sanitation facilities turned into breeding places of disease, vice, and crime. There was as yet no effective municipal administration to cope with these novel problems, and the workers themselves were too poor to improve their condition.

Poor housing was not the only hardship afflicting the early workingman. Since mechanized industry required little skill, there was always an abundance of manpower, and wages were kept at a minimum. The average working day was between twelve and sixteen hours. But even this rarely yielded sufficient pay to support a worker's family, so that women and children had to work as well. Since they were more docile and received less pay, they were much in demand. But women and children also suffered more than men did from the harsh conditions in factories and mines. No provisions were made for the workers' safety, and accidents resulting from machines to which they were not accustomed were frequent. There was no insurance against accidents, sickness, or old age. Furthermore, as more machines were used and as more efficient machines were invented, unemployment added to the worker's hardships. As industrialization spread to the Continent, so did the abuses that accompanied it. Conditions in Belgium and France were almost as bad as those in England.

Middle-Class Indifference

The attitude of much of the middle class toward the misery of the working class was one of indifference. The pioneers of modern industrialization, the new "captains of industry," were tough and ruthless men. They had to be if they wanted to survive because competition was keen and risks were great. For every one of them who made good, there were several who fell by the wayside; the path of early industrialism was lined with bankruptcies. Economic booms burst; wars closed markets; machinery broke down or became obsolete; and the agrarian supporters of the old order fought stubbornly against middle-class efforts to gain economic and political influence.

In order to understand the seemingly callous attitude of the middle class toward the hardships of the workers, we must consider briefly the middle-class philosophy of liberalism, which tried to justify such selfish behavior. It was the belief in economic liberalism that prevented any drastic measures of social

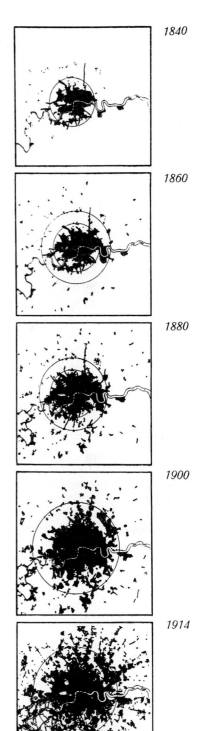

1840

1860

1880

1900

1914

The growth of London from 1840 to 1914. The diameter of the circled zone in 1840 was four miles; in 1914 it was nine and a half.

Children working in a coal mine, illustration from the Shaftesbury Report, 1842. The evidence presented in this report brought about the Coal Mines Act of 1842 and subsequent measures to alleviate industrial abuse.

Child Labor

PRO

I have visited many factories, both in Manchester and in the surrounding districts, during a period of several months, entering the spinning rooms unexpectedly, and often alone, at different times of the day, and I never saw a single instance of corporal chastisement inflicted on a child, nor indeed did I ever see children in ill-humor. They seemed to be always cheerful and alert, taking pleasure in the light play of their muscles—enjoying the mobility natural to their age. The scene of industry, so far from exciting sad emotions in my mind, was always exhilarating. . . . The work of these lively elves seemed to resemble a sport, in which habit gave them a pleasing dexterity. . . . As to exhaustion by the day's work, they evinced no trace of it on emerging from the mill in the evening; for they immediately began to skip about any neighboring playground, and to commence their little amusements with the same alacrity as boys issuing from a school.

CON

The report of the Central Commission relates that the manufacturers began to employ children rarely of five years, often of six, very often of seven, usually of eight to nine years; that the working-day often lasted fourteen to sixteen hours, exclusive of meals and intervals; that the manufacturers permitted overlookers to flog and maltreat children, and often took an active part in so doing themselves. One case is related of a Scotch manufacturer who rode after a sixteen years old runaway, forced him to return running before the employer as fast as the master's horse trotted, and beat him the whole way with a long whip.

From Andrew Ure, *The Philosophy of Manufactures* (3rd. ed.; London: H. G. Bohn, 1961), p. 301; and Friedrich Engels, *The Condition of the Working Class in England in 1844* (New York: J. W. Lovell, 1887), p. 101.

reform in the early part of the nineteenth century. The absence of such reform, in turn, led to various protests on behalf of the worker, of which Marxian socialism became the most effective.

MIDDLE-CLASS LIBERALISM

The term *liberalism* has assumed so many different meanings that it defies clear definition. In the early nineteenth century, however, liberalism had definite meaning and aims. A liberal was a person who believed in freedom—freedom of thought, freedom of religion, freedom from economic restrictions, freedom of trade, and freedom from the political injustices of the old regime. Most of these freedoms had already been demanded by the leaders of the Enlightenment. The *philosophes* held that every man had certain natural rights—life, liberty, and property. These rights the middle class had already demanded before and during the French Revolution, and it continued to demand them. But as time went on, its claims were based not on natural law, as they had been during the eighteenth century, but on the grounds that they were the most sensible and useful way of bringing about the "greatest happiness of the greatest number." This attitude of applying utility to political and social institutions is called "utilitarianism."

"Utilitarianism"

The key figure in the transformation of liberal thought from the Enlightenment to the nineteenth century was the English philosopher and reformer Jeremy Bentham (1748–1832), the founder of utilitarianism. Bentham was a rationalist, but the reasonableness of an institution for him did not depend on its conformity with natural law; it depended on its utility. How was this utility to be determined? Bentham wrote: "For everyone, his own pleasure and his own freedom from pain is the sole good, his own pain and his own unfreedom the sole evil. Man's happiness and welfare consist exclusively of pleasurable feelings and of freedom from pain." Translated into politics, this meant that the best government

Jeremy Bentham (1748–1832), detail from a painting by J. Watts.

John Stuart Mill, 1806–73.

was the one that ensured the most pleasure and gave the least pain to the largest number of people. The type of government most likely to produce that effect, according to Bentham, was a democracy.

Bentham's philosophy found many disciples, especially in England. Many of the British reforms in the 1820s and 1830s were due to the agitation of the "Utilitarians," or "Philosophical Radicals." The most influential follower of Bentham was John Stuart Mill (1806–73). Mill was an active public servant, a leading reformer, and a prolific writer on a wide range of subjects. Among his most famous books was the essay *On Liberty* (1859). Its purpose, according to Mill, was to set forth the basic principle according to which relations between the individual and society, between the citizen and his government, should be regulated. That principle, Mill said, is "that the sole end for which mankind may interfere with the liberty of action of the individual is self-protection. The only purpose for which power can be rightfully exercised over any member of a civilized community, against his will, is to prevent harm to others." Here we have a categorical statement in favor of individual liberty. Mill based his plea not on natural law, as earlier advocates of individual freedom had done, but on utility. "I regard utility," he said, "as the ultimate appeal on all ethical questions."

Mill's emphasis on individual freedom, on the right of everyone to do as he saw fit as long as his actions did not conflict with society, had tremendous appeal to the middle-class industrialist and businessman of the nineteenth century. Here was a philosophy that frowned on any but the most necessary interference by the government in the affairs of the individual. "That government is best that governs least," that leaves the individual free to develop his own abilities. In another essay, *Considerations on Representative Government* (1861), Mill discussed the purpose of government in terms that sounded familiar to businessmen. "Government," he said, "is a problem to be worked like any other question of business. The first step is to define the purpose which governments are required to promote. The next is to inquire what form of government is best

fitted to fulfill these purposes." In answer to the first question, what is the purpose of good government, Mill held that it was "to promote the virtue and intelligence of its people"; and in answer to the second question, what form of government is best, Mill, like Bentham, decided in favor of democracy.

Mill's belief in democracy was not shared by most members of the middle class. Nor were his proposals that the government should intervene to protect working children and improve housing and working conditions. Mill was highly critical of the economic injustices and inequities he found in his own society. He suggested as remedies the formation of trade unions and a share in the profits for workers. He even went so far as to question the sanctity of private property. These were already signs of the new type of liberalism that was ultimately to replace the dogmatic liberalism of the early nineteenth century (see p. 652). But even though Mill showed greater compassion for the fate of the lower classes, his demand that the government leave the individual alone as much as possible clearly expressed the sentiments held by the majority of the middle class throughout the nineteenth century.

Liberalism in Politics

The middle class was primarily concerned with economic matters. (We shall see presently how liberalism developed its own economic doctrine.) But the industrialists, merchants, and bankers also realized that economic freedom was of no value unless it was supplemented by political rights. The main guarantee of such rights in the early nineteenth century was seen in a written constitution, like that of the United States. The first document of this kind in recent European history had been the French Constitution of 1791. There were many others between 1812 and 1849. Most of these constitutions favored limited constitutional monarchy rather than true democracy. To ensure the predominance of the middle class, property qualifications for voting and for holding government office were part of all liberal constitutions. Anyone who found this restriction unjust was told that he needed only

Portrait medal of Adam Smith, 1797. The reverse side shows symbols of Smith's *Wealth of Nations.*

to work hard and improve his economic status in order to gain a share in the government. Only in their guarantee of individual liberty did these constitutions make some concession to the masses as well as to the classes. Freedom of the press, freedom of conscience, freedom of association, and freedom from arbitrary arrest—these were shared by rich and poor alike, at least theoretically. Workers who organized in order to improve their condition through collective bargaining, or socialists who used the press to call attention to existing injustices, would soon find out that the individual liberties guaranteed in the constitutions of the early nineteenth century did not apply to them.

The political ideal of early nineteenth-century liberalism was limited democracy. It has been aptly characterized as government of the wealthy, for the wealthy, by the wealthy. It was this ideal that motivated the middle class in the various revolutions discussed previously and that accounted for the widening rift between the middle and lower classes in these revolutions.

The "Classical Economists"

As for the economic philosophy of liberalism, its roots, too, went back to the eighteenth century. Its basic elements were already contained in the writings of Adam Smith (1723–90). This Glasgow professor, in his *Wealth of Nations* (1776), had argued for a policy of individual self-interest, free from any government interference, as the surest road to economic prosperity for society as a whole. Smith had proposed this policy of laissez faire, of leaving things alone, in order to liberate the individual from the many governmental restrictions that had hampered economic progress under mercantilism. He was the first of several writers who are usually called the classical economists. These men, for the first time, formulated certain general economic laws that seemed to apply at all times and in all societies. The most prominent members of the group were Smith, Robert Malthus (1766–1834), and David Ricardo (1772–1823).

Malthus wrote his famous *Essay on the Principles of Population* in 1798. The book grew out of an argument he had with his father. The elder Malthus, a typical product of the eighteenth century, believed that if the world were reformed along rational lines there would be no end to human progress. Young Malthus did not agree. He pointed to the rapidly increasing population of western Europe in the late eighteenth and early nineteenth centuries as an insurmountable obstacle to progress. "The power of population," he wrote, "is indefinitely greater than the power in earth to produce subsistence for man. Population, when unchecked, increases in a geometrical ratio. Subsistence only increases in an arithmetical ratio." Here was the basic hypothesis of Malthusianism: People multiplied much more rapidly than the supply of food that was needed to keep them alive. Human misery, it seemed, was unavoidable. Poverty rather than progress was the normal state of human society.

Many objections have been raised to the dire prophecies of Malthus. Even in his own day, improvements in agriculture and the opening to cultivation of vast new regions in America and elsewhere were increasing the world's food supply. Since then there have been further changes, especially with scientific farming and the development of birth

---

Adam Smith
on the Limitations of Government 1776

According to the system of natural liberty, the sovereign has only three duties to attend to; three duties of great importance, indeed, but plain and intelligible to common understandings: first, the duty of protecting the society from the violence and invasion of other independent societies; secondly, the duty of protecting, as far as possible, every member of the society from the injustice or oppression of every other member of it, or the duty of establishing an exact administration of justice; and, thirdly, the duty of erecting and maintaining certain public works and certain public institutions, which it can never be for the interest of any individual, or small number of individuals, to erect and maintain; because the profit could never repay the expense to any individual or small number of individuals, though it may frequently do much more than repay it to a great society.

From Adam Smith, *An Inquiry into the Nature and Causes of the Wealth of Nations,* ed. by Edwin Cannan (New York: Random House, 1937), p. 651.

Thomas Robert Malthus,
1766–1834.

control to help maintain the balance between population growth and food supply. In our own day, however, the threat of overpopulation has once again taken on a fearful reality, and the current "population explosion" seems to confirm Malthus' most dire predictions.

To the majority of people in the early nineteenth century, the warnings of Malthus also came as a shock. The future, which only recently had held such promise, now suddenly looked bleak; no wonder the new science of political economy was soon called the "dismal science." Yet it was not dismal to everyone—certainly not to the middle class. As industrialists were growing rich while workers were sinking into misery, some voices now favored a more equitable distribution of profits. Such proposals, however, could not stand up against Malthus' assertion that poverty was inevitable. The poor were already increasing much faster than the rich. Giving them more wages or charity, the middle class could argue, would only result in their having more children. The best solution was to keep the poor as poor as possible. Adam Smith had asked government to keep its hands off business; Malthus advocated a similar attitude of laissez faire in regard to social reform.

The pessimistic note that characterizes the teachings of Malthus is also found in the writings of David Ricardo.

His basic work, *On the Principles of Political Economy and Taxation* (1817), was the first real textbook on economics. One of Ricardo's major contributions to the economic theory of early nineteenth-century liberalism was what his disciples called the "iron law of wages." Labor, to Ricardo, was very much like any other commodity. When it was plentiful, it was cheap; when it was scarce, it was expensive. As long as there is an ample supply of workers, wages will inevitably sink to the lowest possible level of subsistence, just above starvation. To try to remedy this situation by lowering profits and raising wages would be futile, since it would merely increase the number of workers' children and, by limiting the supply of capital, cut down production. "Like all other contracts," Ricardo said, "wages should be left to the fair and free competition of the market, and should never be controlled by the interference of the legislature."

Here was another economic law as dismal in its prospects for the lower classes as Malthus' predictions on the increase of population. If there were people living on the verge of starvation, if wages were low and children had to work sixteen hours a day, that was unfortunate; but it was also, as Malthus and Ricardo had shown, inevitable. Attempts to change the situation through charity or legislation designed to improve wages and hours were opposed by middle-class liberals as interference with the beneficent principle of laissez faire.

Liberalism on the Continent

All the intellectual figures mentioned so far in this discussion of liberalism were British. Since England had a larger and more influential middle class than most continental countries, this is not surprising. But the writings of these men had a deep effect on continental liberalism as well. Adam Smith's *Wealth of Nations* in particular supplied most of the ammunition for the attacks of continental liberals on the economic restrictions and regulations of their governments. There were some differences in the direction or emphasis of these attacks. French liberalism, for instance, was more concerned with economic matters than liberalism in

A large Victorian family,
1878.

Germany, where the problem of national unification overshadowed all other issues. Outside England, France, and Germany, the philosophy of liberalism had few contributors. Liberalism, after all, was the credo of a class that had as yet made little headway outside western Europe.

SOCIAL REFORM

Given the laissez-faire attitude of liberalism, it is not surprising that efforts to solve social problems through government action found little support among the middle class. What social reforms were introduced owed much to the agitation of a few individuals, who were motivated either by humanitarianism or, as in the case of Britain's "Philosophical Radicals," by a desire to be utilitarian and efficient.

Factory Acts

Some of the most effective opposition to early nineteenth-century liberalism came from among the representatives of the old order. For political and economic but also humanitarian reasons, some Tories attacked the new industrial system in its most vulnerable spot, the terrible conditions in the mines and factories. As far back as 1802, Parliament had passed an act that cut down the working hours of apprentices. The first real factory act, passed in 1819, forbade the employment in cotton mills of children under nine years of age and limited the daily labor of children over nine to twelve hours. In 1831 night work was abolished for persons under twenty-one. In 1847 the maximum working day for women and children was set at ten hours. Two acts in 1842 and 1855 made it illegal to employ women and children in the mining industry.

Despite the best intentions on the part of their sponsors, however, these early factory acts were not very effective. They were not strictly enforced, and they applied chiefly to the cotton industry. Not until 1833 was their scope extended to include other industries, and only then was some system of inspection set up to enforce the new provisions.

Social Legislation

There were other reforms in England besides factory acts. The Municipal Corporations Act of 1835 enabled municipalities to cope more effectively with problems arising from rapid urbanization. To ensure some degree of uniformity in matters of public health, Parliament in 1848 set up a system of local boards of health. One of the most pressing social problems was the care of the poor. The New Poor Law of 1834 for the first time brought some order into the complicated system of poor relief. It was, however, a mixed blessing to the poor. The law abolished the traditional practice of "outdoor relief," under which the wages of the poorest workers had been supplemented from public funds. Henceforth, to be eligible for relief, the poor had to report to workhouses; and by making conditions in these establishments as unpleasant as possible, all but those who could not possibly make a living otherwise were discouraged from going on relief. Here was a measure, clearly utilitarian, that delighted the middle class. It discouraged idleness and cut the expense of poor relief.

On the Continent, little was done to reform the abuses of early industrialism. A French law in 1803 prohibited work in factories before 3:00 A.M. Under the reign of Louis Philippe, the employment of children under eight was prohibited and the work of children under twelve was limited to eight hours a day. But enforcement of these laws, in France as in England, was very lax. In Belgium, nothing at all was being done to improve the lot of the workers. The only state with any industry in Germany was Prussia, and the Prussian government, in 1839, introduced a factory law that forbade the employment of children under nine and limited the working hours of children to ten hours.

Liberalism and Education

The only field of social reform in which the Continent was ahead of Great Britain was education. Here, for once, liberalism was a great help. Like the *philosophe* of the eighteenth century, the nineteenth-century liberal was a firm believer in education as a means of improving the world and of helping children get ahead. Any governmental measure in favor of education, therefore, had liberal support. Both France and Prussia had a long tradition of public education, which they maintained during the nineteenth century. There was a brief reaction in favor of religious education under the Bourbons, but the Education Act passed under Louis Philippe again asserted the state's role in education. Britain's first provision of public funds for education was not until 1833. It was increased in subsequent years, but even so the amount set aside for education in 1839 was still only half of what it cost to maintain Queen Victoria's horses. Not until 1870 was the first general education act adopted in England. In the meantime, education depended on private initiative, in which the middle class played a leading and beneficial role.

As this discussion has shown, some genuine attempts were made in the first half of the nineteenth century to cope with the ills of early industrialism through social reform. But such attempts ran counter to the laissez-faire philosophy of liberalism. Economic liberalism was, to some extent, a mere rationalization of selfish interests by the middle class. But there was also in it much of the eighteenth-century belief that the world operated according to certain basic laws that could not be altered and which ultimately made for the greatest happiness of the greatest number.

This passive acquiescence in things as they were, however, could not possibly satisfy the workers. They refused to believe that the only solution to their troubles was to do nothing, to let matters take their course. They demanded that remedial action be taken on their behalf, else they were prepared to act for themselves.

WORKING-CLASS PROTEST

The protest of the working class took various forms. Some of the discontent expressed itself in political action, as in the revolutions of 1830 and 1848. In another form of protest, workers vented their anger and frustration on the very

An early photograph of a classroom in an English school, 1856.

instruments that to them seemed primarily responsible for their plight—the machines. There were sporadic instances of such "machine-breaking" during the early phase of industrialization, both in England and on the Continent. But these acts of despair could not halt the advance of the machine age. Instead of waging war against mechanization, workers increasingly tried to escape industrialization altogether by emigrating to the United States, where virgin lands offered them the opportunity of making a better living.

Early Labor Unions

There was another, more effective way in which the working class tried to fight the injustices of industrialism. As the workers grew in number, they became aware that they constituted a new and separate class whose interests conflicted with those of their employers. This growing class-consciousness among the workers led them to organize their

forces in an effort to gain better treatment for themselves.

The first country in which this trend toward labor unions made any headway was again Great Britain. The British government, impressed by the radicalism of the French Revolution, watched with apprehension labor's early efforts to organize. In 1799 and 1800 Parliament passed the Combination Acts, which prohibited workers from organizing to improve their condition. Labor's continued activities, however, together with the agitation of some middle-class reformers, finally made the government relent. In 1824–25, as we have seen, the Combination Acts were repealed. Henceforth, trade unions in England were no longer illegal, though it was still impossible under the law of conspiracy to engage in strikes and other forms of protest. Even so, under the new dispensation local unions arose throughout Britain. The next logical step was the formation of a large labor organization. This step was taken in 1845, with the organization of the "National Association for the Protection of Labour." In 1859 the Association was instrumental in having

Parliament allow peaceful picketing. In 1868 a Trades Union Congress representing more than 100,000 members met in Manchester. By 1875, trade unions in Britain had won full legal status, including the right to strike and to picket peacefully. The British labor movement had at last come into its own.

On the Continent, labor's efforts at self-help were much less successful. Labor unions were forbidden in Belgium until 1866, and there was no labor movement in Germany to speak of until after 1870. In France, the right of workers to organize had been forbidden even during the Revolution. This ban was reiterated in the Napoleonic Code of 1803. Some French workers organized secret societies that fomented strikes and local uprisings; but these only made the government more determined in its repressive policy. The French banker Casimir Périer expressed the feelings of the government and the middle class when he said, "The workers must realize that their only salvation lies in patient resignation to their lot." Others in France, however, took a less passive view of the worker's fate. If

Slitting room of a pen factory in Birmingham, 1851.

England was prominent in defining the middle-class philosophy of liberalism, France was equally prominent in producing its counterpart, the working-class philosophy of socialism.

THE BEGINNINGS OF MODERN SOCIALISM

Socialism as a mode of life is nothing new. It always existed, and still does, in primitive communities where people work together and share the proceeds of their common labor. Socialism as an economic and social philosophy, on the other hand, is a relatively recent development, closely connected with the rise of modern industrialism. The term *socialism* did not come into common use until the 1830s. Like liberalism, it has assumed a wide variety of meanings. Today almost any kind of government interference with the free play of economic forces is called socialism, whether it be the communist system of Russia or the "welfare state" of the United States.

While there are many varieties of socialism, all share certain fundamental principles. All socialists think that the existing distribution of wealth is unjust, since it gives a few people far more than they possibly need and leaves large numbers of people with barely enough to exist. To close the gap between the haves and the have-nots, socialists advocate common ownership of the resources and means of production that constitute and create society's wealth. The fruits of production—that is, the profits of human labor—socialists propose to distribute in such a way that every member of society receives an equal or at least an equitable share. All schools of socialism agree that there should be far-reaching changes in society in the direction of economic and social as well as political equality.

The Utopian Socialists

Historically, modern socialism is usually divided into pre-Marxian and post-Marxian socialism or, in terms introduced by the Marxists, into "Utopian" and "scientific" socialism. The Utopian socialists earned their epithet because of the unrealistic nature of their schemes. Most of the Utopians were French, and they all came from the middle or upper class. In view of the poverty and lack of education of the working class, this is hardly surprising.

The first Utopian socialist to achieve any prominence was a French nobleman, Count Henri de Saint-Simon (1760–1825). Concerned by the social and economic injustices of a laissez-faire economy, Saint-Simon suggested that the state take a hand in organizing society in such a way that people, instead of exploiting one another, join forces to exploit nature. "The whole society," he held, "ought to strive toward the amelioration of the moral and physical existence of the most numerous and poorest class." Saint-Simon defined the principle according to which this amelioration should operate as: "From each according to his capacity, to each according to his work." In time this became one of the basic slogans of socialism.

Another prominent Utopian was Charles Fourier (1772–1837). Most of the ills of society, Fourier held, were due to the improper social and physical environment in which most people lived. To provide a more favorable environment, Fourier proposed the creation of so-called *phalanges,* or phalanxes. These were to be pleasant communities of some 1,600 to 1,800 people, living on 5,000 acres of land, and forming a self-sufficient economic unit. Fourier's plans never got very far in Europe. But in the United States, where land was cheap and pioneering more common, a number of cooperative establishments were tried. None of them, however, was a lasting success.

The only one among the French Utopians to play an active role in politics was Louis Blanc (1811–82). His reform proposals were a good deal more realistic than those of the other Utopians. Blanc realized that economic reform, to be effective, must be preceded by political reform. Once true democracy had been achieved, the state could initiate the new type of industrial organizations that Blanc proposed. These consisted of social or national workshops—that is, self-supporting units of production, owned

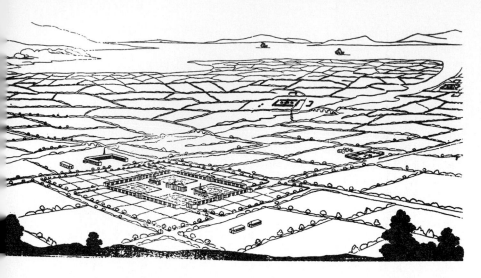

best intentions are not sufficient to re-form society. A more realistic and more militant type of socialism was needed that would use the worker's potential economic and political power to wrest concessions from the middle class. This new kind of socialism was first presented in the writings of Karl Marx (1818–83) and Friedrich Engels (1820–95).

MARXIAN SOCIALISM

One of the reasons for the failure of the Utopian socialists was that they never sparked any substantial movement among the workers. There were some political working-class organizations during the 1830s and 1840s, but they had to operate as secret conspiracies rather than open political parties. In France, Auguste Blanqui founded the "Society of Families" and the "Society of Seasons," both of them socialistic or communistic. Another such society, founded by German exiles, was the "League of the Just." Its program was originally supplied by Wilhelm Weitling, a German tailor who in 1842 published his *Guarantee of Harmony and Freedom.* These various underground organizations were all influenced by the writings of the Utopian socialists, but in their demands for complete economic equality, or communism, they went considerably beyond the demands of the middle-class Utopians.

Communism—that is, the abolition of all private property—ultimately became the basis of most socialist programs. A century ago, of course, the term *communism* did not have the connotations it has assumed since the Bolshevik Revolution. The number of communist socialists in the first half of the nineteenth century was extremely small, and very few people realized the ultimate implications of their aims. In 1844 two young Germans, Karl Marx and Friedrich Engels, established contact with the "League of the Just." Soon thereafter its name was changed to the "Communist League," and from secret revolutionary conspiracy it now shifted to open propaganda. In 1847–48 Marx and Engels supplied the League with its new program, which they called the *Communist Manifesto.*

Below: contemporary drawing of Robert Owen, whose plan for the agricultural and manufacturing villages of Unity and Mutual Cooperation (1817) is shown above.

and operated by the workers on a cooperative, profit-sharing basis. Workshops of this sort were given a brief try by the revolutionary government of 1848, of which Louis Blanc was a member. The experiment failed, however, largely because the original purpose of the workshops was subordinated to the needs of the moment. Instead of self-supporting industrial enterprises, the workshops of 1848 were used for the temporary relief of unemployment.

The most prominent Utopian socialist outside France was the British industrialist Robert Owen (1771–1858). Appalled by conditions he found when he took over the cotton mills at New Lanark in Scotland, Owen gave his workers decent housing, increased their pay, and shortened their working-hours. In the model community he created, both productivity and profits increased, thus bearing out Owen's contention that satisfied workers were also better workers. Owen was less fortunate with a project he attempted on this side of the Atlantic. The community of New Harmony in Indiana, conceived along the lines of Fourier's phalanxes, turned out to be a fiasco.

Utopian socialism, in fact, had little to show for its manifold efforts. Like the *philosophes,* the Utopians believed in the natural goodness of man and the perfectibility of the world. They soon discovered that most men were not naturally good and reasonable. But even the failure of the Utopians contained a useful lesson. It showed that idealism and the

Family photograph of Karl Marx (right), his wife, and two daughters in the 1860s. Friedrich Engels is at left.

failed, he went to England. There he remained until his death in 1883, leading a none-too-happy life, constantly beset by financial worries and ill health. It was while in England that Marx wrote most of his basic works, notably *Das Kapital,* the first volume of which appeared in 1867.

The Communist Manifesto

The basic elements of Marx's social philosophy were contained in the brief and persuasive *Communist Manifesto.* Its fundamental proposition, as restated by Engels in his introduction to a later edition of the *Manifesto,* was

> that in every historical epoch the prevailing mode of economic production and exchange, and the social organization necessarily following from it, form the basis upon which is built up, and from which alone can be explained, the political and intellectual history of that epoch; that consequently the whole history of mankind (since the dissolution of primitive tribal society, holding land in common ownership) has been a history of class struggles, contests between exploiting and exploited, ruling and oppressed classes; that the history of these struggles forms a series of evolutions in which, nowadays, a stage has been reached where the exploited and oppressed class—the proletariat—cannot attain its emancipation from the sway of the exploiting and ruling class—the bourgeoisie—without, at the same time and once and for all, emancipating society at large from all exploitation, oppression, class distinctions, and class struggles.

Here are the two things for which Marx is most famous: his economic, or materialistic, interpretation of history, and his theory of the class struggle. Other thinkers before Marx had recognized the influence of material circumstances and of the environment upon history. But Marx focused his attention on one particular aspect of environment that he considered fundamental: the means of production, the way in which people make a living. It is the economic structure of society, according to Marx,

Karl Marx and Friedrich Engels

Both Marx and Engels came from the middle class that they spent most of their lives attacking. Even as a university student in Germany, Marx had shown a lively interest in social issues and socialism. His early writings brought him into disfavor with the police and in 1843 led to his first exile in Paris. There he met Engels, the son of a wealthy German industrialist with industrial holdings in England. Engels was already a communist, and there developed between the two men a close intellectual partnership. Engels is usually overshadowed by Marx, but his contributions to Marxian doctrine were considerable; besides, Engels through most of his life supported Marx financially.

The first result of the collaboration between Marx and Engels was the *Communist Manifesto,* which appeared during the revolutions of 1848. Marx and his fellow exiles welcomed the revolutions, and Marx himself was present during the upheavals in Paris. When the revolutions

On Understanding Marx

Rigorous examination is one thing Marx's ideas will not stand because they were not rigorously formulated. To do justice to his intent they must often be reinterpreted and qualified. They constitute a mixture of the true, the vague, and the false.

It should be apparent to any sensitive reader that Marx writes primarily as a critic of capitalism, as a man fired with a passionate ideal to eliminate the social inequalities, the poverty, and injustices of his time. Much of what he said makes sense and good sense considered as a description of the capitalist society of his time and as a prediction of the probable historical development of any capitalist system *on the assumption* that nothing outside that system, especially political influences, interferes with its development. Marx's fundamental errors arise from an uncritical extrapolation of what he observed in capitalist societies to all class societies, and from a disregard of the enormous influence which political, national, and moral forces have exerted on the development of capitalism as an economic system.

From Sidney Hook, *Marx and the Marxists: The Ambiguous Legacy* (Princeton: Van Nostrand, 1955), p. 35.

that determines its social, political, legal, and even cultural aspects. Historians before Marx, especially after the eighteenth century, had viewed history as an intellectually determined process. Marx took a diametrically opposite view, recognizing material, economic, nonintellectual forces as the sole determining factors.

To illustrate his economic interpretation of history as well as his theory of the class struggle, in the *Communist Manifesto* Marx gave a brief survey of the history of western civilization as he saw it:

> The history of all hitherto existing society is the history of class struggles. Freeman and slave, patrician and plebeian, lord and serf, guildmaster and journeyman, in a word, oppressor and oppressed, stood in constant opposition to one another, carried on an uninterrupted, now hidden, now open fight, a fight that each time ended either in a revolutionary reconstitution of society at large, or in the common ruin of the contending classes.

Marx then examined the history of western society more closely, beginning with the Middle Ages. At that time, the economy of Europe was predominantly agrarian, with a large class of serfs supporting a small class of feudal nobles. Upon this society, material changes began to work: money, trade, the beginnings of a commercial, capitalist economy. As these changes took hold, a new class, a trading or bourgeois class, was formed. And between the old feudal nobility and the new middle class a struggle arose, which led to some preliminary victories of the bourgeoisie in England and Holland and culminated in the American War of Independence and the French Revolution.

The final victory of the middle class came in the nineteenth century. But this did not end the struggle. Because now a new struggle began, this time between the bourgeoisie and the proletariat. It was brought about by another change in the mode of production, the introduction of the factory system and the rise of industrial capitalism. The workers in this new struggle, which Marx saw going on around him, were now herded together in large factories, under the eyes of their "oppressors." They were held down by the iron laws of capitalist economics to a bare subsistence level. But there was one thing these workers could do, according to Marx: they could organize, they could become class-conscious.

Marx felt certain that the bourgeoisie and the workers were already locked in their death struggle. And the victory of the proletariat in this struggle, Marx held, could be predicted with the certainty of a scientific experiment—hence the term "scientific socialism." By the laws of capitalist competition there were bound to be periodic crises, caused by "epidemics of overproduction." As a result of these crises, the poor would get poorer and the rich would get richer. And there would finally come a time when "it becomes evident, that the bourgeoisie is unfit any longer to be the ruling class in society . . . because it is incompetent to assure an existence to its slave within his slavery. . . . Society can no longer live under this bourgeoisie. . . . Its fall and the victory of the proletariat are equally inevitable."

So much for the collapse of capitalism. What then? What will the world be like after the proletariat has won? On that subject Marx is not too clear. At one point he envisages a kind of transition period—the dictatorship of the proletariat, as he calls it—in which the proletariat by revolution will destroy the existing political machinery of the state, will convert the means of production into public property, and will gradually bring about a classless society. The state, as Engels put it, will gradually "wither away." Then what? "In place of the old bourgeois society, with its classes and class antagonisms," Marx concludes, "we shall have an association in which the free development of each is the condition for the free development of all." This is an idyllic picture, but also rather vague, and not very different from the kind of society certain eighteenth-century writers had envisaged. There was, in fact, a good deal of the eighteenth century in Marxism. It shared the later *philosophes'* belief in progress, in the good life here on earth, and in the natural goodness of man.

The Errors and Contributions of Marx

What about Marx's concept of classes, and of history as a series of class struggles? The concept of class certainly was a useful contribution; and if Marx did not make us class-conscious, he helped our understanding of past and present society by making us aware of classes. But his definition of classes entirely in economic terms is much too narrow; and by denying any influence to the individual, it runs counter to our widely held belief in individualism. As for Marx's view of the past as a series of class struggles, it does not really fit the facts of history, nor does his emphasis on merely two opposing classes. Marx recognized the existence of other classes, but he believed that they would ultimately be absorbed by one or the other of the two contending groups—the bourgeoisie and the proletariat. This prediction, like so many others Marx made, thus far has failed to materialize.

There were, then, a good many blind spots in Marx's socialist theories. While the rich were getting richer, the poor did not necessarily get poorer. The general standard of living in the world's industrial nations was to reach heights undreamed of by Marx. Man, furthermore, does not seem to be motivated exclusively, or even primarily, by economic

What If Marx Had Never Lived?

No one can read the story of Karl Marx or ponder the somber prognostications of Marx the historian or the economist without asking, "Would history have been significantly different if Marx had not lived?"

It is a surprisingly difficult question to answer. To be sure, the trend of world capitalism would not have been deflected by so much as an inch if it had been deprived of the insights of Marx's masterwork, *Das Kapital*. Marxism as a system of thought has exerted virtually no direct influence on the internal economic evolution of American or European capitalism as such. But the influence of Marxism is not so easily summed up when we look at the revolutionary countries: at Russia or China or Cuba or at the bubbling cauldron of the underdeveloped world. And its effects on these countries has, in turn, affected the West.

A first glance would tell us that in these lands Marx was of the greatest importance. Whole political catechisms and, more than that, crucial political guidance have been wrested from the writings of Marx and his collaborator Friedrich Engels, writings which have on many occasions assumed the role of Biblical literature in a fundamentalist community. Even so relatively liberated a Marxist as the Yugoslav spokesman Edvard Kardelj wrote a polemic against the Chinese position on the question of coexistence in 1960 by leaning not so much on facts and empirical evidence as on what Marx or Engels said. If Marx said (or if one can "interpret" Marx to have said) that coexistence was possible, then it is possible; if he said not, it is not.

Thus Marx and Marxism have indubitably left their imprint on the vocabulary, the thought pattern and the discourse of the revolutionary nations. Yet it is difficult to believe that the revolutions themselves would not have occurred or that Communism (by whatever name) would not be a great world presence today had Marx not lived. The forces which finally burst through the crusts of tired and corrupt societies in Russia, China and Cuba—and which threaten to do so again in Latin America and Asia and Africa—may have been guided by Marxism, but they were not generated by Marxism alone. Had Marx never lived or written, old and incapable regimes would have given way to new and vigorous ones, no doubt with all the agonies by which such changes in history are usually accompanied. The world would have been different surely, but not perhaps all that different.

From Robert L. Heilbroner in Isaiah Berlin, *Karl Marx: His Life and Environment* (New York: Time-Life, 1963), pp. xviii-xix.

concerns. Despite Marx's attacks on religion, the established churches have continued to play an important part even in the lives of the lower classes. Another force that increasingly came to command the allegiance of rich and poor alike was nationalism. The great wars of the last century have been fought not between the "oppressed" and their "oppressors," but between the citizens of different nations, including the workers, for the defense or the greater glory of their own country.

Despite errors and shortcomings in his teachings, however, the contributions of Marx to modern thought have been considerable. By bridging the gap between politics and economics, he enriched our understanding of the past. We may not accept the dominant role he assigned to economic factors, but we have come to realize the importance of these factors. Prior to Marx, the division of society into rich and poor, haves and have-nots, was accepted as a natural, unchangeable fact. It was chiefly due to Marx that society was jolted out of such complacent acceptance of the *status quo*. By predicting far-reaching changes, he made people aware that changes were possible. The threat of revolutionary change conjured up in Marx's writings did much to hasten the peaceful evolution that has so markedly improved the condition of the lower classes in all industrial societies. Marxian socialism offered its followers a seemingly logical, scientifically certain answer to the many perplexities of modern society. This explains its appeal to workers and intellectuals alike. The ultimate success of Marxism lay in the almost religious fervor it inspired among its disciples.

OTHER FORMS OF SOCIAL CRITICISM

Marxian socialism, in its ultimate effects on society, turned out to be the most important attack on the capitalist philosophy of laissez faire. There were other critics of this philosophy, however, who tried in various ways to awaken their contemporaries to the social problems created by the industrialization of society.

Humanitarianism

Writers like Victor Hugo and Honoré de Balzac in France and Charles Dickens in England, by dwelling in their novels on the more sordid aspects of the new industrialism, played on human sympathy in the hope of creating a climate favorable to reform. The historian Thomas Carlyle, in his *Past and Present* (1843), showed deep concern over the growing division between the working classes on the one hand and the wealthy classes on the other. He turned against the "mammonism" and the "mechanism" of his age and admonished the new captains of industry to be aware of their responsibilities as successors to the old aristocracy. Benjamin Disraeli, one of the rising young Tories, in his social novel *Sybil* (1845), deplored the wide gap that industrialization had opened between the rich and the poor. It was, he said, as though England had split into two nations "between whom there was no intercourse and no sympathy."

Christian Socialism

Another body of social criticism arose within the Christian churches, first in England and later on the Continent. For centuries past, organized Christianity had been the chief dispenser of charity to the poor and the aged. The beginnings of modern Christian socialism go back to a small group of English clergymen who felt that the best way to attack the evils of industrialism was to reaffirm the gospel of charity and brotherly love. The leader of the Christian Socialist movement was the Anglican theologian Frederick Denison Maurice. Its best-known propagandist was the clergyman and novelist Charles Kingsley. In his famous tract *Cheap Clothes and Nasty* (1850), written under the pseudonym of "Parson Lot," Kingsley attacked the condition of "ever-increasing darkness and despair" in the British clothing industry, whose sweatshops were "rank with human blood." To remedy a situation in which men were like "beasts of prey, eating one another up by competition, as in some confined pike-pond, where the great pike, having dispatched the little ones, begin to devour each other," Kingsley

Charles Dickens (1812–70), at age 47.

The Reverend Charles Kingsley (1819–1875), English author and noted Christian Socialist.

proposed the formation of cooperative enterprises in which everyone would be "working together for common profit in the spirit of mutual self-sacrifice." Christian Socialism, in appealing to the social consciousness of "every gentleman and every Christian," helped to modify the belief in laissez faire and to prepare the soil for the movement of social reform that gained momentum in the second half of the nineteenth century.

Anarchism

One other form of social protest of quite a different nature deserves mention here, even though its effects were not felt until later in the century. Anarchism, like socialism, was intended to overthrow capitalism. But while the socialists were ready to use the state as a stepping stone for the realization of their aims, the anarchists were deeply opposed to any kind of governmental authority and organization. One of the earliest theorists of anarchism was the French publicist Pierre-Joseph Proudhon (1809–65). In his pamphlet *First Memoir on Property* (1840) he asked the question, "What is property?" and replied with the well-known slogan, "Property is theft!" This seeming opposition to private property appeared to align Proudhon with communism and endeared him to Marx. The latter's admiration cooled, however, when he discovered that Proudhon was less interested in overthrowing the middle class than in raising the worker to the level of that class. Proudhon was against any kind of government, be it by one man, a party, or a democratic majority. "Society," he wrote, "finds its highest perfection in the union of order with anarchy."

The most famous proponent of anarchism was a Russian nobleman, Mikhail Bakunin (1814–76). A theorist of anarchism, he also practiced what he preached. Bakunin was involved in several revolutions, was three times condemned to death, and spent long years in prison and Siberian exile. Bakunin attributed most of the evils of his day to two agencies—the state and the Church. He objected to both institutions because of the restrictions they impose on human freedom. His ideal society was a loose federation of local communities, each with a maximum of autonomy. In each of these communities the means of production were to be held in common. The way to achieve this governmentless state of affairs, Bakunin held, was not by waiting patiently for the state to wither away, as Marx had held, but by helping matters along, if necessary by means of terrorism, assassination, and insurrection. The last decade of the nineteenth century, as we shall see, witnessed a whole series of assassinations attributed to anarchists. But anarchism never developed into a well-defined movement, partly because of Bakunin's death in 1876, partly because of the impracticable nature of its doctrine. Traces of it, however, survived into the twentieth century and contributed to another type of social protest, syndicalism (see p. 662).

By the middle of the nineteenth century, the coming of the Industrial Age, with its revolutionary political, social, and economic effects, had made itself felt over most of Europe. It also extended to other parts of the world (see Chapter 27).

Mikhail Bakunin (1814–76).

For the next two decades, people's attention in Europe and the United States became absorbed by momentous political developments. A series of wars radically changed the existing order and overshadowed economic developments.

Once the political situation had become stabilized, however, shortly after 1870, a second wave of economic development swept over Europe and the world, a wave of such magnitude that it is often called a "Second Industrial Revolution."

Suggestions for Further Reading

Note: Asterisk denotes a book available in paperback edition.

General

Historians' views of the "Industrial Revolution" have changed over the years, as is shown in E. E. Lampard's perceptive essay, *Industrial Revolution: Interpretations and Perspectives* (1957). A good recent account of early industrialization is P. Deane, *The First Industrial Revolution** (1965). H. J. Habbakuk and M. Postan, eds., *The Industrial Revolutions and After* (1965) (Vol. VI of *The Cambridge Economic History of Europe*), contains essays by noted specialists. W. W. Rostow's influential book, *The Stages of Economic Growth** (1960), has introduced novel concepts like "take-off" into the debate on industrialization. The widening scope of industrialization is stressed in W. O. Henderson, *The Industrial Revolution on the Continent* (1961). A. P. Usher, *A History of Mechanical Inventions* (1929), and G. Fussell, *The Farmer's Tools, 1500–1900* (1952), discuss the importance of technological change; and A. M. Carr-Saunders, *World Population: Past Growth and Present Trends* (1937), traces the beginnings of the current "population explosion." On urbanization, see L. Mumford, *The City in History* (1961). The same author's *Technics and Civilization* (1934), and S. Chase, *Men and Machines* (1929), view with some alarm the impact of technology on man.

Economic Changes in Britain

Because England was the first country to undergo the transition to modern industrialism, its agricultural and industrial revolutions have been studied most intensively. Both P. Mantoux, *The Industrial Revolution in the Eighteenth Century* (1929), and T. S. Ashton, *An Economic History of England: The Eighteenth Century* (1955), deal with the roots of these developments, although with different emphases. A small volume by T. S. Ashton, *The Industrial Revolution, 1760–1830** (1948), corrects many misconceptions about early industrialism. J. H. Clapham, *An Economic History of Modern Britain*, Vol. I (1926), covers the period between 1820 and 1850. Briefer treatments are W. H. B. Court, *A Concise Economic History of Britain from 1750 to Recent Times* (1954), and A. Redford, *An Economic History of England, 1760–1860* (1947). The changes in British agriculture are the subject of G. Slater, *The English Peasantry and the Enclosure of the Common Fields* (1907); Lord Ernle, *English Farming, Past and Present* (1936); J. L. Hammond and B. Hammond, *The Village Labourer, 1760–1832* (1918); and D. G. Barnes, *A History of the English Corn Laws, 1660–1846* (1930). The following are detailed studies on special aspects of the Industrial Revolution in England: T. S. Ashton, *Iron and Steel in the Industrial Revolution* (1951); W. H. B. Court, *The Rise of the Midland Industries, 1600–1838* (1938); and A. Redford, *Manchester Merchants and Foreign Trade, 1794–1858* (1934). The most important single invention of early industrialism is the subject of H. W. Dickinson, *A Short History of the Steam Engine* (1939), and of J. Lord, *Capital and Steam Power, 1750–1800* (1923).

The Spread of Industrialism

Besides England, only France experienced any noticeable industrial development during the eighteenth century. These beginnings are discussed in H. E. Sée, *Economic and Social Conditions in France During the Eighteenth Century* (1927), and in S. T. McCloy, *French Inventions of the Eighteenth Century* (1954). Later developments in France are treated in A. L. Dunham, *The Industrial Revolution in France, 1815–1848* (1955), and R. E. Cameron, *France and the Economic Development of Europe, 1800–1914** (1961). British influence on economic developments abroad is traced by W. O. Henderson, *Britain and Industrial Europe, 1750–1870* (1954); E. J. Hobsbawm, *Industry and Empire* (1970); and L. C. A. Knowles, *Economic Development in the Nineteenth Century: France, Germany, Russia, and the United States* (1932). Other useful economic histories are: J. H. Clapham, *Economic Development of France and Germany, 1815–1914** (1936); S. B.

Clough, *France: A History of Natural Economics* (1939); W. O. Henderson, *The Zollverein* (1939); P. I. Lyashchenko, *History of the National Economy of Russia to 1917* (1949); and J. Blum, *Lord and Peasant in Russia** (1961).

The Social Effects of Industrialization

The traditional emphasis on the negative effects of early industrialism is evident in J. L. Hammond and B. Hammond, *The Town Labourer, 1760–1832* (1917), *The Skilled Labourer, 1760–1832* (1919), and *The Bleak Age** (1947). That emphasis has found recent confirmation in E. P. Thompson, *The Making of the English Working Class** (1963). A more neutral picture is drawn in A. Briggs, *The Age of Improvement, 1783–1867* (1959); S. G. Checkland, *The Rise of Industrial Society in England, 1815–1885* (1964); and G. Kitson Clark, *The Making of Victorian England* (1962). On urban growth, see A. Redford, *Labour Migration in England, 1800–1850* (1929); and on landed interests, see F. M. Thompson, *English Landed Society in the Nineteenth Century* (1963). The situation in France is dealt with in L. Chevalier, *Working Classes and Dangerous Classes in Paris during the First Part of the Nineteenth Century* (1971).

Economic Liberalism

The best way to study the utilitarians and classical economists is through their writings. The most important of these—J. S. Mill, *Autobiography** and *On Liberty;** T. R. Malthus, *An Essay on Population;** and D. Ricardo, *Principles of Political Economy and Taxation**—are available in several editions. The general development of modern economic thought is presented in C. Gide and C. Rist, *History of Economic Doctrines from the Physiocrats to the Present Day* (1913, 1948), and in E. Roll, *A History of Economic Thought* (1942). The standard work on Bentham and the utilitarians is É. Halévy, *The Growth of Philosophic Radicalism** (1955). More recent treatments are J. Hamburger, *Intellectuals in Politics: John Stuart Mill and the Philosophic Radicals* (1965), and S. H. Letwin, *The Pursuit of Certainty: David Hume; Jeremy Bentham; John Stuart Mill; Beatrice Webb* (1965). There are also pertinent chapters in C. Brinton, *English Political Thought in the Nineteenth Century** (1949).

Social Reform

Social reform in the first half of the nineteenth century was almost entirely restricted to Great Britain. W. M. Thomas, *The Early Factory Legislation* (1948), deals with the period between 1802 and 1853. Other notable reform efforts are dealt with in E. L. Woodward, *The Age of Reform, 1815–1870* (1938); L. Radzinowitz, *A History of English Criminal Law: The Movement for Reform, 1750–1833* (1948); and S. Webb and B. Webb, *English Local Government: English Poor Law History*, 3 vols. (1927–29). For accounts of early attempts by the working class to organize itself politically and economically, see G. D. H. Cole, *British Working Class Politics, 1832–1914* (1941); S. Webb and B. Webb, *History of Trade Unionism* (1920); and H. M. Pelling, *History of Trade Unionism* (1963). A good introduction to social reform is through the biographies of some of the leading reformers: G. D. H. Cole, *The Life of William Cobbett* (1942); G. Wallas, *Life of Francis Place* (1925); G. F. A. Best, *Shaftesbury* (1964); and G. M. Trevelyan, *Lord Grey and the Reform Bill* (1929).

Socialism

Good surveys of the subject are G. D. H. Cole, *Socialist Thought: The Forerunners, 1789–1850* (1962), and H. W. Laidler, *Social-Economic Movements* (1949). Less systematic but more readable is E. Wilson, *To The Finland Station** (1953). G. Lichtheim, *The Origins of Socialism* (1969), is brilliant. R. Owen, *The Life of Robert Owen, by Himself* (1920), gives insights into the thought of this leading Utopian reformer. Among several books on Owen, J. F. C. Harrison, *Robert Owen and the Owenites in Britain and America* (1969), is the most recent. F. Manuel, *The Prophets of Paris** (1962), deals with the French Utopian socialists. The literature on Marxian socialism is vast. A convenient collection of basic sources is available in *Karl Marx and Frederick Engels; Selected Works*, 2 vols. (1951). The easiest way for the layman to become acquainted with Marx's basic concepts is still K. Marx and F. Engels, *The Communist Manifesto** (1848), available in countless editions. G. D. H. Cole, *The Meaning of Marxism** (1948), offers one of many keys to an understanding of Marxist theory. G. Lichtheim, *Marxism** (1961), is an important contribution. There are numerous biographies of Marx, some favorable, like F. Mehring, *Karl Marx: The Story of His Life* (1936), and others hostile, like L. Schwarzschild, *The Red Prussian: The Life and Legend of Karl Marx** (1947). A balanced treatment is I. Berlin, *Karl Marx: His Life and Environment** (1963). The role of Engels in the genesis of Marxian socialism is emphasized by G. Mayer, *Friedrich Engels* (1935). For a discussion of anarchism, see two excellent biographies of its founders: D. W. Brogan, *Proudhon* (1934), and E. H. Carr, *Michael Bakunin** (1937). J. Joll, *The Anarchists** (1965), deals mainly with the later activities of the anarchists.

26

A New Balance of Power, 1850–1871

British officers in the Crimean War, 1854–56.

The keynote of European history during the first half of the nineteenth century had been revolution. In a long series of upheavals that reached its climax in 1848, Europe had tried to find some adjustment between the traditional claims of the old monarchical and aristocratic order and the democratic demands of the rising middle and lower classes. By 1850 the middle class had won some notable victories, and parliamentary government had gained a hold in most of western Europe. East of the Rhine, however, the old regime had stood its ground, and the conflict between the claims of monarchical and popular sovereignty continued.

The nature of this conflict, however, changed during the next few decades. In the past, the issues dividing the defenders of the old order and the advocates of the new had been largely drawn along ideological lines. There had been little common ground between the conservatism of men like Metternich and Nicholas I and the liberal and national aspirations of the middle class. The men who rose to leadership after 1850 were less committed to ideology. They were realists, ready to forgo some of their principles in order to achieve some of their aims. It was in realistic appraisal of the new social and political forces brought to the fore by industrialization that Bismarck gave the German middle class some of the concessions for which it had vainly fought in the past. By the same token, the middle class was ready to give up some of its political aims in order to protect and advance its economic interests. Demands for political reform continued. But the unprecedented economic growth of Europe, especially after 1870, helped to divert the attention of the middle class from politics to economics.

Besides economic growth, there was nationalism to command people's attention. Before 1850, domestic upheavals and international peace had been the order of the day; after 1850, the reverse was true. Five wars involving great powers were fought between 1854 and 1871, all of them prompted by nationalist aims and interests. In the past, whenever the *status quo* reached at Vienna had been threatened or actually changed, the "Concert of Europe" had collaborated to see that peace was speedily restored and that the balance of power was maintained. With the rise of nationalism, however, the European concert became more and more difficult to maintain. Even before 1850 the powers had failed to see eye-to-eye on certain international issues. But it was not until after 1850 that the first major showdown occurred. The Crimean War of 1854–55 was the first in a whole series of conflicts that put at least a temporary end to the Concert of Europe. By 1871, a new balance of power had emerged on the Continent, significantly different from the balance that had existed twenty years earlier.

THE EASTERN QUESTION

The Crimean War was the culmination of the latent crisis caused by the slow disintegration of Turkish rule in the Balkans. The "Eastern Question" had already caused one brief war between Russia and Turkey in 1828–29. To ensure year-round navigation, Russia depended on free access to the Black Sea through the Turkish Straits. This it had gained for its merchant ships in the Treaty of Adrianople (1829). Attempts to gain exclusive passage for Russian warships, however, had run into opposition from the rest of the powers, since such an arrangement would have guaranteed Russian predominance in the Black Sea. Instead the Straits Convention of 1841 affirmed the closure of the Straits to *all* foreign warships.

The Straits were not the only issue involved in the Eastern Question. Both France and Great Britain had considerable commercial interests in the Near East, and the British regarded the eastern Mediterranean as the chief approach to India. These interests, the western powers felt, were threatened by Russia's gradual encroachment on Turkey, as evidenced in its occupation of the Danubian principalities of Moldavia and Wallachia after 1829. While Russia was thus threatening to change the *status quo* in the Ottoman Empire, France and England hoped to maintain it.

A Consultation about the State of Turkey, a contemporary cartoon. The "Sick Man of Europe" (Turkey) is threatened by Death (Russia), while the physicians (France and England) hold their consultation.

between Turkey and Russia, Britain and France sent naval contingents to the entrance of the Straits in 1853. Russia replied by reoccupying the Danubian principalities that it had evacuated two years earlier. The Concert of Europe, acting on Austrian initiative, vainly tried to keep tension from mounting. In October 1853 Turkey, trusting in British and French support, declared war on Russia. Pressure of public opinion and concern over the expansion of Russian influence later brought the western powers into the war on Turkey's side. For the first time in forty years, the great powers had become involved in war with one another.

The Crimean War and the Peace of Paris

The major action of the Crimean War was a year-long siege against the Russian stronghold of Sebastopol on the Crimean Peninsula. It was one of history's costliest operations, with most of the casualties caused by disease. One of its few positive effects was the creation of the first modern nursing and medical services under the direction of Florence Nightingale, from which ultimately arose the International Red Cross.

The Crimean War lined up most of the European powers against the Russians. As the war progressed, Austria drew closer to the western powers and finally concluded an alliance with them. Austria never did any actual fighting, but even so the Russians resented its "ingratitude" for the aid Nicholas I had given the Austrians during the Hungarian uprising in 1849. Prussia outwardly followed Austria's lead but actually maintained a friendly neutrality and secretly aided the Russian cause. The small kingdom of Piedmont-Sardinia also entered the war on the side of the western powers hoping to gain as a reward their support of Italian unification.

After eleven months of siege, the fortress of Sebastopol fell in September 1855. Nicholas I had died in March, and his successor, Alexander II, was now ready to talk peace. The Paris Peace Conference met in the spring of 1856. To curtail Russian influence over the area adjacent to the Ottoman Empire, the

Another source of friction, which ultimately served as the immediate cause for the Crimean War, concerned the so-called Holy Places—that is, those sections of Jerusalem and Palestine that were closely associated with the life of Christ. Christians within the Ottoman Empire had long been guaranteed certain rights by their Turkish masters, and foreign pilgrims had been granted access to the Holy Land. The interests of the western Christians were traditionally championed by France, while Russia considered itself the guardian of eastern, Greek Orthodox rights. Shortly after 1850, conflicts between the two religious groups led to a number of incidents. As a result, the tsar tried to pressure Turkey into officially recognizing Russia's role as protector of Greek Orthodox rights in Turkey. In order to emphasize their interest in the negotiations taking place

A ''cantinière'' (canteen-worker) in the Crimean War, 1855.

The Congress of Paris, 1856. Seated: Baron Hübner (Austria), Ali Pasha (Turkey), Lord Clarendon (Britain), Count Walewski (France), Count Orlov (Russia), Baron de Bourqueney (France), and Lord Cowley (Britain). Standing: Count Cavour (Sardinia), De Villamarina (Sardinia), Count Hatzfeldt (Prussia), Count Vincent Benedetti (France), Mohammed Jemil Bey (Turkey), Baron Brunnov (Russia), Baron Manteuffel (Prussia), and Count Buol (Austria).

Black Sea was neutralized, which meant that Russia could not have any warships or fortifications there. In addition, navigation on the Danube River was declared free and open to all powers, and Russia had to surrender part of Bessarabia at the mouth of the Danube to the Turkish principality of Moldavia.

The Paris Conference also discussed the future of the Danubian principalities. Moldavia and Wallachia, it was decided, were to be under the temporary supervision of the great powers. Each principality was given a separate government. This, however, failed to satisfy the national aspirations of the Rumanians, who made up most of the population of the two regions. In 1858, therefore, both principalities elected the same man, Prince Alexander Cuza, as their ruler. After further consolidation of their common institutions, the principalities were finally recognized by the great powers in 1862 as the single and independent state of Rumania. The principle of nationality had triumphed once again.

Among the other decisions of the Paris Conference was the formal admission of Turkey to the family of powers, upon promise that it would introduce a number of much-needed reforms. The Paris Conference also issued a declaration against privateering and limited the rights of blockade by specifying that, to be effective, a blockade had to be backed by force. This principle of the "freedom of the seas" was intended to safeguard the rights of neutral countries in time of war. Finally, the Congress took notice, at least, of the "Italian Question" by permitting Cavour, the prime minister of Piedmont, to plead the cause of Italian unification before the assembled dignitaries. This was only a gesture, but it was a significant one.

The Peace of Paris, like the Vienna settlement forty years earlier, was an effort by the great powers to remove the sources of tension that had led to war and to restore the balance of power that had been threatened by one of them. But while the Vienna settlement had succeeded in restoring international stability, the Paris settlement left a legacy of unresolved tensions. The Russians, in particular, felt humiliated and henceforth would try to recoup the losses they had suffered in the Crimean War. The French, having won an important victory, took pride in the fact that their emperor had emerged as the leading figure at the Paris Peace Conference. But Napoleon III's role as arbiter of Europe merely whetted his appetite for further foreign

Napoleon III, in the uniform of a major general, *ca.* 1860.

ventures, and he was soon to come up with new plans for revising the map of Europe. The fact, furthermore, that Cavour had been permitted to raise the question of Italy's future at the conference gave fresh hope to Italian nationalists, whose aspirations could be fulfilled only by war against Austria.

The country, other than Russia, to be most seriously affected by the Crimean War was Austria. Whether it realized it or not, Austria had been seriously weakened, not only by its estrangement from Russia but by the coolness that had developed with Prussia. The latter, already restive under the domination that Austria had resumed in German affairs after 1850, was further alienated by Austria's attempts to involve the two leading German powers in the Crimean War. This isolation of Austria from its two traditional friends, Russia and Prussia, was perhaps the most significant result of the war. It was the more ominous because England, having learned a bitter lesson at Sebastopol, once more withdrew from continental affairs. Austria was thus left entirely at the mercy of Italian and German nationalism. The stage had been set for one of the most dramatic periods in European history. The tragic hero of this drama was the French Emperor, Napoleon III.

THE SECOND FRENCH EMPIRE

Louis Napoleon was to guide the destiny of France for the two fateful decades after 1850. To this day, however, he remains very much of an enigma. Was he a dictator, as some people have claimed, or was he a genuine democrat, as he himself claimed? After his fall from power in 1870, there was little doubt in anyone's mind that he was a fraud and a failure. More recently, however, historians have become somewhat more charitable in their judgment. In his domestic policy, Napoleon III gave France some of the happiest years in its history. And if in his foreign policy he showed an unerring instinct for doing the wrong thing, his motives were idealistic, and many of his reverses were due to forces over which he had no control.

Louis Napoleon became emperor by a cleverly managed *coup d'état.* Like most countries after 1848, the Second French Republic experienced a wave of reaction. Socialists were ejected from the legislature, the right to vote was curtailed; public meetings were restricted, and the freedom of the press was curbed. At the same time, however, France's new president, Louis Napoleon, was eager to gain the support of the French masses. In pursuit of this aim, he dissolved the Assembly in December 1851 and called for new presidential elections. There was some street fighting, but his *coup* succeeded. The French people once again endorsed the name Napoleon by a vast majority. A year later, the president finished his overthrow of the Republic by proclaiming himself Emperor of the French, thus pursuing further the historical parallel between himself and his uncle.

The analogy was carried still further in the Empire's political institutions, which closely followed those of the first Napoleon. There were two parliamentary bodies—an appointive senate and a legislature elected by universal male

---

Napoleon III

Napoleon III was, to borrow Gamaliel Bradford's phrase, a "damaged soul"; and, after 1860, a damaged soul imprisoned in a damaged body. Grave, thoughtful, kind, devoted to noble causes, determined withal, fearless, and surprisingly practical, he had in him also the tortuousness of the eternal plotter, the vagueness of the Utopian, the weakened fiber of the sensualist, the fatalism of the gambler. Some characters in history are obvious in their greatness, mediocrity, or turpitude: even though our sympathies may widely differ, we feel we can focus Washington, Victoria, Gladstone, and even Napoleon I. Napoleon III is not one of these. His elusive physiognomy changes altogether with the light that is turned upon it. At one moment, he appears impressive: the only political leader in the nineteenth century whose thought could still be a guide for us today. At other times, the caricature drawn by Kinglake and Victor Hugo seems almost convincing: the middle-aged rake in imperial trappings, sinister even in his futility. The most searching, the most persistent light of all, the one in which he was seen by every one who approached him, reveals him as gentle, not merely in speech and smile, but to the very depths of his being.

From Albert Guérard, *Napoleon III* (Cambridge, Mass.: Harvard University Press, 1943), p. 290.

suffrage—both of which could merely discuss what the emperor saw fit to put before them. By carefully managing elections, furthermore, Napoleon was always in a position to command a parliamentary majority. Most major decisions were reached by the emperor himself in consultation with a Council of State made up of experts with purely advisory functions. The Second Empire, at least during its first ten years, was little more than a thinly disguised dictatorship.

The "Authoritarian Empire"

Despite the absence of political freedom, the authoritarian phase of Napoleon's rule was a happy period. The emperor gave his countrymen what they wanted most—prosperity at home and glory abroad. Like many a dictator since, Napoleon III tried to do something for everyone. The peasants, who had voted him into office and who continued to endorse his policy in numerous plebiscites, were helped by large scale public works and improved credit facilities. The workers, who continued to remain cool to the new regime, were aided by far-reaching social legislation and public housing. But the class with which Napoleon's relations were most harmonious, at least in times of prosperity, was the industrial and commercial middle class.

More than any other statesman of his time, the Emperor of the French realized the importance and implications of modern industrialization, and he did his best to create conditions favorable to industrial growth. As a result, French railway mileage during the 1850s alone increased more than fivefold. A French law of 1863 permitted the formation of "limited liability" companies. By limiting the liability of stockholders to the stock they owned, investment was made less risky and the savings of the proverbially thrifty Frenchman were now attracted to industry. In a series of farsighted commercial agreements, notably the Cobden-Chevalier treaty (1860) with England, Napoleon abandoned the traditional protectionism of France in favor of moderate free trade. As a result, French exports soon exceeded imports. France in 1870 was still the chief industrial competitor of Great Britain. French industrial expansion had some negative aspects as well. There was an air of gaudiness and vulgarity about the newly enriched middle class. Speculation and overexpansion led to periodic crises and depressions. But on the whole the new prosperity was sound and was shared by all classes of the population.

As a symbol of the Empire's prosperity and splendor, Napoleon was instrumental in having the city of Paris transformed into the beautiful work of art it remains to the present day. The center of the city was completely rebuilt, with wide boulevards, stately squares, and lovely parks. Like so many of Napoleon's projects, this "urban renewal program" served a dual purpose. By providing employment and eradicating ugly slums, it aided the workers; but at the same time it did away with the breeding-grounds of radicalism and revolution. The wide avenues of the new city were unsuitable for erecting barricades, and they permitted the use of cavalry and artillery in case there should ever be another popular uprising.

The Second Empire came to an end on the battlefield in war against Prussia in 1870. Before that time, however, domestic discontent had already forced Napoleon to abandon many of the authoritarian practices of his earlier years. Most of this discontent was provoked by his blundering foreign policy. The French people, still smarting from the defeat they had suffered forty years earlier, were not opposed to war, so long as they won. France's involvement in the Crimean War had been popular, and the same was true of a number of small co-

lonial ventures. The occupation of Algeria was completed; new French settlements were established in West Africa; New Caledonia was occupied in 1853; and during the 1860s protectorates were secured over Cambodia and the region later called French Indochina. The French participation in the wars of Italian unification, on the other hand, while it brought some military glory and new territory, was deeply resented by French Catholics, since it deprived the papacy of its territorial holdings. Still more disastrous in French eyes were Napoleon's futile efforts, between 1862 and 1867, to establish a French protectorate over Mexico (see p. 628). The crowning blow to Napoleon's prestige, however, came when he failed to secure territorial compensations for France during Prussia's unification of Germany (see p. 609).

The "Liberal Empire"

To pacify the growing domestic opposition, Napoleon, during the 1860s, attempted a gradual liberalization of French political life. The "Liberal Empire" was initiated in 1860 when restrictions on debate in the legislative body were lifted and parliamentary proceedings were made public. Subsequent decrees extended the powers of the legislature and relaxed the restrictions on public meetings and the press that had existed since 1852. But these concessions only helped to swell the ranks of the opposition. By 1869 the government had so lost its grip that the parliamentary elections of that year returned ninety-three opposition candidates, thirty of whom were republicans. With labor unrest prompting a growing epidemic of strikes, and with the republican program of Léon Gambetta gaining more and more adherents, the government made some sweeping last-minute efforts to save its life. In their totality, these reforms amounted to the establishment of a parliamentary regime. In May 1870 the French electorate endorsed these constitutional changes with a rousing majority. But it was too late. Two months later the war with Prussia broke out, sweeping away the Empire and bringing in the Third Republic.

Paris boulevard, 1860. Detail of one part of a stereographic pair on glass, showing the results of Napoleon III's "urban renewal" program.

THE UNIFICATION OF ITALY

The domestic events in France must be viewed against the background of Napoleon's foreign policy. He had two main motives: to gain glory for France and to win freedom for suppressed nationalities. It was the conflict between the selfishness and the altruism, the realism and the idealism, inherent in these aims that accounts for much of the fateful vacillation in Napoleon's policy. The vacillation first manifested itself in his dealings with Italy.

Italy after 1848

Italy before 1848 had been an unhappy country, ridden by many factions, each hoping to bring about political unification according to its own plans. As a result of the abortive revolutions of 1848, however, unification under the leadership of the kingdom of Piedmont-Sardinia had emerged as the most feasible scheme. The king of Piedmont, Victor Emmanuel II, had been unique in not revoking the liberal constitution granted during the revolution. He did not relent, furthermore, in his hostile policy toward Austria. Turin, the capital of Piedmont, soon became a haven for Italian patriots from all over the peninsula trying to escape the persecutions of their reactionary, pro-Austrian rulers.

The man who realized the unique position of Piedmont and used it to bring about the unification of Italy was Count Camillo di Cavour. At the age of forty, in 1850, Cavour was appointed minister of agriculture and commerce, and in 1852 he became prime minister. Cavour at first was not so much interested in uniting the whole of Italy as he was in extending the power of Piedmont in the North. This, he realized, could be done only against the opposition and at the expense of Austria. To prepare for a showdown with Austria thus became one of his major concerns.

Before Austria could be tackled, however, several things were needed. The first was to create sympathy for the "Italian Question" outside Italy. This was done by having Piedmontese troops participate in the Crimean War and by having the Italian problem discussed by the powers at the Paris Peace Conference. A second prerequisite for a successful war against Austria was the military and economic strengthening of Piedmont. Cavour did his best to improve the armed forces and to further the building of railroads, of whose strategic importance he was very much aware. In a number of commercial treaties, Cavour integrated the economy of Piedmont with that of western Europe. He also fostered legislation improving the structure of business corporations, credit institutions, and cooperative societies. These economic measures alone entitle Cavour to a place of honor in his country's history.

Cavour and Napoleon III

The third requirement for Piedmont to be able to move against Austria was outside military aid. To get such aid, Cavour looked to France and Napoleon III. The French emperor had always held a lingering affection for Italy. To aid Italian unification not only appealed to his idealism but it also might strengthen the prestige of France and of himself. It was considerations like these that led to a super-secret meeting at Plombières in 1858 at which Napoleon promised Cavour his aid if Piedmont should become involved in a war with Austria. Once the war was won, Piedmont would form an enlarged kingdom of Upper Italy, and the whole peninsula was then to be united in a loose federation with the pope as president. France was to be rewarded for its help with the Piedmontese regions of Nice and Savoy. It is important to note that the Plombières agreement did not call for an Italy united under Piedmont.

The main difficulty was finding a pretext for war with Austria. While waiting for an opportunity, the two conspirators continued their preparations. As rumors of an impending war in Italy grew more persistent, the other powers began to show concern. Austria was the least worried. The Austrians were used to recurrent rumors of an Italian war and refused to take them seriously. England and Prussia, on the other hand, were less confident. The former, in the spring of

Count Camillo di Cavour, 1810–61.

1859, came out with a plan for the evacuation of Austrian troops from the peninsula and the creation of an Italian federation. This was such an appealing scheme that Napoleon began to show signs of trying to back out of his agreement with Piedmont. At this point, when Cavour's carefully laid plans seemed about to fail, the Austrian emperor, Francis Joseph, forced a showdown by demanding that Piedmont refrain from any further preparations for war. When Piedmont turned down this ultimatum, Austrian troops, on April 29, 1859, invaded Piedmont. France thereupon joined its ally in the war against Austria.

The War of 1859

Had the Austrians moved quickly, they might have won the war. But by wasting time, they allowed the French to move their forces into Italy. After six weeks of bloody fighting, the French and Italian armies had won two indecisive victories at Magenta and Solferino and had driven the Austrians out of Lombardy. The next obvious step was the liberation of Venetia.

At this point, in July 1859, Napoleon surprised his ally and the world by concluding an armistice with Francis Joseph at Villafranca. There were several reasons for Napoleon's sudden defection: He apparently had been shocked by the bloodshed at Magenta and Solferino; the Austrian army was by no means beaten; there was dissatisfaction among many Frenchmen with a war against another Catholic power; and there was some fear that Prussia might come to Austria's aid. Under the terms of the Villafranca agreement, Napoleon broke his promise that Piedmont should get both Lombardy and Venetia. Austria merely surrendered Lombardy, which Napoleon then offered to Victor Emmanuel. The king, much to Cavour's consternation, accepted.

The First Phase of Italian Unification

Villafranca, however, turned out to be a blessing in disguise for the Italians. Up to this point the war had been waged chiefly for the enlargement of Piedmont.

THE UNIFICATION OF ITALY   1859–70

Now suddenly it became a war for Italian unification. At the start of the war, some of the small states in northern and central Italy had revolted and driven out their rulers. The prospect of their return now led the populace of these regions to raise an army and to proclaim their union with Piedmont. Cavour, in January 1860, asked Napoleon's consent to Piedmont's annexation of the central Italian states. Napoleon agreed, in return for the surrender of Nice and Savoy, which he had been promised at Plombières but which he had forfeited at Villafranca. In March 1860, plebiscites in Parma, Modena, Romagna, and Tuscany confirmed the union of central Italy with Piedmont.

The next act in the drama of unification was dominated not by Cavour but by a man who was his opposite in all respects—a romantic, a republican, an effective leader of men, but a complete political amateur—Giuseppe Garibaldi.

Giuseppe Garibaldi, 1807–82.

The role of this colorful figure in the brief fiasco of the Roman republic in 1849 has already been discussed (p. 563). In May 1860, Garibaldi assembled an expeditionary force at Genoa. Its task was to help complete the liberation of the Kingdom of the Two Sicilies, where an uprising against the reactionary Bourbon regime had taken place. Garibaldi's expedition was a huge success. Aided by the local population, his small force of "Redshirts" defeated an army twenty times its size. By August Sicily was in Garibaldi's hands, and he was ready to cross to the mainland.

Garibaldi's success, however, raised a number of problems. His growing popularity threatened to displace Victor Emmanuel as the leader of a united Italy. Garibaldi might give in to the urgings of Mazzini and surrender the southern half of the peninsula to republicanism; or else he might move against Rome, to complete the unification of Italy. Such a move might lead to a conflict with France, which still considered itself the protector of the papacy. To avert such a crisis, Cavour convinced Napoleon that the only way to stop Garibaldi was for Victor Emmanuel to meet him on the way. Promising to respect the independence of Rome itself, the Piedmontese army now invaded the Papal States, defeated the papal forces, and after bypassing Rome came face to face with Garibaldi's band not far from Naples. The situation was tense. But Garibaldi was too much of a patriot to let selfish ambitions interfere with his hope for a united Italy. Instead, he voluntarily submitted to Victor Emmanuel, thus completing the first phase of Italian unification.

The Kingdom of Italy

The Kingdom of Italy was proclaimed in March 1861. Two months later, Cavour succumbed to an attack of typhoid fever and died, just as his country needed him most. The unification of Italy was by no means completed. Venetia did not become part of the kingdom until after another Austrian defeat, this time by Prussia in 1866; and Rome remained in papal hands until 1870. Other difficulties

Victor Emmanuel II, King of Italy, 1849–78.

beset the new state. Not all Italians were happy with the results of unification. The followers of Mazzini would have preferred a republic to a monarchy, and even many monarchists would rather have seen a loosely federated union than the centralized monarchy that resulted from the "conquest" of the peninsula by Piedmont. Regionalism and particularism also interfered with the integration of the eight or more separate states. Tensions between the North and the South were especially marked. The poverty and illiteracy of the Italian masses, furthermore, made the extension of democracy a slow process, and Italy's parliamentary regime soon became known for its corruption. The wars of unification imposed staggering financial burdens, and taxes now were higher than ever before. At the same time, lack of coal and iron prevented large-scale industrialization, which might have relieved Italy's economic plight. Yet despite these shortcomings, the new Italy considered itself one of the great powers and tried to imitate the wealthier nations by maintaining an army and navy far beyond its means.

Much of the discontent and disillusionment in Italy after unification was blamed on Cavour's hurried policy. But we must remember that the unification of Italy had not really been his goal at the start. Much of his policy was determined by the other two makers of Italy, Napoleon III and Garibaldi. Where we may find fault with Cavour is in the devious methods he employed to achieve his aims. But such *Realpolitik,* as it came to be called, was not considered out of place by an age that gloried in nationalism and worshiped success. Much the same spirit that animated Cavour was to guide Bismarck in his German policy. And just as Cavour had started out in the hope of enlarging Piedmont but ended by creating the Kingdom of Italy, so Bismarck began working for a greater Prussia and wound up with a German Reich.

AUSTRO-PRUSSIAN RIVALRY

The most striking similarity between the unification of Italy and that of Germany was Austria's involvement in both. Austria's defeats in 1859 and 1866 were due in large measure to internal weakness caused by political disunity. Nationalism, which proved a boon to Cavour and Bismarck, was a source of infinite trouble to Francis Joseph and the many capable Austrian ministers who tried to find some way of keeping their empire from falling to pieces.

Nationalism in the Austrian Empire

Prince Schwarzenberg, who had succeeded Metternich in 1848, had given Austria a constitution early in 1849. While calling for a high degree of centralization, it had recognized at least some local and provincial privileges. These mild concessions to the spirit of nationalism, however, were only temporary. Beginning in 1850, all but the centralizing tendencies of the constitution were ignored. Schwarzenberg died in 1852, but his policies were continued. Petty officials, most of them German, directed the affairs of provinces whose language they did not speak and whose customs they ignored. Yet instead of counteracting the centrifugal tendencies of nationalism, this system merely increased the tension between the German ruling caste and the subject peoples.

Austria's defeat at the hands of France and Piedmont in 1859 once again brought home the need for reform. As a result, the excessive centralization of the preceding decade now gave way to some degree of provincial autonomy. In 1861 a new constitution established a central legislature, the *Reichsrat*, made up of delegates from the various regional diets. But the new system, like all earlier ones, had serious flaws. Since the German element was still guaranteed a majority, some of the other nationalities, especially the Hungarians (or Magyars), refused to attend the meetings of the *Reichsrat*. It soon became clear that another effort at solving the nationalities problem had failed. In September 1865 Francis Joseph suspended the constitution of 1861.

At this point the war with Prussia intervened (see below), leaving Austria

still weaker and less able to resist the demands of the Hungarian nationalists. As a result of extended negotiations between Austrian and Hungarian leaders, a compromise, or *Ausgleich*, was finally reached in 1867. Under the new arrangement a Dual Monarchy was established, with Francis Joseph serving both as Emperor of Austria and King of Hungary. Except in such fields as finance, foreign affairs, and war, where joint ministries were set up, the two parts of the monarchy now were entirely autonomous. Yet since neither the Germans nor the Hungarians held a majority in either half of the Dual Monarchy, the *Ausgleich* did not solve the nationalities problem. Subsequent efforts to recognize the Slavic regions by establishing a Triple Monarchy were defeated by opposition from Germans and Hungarians alike. This continued oppression of Slavic nationalism constituted a major threat to the existence of Austria-Hungary and to the peace of Europe.

Prussia after 1850

Prussia presented quite a different picture from Austria. In administrative efficiency, financial soundness, and military strength, Prussia after 1850 was far superior to its Austrian rival. Except for a small Polish minority in the eastern provinces, its population was homogeneous. And while in Austria industrialization had hardly begun, Prussia during the 1850s began to take its place among the leading industrial powers of the Continent.

Like Austria, Prussia had been granted a constitution in 1849. Since it provided for universal suffrage, it had a deceptively democratic appearance. But by dividing the electorate into three classes, according to the taxes each voter paid, the Prussian constitution made certain that the wealthiest citizens controlled a majority in the lower house of the *Landtag*. With this constitutional arrangement it was not surprising that Prussia continued to be one of the most reactionary states in Germany. In 1857 King Frederick William IV was succeeded by his brother, Prince William. William was sixty-two years old and an

Francis Joseph I (1830–1916), Emperor of Austria.

arch-conservative. Having spent most of his life in the army, he had little experience in government. It was due to William's concern over the shortcomings of Prussia's military establishment that Prussia, in 1860, entered upon one of the most serious domestic crises in its history.

Despite a considerable increase in population, Prussia's armed forces in 1860 were still essentially what they had been in 1814. When William tried to correct this situation, however, he ran into opposition from the liberal majority in the *Landtag,* which, under the constitution, had to authorize the necessary funds and which objected to some of the details of the government's reform proposals. By 1862 king and parliament had become deadlocked over the issue. At this point William decided to recall his ambassador to Paris, Otto von Bismarck, and charge him with carrying on the fight with the *Landtag.*

Bismarck and the Constitutional Conflict

The man who was soon to direct the affairs of Germany as first chancellor of the German Reich was then forty-seven years old. He came from an old Prussian family of noble landowners, or *Junkers.* During the revolution of 1848 he had proved himself a devoted royalist. As a reward he had been appointed Prussia's representative to the Frankfurt Diet during the 1850s and later ambassador to St. Petersburg and Paris. In these various assignments he had shown outstanding ability as a diplomat and as a manipulator of men. But he was also known as a fighter. It was this combination that had recommended him to William I.

Bismarck first tried to mediate the conflict between king and parliament. When this proved impossible, however, he did not give in but carried out the proposed army reforms without parliamentary approval, using funds earmarked for other purposes. The conflict was never resolved but was ultimately overshadowed by more spectacular events. Two wars, in 1864 and 1866, not only gave proof of the excellence of Prussia's reformed army but so aroused the patriotism of the *Landtag* delegates that they were ready to forget their liberal principles. When, during the war with Austria in 1866, Bismarck asked parliament for retroactive assent to the unauthorized expenditures of the previous years, the majority of delegates supported him.

The Prussian constitutional conflict had thus been "solved," as Bismarck had predicted, "by blood and iron." But in the process, Prussian and German liberalism had suffered a serious defeat. Liberals in Germany henceforth were split

Prince Otto von Bismarck, 1815–98.

Principles of "Realpolitik"

The state is by nature a realistic politician, if only by virtue of the conditions of its existence, and has therefore always had to suffer being treated as a criminal by political idealists and visionaries. . . . In contrast to the politics of the state, the politics of the people is most susceptible to idealism and fantastication. The causes of this difference are obvious. On the one hand we have the school of political life and the consciousness of responsibility, on the other hand inexperience and yielding to intellectual or emotional whim with little or no thought for the consequences. . . .

For the state, in contrast to the individual, self-preservation is the supreme law. The state must survive at any price; it cannot go into the poorhouse, it cannot beg, it cannot commit suicide; in short, it must take wherever it can find the essentials of life.

Politics, in so far as they are not in the hands of the community, are a mandate which carries responsibility toward the constituency as well as toward the moral law, two responsibilities which need to be weighed against one another.

The right of the politician to sacrifice the welfare of the state to his personal scruples of conscience may be undeniable in simple matters or those of secondary significance, but it may be extremely doubtful in difficult and important cases.

The clash of duties, which the individual can as a rule easily avoid, occurs so often, so unavoidably, and so fatefully in the life of the state that politics is often a matter of choice between two moral evils.

Finally, there occur historic necessities and political acts of nature before which the state and the people resign themselves irresistibly and passively, and to which, therefore, the ethical criterion of human conduct is quite inapplicable. . . .

From A. L. von Rochau, *Grundsätze der Realpolitik* (1869), quoted in W. M. Simon, *Germany in the Age of Bismarck* (New York: Barnes and Noble, 1968), pp. 133–34.

in two factions—a larger one that continued to support Bismarck, putting nationalism above liberalism, and a smaller faction that stuck to its liberal principles. This split within German liberalism was never healed. It was the most fateful legacy of the period of German unification.

Rivalry between Austria and Prussia

Bismarck did not really plan the unification of Germany; it developed more or less accidentally out of Prussia's desire to assert itself against Austria's claims for supremacy in German affairs. The rivalry between Austria and Prussia was of long standing—it went back at least to the days of Frederick the Great and Maria Theresa in the eighteenth century. During most of the intervening period, Prussia had been quite ready to recognize Austria's traditional leadership. The most recent manifestation of Prussia's subjection to Austria had occurred in 1850, when Austria had prevented a scheme advanced by Frederick William IV for a union of German princes under Prussian leadership. Instead, Austria had insisted that the diet of the German Confederation under the presidency of Austria be reconstituted at Frankfurt.

Bismarck, as Prussia's delegate to the Frankfurt Diet, did not object to Austria's leadership in German affairs so long as Austria, in return, recognized Prussia's preeminence in northern Germany. Only after Bismarck realized Austria's unwillingness to cooperate did he decide that the interest of Prussia demanded that Austria be excluded from Germany. Before Prussia could assume leadership in Germany, however, it had to make sure of the good will, or at least the acquiescence, of the great powers. The Italian national movement had enjoyed the sympathy of almost everyone outside Austria, but few people in western Europe wanted to see a Germany united under Prussian auspices. During the Crimean War, Austria had tried to induce Prussia to join in aiding the western powers, but Prussia had remained friendly toward Russia. This was the basis for a close friendship between Prussia and Russia that was to remain a

constant element in international affairs for the next few decades.

The first outward sign of Prussia's emancipation from Austrian tutelage came during the Italian war of 1859. Austria at the time fully expected Prussia to be its ally against Piedmont and France. Prussia was ready to comply, but asked to be put in charge of its own and whatever other German forces might be raised. Austria, still filled with its own importance, refused this understandable request. Prussia's neutrality during the war won the gratitude of both France and Italy. Austria's defeat, on the other hand, clearly showed how much its claim to leadership was based on past prestige rather than present power.

By the end of the 1850s most German liberals were expecting Prussia to take the lead in unifying Germany. The constitutional struggle over the reform of the Prussian army, however, put a temporary damper on their enthusiasm. At the same time, the Austrian constitution of 1861 seemed to indicate more liberal tendencies in the Habsburg Empire. It thus encouraged the Catholic and traditionalist forces, especially in southern Germany, who hoped for a united Germany under Austrian leadership. To take advantage of this shift in opinion, Austria convened a congress in 1863 to consider the reform of the German Confederation in the direction of greater national unity. But Bismarck urged his king to boycott the congress. Without Prussia, the Frankfurt meeting was doomed to failure.

The Schleswig-Holstein Question and the War with Denmark

The final showdown between Austria and Prussia grew out of their involvement in the affairs of the two northern German duchies of Schleswig and Holstein. The Schleswig-Holstein question is famous for its intricacy, and its details need not concern us here. The duchies, largely German but partly Danish, had long been held in personal union by the king of Denmark. In an age of rising nationalism, however, this indeterminate status became increasingly difficult to maintain. The issue had already led to a brief war between Danes and Germans

A cartoon depicting the nature of the European balance.

in 1848, in which Denmark had been defeated. The issue became acute again in 1863, when Denmark tried to annex Schleswig. This time both Austria and Prussia rushed to the defense. Their motives for intervention were complex. Both wanted to pose as defenders of German unity, but Prussia also wanted to expand its power in northern Germany.

The war itself was brief. The Danes suffered a crushing defeat. Under the Peace of Vienna in 1864 Denmark surrendered Schleswig and Holstein to Austria and Prussia. In this joint possession of the duchies lay the seeds of the war that broke out between Austria and Prussia two years later. Although Austria and most of the German states wanted the duchies to go to a German claimant, the Duke of Augustenburg, Bismarck wanted the duchies for Prussia. The question was how to bring about such annexation. In 1865 the victors reached a temporary compromise in the Convention of Gastein, under which Prussia was to administer Schleswig and Austria Holstein, while the future of the duchies was to remain a joint responsibility. But this arrangement solved nothing. As Austria continued to encourage the aspirations of the Duke of Augustenburg, and as Prussia proceeded to make itself at home in Schleswig, it became clear that force might be needed to decide the fate of both duchies.

The War of 1866

In the fall of 1865, Bismarck met Napoleon III at Biarritz to sound him out on France's attitude toward a possible war between Prussia and Austria. The meeting suggests a certain parallel to the Plombières meeting of Cavour and Napoleon, except that Bismarck was not asking for French aid; all he wanted was a promise of neutrality. This Napoleon gave, hinting at some unspecified compensations for France. Bismarck agreed. In the spring of 1866, Prussia concluded an alliance with Italy, to which Napoleon also gave his blessing. The remaining great powers did not present much of a problem. Since England had stood by while Denmark was defeated, Bismarck felt that it would not intervene to save

Area where Bismarck promised to hold a plebiscite. It did not take place until 1920, when part of the region reverted to Denmark.

Austria. And Russia's friendship for Prussia and its antagonism toward Austria left little doubt where it would stand.

With the diplomatic spadework done, Bismarck's next task was to find a cause for war with Austria that would rally the rest of Germany to Prussia's side. This was not easy, since most of the German princes sided with Austria on the future of Schleswig-Holstein. When Bismarck finally used Prussia's differences with Austria over the duchies as an excuse to order Prussian troops into Holstein, the remaining members of the German Confederation joined the Austrian side. The war of 1866 was thus not only a war of Prussia against Austria but against most of the rest of Germany as well.

There was little enthusiasm in either camp at the start of the war. Austria was deeply divided and poorly prepared. The Austrians were further handicapped by having to fight on two fronts, Italy and Germany. The Prussians, on the other hand, were in excellent military form, equipped with the latest weapons and led by a master-strategist, Count Helmuth von Moltke. As the first news of victory arrived, moreover, the attitude of the Prussian people changed from apathy to enthusiasm. The war was over in a few weeks. It was decided almost entirely by one major battle, near Königgrätz and Sadowa, in Bohemia, in which the Austrians were defeated, though not annihilated.

The final peace treaty was signed at Prague in August 1866. Chiefly because of Bismarck's insistence, the settlement was remarkably lenient. Bismarck realized that the rest of the powers, especially France, would not stand for a punitive peace. Austria consented to the dissolution of the German Confederation and recognized the various territorial gains Prussia had made in the North, including Schleswig-Holstein. In a separate settlement Austria surrendered Venetia, which went to Italy. As for Austria's German allies, most of the northern ones were annexed by Prussia, while the southern ones had to pay indemnities and conclude military alliances with Prussia. Prussia thus consolidated its holdings in the North and assumed indirect control over the rest of Germany.

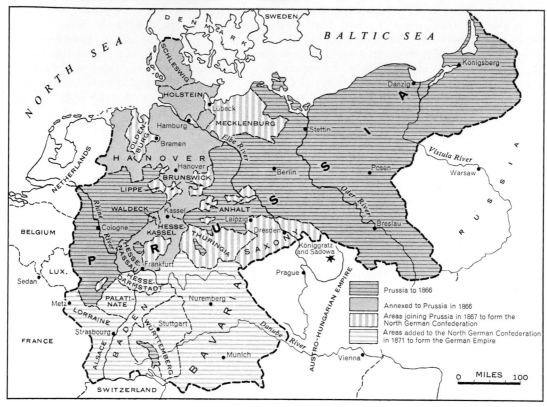

THE UNIFICATION
OF GERMANY

The war of 1866 had been waged for the aggrandizement of Prussia. But in the minds of most Germans it soon appeared as a deliberate stage in the unification of Germany. During the winter of 1866–67, delegates from the states that were left in northern Germany after the peace settlement met in Berlin to form a North German Confederation. The plan had originated with Bismarck, whose aim was to establish Prussia's preponderance over the whole region north of the Main River.

The North German Confederation

The constitution of the North German Confederation established a federal system under which the central government controlled foreign and military affairs. The executive was vested in the king of Prussia as president, assisted by a chancellor—Bismarck. An upper house, or *Bundesrat,* consisted of delegates from the various member states. The lower house, or *Reichstag,* was made up of deputies elected by universal manhood suffrage. Most of the power was vested in the upper house, in which Prussian influence prevailed. There was no ministerial responsibility, since the only minister was the chancellor, and he was responsible only to the president, or king.

The main significance of the North German Confederation's constitution was that it served as a basis for the constitution of the German Empire after 1871. Just as it assured the domination of Prussia in northern Germany after 1867, so after 1871 it perpetuated Prussia's domination over the rest of Germany. How far Bismarck actually foresaw developments beyond 1867 is difficult to say. He never was a German nationalist—his major concern was with the power and security of Prussia. Nor was there much desire among the rulers of South Germany to submit to the king of Prussia. The state of affairs that existed in 1867, therefore, could have lasted for a long time had it not been for the unfortunate machinations of Napoleon III. Like his uncle, Napoleon served as the involuntary agent of German nationalism.

Bismarck and Napoleon III

Napoleon's readiness at Biarritz to let Prussia settle accounts with Austria had been due to his underestimation of Prussian strength. Thinking Prussia and Austria pretty evenly matched, he had expected to throw French power into the balance at the crucial moment. Austria's defeat at Sadowa, therefore, had come as a shock. Together with France's fiasco in Mexico, the defeat of Austria was built up by Napoleon's domestic opponents as a major French defeat. The only way to save French prestige was through some kind of territorial compensations such as France had received during the unification of Italy.

Napoleon should have pressed his demands for compensations while the fate of Austria still hung in the balance. Once Prussia had won the war, Bismarck was no longer in any mood to make concessions. On the contrary, Napoleon's demands served him to good effect in furthering his own policy. He used Napoleon's bid for territories in the west or south of Germany to cement ties with the southern German states as the best possible protection against French designs; and he later used Napoleon's request for Prussian support in the acquisition of Belgium to incriminate France in the eyes of Great Britain. In a third attempt to gain territorial compensation, Napoleon tried to buy the Duchy of Luxembourg. Bismarck at first approved of the deal but later changed his mind.

Napoleon III, faced with mounting criticism at home and frustrated in his efforts to gather laurels abroad, gradually realized that an armed showdown with Prussia might be inevitable. To prepare himself, he began casting about for allies. But neither Austria nor Italy, whom he approached, had any desire to become involved in a war between France and Prussia. Even so, Napoleon assumed that in case of a war with Prussia he could count on the aid of one or both of the Catholic powers.

The War of 1870

The immediate cause of the war between France and Prussia was the offer of the Spanish throne, temporarily vacated by revolution, to a Hohenzollern prince, distantly related to the king of Prussia. Bismarck was instrumental in having the prince accept the Spanish offer; yet there is no clear evidence that he intended to use the affair to provoke a war with France. Moreover, when France protested the Spanish candidacy, the Prussian government urged the prince to abandon the project. But this did not satisfy the French, who demanded an apology from King William and a promise that the candidacy would not be renewed. This unreasonable de-

The balloon in which Léon Gambetta, Minister of the Interior, escaped during the siege of Paris in October 1870 in order to organize resistance in the provinces.

mand was made in a famous interview between the French ambassador and the king at the watering-place of Ems, an interview that William cut short. When news of this incident reached Berlin, Bismarck edited the report in such a way to make it look as though France had suffered a major diplomatic defeat. It was this edited "Ems dispatch" that led France to declare war on Prussia. In this case Bismarck had foreseen the results, and to that extent he may be held responsible for the war of 1870. Yet his action was merely the latest in a whole series of mutual recriminations, and most historians now agree that responsibility for the war must be shared by both sides.

Events in the early summer of 1870 had moved so quickly that all of Europe was taken by surprise. France's precipitate action lost whatever sympathy it had enjoyed among the other powers. England maintained the aloofness it had shown ever since the Crimean War. Russia continued its policy of benevolent neutrality toward Prussia. Italy was preoccupied with completing its unification by taking the city of Rome. And Austria would prove dangerous only if Prussia ran into difficulties. But there was little

chance of that. In numbers, leadership, and morale, Prussia's forces were far superior to those of France. The participation of southern German contingents made this a national German war. The French army fought valiantly, but its leadership was poor and its morale was low. The fact that Napoleon III, worn out by a lingering illness, assumed personal command did not help matters.

The war itself was decided in a series of bloody battles. The climax came on September 2, with Napoleon's capitulation at Sedan. But the fighting continued for several more months and the city of Paris, where a republic had been proclaimed, did not surrender until the end of January 1871. A temporary armistice was concluded on January 28, pending the election of a representative assembly. The National Assembly chose the liberal monarchist Adolphe Thiers as chief executive. The first task of the new government was to negotiate a final settlement with Bismarck.

The Results of the War

The peace signed at Frankfurt on May 10, 1871, was a harsh one. France

French battery in front of Belfort (Alsace), which capitulated to the Germans February 13, 1871, after a siege of 108 days.

had to pay an indemnity of 5 billion francs, and the country was to remain occupied until the indemnity had been paid. In addition, France had to cede Alsace and part of Lorraine, which, for the most part, it had taken from the Holy Roman Empire in the seventeenth century. The inhabitants of Alsace spoke German, but they were pro-French and anti-Prussian in feeling. To take so large a slice of territory in an age of ardent nationalism was a dangerous move. The issue of France's "lost provinces" remained an insuperable obstacle to closer Franco-German relations.

The signing of the peace did not end France's troubles. The new National Assembly had a majority of monarchists, so that the survival of the republic depended on the continued split among the three monarchist factions—Bourbon, Orléanist, and Bonapartist. The republican minority had its main support in the city of Paris. It was here, in March 1871, that fear of a monarchist revival, indignation over a humiliating peace, and general misery resulting from the recent siege of the city led to a violent uprising. The Paris Commune, as the government of the insurgents was called, lasted until the end of May. Its aims, on the whole, were moderate. But the Commune also included a few socialists. This fact, plus some of the excesses committed during the fighting against the troops of the National Assembly, did much to reawaken middle-class fear of a "red peril." After their defeat in the final "Bloody Week" of May, thousands of Communards were executed, imprisoned, or deported. The issue of republic against monarchy continued to hang in the balance for some time.

While the siege of Paris was still under way, another important event had taken place. On January 18, 1871, in the Hall of Mirrors in the palace at Versailles, King William of Prussia was proclaimed German emperor. This ceremony was the climax of long negotiations between Bismarck and the rulers of southern Germany. There had been much hesitation among these Catholic and more liberal states to submit to a confederation dominated by Protestant and reactionary Prussia. Many conservative Prussians were equally hesitant, fearing that Prussia might lose its identity in the larger empire. Even Bismarck, the architect of unification, was not motivated by national enthusiasm. But by fulfilling the German people's dream for unity, he hoped to increase the power and prestige of his beloved Prussia.

The Franco-German War not only completed the unification of Germany; it ended the long struggle for Italian unity. After a plebiscite in October 1870, Rome was annexed to Italy and became Italy's capital. A subsequent effort to mollify the papacy by a generous Law of Papal Guarantees was turned down by the pope, who henceforth considered himself "the prisoner of the Vatican." This state of affairs remained unchanged until 1929 when the signing of the Lateran Treaty put an end to the feud.

The year 1871, like the year 1815, was a landmark in European history. Both

---

Franco-German Agreement on Causes of the War of 1870
1951

A fair judgment on the outbreak of war in 1870 must admit that both sides contributed to an increase of existing tensions:

1. Bismarck by his secret support of the Hohenzollern candidacy for the Spanish throne. He thus hoped to outwit Napoleon and to press him diplomatically so that the fall of the imperial regime might result. He may also have intended to weaken France militarily in case of war by creating a front in the Pyrenees.
2. Napoleon and his cabinet by their exaggerated diplomatic and political counter-offensive since July 6, especially by their demand of a guarantee from King William [that the candidacy would not be renewed]. This put France in the wrong with the rest of Europe, although Napoleon and most of his ministers feared war more than they desired it.
3. Finally Bismarck by the well-known editing of the Ems dispatch, which was not a "falsification" but a conscious aggravation with the aim of forcing France into a serious diplomatic defeat or a declaration of war.

It must be recognized that the German as well as the French peoples went to war in the honest conviction that they were challenged by the other side. Neither of them knew the diplomatic details, which were cleared up only much later.

From "Deutsch-französische Vereinbarung über strittige Fragen europäischer Geschichte," *Internationales Jahrbuch für Geschichtsunterricht*, Vol. II (1951), pp. 81–82.

Animated French map of Europe in 1870. A caption with it explains: "England, isolated, swears with rage and almost forgets Ireland, whom she holds on a leash. Spain frets, propped up by Portugal. France repulses the invasion of Prussia, who reaches with one hand for Holland and the other for Austria. Italy, also, says to Bismarck: 'Take your feet away from there.' Corsica and Sardinia, a regular urchin who laughs at it all. Denmark, who has lost his legs in Holstein, hopes to regain them. European Turkey yawns and wakes up. Asiatic Turkey inhales the smoke of her water pipe. Sweden leaps like a panther, and Russia resembles a bugbear out to fill his basket."

years saw the end of a major war, and both initiated a long period of peace among the major powers. But this is about as far as the parallel goes. Relations among states in 1815 and after had still been conducted according to certain general rules. But the cynical diplomacy of Cavour, Napoleon III, and Bismarck had changed this. From now on, suspicion rather than trust characterized international dealings, and, though there was to be no major war for forty-three years, the threat of war was almost always present.

In 1815 the balance of power had been revived along traditional lines, but by 1871 an entirely new balance had emerged. Austria, Russia, Great Britain, and France had been the leading powers at Vienna, with Prussia lagging far behind and with Italy a mere "geographical expression." By 1871 that order had been thoroughly revised. Both Austria and France now were overshadowed by a Prussianized Germany, and even Italy demanded recognition as a great power. England and Russia continued in their former status; while at Vienna they had taken an active part in shaping the affairs of the Continent, the balance of 1871 had been brought about without their participation. Here, perhaps, lies the major

difference between 1815 and 1871. When Napoleon I had upset the balance of power, the Concert of Europe met at the Congress of Vienna to restore it. There was no such concert in 1871, and hence there was no congress. The Concert of Europe had gone to pieces over the Crimean War. Both Great Britain and Russia had kept out of the subsequent wars of Italian and German unification. It was the passivity of these peripheral powers, as much as the activities of Cavour, Bismarck, and Napoleon III, that helped to bring about the changed European balance of 1871.

ENGLAND'S "VICTORIAN COMPROMISE"

England had always maintained a certain isolation from the Continent, and it had added reason to do so after the middle of the nineteenth century. The British people did not remain immune from the virus of nationalism. But the Crimean War had brought home the futility of military involvement. And besides, it had brought defeat to Russia, whose advances in the eastern Mediterranean had presented the only real threat to British commerce.

The "Workshop of the World"

The twenty years after 1850 were the most prosperous in British history. While wars elsewhere helped retard economic development, Britain's industry and commerce experienced an unprecedented boom. This was the heyday of free trade, a policy from which Britain, as the most advanced industrial nation, profited most. The change in shipbuilding from wood to iron, furthermore, opened up a wholly new field for expansion. By 1870, Britain's carrying trade enjoyed a virtual monopoly. While British engineers were building railroads the world over, Britain's surplus capital sought outlets for investment on the Continent and overseas. Between 1854 and 1870, England's foreign holdings more than doubled.

Though Britain was reluctant to become involved in European politics, it showed no such hesitation overseas. (The next chapter has more to say on British colonial policy.) While in some parts of the British Empire, such as Canada and Australia, the basis for self-government was being laid, elsewhere, notably in India, Britain tightened its reins. In 1859 the rule of the East India Company was taken over by the British government. Commercial expansion in China, begun in the 1840s, made rapid advances in the late 1850s. The new Suez Canal, built by French interests, soon became a major artery for British commerce.

The Second Reform Bill

Britain's prosperity did not do away with political discontent. There had been no major political reforms since 1832. The Tories, now called Conservatives, had acquiesced in the new conditions created by the Great Reform Bill; and the Whigs, now called Liberals, while favoring reforms in other fields, also considered the Reform Bill final. The aims of the two parties had thus become almost indistinguishable. Neither the aristocracy nor the middle class was dominant. Government proceeded by compromise.

Meanwhile, as a result of advancing industrialization, Britain's middle and working classes were growing rapidly. This growth could not help but create a demand for further extension of the franchise. By the 1860s the need for reform could no longer be ignored. Both parties at the time had leaders ready to take charge of the contest over parliamentary reform. Since 1852 the Conservative Benjamin Disraeli and the Liberal William Gladstone had played important roles in cabinets of their respective parties. In 1866 Gladstone introduced a moderate reform bill that was promptly defeated by the Conservatives. An even more radical bill introduced the next year by Disraeli was passed, largely with Liberal support. The Second Reform Bill of 1867, by giving the vote to urban workers, doubled the number of voters. It did not introduce universal suffrage, but it did provide the majority of adult British males with a voice in their government.

Caricature of William Gladstone in 1869, by "Ape" (Carlo Pellegrini).

Gladstone's First "Great Ministry"

The agitation surrounding the Second Reform Bill had ended the Victorian

French satirical drawing of England's Irish problem. Queen Victoria, touring the island, is shielded from seeing unpleasant sights.

Compromise. Both Conservatives and Liberals now tightened their organizations and became parties in the modern sense. When the elections of 1868 returned a Liberal majority, Gladstone formed his first "great ministry." Just as the Bill of 1832 had been followed by a long series of domestic reforms, so the years after 1867 saw many overdue measures enacted. Notable among them was the Education Act of 1870, which, at long last, relieved a situation in which almost half of Britain's children had received no schooling.

One problem concerned Gladstone above all others—the problem of Ireland. That unhappy country, vastly overpopulated, had long been on the verge of starvation. Migration to the United States relieved some of the pressure but also added to unrest. The Fenian Brotherhood, founded in New York in 1858, was responsible for many acts of violence in England and Ireland. Gladstone considered the solution of the Irish problem his major mission. Its roots were partly religious, partly economic. To solve Ireland's religious grievances, the Disestablishment Act of 1869 freed Irish Catholics from having to support the Anglican Church. To improve land tenure, the Land Act of 1870 curtailed the power of absentee landlords to evict their tenants without compensation. But since the Land Act did not heed Ireland's demands for the "three F's"—fair rent, fixity of tenure, and free sale—it was only a half-measure.

Like most of Gladstone's reforms, his Irish policy violated many vested interests and contributed to his defeat in 1874. There were other causes of discontent. Though elected by working-class votes, Gladstone had done little to improve the status of the laborer. Prosperity, meanwhile, had begun to level off, and from 1873 on depression elsewhere made itself felt in Britain as well. Finally, Gladstone's foreign policy—peaceful, sensible, but unexciting—lacked popular support. With Disraeli, who succeeded him in 1874 and who combined social legislation at home with an active imperial policy abroad, a new chapter in British history began.

RUSSIA: REACTION AND REFORM

The second great power on the periphery of Europe, tsarist Russia, pursued its own peculiar course through most of the nineteenth century. The westernization of Russia that had begun during the eighteenth century continued, but very slowly. Because of its vast size and the multiplicity of its backward peoples, Russia faced a number of problems not shared by any of the other great powers. To establish political control in the face of such obstacles required a regime of strict autocracy. The will of the tsar was law. His decrees were translated into action by a huge bureaucracy whose openness to bribery helped somewhat to soften the harshness of tsarist rule. Russia's government has been aptly described as "despotism tempered by corruption."

Aside from autocracy, there were other institutions peculiar to the tsarist empire. Although in western Europe the nobility had lost much of its power, Russia's aristocracy continued to enjoy its traditional privileges. Besides owning almost all the land, the nobles were exempt from taxation and from military service. There was as yet no middle class to speak of, except in the few larger towns. The majority of the tsar's subjects, more than 95 percent, were peasants, and most of them were still serfs. Serfdom in Russia was much more burdensome than it had been in western Europe. Even the legally free peasants, who by 1833 constituted about a third of the population, were kept in a decidedly inferior position. Occasionally, when the misery of the Russian masses became too much to bear, they sought relief in local uprisings. There had been more than 500 such mutinies during the rule of Nicholas I (1825–55). Nicholas actually had introduced some measures aimed at alleviating the worst abuses of serfdom, but to go to the root of the evil and to liberate the serfs would have meant taking land away from the nobility; even the autocratic tsars did not dare do that. Instead, Nicholas continued to preach the principles dearest to his reactionary heart—obedience to autocracy, adherence to the traditional Orthodox religion, and patriotic faith in the virtues of Russian nationality.

"Westerners" versus "Slavophils"

The obstacles that the tsarist government put in the way of education and the restriction it imposed on western ideas helped to keep down the numbers of the Russian "intelligentsia"—that is, those few people whose intellectual interests set them apart from the illiterate masses. Still, by the middle of the nineteenth century this group had grown numerous enough to make its influence felt. There were two clearly defined factions among Russian intellectuals—the "Westerners" and the "Slavophils." The Westerners saw their country as essentially a part of western civilization, merely lagging behind but able eventually to catch up. The Slavophils, on the other hand, held that the difference between Russia and the West was not one of degree but of kind. They pointed to the peculiar foundations of Russian civilization—Byzantine, Slavic, and Greek-Orthodox as compared to the Roman, Germanic, and Catholic roots of western civilization. And they believed that each nation should live according to its own traditions rather than trying to imitate the institutions and practices of other countries. These theoretical differences between Westerners and Slavophils also determined their attitudes toward current problems. While the Westerners favored constitutional government, rationalism, and industrial progress, the Slavophils saw the salvation of Russia in benevolent autocracy, Orthodox Christianity, and the reform of Russia's predominantly agrarian society. This eastern-versus-western orientation henceforth remained a permanent characteristic of Russian political and social philosophy.

The most important political developments during the regime of Nicholas I were in foreign affairs. One of the main aims of Russian policy continued to be the domination, direct or indirect, over the disintegrating Ottoman Empire. Western opposition to Russia's Turkish aspirations had finally led to the Crimean War. More than any previous event, this conflict had shown the inefficiency, corruption, and poor leadership of the tsarist regime. Nicholas had died during the war. His successor, Alexander II (1855–81), was far less reactionary. Though he had little understanding of social and economic problems, he was impressed by the clamor for reform that had set in after the Crimean defeat. The most widespread demand of the reformers was for the emancipation of the serfs.

The Emancipation of the Serfs

Alexander II realized that the alternative to abolishing serfdom from above might ultimately be revolution from below. He therefore initiated a careful study of the situation that finally, in March 1861, led to the Emancipation Edict. Its immediate effects, however, were far from happy. It was of little use for the Russian serf to gain his freedom without at the same time obtaining sufficient land to make a living. Yet to deprive the nobility of its labor force and most of its land would have placed the burden of emancipation entirely upon that class. The solution finally arrived at was a compromise that satisfied no one. The peasants were given almost half the land, not in direct ownership but in large holdings administered by the village community, the *mir*. The *mir* in turn ap-

Serfdom

Few realize what serfdom was in reality. There is a dim conception that the conditions which it created were very bad; but those conditions, as they affected human beings bodily and mentally, are not generally understood. It is amazing, indeed, to see how quickly an institution and its social consequences are forgotten when the institution has ceased to exist, and with what rapidity men and things change. I will try to recall the conditions of serfdom by telling, not what I heard, but what I saw . . . :

Father . . . calls in Makár, the piano-tuner and sub-butler, and reminds him of all his recent sins. . . . Of a sudden there is a lull in the storm. My father takes a seat at the table and writes a note. "Take Makár with this note to the police station, and let a hundred lashes with the birch rod be given him."

Terror and absolute muteness reign in the house. The clock strikes four, and we all go down to dinner. . . . "Where is Makár?" our stepmother asks. "Call him in." Makár does not appear, and the order is repeated. He enters at last, pale, with a distorted face, ashamed, his eyes cast down. . . . Tears suffocate me, and immediately after dinner is over I run out, catch Makár in the dark passage, and try to kiss his hand; but he tears it away, and says, either as a reproach or as a question, "Let me alone; you, too, when you are grown up, will you not be just the same?"

From Prince Peter Kropotkin, *Memoirs of a Revolutionist* (Boston: Houghton Mifflin, 1899), pp. 49–51.

Alexander II, *ca.* 1876.

portioned land use among the village households. The landowners were compensated by the government; but the redemption money that the government paid to the nobles had to be repaid over a period of forty-nine years by each village community.

Emancipation thus freed the individual peasant from servitude to his noble master but subjected him to the communal control of his village. It substituted a new "peasant problem" for the old problem of serfdom. To be freed from the redemption payments and the tutelage of the *mir,* and to get hold of the land still in the hands of the nobility— these remained burning issues for the Russian peasantry into the twentieth century.

Reform, Radicalism, and Reaction

The liberation of the serfs, while the most spectacular of Alexander's acts, was not the only effort he made to strengthen his regime through timely reforms. In 1863 he granted universities a greater degree of academic freedom. In 1864 he reformed the Russian judicial system along western lines. The same year Alexander introduced a measure of local and regional self-government through elected assemblies, or *zemstvos.* The hope of the reformers that this development might eventually culminate in a national assembly was disappointed. But even so, the *zemstvos* provided some opportunity for public discussion and the development of civic responsibility, both hitherto unknown in Russia.

The more changes Alexander introduced, the more hopes he aroused. One of the results of his policy had been to give an impetus to various reform movements among the intelligentsia, whose aims and agitation became ever more radical. Western socialism had been slow to gain a hold in Russia, where industry was still in its infancy. Consequently, Russian socialists like Alexander Herzen tried to appeal to the Russian peasant, whose village community already exhibited many of the collective features cherished by socialists. In the 1860s it became the fashion for members of the intelli-

gentsia to go out and live among the peasants in the hope of arousing them from their apathy and urging them into starting a revolution. This "go-to-the-people" movement (*Narodniki*), however, failed because the peasants were too backward and the authorities too vigilant. In their opposition to everything their government stood for, the younger members of the intelligentsia now began to refer to themselves as "nihilists," believers in nothing. Most of them vented their anger over the existing system merely by expounding radical ideas and by disregarding conventional manners and mores. During the 1870s, however, some of the nihilists fell under the influence of Mikhail Bakunin and his philosophy of anarchism. In 1879 this terrorist faction formed a secret society, "The Will of the People," whose aim was to overthrow the government by direct action and assassination.

Frightened by these manifestations of radicalism, Alexander II reverted to a policy of renewed reaction. Yet by reverting to repression, he merely helped to strengthen the revolutionary forces he hoped to combat. This fact was brought home to him in several attempts on his life, and in 1880 he tried once again to return to his initial policy of reform. But by then it was too late. Alexander II was killed by a terrorist bomb in 1881.

The Primacy of Foreign Policy

During the two decades after 1850 foreign policy in most of Europe overshadowed domestic policy. There were few discernible trends in domestic affairs. Industrialization continued, but its progress was still uneven. Democracy made gains in some countries (notably England), but it suffered reversals in others (notably Germany). Some important reforms helped ease tension—the Emancipation Edict in Russia, the *Ausgleich* between Austria and Hungary, the Second Reform Bill in England. But for each issue resolved, others arose elsewhere—the conflict between monarchism and republicanism in France, the defeat of liberalism in Germany, the tension between North and South in Italy, to mention but a few.

The most significant event in the "era of unification" was the emergence of Germany as a great power. From 1871 to 1945 the influence of that belatedly unified nation made itself felt in every major international crisis and in the history of every country. Compared to German unification, the unification of Italy today seems of minor importance, though it did not appear so at the time. Of much greater consequence was the tragic fate of the Second French Empire. Its defeat at the hands of Prussia sowed some of the seeds that brought forth the great wars of our century. But these events were far off in 1871. At the time it seemed as though the Continent at long last had found the stability that statesmen before 1850 had tried so hard to achieve. The future was to show the precariousness of the new balance of power.

Suggestions for Further Reading

Note: Asterisk denotes a book available in paperback edition.

General

Most of the general works cited after Chapter 24 also cover this later period. An admirably comprehensive view may be gained from R. C. Binkley, *Realism and Nationalism, 1852–1871** (1935). The international affairs of Europe are covered in A. J. P. Taylor, *The Struggle for Mastery in Europe, 1848–1918** (1954).

The Eastern Question

The disintegration of the Ottoman Empire is treated authoritatively in J. A. R. Marriott, *The Eastern Question in European Diplomacy* (1926), and more briefly in M. S. Anderson, *The Eastern Question** (1966). On the background of the Crimean War, see E. Horvath, *Origins of the Crimean War* (1937); H. W. V. Temperley, *England and the Near East: The Crimea* (1936); G. B. Henderson, *Crimean War Diplomacy and Other Historical Essays* (1947); and D. Hopwood, *The Russian Presence in Syria and Palestine, 1843–1914* (1969). B. D. Gooch, ed., *Origins of the Crimean War** (1969), presents various interpretations by different historians. W. E. Mosse, *The Rise and Fall of the Crimean System, 1855–1871* (1967), takes a new look at the larger issues connected with the war. The war itself is vividly portrayed in N. Bentley, ed., *William H. Russell's Despatches from the Crimea, 1854–1856* (1967). The Crimean War also provides a somber background for two fine books by C. Woodham-Smith: *Florence Nightingale, 1820–1919** (1951), and *The Reason Why** (1953).

The Second French Empire

The most thorough studies of Napoleon III's early career are both by F. A. Simpson, *The Rise of Louis Napoleon* (1950), and *Louis Napoleon and the Recovery of France, 1848–1856*, 3rd ed. (1951). The political history of the Empire is covered in O. Aubry, *The Second Empire* (1940), and in J. M. Thompson, *Louis Napoleon and the Second Empire* (1955). A. Guérard, *Reflections on the Napoleonic Legend* (1924), traces the Napoleonic heritage of the emperor. The same author, in his *Napoleon III** (1943), draws a sympathetic picture of a man whom others have called a "herald of fascism." A collection of contrasting interpretations of Napoleon III may be found in B. D. Gooch, *Napoleon III: Man of Destiny—Enlightened Statesman or Proto-Fascist?** (1963). N. N. Barker, *Distaff Diplomacy: The Empress Eugénie and the Foreign Policy of the Second Empire* (1967), deals with the influence of the wife of Napoleon III. Among more specialized studies on the Empire, the following are of interest: T. Zeldin, *The Political System of Napoleon III* (1958); F. C. Palm, *England and Napoleon III: A Study in the Rise of a Utopian Dictator* (1948); L. M. Case, *French Opinion on War and Diplomacy During the Second Empire* (1953); L. M. Case and W. F. Spencer, *The United States and France: Civil War Diplomacy* (1970); C. W. Hallberg, *Franz Joseph and Napoleon III, 1852–1864: A Study of Austro-French Relations* (1955); and D. S. Pinckney, *Napoleon III and the Reconstruction of Paris* (1958). R. L. Williams, *Gaslight and Shadow: The World of Napoleon III** (1957), conveys some of the glamour and excitement of one of the most brilliant periods in French history. The same author's *The French Revolution of 1870–1871** (1969), deals with the end of the Empire. E. S. Mason, *The Paris Commune* (1968), is a balanced account.

The Unification of Italy

The dramatic events of these crucial years are best studied through the lives of the main participants, including Napoleon III. A. J. Whyte, *The Political Life and Letters of Cavour, 1848–1861* (1930), and W. R. Thayer, *The Life and Times of Cavour*, 2 vols. (1914), are standard works. The same holds true for the classic accounts of Garibaldi's colorful exploits in G. M. Trevelyan, *Garibaldi and the Thousand* (1911), and *Garibaldi and the Making of Italy* (1911). More recent are the excellent studies by D. Mack Smith: *Cavour and Garibaldi, 1860: A Study in Political Conflict* (1954); *Garibaldi* (1956); and *Victor Emmanuel, Cavour, and the Risorgimento* (1971). The best biographies of Mazzini are B. King, *The Life of Mazzini* (1902), and G. O. Griffith, *Mazzini: Prophet of Modern Europe* (1932). The role of Napoleon III in the unification of Italy is treated in most of the works on the Second Empire cited above, as well as in L. M. Case, *Franco-Italian Relations, 1860–1865* (1932), and in J. W. Bush, *Venetia Redeemed: Franco-Italian Relations, 1864–1866* (1967). On British policy, see D. E. D. Beales, *England and Italy, 1859–1860* (1961).

The Unification of Germany

The most recent comprehensive account in English of the events culminating in 1871 is O. Pflanze, *Bismarck and the Development of Germany: The Period of Unification, 1815–1871* (1963). T. S. Hamerow, *The Social Foundation of German Unification, 1858–1871* (1969), supplies the domestic background. The Prussian constitutional conflict is the subject of E. N. Anderson, *The Social and Political Conflict in Prussia* (1954). On the war with Denmark, L. D. Steefel, *The Schleswig-Holstein Question* (1932), remains standard. For an understanding of Austro-Prussian rivalry, H. Friedjung, *The Struggle for Supremacy in Germany, 1859–1866* (1897, 1935), is still important. See also C. W. Clark, *Franz Joseph and Bismarck: The Diplomacy of Austria Before the War of 1866* (1934), and E. A. Pottinger, *Napoleon III and the German Crisis, 1865–1866* (1966). Subsequent Austrian developments are covered in A. J. May, *The Hapsburg Monarchy, 1867–1914* (1951), and in R. A. Kann, *The Habsburg Empire* (1957). On the war of 1866, see G. Craig, *The Battle of Königgrätz: Prussia's Victory over Austria, 1866* (1964). On the outbreak of the Franco-Prussian War, see L. D. Steefel, *Bismarck, the Hohenzollern Candidacy, and the Origins of the Franco-Prussian War* (1962). R. Millman, *British Foreign Policy and the Coming of the Franco-Prussian War* (1965), is useful. There are many biographies of Bismarck, none of them wholly satisfactory. E. Eyck, *Bismarck and the German Empire** (1950), is an abbreviation of a much longer German work; A. J. P. Taylor, *Bismarck: The Man and the Statesman** (1955), is more readable but less sound. The international repercussions of German unification are admirably clarified in W. E. Mosse, *The European Powers and the German Question, 1848–1871* (1958). On the war between France and Prussia, see M. E. Howard, *The Franco-Prussian War** (1961).

England

Both A. Briggs, *The Age of Improvement, 1783–1867* (1959), and G. Kitson-Clark, *The Making of Victorian England* (1962), contain authoritative accounts of the mid-Victorian era. E. Longford, *Victoria R. I.** (1964), is based on the queen's personal archives. British foreign policy and its chief maker are vividly presented in D. Southgate, *"The Most English Minister": The Policies and Politics of Palmerston* (1966). H. C. F. Bell, *Lord Palmerston*, 2 vols. (1936), is the best biography. For a brilliant survey of social and intellectual life, see G. M. Young, *Victorian England: Portrait of an Age** (1936). Good monographs on important domestic developments are J. H. Hanham, *Elections and Party Management: Politics in the Time of Disraeli and Gladstone* (1959), and F. B. Smith, *The Making of the Second Reform Bill* (1966).

Russia

The political history of Russia is covered in M. T. Florinsky, *Russia: A History and an Interpretation*, Vol. 2 (1953); and in H. Seton-Watson, *The Russian Empire, 1801–1917* (1967). J. H. Billington, *The Icon and the Axe* (1966), is a comprehensive synthesis of Russian culture. A. Herzen, *My Past and Thoughts*, 6 vols. (1924–27), is a graphic contemporary account by one of Russia's leading intellectuals. On the crucial problem of serfdom, see G. T. Robinson, *Rural Russia Under the Old Regime* (1949), and T. Emmons, *The Russian Landed Gentry and the Peasant Emancipation of 1861* (1968). D. M. Wallace, *Russia** (1912), is still valuable for an understanding of the Russian people. The following discuss two basic trends of Russian life and thought: H. Kohn, *Pan-Slavism: Its History and Ideology** (1953); and N. V. Riasinovsky, *Russia and the West in the Teaching of the Slavophiles* (1953). S. Graham, *Tsar of Freedom: The Life and Reign of Alexander II* (1935), deals sympathetically with a tragic figure. W. E. Mosse, *Alexander II and the Modernization of Russia** (1958), is a brief survey.

27 Europe and the World in the Nineteenth Century

Lord Curzon, Viceroy of India, and Lady Curzon, with Indian notables, *ca*. 1900.

From the "Age of Discovery" until the nineteenth century the world leadership of Europe had remained virtually unchallenged. As European nations established overseas commercial or colonial contacts, the ultimate conquest of the globe by western civilization appeared inevitable. But there had also been signs of a reverse trend, as some regions seemed to grow restive under European tutelage. The United States had been the first European overseas possession to gain independence, and there were soon to be similar movements for independence in the other regions where Europeans had settled. In time this unrest also affected some of the native peoples. Only the Japanese managed to become sufficiently westernized to escape foreign control. But other potentially great powers, notably India and China, wanted to emulate the Japanese. Despite the continued ascendancy of Europe during the nineteenth century, therefore, there were indications that the day of European supremacy was drawing to a close.

This chapter deals only with the major spheres of European expansion—North and South America, the British Empire, and Asia. The African continent was not opened up to European penetration until the end of the nineteenth century, and the resulting rivalry among the powers there will be more profitably discussed in a later chapter. The United States will command far more attention than any of the other regions, mainly because America remains to this day the most important overseas extension of European civilization.

THE UNITED STATES BECOMES A GREAT POWER

In 1815 America was of little concern to most Europeans. A century later, it had emerged as the decisive arbiter in the greatest war Europe had ever fought. The advent of this newcomer on the international stage was long delayed. Through most of the nineteenth century, America remained politically isolated from the rest of the world, so much so that "isolationism" still remains a strong trend in American foreign policy.

America and Europe

In the "Monroe Doctrine" of 1823, America had warned Europe to desist from any further colonization in the Western Hemisphere. On several occasions during the nineteenth century, notably during the 1830s and 1840s, the United States became involved with its neighbors to the north and south over territorial issues. But these localized conflicts had no effect on the European balance of power. Even the international repercussions of the American Civil War did not lead to European intervention. It was only at the close of the nineteenth century, in the war with Spain, that America once again went to war with a European power.

Despite the political isolation in which the United States shaped its destiny, cultural relations between the new republic and the old continent remained close, though America at first was a recipient rather than a contributor in this cultural exchange. In the 1830s and 1840s, foreign travelers still commented on the backwardness and boorishness of American manners and customs. But there were also some friendlier critics, like the young Frenchman Alexis de Tocqueville, whose *Democracy in America* (1835–40) predicted correctly the leading role that the United States would some day play in world affairs.

America had shared the European vogue of Romanticism, and some of Europe's early socialists had tried out their utopian experiments on American soil. By the middle of the nineteenth century American writers like Irving, Cooper, Longfellow, and Poe drew foreign attention to American literature, and the monumental works of the historians Prescott, Parkman, Bancroft, and Motley did the same for American historiography. There were other fields in which American influence made itself felt. The pioneering efforts of American reformers in advocating women's rights, pacifism, and temperance evoked responses overseas; and the gradual adoption in Europe of universal male suffrage and free public education profited greatly from the American example. In technical inventions America already showed the genius that was ultimately

America led the way in invention of better means of communication. Shown above is the tape on which the first telegraph message was received in Baltimore on May 24, 1844. Samuel F. B. Morse had tapped out the message ''What hath God wrought?'' from Washington. Below is a photograph of Alexander Graham Bell's invention in 1876—the telephone.

it the leading industrial nation of the world. The cultural exchange between Europe and the United States thus became less one-sided as time went on. Better means of communication also played their part. By the 1860s, the steamship had begun to compete successfully with the sailing vessel, and the laying of a transatlantic cable in 1858 speeded the exchange of news and ideas.

The Westward Movement

In its domestic development the United States faced many of the same social and economic problems that confronted the nations of Europe. But since America was a new nation, unencumbered by feudal traditions and endowed with a rich and virtually empty continent, it grew into something radically different from Europe. Within one century the territory of the United States increased more than fourfold. To assimilate and integrate these new lands proved to be America's foremost political problem,

and its final solution contributed to the origins of a bloody civil war. Yet the abundance of fertile lands also helped to relieve economic and social pressures that might have had similarly violent repercussions. The result of America's territorial expansion was a superpower marked by vast size, advantageous location, wide variety of climate, and great wealth of natural resources.

Immigration

The territorial growth of the United States was closely related to the phenomenal growth of its population. From less than 4 million in 1790, the population shot up to over 60 million in the course of a hundred years. Much of this increase was due to the ceaseless stream of European immigrants, totaling more than 35 million between 1815 and 1914. Many of them still came to escape political or religious persecution, but there was also the attraction of the seemingly unlimited economic opportunities of the New World. The constant supply of cheap labor provided by immigration was a boon to America's growing economy. The rapid Americanization of these new citizens was aided by the fact that the United States had no privileged classes, no established church, and no military caste. American society had its sectional and occupational groupings, but they were not as rigid as the European hierarchies. Economic opportunity for all, an open society in which ability and hard work brought success—these were the ingredients of the "American dream."

Early Industrialization

Like most European countries, the United States in the first part of the nineteenth century remained predominantly agrarian. It was the abundance of land that attracted land-hungry Europeans. But as in Europe, the vast increase of population required additional eco-

De Tocqueville on Russia and America   1835

There are at the present time two great nations in the world, which started from different points, but seem to tend towards the same end. I allude to the Russians and the Americans. . . . All other nations seem to have nearly reached their natural limits, and they have only to maintain their power; but these are still in the act of growth. . . . These alone are proceeding with ease and celerity along a path which no limit can be perceived. The American struggles against ——les that nature opposes to him; the adversaries of the Rus- ——. The former combats the wilderness and savage life; —— with all its arms. The conquests of the Ameri- —— the plowshare; those of the Russian by —— lies upon personal interest to ac- —— to the unguided strength and —— ussian centers all the authority —— cipal instrument of the former is —— heir starting-point is different and —— et each of them seems marked out —— the destinies of half the globe.

621

——ocracy in America (New York: Knopf, 1953),

Immigrants at Ellis Island,
New York, *ca.* 1912.

nomic outlets, and these were provided by industry. By the middle of the nineteenth century the eastern states had thriving industries. At the same time, the opening up of western territories provided an ever-expanding market. Full-scale industrialization did not take hold until after the Civil War. Prior to 1860, however, many of the social effects of industrialization that were seen in Europe had already made themselves felt. Labor conditions in American factories on the whole were better than those in Europe. During the first half of the nineteenth century there were the beginnings of American labor unions, but a labor movement in the modern sense, in America as in Europe, did not develop until later.

In its economic philosophy, America shared the faith of European liberals in freedom from state control. The American Revolution had been fought against the mercantilist restrictions imposed by the mother country. Once these restrictions had been removed, there remained few obstacles to free enterprise. A philosophy of laissez faire thus came to permeate the economic life of the United States. There was only one field in which American industry not only tolerated but demanded government control, and that was tariff legislation. With the world's largest free-trade area within their own borders, American manufacturers were eager to keep foreign competitors out.

America after 1815

The revolutionary turmoil in Europe after 1815 had its parallel in the unrest that prevailed in the United States during the 1820s. The source of this unrest was economic and social. As America's population increased, and as the new territories acquired with the purchase of Louisiana (1803) and Florida (1819) filled up with new settlers, a number of differences arose between the established interests in the East and the new forces on the frontier. Another source of unrest arose among the new workers of the

East, most of them recent immigrants with little bargaining power and no social standing. Thanks to the growth of the democratic process after the Revolution, this discontent was able to express itself at the ballot box.

Democracy in the United States had been slow to reach all levels of society, and it was not until the late 1820s that male suffrage had been adopted in the majority of states. Largely as a result of this increased democratization Andrew Jackson was elected President in 1828. More than any of his predecessors, Jackson could claim to be the people's choice. He was the first westerner to win the highest office, a popular hero of the War of 1812, and, most important, a man who had risen from poverty by his own efforts. The road from log cabin to White House henceforth became part of the American dream.

The "Age of Jackson"

The "Age of Jackson" was a period of major change in American life, more so even than the 1830s were in western Europe. The democratization of political life continued with the adoption of the patronage or "spoils system," and with the practice of having presidential candidates nominated by national conventions rather than by a handful of party leaders. Closest to Jackson's heart was the further development of the West. In a number of treaties concluded with Indian tribes, the federal government won title to millions of acres of virgin land. These were sold at auction at low cost, after free land for schools, roads, a state university, and other public purposes had been set aside. Jackson's opposition to eastern financial interests, furthermore, made him the advocate of state banks, whose lavish granting of credit helped develop the West.

With the opening of the West, sectional rivalry became one of the major issues in American politics. Not only the West, but the South as well, found itself at odds with the North, especially over tariffs. The South, depending on cotton exports, favored free trade, while the North demanded high tariffs to protect its infant industries. Finding itself more and more overshadowed by the North,

Above: Andrew Jackson (1767–1845), by Thomas Sully. Left: his campaign poster in 1828.

the South used the proposal of a high tariff in 1828 as an occasion for raising the vital question of "states' rights." The relationship between state and federal governments had been an issue in American politics since the early days of the Republic. The Constitution of 1787 had considerably widened the power of the central government over what it had been under the Articles of Confederation, and the policy since then had been to carry this centralization further.

But there was also strong sentiment against this tendency. Critics of centralization took the view that the Constitution was primarily a compact among sovereign states, and that the states had the right to nullify an act of Congress if it violated the terms of that compact. It was this idea of nullification that was used by Jackson's Vice President, John C. Calhoun, a Southerner, to fight the "tariff of abominations." In the ensuing crisis Jackson broke with Calhoun and defended the sovereignty of the Union against the advocates of states' rights. A final showdown was averted by the compromise tariff of 1833. But this did not remove the underlying conflict between federal power and state sovereignty.

Expansionism of the 1840s

In foreign affairs the Jacksonian period was uneventful. As more and more settlers began moving westward, however, it was inevitable that tensions

John C. Calhoun (1782–1850), by Charles Bird King.

would develop with the British in the north and the Mexicans in the south over rival claims to western territories. These intermittent conflicts came to a head and were settled during the 1840s. American-British economic relations were so advantageous that it was in the interest of both to avoid a major crisis over the American-Canadian frontier. By the Webster-Ashburton Treaty (1842), therefore, the northeastern boundary was adjusted to mutual satisfaction. A similar compromise was reached for the Northwest in the Oregon Treaty (1846), which fixed Oregon's northern boundary along the forty-ninth parallel.

Relations with America's southern neighbor, Mexico, were considerably more stormy. The main controversy here arose over Texas. The influx of American settlers into this Mexican border region had begun in 1821. Because of constant difficulties with Mexican authorities, the American settlers first demanded autonomy and then, in 1836, proclaimed their independence. The next logical step, admission of Texas to the Union in 1845, led to war with Mexico. As a result of the Mexican War (1846–48), Mexico relinquished its claims to Texas. Mexico also ceded California and New Mexico in return for $15 million. Eight years later, with the Gadsden Purchase, America acquired another slice of Mexican territory.

The settlement with Mexico, together with the Oregon Treaty, gave the United States an extended frontage on the Pacific. The implications of this development for American foreign policy were to become evident only gradually. For the time being, the most pressing need of the vast regions of the new West was for settlers to substantiate America's claims. In a fitting climax to a decade of expansion, gold was discovered in the Sacramento Valley in 1848. The resulting gold rush profited only a few of the many thousands who streamed to California from all over the world. But these "forty-niners" helped to increase the population of California more than fourfold in a single decade.

The Slavery Issue

The expansionism of the 1840s also aggravated the long-standing sectional conflict between proslavery and anti-slavery forces. What has been said about the democratic nature of American society did not apply to the large number of black slaves in the South or even to free blacks in the North. While almost everywhere in the world slavery was being abolished, it was gaining a new lease on life in the American South. In a nation dedicated to a belief in equality, there now arose an aristocracy of wealthy plantation-owners whose belief in their

Slavery

AN APOLOGIST'S VIEW

The negro slaves of the South are the happiest, and, in some sense, the freest people in the world. The children and the aged and infirm work not at all, and yet have all the comforts and necessaries of life provided for them. They enjoy liberty, because they are oppressed neither by care nor labor. The women do little hard work, and are protected from the despotism of their husbands by their masters. The negro men and stout boys work, on the average, in good weather, not more than nine hours a day. . . . Besides, they have their Sabbaths and holidays. White men, with so much of license and liberty, would die of ennui; but negroes luxuriate in corporeal and mental repose. With their faces upturned to the sun, they can sleep at any hour; and quiet sleep is the greatest of human enjoyments. . . . The free laborer must work or starve. He is more of a slave than the negro, because he works longer and harder for less allowance than the slave, and has no holiday, because the cares of life with him begin when its labors end. He has no liberty, and not a single right.

AN ABOLITIONIST'S VIEW

The slaves in the United States are treated with barbarous inhumanity . . . they are overworked, underfed, wretchedly clad and lodged, and have insufficient sleep . . . they are often made to wear round their necks iron collars armed with prongs, to drag heavy chains and weights at their feet while working in the field . . . they are often kept confined in the stocks day and night for weeks together, made to wear gags in their mouths for hours or days, have some of their front teeth torn out or broken off, that they may be easily detected when they run away . . . they are frequently flogged with terrible severity, have red pepper rubbed into their lacerated flesh, and hot brine, spirits of turpentine, etc., poured over the gashes to increase the torture . . . they are often stripped naked, their backs and limbs cut with knives, bruised and mangled by scores and hundreds of blows with the paddle, and terribly torn by the claws of cats, drawn over them by their tormentors.

From George Fitzhugh, Cannibals All! (1857); and Theodore Dwight Weld, Slavery As It Is (1839).

own superiority and the inferiority of the black race foreshadowed the racist ideologies that were to arise in Europe during the later nineteenth century.

The main concern of southern politicians in the first half of the nineteenth century was to prevent antislavery legislation. This could be done only if an even balance between slave and free states was maintained. Such a balance in the past had been maintained by compromise. But compromise became increasingly difficult as more and more territories were added to the Union. With the petition of California in 1849 for admission as a free state, the issue reached a critical stage. If granted, the admission would upset the existing balance between slave and free states. After prolonged debates, differences were once more patched up. The Compromise of 1850 called for the admission of California as a free state, but it left the question of whether the two new territories of New Mexico and Utah were ultimately to be admitted as free or slave states up to their own decisions. It was this introduction of state option, or popular sovereignty, that injected a new and disturbing element into the slavery controversy.

Beginning in the mid-1850s a series of tragic events and incidents drove the opposing factions on the issue of the expansion of slavery still further apart. The rivalry between proslavery and antislavery forces over whether Kansas was to be a free or slave state soon plunged that territory into a miniature civil war. The Supreme Court's Dred Scott decision (1857), which ruled that slaves were property and thus could not become free by moving to a free state, deeply antagonized the North. On the other hand, an attempt by the abolitionist John Brown to lead slaves on a raid of the arsenal at Harper's Ferry (1859) aroused the specter of a slave revolt in the South. The presidential campaign of 1860 was dominated by the slavery issue. The Democrats were divided into a southern, proslavery wing and a northern faction holding to the compromising policy of popular sovereignty. The Republicans, on the other hand, stood united against any further extension of slavery.

Banner of the Third United States Colored Troops.

THE SLAVERY ISSUE 1861

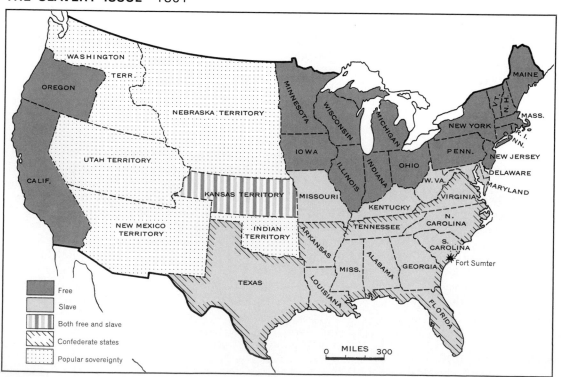

Free
Slave
Both free and slave
Confederate states
Popular sovereignty

WASHINGTON
TERR.
OREGON
NEBRASKA TERRITORY
MINNESOTA
WISCONSIN
MICHIGAN
MAINE
NEW YORK
MASS.
R.I.
CONN.
PENN.
NEW JERSEY
IOWA
ILLINOIS
INDIANA
OHIO
UTAH TERRITORY
CALIF.
KANSAS TERRITORY
MISSOURI
W. VA.
DELAWARE
MARYLAND
VIRGINIA
KENTUCKY
N. CAROLINA
NEW MEXICO TERRITORY
INDIAN TERRITORY
ARKANSAS
TENNESSEE
S. CAROLINA
Fort Sumter
TEXAS
MISS.
ALABAMA
GEORGIA
LOUISIANA
FLORIDA

MILES
0   300

The Republican candidate, Abraham Lincoln, was chosen as President by an electorate divided along sectional lines. Repeatedly in previous years the South had talked of secession as a last resort in defending its way of life. Calhoun, the defender of states' rights had suggested that if compromise proved impossible the states should "agree to separate and part in peace." It was South Carolina, the home of the "great nullifier," that now replied to Lincoln's election by passing its Ordinance of Secession. One after another, most of the slave states seceded from the Union and formed the Confederate States of America. In his inaugural address Lincoln strongly rejected the right of secession and vowed to maintain the Union. But he also left the door open for possible reconciliation.

The issue of peace or war hung in the balance for a while longer. It was decided on April 12, 1861, when Confederate forces opened fire on the federal garrison at Fort Sumter in Charleston Harbor.

The American Civil War

The American Civil War was fought initially to preserve and protect the Union. To that extent it belongs among the great wars of national unification that were being waged in Europe at the same time. The Civil War was expected to be a brief conflict in which the immense advantages of the North would prove decisive. But the South put up a valiant fight, and in the early part of the war won some brilliant victories. Nobody would have predicted that the war would

Union troops in the Civil War stringing telegraph wires on the battlefield.

Garrison of South Carolina Confederate troops, April 1861.

last four years and would turn into one of the most costly military ventures known up to that time.

Among the political developments of the war the most important was Lincoln's Emancipation Proclamation, to take effect on January 1, 1863. The extension of northern war aims to include the abolition of slavery changed the war from a mere political struggle into an ideological crusade. This change was brought about more by the pressure of circumstances than by actual design. Lincoln himself would have preferred a more gradual and voluntary process of emancipation.

The granting of freedom to black Americans inevitably raised the closely related question of granting them equality as well. The abolitionist minority had never made any distinction between the two. But it took endless debates and several years before the country as a whole was ready to implement the gift of freedom with the guarantee of equality. This was done in several constitutional amendments and civil-rights acts. Beginning in the 1870s, however, the United States Supreme Court interpreted this postwar legislation in a way that violated its spirit, if not its letter, and that kept America's blacks in a state of inferiority for decades to come.

Europe and the Civil War

The Emancipation Proclamation made a very strong impression in Europe. The European powers had watched America's westward movement in the early part of the century with disapproval. During the Mexican War Great Britain actually considered joint intervention with France on behalf of Mexico, and during the 1850s these two powers helped to discourage American plans for the acquisition of Cuba from Spain. The outbreak of the Civil War led official European circles to hope that America would be permanently weakened by the secession of the southern states. Both the British and the French governments were decidedly cool toward the North, and on several occasions diplomatic rupture seemed imminent. When a northern warship removed two Confederate commissioners from the British steamer

"Trent" in 1861, a major crisis was averted only by America's readiness to give in to British protests and release the commissioners. Great Britain, on the other hand, had to heed the protests of the North against permitting southern privateers to be outfitted and to operate from British ports.

American relations with France became strained when Napoleon III tried to bolster his position at home by establishing a puppet regime in Mexico. In 1863 French troops occupied Mexico City, and the following year Archduke Maximilian of Austria was proclaimed Emperor of Mexico. This was in open violation of the Monroe Doctrine, but the United States was too preoccupied to make any protest. Once the Civil War was over, however, it demanded the withdrawal of French troops (1866). Left without support, Maximilian could not last long. He was executed by a Mexican firing squad in 1867.

Not all the governments of Europe hoped to profit from America's domestic tragedy. The Prussian government was favorably disposed toward the North and wished to see the Union preserved as a counterweight to Britain's maritime supremacy. Russia took a similar attitude. The Russians had given up their settlements in California in 1844, and American fears that the tsarist government would take advantage of the Civil War to extend its sphere of influence southward from Alaska proved groundless. Russia sold Alaska, its last remaining colony in North America, to the United States in 1867 for a mere $7.2 million. The same year America also occupied the Midway Islands, thus signifying its new interest in the Pacific area.

The most wholehearted support of the northern cause during the Civil War came from the rank and file of Europe's population. To the Germans and Italians the war appeared as a struggle for national unity, and to people everywhere the Civil War was another phase in the universal fight for freedom and independence that had been waged in Europe ever since the French Revolution. Even before Lincoln's Emancipation Proclamation, most Europeans saw the American war entirely in terms of liberating the

Archduke Maximilian of Austria, Emperor of Mexico (1864–67).

southern slaves. The victory of the North was widely hailed as a triumph of democracy, and some historians feel that it contributed to the liberalization of the British and French governments after 1865.

Reconstruction in the South

America's reputation for liberalism and tolerance, however, was considerably tarnished by the Reconstruction period following the Civil War. The assassination of Lincoln had aroused worldwide indignation and sorrow, and the absence of his moderating influence was keenly felt in the American government's efforts to deal with a recalcitrant South. In an attempt to overcome southern resistance to the political and social emancipation of southern blacks, the Reconstruction Acts of 1867 and 1868 placed the South under military rule, from which it could escape only after drafting new constitutions that accepted the constitutional amendments and civil-rights legislation passed since the end of the war.

Added to the political tension were economic problems. The South emerged from the war with many of its cities destroyed, its economy disrupted, and one of its major economic assets, slavery, gone. The influx of northern "carpet-baggers," intent on making personal or political profit out of southern misfortune, kept alive the bitterness generated by war. The distinctive way of life on which southerners had prided themselves was gone forever; but the ideals on which it had rested remained alive. The slow process by which southern blacks were once again disenfranchised and, by a series of "Jim Crow" laws, segregated as well, did not really gain momentum until the 1890s. Its cumulative effect was to perpetuate sectionalism by creating a "solid South" dominated by the Democratic Party and dedicated to keeping the black "in his place."

Economic Growth

While America was trying to heal the wounds of war during the last decades of the nineteenth century, it was also trying to fill in its remaining "open spaces" and to realize its great industrial potentialities. Both these developments were aided by the continued influx of millions of immigrants. Of considerable help in attracting new citizens and in aiding American farmers were the Homestead Act of 1862 and successive land laws, as well as the easy access provided to the West by the construction of transcontinental railroads. The first such line was completed in 1869. American agriculture already had profited from mechanization. The invention of barbed wire in 1873 made possible the fencing in of vast areas for cattle-raising, and the introduction of the refrigerator car proved a boon to the meat-packing industry. As a result of these and other improvements, western farming took on some of the characteristics of an industry, producing on a large scale for distant markets.

Even more important than the growth of America's agriculture after the Civil War was the expansion of its industries. Government procurement of war materials even at the cost of heavy federal deficits had caused an industrial boom, which continued once the war was over. Between 1860 and 1900 the amount of capital invested in American industry increased more than tenfold, and the export of manufactured articles by 1900 was four times what it had been in 1860. By 1890 the United States had emerged as the world's leader in the production

A poster of 1874 advising farmers of "the greatest invention of the age"—barbed wire.

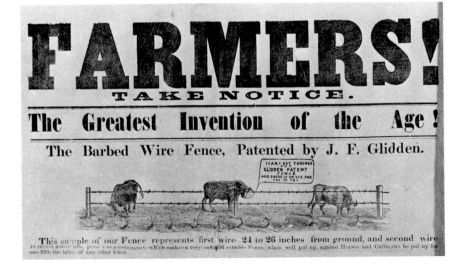

of steel and pig iron, and with close to 200,000 miles of railroads in 1900 America had more mileage than the whole of Europe. America also excelled in mass-production methods based on standardization, interchangeable parts, and ultimately the assembly line.

Government Regulation of Business

As often happens in rapidly expanding economies, America suffered a series of economic crises, of which the Panics of 1873 and 1893 were the most significant. Both had their parallels overseas, and the withdrawal of European capital from American industry in each case precipitated matters. To modify the effects of competition, American heavy industry after 1873 began to combine its resources in order to meliorate the cost of competition, to fix prices, and to control markets. The first of these "trusts" was the Standard Oil Company of John D. Rockefeller (1879). But since these large organizations evoked strong public protests, Congress in 1890 enacted the Sherman Antitrust Law, a gesture, at least, toward remedy. Its enforcement was sufficiently lax, however, to permit the continued concentration of control in industry and banking.

There were other occasions when the federal government had to intervene in order to curb the excesses of unrestricted competition. Contrary to the practice in Europe, where governments had taken an active hand in the construction and operation of railroads, American lines were built through private initiative, aided by lavish grants of public lands. To realize maximum profits, American railroads charged exorbitant rates where there was no competing carrier. There had been various earlier proposals for federal regulation of the railroads, but not until 1887 was the Interstate Commerce Act passed. The new law was chiefly concerned with rates, and it created an Interstate Commerce Commission to enforce its provisions which at first, however, was not very effective.

There was one field in which American business did not mind governmental intervention. Protective tariffs had been a major concern of industrialists during the early nineteenth century. Southern opposition to protectionism, together with Britain's abolition of the Corn Laws in 1846, had brought a brief interval of free trade. But the economic and financial demands of the Civil War reversed the trend. Beginning in 1861 America entered upon a new era of protectionism. Its high point came with the Dingley Tariff Act of 1897, which made the United States the most protectionist country in the world.

The unprecedented industrial expansion of the years after the Civil War gave an air of opulence and optimism to the "Gilded Age." Not all Americans, however, shared in the rise from rags to riches. The South in particular was slow to recover from its defeat and adjust to a world in which cotton was no longer king. The Panic of 1873, moreover, by causing price cuts among farmers and wage cuts among workers, bred widespread discontent. As a result, the 1870s saw the first serious efforts among these potentially powerful groups to assert their influence in national affairs.

Labor and Farm Unrest

There had been a growing awareness among American workers that they might improve their status by combining their small local unions into a more powerful national organization. The first such body to wield any real influence, the Knights of Labor, was founded in 1869. At its height, it had more than 700,000 members. In 1886 a wave of strikes culminated in the Haymarket Square riot in Chicago, in which several policemen were killed. The Knights of Labor, though not directly involved, were nevertheless blamed. There were other reasons for their decline, notably the growing strength of a new national movement, the American Federation of Labor. The A. F. of L. was to be the spearhead of the American labor movement for the next half-century.

Workers' attempts at organization, however, did not at first improve their condition very much. With large numbers of impoverished immigrants swelling the labor market, working conditions

Poster announcing the opening of the Union Pacific Railroad after the railroad had been joined from the Atlantic to the Pacific.

continued to be harsh, hours long, and wages low. Repeated strikes, in which hired strikebreakers fought vicious battles with strikers, further widened the gap between capital and labor. After the Pullman strike of 1894, the Supreme Court ruled that the Sherman Antitrust Act applied to labor unions if they obstructed interstate commerce. It was only after the turn of the century that American workers began to get a "square deal," in large part because of the efforts of their own unions, but also because of the intervention of a more sympathetic government.

Another large body of Americans who felt their interests neglected in a nation that was becoming rapidly industrialized were the farmers. In 1867 the National Grange of the Patrons of Husbandry had been formed, chiefly as a social organization, but also as a platform for agrarian discontent. The main grievance of farmers was the unfair practices of railways. The Interstate Commerce Act (1887) sought to improve the situation, but its initial effectiveness was limited. Suffering increasingly from protectionism abroad and falling prices at home, America's farmers during the 1880s formed regional groupings that ultimately grew into the National Farmers' Alliance and Industrial Union. Its purpose was to aid farmers by cooperative ventures and by bringing pressure against eastern industrial and banking interests who were held responsible for much of the farmer's plight. The climax of the farmers' discontent came with the formation of the People's Party in 1891. The Populists, profiting from the unrest among workers as well, soon emerged as a powerful third force in national politics. Their demands included currency reform, a graduated income tax, and government ownership of the railroads. A particular issue long close to farmers' hearts was the free and unlimited coinage of silver, from which they expected an upturn of farm prices. When the Democratic Party in 1896 adopted some of the Populist platform, including "free silver," the new party joined forces with the Democrats, thus making the latter the spokesmen of agrarian and labor interests.

Foreign Policy after the Civil War

There were few noteworthy events in American foreign policy between the Civil War and the end of the century. In 1889 America signed a treaty with Germany and Great Britain that established tripartite control over the island of Samoa in the South Pacific. The following year Congress adopted a sweeping naval program, calling for a fleet that would place the United States among the world's leading naval powers. Various plans during the 1890s for an American-controlled canal across Central America failed to materialize, as did attempts to annex Hawaii. The islands did not become American until the Spanish-American War in 1898.

Closer to home, the United States improved relations with the nations of the Western Hemisphere. In 1889 the first Pan-American Conference was held in Washington. In 1895, during a border dispute between Venezuela and British Guiana, Secretary of State Olney reaffirmed the principles of the Monroe Doctrine in strong and belligerent tones. A few years later, in 1898, the United States caught the expansionist fever that was driving the European powers into imperialist ventures. From then on American foreign policy became more and more involved with the rivalries of the other great powers. The days of American isolation were almost over.

American Culture

In cultural matters the United States during the second half of the nineteenth century continued to share in the leading trends of Europe. American painters still went to study in Paris, American scholars were trained at foreign universities, and America's symphony orchestras and opera companies depended almost entirely on European talent. But there was some evidence of a native American culture, making up in freshness and originality for what it lacked in refinement. The writings of Walt Whitman and Mark Twain, the paintings of Winslow Homer and Thomas Eakins, the compositions of Edward MacDowell, and the functional architecture of Louis Sullivan all had an

Mark Twain (1835–1910), American humorist of the "Gilded Age."

unmistakably American flavor. The most original and influential of America's intellectual contributions during the late nineteenth century was the philosophy of pragmatism. Its beginnings went back to the early 1870s, but it only attracted general attention with the writing of William James at the turn of the century. In the popular mind pragmatism justified America's preoccupation with practical pursuits and gave moral sanction to the fierce struggle for material success.

Most Americans were proud of this success. Yet there were some critical voices. In a period of progress and prosperity, both seemingly the result of laissez faire, the American journalist Henry George wrote his *Progress and Poverty* (1879), which challenged the free-enterprise system. Thorstein Veblen, in *The Theory of the Leisure Class,* (1899), examined the role of the consumer in the economy of his day and found that such materialistic considerations as "conspicuous consumption" and "conspicuous waste" were exerting an unhealthy influence on the existing price structure. Social criticism also found expression in the novels of Edward Bellamy, Theodore Dreiser, and Frank Norris. All these writers had considerable influence in Europe, where concern over the effects of unrestrained economic liberalism had long agitated socialists and social critics.

In the realm of ideas, as in politics and economics, America at the end of the nineteenth century was making its influence felt far beyond its frontiers. Viewed with a mixture of awe and envy, hope and uneasiness, admiration and condescension, the United States appeared to most Europeans as the black sheep of their family that had struck out on its own and had made good.

LATIN AMERICA: AN AGE OF DICTATORS

When Latin America won its independence from Spain and Portugal in the early nineteenth century, the region comprised nine sovereign states, most important among them Argentina, Brazil, Chile, Mexico, and Peru. By 1850 several of these states had split and their number

had grown to seventeen; on the eve of the First World War there were twenty independent Latin-American nations. These countries had certain things in common. With the exception of Brazil (where Portuguese was spoken), they were Spanish in culture and language; they were all predominantly Catholic; and the majority of their people were Indians, with white minorities that grew larger as more and more immigrants arrived from the Latin countries of Europe. Economically, Latin America throughout the nineteenth century remained predominantly agrarian and backward. Industrialization did not take hold until after the turn of the century, and then only slowly.

One other characteristic all Latin-American countries shared was extreme political instability. Lack of political experience, together with economic difficulties and sectional conflicts, brought an endless succession of dictators. Few countries produced any outstanding leaders. Mexico was an exception, with Santa Anna (1828–55), Benito Juárez (1855–72), and Porfirio Díaz (1877–1911) all gaining fame chiefly through their efforts to resist foreign encroachment.

The weakness and confusion of Latin America seemed to invite such encroachment. The United States, through its Monroe Doctrine, tried to forestall outside intervention. But it was chiefly Britain's support of American policy, combined with a temporary lull in overseas expansion, that kept Europe from challenging the Monroe Doctrine during the first half of the nineteenth century. When the first such challenge was delivered, during the Mexican venture of Napoleon III, the United States was strong enough to take a firm stand. Meanwhile Washington had embarked on its own course of expansion at the expense of Mexico in the 1840s. This first phase of American imperialism was followed by a second round fifty years later (see p. 685). Except for this transitory intervention on the part of the United States, however, Latin America remained free from outside interference. Isolation had its political advantages, but it retarded the economic development of a potentially prosperous region.

THE BRITISH EMPIRE: FROM COLONIES TO DOMINIONS

Prior to 1800 only the American continents had attracted any substantial number of European settlers. Elsewhere, European influence had remained chiefly commercial. It was only during the course of the nineteenth century that Asia, Africa, Australia, and New Zealand were colonized by Europeans. In this process of Europeanization, Great Britain led the way. As the nineteenth century opened, it still had vast holdings on the North American continent and in India. In addition, it had taken the first steps toward opening up Australia and had established claims to New Zealand.

The Empire After 1815

Despite these large possessions, England's colonial enthusiasm after 1815 was at a low ebb. The loss of the American colonies was partly responsible. With the decline of mercantilism, furthermore, the possession of colonies as sources of raw materials and possible markets had lost much of its meaning, since free trade enabled every nation to trade wherever it chose. By 1830 a number of British people were advocating the release of most of the remaining colonies from the control of the mother country. These proposals never got very far, however, mainly because of the agitation of a handful of men usually called the Colonial Reformers. Chief among them were Edward Gibbon Wakefield and the Earl of Durham. Wakefield, in his *Letter from Sidney* (1829), had laid down a plan for the systematic colonization of regions suitable for white settlement. Many of his ideas were subsequently carried out in Australia and New Zealand.

Canada: The First Dominion

Of still greater significance than Wakefield's activities were the proposals made by Lord Durham in his *Report on the Affairs of British North America* in 1839. Canada had been a source of trouble ever since it was taken over from the French in 1763. Its original French settlers re-

Lord Durham (1792–1840), Governor of Canada 1837–40.

sented the influx of large numbers of Britishers, especially after the American Revolution, and efforts to separate the two nationalities by the Canada Act of 1791 had not eased tensions. Discontent with British rule in both Upper and Lower Canada after 1815 had culminated in a brief uprising in 1837. To restore order, Lord Durham was made governor of Canada, and it was on the basis of his first-hand experience that he wrote his famous *Report*. In it he suggested that Upper Canada (Ontario) and Lower Canada (Quebec) be reunited and given responsible self-government. Durham's proposals were incorporated in the Union Act of 1840.

This new arrangement, noted for its granting of self-government, still did not solve the differences between French and British settlers. After long debates among the provincial leaders of Canada, a new federal constitution, the British North America Act, was finally adopted by Britain's Parliament in 1867. Ontario and Quebec were once more separated, and together with the provinces of New Brunswick and Nova Scotia were united in the Dominion of Canada. From the start the Dominion had complete control over its internal affairs, and as time went on it became more and more independent in external matters as well.

Australia, New Zealand, and the Union of South Africa

The evolution of dominion status for Canada was a landmark in the history of the British Empire. A former colony had been set free yet had remained loyal to the mother country. The first step had thus been taken on the road toward what later came to be known as the British Commonwealth. The practice followed in Canada was in time applied to other British settlements overseas. Australia's various states were granted self-government beginning in 1850 and were given dominion status as the Commonwealth of Australia in 1901. In New Zealand, self-government began in 1876 and dominion status was achieved in 1907. Finally, in South Africa various of the smaller territories were joined together in the Union of South Africa in 1910. This

Walter Bagehot
on the Superiority of Englishmen
1869

Let us consider in what a village of English colonists is superior to a tribe of Australian natives who roam about them. Indisputably in one, and that a main sense, they are superior. They can beat the Australians in war when they like; they can take from them anything they like, and kill any of them they choose. . . . Nor is this all. Indisputably in the English village there are more means of happiness, a greater accumulation of the instruments of enjoyment, than in the Australian tribe. The English have all manner of books, utensils, and machines which the others do not use, value, or understand. . . . I think that the plainer and agreed-on superiorities of the Englishmen are these: first, that they have a greater command over the powers of nature upon the whole. . . . Secondly, that this power is not external only; it is also internal. The English not only possess better machines for moving nature, but are themselves better machines. . . . Thirdly, civilized man not only has greater powers over nature, but knows better how to use them, and by better I here mean better for the health and comfort of his present body and mind. . . . No doubt there will remain people like the aged savage who in his old age went back to his savage tribe and said that he had "tried civilization for forty years, and it was not worth the trouble." But we need not take account of the mistaken ideas of unfit men and beaten races.

Walter Bagehot, *Physics and Politics* (New York: Knopf, 1948), pp. 214–16.

completed the list of Britain's original dominions.

The four self-governing dominions thus established were not by any means fully sovereign and independent states. In their foreign affairs in particular, they were still under the control of Great Britain. But such dependence was not felt as a burden. When war broke out in 1914, England did not have to bring pressure to bear on its dominions to join the fight against the Central Powers. The bond of common ideals and institutions had created a community of interest that stood the test of war.

India under the
East India Company

The change from colonies to dominions happened only in those regions that had substantial numbers of white settlers. Elsewhere traditional colonialism continued. This was particularly true in the most valuable of England's possessions, India. As a result of the Seven Years' War, England in 1763 had become the dominant European power in that part of the world. Britain's interests in India, since 1600, had been represented by the East India Company. This was a joint stock company that enjoyed a monopoly of trade and operated with little interference from the British government. Primarily concerned with making profits for its investors, the company systematically exploited the natives.

In time the East India Company's policy began to run into criticism at home, forcing the government to impose restrictions on the company's activities. The Regulation Act of 1773 provided for a governor general appointed by the crown, and the India Act of 1784 placed the company's political activities under the supervision of a Board of Control in London. Later measures restricted and ultimately abolished the East India Company's trade monopoly. The general tendency before the middle of the nineteenth century was to transfer more and more of the company's functions and powers to the British government.

The event that brought the company's rule in India to an end was the Indian Mutiny of 1857. Britain's policy in India during the first half of the nineteenth century, especially under such able governor generals as Lord William Bentinck and the Earl of Dalhousie, had begun to be much more beneficial. India's finances had been overhauled, a system of western education had been introduced, and Indians had been given some participation in their government. Despite these and other improvements, however, there remained a great deal of discontent and unrest. Princes and landlords who had lost their former influence, orthodox Moslems and Hindus who feared the spread of Christianity, intellectuals who objected to the westernization of Indian culture, and the people at large who lived in acute misery—all these elements combined to bring about the "Great Mutiny" that was staged in 1857.

The revolt started over a minor incident among the sepoys—the native soldiers who made up the bulk of England's

Seven Years' War	British East India Company Control (Moguls keep imperial title)	Direct Rule by British Government

1756 1763

Great Mutiny
1857

Indian Independence
1947

armed forces in India. The mutiny was poorly organized and short-lived, but its violence cast a long shadow on Anglo-Indian relations. The British public blamed the East India Company for most of the conditions that helped bring on the rebellion. In 1858, therefore, Parliament took over all the company's duties and obligations. The governor general now became a viceroy, and the place of the old Board of Control was taken by a secretary of state for India within the British cabinet.

British Rule in India

With the assumption of full control by the British government, the history of India entered a new phase. Under the Indian Councils Act of 1861, the viceroy was assisted by legislative and executive councils that included some Indian representation. But the viceroy retained the veto power. It was thus native participation rather than self-government that prevailed in India. Britain's efforts, moreover, to cope with the major problems of a rapidly growing population living in dismal poverty were only partly successful. The Indian farmer, paying exorbitant rents to his landlord and working small plots of exhausted soil, was subject to periodic famines. Industrialization, which might have absorbed much of the surplus population, was discouraged for fear that it might compete with industry back home.

Despite these shortcomings, British rule of India proved a vast improvement over what had existed under the East India Company. With the growth of a native middle class, demands for political

THE BRITISH EMPIRE   Nineteenth century

and social reforms became more vociferous. In 1886 the most important native political party, the National Congress, held its first meeting. At the start the Congress demanded only moderate reforms. But as time went on it became more radical, and by 1907 there was a faction asking for complete independence. To encourage the moderates within the Congress, the British in 1909 made further concessions toward representative government. For the time being these improvements seemed to satisfy India's demands. When war broke out in 1914, India, like the dominions, rallied to the side of the mother country.

The "New Imperialism"

The lack of interest in colonial expansion, which had prevailed in England during the first half of the nineteenth century, came to an end after 1870. The man who helped rekindle the interest of his countrymen in the far-flung possessions of their empire was Benjamin Disraeli. In 1875 he quietly bought a substantial interest in the Suez Canal Company, thus starting Britain's involvement in Egypt. The following year Disraeli had Parliament confer the title of Empress of India upon Queen Victoria, an honor that pleased most of her subjects.

The revival of imperialist sentiment was not confined to England. Almost all the major and some of the minor powers of Europe now started competing for the still unclaimed regions of the world. The reasons for this sudden wave of "new imperialism" were partly political and largely economic. The rivalries resulting from this scramble for overseas possessions were a major factor in the mounting international tension leading up to the First World War. The main spheres of expansion were the newly explored continent of Africa and the ancient empire of China.

HER MOST GRACIOUS MAJE

Our Queen and our Empress
Is greater and wiser
Than all foreign monarchs,
Including "der Kaiser."

British imperialism: cartoon and verse from *Pictures for Little Englanders,* a children's book published in the late nineteenth century.

CHINA AND THE GREAT POWERS

Contacts between China and the western world in the past had been limited. Some commercial relations had developed with Dutch, Portuguese, and British traders, and in the eighteenth century Jesuit missionaries had been welcomed at the court of the Manchu dynasty. Beginning in 1757, however, the Chinese government, antagonized by the conduct of some of the European traders, had closed all its ports except Canton. Henceforth all business had to be transacted there and under narrowly prescribed rules. These irksome restrictions generated most of the tension that ultimately led to the Opium War of 1839.

The Opium War

Various efforts in the early nineteenth century, especially on the part of the British government, to have additional ports opened to foreign trade were unsuccessful. An added source of trouble between Britain and China was the flourishing trade in opium that had developed during the eighteenth century. There were few commodities China was ready to buy from the outside world, and

A French caricature of the causes of the Opium War. The Englishman, backed by troops, is telling China: "You must buy our poison. We want you to deaden yourself so completely that we'll be able to take all the tea we want to drink with our beefsteak."

opium was one of them. The Chinese government had long been alarmed by the flourishing trade in opium and had vainly tried to stop it. In 1839 it moved to confiscate and destroy the vast quantities of the drug stored in Canton. It was this action that started the Opium War with Great Britain.

After three years of intermittent fighting, the Chinese were forced to agree to Britain's terms as laid down in the Treaty of Nanking (1842). Under its provisions, four ports in addition to Canton were opened to British traders and Britain was given the island of Hong Kong as a base. In subsequent treaties, France and the United States received additional concessions that came to be shared by all powers alike. Most important among these was the principle of "extraterritoriality," which placed all foreigners in China under the jurisdiction of their own consular courts.

The "first treaty settlement," as these various Chinese concessions came to be called, was a landmark in that country's history. As more and more "treaty ports" were added in the course of the century, many of them inland cities, the Chinese Empire was gradually opened up by foreign traders and missionaries, with far-reaching effects on China's economy and society. The first effects of this sudden contact between two very different civili-

IMPERIALISM IN CHINA   1842–1901

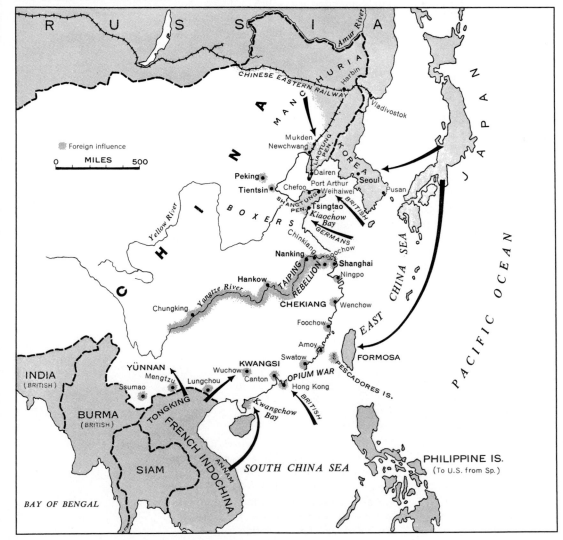

zations were felt in one of the most violent crises in China's history, the Taiping Rebellion (1850–64).

The Taiping Rebellion

The underlying cause of the rebellion was the inefficiency and corruption of the Manchu government and the weakness it had shown in its dealings with the western powers. There had been mounting discontent with a system that exploited the masses of the people for the good of a small ruling clique. With the death of the emperor in 1850, various local manifestations of unrest came together in a general rebellion. In its ideology, the Taiping Rebellion was influenced by Christianity. Its leader was a religious mystic, Hung Hsiu-ch'üan. Its main appeal to the Chinese peasant lay in its abolition of the high land rent.

The Taiping rebels, though antiforeign, nevertheless hoped to gain the support of the European powers in their struggle against the Manchu regime. Tensions between China and the western powers had continued into the 1850s; and as the British and French continued to insist on their treaty rights, a new series of conflicts broke out. The Chinese government thus found itself at war with domestic as well as foreign elements. Had these two opponents joined forces, they could easily have overthrown the Manchu dynasty. As it turned out, however, the European powers, aided by the Taiping rebels, first defeated the Chinese government and then helped the government defeat the Taiping rebels.

After the fall of Canton and the occupation of Tientsin in 1858, Peking was once more ready to come to terms with the powers. Under the Treaties of Tientsin, China opened several more treaty ports, agreed to the establishment of foreign legations at Peking, and permitted foreigners to move freely throughout the country. In addition, the Yangtze River was opened to foreign navigation and the opium trade was legalized. When the Chinese failed to honor these obligations, the French and British briefly resumed hostilities. The climax came with the storming of Peking and the burning of the emperor's summer palace. Under a new convention signed in 1860, China had to make further concessions. Simultaneously the Russians, taking advantage of China's embarrassment, secured for themselves a large slice of territory north of the Amur River, where they founded the port of Vladivostok. This gave them a long-desired outlet to the Pacific.

Once peace had been made, the Manchu government could turn its full force against the Taiping rebels. In this it had the support of the foreign powers. This western attitude has been rightly criticized. The Taiping rebels certainly were far more enlightened and progressive than the reactionary clique that surrounded the Manchu court. Yet the powers were mainly concerned with the preservation of their privileges, which the rebels intended to abolish. Western policy was motivated by self-interest rather than a desire to reform China.

The suppression of the Taiping Rebellion ushered in a period of comparative peace in Chinese affairs. Some efforts were made by the government to modernize China while maintaining its Confucian tradition, but these were not very successful. Beginning in 1877 China established its first diplomatic missions abroad. The telegraph meanwhile helped to bridge the country's vast distances, but the first railroad was not opened until 1888. The great powers did little to further China's reforming efforts. Some Chinese students studied abroad, and Protestant missionaries continued to bring western ideas to China. But frequent incidents in which Chinese crowds attacked foreigners served as convenient excuses for further foreign encroachment. France strengthened its influence over Indochina in 1884, and Britain's protectorate in Burma was recognized by China in 1886. These regions in the past had been tributaries of China.

The Sino-Japanese War

China's first major international conflict after 1860, however, was not with a western power but with an eastern rival, the empire of Japan. Japan had been far more successful than China in adapting to western ways. And the Japanese did not overlook the revelation of China's weakness in its dealings with the European powers. The area over which the two came to blows in 1894 was Korea, the section of the mainland closest to Japan. Korea had long been a tributary of China, but it had also seen gradual encroachment by Japan. It was this encroachment that finally led to war.

The Sino-Japanese War (1894–95) was won by Japan despite Chinese superiority in manpower and naval strength. Under the Treaty of Shimonoseki (1895), China had to recognize the independence of Korea and had to cede to Japan the island of Formosa, the Pescadores Islands, and the Liaotung Peninsula. The European powers, with the exception of England, were much alarmed by Japan's obtaining a foothold on the Chinese mainland. Russia in particular did not want the Japanese in the Liaotung Peninsula. Russia was joined by France, with whom it had recently concluded an alliance, and by Germany, who was eager to get on better terms with Russia, in putting pressure on Japan to forgo annexation of the peninsula. Japan had little choice but to give in. The Japanese got even with Russia ten years later (see p. 642).

The Scramble for Foreign Concessions

China's defeat by Japan came just when the rivalry among the great powers for overseas territory had reached a new height. The weakness of China now served as the occasion for an imperialist feast the likes of which the world had rarely seen. Between 1896 and 1898, all the major European powers received from China spheres of influence, trading rights, railway concessions, naval stations, mining rights, and whatever other forms of direct and indirect control western imperialists could devise. Russia got Port Arthur on the very same Liaotung Peninsula from which it had just ousted Japan; Germany acquired special rights on the Shantung Peninsula; the British secured a naval base at Weihaiwei; and the French obtained a lease of Kwangchow Bay. The United States, preoccupied with its own venture into imperialism during the Spanish-American War,

merely issued a warning to the powers not to interfere with existing treaty ports and other interests in China. This "Open Door" (that is, equal economic opportunity for everyone) note of 1899 had little immediate effect, but it expressed an important principle of future American foreign policy for the Far East.

Reform and Reaction

At the height of the foreign encroachments in 1898, the imperial government made a belated attempt at reform. The short-lived "hundred days of reform," as this effort was called, was inspired and directed by K'ang Yu-wei, China's last great Confucian scholar. He hoped to create a constitutional monarchy, improve the civil service, reform the educational system, and introduce some western technology. The reformers had the support of the emperor, Kuang-hsü, but they were opposed by the established political and military hierarchy, which looked for leadership to the dowager empress Tz'ŭ Hsi. This remarkable lady had long been the center of resistance to all reforms. Discovering in the fall of 1898 that she was about to be arrested, she decided to strike first. She imprisoned the emperor and suppressed the reform movement. Until her death in 1908, the empress dowager ruled supreme.

The victory of reaction in China was aided by a military uprising at the turn of the century, directed primarily against foreigners. The "Fists of Righteous Harmony," or "Boxers," as these antiforeign elements were called, were chiefly active in the North of China. As more and more foreigners were attacked and the foreign legations in Peking put under siege, the great powers decided to strike back. An international expeditionary force descended on China, took Tientsin, and sacked Peking. Only the rivalry among the powers prevented the outright partitioning of the country. Instead, China had to pay a huge indemnity.

China's repeated defeats at the hands of the West had given ample proof that western civilization, at least in its material aspects, was superior to that of the East. As demands for reform within

German caricature of China besieged by Italian, English, German, Russian, French, American, Japanese, and Austrian troops. The caricature is in the form of a postcard, with the inscription: "Friendly Greetings from the Chinese Wall!"

Tz'ŭ Hsi (1854–1908). The dowager empress of China, who resisted foreign encroachment by encouraging the abortive Boxer Rebellion. Shortly after her death the Manchu dynasty came to an end.

China became stronger, the Manchu dynasty was forced into some half-hearted attempts to liberalize the government. In 1908 a draft constitution was published, calling for the election of a national parliament after nine years. Before it could go into effect, however, the Manchu regime was overthrown.

The Revolution of 1911

The leader of the revolution was a Chinese doctor, Sun Yat-sen, generally considered the founder of modern China. His movement—the Kuomintang, or National People's Party, as it was ultimately called—aimed to reform China and to free it from foreign encroachment. Its program consisted of three main points: national independence, democracy, and social justice. Prior to 1911 Sun's organization engineered some abortive local risings. To overthrow the Manchu dynasty, however, added support was needed. This was supplied by some of the provincial governors and military leaders who had long been at odds with the central government. Outstanding among these military figures was Yüan Shih-k'ai, a follower of the empress dowager, who had lost his position when the empress died in 1908. In 1911 the government asked Yüan to help put down a local uprising of Sun Yat-sen's followers at Hankow. Instead, Yüan helped depose the last Manchu emperor. It was this combination of forces that brought about the initial victory of the Revolution. In return for his support, Yüan was made president of the new Chinese Republic.

The main problem facing China after 1911 was how to reconcile the diverse elements in its government. In 1912 a provisional constitution called for a parliamentary government. But meanwhile Yüan Shih-k'ai was trying to extend his own power in the hope of ultimately founding a new dynasty. In 1914 Yüan embarked on a brief period of personal government. He died in 1916. With him China lost a leader who might have prevented the general anarchy and civil war that prevailed throughout the country for the next ten years. China's efforts to set its own house in order had failed.

THE EMERGENCE OF MODERN JAPAN

China's contacts with the West had proved disastrous; Japan's experience was far more fortunate. In the first half of the seventeenth century, Japan had been virtually closed to western influence. It was not until the middle of the nineteenth century that internal weakness and outside pressure brought about the reopening of the island empire. Japan at the time was still being ruled—as it had been for centuries—by the emperor's commander in chief, or shogun. This essentially feudal system, however, was proving increasingly inefficient, and there was fear that unless Japan modernized its ways, it might suffer the fate of China and become a victim of western exploitation.

The Opening Up of Japan

Japan was reopened to the outside world, suddenly and dramatically, through the efforts of the American commodore Matthew Perry. His request in 1853, backed by an imposing fleet of steam warships, that commercial relations be established between the United States and Japan could not be refused, given Japan's military backwardness. In the resulting Treaty of Kanagawa (1854) the first Japanese ports were opened to foreign trade. Commercial and other agreements followed, not only with America but with other nations as well. The long period of Japan's seclusion, thanks to American initiative, had been ended.

Japan, however, did not become a victim but rather a competitor of the western powers in the colonization of the Far East. This it did by a policy of determined modernization and westernization. Japan's rapid transition from feudalism to industrialism did not come about without a major domestic upheaval. The sudden influx of foreigners caused deep resentment among many Japanese. While the shogun had been forced by circumstances to collaborate with the western powers, the emperor and his advisers had advocated resistance. The struggle between these two

Japanese representation of Matthew Perry, printed shortly after his mission to Japan in 1853. Compare this with Perry's photograph on the facing page.

factions was decided in 1867, with the victory of the imperial supporters and the resignation of the last shogun. In 1868 the Meiji emperor had assumed direct control over the nation, moving his capital from Kyoto to Edo, now renamed Tokyo.

The Meiji Period

The Meiji period (1868–1912) saw the emergence of Japan as a modern great power. The outstanding developments during the last decades of the nineteenth century were the abolition of feudalism and the industrialization of Japan. In 1871 an imperial decree abolished the large feudal fiefs and inaugurated a more highly centralized government along western lines. As the power of the old privileged families declined, so did the importance of their retainers, the samurai. When in 1876, the members of this traditional warrior class were forbidden to wear their two swords, the sign of their privileged status, they revolted. The Satsuma Rebellion (1877), involving some 200,000 men, was crushed by troops armed with modern weapons. With it the last resistance of feudal forces came to an end.

The modernization of Japan was most rapid and thorough in the industrial field. Industrialization had to start virtually from scratch, but the imperial government from the beginning took a hand in founding and running essential industries. When financial difficulties after 1880 forced the government to sell its enterprises, they were bought by a few wealthy families, the *zaibatsu*, who from then on dominated the economic life of Japan. The influence of the state over economic affairs, however, continued to be close, and the spirit of laissez faire, so prominent in the West, never gained a comparable hold in Japan.

The modernization of Japan affected every aspect of its life. Together with universal military service, universal education helped to transform illiterate peasants into trained and obedient workers. Buddhism was deemphasized and Christianity was tolerated. There was also renewed interest in the ancient native religion of Japan, the cult of Shinto. With its veneration of the emperor as the Son of Heaven, Shintoism provided a religious basis for Japan's new nationalism. In its efforts to catch up with the West, Japan borrowed freely wherever it could find the institutions best suited to its needs. Its legal system was modernized along French lines, and its financial organization was borrowed from the United States. British officers helped build a new navy, and the new Japanese constitution followed the German model.

One of the main concerns of the Meiji period was the creation of some form of representative government. The emperor had promised a deliberative assembly in his "Charter Oath" of 1868. But it was not until 1884 that the drafting of a Japanese constitution was begun. As promulgated in 1889, the constitution established an Imperial Diet of two houses. The lower house was elected under a restricted franchise that gave the vote to less than half a million Japanese. There was no ministerial responsibility. The emperor could issue decrees with the force of laws, and he could declare war. The Japanese constitution thus did not really affect the traditional power structure. Still, the introduction of parliamentary practices gave some voice and experience to the rising middle class, and the Japanese people gained more political influence than they had ever had before.

Despite its preoccupation with domestic reform, Japan also was able to carry on an active and successful foreign policy. Industrialization called for raw materials and markets, and a growing population called for living space. As early as 1874 Japan sent an expedition to

Commodore Matthew Perry, daguerrotype by M. Brady.

Formosa. In 1876 Japan started the long rivalry with China over Korea that led to the Sino-Japanese War (1894–95). Japan's victory in that war, as we have seen, caused the tension with Russia that in turn led to a still more important war ten years later.

The Russo-Japanese War

The rivalry between Japan and Russia in the Far East went back to the middle of the nineteenth century. At that time Russia began extending its influence over the portion of China facing the Sea of Japan. By the end of the century, the only region opposite Japan still free from Russian domination was Korea. Japan continued to assert its interests in Korea after its victory over China in 1895. At the same time, however, the tsarist empire was stepping up its activities there. In 1902 Japan concluded an alliance with Great Britain, which had long opposed Russia's expansion in Asia. Japan thus was assured of the friendship of another major power with interests in the Far East.

The Russo-Japanese War, long in the making, broke out in 1904. Japan had definite strategic advantages, but even so the world was little prepared for the resounding defeat inflicted on the Russians. After eighteen months of fighting, the mediation of President Theodore Roosevelt ended the war. The treaty of peace signed at Portsmouth, New Hampshire (1905), completed the emergence of Japan as a major power. Its interests in Korea were now recognized. In addition, Japan received control over the Liaotung Peninsula, together with some Russian railroad concessions in southern Manchuria. Russia also ceded to Japan the southern half of the island of Sakhalin.

Japan's victory over Russia marked a turning point in relations between Europe and Asia. For the first time in modern history, one of the so-called backward nations had defeated one of the major powers of the West. The effects of this event were felt in an upsurge of nationalism among the nations of Asia, the ultimate repercussions of which have lasted into our own day.

AN EVALUATION
OF WESTERN IMPERIALISM

The growth of the United States into a major power, the transformation of the British Empire into a worldwide Commonwealth, the opening up of China, and the westernization of Japan—all these were manifestations of the vast influence that western civilization had gained in the course of a single century. One region became almost wholly sub-

Russian propaganda postcard, entitled "Battle Song of the Russian Sailors," shows a Russian sailor punching Admiral Togo during the Russo-Japanese War.

Theodore Roosevelt with the Russian and Japanese representatives at the peace negotiations in Portsmouth, New Hampshire, ending the Russo-Japanese War (1905). Left to right: Sergius Witte, Baron Rosen, Roosevelt, Baron Komura, and Baron Takahira.

servient to western domination during the latter part of the nineteenth century—the continent of Africa (see p. 679).

Much of this expansion of western civilization had taken place in the last decades of the nineteenth century. In an age of ardent nationalism, it was considered a point of honor for any great power to raise its flag over as large an area of the globe as possible. At a time, furthermore, when unprecedented industrial growth created an urgent need for raw materials, markets, and outlets for surplus capital and population, colonies and foreign concessions seemed to provide a ready solution to economic problems. Finally, a civilization that considered itself superior to all others could easily convince itself that its members had a civilizing mission and should assume what Rudyard Kipling called "the white man's burden."

The various motives for imperialist expansion have come in for a good deal of criticism. There can be no doubt about the sincerity with which most western imperialists believed in the advantages that the spread of their civilization would bring to the rest of the world. It was only after the bitter experiences of the twentieth century, when the cause of western imperialism suffered one reversal after another, that this belief began to be shaken. Politically, western domination of colonial regions merely seemed to awaken among the subjected peoples a consciousness of their own national interests and a desire for independence. While this in itself may be a positive achievement, it certainly was not what the imperialists of the last century had envisaged. Economically, the advantages derived from imperialism were limited to small groups within the mother countries. As time went on it became clear that the most advantageous policy in the long run was the economic development rather than the exploitation of backward areas. Such development, however, was slow and expensive, and its ultimate effect was to emancipate rather than subdue colonial areas.

About the civilizing effects of the spread of western civilization, there are divided opinions. There is no need to point out the many advantages that have come to the rest of the world from its contacts with the West. In the field of medicine alone, the lives of millions of people have been saved by western scientists, and the slow but steady rise in the living standards of even the most backward regions would have been impossible without western aid and examples. The fault that has been found with the westernization of the world has been chiefly in the methods employed by western imperialists. Until quite recently the advantages that western civilization brought to many parts of the world were largely incidental to the primarily selfish aims and ambitions of the more advanced nations. The white man's burden, it has been said, has rested heavily on the shoulders of the black, brown, and yellow men who were subjugated by him. Only in our own day have we come to recognize and to correct some of the mistakes made by western imperialism in the past.

Christian missionary in India, *ca.* 1900.

J. A. Hobson on Imperialism   1902

Thus do the industrial and financial forces of Imperialism, operating through the party, the press, the church, the school, mould public opinion and public policy by the false idealization of those primitive lusts of struggle, domination and acquisitiveness, which have survived throughout the eras of peaceful industrial order, and whose stimulation is needed once again for the work of imperial aggression, expansion, and the forceful exploitation of lower races. For these business politicians biology and sociology weave thin convenient theories of a race struggle for the subjugation of the inferior peoples, in order that we, the Anglo-Saxon, may take their lands and live upon their labours; while economics buttresses the argument by representing our work in conquering and ruling them as our share in the division of labour among nations, and history devises reasons why the lessons of past empire do not apply to ours, while social ethics paints the motive of "imperialism" as the desire to bear the "burden" of educating and elevating races of "children." Thus are the "cultured" or semi-cultured classes indoctrinated with the intellectual and moral grandeur of Imperialism. For the masses there is a cruder appeal to hero-worship and sensational glory, adventure and the sporting spirit: current history falsified in coarse flaring colours, for the direct stimulation of the combative instincts. . . . Imperialism is a depraved choice of national life, imposed by self-seeking interests which appeal to the lusts of quantitative acquisitiveness and of forceful domination surviving in a nation from early centuries of animal struggle for existence.

J. A. Hobson, *Imperialism: A Study* (Ann Arbor Paperbacks, 1965), pp. 221–22, 368.

Suggestions for Further Reading

Note: Asterisk denotes a book available in paperback edition.

General   Because of its wide range, there are no general works covering the whole subject matter of this chapter. D. K. Fieldhouse, *The Colonial Empires* (1966), is a useful survey, as is S. L. Easton, *The Rise and Fall of Western Colonialism** (1964). P. T. Moon, *Imperialism and World Politics* (1926), is still a standard work on the expansion of Europe. K. S. Latourette, *A History of the Expansion of Christianity*, Vols. V and VI (1945), deals with an important aspect of Europe's spreading influence. Good general works on the Far East are E. O. Reischauer and A. M. Craig, *A History of East Asian Civilization*, Vol. II: *East Asia: The Modern Transformation* (1965); and G. M. Beckmann, *The Modernization of China and Japan* (1962). C. E. Carrington, *The British Overseas* (1950), deals with British colonization. The motives of modern imperialism are treated in numerous books, among them the classics by J. A. Hobson, *Imperialism: A Study** (1902), and N. Lenin, *Imperialism: The Highest State of Capitalism** (1916). More recent studies and critiques of imperialism are J. A. Schumpeter, *Imperialism and Social Classes** (1955), and E. M. Winslow, *The Pattern of Imperialism* (1948). See also A. P. Thornton, *Doctrines of Imperialism** (1965), and R. Koebner and H. D. Smith, *Imperialism: The Story and Significance of a Political Word, 1840–1960* (1964). The effect of imperialism on the colonial peoples is the subject of F. Fanon, *The Wretched of the Earth** (1969). D. O. Mannoni, *Prospero and Caliban: The Psychology of Colonization* (1956), is unique and provocative. On the spread of Europe's economic influence, see W. Woodruff, *Impact of Western Man: A Study of Europe's Role in the World Economy, 1750–1960* (1967).

The United States   The vast literature on American history during the nineteenth century makes any selection of representative titles difficult. An excellent introduction to the subject are the relevant chapters in J. M. Blum *et al.*, *The National Experience: A History of the United States*, 3rd ed. (1973), written by experts and containing detailed bibliographies. S. E. Morison, *History of the United States* (1965), is considered the master's masterpiece. On the pre-Jacksonian period, see G. Dangerfield, *The Era of Good Feelings** (1952) and *The Awakening of American Nationalism** (1965). The westward movement is discussed in R. G. Athearn, *America Moves West* (1964), and R. A. Billington, *Westward Expansion* (1967). Among studies on slavery, K. M. Stampp, *The Peculiar Institution** (1956), and E. D. Genovese, *The Political Economy of Slavery* (1965), stand out. Industrial development is treated in D. C. North, *The Economic Growth of the United States, 1790–1860** (1961). On the Age of Jackson, see G. G. Van Deusen, *The Jacksonian Era** (1959), and C. M. Wiltse, *The New Nation, 1800–1845** (1961). A. Nevins, *Ordeal of the Union*, 2 vols. (1947), and J. G. Randall and D. Donald, *The Civil War and Reconstruction* (1961), are representative works on the Civil War and its background. The aftermath of the war is treated in K. M. Stampp, *The Era of Reconstruction* (1965), and in C. V. Woodward, *Origins of the New South, 1877–1913** (1951). The following are recommended for their insights into various phases of American thought and society: R. Hofstadter, *The American Political Tradition** (1955); L. Hartz, *The Liberal Tradition in America** (1955); and C. Rossiter, *Conservatism in America** (1955). On relations between the United States and Europe, see J. B. Brebner, *North Atlantic Triangle: The Interplay of Canada, the United States, and Great Britain* (1945), and H. Koht, *The American Spirit in Europe: A Survey of Transatlantic Influences* (1949).

Latin America   One of the best recent histories of Latin America is J. F. Rippy, *Latin America: A Modern History* (1958). Other good standard works are D. G. Munro, *The Latin American Republics* (1950); H. Herring, *A History of Latin America* (1955); and W. L. Schurz, *The New World: The Civilization of Latin America* (1954). F. Tannenbaum, *Ten Keys to Latin America* (1962), deals with the broader aspects and issues of Latin American life. The following cover specific subjects: J. L. Mecham, *Church and State in Latin America* (1934); G. Plaza, *Problems of Democracy in Latin America* (1950); W. C. Gordon, *The Economy of Latin America* (1950); R. Crawford, *A Century of Latin American Thought*, rev ed. (1966); and G. Arciniegas, *Latin America: A Cultural History* (1967). On hemispheric relations, see D. Perkins, *A History of the Monroe Doctrine*, rev. ed. (1955); S. F. Bemis, *The Latin American Policy of the United States* (1943); and A. P. Whitaker, *The Western Hemisphere Idea: Its Rise and Decline* (1954).

The British Empire The most comprehensive work on the subject is J. H. Rose *et al.*, eds., *The Cambridge History of the British Empire*, 7 vols. (1929–40). For additional suggestions, see C. F. Mullett, *The British Empire-Commonwealth: Its Themes and Character* (1961). The four original dominions are treated individually in J. M. S. Careless, *Canada: A Story of Challenge* (1953); M. Clark, *A Short History of Australia*, rev. ed. (1969); K. Sinclair, *A Short History of New Zealand* (1961); and C. W. de Kiewiet, *A History of South Africa: Social and Economic* (1941). Good brief histories of India are W. H. Moreland and A. C. Chatterjee, *A Short History of India* (1957), and P. Spear, *India: A Modern History* (1961). Britain's role in India is evaluated in P. Woodruff, *The Men Who Ruled India*, 2 vols. (1954); R. P. Mansani, *Britain in India* (1961); M. Bearce, *British Attitudes Towards India* (1961); and E. J. Thompson and G. T. Garratt, *Rise and Fulfilment of British Rule in India* (1934). A key event in Indian history is the subject of T. R. Metcalf, *The Aftermath of Revolt: India 1857–1870* (1964).

China Good histories of China are K. S. Latourette, *The Chinese: Their History and Culture*, rev. ed. (1964); W. Eberhard, *A History of China* (1950); and J. A. Harrison, *China Since 1800** (1968). On the later phase of Chinese history, see V. Purcell, *The Boxer Uprising* (1963); M. C. Wright, ed., *China in Revolution: The First Phase, 1900–1913** (1968); and A. M. Sharman, *Sun Yat-sen* (1934). Chinese views of their country's history may be found in Li Chien-nung, *The Political History of China, 1840–1928* (1956), and in I. C. Y. Hsü, *China's Entrance into the Family of Nations: The Diplomatic Phase, 1858–1880* (1960). A useful introduction to Chinese philosophy is H. G. Creel, *Chinese Thought from Confucius to Mao Tse-tung** (1953). F. Michael, *The Taiping Rebellion* (1966), and J. K. Fairbank, *Trade and Diplomacy on the China Coast: The Opening of the Treaty Ports, 1842–1854*, 2 vols. (1953), are pioneering works. Other works dealing with the impact of the West on China are Ssu-yu Teng and J. K. Fairbank, *China's Response to the West: A Documentary Survey, 1839–1923* (1954); R. Dawson, *The Chinese Chameleon: An Analysis of European Conceptions of Chinese Civilization* (1967); A. Iriye, *Across the Pacific: An Inner History of American-East Asian Relations* (1967); and J. K. Fairbank, *The United States and China** (1963).

Japan E. O. Reischauer, *Japan: Past and Present* (1956), and J. W. Hall, *Japan from Pre-History to Modern Times* (1970), are good introductions. One of the best brief histories of the last hundred years is H. Borton, *Japan's Modern Century* (1955). See also A. Tiedemann, *Modern Japan: A Brief History** (1955). Special aspects of Japanese history and culture are treated in W. W. Lockwood, *The Economic Development of Japan* (1954); M. B. Jansen, ed., *Changing Japanese Attitudes Toward Modernization* (1965); H. Passin, *Society and Education in Japan* (1965); D. M. Brown, *Nationalism in Japan: An Introductory Historical Analysis* (1955); N. Ike, *The Beginnings of Political Democracy in Japan* (1950); and W. T. De Bary, ed., *Sources of the Japanese Tradition* (1958). G. B. Sansom, *The Western World and Japan: A Study in the Interaction of European and Asiatic Cultures* (1950), discusses the rest of Asia as well as Japan. Japanese relations with the United States are treated in P. J. Treat, *Diplomatic Relations Between the United States and Japan, 1853–1905*, 3 vols. (1938–1963); R. A. Esthus, *Theodore Roosevelt and Japan** (1967); and R. S. Schwantes, *Japanese and Americans: A Century of Cultural Relations* (1955). Important, though not always accurate, is R. Benedict, *The Chrysanthemum and the Sword: Patterns of Japanese Culture* (1946).

28

The Period of Promise, 1870–1914

The last decades of the nineteenth century in Europe were optimistic years. With economic prosperity at home, with peace abroad, and with rapid advances in all fields of scientific research, the belief in unlimited progress that had prevailed since the Enlightenment seemed happily confirmed. But from a later vantage point and with the knowledge of what happened in 1914, the period looks different. We now realize that despite rising prosperity many Europeans continued to live in poverty. Peace on the European continent was bought at the price of subjugating colonial peoples overseas and suppressing national minorities at home. The preeminence of science, with its stress on material values, makes the pre-1914 period in retrospect appear as a crass and materialistic age.

This chapter is primarily concerned with domestic affairs. Developments in

The Eiffel Tower (1889), proud monument of an age of progress.

various parts of Europe differed, but certain political, economic, and social trends were common to most countries. In politics, Europe after 1870 witnessed the gradual spread of constitutional and democratic government. In economics, most countries shared in the unprecedented industrial growth that is sometimes referred to as the "Second Industrial Revolution." In the social sphere, the labor movement and its doctrine of socialism came to play an increasingly important role in the affairs of almost all nations.

THE GROWTH OF DEMOCRACY

Before 1870 only Switzerland could be called a true democracy. By 1914 almost all the countries of western Europe had become democracies, and universal manhood suffrage, though not as yet parliamentary government, had been introduced even in central Europe. No country had truly universal suffrage. The efforts of a handful of determined "suffragettes" to gain political rights for women were met by staunch male opposition. But in many other respects women by 1914 had been freed from the legal inferiority and some of the economic and social disadvantages from which they had suffered in the past.

The extension of political power from the aristocracy and the upper middle class to the mass of the people was most significant. The virtual eradication of illiteracy, except in Russia and Italy, together with a popular press that profited from the many technical advances of the period, gave public opinion everywhere an increasing influence in the formation of policy. The "Age of the Masses" was drawing near.

Varying Degrees of Democracy

The degree of democracy varied in different countries. In England some 20 percent of the male electorate still could not vote in 1914. In France and Italy universal manhood suffrage existed, but the smooth functioning of democracy was prevented by weaknesses in their respective parliamentary systems. Germany, too, had universal manhood suffrage. But since the chancellor was not responsible to parliament, democracy hardly existed. In Austria-Hungary the main obstacle to democratic government was the perennial problem of nationalities. In Russia the franchise in 1914 was still limited and the National Assembly, or *Duma*, had merely advisory functions.

Democracy and Education

The success of democracy depended to no small extent on the existence of an informed electorate. Consequently the spread of democracy was accompanied almost everywhere by determined efforts to improve education. In England the Education Act of 1870, which introduced general education, was extended by subsequent acts that made instruction free and compulsory. In Germany, already known for its advanced school system, further progress was made, especially in technical training. The main concern of the French Third Republic was to make instruction compulsory and to exclude the Catholic Church from public education. Both aims were accomplished by the so-called "Ferry Laws" in the early 1880s.

The need for popular education was especially acute in countries with high illiteracy rates. To improve the status of some 68 percent of its population who could not read or write, the Italian government passed legislation in 1877 making education compulsory. But this act became effective only after 1911, when the central government took over the financial support of local schools. While all other countries, including the smaller ones, made deliberate efforts to stamp out ignorance, the tsarist government of Russia tried to discourage lower-class education on the grounds that it would "draw people away from the environment to which they belong."

The growth of democracy and general education between 1870 and 1914 did not necessarily bring the many blessings that liberals in particular had expected. Some earlier writers on democracy, like De Tocqueville and Mill, had already warned against imposing the standards

Suffragette, 1908.

of the majority upon society as a whole. Such criticism continued in the late nineteenth century. To Henry Adams, democracy was one of the lower forms of government. The Englishman Walter Bagehot warned that the voice of the people might easily turn out to be the voice of the devil. And the German philosopher Friedrich Nietzsche criticized parliamentary government as a means "whereby cattle become masters." How justified these warnings would turn out to be in some countries was not realized until after the First World War.

THE "SECOND INDUSTRIAL REVOLUTION"

The second general trend shared by most of Europe in the late nineteenth century was an unparalleled increase in the rate of industrial growth. In some respects this "Second Industrial Revolution" was merely a continuation of the first, but it had certain unique characteristics. New sources of power—electricity and oil—competed with steam in driving more intricate machinery. Refined techniques of steel production and the discovery of methods to use lower-grade ores made steel available in greater quantities and at a much lower price. Synthetic products, notably dyes produced from coal tars, became the foundation of whole new industries; and the introduction of dynamite by the Swedish chemist Alfred Nobel in 1867 had repercussions in the military as well as the industrial field.

There were many other novel features of industrialism at the end of the century. New means of communication and transportation helped to speed up business transactions; new methods of promotion boosted sales; a vast increase in the supply of liquid capital aided economic growth; and the rapid expansion of many enterprises led to new forms of industrial organization. All these innovations had one thing in common: They helped to increase the industrial output of Europe beyond anything ever known. The Second Industrial Revolution was mainly a quantitative phenomenon. The total production of the western world, including the United States, more than tripled between 1870 and 1914.

Social Effects

This increased industrialization accentuated earlier trends in society. The population of Europe continued to grow by leaps and bounds. With this growth of population, the shift from rural to urban life continued. While in 1800 most Europeans were still living in the country or in small towns, by 1900 from one-third to one-half of the population in the more highly industrialized countries lived in large cities. As industries expanded, agriculture declined. Through mechanization and chemical fertilizers, farmers were able to achieve remarkable increases in crop yields. But even so, Europe would have gone hungry had it not been for the expanding agricultural economies of Russia, the Americas, and Australia.

Industrialization continued to affect people's lives in many other ways. The invention of labor-saving devices and the mass production of consumer goods helped to make life easier and more comfortable. Central heating, the use of gas and electricity, the low-cost production of ready-made clothing, and the perfection of canning and refrigeration are only a few of the conveniences now enjoyed by most of the population.

But mechanization and mass production also had their negative sides. Sociologists began to worry that the influence that machines gained over man might in time make him the slave rather than the master of his inventions. Mass production tended to standardize and cheapen public taste. Closely related to mass production was the problem of overproduction. To remedy this situation, advertising steadily gained in importance. The production of cheap paper from wood pulp in the 1880s and the resulting growth of popular journalism proved a boon to advertisers. Yet some people deplored the money spent by manufacturers to make people buy at higher cost goods that they did not really need or want.

"Big Business"

One of the characteristics of industrial development since 1870 has been the substitution of "big business" for the smaller factories that had prevailed earlier. As enterprises became fewer, larger, and more competitive, producers found it desirable to form combinations to control production, distribution, and price levels. The "trusts" of the United States, the "amalgamations" of Great Britain, the "cartels" of Germany, and the "syndicates" of Russia differed in specifics but were alike in their efforts to establish some control over the production and distribution of goods. Opponents of this industrial concentration claimed that it tended to create monopolies that kept prices at artificially high levels. In response to such criticism, the United States in 1890 prohibited the formation of trusts, but it was the only major country to do so.

The period of "monopolistic capitalism," as the decades after 1870 are called, was also the heyday of the great industrialists—the Carnegies, Rockefellers, Krupps, Nobels, and others. The huge economic power of these "tycoons" could not help but give them political influence as well. But business leaders did not use their wealth only for their own ends. The ruthlessness that had characterized business during the early days of industrialization was gradually mitigated by signs of social consciousness on the part of some leading capitalists. One of the best examples of this humanitarian attitude was the steel magnate Andrew Carnegie. In his book *The Gospel of Wealth* (1900), Carnegie insisted that wealth was a public trust, not to be handed on within a single family but to be returned to the community from which it had been derived. To practice what he preached, Carnegie gave more than 300 million dollars to worthy causes in the United States and Great Britain. There were also humanitarian capitalists in Europe, where the "Nobel prizes" and the "Rhodes scholarships" commemorate two highly successful businessmen.

THE RISE OF THE WORKING CLASS

A third general trend prevalent in Europe during the period after 1870 was the increasing influence of the working class and its socialist philosophy. Much of the improvement in the worker's condition was due to the political power he came to wield through various socialist parties and to the economic power of his labor unions. As a result of the many efforts on his behalf, the status of the European worker by 1914 had been raised far above what it had been in 1870.

New Varieties of Socialism

The basic aims and ideas of modern socialism as derived from Karl Marx and Friedrich Engels have been discussed (see pp. 586–90). Marx had predicted an increasing concentration of capital, balanced by a growing impoverishment of the masses, leading eventually to the collapse of capitalism. Events during the late nineteenth century, however, failed to bear out Marx's predictions. While much capital was concentrated in a few hands, there was a corresponding diffusion of ownership by means of joint stock companies. And while in recently industrialized countries workers suffered from many of the hardships that had marked the First Industrial Revolution, once industrialization had taken hold their condition improved. By the end of the century it became clear that Marx's prediction had to be adjusted to changed circumstances. The result of this adjustment in Marxian doctrine is called "revisionist," or "evolutionary," socialism.

The leading theorist of revisionism was the German socialist Eduard Bernstein. Bernstein had spent some time in England, where he came in contact with a non-Marxian brand of socialism advocated by a group of intellectuals, among them Sidney and Beatrice Webb, H. G. Wells, and George Bernard Shaw. Their socialism was called "Fabianism" after the Roman general Fabius, who preferred to defeat his enemies by gradually wearing them down rather than by direct attack. In this same manner the Fabian Socialists opposed violent revolution and sought instead to achieve socialization by way of gradual reform. Bernstein, on his return to Germany in the 1890s, began to expound his own revised version of Marxian socialism. One of its chief characteristics was the denial of Marx's concept of the class struggle. In his *Evolutionary Socialism* (1899), Bernstein advocated

Evidence of the growth of advertising—a London bus at the turn of the century.

Beatrice (1858–1943) and Sidney Webb (1859–1947), Fabian Socialists in England.

Marxism, the Russian Vladimir Ilyich Ulyanov, better known by his pseudonym Nikolai Lenin, held that collaboration with capitalism would help to perpetuate a system that would become more and more oppressive to the working class. Only a revolution could overthrow this system, and it was up to a minority within the proletariat, organized into a well-disciplined workers' party, to prepare the way for revolution by keeping alive the idea of class struggle. Except in eastern Europe, this revolutionary brand of "Leninism" found few followers before the First World War.

Marxism as a political movement had its international as well as its national aspects. Marx had believed that the best way to combat capitalism was for the workers of the world to unite their efforts. He had been instrumental, therefore, in founding the International Workingmen's Association in 1864. But the First International, as it was called, was not very successful. Marx's domineering manner, his controversy with Bakunin, who was among the leaders of the International, and the excesses of the Paris Commune in 1871, which were falsely blamed on the socialists, combined to bring about the gradual decline of the First International and its demise in 1876.

With the rise of socialist parties in most major countries during the next decade, however, there was again a need for some kind of international organization, and a Second International was formed in 1889. From the start it was beset by grave internal differences, especially on the issue of revisionism. As time went on, moreover, it became obvious that the national loyalties of most socialists were stronger than their feelings of international solidarity. The Second International opposed war as a means of settling international disputes; but when the test came in 1914 the ideals of international socialism quickly gave way to the stronger appeal of national patriotism.

that instead of waging a revolutionary struggle against the middle class, the working class should collaborate with any group, proletarian or bourgeois, that would help to bring about a gradual improvement in the workers' condition.

The revisionist ideas of Bernstein caused a major stir in Marxist circles. Orthodox Marxists denounced revisionism and reaffirmed their faith in the validity of all Marx's teachings. One of the most determined defenders of pure

The Growth of Labor Unions

In addition to setting up their own political parties, workers tried to improve

Leninism

I assert: [(1)] That no movement can be durable without a stable organization of leaders to maintain continuity; (2) that the more widely the masses are spontaneously drawn into the struggle and form the basis of the movement, the more necessary it is to have such an organization and the more stable must it be (for it is much easier then for demagogues to sidetrack the more backward sections of the masses); (3) that the organization must consist chiefly of persons engaged in revolutionary activities as a profession; (4) that in a country with an autocratic government, the more we *restrict* the membership of this organization to persons who are engaged in revolution as a profession and who have been professionally trained in the art of combating the political police, the more difficult will it be to catch the organization; and (5) the *wider* will be the circle of men and women of the working class or of other classes of society able to join the movement and perform active work in it.

From Nikolai Lenin, "What Is to Be Done?" 1902, *Selected Works* (London: Lawrence and Wishart, 1936), Vol. II, pp. 138–39.

Headquarters of the First International, in a Paris back street.

their lot through the formation of labor unions. In the early part of the nineteenth century, unions had made little progress anywhere except in Great Britain, and even there their activities remained restricted. This situation improved markedly after 1870. In England, in a series of legislative acts in 1874–75, unions were given permission to strike and to engage in peaceful picketing. The most important advance in the history of British organized labor came as a result of the famous London dock strike of 1889. The first major strike among unskilled workers, this event marked the extension of union activity beyond the skilled groups that in the past had made up union membership.

On the Continent the labor movement was slower in gaining momentum. In France labor unions had made little headway by 1870. The bloody events of the Paris Commune of 1871 (see p. 611) cast a shadow on any kind of labor activity, and it was not until 1884 that the Waldeck-Rousseau Law granted full legal status to unions and allowed them to form larger federations. The decisive step in this direction came in 1895, when the

Engraving of London matchworkers protesting poor working conditions, 1871.

General Confederation of Labor (CGT) was organized. It advocated a program of direct action to destroy capitalism by means of sabotage and general strikes.

Germany, too, witnessed little union activity before 1870. Since the German labor movement was closely allied with socialism from the start, it was adversely affected by the antisocialist measures of Bismarck. It thus did not really gain momentum until after 1890. Under the Imperial Industrial Code, German workers were permitted to strike, but an unfriendly government and hostile courts restricted the activities of organized labor wherever possible. Even so, the labor movement in Germany, by exerting pressure on government and employers, helped to improve the condition of German workers.

In the less industrialized countries of Italy, Austria-Hungary, and Russia, trade unionism played a minor role. In Italy the labor movement was split into several factions, the largest of which, the socialist General Italian Federation of Labor, was founded in 1907. Socialist unions also predominated in Austria, though there was hardly any organized labor in agrarian Hungary. Russia had no real labor unions until after 1905, and even then they did not gain much influence.

The "Welfare State"

The agitation of European workers for political, economic, and social reforms did much to make their governments adopt programs of social legislation designed to help the lower classes. Such intervention by the state in the affairs of the individual was a radical departure from the laissez-faire philosophy of early nineteenth-century liberalism. The idea that the state should concern itself with the well-being of its citizens and become, as we would say today, a "welfare state," found acceptance among politicians both in England and on the Continent. The social legislation resulting from this new attitude was so far-reaching that it has been referred to as "state socialism." Its chief purpose was to satisfy the reasonable grievances of the working class and by so doing to preserve the capitalist system.

Similar motives were behind various appeals of the Christian churches, notably the Catholic Church, for collaboration rather than conflict between employers and workers. "Christian Socialism" was nothing new, but it gained significance as the teachings of Marx began to compete with and to undermine the influence of Christianity among workers. The leading pronouncement on Christian social policy was made by Pope Leo XIII in his encyclical *Rerum novarum* in 1891, in which he condemned socialist attacks on private property and the Marxian concept of class struggle and suggested that the state aid its poorer citizens and that employers and workers settle their differences in a spirit of Christian brotherhood.

So much for the general trends—political, economic, and social—that prevailed in Europe between 1870 and 1914. As we now turn to a discussion of the domestic affairs of the major powers, we shall find these trends much in evidence.

ENGLAND: "MOTHER OF DEMOCRACY"

England after 1870 continued along the road of gradual political and social reform that it had followed since the early nineteenth century. The long reign of Queen Victoria reached its halfway mark in 1869. Gladstone's "great ministry" came to an end in 1874. For the next six years Disraeli, Earl of Beaconsfield from 1876, conducted a policy noted chiefly for its successes abroad. Between 1880 and 1895, Liberal and Conservative governments alternated, with Gladstone heading three more ministries and Lord Salisbury serving as his Conservative counterpart. The last two decades before 1914 were equally divided between the two major parties, the Conservatives remaining in power until 1905 and the Liberals leading thereafter. Generally speaking, the Liberals were more active in domestic affairs, where Gladstone's reforming zeal found its successor after the turn of the century in the dynamic David Lloyd George. The Conservatives, on the other hand, were more concerned with foreign affairs, especially England's

overseas interests. Lord Salisbury personally assumed the post of foreign minister in his three cabinets, and he was ably seconded by Joseph Chamberlain as colonial secretary.

The British problem that overshadowed all others was the question of Ireland. Gladstone, who had long been working to improve that country's unhappy condition, sought once again to remedy some of the worst abuses of Irish land tenure in the Land Act of 1881. He failed, however, chiefly because of resistance from Ireland's Nationalists. Under the leadership of Charles Parnell, the Nationalists demanded political rather than economic reforms. Gladstone hoped to satisfy Irish demands by two Home Rule Bills, but he was defeated both times by a coalition of Conservatives and dissident Liberals. Subsequent Land Purchase Acts, under Conservative sponsorship and aimed at helping Irish tenants buy their land, somewhat counteracted the agitation of Irish nationalism. The Irish question became acute once more in 1912 when the Liberals introduced a third Home Rule Bill, which did not become law until September 1914. By that time war had broken out and home rule had to be postponed.

England's ability to resist any really serious crises, except for the perennial Irish question, was largely due to the peaceful adjustments it continued to make to the demands of an increasingly democratic age. The franchise that had been granted to urban workers in the Reform Act of 1867 was extended to rural laborers under the Franchise Act of 1884. A Redistribution Bill in 1885 established uniform electoral districts, and the Parliament Bill of 1911 abolished the veto power of the House of Lords over money bills. Democracy had made considerable progress in Britain by 1914, leaving only some 20 percent of the male population—domestic servants, bachelors living with their parents, and men with no fixed abode—without a vote.

Economic Developments

As we turn from politics to economics, the picture in England looks somewhat less bright. Prior to 1870, British

Gladstone giving a "whistle-stop" speech, 1885. His practice of making political speeches from trains was said to have horrified Queen Victoria.

Victoria's "Golden Jubilee"

Queen Victoria made her historic progress through London on June 22nd, 1887, in brilliant sunshine. As if to put a seal on the legend of "Queen's Weather," the sun came out from a dull sky as the first guns in Hyde Park announced that she had left the Palace, having previously touched an electric button which telegraphed her Jubilee Message round the Empire: "From my heart I thank my beloved people. May God bless them!"

Queen Victoria's account of her reception by London was by no means exaggerated. "No one ever, I believe, has met with such an ovation as was given me, passing through those six miles of streets . . . the crowds were quite indescribable, and their enthusiasm truly marvellous and deeply touching. The cheering was quite deafening, and every face seemed to be filled with real joy."

London's sense of its own greatness, as the metropolis of a far-flung Empire, vied with a poignantly personal affection for the venerable figure who was both a living and a symbolic mother. "Our Hearts Thy Throne," declared a triumphal arch at Paddington; the Bank of England declaimed: "She Wrought Her People Lasting Good." "Go it, old girl!" called an ecstatic voice from the crowd. . . .

Nothing went wrong. Gradually she relaxed in her carriage . . . tears of happiness filled her eyes and sometimes rolled down her cheeks, whereupon the Princess of Wales would lean forward and gently press her hand. . . . She was incomparably the best Queen the world had got and more than one foreign nation, still struggling under the rule of tyranny, self-indulgence or fatuity, wished she were theirs.

From Elizabeth Longford, *Victoria R. I.* (London: Weidenfeld & Nicolson, 1964), pp. 688–90.

industry had enjoyed undisputed leadership, and despite the repeal of the Corn Laws in 1846 British agriculture had been able to hold its own. This situation gradually changed as Germany and the United States became England's chief industrial rivals, and as the influx of cheap agricultural products from overseas caused a rapid decline in British farming.

Germany and America overtook England in the basic iron and steel industries by 1914, and England's share of the world's total trade fell from 23 percent in 1876 to 15 percent in 1913.

Much of this relative decline in England's economic leadership was inevitable, of course, as nations that had once been Britain's customers began to supply their own needs and claim their own share of world trade. But there were other causes for the slowdown in England's economic growth. Scientific and technical education lagged behind that of other nations, notably Germany. England was slow in modernizing its industrial equipment and adopting new methods, and it failed to realize the importance of effective salesmanship. Furthermore, while tariff walls were being erected everywhere else to protect industry and agriculture, Britain clung to its policy of free trade, despite efforts, notably by Joseph Chamberlain at the turn of the century, to change to protectionism.

Labor and Social Reform

Even though its economic leadership was declining, Britain was still the most prosperous nation of the world. This prosperity was shared by the British worker, who was far better off than the workers in most continental countries. Great Britain was the only major European country in which Marxian socialism did not gain any large following. In 1881 an organization advocating Marxist principles was founded, but its advocacy of violence had little attraction for the British workingman. The Fabian Society, founded in 1883, appealed chiefly to middle-class intellectuals. What political influence the British working class exerted before 1914 came chiefly from the British Labor Party. Its origins went back to the early 1890s, but its official beginning dates from 1900, when several groups, including trade unions and Fabians, joined forces behind the Labor Representation Committee. In the general election of 1906, the Labor Party won twenty-nine seats in Parliament. Its program called for the gradual socialization of key industries and utilities, very much along Fabian lines.

Another avenue through which British labor improved its status was union activity. The London dock strike of 1889 was successful, but there were occasional reverses, such as the Taff Vale decision of 1901 and the Osborne Judgment of 1909, both handed down by the House of Lords. Under the Taff Vale decision, labor unions were to be liable for damages resulting from strikes, while the Osborne Judgment made it illegal for unions to pay stipends to Labor members of Parliament. Both restrictions were subsequently removed under the influence of the Labor Party.

While the worker was helping himself, the government also did its share to help him through welfare legislation. There had already been examples of such legislation earlier in the century, especially the several factory acts. Factory legislation was now extended by several acts—in 1878, 1901, and 1908—and a minimum-wage law was passed in 1912. Social insurance was initiated, first against accidents (1880), then against old age (1909), and finally against sickness and unemployment (1911). To finance these expensive measures, which Conservatives and some old-time Liberals termed "socialist," the Liberal government of Lloyd George in 1909 introduced a "People's Budget," which shifted the main tax burden to the rich. It was passed only over the stiff opposition of the House of Lords, whose powers, as we have seen, were subsequently curtailed.

As the result of an enlightened policy at home and a strong position abroad, England in 1914 was at the height of its power. There were some danger signals —in Ireland and India. Britain's economy was going "soft," and its political system needed further reforms. But there was no reason to assume that it would not be able to cope with these issues in the future as it had in the past. Britain, on the eve of the First World War, was contented and confident.

FRANCE: REPUBLIC IN CRISIS

Britain's steady progress toward political and social democracy had no parallel on the Continent. The French Third Republic, after stormy beginnings, developed a system of government that in some ways was more democratic, though far less stable, than that of Great Britain. The French presidency was largely a ceremonial office. The cabinet was responsible to a bicameral legislature, the lower body of which, the Chamber of Deputies, was elected by universal male suffrage. Instead of clearly defined political parties, France had a large number of loosely organized factions, each headed by some outstanding political figure. This feature made the formation of workable majorities in the Chamber of Deputies extremely difficult and led to a long series of coalition cabinets, more than fifty during the forty years before the First World War.

Republicans versus Monarchists

One of the main reasons for the erratic course of French politics after 1870 was the antirepublican sentiment of many Frenchmen. On several occasions in the early years of the Republic, the various royalist factions had come dangerously close to resurrecting the monarchy. But the Third Republic survived, partly because of the lack of unity among its enemies. It was not until 1879 that the French government became wholly republican in its legislative and executive branches.

But the republican elements were no more united than their enemies. A radical faction, led since Gambetta's death in 1882 by Georges Clemenceau, was deeply anticlerical and interested chiefly in revenge against Germany. The moderate republicans, on the other hand, were willing to compromise on domestic and foreign issues. Their chief figure, Jules Ferry, emerged as France's leading statesman in the last decades of the century. During most of the 1880s, radicals and moderates managed to cooperate in launching the Republic on a successful course at home and abroad. Despite their many achievements, however, widespread opposition persisted. Beginning in 1886 this opposition rallied around the recently appointed minister of war, General Georges Boulanger. By early 1889 the popularity of the dashing general was such that he might easily have led a successful *coup* against the Republic, had not his courage failed him at the crucial moment. Nevertheless, the Republic had come dangerously close to being overthrown.

As it turned out, the Boulanger affair helped to strengthen the Republic by drawing the radical and moderate republicans more closely together. But this gain was soon lost again in the so-called Panama Scandal, in which a number of radical republican deputies were found to have accepted large bribes from the corrupt and bankrupt Panama Canal Company. The dust of this affair had still not quite settled when the Third Republic was shaken by an even more serious crisis, the Dreyfus case.

In the fall of 1894, Captain Alfred Dreyfus, a Jew, was accused of having betrayed military secrets to the Germans and was condemned to life imprisonment on Devil's Island. Despite clear evidence of his innocence, it took five years before he was fully vindicated. During this time, the reactionary right—monarchists, Catholics, and the army, together with a handful of anti-Semites —denounced any attempt to clear Dreyfus as an attack on the honor of the

English cartoon of General Boulanger as General Bonaparte (1889), a parody of the famous painting of Napoleon by J.-L. David.

Economic Developments

France, which had enjoyed considerable prosperity before 1870, was set back by the Franco-Prussian War and was slow to profit from the Second Industrial Revolution. The losses in manpower and material, Germany's demand for a heavy indemnity, and especially the surrender of the valuable industrial region of Alsace-Lorraine, severely retarded French industrial growth. The majority of the French, moreover, were still engaged in agriculture, and protective tariffs, such as the Méline Tariff of 1892, mainly aided the farmers. What industry there was consisted largely of small establishments, and only a few industries were affected by the trend toward industrial concentration. French foreign trade almost doubled between 1870 and 1914. But since the commerce of its competitors increased at a much greater rate, France found itself demoted from second to fourth place in world trade. There was one activity in which France led the rest of the world: The amount of French money invested abroad during the thirty years before 1914 rose from 13 to 44 billion francs. These foreign loans were a valuable source of national income, and they were used as an effective instrument to facilitate French foreign policy.

Socialism and Social Reform

Since France was less industrialized than some other nations, its working class was smaller and French socialism never gained the influence it did elsewhere, especially in Germany. Socialism in France, furthermore, had received a serious setback in the disastrous Paris Commune, a setback from which it did not recover until the late 1870s. Like socialists in most other countries, the French were split into moderate and radical factions. The revolutionary group, led by Jules Guesde, and the moderates, led by Jean Jaurès, did not join forces until 1905, when they formed the United Socialist Party. Again like most other socialist parties, the French socialist party was revolutionary in theory but evolutionary in practice. Between 1906 and

Captain Dreyfus in 1899 passing between a ''guard of dishonor,'' soldiers whose backs are turned to him. The reactionary military faction arranged for this practice in order to discredit and humiliate Dreyfus.

nation and the discipline of the army. The radical left, spearheading the defense of Dreyfus, cleared its reputation of the blemish incurred in the Panama Scandal. The Dreyfus case was an extended duel between the two factions that had fought each other since the founding of the Third Republic. While its outcome was a victory of republicanism, the struggle itself testified to the continued strength of the forces of reaction.

The most immediate result of the Dreyfus affair was a shift from moderate to radical republicanism. After winning the elections of 1902, the Radicals formed their first ministry and at long last were able to carry out their own program. Their most drastic measures were directed against the Catholic Church. A bill for the separation of church and state brought to an end the Concordat of 1801, whereby the state had paid the salaries of the clergy and had participated in the selection of priests. The Church, henceforth, was to be entirely on its own. In social reform the Radicals were less successful. With the emergence of socialism in France at the turn of the century, radicalism found a powerful rival with far more sweeping social and economic aims.

1914, its membership in the Chamber of Deputies nearly doubled.

In the realm of social reform, France lagged behind England. A factory law of 1874, amended by subsequent acts, fixed the minimum working age for children at thirteen, restricted working hours for adults to twelve hours, and introduced various other health and sanitation measures. Social insurance did not begin until the end of the century. Accident insurance was introduced in 1898, and old-age pensions were started in 1910. There was no protection against unemployment, and health insurance was left to private initiative under state supervision.

Even though the French working class was not as numerous as its counterparts in England and Germany, the government's failure to solve some of the economic and social problems of the worker caused constant domestic unrest during the years just before 1914. At the same time, the Third Republic continued to be attacked from the right. Royalism and an intense brand of nationalism were kept alive by a few wealthy reactionaries in the *Action Française* of Charles Maurras and Léon Daudet. Yet the majority of the French seemed to approve the programs of reforms at home and peace abroad, which brought resounding victory for the Radicals and Socialists in the elections of 1914. French pacifism, while admirable, came at a most inopportune time, just when Europe was getting ready for a major war. France, on the eve of the First World War, was still a nation divided on many vital issues.

GERMANY: EMPIRE TRIUMPHANT

The new German *Reich* presented a spectacle of wealth, success, and supreme self-confidence. Had its unprecedented industrial growth been paralleled by political changes in the direction of a more liberal parliamentary government, Germany might easily have rivaled England as the most progressive nation in Europe.

We have already discussed the constitutional framework of Germany and of its largest member state, Prussia (see p. 604). Repeated demands of liberals and socialists for the reform of the Prussian three-class franchise and for the introduction of parliamentary government in the Empire were of no avail. The *Reichstag,* to be sure, was elected by manhood suffrage. But the main direction of policy continued to rest with the chancellor (who was appointed by and responsible to the emperor) and the Federal Council, or *Bundesrat,* in which Prussia held a controlling position. Even so, the German electorate might have made its influence felt more decisively had it not been split into five or six major parties, each of which differed in political and economic aims and none of which ever won a majority.

Repression at Home— Aggression Abroad

During its first twenty years, the German Empire was ruled by the strong hand of Bismarck. The "iron chancellor's" claim to fame rests on his foreign rather than his domestic policy. During the 1870s Bismarck antagonized large sections of the German people by his fierce struggle against the Catholic Church. The so-called *Kulturkampf,* while appealing to liberal anticlericalism, failed in its major objective—to prevent the rise of political Catholicism. The Catholic Center Party emerged from its persecution as a potent factor in German politics. Bismarck's attempt, during the 1880s, to prevent the rise of a strong Socialist Party was equally unsuccessful. By enlisting liberal support in his fight against Catholics and socialists, Bismarck perpetuated the political disunity of the German people and contributed further to the decline of German liberalism.

Bismarck had no worthy successor. The unceremonious manner in which the great chancellor was dismissed by William II in 1890 was indicative of the young emperor's desire to be his own chancellor. But William II was utterly unsuited for such a role. Erratic, unstable, and given to rash utterances, especially on matters of foreign policy, the kaiser launched Germany on an expansionist *Weltpolitik* (world policy) that soon lost it the international trust it had gained

Jean Jaurès (1859–1914), at a socialist party rally in 1913.

under Bismarck. More than in any other country, issues of foreign policy played a dominant role in Germany. The army, long powerful in Prussian affairs, remained one of the cornerstones of the empire. Except for its budget, which the *Reichstag* had to grant for several years in advance, it remained entirely free from civilian control.

Within the *Reichstag* there was very little chance for any effective opposition to the government's aggressive policy abroad and its reactionary policy at home. The alliance between prominent industrialists and landowners, initiated under Bismarck, assured the government of a workable parliamentary majority. Both groups profited from tariff protectionism and both were united in their opposition to lower-class demands for political and social democracy. Against this coalition between the industrialist National Liberals and the agrarian Conservatives, the Socialist opposition and the occasionally critical Center and Progressive parties could do very little, especially as they were rarely united among themselves. On a few occasions, notably during the "Daily Telegraph Affair" in 1908, when William II, in an interview to the British press, made some irresponsible statements on Anglo-German relations, it seemed as though public indignation might check the kaiser's erratic rule. But the discipline so deeply instilled in every German, and the economic prosperity the nation enjoyed, kept the public from taking any drastic steps.

Economic Developments

The immediate effect of Germany's unification in 1871 had been a short-lived economic boom, which had come to a sudden halt in the worldwide depression of 1873. It was only during the last two decades of the century that Germany began to show its great economic power, a power based on ample resources of coal and iron and a well-trained and disciplined labor force. Much of Germany's economic success can be attributed to the protective policy that Bismarck initiated in 1879. Germany was not the first nation to abandon free trade, but it was Germany's step that ushered in a period of tariff rivalry among the major powers and thus injected a strong element of nationalism into economic relations.

Germany's rapid economic growth was due in large measure to the development of its domestic market—its population increased from 41 million to 67 million between 1871 and 1914—but German competition was also felt abroad. The main pillars of German prosperity were coal and iron, concentrated in Alsace-Lorraine, the Saar, Upper Silesia, and particularly the Ruhr area, where the firms of Krupp, Thyssen, and Stinnes built their huge industrial empires. Germans took the lead in other pursuits as well, especially the electrical and chemical industries. By 1914 Germany's merchant marine was second only to that of Great Britain, although the British commercial fleet was still more than three times as large as that of Germany.

Imperial Germany—A German Reappraisal

The integral unification of the nation had not been brought about; the Gordian knot was uncut. What had been achieved was paid for through losses to the nation's fabric and damage to the nation's psychology. Revitalized, the hard, Old Prussian character could be superimposed on the soft, amorphous German spirit, and Prussia's militaristic-*cum*-political civilization could form the grand alliance, foreshadowed in the *Zollverein*, with a civilization inspired by economics and technology. The middle classes, caught, as they had been since 1848, between the authoritarianism of the state and the demands of the Fourth Estate, completely lost their self-confidence. The spirit of culture, withering throughout the Occident, could put down no deep roots in the stony landscape of the new structure; and in the unsettled atmosphere, the cultural decline was bound to have more grievous effects than in the long-established countries of the West. The national character coarsened. In 1866, the nation's sense of right and wrong having been thrown into confusion, the success of a daemonic, charismatic statesman remolded that character; in the *Kulturkampf*, it was thrust back from the deep wells of religion, to which the schism had long blocked proper access, and the anti-Socialist law added an element of callousness. The unscrupulous vitality of *Realpolitik* took the place of vanished character traits. Bent on the acquisition of power and wealth, the Germans were at the same time incapable of recognizing the limits of the possible within their policy of realism. Indeed, they were dazzled by sudden good fortune which they failed to understand.

Ludwig Dehio, *The Precarious Balance*, trans. by Charles Fullman (New York: Random House, 1965), p. 221.

Bertha von Suttner (1843–1914), Austrian writer, whose pacifist novel, *Lay Down Your Arms* (1892), inspired Alfred Nobel to establish the Nobel Peace Prize. She was the first woman recipient of the prize in 1905.

Socialism and Social Reform

The main critics of German domestic and foreign policy were the Social Democrats. Theirs was the largest and most influential socialist party in Europe. The origins of the party went back to the 1860s, but it did not become a political force until 1875. At that time a non-Marxian faction, organized by Ferdinand Lassalle in 1864, and a Marxian faction, led by Wilhelm Liebknecht and August Bebel, united to form the Social Democratic Party (SPD). Despite severe restrictions and the persecution of its members by the Bismarckian government, the numbers of the SPD steadily increased until by 1912 it had become the largest party in the *Reichstag*. Its program, first formulated at Gotha in 1875 and revised at Erfurt in 1891, while strictly "orthodox" in tone, nevertheless included a number of "revisionist" demands for specific reforms.

The agitation of the SPD was directed against the political and social rather than the economic inequities of the empire. The phenomenal economic growth of the country could not help but be reflected in a rising standard of living for the workers. The German government, furthermore, through extensive programs of social reform, tried to alleviate the hardships inherent in massive industrialization. In 1878 factory inspection was made compulsory, and in 1891 an Imperial Industrial Code introduced the usual sanitary and safety provisions and regulated working hours for women and children. Germany's pioneering efforts were in the field of social legislation. In a calculated effort to divert German workers from socialism, Bismarck, between 1883 and 1889, introduced far-reaching measures for health, accident, and old-age insurance. These served as models for similar legislation in other countries, notably England.

The German Empire in 1914 was an anomaly among European powers—economically one of the most advanced yet politically one of the most backward. The majority of Germans, though not happy about their political impotence, took comfort in their economic achievements. They might criticize their government's domestic policy—its opposition to parliamentary rule, its refusal to curb the influence of the military, its favoring of the few at the expense of the rest of the population. But most Germans saw little wrong with a foreign policy that demanded "a place in the sun" for Germany. Germany in 1914 was rich, powerful, and self-assertive.

AUSTRIA-HUNGARY: THE RAMSHACKLE EMPIRE

The Austro-Hungarian Empire, ever since the *Ausgleich* of 1867, had been virtually divided into two separate states. Both Austria and Hungary were constitutional monarchies, but their governments were far from democratic. Various attempts before 1914 to improve this situation were complicated by the perennial problem of nationalities. After 1873 the Austrian lower house, or *Reichsrat*, was elected by a complicated four-class franchise, which gave disproportionate influence to the upper classes and the German minority among the population. This system, with some minor changes, lasted until 1907. By that time agitation among the various subject nationalities had become so strong that electoral reform could no longer be put off. The electoral law of 1907 at long last granted universal manhood suffrage. But the return in subsequent elections of a large majority of non-German delegates led to such constant wrangling in the *Reichsrat* that the orderly conduct of democratic government became impossible and rule by decree remained the order of the day. In Hungary the situation was still more hopeless. Here the upper crust of Magyar landowners completely dominated both houses of parliament. The rising protest of Hungary's subject nationalities brought some slight electoral reforms, but Hungary in 1914 remained essentially a feudal state dominated by a Magyar aristocracy.

Conflict of Nationalities

The overriding problem of Austria-Hungary continued to be the conflicts among its many nationalities. In Austria the Czechs were the main problem. The Poles of Galicia formed a compact group that was relatively well treated and enjoyed cultural autonomy. The Czechs, on the other hand, were closely intermingled with Germans. Attempts to introduce Czech, together with German, as the official languages of Bohemia were met by German opposition. German nationalism found a mouthpiece in the German *Schulverein* of Georg von Schoenerer. Meanwhile, the "Young Czechs," led by Thomas Masaryk, fought for the rights of their own people.

While Austria made at least some concessions to its minorities, Hungary followed a strict policy of Magyarization, trying to eradicate rather than appease opposition. The major problem in Hungary was created by the Croats, who looked to Serbia for the lead in forming a Yugoslav—that is, South Slav—federation. The situation was complicated by the fact that the region of Bosnia-Herzegovina, since 1878 under Austrian administration, was also inhabited by Southern Slavs. The heir to the Austro-Hungarian crowns, Archduke Francis Ferdinand, was known to favor reforms that would give the Slavic element within the Dual Monarchy equal rights with Germans and Magyars. Nei-

ther Hungary nor Serbia liked such schemes. The Hungarians wanted to continue lording it over their Slavs, and the Serbs hoped to attract the Southern Slavs away from Austria-Hungary.

Thus, the existing state of affairs in Austria-Hungary had few real supporters. Emperor Francis Joseph, eighty years old in 1910 and the most respected monarch in Europe, tried his best to meet the rising tide of nationalism by appealing to the traditional loyalty to the House of Habsburg. But his efforts were in vain.

Economic Developments

Even though there was considerable industrialization in the Austrian half of the empire, the country as a whole remained predominantly agrarian. As such it suffered increasingly from the competition of the larger agrarian economies of Russia, the United States, and Australia. A high tariff policy, though it protected agriculture, kept living costs high, which in turn made for high wages and prevented Austrian industries from successfully competing abroad. Even so, there was some industrial progress. It would have been greater had the economic interdependence between Austria and Hungary been better utilized. As it was, industrial Austria and agrarian Hungary pursued separate and often contradictory economic policies.

Socialism and Social Reforms

Socialism in Austria did not become a factor to be reckoned with until the end of the century. In 1889, Victor Adler, the most prominent Austrian socialist, unified various socialist factions behind the Austrian Social Democratic party. Socialist agitation, in part, was responsible for the introduction of universal male suffrage in Austria in 1907. This development, in turn, helped the party to grow. The program of the Austrian socialists was revisionist, and their main support came from the working-class population of Vienna. Their major weakness was national diversity: By 1911 the party had split into German, Czech, and Polish factions. There was no socialist movement to speak of in Hungary.

Emperor Francis Joseph (center) relaxing with guests at the wedding party of his great-nephew and heir, Archduke Karl Franz Joseph, in 1911.

The Austrian government, like governments elsewhere, took a hand in improving the workers' lot. A system of factory inspection was set up in 1883, and an Industrial Code in 1907 set the minimum working age at twelve, provided for an eleven-hour working day, and introduced safety and sanitation standards for factories.

The economic and social problems of the Austro-Hungarian Empire in 1914 were still overshadowed by its nationalities problem. Every possible solution for this problem had been proposed and a few had been tried. Since each proposal left one or another of the many nationality groups dissatisfied, a policy of repression always prevailed. The result of this negative policy was the assassination of Francis Ferdinand at Sarajevo on June 28, 1914.

ITALY: GREAT POWER BY COURTESY

In Italy, economic backwardness and widespread illiteracy retarded the growth of democracy, although some superficial progress was made. The Italian constitution, the *Statuto,* which Piedmont had adopted in 1848, still limited the franchise in 1870 to a mere 2.5 percent of the population. Property qualifications and the voting age were gradually lowered, however, and virtually all adult males were permitted to vote by 1914. But this extension of the franchise was a mixed blessing. By giving the vote to the illiterate poor, it enabled a handful of ambitious politicians to manipulate elections and to make Italy's parliament a pliable instrument of their policy. The practice of "transformism"—that is, of avoiding parliamentary opposition by giving the most powerful critics a share in the government—avoided difficulties, but in the long run it proved a serious obstacle to the growth of democracy in Italy.

Political Instability

Despite marked economic improvements, Italy remained a poor and struggling country. A great power by courtesy more than through actual strength, Italy's

frantic efforts to live up to a glorious past led it into military ventures it could ill afford. The conservative forces that had brought about the country's unification remained in power until 1876. Regional opposition to extreme centralization and widespread discontent with heavy taxation then shifted the power to the more liberal factions. From 1886 to 1896, the experienced Francesco Crispi as prime minister provided firm leadership. His attempts to divert the people's attention from discontent at home through colonial ventures abroad suffered a dismal defeat at the hands of Ethiopia in the battle of Adua (1896). The end of the century saw a rising tide of labor unrest, bread riots, and street fighting. In 1900 King Humbert fell victim to an anarchist assassin and was succeeded by the more liberal Victor Emmanuel III.

During the last years before the war, Italy, under the capable but unprincipled Giovanni Giolitti, at long last made some headway in the solution of its worst economic difficulties. Giolitti also managed to effect a partial reconciliation between the Italian government and the Catholic Church. The pope continued to consider himself "the prisoner of the Vatican," but in 1905 he did lift the ban against the participation of Catholics in political affairs.

Economic Developments

Most of Italy's troubles were due to it's poverty. Even more so than France, Italy was still primarily an agrarian nation. But while France was able to produce the bulk of its own food, Italy's soil was too poor and its agricultural methods too backward to support its rapidly growing population. The mounting population pressure could be relieved only through large-scale emigration and increased industrialization. The latter was hampered, however, by lack of essential raw materials and shortage of capital. Attempts at protectionism, furthermore, tended to affect Italy's own exports, and it was only with the conclusion of a series of commercial treaties in the 1890s that Italian exports picked up. With the help of hydroelectric power to make up for its coal shortage, Italy gradually developed

Francesco Crispi (1819–1901), prime minister of Italy (1887–91, 1893–96).

its own textile industry and gained world leadership in the production of silk. But despite these improvements, and despite almost a doubling of its foreign commerce between 1900 and 1910, Italy's balance of trade continued to be unfavorable and Italy depended heavily on foreign loans.

Socialism and Social Reform

As it did almost everywhere else in Europe, industrialization in Italy brought in its wake the rise of socialism. The first socialist party in Italy was organized in 1891. It, too, had its initial difficulties over revisionism, and it was not until 1911 that the radical, "orthodox" element won the upper hand. The Italian socialist party did not gain any mass following until after 1900. Large numbers of Italian workers were attracted by the more violent programs of anarchism and syndicalism. Syndicalism applied the anarchist principle of direct action to economic affairs. The syndicalists hoped to overthrow capitalism by means of industrial sabotage and strikes, culminating in a general strike that would cripple the nation's economy and bring about the political victory of the working class. The first major general strike in Italy took place in 1904. It failed for lack of popular support.

The Italian government tried to cope with the social effects of industrialization by factory acts and social legislation. Accident and old-age insurance were introduced in 1898. But the basic causes of trouble—poverty and illiteracy—could not be erased overnight. Meanwhile the Italian people, inexperienced in the ways of democracy, fell more and more under the influence of extremists of the right or left—the right calling for glorious ventures abroad, the left opposing war and demanding reforms at home. Thus divided, Italy was in no condition to enter a major war in 1914.

RUSSIA:
STRONGHOLD OF AUTOCRACY

Tsarist Russia, to the bitter end in 1917, remained the most autocratic among European states. The brief flurry of reforms under Alexander II during the 1860s had soon given way again to Russia's traditional policy of repression. The reign of Alexander II came to a violent end in 1881, when he was assassinated by members of the terrorist "Will of the People." His son, Alexander III (1881–94), was a reactionary and a Slavophile, not unlike Nicholas I. For well over a quarter-century Alexander III and his son and successor, Nicholas II (1894–1917), followed a policy of darkest reaction. Aided by Vyacheslav Plehve, director of the state police and later minister of the interior, and by Constantine Pobedonostsev, who as "Procurator of the Holy Synod" was the highest official in the Russian Orthodox Church and one of the most powerful men in Russia, the principles of orthodoxy, autocracy, and nationality once again became the watchwords of Russian policy. Catholics in Poland and Protestants in the Baltic provinces were persecuted; the powers of local and provincial councils, established under Alexander II, were curtailed; popular education was discouraged; and nationalism in Finland, Poland, the Ukraine, and elsewhere was suppressed. A particularly shocking feature of Russian policy was its persecution of the Jews. There were hardly any positive achievements during this period of unrelieved repression, except the economic reforms of Count Witte.

Economic Developments

Russia was the last major European power to feel the impact of industrialization. The government's main concern prior to 1890 had been the improvement of farming methods and the cultivation of new lands. Russia's agricultural exports between 1860 and 1900 increased almost fourfold, despite rising tariff barriers. Beginning in the 1890s, Russia also embarked on a program of industrialization, chiefly under the direction of its minister of finance and commerce, Count Sergei Witte. By introducing the gold standard in 1897, Witte stimulated economic activity and made investment in Russian industry more attractive to outsiders. The construction of the Trans-Siberian Railway helped open up the country's rich mineral resources and fur-

"Bloody Sunday" (January 22, 1905). A procession of workers is fired on by tsarist troops on its way to the Winter Palace; seventy people were killed and two hundred forty wounded.

thered the iron industry in the Ural Mountains. As a result Russia by 1900 held fourth place among the world's iron producers and second place in the production of oil. The opposition of agrarian interests to Witte's industrial policy, however, led to his retirement in 1903. Together with an economic depression and the Russian defeat in the war with Japan (1904–05), Witte's departure helped to slow down Russia's industrial development. Lack of capital, the educational backwardness of the Russian worker, and his continued subjection to the village community were chiefly responsible for Russia's failure to realize its tremendous economic potentialities.

Socialism and Social Reform

Because of the government's vigilance toward all manifestations of social and political protest, socialism in Russia was slow to take hold. It was not until 1891 that the first Marxian socialist party was organized by Georgi V. Plekhanov. The activity of the Social Democratic party was largely confined to underground agitation. At a party congress in London in 1903, Russia's socialists split into two groups. The Mensheviks (or minority), under Julius Martov, advocated a gradual evolution to democracy and socialism, while the Bolsheviks (or majority), under Nikolai Lenin, followed the more radical, "Leninist" line. Besides Marxian socialism, which appealed to the rising indus-

trial proletariat, there was also an organization of agrarian socialists in Russia, the Socialist Revolutionaries. Their program harked back to the ideas of Alexander Herzen and to the populist "go-to-the-people" movement. To achieve their goals, the Socialist Revolutionaries advocated terrorism and assassination.

Increased industrialization in Russia brought the usual hardships for the working class. With an ample supply of manpower from landless peasants, wages remained low and the Russian worker had to slave long hours to eke out a meager existence. The government, in time, did regulate the employment of women and children and introduced maximum working-hours. But without a corresponding increase in wages, these restrictions merely tended to lower the total income of workers' families. Moreover, to voice discontent through labor unions was prohibited by law. Even so, unrest among the workers gave rise to frequent strikes of increasing violence.

The Revolution of 1905

The workers were not the only class that was restless at the turn of the century. There were the masses of landless peasants, whose grievances were kept alive by the Socialist Revolutionaries; there was opposition among national minorities against the government's policy of Russification; and there was growing agitation among liberal members of

The march on the Winter Palace on "Bloody Sunday" in 1905 was organized by the priest Georgy Gapon, shown above.

the middle class, who demanded a change to constitutional government. As economic depression was worsening the lot of the workers, the Russo-Japanese war upset the rural economy by requiring that peasants be drafted. With the tide of war turning against Russia, tension mounted and finally erupted in revolution. The Revolution of 1905 began on January 22, "Bloody Sunday," when a peaceful protest march was fired upon by tsarist troops. A general strike soon crippled the major industrial centers, peasants rose against their landlords, and mutinies broke out in the army and navy. In October the Social Democrats and the Socialist Revolutionaries set up a Soviet (or Council) of Workers' Delegates in St. Petersburg.

By that time, however, the revolution had run its course. Tsar Nicholas, after first intending to meet force by force, finally gave in and made a number of political concessions. The "October Manifesto" of 1905 guaranteed individual freedoms and called for the election of a National Assembly, or *Duma*, by almost universal male suffrage. But the promises made by Nicholas under duress were soon forgotten. It took three elections, each under a more restrictive franchise, before a *Duma* was finally elected that satisfied the tsar's wish for an advisory rather than a legislative body. Meanwhile the government had taken savage reprisals against the rank and file of the revolutionaries, executing an estimated fifteen thousand and arresting many times that number. Even so, Russia for the first time in its history now had an elected national assembly that could at least serve as a training-ground in parliamentary procedures. The democratic spirit thus penetrated, if ever so slightly, the last stronghold of autocracy.

Repression and Reform

The outstanding figure of the last decade before the war was Peter Stolypin, chief minister until 1911. A conservative monarchist, he nevertheless believed in a limited degree of representative government. He worked harmoniously with the moderate faction within the third *Duma*, the "Octobrists,"

who in contrast to the more liberal "Cadets" were satisfied with a mere consultative role. Stolypin's policy combined repression with reform. On the one hand he bore down hard on all revolutionary activities by Social Democrats and Socialist Revolutionaries. Their leaders were arrested, driven into exile (as were Lenin and Trotsky), or sent to Siberia (as was Stalin). These negative measures, however, were supplemented by far-reaching reforms. Realizing the desire of Russia's peasants for land of their own, and aware of the support that could be gained from a large class of small farmers, Stolypin started to divide the communal holdings of the villages, distributing the land among the individual members of the *mir*. This was a slow and complicated process, and by 1917 only about one-tenth of Russia's peasants had become independent farmers. Nevertheless, it was a farsighted move, and it might have saved the tsarist regime if land reform had been completed in time.

Stolypin's reformist policy was opposed not only by the advocates of revolution, for whom it did not go far and fast enough, but also by the forces of reaction. The latter again gained the upper hand when Stolypin was assassinated in 1911. Nicholas II was a weak and vacillating monarch, firmly committed to the autocratic beliefs of his father and deeply under the influence of his German wife. The Tsarina Alexandra had fallen under the spell of an evil and ignorant "holy man," Gregory Rasputin. This power-hungry Siberian peasant gained such influence over the imperial family that he became the real power in Russia. Reaction coupled with corruption and inefficiency led to a gradual paralysis of Russia's government, making it doubly vulnerable to any major crisis. Such a crisis arose with the First World War.

THE "CULT OF SCIENCE"

This discussion of the domestic affairs of the major powers between 1870 and 1914 thus far has dealt entirely with political, social, and economic events. Now it is necessary to outline the intellectual climate in which these developments took

Gregory Rasputin, the "holy man" who became the power behind the tsarist regime.

place. The title of this chapter—"The Period of Promise"—fits particularly well the intellectual and cultural trends of these years. Their outstanding characteristic may be described as an overriding interest and a deep belief in science. Man had been interested in science before. But it was only in the second half of the nineteenth century that a veritable "cult of science" developed. Science offered a positive alternative to the seemingly futile idealism and Romanticism of the early nineteenth century. Scientific research, in the past the domain of a few scientists and gentleman scholars, now became the concern of large numbers of people, especially as the application of science to industry gave an incentive for new inventions. "Pure" science continued to be of fundamental importance. But "applied" science—the "marriage of science and technology" so characteristic of the Second Industrial Revolution—now took precedence in the minds of most people. A virtually endless series of scientific inventions seemed to provide tangible evidence of man's ability to unlock the secrets of nature. If support was needed for the optimistic belief in unlimited progress, science provided it.

Materialism and Positivism

The growing concern of modern man with the material aspects of his civilization was also reflected in late nineteenth-century thought. A few basic scientific discoveries served as a foundation for an essentially materialistic philosophy that appealed to the educated middle class. Chemists and physicists earlier in the century had found matter and energy to be constant and indestructible. These scientific findings were translated by certain "popularizers of science"—writers who interpreted the discoveries of scientists to the average layman—into a philosophy of materialism. An early exponent of this philosophy was the German philosopher Ludwig Feuerbach. More influential, however, was the German physician Ludwig Büchner, whose book *Force and Matter* (1855) went through twenty-one editions and was translated into all major languages. Proclaiming the eternity of force

(i.e., energy) and matter, Büchner concluded that it was "impossible that the world can have been created. How could anything be created that cannot be annihilated?" Another influential scientific writer was the German biologist Ernst Haeckel, whose most famous book, *The Riddle of the Universe at the Close of the Nineteenth Century* (1899), became an international best-seller. Haeckel's "monistic philosophy" was entirely concerned with the material world, emphasizing not merely the eternity of matter and energy but insisting that even the human mind and soul had their material, physical substance. As for the riddles of the universe, Haeckel declared with the optimism typical of his age that all but one of them had been solved; and the remaining one, "what the pious believer called Creator or God," was not worth troubling with, since there was no means of investigating it.

More lasting in its effect on western thought than materialism was another philosophy concerned with the impact of modern science on society—positivism. This philosophy had been worked out in the first half of the nineteenth century by the Frenchman Auguste Comte, but its influence was not felt until later. According to Comte, man in his development had passed through two well-defined phases, the theological and the metaphysical, and had now entered a third, the scientific or positive, phase. In this last phase man no longer concerned himself with ultimate causes, as he had during the metaphysical stage, but was satisfied with the material world and with whatever he might learn from observing it. Here was a philosophy that accepted science as its only guide and authority and which for that reason was eminently suited to the late nineteenth century.

THE DARWINIAN REVOLUTION

The scientific development that had the most revolutionary impact on almost every facet of western thought and society in the second half of the nineteenth century occurred in biology. It is concerned with the theory of evolution, and

Charles Darwin (1809–82).

its major exponent was the British scientist Charles Darwin.

The idea of evolution was nothing new. Both in the general sense of a gradual development of human society from simple to more complex institutions, and in the more narrow biological sense that all organisms had evolved out of more elementary forms, the concept of evolution had earlier roots in western thought. Darwin's major contribution was to provide a scientific basis for what had previously been a mere hypothesis.

Darwinism

Darwin was influenced in the formulation of his theory by the writings of the geologist Charles Lyell and by Robert Malthus' *Essay on Population.* Lyell, in his *Principles of Geology* (1830), had restated the thesis advanced some fifty years earlier by James Hutton that the earth's physical appearance was the result of the same type of geological processes that are still active today. This idea of vast changes brought about by natural causes, which Lyell had applied to the inorganic world, Darwin applied to the world of organisms. In searching for an explanation of organic evolution, Darwin was impressed by Malthus' account of the intense competition among mankind for the means of subsistence.

The essence of Darwinism is stated in the full title of his basic work: *On the Origin of Species by Means of Natural Selection, or the Preservation of Favored Races in the Struggle for Life* (1859). His theory was subsequently elaborated and applied to the human species in *The Descent of Man* (1871). According to Darwin, life among all organisms is a constant "struggle for existence." In this struggle only the fittest survive. This survival of the fittest, Darwin held, was due to certain favorable variations within the given organism that proved of particular advantage in its competitive struggle with other organisms. These lucky variations, handed on to subsequent generations and enhanced by further variations, would in time evolve an entirely new organism, so radically different from its ancestor as to be considered a new species. This "natural selection," Darwin suggested, was fur-

ther aided by "sexual selection"—that is, the mutual attraction and consequent mating of the fittest members of a species to bring forth the fittest offspring. Darwin also accepted the notion that certain "acquired characteristics"—the long neck of the giraffe, for example—may be inherited.

Many contemporary scientists accepted Darwin's theories only reluctantly. Yet his main idea—that all existing forms of life have evolved out of earlier and simpler forms—remains valid to this day. Only his explanation of the actual process of evolution has been challenged. The idea of the inheritance of acquired characteristics had been pretty well shaken by the end of the nineteenth century. Darwin's concept of evolution as a cumulative result of many minute changes, furthermore, has gradually given way to the view that evolution proceeds by way of larger and more sudden changes, or "mutations." These modifications came later, however, and thus could not affect the revolutionary impact of Darwin's theories when they were first announced. More than any other single idea of the nineteenth century, the concept of evolution has left its mark on modern thought and society.

The Impact of Darwinism

By applying the idea of evolution to all living organisms, including man, Darwin destroyed many of the most cherished beliefs of his contemporaries. Yet to an age that worshiped science, the thought that man was just as much subject to the logic of science as was everything else in nature also held a great fascination. Underlying much of Darwin's work was the idea of progress, an idea dear to the nineteenth century. History, the study of man's past, suddenly appeared in a new light—as a march toward some far-off, lofty goal. The gentle and retiring scientist himself took little part in the excitement and controversy stirred up by the doctrine that bore his name. The popularization of Darwin's thought was due chiefly to the efforts of other men, especially his friend Thomas Huxley. The application of the evolutionary concept to every aspect of human society, from physics to ethics, was carried out by another admirer of Darwin, Herbert Spencer. Spencer's ten-volume *Synthetic Philosophy*, published between 1860 and 1896, was hailed at the time as a brilliant synthesis of all existing scientific knowledge. Today it has been practically forgotten.

Of all Darwin's new ideas, the concept of life as a struggle for existence in which the fittest would survive had particular appeal to his contemporaries. The philosophy of laissez faire, with its emphasis on competition, had long been hailed as the root of economic success. Darwinism seemed to give scientific sanction to this belief in laissez faire. Big business, according to John D. Rockefeller, was "merely a survival of the fittest . . . the working out of a law of nature and a law of God." But not only the capitalists derived great comfort from Darwin. His emphasis on the importance of environment for the improvement of man also gave hope to the socialists in their demands for social and economic reform. More than ten years before Darwin published his *Origin of Species*, Karl Marx, the "Darwin of the social sciences," had already sketched the evolution of society through a series of struggles among social classes.

The emphasis on struggle as a necessary condition for progress, however, was a narrow and one-sided interpretation of Darwinism, not shared by its author. In his *Descent of Man*, Darwin had emphasized that a feeling of sympathy and coherence, social and moral qualities, were needed for the advancement of society. But to the majority of people the struggle for existence assumed the validity of a natural law, a law, moreover, that applied not just to relations among individuals but to relations among groups.

"Social Darwinism"

Herbert Spencer was one of the first to apply the theory of evolution to groups and states. History to Spencer was a struggle for existence among social organisms leading, as in the case of the struggle among individuals, to the "survival of the fittest." The classical statement of what came to be called "Social

Darwin testing the speed of an elephant tortoise in the Galapagos Islands during his voyage on the surveying ship "Beagle," 1831–36. This journey provided most of the observations for his theory of evolution. Drawing by Meredith Nugent.

Darwinism" was made by the English banker and political scientist, Walter Bagehot, in his book *Physics and Politics: Thoughts on the Application of the Principles of Natural Selection and Inheritance to Political Science* (1872). According to Bagehot, the struggle for existence had always applied to groups as well as individuals, and in this struggle "the majority of the groups which win and conquer are better than the majority of those which fail and perish." In other words, among nations as among individuals, the strongest survive and the strongest, for that reason, are the best. Needless to say, this restatement of the well-known maxim that "might makes right" had little to do with Darwin's original theory.

Social Darwinism has been described as a blending of evolutionary and nationalist elements. To a generation that had recently experienced several major wars and that was actively engaged in numerous expeditions against colonial peoples overseas, Social Darwinism, with its glorification of war, came as a welcome rationalization. "The grandeur of war," Heinrich von Treitschke, one of Germany's most popular historians, told his students, "lies in the utter annihilation of puny man in the great conception of the state. . . . In war the chaff is winnowed from the wheat." It is not surprising to find such views in a country that owed so much to war. But war also found advocates elsewhere. The Frenchman Ernest Renan praised it as "one of the conditions of progress, the sting which prevents a country from going to sleep";

and President Theodore Roosevelt held that war alone enabled man to "acquire those virile qualities necessary to win in the stern strife of actual life."

The influence of Social Darwinism may also be seen in the injection of racialism into nationalism. If being victorious meant being better, what was more natural than to view the triumph of one nation or race over another as a sign of the victor's inherent superiority? Among the earliest writers on racialism was the French count Arthur de Gobineau. His *Essay on the Inequality of the Human Races* (1853–55) proclaimed the superiority of the white race and distinguished within that race between the superior Germanic "Aryans" and the inferior Slavs and Jews. Gobineau's racial doctrine, wholly unscientific, found its main echo in Germany. But the idea of white, specifically Anglo-Saxon, superiority was also popular in England and America. It provided an ideological justification for the imperialist expansion of the late nineteenth century.

The "Warfare of Science with Theology"

The most violent repercussions of Darwinism were felt in the religious field. The controversy between Darwinism and religion was part of a larger conflict that has been described as "the warfare of science with theology." The religious revival during the Age of Romanticism had soon given way to a noticeable decline in religious interest. As the state took over the functions of the churches in social welfare and education, and as some of the material benefits of industrialization spread among the lower classes, the need for the aid and comfort that religion had given in the past was no longer so acute. The tendency of the churches, furthermore, to favor the political *status quo* antagonized many liberals, and political anticlericalism became an important issue in most countries. Finally, there was the appeal that nationalism, socialism, and materialism came to have for many people. Both socialism and materialism were avowed enemies of religion.

Although these causes go far to explain the decline in religious interest in the second half of the nineteenth century, the most important reason was the effect modern science had on Christianity. Many scientific discoveries, especially in geology and biology, contradicted Christian beliefs, and the methods of scientific inquiry, when applied to Christianity itself, produced some disturbing results. In biblical or "higher" criticism, for instance, scholars studying the origins of the Bible discovered that most of its books had been written long after the events they described, and that few biblical writings existed exactly as they had originally been written. Other scholars, concerned with the study of comparative religion, detected striking similarities between Christianity and other religions. They found that there

Darwin on Man's Moral Qualities

The development of the moral qualities is a more interesting problem. The foundation lies in the social instincts. . . . A moral being is one who is capable of reflecting on his past actions and their motives—approving of some and disapproving of others; and the fact that man is the one being who certainly deserves this designation, is the greatest of all distinctions between him and the lower animals. But in the fourth chapter I have endeavoured to show that the moral sense follows, firstly, from the enduring and ever-present nature of the social instincts; secondly, from man's appreciation of the approbation and disapprobation of his fellows; and thirdly, from the high activity of his mental faculties, with past impressions extremely vivid; and in these latter respects he differs from the lower animals. . . .

Social animals are impelled partly by a wish to aid the members of their community in a general manner, but more commonly to perform certain definite actions. Man is impelled by the same general wish to aid his fellows. . . . The moral nature of man has reached its present standard, partly through the advancement of his reasoning powers and consequently of a just public opinion, but especially from his sympathies having been rendered more tender and widely diffused through the effects of habit, example, instruction, and reflection. It is not improbable that after long practice virtuous tendencies may be inherited. With the more civilized races, the conviction of the existence of an all-seeing Deity has had a potent influence on the advance of morality. . . . Nevertheless the first foundation or origin of the moral sense lies in the social instincts, including sympathy; and these instincts no doubt were primarily gained, as in the case of the lower animals, through natural selection.

From Charles Darwin, *The Descent of Man*, rev. ed. (New York: D. Appleton and Company, 1886), pp. 610–12.

were few differences in dogma and ritual between early Christianity and some of the many mystery cults that had flourished in the eastern Mediterranean at the time of Christ. Christianity, it seemed, was merely the one among many similar religions that had survived.

These discoveries concerning the origins of Christianity became more widely known when they were used in modern accounts of the life of Christ. A German scholar, David Friedrich Strauss, as early as 1835 had written a *Life of Jesus* that denied the divinity of Christ. Less scholarly and more popular was the *Life of Jesus* (1863) by the French writer Ernest Renan. Both works recognized Christ as a superior human being, but they denied that He had performed miracles or had risen from the dead.

Darwinism and Religion

Far more drastic in their effect on the faithful than these attempts to humanize Christ were the findings of Darwin. Not only did Darwin and Lyell challenge the biblical view of creation, but by making man a part of general evolution Darwin dethroned the lords of creation from the unique position they had hitherto occupied. Why, one might ask, should man alone of all creatures possess an immortal soul, and at what stage of his evolution was he endowed with it?

The Catholic Church, because it was more tightly organized and in its doctrine placed less exclusive emphasis on the Bible, was able to take a firmer and more consistent stand in this controversy than the various Protestant churches. In 1864 Pope Pius IX issued "A Syllabus of the Principal Errors of our Times," which condemned most of the new political, economic, and scientific tendencies. Six years later a general church council, in an effort to strengthen the pope's position, proclaimed the dogma of papal infallibility. The pope henceforth was to be infallible in all statements he made *ex cathedra*—that is, officially—on matters of faith and morals. The new dogma ran into some opposition among Catholics and it also contributed to the struggle between Church and state in Germany, Italy, and France.

The succession of the more conciliatory Leo XIII to the papacy in 1878 helped pacify matters. Leo was able to make peace with the German and, to a lesser extent, the French governments, and in the social and economic sphere, he tried to steer a middle course between capitalism and socialism. In science, Leo did not oppose discoveries that did not affect Catholic doctrine. Only on the subject of evolution did the papacy persist in its rigid opposition. Some Catholics had begun searching for ways to reconcile the contradictions between science and theology. This "modernism," as such attempted compromise was called, was considered a heresy by the Church. Only after the First World War did the Church gradually take a more tolerant view.

In contrast to Catholicism, Protestant (and to some extent Jewish) doctrine and ritual were almost entirely based on the Bible. The effect of scientific discoveries at variance with biblical statements, therefore, was felt more deeply. The fact, furthermore, that Protestantism was split into almost three hundred sects made any uniform stand in the warfare between science and theology very difficult. At the same time, however, Protestant emphasis on the freedom of the individual to work out his own relations with God made it possible for many Protestants to reach their own compromise between faith and reason. A minority of Protestants, called "Fundamentalists," less influential in Europe than in the United States, continued to cling to a literal interpretation of the Bible and insisted on the validity of the account of creation as given in the Book of Genesis.

Despite the confusion it caused not only among Christians but among Jews, the conflict between science and theology did not seriously interfere with the progress of science. The world in 1914 was still viewed as the intricate mechanism that Newton had supposedly shown it to be, a mechanism whose secrets would gradually yield to scientific inquiry. Only a handful of scientists realized that new developments—the discovery of X rays (1895), the isolation of radium (1898), and, most important, the formulation of the theory of relativity (1905)—had opened up an infinite number of new mysteries and had brought the world to the threshold of another scientific revolution.

ART IN THE AGE OF SCIENCE

The cult of science that dominated the intellectual climate at the end of the nineteenth century also had its devotees in art and literature. It is difficult in dealing with any period, especially one as diverse as the one described in this chapter, to single out those artistic trends that most clearly reflect the spirit of the age. To call the early nineteenth century an Age of Romanticism and the late nineteenth century an Age of Realism is very much an oversimplification. There were Realists and Romanticists in both these "ages," and some artists combined the characteristics of both periods in their work.

The Romantic artist, as we have seen, had preferred an ideal world of his imagination to the real world in which he lived. He had set his concept of natural beauty against the ugliness of early industrialism. And he had escaped from a harsh present to a more rosy past. Before the middle of the nineteenth century, however, some artists had already begun to be interested in the world as it was, not as they felt it ought to be. This shift from Romanticism to Realism was most evident in literature; it was less pronounced in painting, and there were hardly any signs of it in music.

Realism and Naturalism

The novel, hitherto a neglected literary form, now became the favorite medium in literature. And while the Romantic writer had been primarily interested in the unusual individual, the realistic novel was concerned with typical everyday society. Most of the great novels of the nineteenth century—from Dickens and Thackeray in England to Balzac and Flaubert in France, Fontane in Germany, and Turgenev and Tolstoy in Russia—fall into the category of social novels. Not only did these authors describe the society in which they lived;

Henri de Toulouse Lautrec (1864–1901) at work in the garden of his Montmartre studio in Paris.

they dwelled on the problems of that society. Literature was becoming increasingly a form of social criticism.

The shift toward Realism reached its climax in the late nineteenth century in a literary movement called Naturalism. Naturalism represented the conscious effort of some writers to apply scientific principles to art. Naturalistic writers like Émile Zola in France, Henrik Ibsen in Norway, and Gerhart Hauptmann in Germany were not interested so much in beauty as they were in truth. To get at truth they discarded subjective intuition and strove to describe objectively what they had learned from study and observation. The Naturalist was much impressed with the discoveries of modern science, especially in biology and such new fields as sociology and psychology, and he made use of this new knowledge in his writing. The Naturalist felt it was one of his chief functions to call attention to existing evils and abuses. If this meant focusing his artistic efforts on the seamy side of life, he did so, hoping that by serving as diagnostician of society's illness he might help cure it.

Impressionism

The change from Romanticism to Realism was far less pronounced in painting than in literature, though some new trends did appear. In the past artists had been concerned with the unusual and beautiful, but now they turned more to ordinary and often ugly everyday subjects heretofore considered unworthy of their attention—farmers, laborers, and urban scenes.

The real innovation in nineteenth-century painting, however, was not so much in subject matter as in technique. As Naturalism did to literature, so Impressionism applied scientific principles to painting. Influenced by scientific discoveries about the composition of light, painters like Camille Pissaro, Claude Monet, and Auguste Renoir used short strokes of pure color to depict nature in its ever-changing moods, not as it appeared to the logical mind but as it "impressed" the eye in viewing a whole scene rather than a series of specific objects. An Impressionist painting, examined at close range, thus appears as a maze of colored dabs that, viewed from a distance, merge into recognizable objects with the vibrant quality imparted by light.

In trying to find the scientific temper of the late nineteenth century reflected in literature and art, however, one must guard against oversimplification. A relationship between art and science certainly existed. But it would be wrong to assume that the majority of people at the time were aware of this relationship. The average European probably had little use for social novels or Impressionist paintings. He liked pictures that "told a story," preferably a sentimental one. And he liked second-rate novels of love and adventure by authors long since forgotten.

Symbolism

If these cultural interests of the average man expressed an unconscious desire to escape the realities of the present, a similar tendency may be noted among a few highly sensitive writers. They deplored their generation's preoccupation with material values, and far from singing the praises of the industrial age they spoke out against its dirt and vulgarity. Earlier in the century, the Englishmen Matthew Arnold and John Ruskin had lamented the materialism and the loss of esthetic values resulting from industrialization. Their complaints were echoed later by their compatriot William Morris, who would have preferred to withdraw from the machine age with its cheapening of taste and return to the simplicity and dignity of the Middle Ages.

There was a note of romanticism and escapism in this longing for beauty in an age of slums and soot. Naturalism had little use for beauty; to the Naturalist, art had to serve a purpose and preach a message. In protest against this arid view, a group of French writers at the end of the century proclaimed that art was sufficient unto itself—"art for art's sake." Art to these neo-Romantic, or Symbolist, poets—Stéphane Mallarmé, Paul Verlaine, and others—was not for everyone but only for the select few to whom it spoke in "symbols," using words not so much for their meaning but for the images and analogies they conveyed, often by sound alone. Symbolism, like Romanticism before, was deeply subjective and thus difficult to define. It is significant as an indication that there were people before 1914 who did not find all things perfect in a society that gloried in its material achievements and accepted the struggle for wealth as a sign of progress.

The Symbolists were not alone in their criticism. The most outspoken critic of the generation before 1914 was the German philosopher Friedrich Nietzsche. In a series of beautifully written, epigrammatic books in the 1880s, Nietzsche attacked almost everything his age held sacred—democracy, socialism, nationalism, racialism, imperialism, militarism, materialism, intellectualism, and especially Christianity. Little understood by his contemporaries and much misunderstood since, Nietzsche's influence was felt more after than before the First World War. Few people today would agree with his wholesale condemnation of his age. Yet in striking out blindly, Nietzsche could not help but hit on many of the weaknesses we have since come to recognize in an age characterized above all by smugness and misplaced self-confidence.

Friedrich Nietzsche (1844–1900).

Suggestions for Further Reading

Note: Asterisk denotes a book available in paperback edition.

General   Two good broadly conceived works that treat European civilization as an entity are C. J. H. Hayes, *A Generation of Materialism, 1871–1900* (1941), and O. J. Hale, *The Great Illusion, 1900–1914* (1971). National events are well covered in R. C. K. Ensor, *England, 1870–1914* (1936); D. W. Brogan, *The Development of Modern France, 1870–1939,* Vol. I rev. ed. (1966), K. S. Pinson, *Modern Germany, Its History and Civilization,* 2nd ed. (1966); D. Mack Smith, *Italy: A Modern History* (1959); A. J. May, *The Hapsburg Monarchy, 1867–1914* (1951); and H. Seton-Watson, *The Decline of Imperial Russia, 1855–1914* (1952).

The Growth of Democracy   The progress of political and social democracy is treated in A. Rosenberg, *Democracy and Socialism* (1939), and in H. S. Hughes, *Consciousness and Society: The Reorientation of Social Thought, 1850–1930* (1958). Other relevant works are J. Bowle, *Politics and Opinion in the Nineteenth Century* (1954); C. Moraze, *The Triumph of the Middle Classes* (1966); and C. Cipolla, *Literacy and Development in the West* (1969). Problems of parliamentary government in western Europe are discussed in É. Halévy, *History of the English People in the Nineteenth Century,* Vols. V and VI (1936), and D. Thomson, *Democracy in France Since 1870,* 4th ed. (1964). The peculiar situation in Germany is analyzed in two valuable studies: A. Rosenberg, *The Birth of the German Republic, 1871–1918* (1931); and A. Gerschenkron, *Bread and Democracy in Germany* (1943). Habsburg attempts to cope with the nationalities problem are disentangled in O. Jászi, *The Dissolution of the Habsburg Monarchy* (1929), and with emphasis on individual national groups in R. A. Kann, *The Multinational Empire,* 2 vols. (1950). The halfhearted efforts at political reform in Russia are discussed in G. Fischer, *Russian Liberalism from Gentry to Intelligentsia* (1958), and in B. Pares, *The Fall of the Russian Monarchy* (1939). Women's efforts for equal rights are the subject of W. L. O'Neill, *Woman Movement: Feminism in the United States and in England* (1969).

The "Second Industrial Revolution"   Several of the books mentioned in the reading list for Chapter 25 also cover this later period. D. Landes, *The Unbound Prometheus: Technological Change and Industrial Development in Western Europe from 1750 to the Present* (1969) is a major recent contribution. Additional treatments for the leading industrial countries are A. L. Levine, *Industrial Retardation in Britain, 1880–1914* (1967); W. W. Rostow, *The British Economy in the Nineteenth Century* (1948); S. B. Clough, *France: A History of National Economics, 1789–1939* (1939); and G. Stolper, K. Häuser, and K. Borchardt, *The German Economy—1870 to the Present* (1967). M. S. Miller, *The Economic Development of Russia, 1905–1914* (1926), is more detailed, and W. L. Blackwell, *The Industrialization of Russia: An Historical Perspective* (1970), covers a longer period. On European economic expansion overseas, see H. Feis, *Europe, the World's Banker, 1870–1914* (1930).

The Rise of the Working Class   A brief introduction to European radicalism is D. Caute, *The Left in Europe Since 1789* (1966). On evolutionary socialism, see P. Gay, *The Dilemma of Democratic Socialism: Eduard Bernstein's Challenge to Marx* (1952), and A. M. McBriar, *Fabian Socialism and English Politics, 1884–1918* (1962). The best book on German Social Democracy is C. Schorske, *German Socialism, 1905–1917* (1955). Good surveys of international socialism are J. Joll, *The Second International, 1889–1914* (1955), and M. Beer, *Fifty Years of International Socialism* (1937). On the growth of organized labor, see W. A. McConagha, *The Development of the Labor Movement in Great Britain, France, and Germany* (1942), and H. Pelling, *The Origins of the Labour Party, 1880–1900,* 2nd ed. (1964). Social legislation before 1914 is covered in K. de Schweinitz, *England's Road to Social Security* (1943), and W. H. Dawson, *Social Insurance in Germany, 1883–1911* (1912). The influence of individual reformers in England is discussed in H. Ausubel, *In Hard Times: Reformers Among the Late Victorians* (1960), and in M. Richter. *The Politics of Conscience: T. H. Green and His Age* (1964). On the role of the churches in the field of social reform, see D. O. W. Wagner, *Church of England and Social Reform Since 1854* (1930); J. N. Moody, ed., *Church and Society: Catholic Social and Political Thought and Movements, 1789–1950* (1953); and K. S. Inglis, *Churches and the Working Class in Victorian England* (1963).

**Domestic Affairs
of the Major Powers**

Much of this subject is covered in the works already cited. An interesting way of supplementing the more general accounts is through biographies. Among the standard lives of the great, L. Strachey, *Queen Victoria** (1921), is a classic, though E. Longford, *Victoria R. I.** (1965), is more reliable. R. Blake, *Disraeli* (1967), and P. Magnus, *Gladstone* (1955), are more readable than earlier standard accounts. Two great French leaders are commemorated in G. Bruun, *Clemenceau** (1943), and J. H. Jackson, *Jean Jaurés; His Life and Work* (1943). There are no really satisfactory works on the continental monarchs. M. Balfour, *The Kaiser and His Times* (1964), is entertaining but not definitive. J. Redlich, *Emperor Francis Joseph* (1929), lacks color; and neither Nicholas II of Russia nor the kings of Italy have been found worthy of major scholarly biographies.

B. D. Wolfe, *Three Who Made a Revolution** (1955), tells about the future rulers of Russia—Lenin, Trotsky, and Stalin—before their rise to power. The nineteenth-century background of Russia's revolutionary movement is described in E. Lampert, *Studies in Rebellion* (1957) and *Sons Against Fathers* (1965). See also A. Yarmolinsky, *Road to Revolution* (1957). T. H. von Laue, *Sergei Witte and the Industrialization of Russia* (1963), is important for Russian economic history.

Significant monographs on German history include P. G. J. Pulzer, *The Rise of Political Anti-Semitism in Germany and Austria** (1964); J. C. G. Röhl, *Germany Without Bismarck* (1967); M. Kitchen, *The German Officer Corps, 1890–1914* (1968); G. Roth, *Social Democrats in Imperial Germany* (1963); and F. Stern, *The Politics of Cultural Despair** (1965). For a balanced view of the most crucial event in French politics, see D. Johnson, *France and the Dreyfus Affair* (1967). Other phases of French politics are treated in E. Weber, *Action Française* (1962); M. Curtis, *Three Against the Third Republic* (1959), which deals with Sorel, Barrès, and Maurras; and R. Byrnes, *Anti-Semitism in Modern France* (1950). Britain on the eve of the First World War is the subject of C. Cross, *The Liberals in Power, 1905–1914* (1963), and G. Dangerfield, *The Strange Death of Liberal England** (1961). The Italian scene is described in J. A. Thayer, *Italy and the Great War: Politics and Culture, 1890–1915* (1964), and in C. Seton-Watson, *Italy from Liberalism to Fascism, 1870–1925* (1967).

Intellectual History

The general works by J. H. Randall, *The Making of the Modern Mind* (1940), and C. Brinton, *Ideas and Men** (1950), have good chapters on the intellectual life of the late nineteenth century. E. Weber, *Paths to the Present: Aspects of European Thought from Romanticism to Existentialism** (1960), contains unusual selections of readings. On the history of science, see A. E. E. McKenzie, *The Major Achievements of Science*, 2 vols. (1960), and W. C. Dampier, *A Shorter History of Science** (1957). The all-pervasive influence of Darwin is shown in P. B. Sears, *Charles Darwin: The Naturalist as a Cultural Force* (1950), and J. C. Greene, *The Death of Adam: Evolution and Its Impact on Western Thought* (1959). On the contemporary impact of Darwinism, see W. Irvine, *Apes, Angels, and Victorians* (1955). J. Barzun, *Darwin, Marx, Wagner** (1958), stresses similarities in three outwardly different contemporaries. W. Bagehot, *Physics and Politics** (1956), the work of a leading Social Darwinist, is still important. The wide appeal of Social Darwinism is shown in R. Hofstadter, *Social Darwinism in American Thought** (1955). W. Kaufmann, *Nietzsche: Philosopher, Psychologist, Antichrist** (1956), is a leading interpretation of the most influential philosopher of the period.

The classic study on the literature of the nineteenth century is G. Brandes, *Main Currents in Nineteenth-Century Literature*, 6 vols. (1923). Briefer and more pertinent is E. Wilson, *Axel's Castle: A Study in the Imaginative Literature of 1870–1930** (1958). For the impact of science on literature, see M. Nicolson, *Science and Imagination* (1956). The beautifully illustrated volume by R. Raynal, *The Nineteenth Century: New Sources of Emotion from Goya to Gauguin* (1951), shows the transition from traditional to modern art. See also F. Mathey, *The World of the Impressionists* (1961). H. Leichtentritt, *Music, History, and Ideas* (1938), and C. Gray, *History of Music* (1947), discuss new musical trends. On "popular culture," see R. Williams, *Culture and Society, 1780–1950** (1958), and B. Rosenberg and D. M. White, eds., *Mass Culture** (1959).

29 The Struggle for a European Equilibrium, 1871–1914

The diplomatic history of Europe and the world between 1871 and 1914 must be viewed in the context of the political, economic, and cultural trends noted in the preceding chapter. The spirit of competition that pervaded relations among individuals and classes had its parallel in the political and economic rivalry among nations. Many international crises arose directly out of domestic tensions. Had the internal affairs of the powers before 1914 been more harmonious, international affairs might possibly have been more peaceful.

Our view of international relations after 1870 is conditioned by knowledge of what happened in 1914. Most historians agree that, while some of the immediate causes that brought about war in 1914 could have been avoided, its real causes were deeply rooted. To understand how deeply, we must remember the far-reaching effects that the unification of Italy and Germany had had on the European balance of power. Two regions that heretofore had been mere pawns in international affairs suddenly emerged as great powers. The political and territorial framework of the Continent thus lost much of its former elasticity. The only region in Europe where major changes were still possible was the Balkan Peninsula. Austria-Hungary, now excluded from German and Italian affairs, claimed the Balkans as its natural sphere of influence. Since Russia and, to a lesser extent, Italy made the same claim, the Balkans became the scene of recurrent international crises.

Another source of international tension was the growing colonial rivalry among the powers. With opportunities for territorial expansion on the Continent restricted, and with expanding economies clamoring for markets and raw materials, colonial conflicts injected an element of perennial friction into international affairs. An added cause for tension was nationalism. As long as members of one nationality were subjected to domination by another, as was the case in Austria-Hungary, Turkey, and, to a lesser extent, Germany, the peace of Europe remained precarious at best.

Bismarck (left) with a visiting Kaiser William II at the time of their "reconciliation" in 1894.

THE AGE OF BISMARCK, 1871–90

Despite the unsettling effects of Italian and German unification, Europe at first managed to adjust peacefully to the changed situation. The chief credit for the relative stability that prevailed for the two decades after 1871 belongs to Count Bismarck. The fundamental aim of the German chancellor was the consolidation of the new German *Reich*. For this he needed peace. Bismarck considered Germany a "satiated" power, with no further territorial ambitions. The main threat to its security was France's desire for revenge. To keep France isolated, therefore, became the guiding principle of Bismarck's foreign policy.

The basic moderation of the German chancellor's aims and the consummate skill of his diplomacy rightly command respect. They show that *Realpolitik* need not necessarily rely on "blood and iron" but can use with equal effect peaceful pressure and persuasion. Yet in merely trying to maintain existing conditions and ignoring those forces that were straining against the *status quo*—notably nationalism and imperialism—Bismarck showed the same blindness that had characterized Metternich before him. Admirable as the Bismarckian system was, it was to fall to pieces as soon as the masterful guidance of its creator was removed.

The "Three Emperors' League"

The first of Bismarck's many international agreements was concluded in 1872 among Germany, Austria, and Russia. The *Dreikaiserbund* tried to revive the collaboration that had existed in the days of the "Holy Alliance." But the feeling of solidarity that had animated the three conservative powers in the days of Metternich had since given way to mutual rivalries. Russia, in particular, had never forgiven Austria its "ingratitude" during the Crimean War, and it now resented the leadership that Germany assumed within the new Three Emperors' League. A first sign of disagreement between Germany and Russia appeared during the so-called "war-in-sight" crisis of

1875, when rumors that Germany was planning a preventive war against France brought protests from England and Russia. Bismarck's role in fomenting the crisis is not quite clear, though there is no evidence that he was seriously considering war against France. Russia's action, therefore, seemed unnecessarily meddlesome, especially in view of its traditional friendship with Prussia. The monarchical front had shown itself far from solid.

The Russo-Turkish War and the Congress of Berlin

A far more serious rift within the Three Emperors' League developed out of Russia's ambitions in the Balkans. The inefficiency and corruption of the disintegrating Ottoman Empire had invited intervention several times before, most recently during the Crimean War. In 1875 new revolts against Turkish misrule broke out in the Balkans. The Turks acted with their usual ferocity in putting down these nationalist uprisings and would have held the upper hand if Russia, in the spring of 1877, had not joined the insurgents. It did so after making sure of Austrian neutrality and recognizing in return Austria's right to occupy the Turkish provinces of Bosnia and Herzegovina. In addition, Russia promised not to support the formation of any large Balkan state.

The Russo-Turkish War, after some reversals, ended in Russian victory. In a treaty signed at San Stefano in March 1878, several of Turkey's subject nationalities were granted independence. Among them was to be a large Bulgarian state, which Russia was to occupy for several years. In addition, Russia was to get some territorial compensations. This startling increase of Russian influence in the Balkans deeply alarmed the other great powers. Their pressure induced Russia finally to agree to submit the settlement to an international conference at Berlin in June 1878.

Most of the important decisions of the Congress of Berlin were actually reached in preliminary agreements, which the Congress then confirmed. The proposed Greater Bulgaria was divided into three parts, leaving only a small Bulgarian state; Serbia, Montenegro, and Rumania were granted full independence; Austria was given the right to occupy and administer Bosnia and Herzegovina; and England was given control over the island of Cyprus. Russia rightly felt that it had been cheated out of its victory. While England and Austria made substantial gains, Russia had to be satisfied with Bessarabia and some gains in the Caucasus. The Russians blamed their defeat on Bismarck, who, they held, had violated his self-styled role as "honest broker" by favoring the interests of Russia's adversaries. The Congress of Berlin provoked a serious crisis in the relations between Germany and Russia and ended the Three Emperors' League.

The Austro-German Alliance

The breakup of the Three Emperors' League forced Bismarck to find a substitute. This he did in a secret alliance with Austria. The Dual Alliance of 1879 was the climax of Germany's *rapprochement* with Austria that had been Bismarck's concern since 1866. The alliance was renewed periodically and remained in

Bismarck

PRO

Bismarck is generally described in the textbooks as the first *Realpolitiker*; but unfortunately so much has been written about *Realpolitik* that its meaning has become obscure and mixed up with blood and iron and incitement to war by the malicious revision of royal telegrams. . . . It may be permissible to suggest that the essence of Bismarck's realism was his recognition of the limitations of his craft, and that it was this, coupled with the passion and the responsibility that he brought to his vocation, that made him a great statesman.

CON

Himself always plotting combinations against others, Bismarck was convinced that all the world was plotting combinations against him and lived in a half-mad imaginary world in which every statesman was as subtle and calculating, as ruthless and assiduous as he was himself. . . . At bottom he was a barbarian of genius, mastering in the highest degree the mechanical and intellectual side of civilization, altogether untouched by its spirit.

From Gordon A. Craig, *From Bismarck to Adenauer* (Baltimore: Johns Hopkins, 1958), p. 28; A. J. P. Taylor, *The Course of German History* (New York: Coward-McCann, 1946), pp. 95–96.

THE TREATY OF SAN STEFANO   1878

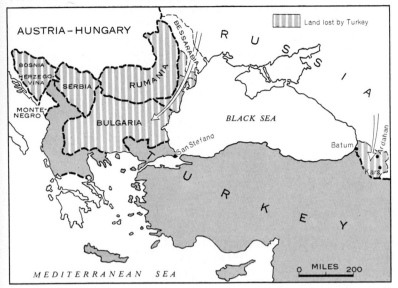

THE CONGRESS OF BERLIN   1878

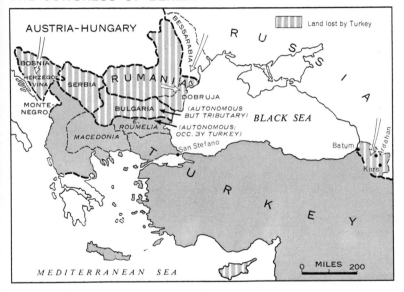

marck expected that Russia, unable for ideological reasons to draw closer to republican France, and separated from England by rivalries in Asia, would feel sufficiently isolated to desire a renewal of its former ties with Germany. Bismarck's assumption proved correct.

The Second "Three Emperors' League"

Russia would have preferred a treaty with Germany alone, but Bismarck insisted that Austria be included as well. A new Three Emperors' League was finally concluded in 1881. It provided that in case one of the members became involved in war with a fourth power, the other two would remain neutral. In this way Bismarck relieved his fear that Russia might join France in a war against Germany. The most important provisions of the treaty dealt with the Balkans: Any territorial changes in that region henceforth were to require the consent of all three powers; Austria reserved its right to annex Bosnia and Herzegovina at a time of its own choosing; and Russia's wish for the eventual union of Bulgaria and Eastern Roumelia (one of the regions separated from Greater Bulgaria at Berlin) was recognized. By dividing the Balkans into spheres of influence, the three powers seemed finally to have brought the Balkan problem under control. The new arrangement, however, overlooked the national aspirations of the Balkan peoples themselves.

The Triple Alliance

Before the Balkan question became acute once more in 1885, Bismarck had further extended his diplomatic network with the Triple Alliance of Germany, Austria, and Italy in 1882. The initiative this time came from the Italians. Italy for some time had hoped to enhance its status as a great power by occupying the Turkish region of Tunis in North Africa. It was deeply distressed, therefore, when the French took Tunis in 1881. To strengthen its diplomatic position for the future, Italy sought closer ties with Austria and Germany. Like the rest of Bismarck's treaties, the Triple Alliance was primarily defensive. Bismarck never took

force until 1918. Its provisions were purely defensive, calling for mutual aid if either member was attacked by Russia. Bismarck has been criticized for tying Germany's fate to the ramshackle Dual Monarchy. But he did not necessarily envisage the alliance as permanent, and he thought Germany strong enough to keep Austria's ambitions in the Balkans in check so as to avoid a showdown with Russia. Nor did the union with Austria mean that Germany was ready to sever relations with Russia altogether. Bisit very seriously, except for the fact that it contributed to the diplomatic isolation of France.

The years immediately after 1882 mark the high point of Bismarck's influence in Europe. French nationalism appeared to have been successfully diverted into colonial channels in North Africa; the situation in the Balkans appeared under control; and Austria's position had been strengthened by a secret treaty with Serbia in 1881 that made Austria the protector of its small neighbor. In 1883 Rumania concluded an alliance with Austria, to which Germany adhered later. The treaty was chiefly directed against Russian ambitions in the Balkans, where a new crisis flared up in 1885.

The Reinsurance Treaty

This latest Balkan crisis was touched off by an upsurge of Bulgarian nationalism in Eastern Roumelia, leading to the reunion of that region with Bulgaria. During the ensuing wrangle the Three Emperors' League met its final fate. For some time Russian nationalists, resenting German support of Austria in the Balkans, had demanded that Russia seek the friendship of France. Bismarck's worst fears seemed about to come true. But the tsarist government was reluctant to cut its connections with Berlin. Russia, therefore, proposed to the Germans that they enter into an agreement without Austria. The upshot was the so-called Reinsurance Treaty of 1887, which provided for benevolent neutrality in case either partner became involved in war, unless Germany attacked France or Russia attacked Austria. The Reinsurance Treaty also recognized Russia's interests in Bulgaria and the Turkish Straits.

This last of Bismarck's major treaties has been both hailed as a diplomatic masterpiece and condemned as an act of duplicity. It certainly did run counter to the spirit, if not the letter, of the Dual Alliance. But while Bismarck encouraged Russia's Balkan ambitions, he at the same time put an obstacle in the way of these ambitions by sponsoring the so-called Mediterranean Agreements between England, Italy, and Austria. Signed also in 1887, these agreements called for the maintenance of the *status quo* in the Mediterranean, including the Balkans. Any assurances Bismarck had given to Russia about Bulgaria and the Straits were thus successfully neutralized.

In making a fair appraisal of Bismarck's diplomacy, it is necessary to go beyond a mere comparison of treaty texts and consider the motives behind his treaties. These invariably were to maintain peace. Bismarck hoped to achieve this aim by isolating France and balancing the rest of the powers so that any unilateral disturbance of the peace would automatically result in a hostile coalition against the aggressor. Seen in this light, Bismarck's policy was less crafty than it appeared when the world first learned about the Reinsurance Treaty after the chancellor's retirement. A valid criticism of Bismarck's policy is that it was far too complicated to be successful in the long run and that it rested more on the attitudes of Europe's statesmen than on the sentiments of their peoples. Such disregard of public opinion became increasingly difficult in an age of democracy and nationalism.

FROM EUROPEAN TO WORLD POLITICS

One of the most important trends in international affairs after Bismarck has been the growing involvement of Europe in world affairs. This development had started much earlier, of course; but it was only at the end of the nineteenth century that events in Europe and overseas became so intricately interwoven that the histories of Europe and the world could no longer be treated separately.

The "New Imperialism"

The expansion of European influence in the late nineteenth century is often called the "new imperialism," to distinguish it from earlier phases of overseas expansion. Its motives were similar to those found earlier in the century, although they now operated with far greater intensity. Imperialism in the past had been chiefly limited in its appeal to the upper classes. Now suddenly it became of vital concern to everyone. More than any other movement, the new imperialism expressed the general climate of the period before 1914. Aggressive nationalism, ruthless economic competition, the restless struggle for success, all found an outlet in the scramble for overseas colonies and concessions, protectorates and spheres of influence. Here was an opportunity for men of daring and initiative to suffer hardships in distant lands not merely to advance their own fortunes but also, as they never tired telling the world, to undertake a "civilizing mission" for the good of mankind. Of the many driving forces behind the new imperialism, this "aggressive altruism" was one of the most potent.

England continued to lead in the new imperialism as it had in the old. After a period of declining interest in overseas expansion, Britain resumed its imperialist course after 1870. By 1914 it controlled one-fifth of the world's land and one-fourth of its population. The second largest colonial empire in 1914, that of France, had been acquired almost entirely during the nineteenth century. In its expansion into North Africa, France became involved first with Italy over Tunis, then with England over Egypt and the Sudan, and finally, after the turn of the century, with Germany over Morocco. Germany, prior to 1880, had no overseas possessions, and Bismarck was slow to enter the colonial race. When he finally did, beginning in 1884, it was in part to enhance Germany's bargaining position in Europe. It was William II who launched Germany in earnest on a course of *Weltpolitik*, in pursuit of which it provoked several international crises. Similar friction was caused by Italy's belated claims to colonies. Russia, as in the past, confined its expansion to adjacent areas in Asia. The only major power refraining from colonial expansion was Austria.

THE CONQUEST OF AFRICA

The most spectacular expansion of European influence after 1870 took place in Africa. In order to simplify the involved story of the scramble for African territory, events in the northern, central, and southern regions will be discussed separately. But it must be remembered that

many of these developments actually happened simultaneously.

North Africa

The Mediterranean coast of Africa, since the seventh century, had been under the influence of Moslem civilization; since the early sixteenth century, it had been under the direct or indirect rule of the Ottoman Empire. France gained its first foothold in North Africa with the acquisition of Algiers in 1830. In the course of the century France extended its sphere of influence inland and in time Algeria became an integral part of France. The next major move came with the establishment of a French protectorate over Algeria's eastern neighbor, Tunis, in 1881. Subsequently France began extending its influence westward over the sultanate of Morocco. The situation here was complicated by the fact that several other powers, notably Germany, also had economic interests in that region. A French protectorate over Morocco was thus not won until 1911, and then only after two major international crises (see pp. 689–91).

Egypt, the Sudan, and Tripoli

While France was establishing itself in the western half of North Africa, Britain was doing the same in Egypt and the Sudan. Egypt in 1870 was still nominally part of the Turkish Empire. Its gradual subjugation to foreign control was due to

Algerian officer in the French army, 1886.

The Sphinx is neck-high in sand and British soldiers in this photograph taken in 1882, after the bombardment of Alexandria.

IMPERALISM IN AFRICA   1884 and 1914

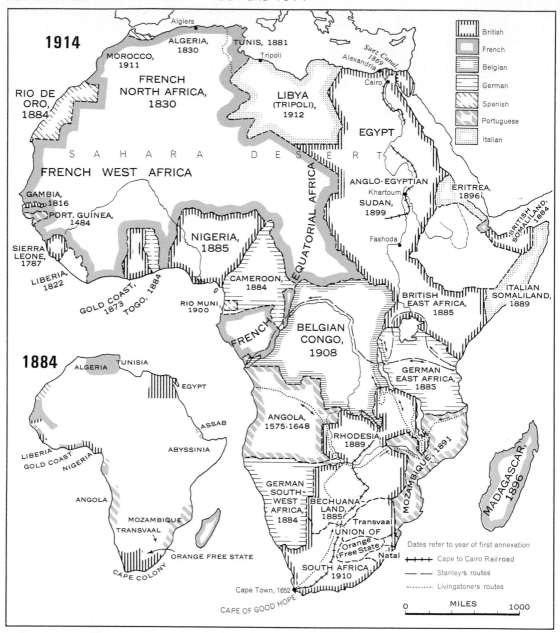

1914

Algiers
ALGERIA, 1830
TUNIS, 1881
Tripoli
MOROCCO, 1911
FRENCH NORTH AFRICA, 1830
LIBYA (TRIPOLI), 1912
Suez Canal 1869
Alexandria
Cairo
EGYPT

RIO DE ORO, 1884

S A H A R A   D E S E R T

FRENCH WEST AFRICA

ANGLO-EGYPTIAN SUDAN, 1899
Khartoum
ERITREA 1896
Fashoda
BRITISH SOMALILAND, 1884

GAMBIA, 1816
PORT. GUINEA, 1484
SIERRA LEONE, 1787
LIBERIA, 1822
GOLD COAST, 1873
TOGO, 1884
NIGERIA, 1885
CAMEROON, 1884
RIO MUNI 1900
FRENCH EQUATORIAL AFRICA
BELGIAN CONGO, 1908
BRITISH EAST AFRICA, 1885
ITALIAN SOMALILAND, 1889
GERMAN EAST AFRICA, 1885

1884

ALGERIA
TUNISIA
EGYPT
ASSAB
ABYSSINIA
LIBERIA
GOLD COAST
NIGERIA
ANGOLA, 1575-1648
ANGOLA
RHODESIA 1889
MOZAMBIQUE 1891
MADAGASCAR 1896

GERMAN SOUTH-WEST AFRICA, 1884
BECHUANA-LAND, 1885
Transvaal
UNION OF Orange Free State
Natal

MOZAMBIQUE
TRANSVAAL
ORANGE FREE STATE
CAPE COLONY

SOUTH AFRICA 1910
Cape Town, 1652
CAPE OF GOOD HOPE

British
French
Belgian
German
Spanish
Portuguese
Italian

Dates refer to year of first annexation
Cape to Cairo Railroad
Stanley's routes
Livingstone's routes

0   MILES   1000

reckless borrowing of foreign money at prohibitive interest rates. When, in 1876, the Egyptian government suspended interest payments on some of its foreign obligations, Britain and France, the leading creditors, established a dual control over Egypt's finances. The subsequent rise in taxes infuriated the Egyptian taxpayer. To counteract a rising tide of Egyptian nationalism, Britain occupied Egypt in 1882. As a result, Anglo-French dual control over Egypt came to an end.

France, needless to say, resented its exclusion from Egypt and on every occasion tried to put obstacles in England's way. Tension between the two powers was aggravated by their rivalry over the Sudan. This Egyptian dependency had won temporary independence in 1885. But when France and Belgium began advancing toward the Sudan from central Africa, British and Egyptian forces in 1896 started to retake the region. The climax of their expedition came in 1898

The influence of African art on European art: at top, wood doll from Ghana, late nineteenth century; below, *Head,* by Modigliani, *ca.* 1913.

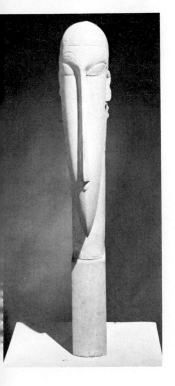

when British and French forces met at Fashoda on the Upper Nile. As both Britain and France laid claim to the Sudan, war seemed imminent. But the French government, troubled by the Dreyfus affair at home and inferior in naval strength, finally gave in and left England in control. In 1899 Egypt and England established joint control over what came to be known as the Anglo-Egyptian Sudan.

One stretch of land along the Mediterranean had not as yet come under foreign control—the region of Tripoli between Egypt and Tunis. It was of little value, consisting largely of desert. But in an age when overseas expansion was a matter of prestige, even so poor a prize seemed worth taking. After making certain of French support by recognizing France's claims in Morocco, Italy in 1911–12 waged war against Turkey and annexed Tripoli. The Italian colony of Libya, as it was called, was one of the least lucrative of imperialist ventures. But it was a source of great pride to the Italians.

Central Africa

Very little of central Africa had been explored before the second half of the nineteenth century. Among the most famous explorers of the region were David Livingstone and Henry Morton Stanley. Livingstone, a Scottish missionary, spent almost thirty years in Africa. When he failed to return from his third and last major expedition in 1871, Stanley, a British-born American journalist, was sent to find him. Stanley's successful search for Livingstone gave him a taste for exploration that made him the leading explorer of the Congo region. After vainly seeking to interest the British in his plans for opening up the Congo, Stanley found a sponsor in King Leopold II of Belgium. Leopold's claims to the Congo Free State were recognized by an international conference at Berlin in 1885. For the next twenty years a policy of the most ruthless colonial exploitation made a vast fortune for Leopold's various personal enterprises in the Congo. Only after these brutal methods were revealed was control over the region transferred to the Belgian state in 1908.

The practice whereby enterprising individuals staked out claims that were later protected by their governments was also used to great advantage by the Germans. Beginning in 1884 the German government took over the rights that various German merchants and explorers had staked out over large parts of southwest, central, and east Africa. The British tried to discourage these German moves. When this attempt proved fruitless, they moved quickly to stake out their own claims for the interior of the continent. France, meanwhile, extended its holdings in central and west Africa and in 1896 proclaimed possession of the island of Madagascar. Italy acquired Eritrea and Somaliland at the southern end of the Red Sea in 1890. Italy's attempts to extend its holdings inland into Abyssinia were stopped by Ethiopian forces in the Battle of Adua (1896).

South Africa

Some of the most valuable colonial prizes were to be found in the southern part of the African continent. Britain had acquired the Dutch Cape Colony there in 1806. As a result of tension between the new British immigrants and the original Dutch settlers, or Boers, the latter, beginning in the 1830s, had moved northward and founded two new Dutch colonies, the Orange Free State and the Transvaal. Britain recognized the independence of these republics in 1852. With the subsequent discovery of diamonds and gold in these regions, however, the inhabitants of the Cape Colony began to call for an extension of British sovereignty over the Orange Free State and the Transvaal.

The leading advocate of Britain's South African interests in the late nineteenth century was Cecil Rhodes. A typical "empire builder," Rhodes owned extensive interests in South Africa's diamond and gold fields. He became prime minister of the Cape Colony in 1890. Meanwhile a new discovery of gold in the Transvaal in 1886 had touched off a veritable British invasion into the region. To discourage this foreign influx, the president of the Transvaal, Paul Krüger, placed heavy restrictions on British immigrants. One of the more

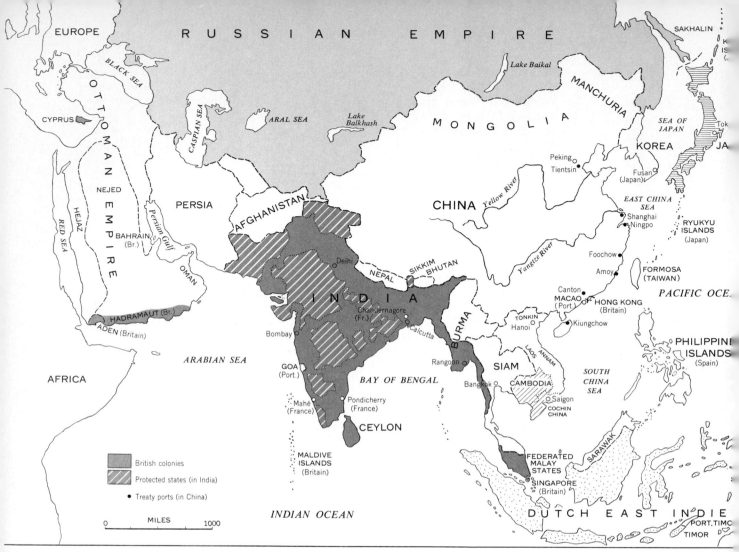

ASIA IN 1880

spectacular incidents in the growing tension between Britons and Boers was the abortive Jameson Raid at the turn of the year 1895–96, an attempt by one of Rhodes' associates to start a revolution among the British minority in the Transvaal. An ill-advised and well-publicized telegram from the German kaiser congratulating Krüger on his defeat of the plot cast a deep shadow on Anglo-German relations at the time.

Finally, in 1899, tension between the Boers and the British led to war. It took Britain two and a half years to defeat the tenacious Boers. Not until 1902 did the Boers lay down their arms, and then only on the promise of very lenient peace terms. As a result of this leniency, the issues of the past were quickly forgotten. When the Union of South Africa was formed in 1910, a former Boer general became the first prime minister of this newest self-governing dominion.

THE NEW IMPERIALISM IN ASIA AND THE PACIFIC

The sudden outburst of imperialism after 1880 also affected Asia and the Pacific. In contrast to Africa, large parts of this region had been under European domination for some time. Developments in India and China have already been discussed (see pp. 634–40); we shall now turn to the rest of the Asian continent and to the Pacific islands.

Russia in Asia

One of the principal powers with interests in Asia was Russia. Its advances

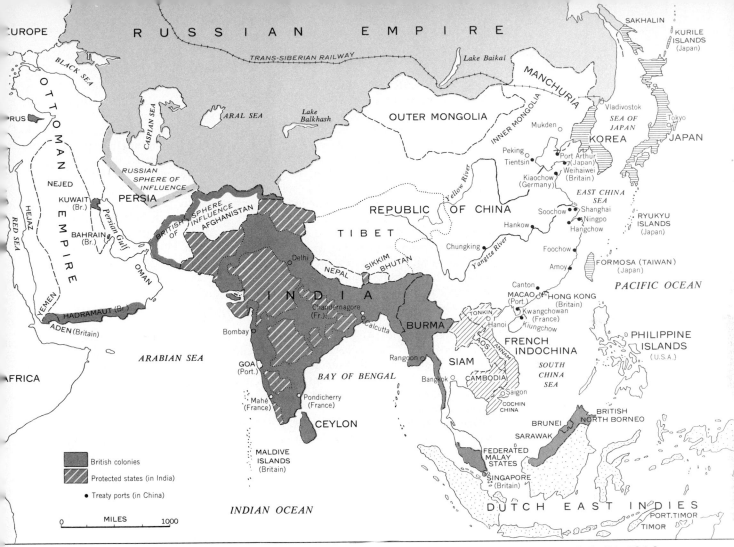

ASIA IN 1914

there took three main directions: to the southwest into the Near East—the Ottoman Empire and especially the region around the entrance to the Black Sea; to the Far East—Siberia and the adjacent coastal regions of China; and to the Middle East—Afghanistan and Persia. Foremost among Russia's aims in the Near and Far East was to find outlets to the sea and ice-free harbors that would enable it to escape its land-locked position. Attempts to do so in the Near East, as we have seen, were met by resistance from the other great powers, notably England. Whenever it met with a setback, as in 1878, Russia shifted its attention from west to east, from Europe to Asia.

Russian expansion into Siberia had proceeded slowly but steadily for more than three centuries. It was greatly facili-

tated by the acquisition of a section of China's coast along the Sea of Japan in 1860 and the founding of the Pacific port of Vladivostok. Russia's aim was to expand southward across the Amur River into Manchuria and then into Korea. But its plans were foiled by the conflicting interests of Japan. As a result of the Russo-Japanese War, Russia's territorial position in the Far East in 1905 was substantially what it had been fifty years earlier. Its failures in the Far East in part explain Russia's renewed interest in the affairs of Europe and the Near East during the last decade before the First World War.

Anglo-Russian Rivalry

In the third sphere of Russian expansion, the Middle East and central Asia,

Russia made considerable progress during the nineteenth century. By 1880 the whole region north of Persia and Afghanistan had become Russian. This extension of Russian power was watched with growing apprehension by Great Britain, which feared that Russia's advance was ultimately directed at India. The mountainous country of Afghanistan served as a buffer against a possible invasion of India from the northwest. In 1879 England had overthrown the pro-Russian ruler of Afghanistan and had occupied most of the country. But British-Russian rivalry continued. It was not resolved until 1907, when Russia finally recognized England's predominant position in Afghanistan.

Another scene of Anglo-Russian rivalry was Persia. The contest here was primarily economic, with both Russian and British interests seeking concessions. But England also feared that Persia might serve as another approach to India. Differences in Persia, as in Afghanistan, were negotiated by the Anglo-Russian Entente in 1907 (see p. 689).

This encroachment of the great powers on hitherto sovereign states was typical of much of European imperialism in Asia. The gradual subjection of China to foreign tutelage during the second half of the nineteenth century was an example. Another example was Siam. The French, after extending their protectorate over Indochina during the 1880s, turned their attention westward. Here they came in conflict with the English, who were interested in Siam because it bordered on Burma, which Britain had taken in 1852. After a certain amount of controversy, Siam in 1896 was made into a neutral buffer state between Burma and Indochina.

The Pacific

The most valuable islands of the Pacific were taken long before 1870. The rivalry of the powers over the few remaining small islands was a sign of how intense the imperialist urge had become. The main contestants in the Pacific were England and Germany, with the United States and France intervening occasionally. It is unnecessary to enumerate all the bits and pieces of land picked up by these powers. The most important, besides America's annexation of the Philippines, was the acquisition of eastern New Guinea by England and Germany in 1884. The most serious crisis arose over the Samoan Islands, which were claimed by Britain, Germany, and the United States. After ten years of intermittent dispute, the islands were divided in 1899 between the United States and Germany, with England receiving compensations in the Solomons.

THE UNITED STATES AS A WORLD POWER

Developments in the United States during the period before 1914 were remarkably similar to developments in Europe. In the purely political sphere, there was less need for further democratization than there was in some European countries, although the agitation of the Populists in the 1890s and of the Progressive Party in 1912 showed that many Americans felt their interests were neglected under the two-party system. In the economic sphere, the United States shared

---

President McKinley and the Philippines

I have been criticized a good deal about the Philippines, but I don't deserve it. The truth is, I didn't want the Philippines, and when they came to us, as a gift from the gods, I did not know what to do with them. . . . I walked the floor of the White House night after night until midnight; and I am not ashamed to tell you, gentlemen, that I went down on my knees and prayed Almighty God for light and guidance. And one night late it came to me this way—I don't know how it was, but it came: (1) That we could not give them back to Spain—that would be cowardly and dishonorable; (2) that we could not turn them over to France or Germany—that would be bad business and discreditable; (3) that we could not leave them to govern themselves—they were unfit for self-government . . . and (4) that there was nothing left for us to do but to take them all, and to educate the Philippinos, and uplift and civilize and Christianize them, and, by God's grace, do the very best we could by them, as our fellow men for whom Christ also died. And then I went to bed, and went to sleep, and slept soundly, and next morning I sent for the chief engineer of the War Department (our map-maker), and told him to put the Philippines on the map of the United States.

William McKinley, quoted in G. A. Malcolm and M. M. Kalaw, *Philippine Government* (Manila: Associated Publishers, 1923), pp. 65–66.

American forces landing at a Cuban port in 1898, during the Spanish-American War.

fully in the industrial expansion that took place in Europe, and by 1914 America led the world in the production of coal, iron, and petroleum.

In trying to cope with the social and economic problems resulting from rapid industrialization, the activities of both the labor unions and the government, in America as in Europe, brought a marked improvement of the worker's status. The efforts of Theodore Roosevelt, after the turn of the century, to secure a "square deal" for the workingman, and his attempts at "trust busting," helped to bridge the gap between capital and labor. Despite the opposition of many Americans to governmental intervention in economic affairs, the United States showed the same tendency toward becoming a "welfare state" that prevailed in most European countries. In the one field in which American business had welcomed government interference—tariff legislation—the trend by 1914 was in the direction of lower tariffs. This was seen by some as a sign that American industry had come of age and was ready to compete with foreign imports on the home market.

The Spanish-American War

America at the end of the nineteenth century thus shared most of the major trends of Europe. This was nowhere more evident than in foreign affairs. Agitation during the 1890s to annex Hawaii and to construct a canal across Central America ran parallel to European expansionism during the same period. Under the administration of Grover Cleveland, such expansionist sentiments were kept under control. His successor, William McKinley, however, was less able to resist the pressures of American nationalism. One of the main subjects of agitation at the time was Cuba, where a revolt against Spanish rule had started in 1895. American sentiment sided with the Cuban rebels and demanded that the United States go to their aid. When the U.S.S. "Maine" mysteriously exploded in Havana harbor in early 1898, the clamor for war became too strong to be resisted any longer.

The Spanish-American War was the first war between the United States and a European power since 1814. The United States had little difficulty in winning the "splendid little war" against Spain. In the peace treaty signed at Paris

Soldier of the Spanish-American War. From a stereo, "A Letter from Home."

in December 1898, the United States obtained Puerto Rico, the Philippines, and Guam. Cuba received its independence, though the Platt Amendment, adopted by Congress in 1901, made it a virtual American protectorate.

America made its influence felt in the Far East and elsewhere in other ways as well. In 1898 the United States finally annexed Hawaii and in the following year divided the Samoan Islands with Germany. Also in 1899, Secretary of State John Hay proclaimed the "open door" policy, which called for equal opportunity in China for all powers, and in 1900 an American contingent participated in a joint expedition of the powers to put down the Boxer Rebellion in China (see p. 639). The United States also sent delegates to the First Hague Peace Conference in 1899, at which a Permanent Court of International Arbitration was created; and in 1905 President Roosevelt helped settle the Russo-Japanese War in the Treaty of Portsmouth.

The United States and Latin America

America's first and foremost concern, however, was with affairs closer to home.

Theodore Roosevelt in particular had long favored an active American policy in Central America. The Hay-Pauncefote Treaty of 1901 secured British consent for the construction of an American canal across the isthmus. In 1903 Panama, in a revolt sponsored by American interests, seceded from Colombia, and the United States was able to acquire the necessary land for its canal. The Panama Canal was opened shortly after the outbreak of war in 1914.

One of the chief dangers to peace in Latin America came from the loans that European investors in search of large profits had granted to the dictators of that region. Failures to meet payments invariably led to foreign intervention and threatened violations of the Monroe Doctrine. In 1902, Germany, Italy, and Great Britain sent warships to force Venezuela to pay its debts. Two years later another group of powers moved against the Dominican Republic. As a warning, and to forestall European intervention, President Roosevelt, in 1904, proclaimed a Corollary to the Monroe Doctrine. It gave the United States the exclusive right to exercise international police power in the Western Hemisphere. In line with its new policy, America sent marines to Cuba in 1906 and to Nicaragua in 1912.

The motive for America's intervention on these occasions was not merely to maintain order but also to protect its own financial interests. This "dollar diplomacy," as its opponents called it, caused much resentment in the countries concerned and among the other great powers. America's policy, its Latin American neighbors charged, despite idealistic pronouncements, was every bit as imperialistic as that of the European powers.

THE FORMATION OF THE TRIPLE ENTENTE 1890–1907

The events outside Europe discussed in the preceding pages provide the background for the diplomatic realignment of Europe after 1890 and the succession of international crises that culminated in the First World War.

Cartoon of Theodore Roosevelt "walking softly and carrying a big stick" as he tows American ships through the Caribbean.

The Franco-Russian Alliance

When Bismarck was dismissed in 1890, his complicated diplomatic system did not long survive. To start with, William II followed the advice of some of Bismarck's more timid underlings and refused to renew the Reinsurance Treaty with Russia. The cutting of Bismarck's "wire to St. Petersburg" did not by itself make the subsequent *rapprochement* between Russia and France inevitable. Only when Germany continued to show deliberate coolness toward its former friend while drawing closer to England did Russia begin to listen to French suggestions for a better understanding. The Anglo-German Heligoland Treaty of 1890, by which Germany surrendered large claims in East Africa to England in return for the small strategic island of Heligoland in the North Sea, was generally interpreted as a sign of German eagerness to oblige England. At the same time, a tariff war was impairing Russo-German commercial relations, and an increase in Germany's armed forces was seen as preparation for a possible war on two fronts. Germany's policy toward Russia, it seemed, was undergoing a complete reorientation.

Even so, Russia was slow to respond to France's overtures. The main obstacle was the differences between their autocratic and republican systems of government. It took four years of deliberations before a final agreement was reached. On January 4, 1894, France and Russia signed a secret military convention that amounted to an alliance. It was designed as a counterpart to the Triple Alliance between Germany, Austria, and Italy. Like the latter, the Franco-Russian alliance was defensive. It protected France against an attack by Germany, or by Italy supported by Germany; and it protected Russia against an attack by Germany, or by Austria supported by Germany.

By the middle of the 1890s, therefore, two sets of European alliances existed. This did not mean, however, that the Continent had been split in two. There were many subsequent occasions when Russia cooperated with Germany and Austria, or when Germany cooperated with Russia and France. International rivalries for the next decade shifted almost entirely to regions outside Europe. Both French and Russian interests in many parts of the world conflicted with those of Great Britain; and Germany, unable to tie England as closely to its side as it wished, now frequently joined the two in opposing British aims. Faced by the discomforting possibility of a continental alliance against it, Britain, rather than Germany, had cause to be alarmed by the new alignment of powers.

Britain's Colonial Rivalries

The regions over which Britain came into conflict with one or several of the continental powers during the 1890s were chiefly the Near and Far East, the Sudan, and South Africa. In the Near East the source of trouble, as usual, was the disintegrating Ottoman Empire. Beginning in 1894 a series of Armenian uprisings against Turkish repression were put down with the massacre of thousands of Armenians. England tried repeatedly to intervene, and Lord Salisbury on two occasions suggested plans for partitioning the Ottoman Empire. But rival interests among the powers and suspicion of British motives prevented what might well have been a final solution of the troubles of the Near East. The situation was further complicated in 1897 by an insurrection against Turkey on the island of Crete in favor of union with Greece. In the resulting war between Greece and Turkey, the British supported the Greeks, but the rest of the powers prevented any aid from reaching Greece. The Turks were victorious, although the powers succeeded in obtaining autonomy for Crete.

While Britain thus found itself at cross-purposes with the rest of Europe in the Near East, Germany took advantage of the various crises in that region to advance its own economic interests. The main instrument of its push to the southeast was to be a Berlin-to-Baghdad railway, for which the sultan granted a concession in 1899. In 1898, Emperor William, on a visit to Damascus, proclaimed himself the friend of the world's

In this German cartoon, Queen Victoria is flattened by the Boer leader, Paul Krueger, as the South African imperialist Cecil Rhodes looks on with dismay.

300 million Moslems. Germany appeared well on the way toward replacing England as the protector of Turkey.

In the Far East the first serious differences between England and the three continental powers came as a result of the Sino-Japanese War in 1895 (see p. 639). When Russia, Germany, and France asked British participation in forcing Japan to give up most of the territory it had taken from China, Britain refused. In the subsequent scramble for concessions from China, France, Germany, and especially Russia gained at the expense of England's hitherto unchallenged dominance there.

All the time that Britain was losing ground in the Near and Far East, its situation in Africa was even more serious. First there was the trouble with Germany over the kaiser's "Krüger telegram" (see p. 682); then came the showdown with France over the Sudan; and finally, in 1899 the Boer War broke out. During that war Britain was without a single friend, and it is surprising that Russian proposals for a continental coalition in favor of the Boers did not materialize. The plan failed because of Germany's insistence that the three powers first guarantee each other's own territories in Europe. This would have meant French renunciation of Alsace-Lorraine.

In view of England's many predicaments, it is understandable that it should look for some way out of its no longer splendid isolation. The obvious choice for a possible ally, considering Britain's many points of friction with France and Russia, was Germany. So in 1898 England began to sound out Germany on a closer understanding.

Britain Abandons Isolation

The Anglo-German negotiations failed. And the main reason for the failure was the reluctance of the Germans to abandon what they considered an unusually favorable position between the Franco-Russian and British camps. Overestimating Britain's eagerness to come to an understanding and underestimating Britain's ability to find friends elsewhere, Germany's foreign secretary Bernhard von Bülow, and his chief adviser, Baron

Holstein, made demands on England that it was unwilling to meet. Britain was primarily interested in enlisting German support against further Russian encroachment in the Far East. Germany, on the other hand, was chiefly worried about a war between Russia and Austria in which Germany might become involved and for which it wanted British aid. Britain, however, refused to extend its commitments to eastern Europe, where, as a naval power, it could not be of much use.

When Anglo-German negotiations finally broke down in 1901, England turned elsewhere. In 1902 it concluded an alliance with Japan. This did nothing to end England's isolation in Europe, but it fulfilled a main purpose—to stop Russia's advance in the Far East. Two years later Japan took advantage of this situation and in the Russo-Japanese War destroyed Russian sea power in the Pacific (see p. 642). In this way Japan emerged as the dominant power in the Far East.

Before the showdown between Russia and Japan, England had already taken a step in Europe to escape its isolation—*rapprochement* with France. England had long been irked by its dependence on Germany, which the latter used on every possible occasion to wring concessions from the British. By settling its long-standing differences with France, Britain not only hoped to find support against Germany but also to allay once and for all its fear of a continental alliance against it. France also felt a need for new friends. Its alliance with Russia had proved disappointing, especially during the Fashoda crisis, when the Russians had refused to back up their ally (see p. 681). After Fashoda, France had turned its attention once more to the Continent. The aim of its nationalistic foreign minister, Théophile Delcassé, was to strengthen France's position by improving its relations with powers other than Germany. He had taken a first step in this direction in 1902 by concluding a secret agreement with Italy. In return for French support of Italian ambitions in North Africa, the Italians promised to support French aims in Morocco, and to remain neutral in case France became involved in a defensive war, even if

France "as the result of a direct provocation" should find it necessary to declare such a war itself.

A far greater achievement of Delcassé, however, was the Entente Cordiale between France and England. The Anglo-French agreement of 1904 settled the main colonial differences that had disturbed relations between the two countries, especially in Africa. Most important was France's recognition of British interests in Egypt and Britain's recognition of French interests in Morocco. The agreement was merely a "friendly understanding." It was not an alliance, and it need never have assumed the character of one had it not been for the careless actions of Germany.

The First Moroccan Crisis

Germany, which was understandably alarmed by the agreement between France and Britain, decided to test the strength of the Entente. In March 1905 William II, on a visit to Tangier in Spanish Morocco, proclaimed Germany's continued support of Moroccan independence and served notice that Germany, too, had an interest in Morocco. The ensuing crisis forced the resignation of Delcassé, and Germany seemed ready to go to war. Franco-German differences were finally brought before an international conference at Algeciras (1906). Here the independence of Morocco was reaffirmed; but in settling specific questions of Moroccan internal administration, the majority of the powers supported the French. Only Austria-Hungary stood by its German ally. Germany's attempt to split the Anglo-French Entente had backfired.

Actually, the first Moroccan crisis brought the French and British still closer together by inaugurating conversations between French and British military and naval authorities concerning possible cooperation in case of war. These conversations continued intermittently until 1914. Beginning in 1912, furthermore, the British navy concentrated its forces in the North Sea, permitting the French to shift their own warships to the Mediterranean. England thus assumed at least a moral obligation for protecting France's northern coast in case of war. The Entente Cordiale, in spirit if not in fact, had been transformed into a virtual alliance.

The Triple Entente

England's close affiliation with France quite naturally raised the question of its relations with France's ally Russia. As a result of Russia's war with Japan, the threat of Russian predominance in China had been removed and there was now no reason why England should not try to settle its colonial differences with Russia as it had with France. This was done in the Anglo-Russian Entente of 1907, which settled the long-standing rivalries of the two powers in Afghanistan, Persia, and Tibet.

The formation of the Triple Entente, as the agreements of 1904 and 1907 together are called, amounted to a diplomatic revolution. A situation that only a few years earlier Germany had considered impossible had now come to pass: England had settled its differences with France and Russia, and the Triple Alliance had found its match in the Triple Entente. The latter was no more aggressive in its initial intent than the Triple Alliance had originally been. But as areas for compromise outside Europe became fewer with the annexation of the remaining colonial spoils, the scene of international rivalries once more shifted to Europe and especially to the Balkans. In the past, Russia's ambitions in this area had been held in check by the rest of the powers. Now it could count on French and British support against Germany and Austria. Germany, on the other hand, left with only Austria as a reliable friend, could no longer restrain Austria's Balkan policy as it had in the past. Any change in the *status quo* of the Balkans, therefore, was sure to lead to a major crisis.

THE MOUNTING CRISIS 1908–13

This brings us to the last fateful years before 1914, when growing international tension, at least in retrospect, appears as a fitting prelude to an inevitable showdown.

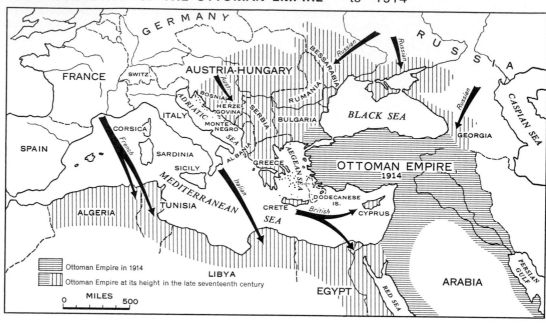

Revolution in Turkey and the Bosnian Crisis

The Balkans became the scene of international complications in 1908 when a revolution broke out in the Ottoman Empire. Turkey's ruler since 1876, Abdul-Hamid II, had never lived up to his repeated promises of reform. Opposition to the sultan's corrupt and decadent regime centered in a group of liberal patriots, the "Young Turks." Their aim was to reform Turkey along the lines of a liberal constitution that had been granted in 1876 but had been completely disregarded afterward. The revolutionaries had a large following among the Turkish army, and the government's resistance to the uprising in 1908 soon collapsed. The Young Turks, however, though liberal in some respects, were extremely nationalistic in their dealings with Turkey's many national and religious minorities. Persecution of Greek Orthodox Christians and efforts to assimilate Turkey's subject peoples soon led to further disruption of the empire: Bulgaria proclaimed its independence in 1908; Crete completed its union with Greece in 1912; and Albania, after a series of bloody uprisings, finally gained its independence from the Ottoman Empire in 1913.

The most important event connected with the Turkish revolution, in its effects upon relations among the great powers, was Austria's annexation of Bosnia and Herzegovina in 1908. There had been no serious tension between Austria and Russia over the Balkans for some twenty years. But this peaceful situation changed after 1905, as Russia once again turned its attention from the Far to the Near East. Russia's foreign minister, Alexander Izvolsky, was an unusually ambitious man, and he found a kindred spirit in his Austrian colleague, Count Aehrenthal. Russia had long hoped to lift the closure of the Turkish Straits to Russian warships; Austria, for its part, had been looking forward to annexing Bosnia and Herzegovina, which it had been administering since 1878. Encouraged by the Turkish revolution, Izvolsky and Aehrenthal met at the latter's castle of Buchlau in September 1908 and there pledged mutual support for their respective aims.

The Bosnian crisis was precipitated when shortly after the Buchlau Agreement Austria went ahead and proclaimed the annexation of Bosnia and Herzegovina without waiting for Russia to act in the Straits. Russia, thereupon, backed by France and England, demanded that Austria's action be brought before an international conference. Germany, on

Abdul-Hamid II, known as "Abdul the Damned" for his cunning and cruelty, was chiefly responsible for the continued backwardness and corruption of the Ottoman Empire during his long rule from 1876 to 1909.

the other hand, supported Austria in opposing a conference unless the annexation of Bosnia-Herzegovina was recognized beforehand. The situation was made more serious because Serbia also had hoped one day to take Bosnia-Herzegovina. Encouraged by Pan-Slav propaganda emanating from Russia, Serbia now demanded compensation from Austria. Since Russia, however, was in no position to fight a war at this time, it had to bring pressure on Serbia to recognize the *fait accompli* in Bosnia and Herzegovina. This the Serbs did under protest.

The Bosnian crisis left a legacy of tension that lasted until the First World War. Both Russia and Serbia had been humiliated. To prevent the recurrence of such a defeat, Russia now began to prepare in earnest for the showdown that seemed inevitable, while Serbia stepped up its agitation among Austria's southern Slavs. Austria had been the real culprit in the affair. But even it would have had to back down if it had not had the support of Germany. The fact that such support had been given only reluctantly was not known to the rest of the world. Italy, finally, was hurt not to have been consulted by Austria about the annexation of Bosnia and Herzegovina and not to have received compensations, both of which it felt entitled to under the Triple Alliance. In October 1909 Italy entered into a secret understanding with Russia, the Racconigi Agreement, in which it promised to support Russia's interests in the Straits while Russia agreed to back Italy's designs in Tripoli. Italy thus had taken another step away from the Triple Alliance.

The Second Moroccan Crisis

Europe had barely recovered from the Bosnian affair when another crisis arose, this time in North Africa. Despite the Act of Algeciras of 1906, friction in Morocco between French and German interests had continued. When native disturbances in Morocco in 1911 led to the intervention of French troops, Germany protested against what it considered a violation of Moroccan independence. To make up for France's increased influence in Morocco, Germany now claimed compensations elsewhere. And to give weight to its demands, it sent a German gunboat, the "Panther," to the Moroccan port of Agadir, ostensibly to protect German lives and interests. For the most part it was British intervention that finally forced Germany to modify its claims and settle the crisis. But meanwhile Europe had once again been brought to the brink of war.

Anglo-German Naval Rivalry

England, throughout the crisis, suspected that Germany's real aim was to secure a naval base in Morocco, which would have posed a threat to Britain's base at Gibraltar. Anglo-German naval rivalry had by now become a matter of deep concern to the British. Naval expansion was closely related to imperialism. A powerful fleet was considered necessary to protect overseas possessions, and overseas possessions in turn were needed as naval bases and coaling stations. As a precaution against the naval increases of the rest of the world, England in 1889 had adopted a "two-power standard," which called for a British fleet 10 percent stronger than the combined naval forces of the two next-strongest powers.

The most serious challenge to Britain's naval power came from Germany. Beginning in 1898, Germany entered upon a course of naval expansion that, by 1914, had made it the second-strongest naval power in the world. Germany's secretary of the navy, Admiral Alfred von Tirpitz, knew that he could not possibly expect to catch up with the British. What he tried to do was to build a navy strong enough that no other country would dare risk getting into a fight with Germany. The German navy was built not so much for a possible showdown with England as for reasons of prestige.

It was difficult for England to see matters in quite the same light. The British felt that Germany, primarily a land power, did not really need a navy, especially since it already had a powerful army. If the Germans went to the great expense of building a navy, this could only mean that they expected some day to challenge Britain's naval supremacy.

Turkish infantry during the Balkan War, 1912.

great powers, its war with Turkey in 1911–12 did not by itself cause any major crisis. As we have seen, it brought Italy its long-coveted North African colony. The Tripolitanian War, however, encouraged several small Balkan states to move against Turkey and thus to reopen the Balkan question.

The chief motive behind the First Balkan War (1912) was the desire of Bulgaria, Serbia, and Greece to gain further concessions at the expense of Turkey. Together with Montenegro, these countries had formed a Balkan League in early 1912. Taking advantage of the war over Tripoli, they invaded the Ottoman Empire in October of that year. Turkey was decisively defeated, and under the Treaty of London (May 1913) it lost all its European possessions except the region adjacent to the Straits.

The peace was less than a month old when a Second Balkan War broke out, this time among the victors over the distribution of the spoils. Under arrangements made before the first war, Serbia was to receive an outlet to the Adriatic in Albania. This met with Austrian and Italian protests, however. As compensation for its loss, Serbia now demanded some of the territory that Bulgaria had received in Macedonia; and when the Bulgarians refused, war ensued between Bulgaria on the one hand and Serbia, Greece, Montenegro, Rumania, and Turkey on the other. Against such an overwhelming coalition, the Bulgarians proved powerless. In the Treaty of Bucharest (August 1913), Bulgaria kept only a small part of Macedonia, the Greeks and Serbs taking the rest.

The Balkan Wars caused deep anxiety among the great powers. A Conference of Ambassadors was convened in London to deal with the Balkan problem, notably the controversy between Austria and Serbia over the latter's aspirations in Albania. As in the past, Russia backed Serbia. Germany, on the other hand, served as a brake on Austria's desire to intervene against Serbia. Since England and Italy also favored the independence of Albania, Russia finally withdrew its support from Serbia and peace was preserved. In the course of events, however, Austria and Russia, together with their

Again and again, notably in 1908 and 1912, Great Britain urged Germany to slow down its naval construction, offering in return to support German colonial aspirations. But William II and Tirpitz saw these efforts merely as a confirmation of their "risk theory" and looked forward to the day when England would be forced to seek an agreement on Germany's terms. More than any other issue, this naval race was responsible for the growing tension between Germany and England during the last decade before the war.

The Balkan Wars

The Moroccan crisis of 1911—besides further strengthening the Anglo-French Entente—also helped to start a series of small wars aimed at the further disruption of the Ottoman Empire. The first of these broke out in the fall of 1911 when Italy, encouraged by France's success in Morocco, decided to embark on the annexation of Tripoli. Since Italy had carefully secured the prior consent of all the

allies, had again come close to war. Serbia had suffered another defeat, for which it blamed Austria and for which even its gains in Macedonia could not be consolation enough. Serbia's outraged nationalism sought revenge a year later in the assassination of the Austrian Archduke Francis Ferdinand at Sarajevo.

THE OUTBREAK
OF THE GREAT WAR

In discussing the origins of the First World War, historians distinguish between underlying and immediate causes. In the first category belong all those factors that contributed to the acute state of international tension before 1914: nationalism, territorial disputes, economic competition, and imperialist rivalries. Some of the tension has also been blamed on the secret diplomacy of the powers, which led to secret alliances that involved nations in conflicts not of their making. But it has also been held that there was not enough secret diplomacy, that a "summit" meeting of Europe's

leading statesmen in the summer of 1914, away from the clamor of their nationalistic press, might have resolved the differences that instead led to war. There had been many instances in the past when such joint action on the part of the Concert of Europe had proved effective. By 1914, however, the feeling of European solidarity that had animated the great powers in the days of Metternich and even Bismarck had everywhere given way to the powerful and divisive force of nationalism. The absence of any effective international agency to preserve peace, more than anything else, caused the catastrophe of 1914.

The story of why and how the war came about has been told many times and in great detail. But to this day information is missing on some important points, and there are still wide differences among historians in the evaluation of the available evidence. It is quite possible that a different action by one or another of the statesmen in the summer of 1914 might have once more prevented a general war. Yet it seems unlikely that such a war could have been postponed

Archduke Francis Ferdinand of Austria and his wife at Sarajevo on June 28, 1914, about to enter the automobile that carried them to their deaths.

The arrest of the assassin.

much longer. If ever there was a time that seemed ripe for war, it was the summer of 1914.

Sarajevo

As we turn from the underlying to the immediate causes of the war, the most important was the assassination of Austrian Archduke Francis Ferdinand at the Bosnian town of Sarajevo, on June 28, 1914.

The assassination of the archduke and his wife was carried out by an Austro-Bosnian citizen of Serb nationality, Gavrilo Princip. The crime had been planned and its execution aided by a secret society of Serb nationalists, the "Black Hand." The archduke had been chosen as victim because he was known to favor reconciling the southern Slav element in the Dual Monarchy, a policy that interfered with the aspirations of Serb nationalism, which hoped for the ultimate union of all southern Slavs under Serbian rule. There is no evidence that the Serbian government had any hand in the plot itself; but Serbia's prime minister, Nicholas Pashitch, had general knowledge of it. Austria, taking for granted that the Serbian government was involved, decided once and for all to settle accounts with Serbia. This it hoped to do in a localized war. But Austria's foreign minister, Count Berchtold, did not seem averse to a larger war if it was necessary to achieve Austria's aim.

European reaction to the assassination at first was one of deep shock and genuine sympathy for Austria. In indignation over the horrible crime, Germany gave Austria that fateful promise to "stand behind it as an ally and friend" in anything the Austrian government should decide to do. As it became clear, however, that Austria intended to use the Sarajevo incident to punish Serbia, the powers became alarmed. Russia warned the Austrians that it "would not be indifferent to any effort to humiliate Serbia." At the same time, France's President Raymond Poincaré assured the Russians of French support in any action they took on behalf of Serbia. By the middle of July, it was clear that Austria, backed by Germany, was ready to move against Serbia, and that Russia, backed by France, was equally ready to protect Serbia.

The Eve of War

The situation thus far was serious, but it was not as yet critical. It became so when Austria, on July 23, presented a stiff ultimatum to Serbia. The latter's reply, while not wholly complying, nevertheless was favorable enough to justify further negotiations. Instead, Austria broke off diplomatic relations and on July 28 declared war on Serbia. Germany had little choice but to live up to its earlier "blank check" and to support Austria. By doing so, the Germans hoped to discourage Russia from helping Serbia and thus to localize the Austro-Serbian conflict. But the Germans were also ready to stand by Austria if the conflict should develop into a general war.

June 28, 1914

My last visit to Germany was in June-July 1914. The Actons were staying at Badenweiler in the Black Forest, and asked me to spend a week with them. On the Sunday afternoon of 28 June we were sitting at tea on the long terrace of the hotel. The place was crowded. Badenweiler has a reputation for radio-active baths; the clientèle was therefore mainly of the cosmopolitan rich. . . . While we were talking I noticed that the head waiter was going round telling people here and there some startling news. The news was that the Archduke Franz Ferdinand had been assassinated at Sarajevo. I did not know who the archduke was, or whether Sarajevo was in Bosnia or in Serbia, . . . but I could see at once that this assassination had an importance far beyond that of an ordinary anarchist plot. I could see this because the other people on the terrace became very excited. They showed their excitement by forming little groups which seemed to sort themselves out according to nationality. I remember listening to a group of Russians; listening, not eavesdropping, because I could not understand a word of what they were saying.

I knew that something very grave had happened, and I was not in the least surprised when Acton began a sentence: "If there is a European war . . ." After about an hour this strange wave of emotion ebbed away. I spent the rest of the time before dinner in the open-air swimming bath. I still felt a little uneasy and bewildered, but I was not really nervous about the prospect of general war. At dinner a rather tiresome orchestra played as usual; no one seemed to be worrying.

From E. L. Woodward, *Short Journey* (New York: Oxford University Press, 1946), pp. 67–68.

The decision whether the war was to be a local or a general one rested primarily with Russia. Germany's action throughout the crisis had given the impression, not unjustifiably, that far from trying to discourage Austria, the German government was actually urging it on into the showdown with Serbia. Since an Austrian victory over Serbia would be tantamount to a Russian defeat, Russian military authorities now began calling for mobilization. The question was: should such mobilization be partial, against Austria-Hungary only, or should it be general, against Germany as well? Plans for a partial mobilization had been abandoned some time ago and in any case would have entailed considerable disadvantages in case general mobilization should become necessary later on. But a general mobilization, it was understood, would make a European war inevitable. The internal debate over this issue went on for several days. Only when the tsar finally became convinced, on July 30, that efforts to restrain Austria were futile, was the decision to go ahead with a general mobilization mode.

The Outbreak of War

Germany's chief of staff, General Helmuth von Moltke, nephew of the great Moltke of Bismarckian times, was worried by reports from Russia. He therefore urged Austria, behind his government's back, to mobilize against Russia, promising unconditional German support. Austria ordered general mobilization on July 31, thus killing any chance for last-minute peace efforts. The same day Germany sent Russia an ultimatum demanding that the latter cease its preparations for war. When the tsar's government replied that this was impossible, Germany, on August 1, mobilized its own forces and a few hours later declared war on Russia. France, meanwhile, had also begun military preparations. To a German inquiry about its attitude in a Russo-German war, France replied that it would "act in accordance with its interests." On August 3, Germany declared war on France.

The reason for Germany's haste in declaring war lay in the plans that its general staff had worked out for a war

on two fronts. The basic idea of the "Schlieffen Plan"—named after its originator, Count Schlieffen, who had been chief of the general staff from 1891 to 1906—was for Germany's main forces to turn west, deliver an annihilating blow against France, and then turn east against the slowly mobilizing Russians. To succeed with its plan, Germany not only needed to mobilize as quickly as possible, but it also had to invade France at its most vulnerable spot, the northeastern frontier between France and Belgium. The Schlieffen Plan, in other words, called for German violation of Belgian neutrality, which, together with the rest of Europe, the Germans had guaranteed in 1830.

Germany's invasion of Belgium on August 3 brought England into the war the next day. Great Britain has subsequently been reproached for not making its position in the crisis clear enough from the start, the argument being that if it had come off the fence earlier it would have deterred the Austrians from going to war against Serbia. Through the Entente Cordiale, especially its secret military and naval understandings, England was deeply committed to France. On the other hand, there had been a marked improvement in Anglo-German relations in the early months of 1914; and England's Entente with Russia had never been very popular. For reasons of its own security, Britain could not possibly afford to stand idly by while Germany won victories over France and Russia that would make it the dominant power on the Continent. But to get the British public to approve involvement in the war, some event was needed to dramatize the German danger. Such an event was Germany's violation of Belgian neutrality. Almost overnight it helped to convert Britain's indecisive neutrality into determined belligerency.

"War Guilt"

A word remains to be said about the question of "war guilt," a subject of controversy to the present day. Most historians agree that Germany, Austria, and Russia bear a major share of the responsibility. England clearly belongs at the other extreme, its errors being chiefly of

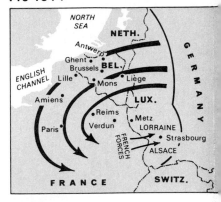

THE UNEXECUTED SCHLIEFFEN PLAN, Pre-1914

The Unexecuted Schlieffen Plan.

omission; and France stands somewhere in between. This much is certain: no one power alone was responsible for the war and none of the great powers was entirely free from responsibility. Many Europeans actually welcomed the war as a relief from the almost unbearable tension that had preceded it. Yet most of the leading statesmen, when faced with the certainty of war, were overcome by fear and desperation. It was as though they had a foreboding that the war they had failed to avert would be far more terrible than they could imagine, and that the world they had known would never be the same again.

Suggestions for Further Reading

Note: Asterisk denotes a book available in paperback edition.

General

Among the major studies on the diplomatic background of the First World War, L. Albertini, *The Origins of the War of 1914*, 3 vols. (1952–57), is generally considered the best. A. J. P. Taylor, *The Struggle for Mastery in Europe, 1848–1918** (1954), is shorter and less objective. J. Remak, *The Origins of World War I, 1871–1914** (1967), is the briefest and most readable account. L. Lafore, *The Long Fuse** (1965), emphasizes the disintegration of Austria-Hungary as a cause of war. Recent monographs on the foreign policy of individual powers are F. R. Bridge, *Great Britain and Austria-Hungary, 1906–1914* (1972); M. Foot, *British Foreign Policy since 1898* (1956); J. A. S. Grenville, *Lord Salisbury and Foreign Policy: The Close of the Nineteenth Century* (1964); and C. Howard, *Splendid Isolation* (1967).

The Age of Bismarck

The leading book in English is still W. L. Langer, *European Alliances and Alignments*, 2nd ed. (1950). The Near Eastern crisis of the seventies is discussed in B. H. Sumner, *Russia and the Balkans, 1870–1880* (1937), and its outcome in W. N. Medlicott, *The Congress of Berlin and After* (1938). For the formation of Bismarck's system of alliances, see A. C. Coolidge, *The Origins of the Triple Alliance* (1926). P. B. Mitchell, *The Bismarckian Policy of Conciliation with France* (1935), rounds out the picture in the West. Germany's first colonial ventures are described in M. E. Townsend, *The Origins of Modern German Colonization, 1871–1885* (1921), and in A. J. P. Taylor, *Germany's First Bid for Colonies** (1938). The closing years of Bismarck's career are studied critically in J. V. Fuller, *Bismarck's Diplomacy at Its Zenith* (1922). The chancellor's dismissal is dealt with in K. F. Nowak, *Kaiser and Chancellor* (1930). G. A. Craig, *From Bismarck to Adenauer: Aspects of German Statecraft** (1958), offers a sympathetic appraisal of Bismarck the diplomat.

Imperialism in Africa and Asia

Some of the works cited in the suggested reading list in Chapter 27 are also relevant here. The authoritative work on the imperialist rivalries of the great powers is W. L. Langer, *The Diplomacy of Imperialism, 1890–1902*, 2 vols., 2nd ed. (1951). The colonization of Africa is covered in R. Robinson and J. Gallagher, *Africa and the Victorians** (1961); E. A. Walker, *A History of Southern Africa* (1957); R. L. Tignor, *Modernization and British Colonial Rule in Egypt, 1882–1914* (1966); P. Gifford and W. R. Louis, eds., *Britain and Germany in Africa* (1967); and H. R. Rudin, *Germans in the Cameroons, 1884–1914* (1938). See also N. Ascherson, *The King Incorporated: Leopold II of the Belgians* (1963), and J. Duffy, *Portuguese Africa* (1959). On the Far East, G. P. Hudson, *The Far East in World Politics* (1939), is the best brief book. See also J. T. Pratt, *The Expansion of Europe in the Far East* (1947); P. Joseph, *Foreign Diplomacy in China, 1894–1900* (1928); and B. H. Sumner, *Tsardom and Imperialism in the Far East and Middle East* (1942). For the economic penetration of the Middle East, see S. N. Fisher, *The Middle East* (1959), and J. B. Wolf, *The Diplomatic History of the Baghdad Railway* (1936). Financial imperialism is treated in H. Feis, *Europe, the World's Banker, 1870–1914** (1930), and in E. Staley, *War and the Private Investor* (1935). Good recent general treatments of the colonial policy of some of the great powers include M. Beloff, *Imperial Sunset: Britain's Liberal Empire, 1897–1921* (1969); H. Brunschwig, *Myths and Realities of French Colonialism, 1871–1914* (1966); and R. F. Betts, *Europe Overseas: Phases of Imperialism* (1968). The following monographs are based on fresh archival sources: A. White, *The Diplomacy of the Russo-Japanese*

War (1964); G. N. Sanderson, *England, Europe and the Upper Nile, 1882–1899* (1965); R. G. Brown, *Fashoda Reconsidered* (1970); and I. H. Nish, *The Anglo-Japanese Alliance: The Diplomacy of Two Island Empires, 1894–1907* (1966).

The United States as a World Power

America's share in the scramble for overseas possessions is treated in A. K. Weinberg, *Manifest Destiny* (1935); J. W. Pratt, *America's Colonial Experiment* (1950); and H. K. Beale, *Theodore Roosevelt and the Rise of America to World Power** (1956). The best books on the Spanish-American War are J. W. Pratt, *Expansionists of 1898** (1936); F. B. Freidel, *Splendid Little War** (1958); and H. W. Morgan, *America's Road to Empire: The War with Spain and Overseas Expansion** (1965). Other phases of American foreign policy are dealt with in E. H. Zabriskie, *American-Russian Rivalry in the Far East* (1946); H. Sprout and M. Sprout, *The Rise of American Naval Power, 1776–1918* (1939); and R. H. Heindel, *The American Impact on Great Britain, 1898–1914* (1940). For a seasoned diplomat's analysis of America's involvement in world affairs since 1898, see G. F. Kennan, *American Diplomacy, 1900–1950** (1951).

The Formation of the Triple Entente

W. L. Langer, *The Franco-Russian Alliance, 1890–1894* (1929), is another authoritative study by this distinguished diplomatic historian. On the formation of the Entente, see J. J. Mathews, *Egypt and the Formation of the Anglo-French Entente of 1904* (1939); P. J. V. Rolo, *The Entente Cordiale* (1969); G. Monger, *The End of Isolation: British Foreign Policy, 1900–1907* (1963); C. Andrew, *Théophile Delcassé and the Making of the Entente Cordiale* (1969); and R. P. Churchill, *The Anglo-Russian Convention of 1907* (1939). Also still relevant is E. N. Anderson, *The First Moroccan Crisis* (1930). S. R. Williamson, *The Politics of Grand Strategy: Britain and France Prepare for War, 1904–1914* (1969), deals with the military conversations growing out of the Entente Cordiale. There is no satisfactory general work on Anglo-German relations during this period, but the following discuss various aspects of the problem: R. J. Sontag, *Germany and England: Background of Conflict, 1848–1894** (1938); R. J. S. Hoffman, *Great Britain and the German Trade Rivalry, 1875–1914* (1933); and P. R. Anderson, *The Background of Anti-English Feeling in Germany, 1890–1902* (1939). The influence of sea power on diplomacy is treated in E. L. Woodward, *Great Britain and the German Navy* (1935); A. J. Marder, *The Anatomy of British Sea Power* (1940); and by the same author, *From the Dreadnought to Scapa Flow: The Royal Navy in the Fisher Era, 1904–1919,* 3 vols. (1961–66). See also P. G. Halpern, *The Mediterranean Naval Situation, 1908–1914* (1971). A good deal of diplomatic history can be found in N. Rich, *Friedrich von Holstein: Politics and Diplomacy in the Era of Bismarck and William II,* 2 vols. (1965).

The Mounting Crisis

The events of the last decade before the war are summarized in G. L. Dickinson, *The International Anarchy, 1904–1914* (1926). On individual phases of the mounting crisis, see B. E. Schmitt, *The Annexation of Bosnia* (1937); I. Barlow, *The Agadir Crisis* (1940); W. C. Askew, *Europe and Italy's Acquisition of Libya, 1911–1912* (1942); E. C. Helmreich, *The Diplomacy of the Balkan Wars* (1938); and E. C. Thaden, *Russia and the Balkan Alliance of 1912* (1965). The influence of public opinion on foreign policy during the prewar era is explored in O. J. Hale, *Publicity and Diplomacy* (1940), and in E. M. Carroll, *Germany and the Great Powers, 1866–1914: A Study in Public Opinion and Foreign Policy* (1939), and *French Public Opinion and Foreign Affairs, 1870–1914* (1930).

The Outbreak of War

V. Dedijer, *The Road to Sarajevo* (1966), is the last word on this subject. The assassination of the Austrian archduke is dramatically told in J. Remak, *Sarajevo** (1959). Although the crisis thus set in motion has been more carefully studied than any comparable event in history, historians still do not agree on who was responsible for the war. S. B. Fay, *The Origins of the World War,** 2 vols. (1932), puts the major blame on Serbia and Russia. B. E. Schmitt, *The Coming of the War, 1914,* 2 vols. (1930), is more severe toward Germany and Austria. The German case is presented in E. Brandenburg, *From Bismarck to the World War: A History of German Foreign Policy, 1870–1914* (1927), and the French position is stated in P. Renouvin, *The Immediate Origins of the War* (1928). More recently, two German historians have placed the major blame on their own nation: F. Fischer, *Germany's Aims in the First World War** (1967); and I. Geiss, ed., *July 1914: The Outbreak of the First World War** (1968). Their works have touched off a major controversy among historians.

30 War, Revolution, and Peace, 1914–1929

The "Great War," as it was called at the time, only gradually turned into a "World War." It was not the first worldwide conflict, but it was the largest. Before the war ended in November 1918, 49 million men had been mobilized in the "Allied" camp, against 25 million among the "Central Powers." It was truly war on an unprecedented scale. Also, more than any previous conflict, this war involved everyone, not only soldiers. The concept of "total war" was born in the First World War. The war lasted much longer than anyone had thought a modern war could, and it brought far more sweeping changes than

anyone would have thought possible. Traditional empires collapsed and new nations arose from the wreckage. The "New World," hitherto of little significance in European affairs, suddenly emerged as decisive to an Allied victory. Europe, which in the past had always settled its own affairs, apparently was unable to do so any longer.

The Great War was part of a transitional phase in modern history, which is how it will be treated here. There was no clear-cut end to the war—certainly not the peace settlements of 1919–20. The problems that the statesmen at Paris wrestled with then continued to plague Europe and the world for at least a decade thereafter. The ways in which these problems were tackled were still very much reminiscent of the nineteenth century. It took a new series of crises, touched off by the Great Depression of

1929 and culminating in another World War, to complete the transition from nineteenth to twentieth century.

THE COMPARATIVE STRENGTH OF THE POWERS

Despite differences in numbers, the actual military strength of the Allies and the Central Powers at the start of the war was quite evenly balanced. The impressive size of the Allied armies was due chiefly to the ill-trained and poorly equipped Russian army. Germany's forces, on the other hand, were the best in the world. France and Britain matched the Germans in numbers, but the Germans excelled in the quality and quantity of their equipment. The Austrian army was inferior to that of Germany and was weakened by its large Slav contingent. But since the main showdown was expected in the West, this handicap did not seem serious.

The Central Powers had other advantages, aside from their superior strength on land. Command of the interior lines of communication enabled them to shift their forces rapidly from one theater of war to another. The Allies, on the other hand, were widely separated; Russia in particular, with the closing of the Baltic and Black Seas, was cut off from much-needed aid. German industry, furthermore, was more readily converted to war production than the industries of its opponents. The Central Powers had more than enough coal and iron, and territories seized on the western front increased their resources. In their supplies of foodstuffs, however, Austria and Germany fell seriously short of their needs.

Had the war been as brief as most wars of the nineteenth century, Germany and Austria might have won it. But as the fighting dragged on, Allied inherent superiority made itself felt. Their manpower was greater; their industrial potential was superior; and, thanks to Great Britain, the Allies enjoyed naval supremacy. By keeping the sea lanes open, the British navy assured the uninterrupted flow of men and material; and by clamping a tight blockade upon Central Europe, Britain aggravated Germany's and Austria's food problems.

Confident of a quick victory, the French rejoiced at the outbreak of the First World War. Later, as the war slipped into a stalemate, despair took over.

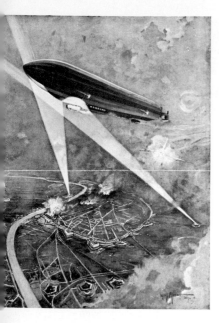

German Zeppelin attacking Antwerp in 1914. Painting by W. Moralt.

British soldiers "go over the top" to attack German lines.

Each side tried to strengthen its position further by seeking additional partners. Since the Allies usually had more to offer, they were more successful in this contest. At the end of the war, thirty "Allied and Associated Powers" were ranged against the Central Powers—Germany, Austria-Hungary, Turkey, and Bulgaria.

The most important additions to the Allied camp, aside from the United States, were Japan, Italy, Rumania, and Greece. Japan's entry into the war in August 1914 proved to be a most profitable move. Without delay the Japanese seized Germany's holdings in China's Shantung Province and occupied Germany's Pacific islands north of the equator. Italy did not join the war until 1915. It had refused to honor its obligations under the Triple Alliance, claiming that its terms did not apply. To balance possible Austrian gains in the Balkans, moreover, the Italians had demanded territorial concessions from Austria. The Austrians agreed to some of Italy's demands, but the Allies were able to offer more. By the secret Treaty of London in April 1915, England, France, and Russia promised Italy not only the Austrian re-gions inhabited by Italians but also considerable territory along the eastern Adriatic and in Asia Minor and Africa. Having received these promises, the Italians declared war against Austria-Hungary in May 1915, and against Germany in August 1916. At that time, Rumania also joined the Allies, and Greece followed in June 1917. In both these cases the pressure of military events and the hope for territorial gains were decisive.

The only two countries that joined the Central Powers were Turkey and Bulgaria. The Ottoman Empire had long maintained close economic ties with Germany and its army had been trained by German officers. In August 1914 Turkey concluded an alliance with Germany; three months later a Turkish naval squadron bombarded Russia's Black Sea ports; and in early November 1914 the Allies declared war on the Ottoman Empire. As for Bulgaria, it had been wooed by both sides. But the Central Powers were able to promise more, and in October 1915 Bulgaria joined the Germans and Austrians in a major drive against Serbia.

THE GREAT STALEMATE 1914–16

Both sides had prepared plans for a brief offensive war. In its grand simplicity, however, the German Schlieffen Plan was far superior to France's Plan XVII, which called for an invasion of Alsace-Lorraine.

1914: The Allies Ahead

From the start of hostilities on the western front, Germany held the initiative. After one month of fighting, German forces had advanced to within twenty-five miles of Paris. In early September 1914, however, the German drive was halted at the river Marne. The battle of the Marne was one of the decisive events of the war, since it dashed Germany's hope for an early victory. There were many reasons for Germany's disappointment. Belgium had put up more resistance than had been expected. Germany, furthermore, had failed to con-

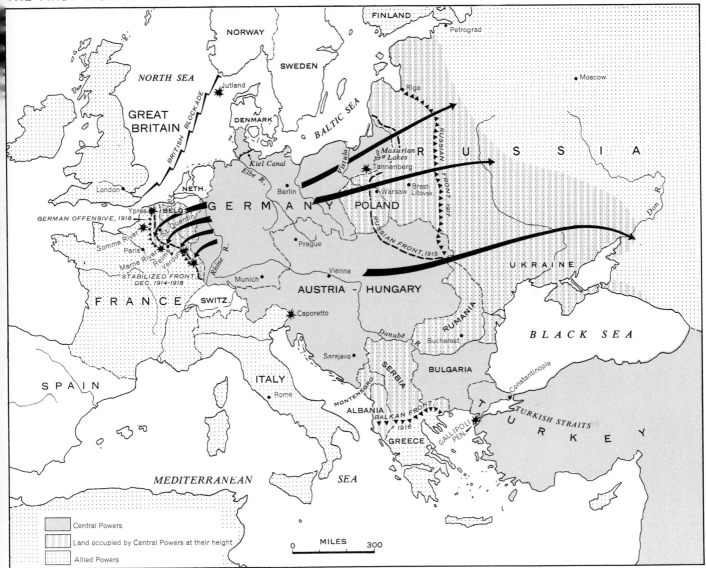

Central Powers

Land occupied by Central Powers at their height

Allied Powers

MILES 0 ——— 300

centrate sufficient forces on the right wing of its invading armies to make possible the gigantic enveloping move that was to strike at the rear of France's forces southeast of Paris. The Schlieffen Plan depended on the closest possible communications between field commanders and the high command, and on rapid lines of supply; neither of these had been provided for.

The battle of the Marne was followed by a series of engagements in which each side hoped to outflank the other, and in the course of which the front was gradually extended to the sea. By November 1914 the fighting in the West had changed from a war of movement to a war of position. Until the spring of 1918 the western front, except for an occasional thrust of a few miles in one direction or the other, remained unchanged.

With the bulk of Germany's forces tied down in the West, Russia was able to score some unexpected successes in the East. In mid-August 1914 two Russian armies invaded East Prussia and within a few days overran almost half of Germany's easternmost province. At the height of danger, the kaiser recalled from retirement General Paul von Hindenburg, a specialist on conditions in the East, and appointed as Hindenburg's chief of staff the younger and more capable Erich Ludendorff. These men soon reversed the situation on the eastern front. In two major battles, at Tannenberg and the Masurian Lakes, Russia lost close to 250,000 men. Russia's reversals in the north were balanced by successes in the southeast against Austria. In a sweeping campaign under Russia's commander in chief, Grand Duke Nicholas, Russian forces in September took most of Galicia and advanced to the Carpathian frontier of Hungary.

In the East, as in the West, the end of 1914 found the Allied and Central Powers locked in a stalemate. But since Germany had failed to deliver a knock-out blow in the West and appeared to be stalled in the East, the advantage was felt to lie with the Allies. In addition, British naval superiority had been responsible for the sinking of a German naval squadron off the coast of South America and for the seizure of most of the colonies that had belonged to Germany.

1915: Allied Reverses

But Allied dreams of victory proved premature. The new Italian ally they gained in the spring of 1915 proved to be of little use. Furthermore, a British attack against the Gallipoli peninsula and the Turkish Straits failed. Had it succeeded, Turkey would have been seriously weakened and the Black Sea opened to Allied shipping. Instead, the Straits remained closed for the rest of the war.

The most serious Allied reverses during 1915 were on the eastern front and in the Balkans. In the spring and summer, German forces in the North and combined Austro-German forces in the South advanced in a series of offensives that cost the Russians Poland, Lithuania, and Courland, drove them out of Galicia, and lost them almost a million men. All of central and eastern Europe was now in German and Austrian hands. In October the Central Powers turned against Serbia; and in November they moved into Montenegro and Albania.

By the beginning of 1916 the tide of war on land seemed definitely to have turned against the Allies. Even on the high seas the Germans were able to make some gains. To counteract Britain's blockade, the German government, in early 1915, imposed a submarine blockade against the British Isles. The first phase of German submarine warfare came to a head with the sinking of the British liner *Lusitania* in May 1915. The loss of 139 American passengers caused a serious crisis in American-German relations. It was settled only after Germany promised to restrict its submarine tactics in the future.

1916: Stalemate

Since time was clearly on the side of the Allies, it seemed imperative to the Germans to force a major showdown. In February 1916, therefore, they launched an all-out offensive against the French stronghold of Verdun. The battle of Verdun was the most famous battle of the war. It lasted more than four months and caused more than 700,000 casualties; yet it ended undecided. Its chief hero on the French side was General Henri Philippe Pétain. Like Hindenburg after the battle of Tannenberg, Pétain became the idol of his people. Both men were to play fateful roles in later years. The battle of Verdun led to an Allied counteroffensive along the Somme River. But the battle of the

The Sinking of the Lusitania

The full horror of the sinking of the *Lusitania* has now been revealed; and it has stirred the people of this country more deeply than even the poison clouds, or any other of the wanton and murderous acts committed by the Germans. . . . By thousands of dastardly crimes the Germans have demonstrated that they are determined to wage this war under conditions of cold-blooded and deliberate murder and outrage, of destruction and brutality, such as the world has never known. . . . Never before, since the world began, has there been witnessed the spectacle of a whole race, numbering many millions, scientifically organised for the objects of wholesale murder and devastation. . . . It is universally seen now that the Germans are a nation apart, that their civilisation is a mere veneer, that they have fallen immeasurably lower than their tribal forbears, and that their calculated and organised barbarity is without precedent in history. Nations, we perceive, can sink to unprecedented depths. No nation has ever fallen so low in infamy. . . .

From an editorial in *The Times* (London), May 10, 1915.

Advertisement placed by Ger-
many in American papers to
warn neutral travelers of the
risks of crossing in the British
vessel *Lusitania*.

Somme, like that of Verdun, failed to force a final decision in the West.

Events elsewhere during 1916 were equally indecisive. In June, Russian forces under General Brusilov started a major drive against the Austrian lines and within a few weeks had taken most of eastern Galicia. These successes brought Rumania into the war. But its participation only made matters worse for the Allies. In late September, Austro-German forces invaded Rumania, and by January 1917 most of that country's rich resources were in the hands of the Central Powers. In the East as in the West, the outcome of the war continued to hang in balance.

The year 1916 also saw the one great naval battle of the war between Germany and Britain. The German navy, to have a chance of success, had to fight in its home waters. But the British refused to venture forth that far. On several occasions the Germans went out into the North Sea, hoping to entice the British into battle. It was on one of these sallies that the two fleets made contact off the coast of Jutland in May 1916. The battle of Jutland was costly and indecisive. The British lost more naval tonnage than the Germans, but they could better afford to. The German fleet henceforth remained safely at home.

By the end of 1916 a stalemate had been reached on all fronts, and victory for either side seemed far away. Meanwhile losses and material costs of the war had been staggering, and the strain of war had begun to tell on the home fronts as well as on the battlefields.

THE HOME FRONTS

People everywhere had greeted the outbreak of war with enthusiastic demonstrations of national unity. Each side believed that it was fighting a "just war." In addition, the war was expected to be short. The Germans hoped to be in Paris before the summer of 1914 was out, and the French were looking forward to Christmas in Berlin. When instead the war dragged on for two years, with no end in sight, enthusiasm gave way to deep depression.

One of the important conditions for victory was effective leadership. Both France and England found outstanding civilian leaders—the British in David Lloyd George, and the French in Georges Clemenceau. In Germany, Austria, and Russia, on the other hand, where the monarch was both chief executive and symbol of national unity, much depended on the leadership he provided. In none of the three countries did the ruler measure up to expectations. William II had neither the ability nor the energy to cope with the problems of a total war. As he gradually faded into the background, his role was taken over by Hindenburg and Ludendorff. In Austria, Francis Joseph was too old and his grand-nephew Charles, who succeeded him in 1916, was too inexperienced to keep the crumbling empire together. The saddest figure among Europe's conservative monarchs was Nicholas II of Russia. In 1915 he assumed personal command of his armed forces, leaving the government in the hands of his wife and her sinister adviser, Rasputin.

Total War

The demands of total war presented many new and difficult problems. All the powers experienced periodic munitions shortages. Labor was scarce. Women were employed in growing numbers and Germany "recruited" workers from Belgium and France. Except for the Russians, who were almost completely isolated, the Allies were able to supplement their domestic production of food and war materials with overseas imports. The Central Powers, on the other hand, cut off by the blockade, were chiefly dependent on their own resources. The Germans tackled the problem with customary efficiency, devising scores of ersatz, or substitute, products and perfecting new processes to obtain scarce materials. Austria-Hungary was far less successful in these respects. Its difficulties were made worse by continuous economic feuds between Austria and Hungary.

The most serious shortages of the Central Powers were in food and clothing. Germany began rationing in 1915,

German women working in a government munitions factory during the war.

but rationing did not increase available supplies. Shortages of labor and transportation reduced the coal supply, adding the misery of cold to hunger. Faced with these hardships, many Germans, especially among the working class, hoped for a speedy end to the war, even without victory.

War Aims and Peace Proposals

Neither side ever stated its war aims openly, except in the most general terms. Secretly, however, the Allies had agreed on the following distribution of spoils: Russia was to get most of the Polish regions under German and Austrian rule, as well as control over the Turkish Straits; France was promised the whole left bank of the Rhine; England was allotted the German colonies; and Italy was to have parts of Austria and territories elsewhere. In supplementary agreements most of the Ottoman Empire was divided into Russian, French, and British spheres of interest.

The war aims of the Central Powers called for the "liberation" of the Poles and the Baltic peoples from Russian domination, the setting up of small satellite states under German and Austrian control, and the annexation of some regions outright. In the West, Germany hoped for additional regions rich in iron ore from France and political and economic control over Belgium. There were also ambitious schemes for a central European federation under German leadership, a *Mitteleuropa,* and for a compact central African colony.

In view of these far-reaching Allied and German war aims, it is not surprising that efforts to reach a compromise peace proved fruitless. The Central Powers took the first official step in December 1916, informing President Wilson that they were ready to enter into peace negotiations. Wilson thereupon asked both sides to state their terms. But this the Germans refused to do. There were other peace moves, notably one inaugurated by Pope Benedict XV in August 1917. All these efforts failed. Both sides wanted peace, but neither side wanted it badly enough to make any real concessions.

THE UNITED STATES ENTERS THE WAR

The United States at first had made every effort to remain neutral. Isolationism was still a strong force; and although there were many Anglophiles in the East, there were also large numbers of German-Americans in the Middle West. America's abandonment of neutrality had several causes. Effective Allied propaganda was one. Another was the growing financial involvement of many Americans in the Allied cause. But more important than either of these factors was Germany's resumption of unrestricted submarine warfare early in 1917.

Unrestricted Submarine Warfare

Germany reached its decision to step up the submarine campaign after its peace move of December 1916 had failed. Germany's civilian authorities opposed unrestricted submarine warfare, fearing that it might bring America into the war. But the real power now lay with the military. With time on the Allied side, Hindenburg and Ludendorff felt that only drastic submarine action could still win the war. They realized that this might lead to American intervention, but they thought England would be defeated long before such intervention would become effective.

Unrestricted submarine war began on February 1, 1917. America broke off diplomatic relations with Germany on February 3. As German submarines began sinking American ships, public opinion became more and more interventionist. The publication of the intercepted "Zimmermann Telegram," a note sent by Germany's foreign secretary urging Mexico to make war on the United States, did the rest. On April 6, 1917, Congress declared war on Germany.

THE RUSSIAN REVOLUTION

America's entrance into the war was made more urgent by changes in Russia that weakened the Allied cause. Events there had long been pointing toward a major domestic upheaval. At first the

Russian people had loyally supported their government's war effort. But the sufferings of war soon dampened their spirit. With insufficient arms and a chronic shortage of munitions, the army lost more than a million men during the first year of the war. While the armies lacked essential materials, the civilian population suffered from food shortages, despite the fact that Russia's economy was primarily agrarian. The blame for all these ills was rightly placed on the inefficiency and corruption of the government. The elected assembly, the *Duma*, repeatedly urged the adoption of reforms; but the tsar continued to meet discontent with repression.

The ''February Revolution'' and Provisional Government

The overthrow of the tsarist regime was the climax of a gradually mounting wave of popular protest. By 1917 more than a million soldiers had deserted the armed forces; in the cities, food shortages led to repeated strikes and riots; and in the countryside, landless peasants began to seize the land of their noble landlords. In early March street demonstrations broke out in Petrograd (the name given to St. Petersburg at the beginning of the war). In the past the government had always been able to use the army against such disturbances. But the troops now fraternized with the rioters. From the capital, insurrection spread to the provinces. On March 12—or February 27 in the Russian calendar, hence the term ''February Revolution''—the *Duma* established a Provisional Government under the premiership of a liberal aristocrat, Prince George Lvov. Three days later, Nicholas II abdicated. He and his family were later moved to Siberia, where they were murdered by the Bolsheviks in the summer of 1918.

The new Provisional Government was faced with problems for which it was completely unprepared. To meet the discontent of the masses some immediate reforms were introduced, but these did not go far enough. The situation was complicated by the existence of a rival government, the Petrograd Soviet of Workers' and Soldiers' Deputies, con-

Alexander Kerensky, studying a map, November 1917. Kerensky himself took over the supreme command of Russian forces.

sisting of Socialist Revolutionaries, Mensheviks, and some Bolsheviks. Because of its popular support, the Soviet was the more powerful of the two groups.

The Provisional Government's main difficulty arose from its desire to continue the war. In July the new minister of war, Alexander Kerensky, launched a futile offensive against the Austrians in Galicia. Its failure led to further riots in Petrograd. To restore order Kerensky, on July 25, replaced Prince Lvov as prime minister. To strengthen his position, Kerensky appointed as commander in chief General Lavr Kornilov, who was popular with the army's rank and file. Kornilov succeeded in restoring some discipline but was unable to halt a German offensive against Riga. When there were signs that Kornilov wanted to make himself military dictator, he was arrested, and on September 14 Kerensky himself assumed supreme command of the army.

The revolution, meanwhile, which thus far had been free from terrorism, became increasingly violent, as workers sacked stores, peasants burned manor houses, and soldiers killed their officers. Revolution in the borderlands, furthermore, threatened the unity of the country. Finally, the Petrograd Soviet, which until then had tolerated the Provisional

Government, was gradually falling under the control of its most radical faction, the Bolsheviks.

The "October Revolution"

The exiled Bolshevik leaders—Lenin, Trotsky, Stalin, and others—had returned from abroad or from Siberia after the February Revolution. Their immediate aim was to gain control of the soviets in Petrograd and elsewhere. At first they only commanded a small minority within the Petrograd Soviet. Lenin advanced his radical program—immediate peace, seizure of land by the peasants and of factories by the workers—against the do-nothing policy of the Mensheviks and the Socialist Revolutionaries. Constantly reiterating this program, the Bolsheviks gradually increased their following within the Soviet and without. As a result, the balance slowly shifted. By September the Bolsheviks controlled the soviets in Petrograd, Moscow, and several other cities.

The only way for the Bolsheviks to gain control of the government was to use force. When Kerensky got wind of the Bolshevik plot and ordered the arrest of their leaders, Bolshevik forces began occupying strategic points in Petrograd on November 6. The main fighting took place around the Winter Palace, seat of the Provisional Government. On November 7 Kerensky took flight, first to the front, and later abroad. The same afternoon an All-Russian Congress of Soviets convened. The majority of its delegates were Bolsheviks. As a first move they formed a new executive, the Council of People's Commissars, with Lenin as Chairman, Trotsky as Foreign Commissar, and Stalin as Commissar for National Minorities.

The "October Revolution"—so named because November 7 was October 25 old-style—was only the first stage on the road to a Bolshevik victory. The followers of Lenin still numbered only a small percentage of the Russian people. When the constituent assembly was elected in late November, less than one-fourth of the delegates were Bolsheviks. But this was to be the first and last free election in Russia. When the assembly met for the first time in January 1918, it was dispersed by Bolshevik forces.

The Treaty of Brest-Litovsk

The most important immediate result of the October Revolution was to end the war on the eastern front. On December 5, 1917, the Bolsheviks concluded an armistice with Germany, and on December

Lenin in 1919.

Lenin
November 7, 1917

It was just 8:40 when a thundering wave of cheers announced the entrance of the presidium, with Lenin—great Lenin—among them. A short, stocky figure, with a big head set down in his shoulders, bald and bulging. Little eyes, a snubbish nose, wide, generous mouth, and heavy chin; clean-shaven now, but already beginning to bristle with the well-known beard of his past and future. Dressed in shabby clothes, his trousers much too long for him. Unimpressive, to be the idol of a mob, loved and revered as perhaps few leaders in history have been. A strange popular leader—a leader purely by virtue of intellect; colourless, humourless, uncompromising and detached, without picturesque idiosyncrasies—but with the power of explaining profound ideas in simple terms, of analysing a concrete situation. And combined with shrewdness, the greatest intellectual audacity.

From John Reed, *Ten Days That Shook the World* (New York: International Publishers, 1919), p. 125.

Bolshevik propaganda poster: the tired Russian soldier.

22 peace negotiations began at Brest-Litovsk. The Bolsheviks wanted "a just, democratic peace without annexations or indemnities." But the Germans were in no mood to forgo their advantages. At one point the Russians broke off negotiations, whereupon the Germans resumed their advance. On March 3, 1918, the Russians gave in and accepted Germany's terms.

Under the Treaty of Brest-Litovsk, Russia was to lose a quarter of its European territory, a third of its population, more than half of its coal and iron, and a third of its industry. The treaty was later invalidated because of the Allied victory in the West. But, for the moment, the Central Powers were freed from the burden of a two-front war and won access to the vast economic resources of eastern Europe. Their position was further strengthened by a peace treaty forced on Rumania at Bucharest on March 5, 1918, under which Germany received a ninety-year lease on that country's oil wells. The triumph of German expansionist aims served to warn the Allies of what to expect in the event of a German victory.

CONTINUED STALEMATE IN THE WEST, 1917

With the Central Powers victorious in the East, the Allies more than ever depended on aid from the United States. A first small contingent of American troops under General John J. Pershing had landed in France as early as June 1917. But it was not until spring of 1918 that American units took any real part in the fighting. Of far greater importance was America's material aid. To meet the submarine danger, a vast shipbuilding program was initiated. Unrestricted submarine warfare at first was a serious threat to the Allied cause. But in time various ways of countering the submarine menace were devised, notably the convoy system.

While the Allies were holding their own at sea, the Central Powers were successfully resisting Allied attempts to force a decision on land. The campaigns on the western front in 1917 were among the bloodiest in the whole war. Yet the lessons of Verdun and the Somme still seemed to hold true—a decision on the western front was impossible. The Central Powers, meanwhile, scored one of their greatest victories on the Italian front. The battle of Caporetto in October 1917 cost Italy close to half a million men in casualties, prisoners, and deserters. Only French and British reinforcements averted a still greater disaster.

The Decline of Civilian Morale

Continuous heavy losses at the front and deprivations at home caused a serious decline in civilian morale. The British, suffering least among Europeans, bore up best. The French, on the other hand, experienced a major military and political crisis. In May 1917 the senseless bloodshed in the West led to open mutiny among troops at the front. The French home front, too, was becoming more and more defeatist. In Italy, where a strong faction had opposed the war from the start, shortages of food and coal brought on a series of strikes. It was only the disaster of Caporetto that made people rally to the support of the government, realizing that the future of their country was at stake.

The Central Powers underwent similar crises. In Germany, differences between civilian and military leaders caused the resignation of chancellor Bethmann Hollweg and the assumption of virtually dictatorial control by Hindenburg and Ludendorff. In Austria the war gave new momentum to the separatist tendencies of the empire's many nationalities. The Czechs and the Yugoslavs set up organizations abroad to work for Allied recognition of their cause, and Polish, Czech, and Yugoslav prisoners in Allied hands were formed into national legions to fight against their homeland.

The general weariness that affected all the belligerents after three years of war quite naturally gave rise to further peace efforts. Like all the earlier attempts, however, they failed, since neither side was ready to make the necessary concessions. The Bolsheviks published the secret treaties revealing

Allied war aims, and western statesmen made highly idealistic pronouncements to counteract these revelations. In January 1918 President Wilson, in an effort to dissociate America from agreements to which it had not been a party, stated his famous Fourteen Points as the basis for a just peace. Briefly stated, they were:

(1) "Open covenants of peace" and an end to secret diplomacy; (2) freedom of the seas in peace and war; (3) "the removal . . . of all economic barriers and the establishment of an equality of trade conditions"; (4) the reduction of armaments "to the lowest point consistent with domestic safety"; (5) the "impartial adjustment of all colonial claims"; (6) the "evacuation of all Russian territory" and an attitude of "intelligent and unselfish sympathy" toward Russia; (7) the evacuation and restoration of Belgium; (8) the freeing of the invaded portions of France and the restoration to it of Alsace-Lorraine; (9) the "readjustment of the frontier of Italy . . . along clearly recognizable lines of nationality"; (10) "the freest opportunity of autonomous development" for the peoples of Austria-Hungary; (11) the evacuation and restoration of Rumania, Serbia, and Montenegro; (12) autonomy for the non-Turkish nationalities of the Ottoman Empire and the permanent opening of the Dardanelles to all nations; (13) the creation of an independent Poland, including "the territories inhabited by indisputably Polish populations," and assurance to Poland of "a free and secure access to the sea"; and (14) the formation of "a general association of nations . . . for the purpose of affording mutual guarantees of political independence and territorial integrity to great and small states alike."

The Fourteen Points were to play an important role in the later negotiations for an armistice and peace, but for the time being they had little effect. The only way to get a satisfactory peace, leaders on both sides felt, was to win the war. With time running against it, Germany, in the spring of 1918, decided to make an all-out bid for victory.

THE COLLAPSE OF THE CENTRAL POWERS

Ludendorff's plan for a large-scale spring offensive had some chance of success. The Germans were able to move large numbers of troops from the East. The Allies, on the other hand, were still suffering from the heavy losses of their 1917 offensives, and reinforcements from America were only just beginning to arrive in sufficient numbers.

The Last Offensives

The gigantic "Emperor's Battle" was launched in March 1918. At first it was overwhelmingly successful. Within three months the Germans once again stood on the Marne, only fifty miles from Paris. But despite brilliant victories, they failed to breach the Allied front. On July 15, when the Germans mounted their last major drive, in the vicinity of Reims, the Allied front was held largely with the aid of American forces.

On July 18, the Allies began their counteroffensive. Ludendorff at first was able to withdraw his forces in good order. But on August 8, the German army suffered its "black day." Using for the first time large numbers of tanks, the British advanced almost eight miles. From here on the Allies never gave the Germans a moment's rest. By the end of September the German army had lost a million men in six months. Morale was low and desertions mounted. Germany's allies, moreover, were showing signs of imminent collapse. On October 4, finally, Germany and Austria appealed to President Wilson for an armistice based on the Fourteen Points.

British tanks at Amiens in 1918. In the final months of the war the Allies effectively used large numbers of tanks under a smoke screen as a cover for advancing infantry.

Chaos in Central Europe

By the time prearmistice negotiations were completed a month later, all the Central Powers had collapsed. The first to give up was Bulgaria. The Bulgarian lines were broken in late September, and before the month was out the government had sued for an armistice. Next came Turkey. During the last year of the war, British forces had steadily advanced from the Persian Gulf into Mesopotamia and from Egypt into Palestine and Syria. With Bulgaria out of the war, Turkey was threatened from the north as well. On October 30 it concluded an armistice.

The Austro-Hungarian Empire, meanwhile, was falling to pieces. On October 21, 1918, the Czechoslovaks declared their independence and a week later the Yugoslavs followed suit. On November 1 Hungary established an independent government. Ten days later, Emperor Charles renounced his throne, and by the middle of November both Austria and Hungary had proclaimed themselves republics.

In Germany the government had reformed itself, in the hope of obtaining more favorable armistice terms. But the Allies would have no dealings with the kaiser. On November 3 mutiny broke out among German sailors at Kiel. Within days the revolt spread through most of northern Germany. On November 7 revolution broke out in Munich and the king of Bavaria abdicated. On November 9, finally, revolution in Berlin overthrew the monarchy and a German Republic was proclaimed.

The Allies, meanwhile, had agreed to accept the Fourteen Points as a basis for an armistice. Under its provisions Germany had to withdraw its forces beyond the Rhine; it had to renounce the treaties of Brest-Litovsk and Bucharest; and it had to surrender large quantities of strategic materials. The terms were so designed as to make any resumption of hostilities impossible. Fighting was officially ended on November 11, at 11 A.M.

The war that was to have been over in four months had lasted more than four years. At its height it had involved some thirty-four nations. It had killed close to 10 million soldiers, wounded twice that number, and caused close to a million civilian deaths. Its total cost has been estimated at over $350 billion. It had brought revolution to central and eastern Europe and had swept away the last remnants of autocratic monarchism. The war's initial purpose—to determine the future of Serbia—had long since given way to far bigger aims. Germany had dreamed of hegemony in Europe and perhaps the world. The Allies had hoped to avert that German threat and in the process to round out their own possessions. Only the United States was seeking no selfish gains. The Peace Conference was to show whether American idealism would prevail against the hardheaded nationalism of European Allies.

THE PARIS PEACE CONFERENCE

The Peace Conference opened on January 18, 1919. All the belligerents were present, except the Central Powers and Russia. As in most major peace conferences, the important decisions were made by the great powers who had contributed most to winning the war. The peace was thus made by a handful of men, the "Big Four": Wilson, Lloyd George, Clemenceau, and Orlando.

The star of the conference was Woodrow Wilson. The favorite aim of the American President was to set up a League of Nations. But his position had

Wilson arriving at Dover, England, on his way to the Peace Conference.

Clemenceau, Wilson, and Lloyd George leaving the palace at Versailles after signing the peace treaty.

been weakened by the return of a Republican majority in the recent congressional elections. Great Britain was represented by its Prime Minister, David Lloyd George, the mercurial Welsh politician. Although his views on the peace were fairly moderate, he had recently won an election on the promise of a harsh peace—a promise that was to haunt him throughout the peace negotiations. The most impressive figure of the conference was France's premier Georges Clemenceau. He hated the Germans, and his foremost aim was to protect France by weakening its former enemy in every possible way. Italy's representative, Prime Minister Vittorio Orlando, played only a minor role. Far more important was his foreign minister, Sidney Sonnino, who was determined to hold Italy's allies to the far-reaching promises they had made in 1915.

Problems of Peacemaking

The problems before the Paris conference were without precedent. The last comparable meeting had been held at Vienna a century earlier. But while the Congress of Vienna had been concerned only with reordering the affairs of Europe, the problems before the Paris conference ranged over the whole world. The Allies as well as the Central Powers had accepted the Fourteen Points as a basis for peace, but many of Wilson's principles differed from the provisions of the Allies' secret treaties. Other complications arose from the many foreign and domestic disturbances while the conference was in session, the popular clamor in the Allied countries for a speedy settlement, and the physical and nervous strain under which the delegates labored. It is not surprising that the peace they made was not perfect.

So long as the victors agreed among themselves, negotiations at Paris went smoothly. But there were several questions on which they did not see eye to eye. The most important were Germany's colonies, the Rhineland, reparations, Fiume, and the Shantung Peninsula.

The Allies agreed that Germany's colonies should not be returned, but they did not agree on what to do with them. France, Japan, and Great Britain and its dominions wanted to annex Germany's holdings. President Wilson, on the other hand, felt that this would violate his Fourteen Points. The impasse was finally resolved by the adoption of the "Mandate Principle," which provided that the German colonies as well as a large part of the Ottoman Empire were to be placed under foreign control, subject to supervision by the League of Nations. Germany later attacked this solution as "veiled annexation" and a violation of the fifth of Wilson's Fourteen Points.

The crisis over the future of the Rhineland almost broke up the conference. The French, for reasons of security, demanded that the left bank of the Rhine be made into an autonomous buffer state. Such an arrangement, however, ran counter to Wilson's principles. The compromise arrived at after long and acrimonious debate called for the permanent demilitarization of the Rhineland and its occupation by Allied forces for fifteen years. In addition, the territory of the Saar was to remain under League administration for fifteen years and France was given the region's coal mines. Finally, Great Britain and the United States promised France an alliance against possible German aggression.

In the discussion of reparations, an argument arose over the extent to which

Germany was to make good damages done to the civilian population of the Allies. Wilson finally gave way to the pressure of his European colleagues and agreed that this should include pensions to victims of war and allowances to their families. To justify so vast a claim, the Allies affirmed that German aggression had been responsible for starting the war. The controversial issue of "war guilt" was thus injected into the peace treaty.

The crisis over Fiume arose from Italy's demand that it be given the Adriatic port in place of the Dalmatian coast, which it had been promised in the Treaty of London but which had been incorporated into Yugoslavia. The Yugoslavs, on the other hand, claimed Fiume as an essential outlet to the sea, and in this they found Allied and American support. When Prime Minister Orlando finally left Paris in protest, the united Allied front showed its first open rift. Italy felt that it had been cheated out of its just reward.

The issue of Shantung involved Japan and China. China had entered the war on the Allied side in 1917. Japan's claim to succeed to Germany's former rights in the Shantung Peninsula clearly conflicted with China's own rights and with Wilson's principles. But the President had only just managed to resist French demands in the Rhineland, and the Fiume crisis was still at its height. So he gave in to Japan's demands, for fear that the Japanese might otherwise refuse to join the League of Nations. The Shantung solution was a serious defeat for the American President, and it lost the United States the traditional friendship of China.

While the negotiations at Paris were in their final stages, the German delegation arrived at Versailles. The Germans were handed a draft of the treaty on May 7 and were given fifteen days in which to present their written observations. These resulted in only a few minor changes. The Germans, therefore, charged that this was a dictated settlement. The signing of the treaty took place on June 28, 1919, at Versailles, five years to the day after the assassination of the Austrian archduke at Sarajevo.

THE TREATY OF VERSAILLES

The peace treaty with Germany contained territorial, military, and economic clauses. It also called for the punishment of "war criminals," including the kaiser. Under the territorial terms of the treaty, Germany had to surrender 13 percent of its prewar area and population. This meant a loss of more than 15 percent of its coal, close to 50 percent of its iron, and 19 percent of its iron and steel industry. Besides giving up its colonies, Germany also had to recognize the independence of Austria. This last provision was to prevent a possible *Anschluss,* or union, for which there was much sentiment in both countries.

The military clauses of the treaty called for the reduction of Germany's army to 100,000 volunteers. The German navy was limited to six battleships of 10,000 tons and a few smaller ships. Germany was to have no offensive weapons—submarines, aircraft, tanks or heavy artillery—and its general staff was

The Disillusionment of Peace

We came to Paris confident that the new order was about to be established; we left it convinced that the new order had merely fouled the old. We arrived as fervent apprentices in the school of President Wilson: we left as renegades. I wish to suggest in this chapter (and without bitterness), that this unhappy diminution of standard was very largely the fault (or one might say with greater fairness 'the misfortune') of democratic diplomacy.

We arrived determined that a Peace of justice and wisdom should be negotiated: we left it, conscious that the Treaties imposed upon our enemies were neither just nor wise. To those who desire to measure for themselves the width of the gulf which sundered intention from practice I should recommend a perusal of the several Notes addressed to the Supreme Council by the German Delegation at Versailles. . . . It is impossible to read the German criticism without deriving the impression that the Paris Peace Conference was guilty of disguising an Imperialistic peace under the surplice of Wilsonism, that seldom in the history of man has such vindictiveness cloaked itself in such unctuous sophistry. Hypocrisy was the predominant and unescapable result. Yet was this hypocrisy wholly conscious, wholly deliberate? I do not think so. . . . We did not realise what we were doing. We did not realise how far we were drifting from our original basis. We were exhausted and overworked.

From Harold Nicolson, *Peacemaking, 1919* (New York: Harcourt, Brace & World, 1933), pp. 187–88.

to be dissolved. To supervise German disarmament, an Allied Military Control Commission was appointed.

In the economic field, the precise amount of reparations to be paid by Germany was left for a Reparations Commission to decide. In the meantime Germany was to pay $5 billion in cash or in kind. France was to receive large amounts of coal to make up for the wanton destruction of its coal mines by Germany's retreating armies. Britain was given quantities of ships to compensate for the losses suffered from submarine warfare. German foreign assets of some $7 billion were confiscated; most of its rivers were internationalized; many of its patents were seized; and it was prohibited from raising tariffs above their prewar level. In short, everything possible was done to avert the threat of a renascent and vengeful Germany. The treaty was no worse than the treaties of Brest-Litovsk and Bucharest, which Germany had imposed on Russia and Rumania. Nor was it much better.

THE TREATIES WITH GERMANY'S ALLIES

The supplementary treaties with the smaller Central Powers were signed in 1919 and 1920. The Treaty of St. Germain with Austria was almost as harsh as that of Versailles. It called for the surrender of large territories to Czechoslovakia, Poland, Yugoslavia, and Italy. Not counting Hungary, the prewar area of the former empire was cut to less than one-third and its population to one-fifth. In addition, Austria's army was limited to 30,000 men. It also had to pay large reparations and agree not to become part of Germany.

Hungary, now separated from Austria, signed its own treaty. Because of a brief communist interregnum under Bela Kun, Hungary did not sign the Treaty of Trianon until the middle of 1920. Its territorial provisions were the most severe of all the postwar treaties. After ceding lands to all its neighbors, including Austria, Hungary was left with little more than a quarter of its former territory and a third of its population. It also had to pay reparations and reduce its army.

Bulgaria, in the Treaty of Neuilly, lost the outlet to the Aegean it had gained in 1913, agreed to reparations, and had to cut its armed forces.

Turkey concluded two peace treaties, one at Sèvres in 1920 and a later one at Lausanne in 1923. The first, which called for a virtual partition of the country, was superseded by the later agreement. In the interim, a revolution of Turkish nationalists under Mustapha Kemal Pasha had completed the revolution begun by the Young Turks in 1908 and overthrown the regime of the Sultan. The Allies had favored the dismemberment of Turkey and in 1919 supported the invasion of Asia Minor by Greek forces. But Turkish re-

THE PEACE SETTLEMENTS IN EUROPE   1919–20

Revolutionaries drive through the streets of Budapest, January 1919, in a demonstration preceding the Communist takeover in March.

sistance under Mustapha Kemal finally convinced the powers that their aim was unattainable. The Allies, therefore, revised the earlier peace settlement. Under the Treaty of Lausanne, signed in July 1923, Turkey gave up everything except Asia Minor and a small foothold in Europe. It did not have to pay any reparations, and the "capitulations"—rights and privileges granted centuries ago to foreign powers—were abolished. The Straits were demilitarized and opened to ships of all nations in time of peace, but they could be closed if Turkey itself was at war. Alone among all the defeated countries, Turkey had thus been able to enforce a radical change in an initially harsh peace settlement. In October 1923 it was proclaimed a republic, with Mustapha Kemal "Atatürk" as first president.

THE AFTERMATH OF WAR

Events in Europe after 1919 were a prolonged effort on the part of all nations to overcome the effects of the war. As might be expected, the defeated countries, foremost among them Germany, were deeply opposed to the postwar settlement. They attacked it not only as too harsh but also as unjust, since it violated several of Wilson's Fourteen Points. In its attempt to sort out the hopelessly intermingled peoples of central Europe, for instance, the principle of self-determination was as often ignored as adhered to.

In countries like Poland, Czechoslovakia, and Rumania, from one-fourth to one-third of the population consisted of alien minorities, mostly Germans or Hungarians. The problem of national minorities, a source of much unrest before 1914, had not been solved by the war.

The situation looked more hopeful with respect to another prewar problem: The war, outwardly at least, had brought the victory of democracy. Popular governments replaced autocratic monarchy in central and eastern Europe and Turkey. But since the political changes in countries like Germany, Austria, and Hungary were closely associated with military defeat, democracy in these countries carried a blemish that only time and success could erase. The tense and tumultuous atmosphere of postwar Europe, however, was not conducive to the peaceful consolidation of democracy. The chaos left behind by war and revolution soon proved too much for the new and inexperienced parliamentary governments of central and eastern Europe. In their place there emerged new kinds of dictatorial and totalitarian regimes, better suited, it seemed, to cope with the emergencies of a world in crisis (see Chapter 31).

The first of these authoritarian systems arose in Russia during the 1920s. The victory of communism in that powerful Eurasian country brought an entirely new and disturbing element into international affairs. The founding of the

NATIONAL MINORITIES IN CENTRAL EUROPE   1919

▨ Polish	
■ German	▨ Bosnian
∷ Russian	▦ Macedonian
▨ Serbian	▦ Bulgarian
▥ Croatian	▨ Hungarian
▤ Slovenian	▥ Rumanian ▦ Albanian
	∷ Czechoslovakian

MILES 0 — 200

Third Communist International ("Comintern") in 1919 by Lenin's lieutenant, Grigori Zinoviev, seemed to confirm the western fear that communism was not content to confine its influence to one country. Short-lived communist regimes in Hungary and Bavaria at the end of the war showed that communism thrived on domestic disorder. After several other attempts to engineer communist risings in Germany, Lenin finally decided to concentrate his efforts on the communization of his own country. But the threat of communist Russia continued to frighten the statesmen of Europe until it was overshadowed in the 1930s by the more immediate threat posed by Nazi Germany.

The tripartite division of Europe into victors, vanquished, and the Soviet Union was the cause of much international unrest. To remedy this situation the Allies had created the League of Na-

tions. Here was something entirely new in European history, a parliament of nations in which international problems could be discussed and solved. That was how the founders of the League had envisaged its mission. But events soon proved otherwise. When the League opened its first session at Geneva in 1921, several of the great powers were missing: Germany was not admitted until 1926, the Soviet Union became a member eight years later, and the United States never joined.

The failure of the United States to ratify the Treaty of Versailles, which also embraced the Covenant of the League of Nations, showed that Americans were not yet ready to assume the role they were destined to play as the world's most powerful nation. America's absence from the League could not help but have unfortunate results. In an assembly dominated by the European victors, the United States would have served as an impartial arbiter. The League of Nations had many shortcomings; but none was as crucial as the void left by America's refusal to become a member.

THE LEAGUE OF NATIONS AND COLLECTIVE SECURITY

The general purpose of the League was "to promote international cooperation and to achieve international peace and security." It was founded on the concept of collective security, under which peace was to be maintained by an organized community of nations rather than by an uncertain "Concert of Europe." The specific tasks of the League were: to work for international disarmament; to prevent war by arbitration of international disputes; to apply sanctions against aggressors; and to register and revise international agreements. In very few of these tasks was the League successful.

Disarmament

The Treaty of Versailles had stated that the disarmament of Germany was intended "to render possible the initiation of a general limitation of the armaments of all nations." But despite this

Will It Work?

"Will it work?"—a cartoon portraying League of Nations sanctions against Italy as a robotlike contraption constructed by League members. The sanctions against Italy for its invasion of Abyssinia in 1935 did not work.

implied promise, general disarmament was tackled most hesitantly. Only in 1926 did a Preparatory Commission begin discussions of a Disarmament Conference, and the Conference itself did not meet until 1932. Its deliberations at that time proved entirely fruitless.

There were several causes for this failure. Shortly after the war, the Allied Military Control Commission began to report a long series of German violations of the Versailles disarmament provisions. Most important were secret contacts between the new German *Reichswehr* and the Russian Red Army. The evidence of these German violations was sketchy, but it was alarming enough to keep the Allies from reducing their own military forces. Another reason for Allied failure to disarm was the difficulty of finding a valid basis for determining a nation's military power. Geographic location, manpower, industrial development, and raw materials, it was felt, were far more significant factors than the actual size of armies. In most of these factors Germany and the Soviet Union excelled, and any general disarmament would have been greatly to their advantage.

Arbitration of International Disputes

The second task of the League was to arbitrate international disputes. Members promised to bring any dispute "suitable for submission to arbitration" before the League Council. Any decision by the Council had to be "unanimously agreed to by the members thereof." If the

Council's decision was not unanimous, League members were free to take whatever action they deemed appropriate. Despite the vagueness of these provisions, the League was able to settle a number of international conflicts. Of some thirty cases submitted during the 1920s, the majority were arbitrated. The League was most effective in settling disputes between small powers. As soon as a major power was involved, however, the League proved quite powerless. In the "Corfu incident" of 1923, for instance, when Italy bombarded and occupied the Greek island of Corfu in retaliation for the murder of some Italians, the Italian government refused to acknowledge the League's competency.

Sanctions against Aggression

The League's procedure for dealing with military aggression was laid down in Article 16 of the Covenant. As major punishment it provided for economic sanctions against the guilty party. To be effective, this policy needed the cooperation of all the great powers. But since two or more of them usually were outside the League, the application of strict economic sanctions proved impossible. This became evident at the time of Japan's invasion of China in 1931 and Italy's war against Abyssinia in 1935. Article 16 also provided for military sanctions, but these were left entirely to individual members. The League itself maintained no armed forces.

Treaty Revision

The registration and publication of international agreements, called for under Article 18 of the Covenant, was intended to prevent the "secret diplomacy" that Wilson had blamed for helping to start the war. Even so, most serious diplomatic negotiations after the war still went on behind closed doors, and the fear of secret treaties persisted. More significant than the publication of treaties was the provision made in Article 19 of the Covenant for the revision of existing treaties. Here was a possibility for peaceful changes in the peace treaties, once the hatreds of war had cooled down. Had the powers availed themselves of this opportunity, Europe and the world might have been spared the Second World War.

Clearly the League of Nations suffered from many weaknesses. Most of these could have been eliminated had the great powers been ready to do so. But since each of them was primarily concerned with its own selfish aims, the hopeful experiment of the League turned out a failure. Only in fields that involved none of the vital interests of the great powers did the League score any gains. The League's Mandate Commission was able to improve the standard of colonial administration. The International Labor Organization, affiliated with the League, did much to raise the status of workers everywhere. Various other League agencies concerned themselves with matters of health, the illicit drug traffic, the international arms trade, and so forth. These agencies set important precedents for the far-reaching activities of the United Nations today.

THE ''WAR AFTER THE WAR,'' 1919–23

For several years after the Peace Conference, Europe underwent so many major and minor international crises that people sometimes wondered if the war had really come to an end. Until the fall of 1919, the Allies intervened against the Bolshevik regime in Russia. Poland fought with Lithuania over the town of Vilna, with Czechoslovakia over the region of Teschen, and with Russia over its eastern frontiers. Polish and German irregular forces fought bloody battles over Upper Silesia in 1922. Intermittent conflicts between Italy and Yugoslavia over Fiume lasted until 1924. The Greeks invaded Turkey between 1919 and 1922 and almost came to blows with Italy in 1923. Austria and Hungary clashed over the Burgenland region in 1921. And in 1923 Germany's default in reparation payments led to the invasion of its key industrial region, the Ruhr district, by French and Belgian troops. These were only the more noteworthy among an unending series of international incidents during the early postwar period.

*The French Search
for Security*

The greatest danger to peace was Germany's desire to escape the restrictions of Versailles. This worried the French in particular. The alliance between France and the Anglo-Saxon powers that had been envisaged at the Peace Conference failed to materialize when America withdrew from the peace settlement. Since Germany was still far superior in human and industrial resources, the French felt that their security demanded the strictest fulfillment of the peace terms. But this insistence on fulfillment caused a growing rift between France and Great Britain. The British now were trying to dissociate themselves from continental affairs and to devote their attention to overseas interests. Germany was no longer a serious economic and naval rival; and since it had been one of England's best customers before the war, Britain wanted it to get back on its feet. Moreover, England felt that a healthy Germany was the best protection against the westward spread of communism. When France invaded the Ruhr in 1923, therefore, Britain expressed its disapproval. It had no desire to see the French assume hegemony over the Continent.

The loss of British support forced France to look elsewhere for security. With Russia disqualified by communism and Italy dissatisfied with the peace settlement, only the smaller "succession states" of central Europe were left. In 1921 France concluded an alliance with Poland, in 1926 with Rumania, and in 1927 with Yugoslavia. In addition, Rumania, Yugoslavia, and Czechoslovakia began to organize the "Little Entente" in 1921. All these countries were interested in maintaining the *status quo,* which was being threatened by the revisionist agitation not only of Germany but of Hungary and Russia as well. Outwardly this French alliance system looked quite impressive. But the total military strength of these small powers was less than a million men, and they required a great deal of French financial aid. As an attempt, furthermore, to isolate Germany, the French system was doomed from the start, for the two outcasts of Europe—Germany and Russia—began to draw together in 1922.

The Russo-German Rapprochement

Russo-German relations after the war at first were strained. The Russians still remembered Brest-Litovsk, and the Germans resented Russia's repeated attempts to stir up revolutions in Germany. Common economic and military interests, however, gradually led to a political *rapprochement*. The first outward sign of this understanding was a treaty of friendship concluded at Rapallo in April 1922. The world was startled and disturbed by what it suspected of being a military alliance. But the Treaty of Rapallo was merely a promise of cooperation between the two partners, important chiefly because it helped Germany escape its diplomatic isolation. There were people in both Germany and Russia who hoped that the treaty would some day develop into something more. But this hope was never fulfilled. Economically the two countries were quite complementary and both stood to gain from mutual trade. But their economic systems were far too different to make such an exchange possible. Despite some later economic and neutrality agreements, Russo-German relations throughout the 1920s remained decidedly cool.

The Ruhr Occupation

The French occupation of the Ruhr in 1923 marked a turning point in the history of postwar Europe. Deprived of its major industrial region, Germany was thrown into an economic crisis, which was made more serious by the passive resistance the people of the Ruhr put up against the French. The German government, faced with paying the Ruhr workers' wages, ran the printing presses overtime to "make money," thereby escalating an already severe inflation. By cutting the coal France hoped to get from the Ruhr, the resisters in the Ruhr contributed to French economic difficulties as well. The German government, which feared for the nation's existence, called off the passive resistance and so ended the Ruhr struggle. There were communist disturbances in central Germany and separatist uprisings in the Rhineland. In the South an unknown ex-corporal, Adolf Hitler, was getting ready to make his first try for power.

The Ruhr episode taught an important lesson to both French and Germans. It showed that rigid insistence on the fulfillment of the Versailles Treaty on the one hand, and stubborn resistance against such fulfillment on the other, helped neither side. Both, it seemed, had to give way if Europe was to be saved from chaos. For the next six years a group of dedicated statesmen devoted their efforts to bringing about such a compromise.

THE "ERA OF LOCARNO" 1924–29

The year 1924 saw important political changes in both France and England. In France the rightist cabinet of Raymond Poincaré, known for his vengeful attitude toward Germany, was replaced after the Ruhr fiasco by a left-wing coalition in which Aristide Briand was foreign minister. In England the Labor Party had a brief inning in 1924 but soon gave way to a Conservative government with Austen Chamberlain as foreign secretary. In Germany the direction of foreign policy after the Ruhr crisis was in the hands of Gustav Stresemann. Together, Briand, Chamberlain, and Stresemann brought Europe a brief respite from fear and uncertainty.

A trainload of coal on its way to France during the occupation of the Ruhr in 1923.

The Locarno Pact

Europe's brief return to stability after 1924 was chiefly due to a more efficient handling of the reparations problem. Without these economic developments, the *rapprochement* between Germany and the western powers would hardly have come about. The first political result of this *rapprochement* was the Locarno Pact.

Under the terms of the Treaty of Versailles, the Allies were to end their occupation of the Rhineland in three phases, beginning in 1925. But since the Allied Military Control Commission had found Germany guilty of disarmament violations, the Allies refused to leave. Stresemann realized that the basic reason for this refusal was France's fear of Germany. To dispel this fear once and for all, he now proposed a treaty by which not only France and Germany, but also England, Italy, and Belgium would guarantee the *status quo* in western Europe. Such a treaty was signed at Locarno in October 1925.

To a world torn by international strife for more than a decade, the Locarno Pact came as a harbinger of a new age in which peace and good will rather than war and suspicion would prevail. "We are citizens each of his own country," Stresemann said at Locarno, "but we are also citizens of Europe and are joined together by a great concept of civilization." This seeming conversion of Stresemann from a rabid German nationalist into a "good European" commanded the admiration of his contemporaries. But Stresemann was less of an idealist than people thought. He was every bit as eager to abolish the restrictions of Versailles as were his nationalist compatriots. Where Stresemann differed was in his realization that the revision of Versailles could not be achieved by force but only through patient negotiation, once Germany had regained the confidence of the world.

The *rapprochement* between Germany and the West, meanwhile, was causing growing apprehension in the Soviet

German Foreign Minister Dr. Gustav Stresemann addressing the League of Nations for the last time, September 9, 1929, shortly before his death.

Union. Despite Russia's resumption of diplomatic relations with France and England in 1924, it had remained an outsider in international affairs. England in particular resented the propagandist activities of the Comintern, and in 1927 once again severed its connections with the Soviets. What Russia feared most was that Germany, as a member of the League, might some day be forced to participate in sanctions against the Soviet Union. To quiet these Russian fears Stresemann, at Locarno, had obtained a modification of Article 16 of the League Covenant, allowing Germany to abstain from participating in any sanctions that endangered its own security. When this still did not satisfy the Russians, Stresemann in April 1926 signed a treaty of neutrality with them. Some saw this Treaty of Berlin as an attempt on Germany's part to play a double game between the East and the West. But there is no doubt that Stresemann's foremost concern was always for closer and stronger relations between Germany and the West.

The Kellogg-Briand Pact

The efforts of the powers to guarantee Europe's security by treaties that would bolster the collective security system of the League climaxed in the signing of the Pact of Paris, or Kellogg-Briand Pact, in August 1928. Its sixty-two signatories, which included the United States, promised "to renounce war as an instrument of national policy." Nothing was more characteristic of the spirit of hopefulness that pervaded the world after Locarno than this attempt to banish war simply by signing a treaty. The Soviet Union was the only major power not present in Paris, but it joined the pact soon thereafter. If security depended on treaties, the world had nothing more to fear.

THE ECONOMIC CONSEQUENCES OF THE WAR

The economic consequences of the war were even more serious than its political aftermath. The territorial losses of Germany and the dismemberment of Austria-Hungary by themselves caused a major economic shock among the defeated powers. The Allies added to their distress by making seemingly limitless demands for reparations. But the victors, too, found the going far from easy. In the West, France and Belgium suffered from the devastation of their industrial regions. In eastern Europe, lack of seed, fertilizers, and agricultural implements resulted in a marked decline of farm production. All the powers, England in particular, had lost important foreign markets. And a general return to protective tariffs retarded recovery everywhere.

The Kellogg-Briand Pact

Secretary of State Frank B. Kellogg came to Paris with a bouquet of white lilies in one hand and in the other a pen to sign a pact. He was a little old man who looked like a little old woman who resembles a little old man. . . . Stresemann came too; this was the first time a German foreign minister had visited Paris since the Franco-Prussian War of 1871. But he was gravely ill, and when he went to pay his respects to Prime Minister Poincaré, a doctor waited in the anteroom. After an hour the doctor sent a written message to Poincaré beseeching him to order Stresemann home to bed.

The Kellogg-Briand Pact was signed on August 27, 1928, at the Quai d'Orsay in the Salle de l'Horloge, amid an orgy of marbles, velvets, silks, all exquisitely blended, spiced with silver and gold. . . . The scenery must have been pleasing to Richelieu's ghost; but this was an American affair . . . Now for the first time I saw Hollywood intrude into the plush-carpeted sanctum of a Foreign Office . . . platoons of sweating technicians in shirtsleeves installed 35-millimeter film howitzers that spied down upon the horseshoe table where "those guys" (as I learned engineers refer to ministers) would perform. As the statesmen entered the room (Poincaré stumbling over the cables), the klieg lights exploded in a pink glow, and all the eighteenth-century Venetian luster of crystal and candles was snuffed out by the crude and sober floodlight of twentieth-century technology.

The pact was signed by fifteen nations, with a heavy gold fountain pen especially manufactured for the occasion. It bore the inscription: "If you want peace, prepare for peace." Kellogg took up the pen with trembling hand, but it was too heavy for the old man, and a French secretary had to help him affix his name.

The Kellogg-Briand Pact has been ineffective in practice every time it has been invoked. . . . It was not a pact, after all, so much as a declaration against sin.

From Emerey Kelen, *Peace in Their Time* (New York: Knopf, 1963), pp. 168–69.

The effects of the postwar economic crisis were felt in many ways. Five years after the war Europe's total industrial production was still at only two-thirds of its prewar level. Unemployment, never much of a problem in the past, now assumed alarming proportions. Another repercussion of the crisis was felt in financial matters. All the major countries of Europe suffered from severe inflation. In Germany, Austria, and Russia, this inflation led to total devaluation of the currency.

The Reparations Problem

Much of the responsibility for Europe's economic difficulties rested with the peacemakers of 1919. In their efforts to solve the Continent's political problems, they often ignored the economic effects of their decisions. They carved new states out of old empires without regard to economic consequences. They even failed to examine the probable effects of the purely economic terms of the peace. A member of the British peace delegation, the economist John Maynard Keynes, called attention to these oversights in his book *The Economic Consequences of the Peace* (1920), a sweeping indictment of the Versailles settlement on economic grounds. The most troublesome part of the treaty, as Keynes foresaw, turned out to be the reparations provisions. In order to pay the large sums called for, the defeated nations needed surplus capital. This they could gain only through increased exports. But such exports competed with the products of the very nations who hoped to profit from reparations. The transfer of large amounts of capital, furthermore, had unsettling effects on the economies of debtors and creditors alike. It was easy, in other words, to ask for huge reparations, but it was difficult to devise sound, workable methods of paying them.

The reparations problem was further complicated by the mutual indebtedness of the victors. The easiest way out would have been the cancellation of all inter-Allied debts. This solution was proposed by Britain and France but was rejected by the United States, who would have

ended up paying for the whole war. America's refusal made the European Allies more than ever dependent on reparations.

The main source of reparations was Germany. The total amount of Germany's obligations had been left open at the Peace Conference. It was later settled at $32 billion. From the start Germany fell behind in its payments. The French, who were to receive more than half of the reparations, were adamant in their demands for prompt payment. The climax of France's insistence on fulfillment came with the invasion of the Ruhr in 1923.

The Dawes Plan
and the Young Plan

Prior to this time, America had suggested that the whole reparations issue be studied by an international committee of experts. With the failure of the Ruhr venture, such a committee was appointed late in 1923. It worked out a plan, named after its chairman, the American financier Charles G. Dawes, which went into effect in September 1924. Under the Dawes Plan, Germany was to pay gradually rising amounts that were to reach a "standard annuity" in 1929. The Dawes Plan worked well. But, more than was generally realized, Germany's ability to pay depended on the influx of foreign loans. With the return of general confidence in its economic stability, Germany began to

Runaway inflation in Germany. Top: a two-billion mark note; below: marks being baled as waste paper.

attract large amounts of capital, especially from the United States. This flow continued until 1929, when American investors began to speculate at home. Since at the same time Germany's yearly payments under the Dawes Plan were about to reach the "standard annuity," and since no time limit had been set on such payments, it seemed a good time to reconsider the whole reparations question.

A series of meetings between German and foreign experts during 1929 finally led to the Young Plan, named after the American expert Owen D. Young. It fixed Germany's total obligations at $29 billion, to be paid over fifty-nine years. But the Young Plan never went into effect. As the Great Depression spread from the United States to Europe, Germany ceased its payments altogether. At a final conference in Lausanne in 1932, Germany was relieved of any future obligations. Opinions differ widely on the total amount of reparations actually paid by Germany. A likely estimate puts it at $6 billion. This was not only far less than originally demanded, but in return Germany had received a far larger amount in foreign loans. The history of reparations has been compared to a merry-go-round: Germany borrowed American funds to pay reparations to the Allies, who used the money to repay their debts to the United States, who lent the money back to Germany.

EUROPEAN RECOVERY

American capital played an important role in the economic life of Europe. Most of America's loans were private and short-term. Their repayment was made even more difficult by the American government's tariff policy. Instead of helping foreign debtors to meet their obligations through increased exports, the United States surrounded itself with high tariff walls. This policy soon provoked a worldwide wave of protectionism. Insistent warnings by European economists against such shortsightedness finally led the League of Nations to call a World Economic Conference in 1927. In their final report, the delegates of the more than fifty participating nations urged their governments to lower tariffs as soon and as much as possible. Before this advice was taken, the Great Depression began. Not least among its causes was the protectionist policy of the postwar years.

Except for its warning on tariffs, however, the World Economic Conference was quite optimistic. Europe's economy after 1925 seemed to justify such optimism. France had rebuilt its destroyed regions, had modernized its industry, and had stabilized its currency. Germany had recovered from the shock of inflation and with the aid of foreign loans had improved its industries so that once again it was the industrial leader of Europe. England's recovery was made much slower by its adherence to the gold standard, its antiquated production methods, and the high living standard of its workers. In Italy, the Fascist government of Benito Mussolini successfully raised the nation's food production. Even in Russia the "New Economic Policy," with its partial return to capitalist practices, brought gradual economic recovery and some relief from the aftermath of war and revolution.

But this apparent economic recovery also had its weak points. It was chiefly restricted to industry. Agriculture continued to suffer from overproduction and foreign competition. The resulting decline of rural buying power reacted upon industry. Some producers, tempted by American loans and the example of American mass-production methods, expanded far beyond the need of their markets. When, after the crash of the American stock market in October 1929, American loans to Europe ceased and old loans were recalled, Europe's economy, deprived of this financial infusion, collapsed.

Within one decade, Europe had thus come full cycle from despair through hope and back to despair. In the early twenties it had seemed that the German Oswald Spengler had been right in his best seller *The Decline of the West* (1918), which predicted the impending doom of European civilization. But then in the mid-twenties a "silver lining" had appeared on the horizon. The optimism of

Unemployment in Britain in 1930 afflicted all levels of society.

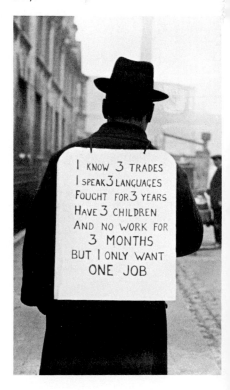

the "Era of Locarno" may appear unjustified in retrospect. But to contemporaries the decrease of international tension, the economic recovery, and the general air of well-being and stability seemed quite real. They were seen as proof that Europe at long last had found the peace it had so long been looking for. One may rightly wonder what would have happened if the recovery of Europe had lasted for another decade. In any attempt to find the causes of the unhappy events of the thirties and forties, the Great Depression will always loom large.

Suggestions for Further Reading

Note: Asterisk denotes a book available in paperback edition.

General

There are many volumes covering world history since 1914. One of the most interesting and original is C. Quigley, *Tragedy and Hope: A History of the World in Our Time* (1966). Other recommended books are F. P. Chambers, *This Age of Conflict: The Western World—1914 to the Present*, 3rd ed. (1962); and, for the years between the two World Wars, R. J. Sontag, *A Broken World, 1919–1939** (1971). D. Thomson, ed., *The Era of Violence, 1898–1945* (1960), Vol. XII in the *New Cambridge Modern History* series, includes contributions by noted specialists on every facet of European and world history. The declining influence of Europe in world affairs is the theme of a small volume by H. Holborn, *The Political Collapse of Europe* (1954). R. Aron, *The Century of Total War** (1955), is a thoughtful analysis of world events in the twentieth century; and G. Barraclough, *An Introduction to Contemporary History** (1964), presents a stimulating discussion of modern issues.

The First World War

The military side of the war is told in B. H. Liddell Hart, *The War in Outline** (1936), and in C. Falls, *The Great War, 1914–1918** (1936). On the home fronts, see F. P. Chambers, *The War Behind the War, 1914–1918: A History of the Political and Civilian Fronts* (1939); G. D. Feldman, *Army, Industry, and Labor, 1914–1918* (1966), which deals with Germany; A. J. May, *The Passing of the Hapsburg Monarchy*, 2 vols. (1966); A. Fontaine, *French Industry During the War* (1962); E. L. Woodward, *Great Britain and the War of 1914–1918** (1967); and A. Marwick, *The Deluge: British Society and the First World War** (1965). There is no comprehensive diplomatic history for the war years. The problem of war aims is treated in F. Fischer, *Germany's Aims in the First World War** (1967); H. W. Gatzke, *Germany's Drive to the West** (1950); and W. R. Louis, *Great Britain and Germany's Lost Colonies, 1914–1919* (1967). America's involvement in the war is discussed in A. S. Link, *Wilson the Diplomatist** (1957), and E. R. May, *The World War and American Isolation* (1959). For a briefer assessment, see D. M. Smith, *The Great Departure: The United States and World War I** (1964). The following are important monographs on various aspects of the war: J. C. King, *Generals and Politicians: Conflict between France's High Command, Parliament and Government, 1914–1918* (1951); P. Guinn, *British Strategy and Politics, 1914 to 1918* (1965); M. C. Siney, *The Allied Blockade of Germany, 1914–1916* (1957); and J. M. Read, *Atrocity Propaganda, 1914–1919* (1941). For a more vivid impression of the war, the following are highly recommended: B. W. Tuchman, *The Guns of August** (1962); L. Wolff, *In Flanders Fields: The 1917 Campaign** (1958); and A. J. P. Taylor, *The First World War: An Illustrated History* (1963).

The Russian Revolution

W. H. Chamberlain, *The Russian Revolution, 1917–1921*, 2 vols. (1952), is a standard work. E. H. Carr, *A History of Soviet Russia: The Bolshevik Revolution, 1917–1923*,* 3 vols. (1950–53), is scholarly but controversial. G. Katkov, *Russia 1917: The February Revolution* (1967), is an important study. The background of the revolution is treated authoritatively in A. B. Ulam, *The Bolsheviks: The Intellectual and Political History of the Triumph of Communism in Russia* (1965). The peace negotiations between Russia and the Central Powers are described by J. W. Wheeler-Bennett, *Brest Litovsk: The Forgotten Peace, March 1918** (1939). Allied intervention is dealt with in G. F. Kennan, *Russia Leaves the War** (1956) and *The Decision to Intervene** (1958); and in R. H. Ullman, *Anglo-Soviet Relations, 1917–1921*,* 2 vols. (1961, 1968). On developments among Russia's national minorities, see R. Pipes, *The Formation of the Soviet Union: Communism and Nationalism, 1917–1923* (1954). O. H. Radkey, *Agrarian Foes of Bolshevism* (1958), deals with the Socialist Revolutionaries during the revolution. Several participants have provided their own version of events: L. Trotsky, *The History of the Russian Revolution*, 3 vols. (1932); V. M. Chernov, *The Great Russian Revolution* (1936); N. N. Sukhanov, *The Russian Revolution 1917: A Personal Record* (1955); A. F. Kerensky, *The Kerensky Memoirs* (1966); and P. T. Wrangel, *The Memoirs of General Wrangel* (1929). A vivid eye-witness account by a young American communist is J. Reed, *Ten Days That Shook the World** (1919).

Revolution in Central Europe

The last days of the war are treated in H. R. Rudin, *Armistice, 1918* (1944); F. Maurice, *The Armistices of 1918* (1943); and K. F. Nowak, *The Collapse of Central Europe* (1924). On the overthrow of the Hohenzollern and Habsburg dynasties, see A. J. Ryder, *The German Revolution of 1918* (1967), and Z. A. B. Zeman, *The Break-Up of the Habsburg Empire, 1914–1918* (1961). Both A. Rosenberg, *The Birth of the German Republic** (1931), and O. Jászi, *The Dissolution of the Habsburg Monarchy** (1929), put events in their respective countries into historical perspective. H. Seton-Watson, *Eastern Europe Between Two Wars, 1918–1941** (1945), and S. Borsody, *The Tragedy of Central Europe** (1960), deal with the problems of the small successor states.

The Peace Treaties

The standard history of the Peace Conference is H. W. V. Temperley, *A History of the Peace Conference of Paris*, 6 vols. (1920–24). A. J. Mayer, *Politics and Diplomacy of Peacemaking** (1967), emphasizes the peacemakers' fear of communism, as does also J. M. Thompson, *Russia, Bolshevism, and the Versailles Peace* (1966). H. Nicolson, *Peacemaking, 1919** (1933), vividly captures the atmosphere of the negotiations. The following deal with inter-Allied relations before and during the Peace Conference: H. I. Nelson, *Land and Power: British and Allied Policy on Germany's Frontiers, 1916–1919* (1963); S. P. Tillman, *Anglo-American Relations at the Paris Peace Conference of 1919* (1961); and A. J. Mayer, *Political Origins of the New Diplomacy, 1917–1918** (1959). The classic indictment of the Versailles settlement is J. M. Keynes, *The Economic Consequences of the Peace* (1920). It is challenged in E. Mantoux, *The Carthaginian Peace, or the Economic Consequences of Mr. Keynes** (1946). P. Birdsall, *Versailles Twenty Years After* (1941), is a judicious reappraisal of the treaty. See also R. B. McCallum, *Public Opinion and the Last Peace* (1944). On the peace settlements with Austria and Hungary, see N. Almond and R. H. Lutz, *The Treaty of St. Germain* (1939), and F. Deák, *Hungary at the Paris Peace Conference* (1942). America's part in the negotiations is reassessed in T. A. Bailey, *Wilson and the Peacemakers* (1947). See also V. S. Mamatey, *The United States and East Central Europe, 1914–1918* (1957).

The Aftermath of War

There is no satisfactory general work in English on international relations between the two wars, although E. H. Carr, *International Relations Between the Two World Wars, 1919–1939** (1947), is an admirable summary. It should be supplemented by the same author's thoughtful analysis of international politics in *The Twenty Years' Crisis, 1919–1939** (1946). H. W. Gatzke, ed., *European Diplomacy Between Two Wars, 1919–1939** (1972), is a collection of articles on various aspects of postwar European diplomacy. On British foreign policy, see F. S. Northedge, *The Troubled Giant: Britain Among the Great Powers, 1916–1939* (1946); and W. N. Medlicott, *British Foreign Policy Since Versailles, 1919–1963,** rev. ed. (1968). Differences between the western powers are treated in A. Wolfers, *Britain and France Between Two Wars** (1940), and in W. M. Jordan, *Great Britain, France, and the German Problem, 1918–1939* (1943). See also L. Kochan, *The Struggle for Germany** (1963). Russo-German relations are covered in K. Rosenbaum, *Community of Fate: German-Soviet Relations, 1922–1928* (1965), and in H. Dyck, *Weimar Germany and Soviet Russia, 1926–1933* (1966). Germany's relations with the western powers are the subject of J. Jacobson, *Locarno Diplomacy: Germany and the West, 1925–1929* (1972). German agitation over "war guilt" is criticized by L. Fraser, *Germany Between Two Wars: A Study of Propaganda and War Guilt* (1944). On Germany's attempts to evade the disarmament restrictions of Versailles, see H. W. Gatzke, *Stresemann and the Rearmament of Germany** (1954). The reparations problem is surveyed in the book by E. Mantoux, cited in the section above, and in K. Bergmann, *The History of Reparations* (1927). The standard history of the League of Nations is F. P. Walters, *A History of the League of Nations*, 2 vols. (1952). G. A. Craig and F. Gilbert, eds., *The Diplomats, 1919–1939** (1953), is a collection of lively essays on the making and makers of interwar diplomacy.

31 Democracy in Crisis

As in international affairs, the Great War also brought about deep changes in the domestic affairs of the major powers during the "long armistice" between 1919 and 1939. Before 1914 the countries of Europe, despite national differences, still had much in common. What feeling of European unity there had been was gone in 1919.

The Continent was divided into victors and vanquished, "have" and "have-not" nations. Among the latter were not only the countries that had lost the war but countries, like Italy and Russia, that felt dissatisfied with the peace settlements. It was in these "revisionist" powers that a new type of totalitarian government arose that, more than anything else,

Scene from the ballet *The Green Table* by the German choreographer Kurt Jooss. An example of Germany's cultural renaissance after the First World War, the ballet satirized the futile efforts of the diplomats to prevent war by their interminable talks around the conference table.

helped to destroy the traditional unity of Europe (see Chapter 32).

The Continent's unique role in world affairs was also beginning to be challenged. As the United States gradually emerged from its isolation, and as regions that hitherto had been firmly dominated by Europe began to play a role of their own, Europe's longstanding predominance faded. World politics gradually overshadowed European politics.

THE AFTERMATH OF WAR 1919–29

One of the major war aims of the western powers had been the triumph of democracy over autocracy. This aim seemed to have been achieved with the rise of new democratic governments everywhere east of the Rhine. But the war left behind so many unsolved problems that even countries with a democratic tradition, like France and England, found it difficult to return from the semiauthoritarian and efficient conduct of war to the more democratic and less efficient pursuits of peace. It is not surprising, therefore, that some of the new democratic nations found it hard to cope with the aftermath of war and that their new democracy in many cases turned out to be short-lived.

Stability in Great Britain

Among the western powers, Great Britain enjoyed by far the most stable domestic development. Democracy scored a success when Britain's franchise was extended to all adults in two further reform acts in 1918 and 1928. Transition from war to peace was made easier by the reelection of Lloyd George's coalition cabinet in 1918 and by a brief industrial boom. Beginning in 1920, however, England underwent an extended economic crisis. Its political effect was to shift power away from the Liberals, first toward the Conservatives and later to Labor.

During most of the 1920s Britain was ruled by the Conservatives, who tried valiantly but vainly to tackle the perennial problems of a large deficit and widespread unemployment. In the elections of 1929 Labor finally won its first major victory. But even this did not give it sufficient strength to introduce decisive economic reforms. The solution of England's economic difficulties had to wait until after the Great Depression.

Despite its unsettled economy, Britain had no serious domestic disturbances. There was some unrest among the workers, and in 1926 trouble in the coal mines led to a general strike. But there was no violence. A certain innate moderation seemed to make the average Englishman poor material for radical agitation from either Right or Left. The Labor Party, though accused of being "soft" on communism, was always moderate in its program and policy; and the Conservatives, though eager to curb the power of the labor unions, were sincerely concerned about the workingman's welfare. The government's policy of maintaining a stable currency was detrimental to British trade, since it hampered competition on the world market. But it also saved Britain's middle class from the demoralizing effects of inflation that were felt in most continental countries.

Instability in France

France led a far more hectic existence after the war. It was worse off economically, having suffered greater losses than Britain. Moreover, the French electoral system of proportional representation, introduced after the First World War, aggravated the excessive factionalism of French politics and caused great instability. There were more than forty different cabinets during the interwar period. For the first five years after the war France was governed by a "national bloc" of rightist and center parties, with Raymond Poincaré as the leading figure. In 1924 reversals in foreign policy, notably the Ruhr fiasco, brought to power a "Cartel of the Left," in which Édouard Herriot and Aristide Briand were prominent.

The most urgent task before the French government was the reconstruction of the devastated regions along the northeastern frontiers. Since Germany, until 1924, remained behind in its reparations payments, France had to pay for

Emergency transport in England during the general strike of May 1926.

A Nazi coalition poster of 1924 addressing an anti-Semitic appeal to the "exploited" working class in Germany.

disorder. Early in 1919 a constituent assembly at Weimar had drawn up an admirably democratic constitution. One of its less happy features, however, was the adoption of proportional representation. As in France, this scheme contributed greatly to political instability. During the fourteen years of its existence, the Weimar Republic saw more than twenty different cabinets. The heavy legacy of war required a government that had the full support of its citizens. Throughout most of its brief life, the Weimar Republic failed to win such support.

The most loyal friends of the republic were the workers who had suffered most from political discrimination under the empire. The German working class, however, was no longer united. It had been split before and during the revolution of 1918 into a moderate majority of Social Democrats and a radical minority that later formed the German Communist Party. The latter openly threatened to overthrow the republic and on several occasions between 1919 and 1923 tried to carry out its threat.

Most of the bourgeois parties of the Weimar Republic professed loyalty to the new regime, although the parties of the right were known to be hostile to it. This hostility was nourished by nationalist propaganda, which blamed the republic both for Germany's defeat and for the signing of the *Diktat* of Versailles. Soon after the war, rabidly nationalistic groups of "free corps" and veterans' organizations embarked on a series of uprisings against the hated republic.

Considering the many attacks from every direction, it is surprising that the Weimar Republic was able to survive. But even though most Germans were not very enthusiastic about the new state, they were even less enthusiastic about the extremists who threatened to overthrow it. In the early twenties the moderate antirepublican parties of the right were able to attract almost 30 percent of the votes. The most critical year in the postwar decade was 1923, when the French invasion of the Ruhr, antirepublican risings on the right and left, and the total devaluation of the currency threatened the country's very existence. But as Germany's economy improved after

this reconstruction. Attempts to raise the necessary funds through increased taxation ran into opposition from the parties of the right. Only the threat of runaway inflation and the pressure of public demonstrations finally led to drastic action. In 1926 a cabinet of "national union" under Poincaré was able to stabilize the currency and put France on the road to recovery. With reconstruction completed and German reparations coming in regularly, France's economy improved rapidly. By 1928 the budget began to show a surplus, unemployment had vanished, and increased wages together with benefits from social legislation gave the lower classes a greater share than before in the nation's economy. France seemed well on the way toward resolving the long-standing conflicts between its rich and its poor.

The Weimar Republic

The new German republic was from the beginning plagued by disunity and

1924, the prorepublican parties made significant gains at the expense of the opposition. Had this recovery lasted longer, the Germans might yet have become reconciled to their new republic.

The New Nations of Eastern Europe

If democracy found the going rough in Germany, it faced even greater difficulties in eastern Europe. Most of the states in this area had gained their independence as a result of the war, and most of them faced similar problems. With the exception of Austria and Czechoslovakia, their economy was predominantly agrarian, and the division of large estates among the peasantry had long been a major issue. Where such land reform was carried out successfully, as in the Baltic states, the rise of independent small proprietors contributed greatly to political stability. In Poland and Hungary, on the other hand, where reform was obstructed by the landed aristocracy, domestic peace remained precarious.

Economic recovery in most of eastern Europe was slow. Widespread illiteracy, antiquated agricultural methods, and lack of capital funds for industrialization were the main obstacles. Efforts at economic collaboration, especially among the Austrian succession states, ran into strong nationalist opposition. Nationalism in eastern Europe was intensified by the problem of minorities. Almost all the new nations included large numbers of foreign nationals.

All the new states started out with modern constitutions and parliamentary governments. But this democratic trend was soon reversed. The first to change was Hungary. After a brief communist interlude under Bela Kun in 1919, conservative forces restored order under Admiral Nicholas Horthy, who founded Europe's first postwar dictatorship of the right. In Poland the rise of authoritarian rule came with Marshal Joseph Pilsud-

ski's seizure of power in 1926. Elsewhere "strong men" suspended constitutions and silenced political opposition. With no democratic experience and hopeless economic conditions, firm rule seemed to be the only alternative. None of these regimes was as totalitarian as the communist dictatorship in Russia or the fascist dictatorship in Italy. It was only after Hitler's rise in the 1930s, when fascism gained control over most of central Europe, that the rule of these small dictators became increasingly arbitrary (see Chapter 32).

Of the few countries in eastern Europe where democracy took hold after the war, the most important were Czechoslovakia and Austria. Czechoslovakia,

German Inflation

The prewar value of the German mark was twenty-five cents. When I first went to Munich at the end of 1921, I already could get about a hundred marks for a dollar. A year later I was getting about sixty-five hundred marks for the dollar. Then, in January 1923, French armies marched into Germany's richest industrial region, the Ruhr, and the German Government decided to finance passive resistance to such foreign military occupation. . . . and for this purpose printed enormous additional amounts of paper money. A month after the occupation of the Ruhr, I was getting more than forty thousand marks for a dollar, and the bottom of the money market began to drop out completely. By August a dollar was buying millions, in September billions, in October trillions of marks. A sad cartoon appeared in a Munich paper showing a little girl sitting beside two huge bundles of paper money, crying pitifully. A passerby was saying: "Why are you crying, little girl?" She answered: "Someone stole the leather straps off my money!" I occasionally played a dollar limit poker game for German marks. When we began that game, the limit was one hundred marks; in October 1923, one trillion marks. It was quite a thrill to raise a trillion.

Finally, that month, the German Government virtually repudiated its enormous public debt by introducing a new unit of value called the rentenmark. . . . This meant that every German who had sacrificed and saved to provide for his old age and for his family was ruined.

From Robert Murphy, *Diplomat Among Warriors* (New York: Doubleday, 1964), pp. 37–38.

ably led by Thomas Masaryk and Eduard Beneš, was generally considered the model among the new democracies. Here land reform was carried out successfully, and with almost half of Austria's former industry under Czech control the country enjoyed a balanced economy. Czechoslovakia's major problem was the desire for greater autonomy among its numerous minorities, which amounted to almost one-third of its population. Especially troublesome were the 3 million Germans living in the Sudeten region.

Austria, since the war, had only Germans within its borders. But even so the new republic was deeply divided along social and economic lines between the urban, industrialized, and radical workers of Vienna, and the rural, agrarian, and conservative peasants of the provinces. Economically, Austria suffered greatly from the consequences of partition. In 1922 the situation became so serious that the League had to step in and grant substantial loans for Austrian reconstruction. By 1926 Austria seemed to be out of danger. But the real cause of her difficulties—the loss of her economic hinterland—had not been removed. As the least viable among the new states of Europe, Austria was to be the first to feel the effects of the Great Depression that spread from the United States to Europe during the early thirties.

THE UNITED STATES AND EUROPE

The recovery of Europe, though uneven, seemed well under way by 1929. It would have been still further advanced had the United States been more aware of its new responsibilities as the world's leading economic power. But America at first preferred to keep aloof from European affairs.

Isolationism and Nationalism

Most Europeans considered this policy of isolationism extremely selfish. America, after all, had suffered much less from the war than Europe had. As a matter of fact, the United States had gained from the war economically, not merely by supplying the Allies but by penetrating into regions formerly controlled by European commerce. The least America could do, or so many Europeans felt, was to forget the loans it had made to its allies during the war. But this the United States refused to do.

There were other sources of friction between the United States and its wartime friends. The French resented America's refusal to honor President Wilson's promise for a joint guarantee, together with Britain, of French security; the British were alarmed by America's growing commercial and naval competition; and neither France nor Britain welcomed the evident *rapprochement* between the United States and Germany. A further cause for concern among Europeans was America's obvious intent of isolating itself not only politically but economically. In an effort to protect American industry against the competition of cheap foreign labor, America during the 1920s introduced some of the highest tariffs in its history.

America's isolationism had its domestic roots in a growing opposition to "foreign" and "radical" influences. This American nationalism manifested itself in several ways. The Ku Klux Klan soon after the war claimed wide support for its persecution of racial and religious minorities; fear of radical elements caused a "red scare" that led to the arrest of several thousand suspects; and, most important, restrictions on foreign immigration severely restricted the flow of immigrants from backward and hence less desirable regions.

American Involvement in Europe

But no matter how much the United States tried to isolate itself, its humanitarian conscience and its economic interests could not help but lead to renewed involvement in international affairs. Americans had already proved themselves far from isolationist as far as charity was concerned. Various relief organizations right after the war had dispensed millions of dollars' worth of supplies wherever they were most needed, even in the Soviet Union. Beginning in 1924 American experts also took

New Members (kneeling in front) being sworn into the Ku Klux Klan, June 1922, in Maryland.

the lead in tackling the reparations problem. With the return of economic stability, American investors during the next five years lent vast amounts to various European countries, especially Germany, Italy, and the smaller nations of central Europe.

In the political sphere America shared the hope of the rest of the world for peace and security. The warm reception that the American people gave the Pact of Paris for "the outlawry of war" was seen by some as a hopeful sign that America had outgrown its isolationism. But in other respects the country remained aloof. Even though many Americans had come to favor the League of Nations, the government refused to participate in any except the League's cultural and social work.

America was also concerned over disarmament, not so much on land as on sea. The rising influence of Japan in the Pacific posed a threat to American interests, and the large increase in Japanese naval expenditure made some limitation of naval forces seem highly desirable. Agreement on this point was reached at a naval conference in Washington in 1921–22. It called for a ten-year naval holiday, the scrapping of large numbers of ships, and a fixed ratio of 5:5:3 respectively for the capital ships of the United States, Britain, and Japan. Simultaneous political agreements guaranteed the *status quo* in the Pacific, reaffirmed the "open door" policy for China, and ended the Anglo-Japanese alliance of 1902. Subsequent efforts at Geneva in 1927 to extend the naval agreement to small ships failed because the British refused to recognize America's claim to parity for all categories. The issue was finally settled to American satisfaction at a third conference in London three years later. But because Japan, France, and Italy remained dissatisfied with the results, these attempts at naval limitation were only partly successful.

AMERICA DURING THE "ROARING TWENTIES"

Although the United States had come out of the war unscathed, it found adjustment to peacetime conditions far from easy. American industry had expanded far beyond its prewar capacity, and the sudden cancellation of government contracts deeply upset the economy. As European industries resumed production, furthermore, United States exports declined. Attempts to cut production costs by lowering wages met with strong opposition from the workers and once the wartime ban on strikes was lifted, labor unrest revived.

Return to "Normalcy"

In domestic as in foreign affairs, the American people were looking back with nostalgia to the peace and prosperity they had known before the war. The man who promised a return to such "normalcy" was the Republican Warren G. Harding, who was elected President by a large majority in 1920. It was under Harding's administration that America entered upon the era of hectic prosperity for which the 1920s are best remembered. The heyday of the "Roaring Twenties" came under Calvin Coolidge.

The Republican administration's overriding concern was with aiding the American business community. High tariffs, the repeal of the excess-profits tax, the lowering of taxes on corporations and on high incomes, injunctions against strikes, and even the persecution of "radicals" and the restriction of foreign immigration—all these measures directly or indirectly benefited big business. America's phenomenal business expansion was also due to the ample capital resources and growing investments that were available from a broader segment of society. Big business, so it seemed, was becoming everybody's business.

President Calvin Coolidge at work on his Vermont farm, *ca.* 1925.

Monte Ryan and the Percival Mackey jazz band rehearsing on a London roof, *ca.* 1930.

countries to retaliate by cutting down their imports of American grain.

The "Jazz Age"

There was an air of restlessness about America's frantic pursuit of business and pleasure during the "Jazz Age" of the 1920s. As is common in periods of rapid economic expansion, America had its share of private and public corruption. The Eighteenth Amendment of 1920, by its rigorous prohibition of alcoholic beverages, almost invited violation of the law by the average citizen. The "speakeasy" and the "bootlegger" became part of American life, and "racketeering" was a common form of crime.

These, unfortunately, were the features that made the deepest impression abroad. Europeans professed to be shocked by the "materialism" of their *nouveau riche* American cousins. But Europe did not remain entirely immune to American influences. American products and production methods found ready imitators abroad, and American styles and American jazz had their admirers among the young. For the first time in history Europe showed signs of becoming Americanized.

The American people themselves seemed well satisfied with their country's apparently endless progress. In 1928 they voted overwhelmingly for another Republican President, Herbert Hoover. Some developments, however, should have caused alarm. Already before 1929 expansion in some basic areas had begun to slow down. Commodity prices had declined steadily from their peak in 1925 and agricultural prices continued to fall. These signs of recession were obscured by a continuing boom on the American stock market. Here prices were bid up by speculators, mostly with borrowed funds, to levels far out of proportion to dividends and earnings. The first danger signals came in mid-September 1929, when stock prices showed some decline. Failures of speculative companies in London later in the month caused some tremors on Wall Street, but still no panic. The collapse of the American stock market came suddenly, on October 23. The next day, "Black Thursday," American investors sold close to 20 million shares

It was not quite everybody's, though. Neither the worker nor the farmer was getting his due share of prosperity. Labor had suffered from the postwar depression and from the popular hysteria that equated union protest with communism. As a result, union membership during the 1920s declined from its wartime high. The American Federation of Labor held its own among skilled workers, but there was no similar organization for the mass of unskilled labor. Even so, most workers in time benefited from the nation's rising economy through almost full employment and better wages.

The stepchild of the American boom was the farmer. He, too, had expanded his operations during the war, borrowing large funds to buy additional land and equipment. As a result, America's farm output by 1919 had more than doubled. Then, as foreign demand decreased and surpluses accumulated, prices dropped and never regained their former level. The government tried to help farmers by creating additional credit facilities and encouraging cooperatives, but the Republican administration shrank away from anything that smacked of direct subsidies. Protective tariffs, furthermore, raised the price of industrial products needed by the farmer and led foreign at a total loss of $40 billion. The Great Depression was on its way.

THE GREAT DEPRESSION

With the rise of industrialization, "business cycles"—that is, alternating phases of prosperity and depression—had become a recognized feature of modern capitalism. But there had never been a depression quite so severe as the one following the American stock market crash. The basic cause of the depression was the world's failure to solve the economic problems inherited from the First World War. Neither at the Peace Conference nor afterward was there any real awareness of how interdependent the world had become economically. Industrial expansion continued full force after the war and soon led to overproduction. Beginning in 1924 a brief period of recovery set in. But that recovery was artificial. As neither farmers nor workers really shared in the economic rise, purchasing power failed to keep up with production. In countries like Germany and Austria, furthermore, industrial expansion was largely stimulated by foreign credits. As these credits dried up, recovery ceased and the economy of these nations collapsed.

This, however, did not happen until the spring of 1931. In the meantime the situation in central Europe had become serious enough to demand radical remedies. One solution proposed in early 1931 was for an Austro-German customs union. But this proposal met with strong opposition from the French, who regarded it as a first step toward an eventual political *Anschluss.* To put pressure on the Austrians, France began to withdraw some of its short-term credits. In May 1931 Austria's largest private bank collapsed. This is generally seen as the beginning of the European phase of the Great Depression. In July the first German bank suspended payments. In September the British government abandoned the gold standard. As other nations followed Britain's example, the only major European power to cling to the gold standard was France. Here the depression was not seriously felt until 1932.

Effects of the Depression

It is difficult to convey the staggering economic blow that the world suffered in the brief span of three or four years after 1929. World industrial production declined more than one-third, prices dropped more than one-half, and more than 30 million people lost their jobs. Some countries were harder hit than others. Germany's industrial production declined by almost 40 percent, and at the height of the depression only one-third of Germany's workers were fully employed. In the United States, industrial production and national income by 1933 had decreased more than one-half, and the unemployment figure was estimated at 14 million.

Because of the worldwide scope of the depression, any attempt to counteract it demanded cooperation among all the major powers. As debtor nations began to default on their obligations, President Hoover in 1931 initiated a year's moratorium on all reparations and war debts. But this proved to be only a stopgap. A year later an economic conference at

Soup kitchen in New York City during the Great Depression, 1931.

President-elect Roosevelt greets President Hoover on the way to the Inauguration, March 4, 1933.

Roosevelt's New Deal

In our day these economic truths have become accepted as self-evident . . . :

The right to a useful and remunerative job in the industries or shops or farms or mines of the nation;

The right to earn enough to provide adequate food and clothing and recreation;

The right of every farmer to raise and sell his products at a return which will give him and his family a decent living;

The right of every businessman, large or small, to trade in an atmosphere of freedom from unfair competition and domination by monopolies at home or abroad;

The right of every family to a decent home;

The right to adequate protection from the economic fears of old age, sickness, accident and unemployment;

The right to a good education.

All of these rights spell security. . . . For unless there is security here at home there cannot be lasting peace in the world.

Franklin D. Roosevelt, message to Congress, January 11, 1944.

Lausanne all but buried the troublesome problem of intergovernmental debts. To save Germany from complete chaos, "standstill agreements" in 1931 temporarily stopped the panicky withdrawal of short-term loans from that country; but this did not halt the country's economic decline. Finally, a World Economic Conference in London in 1933 sought to stabilize currencies. It failed when America refused to adopt its proposals.

International efforts to pull the world out of its economic slump thus turned out to be either too little or too late. In the meantime governments everywhere reverted to the same practices that had helped to bring on the depression in the first place. As America raised its tariffs to unprecedented heights, the rest of the powers followed suit, with even Britain abandoning its traditional policy of free trade in 1932. These and other measures of economic nationalism hindered the revival of international trade.

THE DEMOCRACIES ON THE EVE OF THE SECOND WORLD WAR

The Great Depression belonged to both world wars—its roots went back to the First, and its effects contributed to the Second. While governments were still trying to repair the damages of the upheaval of 1929, clouds were already gathering for the far greater catastrophe of 1939. In this mounting crisis, resolute political leadership was imperative. In countries like Germany and the successor states of central Europe, democratic governments were no longer able to provide such leadership. As authoritarian regimes gained the upper hand, these nations were lost to the democratic cause. But even among the western democracies the crisis of the 1930s called for firm guidance of political and economic affairs. The need for such guidance was felt particularly strongly in the United States.

The United States: The "New Deal"

The Hoover administration, unwilling to interfere with free enterprise, had done too little to help relieve the economic crisis. Discontent with Republican half-measures was chiefly responsible for the Democratic sweep in the elections of 1932. For more than twelve years thereafter, the United States was guided by Franklin D. Roosevelt. The new President was a superb politician and an inveterate optimist, who met the most difficult domestic and foreign emergencies with a boldness and confidence that earned him the admiration of the majority of Americans.

Many of Roosevelt's measures were intended for immediate relief and were thus of passing significance, but many others remain in effect to the present day. Republicans at the time charged that government interference with free enterprise, together with vast "give-away programs," tended to corrupt America's pioneering spirit of self-reliance and would ultimately lead to socialism and bankruptcy. In taxing the rich and aiding the poor, America certainly went far toward repudiating its traditional faith in laissez faire. But the rising standard of living of the masses tended to hasten rather than retard the growth of American business; and if the "New Deal" entailed staggering financial burdens, the nation as a whole seemed willing and able to bear them. The unanimity with which the American people supported the country's war efforts during the Second World War was certainly due in no small measure to the peaceful social and economic revolution of the preceding decade.

Great Britain: Slow Recovery

The most successful holding action against the depression in Europe was waged in Great Britain. In the hope of rallying parliamentary support, Ramsay MacDonald in 1931 transformed his Labor cabinet into a national coalition government. Subsequent elections, however, returned overwhelming Conservative majorities, and in 1935 Stanley Baldwin took over as Prime Minister. He was succeeded two years later by Neville Chamberlain. As might be expected from a predominantly Conservative regime, Britain sought to solve its economic problems by retrenchment rather than

reform. Taxes were raised, government expenditures were cut, and interest rates were lowered. The devaluation of the pound stimulated exports. By the Imperial Duties Bill of 1932 the Conservatives at long last won their battle for protectionism. Subsequent trade agreements with Germany, the Scandinavian countries, and Russia improved British sales abroad. The overall effect of these measures was a modest but steady recovery. This was due more to the strength of the nation's capital reserves, however, than to any farsighted government policy. The Conservatives were deeply opposed to governmental economic planning. Instead, they preferred to have industry help itself. National income, to be sure, increased; but the basis of Britain's economy, its export trade, did not increase commeasurably.

There were few important events in British politics during the 1930s. King Edward VIII abdicated in 1936 to marry an untitled divorcee. By catering to the average Briton's innate conservatism, his abdication seemed to strengthen the monarchy rather than weaken it. Economic improvement helped to keep labor unrest at a minimum. Britain's main concern was with developments abroad, where Italy and Germany had started on the course of aggression that was to culminate in the Second World War.

France: A House Divided

In contrast to England and the United States, where democracy successfully withstood the severe test of depression, the French Third Republic during the 1930s was shaken to its very foundations. With a high degree of self-sufficiency, a huge gold reserve, and no unemployment to speak of, France until 1932 was an island of prosperity in a sea of economic misery. But when disaster came it struck swiftly. By 1935 French industrial production had fallen almost one-third, exports were declining rapidly, and capital was fleeing the country at an alarming rate. Things looked up briefly after the government devalued the franc in 1936, but the rise in domestic prices soon neutralized any advantage.

It was not so much the severity of the economic crisis as the inability of the

Ramsay MacDonald and Stanley Baldwin at a press conference in 1931, during their national coalition government.

The Stavisky Riots of early February 1934, in which thousands of persons were injured and a number killed.

French government to cope with it that accounts for the political chaos that ended with the fall of France in 1940. The Third Republic had been deeply divided from the start. As time went on and France became more and more industrialized, economic differences accentuated political divisions. Workers and petty employees were virtual outcasts from French society, while the right-leaning wealthy classes and peasants had little enthusiasm for the Republic. The war had temporarily drawn the nation together, and once the difficult postwar transition had been made French domestic tensions at long last seemed to have eased. But at this most critical point, the depression intervened, reopening wounds that had only just begun to heal.

Discontent with the government's handling of the economic crisis flared up with sudden violence during the Stavisky scandal in early 1934. Rumors that the machinations of an unsavory promoter, Alexander Stavisky, had enjoyed support from persons high in the government touched off a major riot among rightist elements in Paris. Many of the rioters were members of various fascist leagues, right-wing and royalist organizations, which in aims and tactics were similar to Hitler's storm troopers and Mussolini's Blackshirts. Fascism, like communism, was apt to strike any country weakened by internal discord.

The government's efforts to meet the emergency by rallying the country behind a cabinet of national union, such as Poincaré had formed in 1926, proved fruitless. In 1936 the parties of the left—Radical Socialists, Socialists, and Communists—became sufficiently alarmed over the fascist threat, both at home and abroad, to bury their longstanding differences. Their "Popular Front" won a decisive popular victory in the subsequent elections.

For almost two years various leftist coalitions, in which the Socialist Léon Blum was the leading figure, tried their best to halt the disintegration of the Republic. Blum introduced more far-reaching reforms than any government since the war. But to succeed, Blum's program of social reform needed the cooperation of French businessmen and bankers. And that cooperation was not forthcoming. There were other obstacles to recovery, notably the unsettled state of international affairs, which called for costly rearmament. But the basic reason for Blum's failure was that he was too radical for the right and not radical enough for the left.

While the Germans were preparing to fight the world, the French were fighting one another. Successive waves of "sit-down" strikes—a French innovation—and a rigidly enforced forty-hour week slowed down industry when it should have been working overtime. In April 1938 a slight shift to the right brought Édouard Daladier to the premiership, with far-reaching powers to rule by decree. But Daladier could not do what many abler men before him had failed to do: heal the breach between right and left, bourgeoisie and workers, capitalists and socialists, rich and poor. It was a deeply divided France that went to war in September 1939, and that Hitler found in the spring of 1940.

THE TWILIGHT OF IMPERIALISM

This discussion of events between the two world wars has dealt thus far only with Europe and the United States. But there were important developments elsewhere in the world that affected especially those countries that had colonial possessions. Beginning with the First World War, western imperialism entered upon a slow but steady decline. Economists had long questioned the advantages of colonies to the mother country, and historians had claimed that colonial rivalry had been one of the major causes of the war. The war itself had weakened the great powers and had aroused a feeling of nationalism among the colonial peoples. Just as the desire for independence among European nations had made for international unrest during the nineteenth century, so colonial nationalism was a major cause of international tension in the twentieth.

The Mandate System

The powers had shown signs of a more enlightened attitude toward colonies at the Paris Peace Conference, when they made the mandate system part of the League of Nations Covenant. The former German colonies and certain territories taken from Turkey were to be administered by mandatory powers responsible to the League. In theory this first experiment in international supervision over backward regions was a worthy innovation. But in practice the former German colonies became almost indistinguishable from the mandatory powers' own colonies; and of the more advanced Turkish regions that were promised ultimate independence, only Iraq became a sovereign state. Transjordan, under British tutelage like Iraq, was considered too weak to stand on its own feet. The French mandates, Syria and Lebanon, made some progress toward self-government, but the constitutions granted these countries assured French control.

A special case among Turkey's former possessions was the British mandate of Palestine. The root of the trouble in that area was the conflicting national aspirations of Arabs and Jews. Nationalism among the Jews went back to the Zionist Organization, founded by Theodor Herzl in 1897 to provide a home for the Jews in Palestine. In 1917 the British government, in the so-called Balfour Declaration, had backed these Zionist aspirations, with the qualification "that nothing shall be done which may prejudice the civil and religious rights of existing non-Jewish communities in Palestine." Both Arabs and Jews at first seemed ready to cooperate in joint plans for the future of Palestine. But as more and more Jews migrated to Palestine, the Arabs feared that the Jews would emerge as the dominant faction. In 1929 the first major riots broke out among Arabs and Jews. With the advent of Hitler in 1933, Palestine became a refuge for thousands of Jews and immigration increased manyfold. The result was further tension and intermittent violence between Arabs and Jews. On the eve of the Second World War, the future of Palestine was still far from settled.

The British Commonwealth

The mandate system was not the only innovation in colonial administration after the First World War. There were also important changes within the British Empire. During the nineteenth century those regions of the empire inhabited chiefly by white settlers had gradually changed from colonies into self-governing dominions. This emancipation from British influence continued after the war. The dominions had served loyally at the side of the mother country during the war. But at the Peace Conference, on matters concerning their own interests, they had shown considerable independence. When the dominions refused to follow Britain's lead, on several other occasions during the 1920s, it became clear that the relationship needed clarification. This was achieved at the Imperial Conference of 1926. The formula agreed upon at that time stated that Great Britain and the dominions were to be completely equal in status, united only through common allegiance to the crown. The British Commonwealth of Nations thus established was officially launched by the Statute of Westminster in 1931. The dominions became fully sovereign states, bound to the mother country merely by ties of blood, sentiment, and economic self-interest.

Even so tenuous a relationship, however, was too much for one member of the Commonwealth—Ireland. Efforts to extend home rule to that unhappy island had been interrupted by the outbreak of

Theodor Herzl in 1904.

war in 1914. During the war, the anti-British Easter Rebellion of 1916, spear-headed by the Republican Sinn Fein movement, had been put down with undue severity. From that point on, Sinn Fein became the most dynamic force in Irish politics. In 1921 Britain set up the Irish Free State, which held dominion status and thus shared in the transition from Empire to Commonwealth. Yet in the midst of this hopeful development the depression came, and with it a resurgence of radicalism. In the elections of 1932 the Republicans gained a majority and their leader, Eamon De Valera, became president. During the next few years Ireland severed most of its connections with Great Britain. A new constitution in 1937 completely ignored crown and Commonwealth.

India

Another part of the British Empire that was clamoring for independence was India. Like the dominions, India had stood by Great Britain during the war. As a reward for this support, India expected to be given self-government. A new Government of India Act in 1919, however, still fell far short of home rule. The extremists in the National Congress Party, therefore, refused to cooperate. The new leader of the Congress Party was Mohandas K. Gandhi. A lawyer educated in England, Gandhi had supported the British during the First World War, only to become their most persistent foe thereafter. The keynote of his policy was "noncooperation," an attempt to bring about the breakdown of British rule through passive resistance.

England entered into many fruitless conferences and proposals to try to solve the Indian problem. Since all of them fell short of granting at least dominion status, the National Congress turned them down. The claim of the Congress Party that it represented all of India was denied by the Moslem League of Mohammed Ali Jinnah. This religious split was India's most burning problem. But there were others—economic crises, natural catastrophes, riots, strikes, and famines—all of them adding to the country's extreme instability. When war began in 1939, India's entrance into the family of Com-

Mohandas Ghandi arriving at an Indian conference in London, 1931.

monwealth nations seemed as far away as it had been twenty years earlier.

Colonial Nationalism

The colonial nationalism that caused so much trouble in India was felt elsewhere in the British Empire and in the overseas possessions of the other powers. Britain's protectorate over Egypt was officially terminated in 1922, but continued British control over the Sudan and the Suez Canal gave the Egyptian nationalist "Wafd" party ample cause for agitation. France, in theory at least, had for some time granted French citizenship and representation in the French parliament to some of its colonies. But the French method of centralized rule discouraged the growth of colonial self-government. In advanced regions like North Africa and Indochina, native nationalists rebelled against Frenchification and demanded a voice in running their own affairs. Similarly, in the Netherlands East Indies a swiftly growing nationalist movement opposed the enlightened but paternalistic rule of the Dutch.

The End of American Colonialism

One country that was in earnest about abandoning its imperialist practices was the United States. America had only one real colony, the Philippines. After repeatedly promising independence to the islands, Congress in 1934 provided for American withdrawal after a transition period of ten years. In 1946 the Philippines became a sovereign nation. In Latin America, American "dollar diplomacy" continued briefly after the First World War. But in time the United States adopted a more benevolent "good neighbor policy," especially in economic matters. In 1930 the Clark Memorandum abandoned the Roosevelt Corollary to the Monroe Doctrine, which had been used in the past to excuse United States intervention in Latin America.

THE FAR EAST: PRELUDE TO WAR

Almost everywhere in the world, colonialism after the First World War found itself on the defensive against native nationalism. The only region where imperialism still thrived was in the Far East. There Japan, between the two world wars, embarked on a wholly new phase of expansion, mainly at the expense of China. During the war the Chinese Republic had already felt the threat of its powerful neighbor: The Twenty-one Demands of 1915 had established a Japanese sphere of influence over the mainland opposite Japan; and Chinese efforts at the peace conference to enlist Allied support in regaining the Shantung Peninsula had proved in vain. Only when the powers realized that Japanese expansion might threaten their own interests did they become alarmed. The Washington Conference of 1921–22, while dealing primarily with naval disarmament, had also discussed the future of China. The powers at Washington reaffirmed the "open door" principle and promised to respect China's integrity and independence. In effect things after the war were where they had been before 1914.

China under the Kuomintang

China's domestic affairs, since the death of General Yüan in 1916, had been chaotic, with powerful warlords ruling various provinces. The only group that held any promise for the future was the Chinese Nationalist Party, or Kuomintang. But although its leader, Sun Yat-sen, was elected president in 1921, his influence was restricted to a small region around Canton. His program of freeing China from outside influences needed foreign help. Since he had been rebuffed by the West in the past, Sun Yat-sen in 1923 turned to the Russians for aid.

The Soviet Union welcomed the Chinese Republic not only as an ally against Japan but also as a possible convert to communism. A small Chinese Communist Party had been founded in 1921. As a result of its collaboration with the U.S.S.R., the Kuomintang, hitherto a small organization, now became a mass movement. To provide the trained military forces necessary to unite China, a military academy was founded under the direction of an able young officer and ardent follower of Sun Yat-sen, Chiang Kai-shek. Sun Yat-sen himself did not live to see the initial success of his movement for unification. He died in 1925 and to this day remains the saint and symbol of the struggle for Chinese unity.

The campaign against the northern warlords was led by Chiang Kai-shek. It began in 1926 and was successful. By 1929 the Nationalist government controlled the whole country from its headquarters at Nanking. But except for the lower Yangtze region, its control was at best nominal. In the West and North the provincial warlords maintained their power; and to the south, in Kiangsi and Fukien provinces, the Chinese Communists under Mao Tse-tung and Chu Teh were busy organizing the landless peasants in opposition to the Nanking regime. The breach between Chiang Kai-shek and the Communists had come in 1927 when Chiang, in a sudden purge, had freed himself from Russian and Communist influence. Here were the seeds of the domestic conflict that was to have such serious consequences after the Second World War.

In the meantime the Nationalist regime had begun to tackle the many problems it had inherited from the past. The western powers assisted by making a few concessions, although most of these did not go far enough. In 1929

Chiang Kai-shek (above) succeeded Sun Yat-sen to the leadership of the Kuomintang in 1925 and led the Nationalist government in Nanking. Mao Tse-tung (below) led the Communist faction in southern China in opposition to the Nationalists.

Chiang Kai-shek terminated unilaterally the obnoxious treaties granting extraterritoriality to western nations. Railroad construction, a uniform currency, legal reform, and an income tax all tried to help overcome the country's regionalism and backwardness. But the failure of the Nationalist government to introduce an effective agrarian program left the Chinese masses discontented and open to communist agitation. Added to domestic discord and disunity was the constant threat of Japanese intervention.

Moderation in Japan

Japan, in contrast to China, had fared well during the First World War. The country had profited economically from the increased demand for Japanese goods; it had gained territorially from the seizure of German colonies; and it had established a veiled protectorate over part of China. Any desire for further expansion among Japan's militarists was checked by Allied resistance at the Washington Conference in 1921–22. A terrible earthquake in 1923, furthermore, tied down the nation's energies at home. The 1920s were taken up chiefly with domestic developments. The outward westernization of Japan continued, especially among the middle class. In 1925 universal manhood suffrage was introduced. Apathy among the voters, however, together with the limited powers of the Diet, retarded further democratic growth.

The comparative moderation of Japan's policy was especially apparent in the country's relations with China. In 1922 Shantung was returned to China, with Japan retaining only its commercial privileges. A number of moderate Japanese premiers recognized China's right to organize its own affairs and did not hinder the Kuomintang's policies so long as they did not affect Japan's interests. Only when Chiang Kai-shek's move into northern China threatened Japan's sphere of interest in Manchuria were Japanese troops once more sent to Shantung. As late as 1930, however, Japan still recognized China's tariff autonomy; and in October of that year the government, over the violent protests of Japanese pa-

triots, ratified the London Naval Treaty, which further limited naval construction. But this was the end of the era of moderation. The depression began to hit Japan with disastrous results. The need for cuts in military spending particularly alarmed the militarists, who now came to the fore again, advocating their own brand of totalitarianism. In 1931 they urged Japan into the invasion of Manchuria, which touched off a sequence of events that ended in the Second World War.

AN AGE OF UNCERTAINTY

The years from 1919 to 1939 in retrospect appear as a succession of political and economic crises that were almost bound to lead to another major war. There had been a brief return to normality during the mid-twenties, but even then the world had not regained the feeling of optimism that had characterized the period before 1914. The war and its aftermath had shaken many traditional beliefs and had disappointed many cherished hopes. National self-determination and democracy, it seemed, did not necessarily solve Europe's political problems; nor did rugged individualism and

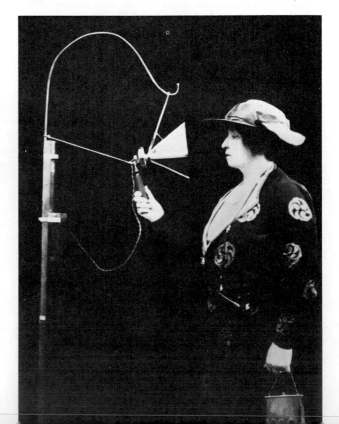

A "miracle" of the twenties: a radio broadcast (featuring operatic soprano Dame Nellie Melba).

laissez faire provide the answer to the world's economic ills. The hope that human reason would solve the few remaining "riddles of the universe" was being undermined by new scientific discoveries, and the widely held belief in unlimited progress seemed open to serious question. As a result of growing doubts about hitherto accepted values, the intellectual climate during the postwar era changed from its prewar feeling of confidence to one of uneasiness and uncertainty.

Material Progress

Not everyone, of course, was equally sensitive to these changes. The majority of people, once they had overcome the hardships of war, were ready to enjoy the spectacular achievements that engineering science had in store for them. Material progress certainly seemed as promising as ever. Not only were there such new "miracles" as the radio, the talking picture, and ultimately television, but constant improvements in production and marketing made these and earlier inventions, like the automobile, available to the average person. The veritable avalanche of laborsaving devices and gadgets that combined to make up a "high standard of living" did not necessarily make life richer, but they certainly made things more comfortable.

Other technological and scientific achievements changed man's everyday life. Improvements in the field of transportation virtually eliminated distance as a barrier. The Old World and the New, up to then days apart, became separated only by hours. Some of the most spectacular developments took place in medicine. A concentrated attack—through research, public hygiene, and improvements in nutrition—brought some of the most deadly diseases under control. This accomplishment in turn led to a lengthening of the average lifespan in the more advanced countries from less than fifty years at the beginning of the century to almost sixty-five years by 1939. Modern science and industry thus continued to fulfill their promise of enabling people to live both better and longer than at any earlier time in history.

Critics of Mass Culture

But material progress was not without its drawbacks, as a few social critics were beginning to point out. The growth of population prior to the Second World War was seen as a threat to cultural values more than to the world's food supply. The Spanish philosopher Ortega y Gasset, in his book *The Revolt of the Masses* (1932), warned that the increase in human beings was so rapid that it was no longer possible to educate modern man in the traditions of his civilization. As a result, the gap between the cultured few and the superficially educated many was wider than ever and becoming more so. And since it was the masses who really exerted political and economic power, their low standards would henceforth be imposed upon society as a whole.

Other voices were raised against the dangers of a civilization that envisaged progress entirely in material terms. One of the most perceptive critics was the British novelist Aldous Huxley, who, in his satirical novel *Brave New World* (1932), predicted with uncanny foresight many later "triumphs" of human ingenuity, from tranquillizer pills to brainwashing. The picture Huxley painted was of a well-adjusted society whose members were scientifically conditioned to whatever status they occupied, existing like animals or vegetables on a well-tended experimental farm. Man as a slave to his technological inventions, as a mere cipher in a collectivist society, as a rootless, lonely, and lost being in a world of bewildering complexity—such were the subjects that increasingly occupied social critics, novelists, and poets.

The "Behavioral Sciences"

The study of man, both as an individual and as a member of society, had

Other "miracles" of the 1900s: a 1932 Ford motor car; an automatic two-slice toaster, manufactured in 1928, that rings a bell when the toast is ready and automatically turns off the current; and an "easily wheeled" Vortex vacuum cleaner, *ca.* 1920.

Sigmund Freud, on the occasion of his only trip to America, September 1909.

for some time past been the task of the social sciences. This term had at first been used only for the traditional subjects: history, political science, and economics. But in time the field had been widened to include the new "behavioral sciences": psychology, sociology, and cultural anthropology.

The beginnings of modern psychology are associated with the name of Sigmund Freud, a Viennese doctor who began formulating his theories at the turn of the century. There had been psychologists before him. True to the spirit of materialism that prevailed at the end of the nineteenth century, men like the German Wilhelm Wundt and the American William James had tried to discover the organic roots of human behavior, assuming that the brain, like any other organ, performed purely biological functions. Freud's approach was radically different. Basic to his teachings was the idea that human behavior is directed by subconscious instincts, or "drives," of which the most repressed is the sexual impulse. These drives are inhibited, usu-

ally in early childhood, and such inhibition leads to various degrees of frustration, which in turn may cause serious neuroses. In an effort to cure his patients, Freud developed a technique called "psychoanalysis," which consisted of an extended and deep probing of the patient's mind to get at the subconscious layers ordinarily revealed only in dreams. The purpose of such probing was to make the patient understand the conflicts that caused his abnormal behavior and by such understanding remove the causes of his mental disturbance.

Freud was not the only pioneer in modern psychology; there were others, notably the Russian Ivan Pavlov. All of them tried to discover at long last what made people act the way they did. The knowledge they gained should have been a source of great satisfaction. But actually, in the beginning at least, the opposite was true. Ever since the Age of Enlightenment man had gloried in the belief that he was a wholly intelligent and rational being. Now suddenly he was faced by the realization that he was subject to dark instincts and drives, and that it was these forces rather than his intellect that determined his behavior. Far from increasing man's self-confidence, modern psychology merely added to his feeling of bewilderment and uncertainty.

The second of the behavioral sciences, sociology, had its beginnings in the nineteenth century with men like Auguste Comte, Karl Marx, and Herbert Spencer. But here, too, the twentieth century introduced new methods and provided many new insights. One of the most important modern sociologists was the Italian Vilfredo Pareto, whose *Mind and Society* was published in English in 1935. Pareto accepted the findings of the psychologists that men were swayed by emotion rather than guided by reason. The ideals or rationalizations that social groups set up were to him mere fronts, or "derivations," which screened the basic irrational motives, or "residues," that really moved people to act. Pareto held that any clever leader or any elite capable of seeing through this human self-deception could use the basic aims of their fellow men to gain supremacy

The Freudian Revolution

Freud's extraordinary achievement was to show us, in scientific terms, the primacy of natural desire, the secret wishes we proclaim in our dreams, the mixture of love and shame and jealousy in our relations to our parents, the child as father to the man, the deeply buried instincts that make us natural beings and that go back to the forgotten struggles of the human race. Until Freud, novelists and dramatists had never dared to think that science would back up their belief that personal passion is a stronger force in people's lives than socially accepted morality. Thanks to Freud, these insights now form a widely shared body of knowledge.

In short, Freud had the ability, such as is given to very few individuals, to introduce a wholly new factor into human knowledge; to impress it upon people's minds as something for which there was evidence. He revealed a part of reality that many people before him had guessed at, but which no one before him was able to describe as systematically and convincingly as he did. In the same way that one associates the discovery of certain fundamentals with Copernicus, Newton, Darwin, Einstein, so one identifies many of one's deepest motivations with Freud. His name is no longer the name of a man; like "Darwin," it is now synonymous with a part of nature.

From Alfred Kazin, "The Freudian Revolution Analyzed," *The New York Times Magazine*, May 6, 1956.

Margaret Mead visiting a
school in New Guinea.

and to establish an authoritarian system in which the masses would obey slogans that appealed to their inner instincts. Pareto thus seemed to provide a "scientific" explanation of fascist totalitarianism. His analysis, if correct, certainly held little hope for a rationally ordered, democratic society.

The third behavioral science, cultural anthropology, likewise tried to find answers to the question of what determined human behavior. By carefully studying primitive tribes, chiefly American Indians and the natives of Pacific islands, anthropologists like Ruth Benedict and Margaret Mead hoped to determine what role environment played in shaping a given culture. One of their discoveries was that differences between cultures were due chiefly to environmental influences rather than to inherent biological factors and that there was no basis for the belief—so dear to many people before 1914—in "superior" and "inferior" races. It was one thing, however, to study a small primitive tribe and another to apply the same research techniques to larger and more complex cultures. But some promising beginnings were made. Students in the field of "human relations," through detailed case studies, were able to gather valuable data on small segments of their own society, in the hope of determining what motivated its members.

Spengler and Toynbee

Most social scientists were concerned with the present rather than the past. Even historians dealing with past events often did so to gain a better understanding of the present. Some of them, notably the German Oswald Spengler and the Englishman Arnold Toynbee, studied the rise and fall of past civilizations in order to predict the future of their own civilization. In the past, history had usually been viewed as a linear process, moving onward and upward toward some faraway goal. These historians presented a different view, according to which history seemed to repeat itself. Civilizations, they held, had always risen and fallen in cycles or curves—from birth to death, from spring to winter,

from morning to night. These grandiose views of history tried to supply at least some answer to men's anxious questions about where their civilization was going. The answer that they supplied was far from hopeful.

Oswald Spengler's *The Decline of the West* (1918) was written during the First World War. With an immense display of erudition the author compared some twenty past "cultures," tracing each through identical phases down to a final phase that Spengler called "civilization." Europe, according to Spengler, was in the midst of this final phase. And like all other cultures before it, European culture would soon disintegrate and collapse. This prophecy of impending doom held a morbid fascination for the generation between the two wars. Historical scholars, to be sure, warned that this "morphology of cultures" was far too sweeping, based on evidence often incomplete or incorrect. Yet it could not be denied that in his comparative study of "cultures," Spengler had uncovered many suggestive parallels, and in his predictions of things to come he seemed to be remarkably correct.

It was largely due to Spengler's inspiration that the historian Arnold Toynbee embarked on his own monumental work, *A Study of History* (1934–54). Like Spengler, Toynbee assumed that there are parallel phases in the development of major civilizations. The birth of a civilization Toynbee saw in man's successful "response" to a "challenge," usually supplied by geography or climate. The growth of a civilization consists in man's gradually solving his physical problems, thus freeing his energies for more elevated intellectual and spiritual pursuits. Not every member of society shares in this process. It is rather a creative minority that takes the lead and makes its views prevail over the passive majority. The breakdown of a civilization, according to Toynbee, occurs when this minority can no longer muster enough creative force to meet a particular challenge. Europe, Toynbee said, was in the midst of this final phase, which he called the "Time of Troubles." He thus arrived at substantially the same prognosis as Spengler of what the future held in store.

Marie Curie in her laboratory, 1906.

Albert Einstein in Berlin, 1920.

The "New Physics"

While the social sciences were giving little comfort in an age of uncertainty, the natural sciences for some time past had been demolishing the simple, rational, and mechanistic view of nature that had prevailed since the days of Newton. Physical science in the late nineteenth century still viewed the universe substantially in Newtonian terms. Before the end of the century, however, the findings of scientists like Konrad Röntgen, Pierre and Marie Curie, Ernest Rutherford, and Max Planck had already raised doubts concerning these hypotheses. They made it clear that a major new explanation, a whole new system of physics and mathematics, was needed to supply the answers to questions on which Newton had been silent. Such a new system appeared in 1905 when the young German physicist Albert Einstein advanced his "theory of relativity."

According to Einstein's theory time and space were not absolute, as Newton had assumed, but relative to the observer. Later he included gravitation and motion in his calculations. Mass in Einstein's universe was thus a variable. The mass of a body depended on its rate of motion; its mass increased as its velocity increased, with the speed of light as the theoretical limit. It was the velocity of light, therefore, rather than time and space, that now emerged as absolute in the "new physics."

A further radical departure from accepted theory was Einstein's assumption of the equivalence of mass and energy. Experiments in nuclear physics already had shown that the dividing line between mass and energy was far from clear, and that matter slowly disintegrated into energy by way of radiation. The amount of matter thus lost was infinitesimal compared to the resulting energy. Einstein expressed this relationship between mass and energy in his famous formula $E = mc^2$, E being energy, m mass, and c the velocity of light. The implication of this formula was that if a process could be devised by which matter could suddenly be transformed into energy, only a small amount of matter would be required to produce a vast quantity of en-

ergy. A practical demonstration of the validity of Einstein's formula came with the first atomic explosion in 1945.

These and other revolutionary developments in science did not immediately affect the outlook of the average person. But as scientists began speaking of the "limitations of science," admitting that they no longer knew all the answers, some of their feeling of uncertainty could not help but enter general consciousness. Instead of living in a rational world with few remaining riddles, man, in the words of Britain's astronomer Sir Arthur Eddington, was faced by a universe in which "something unknown is doing, we don't know what." A mysterious world (as the physicists said it was), inhabited by irrational man (as the psychologists said he was), caught in a civilization predestined for decay and disintegration (as Spengler and Toynbee said our civilization was)—this was a far cry from the happy and confident prospect that had existed only a short time before.

New Cultural Trends

The uncertainty of the age was also reflected in its literature and art. Social criticism among writers was nothing new. But while the Naturalists of the late nineteenth century had hoped to bring about much-needed reforms by their attacks upon society, there was little such hope behind the criticism of the postwar era. Its common denominator was disillusionment—as seen in T. S. Eliot's *The Waste Land* (1922), Thomas Mann's *Magic Mountain* (1924), Theodore Dreiser's *An American Tragedy* (1925), and Sinclair Lewis' *Main Street* (1920). Some of the greatest literature of the years between the wars was escapist—the poetry of Rainer Maria Rilke, the tales of Joseph Conrad, and even the stories of Ernest Hemingway, whose romanticism was concealed behind a tough exterior. The French novelist Marcel Proust, in his *Remembrance of Things Past* (1913–27), looked back with nostalgia on a French society long since gone. And Thomas Wolfe, in *Look Homeward, Angel* (1929), escaped into a less glamorous past.

Yet postwar literature, even though deeply tinged with frustration, was also immensely creative. The insights of modern psychology into the hidden motives of human behavior proved a boon to writers in their age-old quest for an understanding of human nature. There had been psychological novels before, but it was only in this century that almost every writer, consciously or unconsciously, came under the influence of modern psychology, and especially of Freud. The Irishman James Joyce, in his novel *Ulysses* (1922), introduced a method known as "stream-of-consciousness." The search into the subconscious, so typical of Joyce, also motivated dramatists like the Italian Luigi Pirandello and the American Eugene O'Neill. One of the effects of Freudian psychology was to call attention to the role of sex as a force in man's life. As a result, sexual matters were now written about with far more candor than earlier generations would have thought permissible. Still, a book as outspoken on the subject as *Lady Chatterley's Lover* (1928), by the Englishman D. H. Lawrence, could not be published, except in expurgated form, until over thirty years later.

The incongruent mixture of uncertainty and creativity that characterized literature between the two wars also prevailed in painting. Some artists still dealt with recognizable subjects, but more and more of them rebelled against the realism and impressionism of the prewar era. Instead, painters like Paul Klee, Vassily Kandinsky, Erich Heckel, and Ernst Ludwig Kirchner expressed on canvas their inner feelings and impulses, often in styles that reflected the chaotic world in which they lived. These "expressionists," as they were called, in time became so nonobjective and abstract that it was impossible any longer to recognize in them common aims and interests. Each artist had become a law unto himself.

This same creative uncertainty, this search for new means of expression, had its parallel in modern music. Some composers—Jan Sibelius, Sergei Rachmaninov, Richard Strauss, and Ralph Vaughan Williams—continued to use traditional methods, inspired by the heritage of their various cultural backgrounds. But others—Arnold Schönberg, Arthur Honegger, Béla Bartòk, and Paul Hinde-mith—departed from familiar forms and in some cases, by adopting new scales and chords, developed a wholly new musical idiom, which sounded dissonant to most of their contemporaries.

Because so much modern art and music was highly individualistic, it appealed to only a few. Modern architecture had a somewhat wider following. Most architecture in the nineteenth century had been a mere imitation or a mixture of earlier styles. New building materials, steel and concrete, had been developed; but the inherent possibilities of these materials had been ignored by all but a few pioneers, such as the Americans Louis Sullivan and Frank Lloyd Wright. All this changed after the First World War. Architects became increasingly concerned with the function as well as the appearance of their buildings and by striving for simplicity and utility were able to produce structures of great beauty. The doctrine of "functionalism" found its European exponents in Le Corbusier, Walter Gropius, and Mies van der Rohe. It took some time, however, before the general public abandoned its preference for traditional and more ornate styles in favor of contemporary simplicity.

Anti-Intellectualism

It is difficult to gauge correctly the temper of a period as brief as the twenty years between the two world wars. Many of its accomplishments, especially in science, were impressive. But there was a puzzling paradox behind this extension of human knowledge. The more man found out about the world, the more he realized how little he had known before. From a feeling of supreme self-importance at the end of the nineteenth century, man's view of himself was pushed to the opposite extreme: he felt uncertain and insignificant, a creature of instinct, no longer able to shape his own destiny.

It is not surprising that this uncertainty should turn many people against the rationalist philosophy that had prevailed for the past two hundred years. There had been a similar revolt against reason a century before. And like Romanticism then, antirationalism now

Pablo Picasso, *Woman* (study for *Guernica,* 1937).

sprang from the disillusionment that followed a seemingly futile war. Modern anti-intellectualism, as it is called, took several forms. It brought a revived interest in religion, even among scientists, who had not long ago been ardent defenders of materialism. But far larger numbers turned elsewhere for guidance. There were many reasons for the sudden rise of totalitarianism after the First World War. Not the least among them was that it provided its followers with simple beliefs in an age of bewildering uncertainty.

Suggestions for Further Reading

Note: Asterisk denotes a book available in paperback edition.

Great Britain and France

A. J. P. Taylor, *English History, 1914–1945* (1965), and C. L. Mowat, *Britain Between the Wars* (1955), are the best general books on the subject. R. Graves and A. Hodge, *The Long Weekend: A Social History of Great Britain, 1918–1939** (1940), recreates the moods and manners of British society during the period. The same is done for the British "establishment" in H. Nicolson, *Diaries and Letters,* 3 vols. (1966–68). There are some excellent biographies of the leading political figures: K. Morgan, *David Lloyd George: Welsh Radical as World Statesman* (1963); R. Blake, *The Unknown Prime Minister: The Life and Times of Andrew Bonar Law* (1955); G. M. Young, *Stanley Baldwin* (1952); G. E. Elton, *The Life of James Ramsay MacDonald* (1939); K. Feiling, *The Life of Neville Chamberlain* (1946); and H. Nicolson, *King George V* (1952). C. R. Attlee, *The Labour Party in Perspective* (1949), is a review of the party's development between the wars by its leader. C. F. Brand, *The British Labour Party: A Short History* (1964), is a useful survey. The best introduction to French postwar history is D. W. Brogan, *France Under the Republic** (1940). E. J. Knapton, *France Since Versailles** (1952), is a brief survey; and A. Werth, *The Twilight of France, 1933–1940* (1942), describes the mounting crisis on the eve of the Second World War. D. Thomson, *Democracy in France** (1946), is helpful for understanding French politics. For biographies of major politicians, see: G. Bruun, *Clemenceau* (1943); G. Wright, *Raymond Poincaré and the French Presidency* (1942); V. Thompson, *Briand: Man of Peace* (1930); and J. Colton, *Léon Blum: Humanist in Politics* (1966).

Germany

The best political history of the Weimar Republic in English is E. Eyck, *A History of the Weimar Republic,** 2 vols. (1962). A Rosenberg, *A History of the German Republic* (1936), combines insight with criticism. On the dissolution of the Republic, see A. Brecht, *Prelude to Silence: The End of the German Republic* (1944), and the collection of essays by German scholars entitled *Path to Dictatorship, 1918–1933** (1966). The two leading personalities of the period are discussed in H. Turner, *Stresemann and the Politics of the Weimar Republic* (1963), and A. Dorpalen, *Hindenburg and the Weimar Republic* (1964). F. L. Carsten, *The Reichswehr and Politics, 1918 to 1933* (1966), deals with a significant phase of the Republic's history.

The Small Powers

Good general surveys are: H. Seton-Watson, *Eastern Europe Between the Wars, 1919–1941** (1945); R. L. Wolff, *The Balkans in Our Times* (1956); and B. A. Arneson, *The Democratic Monarchies of Scandinavia* (1939). On individual countries, see M. MacDonald, *The Republic of Austria, 1918–1934* (1946); H. Roos, *A History of Modern Poland* (1966); C. A. Macartney, *October Fifteenth: A History of Modern Hungary, 1929–1945,* 2 vols. (1957); and R. W. Seton-Watson, *A History of the Czechs and Slovaks* (1943).

The United States

Two very good studies of the pre-Roosevelt era are A. M. Schlesinger, Jr., *The Crisis of the Old Order, 1919–1933* (1957), and W. E. Leuchtenburg, *The Perils of Prosperity, 1914–1932** (1958). The Roosevelt years are covered in several excellent works: A. M. Schlesinger, Jr., *The Coming of the New Deal** (1959), and the same author's *The Politics of Upheaval* (1960); D. W. Brogan, *The Era of Franklin D. Roosevelt* (1951); W. E. Leuchtenburg, *Franklin D. Roosevelt and the New Deal, 1932–1940* (1936); and J. M. Burns, *Roosevelt: The Lion and the Fox** (1956). E. F. Goldman, *Rendezvous with Destiny: A History of American Reform** (1952), and R. Hofstadter, *The Age of Reform** (1955), deal with the American liberal and progressive movements. F. L. Allen, *Only Yesterday** (1940) and *The Big Change** (1952), are lively social histories of the period. Among memoirs and biographies of New Dealers, the following stand out: R. E. Sherwood, *Roosevelt and Hopkins** (1948); J. M. Blum, *From the Morgenthau Diaries*, 3 vols. (1959–67); R. G. Tugwell, *The Democratic Roosevelt* (1957); and E. Roosevelt, *This I Remember** (1949).

The Great Depression

J. P. Day, *An Introduction to World Economic History Since the Great War* (1939), puts the world economic crisis in its long-range perspective. The crisis itself is studied in J. K. Galbraith, *The Great Crash, 1929** (1955). See also D. A. Shannon, ed., *The Great Depression** (1960), and M. J. Bonn, *The Crumbling of Empire: The Disintegration of World Economy* (1938). H. W. Arndt, *The Economic Lessons of the Nineteen-Thirties* (1944), is an attempt to learn from the past. A major aspect of the international repercussions of the financial crisis is the subject of E. W. Bennett, *Germany and the Diplomacy of the Financial Crisis, 1931* (1962).

The Twilight of Imperialism

Typical of western disillusionment with imperialism are the books by G. Clark, *The Balance Sheets of Imperialism* (1936) and *A Place in the Sun* (1936). The changes in the British Empire and Commonwealth are discussed in K. Robinson, *The Dilemma of Trusteeship: Aspects of British Colonial Policy Between the Wars* (1965). H. Mukerjee, *India Struggles for Freedom* (1948), traces the long road to Indian independence. Earlier stages on this road are related in M. K. Gandhi, *Autobiography** (1948), and in two autobiographical works by J. Nehru, *Toward Freedom** (1941) and *Glimpses of World History** (1942). On events in the Far East, see A. Iriye, *After Imperialism: The Search for a New Order in the Far East, 1921–1931** (1965); R. Gould, *China in the Sun* (1946); and S. Chen and P. S. R. Payne, *Sun Yat-sen: A Portrait* (1946). The situation in the Middle East is discussed in G. Antonius, *The Arab Awakening: The Story of the Arab National Movement* (1939); and the first stirrings of unrest in Africa are treated in R. L. Buell, *The Native Problem in Africa* (1928). See also W. E. B. DuBois, *The World and Africa* (1947).

Intellectual History

Books dealing with the intellectual ferment of the "age of uncertainty" are legion. H. S. Hughes, *Consciousness and Society: The Reorientation of European Social Thought, 1890–1930** (1958), is a fine general study. J. Barzun, *The House of Intellect** (1959), covers the more recent period. Other attempts to see the crisis of our civilization in historical perspective are R. Niebuhr, *The Irony of American History** (1952), and R. Williams, *Culture and Society* (1958). J. Ortega y Gassett, *The Revolt of the Masses** (1932), is a classic criticism of our mass society. The modern trend toward conformity is analyzed in W. H. Whyte, *The Organization Man** (1956), V. O. Packard, *The Status Seekers** (1959); and A. C. Valentine, *The Age of Conformity* (1954). Other dangers to democratic freedom are pointed out by F. A. Hayek, *The Road to Serfdom** (1944), and K. R. Popper, *The Open Society and Its Enemies** (1950).

The basic work on Freud and psychoanalysis is E. Jones, *The Life and Work of Sigmund Freud,** 3 vols. (1953–57). See also G. Costigan, *Sigmund Freud: A Short Biography* (1965). The wide impact of Freudianism is treated in P. Reiff, *Freud: The Mind of the Moralist** (1959), and F. J. Hoffmann, *Freudianism and the Literary Mind** (1957).

New trends in the social and behavioral sciences are exemplified in T. Parsons, *The Structure of Social Action* (1949); E. Fromm, *Escape from Freedom** (1941); C. Kluckhohn, *Mirror for Man** (1949); B. L. Cline, *The Questioners* (1965); and in the studies of American society by D. Riesman, *The Lonely Crowd** (1953) and *Individualism Reconsidered** (1955). See also the essays by noted social scientists in R. Linton, ed., *The Science of Man in the World Crisis* (1945). For the influence of science on society, see B. Barber, *Science and the Social Order** (1952); B. F. Skinner, *Science and Social Behavior** (1956); J. Russell, *Science and Modern Life* (1955); and W. Esslinger, *Politics and Science* (1955).

The "prophets of doom" are evaluated in H. S. Hughes, *Oswald Spengler: A Critical Estimate** (1952), and in M. F. Ashley-Montagu, *Toynbee and History* (1956). On the scientific revolution of our century, see L. Infeld, *Albert Einstein** (1950); L. Barnett, *The Universe and Dr. Einstein** (1952); W. Heisenberg, *The Physicist's Conception of Nature* (1958); and M. Planck, *Scientific Autobiography and Other Papers* (1949).

Modern literature is covered in M. Colum, *From These Roots: The Ideas That Have Made Modern Literature* (1944), and in C. Mauriac, *The New Literature* (1959). On modern art, see E. Langui, ed., *Fifty Years of Modern Art** (1959); W. Haftmann, *Painting in the Twentieth Century*, 2 vols. (1965); and J. Joedicke, *A History of Modern Architecture* (1959). P. Collaer, *A History of Modern Music** (1961), is an introduction to the subject.

32 The Rise of Totalitarianism

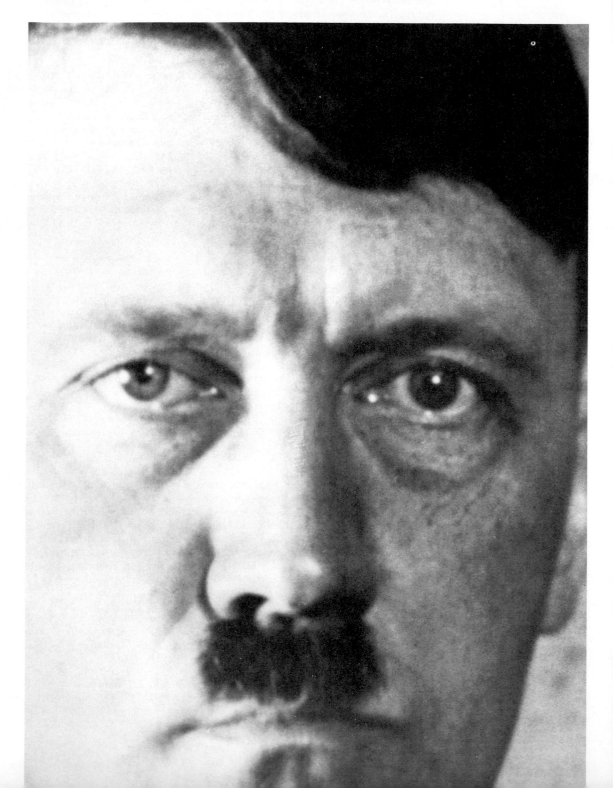

The Communist and Fascist regimes that arose in Europe and Asia during the years between the two world wars have been variously described as autocratic, authoritarian, dictatorial, and totalitarian. These terms do not all mean the same thing. There had been autocratic and authoritarian regimes in the past, most recently in tsarist Russia and imperial Germany; and there have been dictatorships from ancient times to the present. But none of these deserved to be called totalitarian. What we mean by a totalitarian regime is a regime in which a determined minority, by use of threat or force, imposes its will upon the total life of a society. The aims of this ruling clique are usually rooted in some all-embracing ideology. The origins of these totalitarian ideologies go back at least to the nineteenth century, with the appearance of the two creeds that contributed most to totalitarianism: socialism and nationalism. Their growth and spread were aided by industrialism, which gave birth to the mass society in which totalitarianism thrives, and which provided the technical means whereby total domination by a ruling clique was made possible.

There were many ideological differences between the totalitarianism of the Right and the Left—fascism and communism. Communism owed much of its success to the fervor that Marxian socialism inspired among its followers. There was no room for nationalism in Marxism, although nationalism in time became an ingredient of communism. Fascist ideology, by comparison, was less coherent. A mixture of warmed-over nineteenth-century "isms"—Romanticism, Social Darwinism, racialism, militarism, and so forth—its outstanding characteristic was nationalism. Fascism, too, professed a belief in socialism, but it was an extreme form of state socialism from above rather than the Marxian concept of popular socialism from below.

Despite these ideological differences, fascism and communism were alike in many ways. Both exercised the most minute control over the life of every individual; both ruled through a mixture of propaganda and terror; both segregated and persecuted their opponents in concentration and slave-labor camps; and

both sought to extend their power abroad through force or subversion. Why should totalitarian regimes have arisen at the time and in the countries they did? As we shall see, the circumstances differed considerably from country to country, but there were also certain similarities. Totalitarianism arose only in nations with little or no democratic tradition. Most of these countries had undergone lengthy domestic crises caused by the First World War or the Great Depression. In all cases a resolute minority, posing as saviors, initiated changes amounting to a revolution. And as a rule this minority was headed by a leader with great demagogic gifts.

COMMUNISM IN CRISIS 1917–28

It took several years for communism to gain full control in Russia. As we have seen, a Bolshevik minority under Lenin had seized power in the "October Revolution" of 1917. The initial difficulties faced by the new Soviet Republic were so severe that its survival seems almost miraculous. What the Bolsheviks lacked in numbers they made up in revolutionary zeal. To create a new world they tried to make a clean sweep of the old.

"War Communism" and Civil War

In a series of decrees, "War Communism" eradicated "tsarism." It decreed the socialization of the nation's economy, enforced, if necessary, through terror. From its very start the new secret police, or *Cheka*, was a deadly, efficient instrument of Bolshevik rule. The revolutionary fervor of bolshevism was also reflected in its foreign policy. To Lenin, revolution in Russia was but the prelude to world revolution; and the success of the latter was necessary to guarantee the survival of bolshevism at home. Sporadic Communist uprisings in Budapest, Vienna, Munich, and Berlin led to the founding, in March 1919, of the Soviet-controlled Third Communist International (Comintern) as a permanent agency dedicated to inciting world revolution.

Adolf Hitler (1889–1945)

But these Bolshevik attempts to conquer Russia and the world simultaneously turned out to be premature. "War Communism," instead of bringing relief, actually brought further economic misery leading to unrest and civil war. Opposition to the new regime was helped by Allied intervention. Its chief motive was to revive Russian resistance against Germany. During the spring and early summer of 1918, Allied forces landed at various points along Russia's periphery. A Czech legion, made up of prisoners of war, simultaneously fought Communist forces along the Siberian railroad. The Germans, still in control of much of Russia, encouraged separatist movements in the Ukraine and along the Baltic. And to complete the troubles of the Bolsheviks, the Allies imposed a tight naval blockade.

As the antirevolutionary White armies converged on the Soviet heart of Russia, the sphere of Bolshevik influence shrank to the region around Moscow and Petrograd. Yet despite hopeless odds, the Bolsheviks were able to hold their own. The main reason for their survival was the disunity and dispersion of their opponents. Allied intervention was at best half-hearted. The White armies were suspected of trying to restore the old order and therefore lacked popular support. The fact that the Whites enjoyed Allied help further weakened their cause, since it enabled the Bolsheviks, or Reds, to pose as champions of national resistance against foreign intervention. The White armies, finally, operated on widely separated fronts and under divided leadership. For all these various reasons, the White armies were no match for the newly created Red army. By the beginning of 1920, the Bolsheviks had defeated all the White forces except those in southern Russia under General Wrangel.

At this point a new danger arose. The Poles, who wanted to extend their frontier eastward beyond the Curzon Line, the boundary assigned to them at the Peace Conference, now joined forces with Wrangel in a concerted drive against the Red army. This was no longer a civil but a national war, and in an upsurge of patriotism the Russian people rushed to the defense. In a brilliant counterattack,

the Polish army was driven out of Russia and pushed back to the gates of Warsaw. Poland was saved in part by French aid. In the "Miracle of the Vistula," in August 1920, the Red army was halted and thrown back. Under the subsequent peace of Riga, Poland advanced its borders some 150 miles eastward into regions inhabited chiefly by Russians. Another "minorities problem" had been created.

Lenin's "New Economic Policy"

The end of civil and foreign war did not relieve Russia's misery. To add to the nation's calamities, droughts and crop failures in 1920–21 brought one of the worst famines in Russian history. The desperate situation called for drastic measures. In March 1921, therefore, Lenin initiated his "New Economic Policy," or NEP, which called for a radical departure from "War Communism" and a partial return to prewar, capitalist practices. Lenin's more orthodox comrades, notably Trotsky, were against such a retreat from Marxian doctrine. But as it turned out, Lenin's policy was justified by its results. In the seven years during which NEP was in effect, agriculture and industry returned to their 1913 levels. As a result, most Russians were able to get at least the food and clothing they needed and to enjoy a slight rise in wages and standard of living.

The moderation of Soviet policy at home had repercussions abroad. The failure of Communist uprisings in central Europe had shown that world revolution was not as imminent as the Communists had hoped. And with Russia's economic recovery depending heavily on foreign trade and capital, the Soviet Republic was eager to resume normal relations with the rest of the world. In this aim the New Economic Policy proved helpful, since it was interpreted abroad as a sign that the Bolsheviks had begun to see the error of their ways and in time would abandon their Communist "experiment." There was no reason, therefore, why foreign interests should not avail themselves of the opportunities offered by Russia's vast market and resources. Economic *rapprochement* between Russia and the

Russian poster published around 1920. It illustrates suffering during the grain famine; the caption reads "HELP."

West began in 1921. By 1925 diplomatic recognition had been granted the Soviet Union by all major powers except the United States.

But despite such hopeful beginnings relations between Russia and other countries never became really close. The major obstacle to Russia's reintegration into the international community was the well-founded suspicion that the Soviets had not really abandoned their aim of world revolution. As repeated incidents during the 1920s showed, the Comintern was merely marking time.

Lenin did not live to see the results of his New Economic Policy. In 1922 he suffered a paralytic stroke and in 1924, at the age of fifty-three, he died. He had been a remarkable man, with a great mind and superior talents as an agitator and organizer. His unaffected manner set him apart from most other dictators. With a rare mixture of fanaticism and realism, he had always known how to adjust his policy to changed circumstances. Without his leadership it is doubtful that Russia's revolution would have succeeded.

Stalin versus Trotsky

The death of Lenin brought into the open a struggle for power that had been going on behind the scenes for some time. The two chief contenders were Trotsky and Stalin. In their aims they were not unlike: Both looked forward to the ultimate victory of world communism. Where they differed was in the policy they advocated. Trotsky believed that Bolshevik Russia could not survive unless the rest of the world became communist too. Russia, therefore, should concentrate on fomenting and supporting revolutions elsewhere. Stalin, on the other hand, felt that communism should first gain a firm hold in Russia and only then should pursue its goal of aiding Communist movements elsewhere.

In the struggle that developed between Trotsky and Stalin, the personality and tactics of the two turned out to be decisive. Both men had served the revolution well. But while Trotsky's importance as Commissar of War declined once victory had been won, Stalin's in-

fluence continued to grow. He won his most important position in 1922, when he became general secretary of the Communist party. This gave him control over the entire party apparatus. Trotsky's doctrine of "permanent revolution," meanwhile, found little response in a nation exhausted by foreign and civil war. And while Trotsky's often high-handed manner offended his comrades, Stalin was careful to make friends with such "Old Bolsheviks" as Leo Kamenev, the party's chief ideologist, and Grigori Zinoviev, the head of the Comintern.

In 1925 Stalin's policy of conciliation and cunning succeeded in forcing Trotsky to resign from the Ministry of War. Soon thereafter, Kamenev and Zinoviev quarreled with Stalin and joined Trotsky in opposition. But Stalin proved the stronger. Allying himself with two other Old Bolsheviks, Alexei Rykov and Nikolai Bukharin, he had the "Trotskyites" expelled from the leadership of the party and ultimately from the party itself. Trotsky was banished, first to Siberia and after 1929 abroad. He was assassinated in Mexico in 1940. In the meantime Stalin, in 1929, had ousted Rykov and Bukharin, whose gradualist approach to socialization no longer fitted into his schemes. With the last of his potential rivals out of the way, Stalin had emerged supreme.

COMMUNISM TRIUMPHANT 1928–41

The Soviet government in 1928 already was a highly complex system. It received its final form under the "Stalin Constitution" of 1936. The Soviet Union was a federation of states, whose number increased from four in 1922 to sixteen in 1941. Each state at first retained a large measure of cultural autonomy but was under the strict political control of the Supreme Soviet in Moscow. The Supreme Soviet consisted of two chambers, the Soviet of the Union and the Soviet of Nationalities. When they were not in session, their functions were exercised by a Presidium of some twenty-seven members. More important, however, in directing national affairs was the Council

Joseph Stalin (1879–1953), in 1919.

Leon Trotsky (1879–1940), as Commissar for War, 1923–24.

Harvest time on a collective farm in the Ukraine in the 1920s. A propaganda newspaper, "The Collective Farmer," is being printed on the back of the truck for distribution to the peasants.

of People's Commissars, appointed by the Supreme Soviet.

Actual power rested in the hands of only a few people. But a multiplicity of local, regional, and provincial soviets, together with the Supreme Soviet, gave at least an appearance of representative government. Other features of the Russian constitution were also intended to make it appear democratic. Franchise was universal, and a bill of rights guaranteed all kinds of rights and freedoms. The only trouble was that these rights had to be exercised "in the interests of the working people." And the agency that interpreted what these interests were was the Communist party.

The Communist Party

The membership of the Russian Communist party in 1918 was estimated at 200,000. Ten years later, it had increased to over a million. But while it continued to grow, it never became a mass party. Its function was rather to serve as an elite, "the vanguard of the working class." Undeviating faith in Marxian doctrine as interpreted by the

party's leaders, together with blind obedience to orders from above—these were the basic demands made of all party members. Party organization resembled the structure of the Soviet state, from "cells" at the bottom to the All-Union Party Congress at the top. The Congress selected the Central Committee as the chief policy-making organ, and the Central Committee in turn delegated power to the Politburo, the party's highest authority.

The self-abnegation demanded by party membership was highly rewarded by the Soviet state. All the leading positions in the bureaucracy went to party members, and they alone could hold political office. The upshot of this system was the growth of a new ruling caste of Communist functionaries. With the Communist party as the dominant force in Soviet life, control of the party ensured domination of the state. Stalin owed his absolute power to his leading role in the Communist party rather than to any governmental position. And beginning in 1928 he used this absolute power to carry the Communist revolution to its final triumph.

The Five-Year Plans

In order to survive in a hostile world of capitalist powers, Stalin felt the Soviet Union had to realize as rapidly as possible its inherent economic power. Stalin hoped to achieve this goal in three Five-Year Plans. Their aim was the large-scale development of basic industries and the increase of agricultural production through collective farming.

The first Five-Year Plan was launched in 1928. Even if one discounts the exaggerations of Communist propaganda, the achievements of Stalin's policy were most impressive. Between 1928 and 1940 Russia's industrial output grew more than sevenfold. On the eve of the Second World War, the Soviet Union had become one of the leading industrial powers of the world.

Collectivization was less successful. Agriculture in Russia was hampered by small holdings and antiquated methods. The solution to the problem was seen in large-scale farming and mechanization. But the conservative Russian peasant was opposed to any drastic changes and resorted to passive resistance. To break this opposition, the authorities used force. Executions and deportations, added to a severe famine in 1932–33, caused the death of some 4 million people. But even strong-arm methods did not bring the desired results. While by 1940 most of Russia's land had been converted into collective farms, the problems of Russian agriculture had by no means been solved.

Stalin's Five-Year Plans completed the victory of communism in Russia. But that victory was won at the price of untold sacrifices on the part of the Russian people. Millions perished, others languished in labor camps, and the rest led a regimented and drab existence, spurred by alternate waves of propaganda and terror.

The lot of the average Russian gradually improved before the war. Free medical care and other social services, to-gether with full employment, provided the Russian worker with security at the expense of freedom. At the same time, some of the changes introduced shortly after the revolution were now abandoned. The family, at first deemphasized, now again became the basic unit of society. Education became less progressive but more universal. Religion, once persecuted, was at least tolerated. One of the most surprising reversals of the Stalinist era was the renewed veneration of Russia's past. During the Second World War in particular this new Russian nationalism turned for inspiration to the great events of Russian history, thus ignoring Marx's admonition that the proletariat had no fatherland. Stalin's motive in blending the old with the new was to strengthen his regime by rooting it more firmly in the past.

The Sabotage and Treason Trials

Although communism under Stalin gained a firm hold in Russia, there were nevertheless frequent signs of internal unrest. Among the manifestations of such unrest were the so-called sabotage trials of 1928–33 and the treason trials of 1934–38. The sabotage trials involved several groups of Russian and foreign engineers who were accused of sabotaging Russia's industrial efforts. The foreigners in each case denied these charges, but the Russian defendants readily confessed their guilt. Opinion outside Russia was that these trials were staged by the government to try to hide or excuse the many instances of waste and inefficiency revealed during the early years of the Five-Year Plans.

The same explanation, however, did not hold for the treason trials. These amounted to a major purge of thousands of leading figures of the Soviet regime. The reason given for the Great Purge was an alleged conspiracy, instigated by Hitler and Trotsky and ultimately directed at Stalin. The purge was touched off by

A Soviet poster, ''Knowledge breaks the chains of slavery,'' used in a campaign against illiteracy

the assassination of Sergei Kirov, party chief of Leningrad, in December 1934. In January 1935 Zinoviev and Kamenev were accused of conspiracy in the murder and were sentenced to imprisonment. They were condemned to death, together with fourteen other "Trotskyites," in 1936. Many others followed, including Rykov and Bukharin. In 1937 the purge spread to the Red army and throughout the entire Soviet hierarchy. Tens of thousands were arrested, executed, or exiled.

Foreign observers were bewildered and horrified by this spectacle of the revolution "devouring its children." The Great Purge was generally seen as a sign of Russian weakness. The significance of the fact that the Soviet state was strong enough to survive so tremendous a blood-letting was overlooked at the time. That there was opposition in Russia cannot be doubted. In spreading his net as wide as he did, Stalin destroyed any possible danger of a future conspiracy. Such drastic action may well have assured the survival of the Soviet Union in the Second World War.

Russia and the West

Prominent in Stalin's repressive policy at home was the fear of possible intervention from abroad. The memory of such intervention during the revolution was never forgotten. Outwardly, Russia's relations with the West improved markedly during the 1930s. The Soviet Union was the only major power not affected by the Great Depression, and the Russian market offered commercial opportunities that existed nowhere else. The rising threats of Nazi Germany in Europe and of Japan in Asia established a further bond of interest between the Soviet Union and the democracies. In 1933 the United States finally recognized the U.S.S.R.; the following year Russia was admitted to the League of Nations; and in 1935 the Soviets joined France and Czechoslovakia in military agreements against Germany. But despite this apparent *rapprochement*, Russia continued to distrust the West and the West continued to distrust the Russians. This mutual suspicion had tragic consequences on the eve of the Second World War.

THE FASCIST REVOLUTION IN ITALY

The rise of fascism, first in Italy and later in Germany, was in part a reaction to the real or imaginary threat of communism. But even without such a threat, conditions in Italy after the First World War made major changes imperative. The Italian people had been divided about intervention in the war. But once the nation joined the Allies, hopes for territorial rewards ran high. Such expectations were bitterly disappointed at the Peace Conference. Popular discontent was heightened by postwar economic problems. Riots and strikes, together with a sharp increase in the Socialist vote, made Italy's propertied elements fear that a communist revolution was at hand. Various democratic governments tried to cope with this hopeless situation but with little success. Parliamentary democracy had never worked well in Italy. Here, then, was a situation in which some able and unscrupulous demagogue could come along and promise a solution to Italy's problems. The man who saw and seized this opportunity was Benito Mussolini.

Khrushchev on the Great Purge

Stalin originated the concept "enemy of the people." This term automatically rendered it unnecessary that the ideological errors of a man or men engaged in a controversy be proven; this term made possible the usage of the most cruel repression, violating all norms of revolutionary legality, against anyone who in any way disagreed with Stalin, against those who had bad reputations. This concept "enemy of the people" actually eliminated the possibility of any kind of ideological fight or the making of one's views known on this or that issue, even those of a practical character. In the main, and in actuality, the one proof of guilt used, against all norms of current legal science, was the "confession" of the accused himself; and, as subsequent probing proved, "confessions" were acquired through physical pressures against the accused. This led to glaring violations of revolutionary legality and to the fact that many entirely innocent persons, who in the past had defended the party line, became victims.

From *The Crimes of the Stalin Era: Special Report to the 20th Congress of the Communist Party of the Soviet Union* by Nikita S. Khrushchev, ed. by Boris I. Nicolaevsky (New York: The New Leader, 1956).

Benito Mussolini

It has been said that Mussolini was Italian fascism personified, and the movement certainly would have been unthinkable without him. Born in 1883, son of a Socialist blacksmith, Mussolini himself had become a Socialist in his youth. He had worked abroad as an agitator, had been jailed in 1911 for opposing Italy's war with Turkey, and in 1912 had become editor of *Avanti,* Italy's leading Socialist newspaper. When war broke out in 1914, Mussolini was still a pacifist. But he soon changed and advocated Italian intervention on the Allied side. Here is the first of many radical reversals in the life of this accomplished opportunist.

Mussolini's first *Fasci di Combattimento,* or "groups of combat," were formed in the spring of 1919. Their name was derived from the old Roman fasces, a bundle of rods symbolizing unity and authority. Initially made up chiefly of discontented veterans, the number of these "Black Shirts," rapidly increased from a few hundred to many thousands. Their aims were mostly negative: they were against the monarchy, the Church, the Socialists, and the capitalists. In the elections of 1919 the Fascists failed to get a single seat. But two years later they won thirty-five. Capitalizing on the fears of the middle class by posing as the defender of law, order, and property, Mussolini was able to seize power in the fall of 1922.

The ''March on Rome''

Mussolini's boast of having saved Italy from the danger of a Communist revolution was false. That danger, if it ever existed, had run its course by 1922. In the meantime, the Black Shirts were waging a virtual civil war against Socialists and labor unions, and Mussolini was mending his fences in preparation for his *coup.* First he changed his revolutionary movement into a regular political party. Then he proclaimed his loyalty to the monarchy and the Church. And finally he made certain that the army would not oppose him. When everything was ready, in October 1922, Mussolini mobilized his Black Shirts for a dramatic "March on Rome." But King Victor Emmanuel had been well prepared and gave way easily. On October 29, 1922, Mussolini was invited to form a new government, and the following day he made his triumphal entry into Rome by train.

The change from democratic to totalitarian rule in Italy took several years. At the start, Mussolini was given full emergency powers for only one year. He used these powers to tighten Fascist control. To make certain of Fascist victories in future elections, a new electoral law in 1923 provided that any party that gained a plurality of votes would automatically receive two-thirds of the parliamentary seats. Even so, opposition in the Cham-

Mussolini (in suit in center) with Fascist followers in 1922 during the famous ''March on Rome.''

ber continued. In June 1924 one of Mussolini's most fearless critics, the Socialist leader Giacomo Matteotti, was kidnapped, "taken for a ride," and murdered. At first it seemed as though popular indignation would sweep the Fascists from power. Mussolini, pretending to be deeply shocked by the crime, promised severe punishment of the guilty. But when he realized how little united his opponents were, he reversed his course. A new secret police, the OVRA, was founded, and in a wave of persecution enemies of the state were brought before a special tribunal and sentenced to prison or exile. Non-Fascist members of the cabinet were dismissed, and Mussolini was once again given power to rule by decree. In 1926 all opposition parties were outlawed. The Matteotti affair, far from bringing about the fall of fascism, served to cap its victory.

Mussolini gives the Fascist salute to German Hitler youths who visited Rome in 1936.

The Fascist State

Like communism, Italian fascism created its own system of government. Political power, in Mussolini's "corporative state," was vested in some thirteen "syndicates." These confederations, which included both workers and employers, were initially organized to regulate labor conditions. Strikes and lockouts were declared illegal, and the final word in labor disputes rested with the government. Beginning in 1928 this corporate system was made the basis of Italy's political organization. Under a new electoral law, the syndicates drew up a list of candidates for the Chamber of Deputies. Their final selection, however, rested with the Fascist Grand Council, a body of some twenty party leaders appointed by Mussolini. As under communism, the party thus wielded complete political control. Parliament, under this new system, lost most of its former functions. In 1938 even the outward forms of democracy disappeared when the Chamber of Deputies was replaced by a new Chamber of Fasces and Corporations. Since all its members were appointed, there was no longer any need for elections.

The Fascist party, again like its Communist counterpart, considered itself an elite. Its membership in 1934 was about 1.5 million. Its leader, or *Duce*, was Mussolini. Fascist youth organizations took care of indoctrinating the young. The press, radio, and movies were under strict censorship, and every facet of intellectual and artistic life was made to fit in with party propaganda. Only in his relations with the Church did Mussolini show a certain leniency. One of the major achievements of his regime was the Lateran Treaty of 1929, which settled the long-standing feud between the Italian government and the papacy.

The major efforts of Mussolini's policy at home were aimed at improving Italy's economic position. Reduction of government spending, suppression of strikes, and increased taxation brought some financial stability. Italy also shared in the general economic recovery of the late twenties. The Great Depression, however, undid these gains. Even though the Italian government by then had assumed full control over economic affairs, its policy was far less successful than Russia's planned economy under the Five-Year Plans. Not only was Mussolini less ruthless than Stalin, but Italy lacked the Soviet Union's vast natural resources.

Beginning in 1935, furthermore, Mussolini embarked on a costly war, the burden of which had to be borne by the Italian people.

One sure way of diverting domestic discontent is through a strong and successful foreign policy. Mussolini first tried this remedy in 1923, when he ordered the Italian navy to bombard the Greek island of Corfu. But his ardor had been somewhat dampened by the protest of the great powers. For the next ten years, therefore, Mussolini was careful not to appear too aggressive. Italy concluded treaties of friendship with a number of countries, especially those that, like Austria and Hungary, shared its opposition to the peace treaties. In 1924 Yugoslavia, in return for concessions elsewhere, agreed to Italy's annexation of Fiume. Relations with Germany, even after Hitler's rise to power, remained cool, chiefly because of Germany's desire for *Anschluss* with Austria. Mussolini's restoration of domestic order, meanwhile, endeared him to foreign visitors; his opposition to communism made him appear the ally of anti-Communists everywhere; and his improved relations with the Church won him Catholic support. As a result, the new Italy and its leader commanded considerable respect abroad, at least until 1935. Only then did the world begin to realize the danger that fascism posed to world peace.

Fascist Ideology

When Mussolini founded his movement in 1919 he had, by his own admission, "no specific doctrinal plan." He was, as has been said, a born opportunist. In his formative years, Mussolini had come under the influence of a variety of writers, from Machiavelli to Pareto, including Nietzsche, Sorel, and even Marx. Fascism also had its own philosophers, men like Giovanni Gentile and Alfredo Rocco. But one looks in vain for an exposition of Fascist doctrine as clear as that provided for communism by Marx or even as rambling as that provided for nazism by Hitler. Fascism was a dynamic movement, devoted to action rather than thought. Its motto was "Believe, Obey, Fight." "Believe" covered a wide range of romantic ideals, from the glories of Rome to the irrational creed of modern nationalism. "Obey" meant subjection to the authority of the state and its leader, the *Duce.* To "fight" was the noblest aim of all. War alone, Mussolini said, "puts the stamp of nobility upon the people who have the courage to meet it." This belief in war for war's sake was the essence of Italian fascism.

THE RISE OF NATIONAL SOCIALISM IN GERMANY

Mussolini's success in Italy was observed with keen interest in Germany, where a movement akin to Italian fascism had been active since the early twenties. Its leader was an obscure Austrian rabble-rouser, Adolf Hitler, the moving spirit behind the National Socialist German Workers' Party (NSDAP). The brown-shirted members of the party—or "Nazis," as their opponents called them—were similar to Mussolini's first Black Shirts. Most of them were disgruntled war veterans. Like their Italian counterparts, they hoped to seize power by a *coup d'état.* But their Munich *Putsch* in November 1923 had failed. For the next few years Adolf Hitler all but disappeared from the public eye.

Adolf Hitler and His Aims

The man who was soon to determine the fate of the whole world was still not taken very seriously outside the Nazi movement. Born in 1889, the son of an Austrian customs official, Hitler had gone into politics after the First World War, in which he had fought as a German soldier. Considering his humble background and haphazard education, his subsequent rise to power was remarkable. Circumstances played their part, but even they needed a master. The *Führer,* or leader, of the Nazi Party was neither physically nor intellectually impressive. Yet he had certain qualities and abilities that enabled him to subject to his power first a whole people and ultimately a whole continent. One hesitates to call someone "great" who was at the same time so evil. But there was a certain diabolical greatness about this monstrous man. Rarely has anyone inspired such extremes of hatred and adulation as did Adolf Hitler.

As far as Hitler's aims were concerned, National Socialism, in contrast to Italian fascism, had a detailed, if internally contradictory, program. Its twenty-five points offered something to everyone. The worker was promised a share in the profits of industry and the nationalization of the big trusts; the peasant was tempted by land reform and the scrapping of mortgages; and the rest of the people were told to look forward to "the creation and preservation of a healthy middle class." German national honor was to be avenged by breaking the fetters of Versailles. The country was to be strengthened by the union of all Germans in a Greater Germany. The Jews were to be excluded from political life. The parliamentary system was to be abolished. And "positive Christianity" was to replace religious diversity. This program, of course, was never completely implemented, and provisions that might scare off prospective supporters were soon explained away. Yet with its pan-German nationalism, its anti-Semitism, and its opposition to democracy, it clearly foreshadowed future Nazi policy. A still more important prediction of things to come was given in Hitler's autobiography, *Mein Kampf* (My Battle), which he began in 1924. Besides Judaism and Marxism, bolshevism now emerged as a major target, and Russia was singled out as the chief victim of future German expansion.

Much of Hitler's ideology, especially its racism and pan-Germanism, had its roots in nineteenth-century Austrian and German thought. Because of such antecedents, and because Hitler's policy, notably in eastern Europe, seemed like a continuation of earlier trends in German history, the rise of National Socialism has been seen as a natural, almost inevitable, and peculiarly German development. There can be no doubt that Germany's past and the characteristics of its people help to explain the rise of Hitler. But of equal if not greater significance were the evil genius of Hitler himself and the specific circumstances in the early 1930s that made his victory possible.

Hitler's Rise to Power

Before Germany had found time to recover from the results of a lost war and a runaway inflation, it was plunged once more into a major economic crisis—the Great Depression. With millions of unemployed barely existing on a meager dole, political extremism flourished. Between 1928 and 1932 the number of Nazi delegates in the *Reichstag* rose from 12 to 230, and Communist strength increased from 54 to 89. This radicalization made the orderly conduct of government by moderate parties impossible. Democracy, which never had taken firm hold in Germany, broke down. Economic and political chaos, the threat of communism, and constant nationalist agitation against the Peace Treaty—these were the elements

Adolf Hitler

Hitler cannot be confined within a simple formula. For my part I knew three facets of his personality, each corresponding to a like facet in his nature.

His first aspect was one of pallor; his jumbled complexion and vague globular eyes, lost in a dream, lent him an absent, faraway air, the troubled and troubling face of a medium or somnambulist.

The second aspect was animated, colored, swept away by passion. His nostrils would twitch, his eyes dart lightning; he was all violence, impatience of control, lust for domination, abomination of his antagonists, cynical boldness, with a fierce energy ready at no provocation to pull down the universe about his ears. Then his "storm and assault" face was the face of a lunatic.

Hitler's third aspect was that of a naïve, rustic man, dull, vulgar, easily amused, laughing boisterously as he slapped his thigh; a commonplace face without any distinguishing mark, a face like thousands of other faces spread over the face of the earth. . . .

These alternate states of excitement and depression, these fits mentioned by his familiars, ranged from the most devastating fury to the plaintive moanings of a wounded beast. Because of them, psychiatrists have considered him a "cyclothimic"; others see in him the typical paranoiac. This much is certain: he was no normal being. He was, rather, a morbid personality, a quasi-madman, a character out of the pages of Dostoevski, a man "possessed."

From André François-Poncet, *The Fateful Years: Memoirs of a French Ambassador in Berlin, 1931–1938*, trans. by J. LeClerq (New York: Harcourt Brace Jovanovich, 1949), pp. 289–91.

that helped prepare the ground for the rise of dictatorship in Germany, just as they had done ten years earlier in Italy.

Hitler's actual assumption of power was through perfectly legal means. Like Mussolini before him, he was asked—on January 30, 1933—to form a coalition government. The men who helped Hitler gain power—the aged President von Hindenburg and his political advisers—felt confident that they would be able to use the Nazi movement to achieve their own ends: the establishment of a conservative and authoritarian regime. They failed to realize that Hitler was not a man to let himself be used.

To strengthen his position, Hitler first held new elections for the *Reichstag*. But despite the intimidation of political opponents, only 44 percent of the German people voted National Socialist. As a next step, Hitler manipulated the *Reichstag* into passing an Enabling Act that gave the government full dictatorial powers for four years. These powers were then used to prohibit those political parties that did not dissolve themselves. By July 1933 the National Socialists had emerged as the only legal party in Germany. The following November a solidly Nazi *Reichstag* was elected. In the meantime, Hitler had changed his cabinet to include mostly National Socialists. President von Hindenburg, who became increasingly senile toward the end, died in August 1934. Hitler now combined the office of president with that of chancellor, assuming the title of *Führer und Reichskanzler*, leader and chancellor. The transition from democracy to dictatorship was complete.

NATIONAL SOCIALISM IN POWER

Unlike Communist Russia and Fascist Italy, Nazi Germany did not introduce any sweeping constitutional changes. The *Reichstag* continued to meet, though infrequently, to endorse all measures put before it. There were no more elections, but occasionally the German people were asked in a plebiscite to support an act of the *Führer's*. Needless to say, they always did so by a rousing majority. The organization of the civil service was maintained, though it was purged of Jews

President von Hindenburg in 1933. Visible directly behind him is Adolf Hitler, next to a heavily decorated Hermann Göring.

and political opponents. The legal system was overhauled, and traditional concepts of law were abandoned in favor of a new kind of justice that elevated the welfare of the people and the state above the rights of the individual. To ferret out enemies of the state, a secret police, the Gestapo, was given sweeping powers of arrest and investigation.

Nazism at Home

As was the case in other totalitarian states, the Nazi Party in Germany controlled every aspect of national life. In his struggle for power Hitler had been aided by a number of capable lieutenants. These were now rewarded with leading positions in the government. But some of Hitler's old comrades failed to get what they expected. And others felt that Hitler had broken his word by not carrying out the more radical promises of the early Nazi program. To forestall any "second revolution" on the part of these malcontents, Hitler, on June 30, 1934, instituted a major "Blood Purge." In a lightning move the *Führer* arrested and summarily had executed several hundred of his possible opponents.

With the government and the party now under his firm control, there remained only one sphere in which the *Führer* did not wield complete authority, and that was the military. The armed forces had sworn personal allegiance to him after Hindenburg's death, and Hitler's renunciation of the disarmament clauses of the Peace Treaty in March 1935 had further enhanced his standing with the army. But it was not until 1938, after a thorough-going purge of the army's top echelons had removed the generals about whose loyalty Hitler felt uncertain, that the *Führer* felt he had a force on which he could fully rely. Henceforth Hitler himself was to be commander-in-chief of all Germany's armed forces.

The same process of *Gleichschaltung,* or "coordination," that was in government, party, and army extended to every other phase of German life. In many of his innovations, Hitler consciously imitated Mussolini. This was true not only of the symbols and ceremonies of the "Third Reich" but of many of its policies. Like Mussolini, Hitler tried to make his country's economy as strong and self-sufficient as possible. The most spectacular sign of German recovery was the reduction of unemployment. Public works, rearmament, and military conscription ultimately created an actual labor shortage. In 1934 the *Führer* launched the first of two Four-Year Plans to prepare Germany's economy for war. To finance such costly ventures, huge funds were needed. These funds were raised through increased taxation, special levies, and rigid control of prices and profits.

The main sufferer of this policy of "guns instead of butter" was the German worker. His wages were low, his hours long, and his movements restricted. A German "Labor Front" took the place of the former unions. Like the Italian "corporations," it included both workers and employers. Strikes were forbidden, and all labor relations were controlled by the

state. The farmer fared somewhat better. He was given various kinds of subsidies and was protected against foreclosure. Food production increased, although Germany did not become self-sufficient. One of Hitler's aims was a large and healthy rural population. In Nazi mythology "blood and soil" were considered the source of a nation's strength. Artists and writers, regimented like everyone else in Germany's totalitarian society, were called upon to glorify the "nobility of labor," and Nazi propaganda urged each and every German to place the welfare of the community before the good of the individual.

The majority of Germans readily complied with this appeal to make personal sacrifices and to work hard. Not that the German people were all ardent Nazis. The Nazi Party, like its counterparts in Russia and Italy, considered itself an elite, and its membership was limited. The average German was, in his own words, *unpolitisch* (nonpolitical). He welcomed what he considered the "positive" features of the Nazi regime, and he secretly grumbled about the things he did not like. There was even some active opposition—the thousands of prisoners in the concentration camps testified to that. Hitler's efforts to force all Protestants under the control of a "German Christian" church, and his evasion of the concordat he had concluded with the Catholic Church in 1933, brought strong and courageous protests from religious leaders of both confessions. There were other circles of resistance. But these groups were only a minority. Before the outbreak of the Second World War, Hitler's many admirers abroad praised him, like Mussolini, for the miraculous improvements he had brought about, and in particular for the firm stand he had taken against communism at home and abroad.

Anti-Semitism

One aspect of Nazi policy, however, from the start stirred deep concern among observers abroad, and that was the persecution of the Jews. Anti-Semitism had been one of Hitler's earliest obsessions, and it was the aim that

Hitler speaks.

Nazi picket during the boycott of Jewish-owned shops in 1933. The placard reads: "Germans! Strike back! Don't buy from Jews!"

he pursued most persistently and ruthlessly to the bitter end. The first measures against Germany's Jews—fewer than 600,000, or one percent of the population—were taken shortly after the Nazis came to power. In April 1933 all Jews were excluded from the civil service, and a national boycott was imposed on Jewish businesses. Soon thereafter the Jews were excluded from the universities, and lawyers and doctors were barred from practice. The next major step came with the "Nuremberg Laws" of 1935, which deprived all Jews of their citizenship and forbade their marriage to non-Jews. As a result of this "cold pogrom," many Jews went into exile. But worse was yet to come. In November 1938 the assassination of a German diplomat in Paris by a young Polish Jew was made the occasion for a "spontaneous" demonstration against the Jews. Synagogues were burned, shops looted, Jewish homes invaded and their occupants beaten up or killed. Jews henceforth had to wear the yellow Star of David and had to live in segregated ghettos.

The intensification of Jewish persecution in 1938 was merely another sign that Hitler was getting ready for war. Most of Germany's domestic policies since 1933 had been geared to that purpose, no matter how ardently the *Führer* might proclaim his peaceful intentions. Hitler's ultimate aim was a "New Order" for Europe, under which the German people would expand into the unlimited *Lebensraum* ("living space") of the East and rule over the "inferior" Slavic peoples of that region. The unbounded ambition of Hitler's megalomania plunged the world into the most frightful war it had ever seen.

THE SPREAD OF AUTHORITARIANISM

One of the dangers of totalitarianism, in the eyes of the free world, was its tendency to spread to nations that had been weakened by economic crises and political unrest. The rise of communism was generally considered the greater threat, and many a dictatorship of the Right gained power in order to prevent a dictatorship of the Left. The Soviet Union tried its best, with the aid of the Comintern, to help Communist parties abroad. But its numerous attempts at fomenting leftist plots in central Europe and in the Far East remained unsuccessful. Nowhere outside the Soviet Union did communism gain a decisive victory during the interwar period.

Authoritarianism in Europe

Efforts to set up rightist dictatorships, on the other hand, proved more successful. We have already seen the rise of strong men in most of the smaller nations of central Europe during the aftermath of the First World War. Similar regimes arose in Spain and Portugal. In some countries—Yugoslavia, Albania, Bulgaria, Greece, and Rumania—kings turned into dictators. In others—Hungary, Poland, and Spain—power was wielded by an alliance of military and agrarian groups. In still others—Austria and Portugal—authority rested with parties supported by the Catholic Church. As in the case of Russia, Italy, and Germany, all these small nations lacked a strong democratic tradition. Their new regimes were authoritarian rather than totalitarian. In some instances Germany and Italy tried to aid the rise of such authoritarian regimes. In Austria a Nazi *Putsch* in July 1934 failed, and Nazi victory was postponed until the *Anschluss* four years later. In Spain, on the other hand, General Francisco Franco defeated the republican government with the help of Italy and Germany. Like communism, fascism had followers in the democracies as well. But with the exception of France, these native Fascist parties never posed a serious threat. It was only during the Second World War that the Fascist "Fifth Column" became a real danger.

Japanese Fascism

In one nation outside Europe—Japan—economic crisis, rabid nationalism, and the failure of democracy gave rise to a totalitarian regime. The impact of the Great Depression on that heavily industrialized nation had increased the smoldering discontent with the government's inefficiency at home and moderation abroad. The opposition in Japan was centered in the army, particularly among its junior officers. Their aims were expressed in the writings of a young radical, Ikki Kita, who opposed the big industrialists and their political allies and advocated an almost socialist program: restriction of private property, nationalization of industries, and virtual abolition of parliamentary government. With the empire thus revolutionized, he envisaged Japan taking the lead in a crusade against western imperialism and ultimately extending its influence throughout Asia.

The military clique itself had no clear program of action other than to gain control of the government. This they hoped to achieve through pressure, mainly by assassinating moderate politicians. Early in 1936 these activities culminated in a mutiny and the murder of several high officials. The army high command took energetic counter-measures and executed the ringleaders. But at the same time the government made a number of concessions that assured the domination of the military in national affairs. In November 1936 Japan joined Germany and Italy in a treaty against communism, the Anti-Comintern Pact. Fascism had thus founded its own "International."

Japanese fascism differed in several respects from its European counterparts. It was not a well-organized movement under a single leader but rather a small pressure group; and it did not attempt to change the existing system of government but rather to dominate it. Yet in its demands for the submission of the individual to the state, and in its veneration of tradition as embodied in the person of the emperor, Japan's militarism showed definite fascist traits. Most pronounced was the similarity of the foreign policies of the three Fascist powers. Each sought solution of domestic difficulties through foreign expansion; each based the right to such expansion on claims of inherent superiority; and each looked to a special sphere of influence beyond its frontiers. In the case of Japan that sphere was the mainland of China.

THE MARCH OF FASCIST AGGRESSION, 1931–37

The series of international crises that culminated in the outbreak of the Second World War began as far back as 1931 in the Far East.

Japan against China

Japan, for some time past, had been trying to gain control over Manchuria, China's border province in the northeast. The region was rich in iron and coal; it adjoined Korea, where a Japanese protectorate had been established in 1907; and it was not under the direct control of Nationalist China. In September 1931 the Japanese army, using a minor incident along the South Manchurian Railway as an excuse, seized the Manchurian city of Kirin and surrounding territory. Local Chinese forces proved no match for the aggressors, and within a few months most of Manchuria had come under Japanese domination. In 1932 the victorious Japanese renamed their conquest Manchukuo and declared it a protectorate of Japan.

The Chinese government meanwhile protested to the League of Nations and to the United States against this Japanese act of force. The League appointed a special commission of inquiry under Lord Lytton, onetime viceroy of India. Its report condemned Japan's aggression and proposed the establishment of an autonomous Manchuria under Chinese sovereignty. The United States, in its "Stimson Doctrine," declared that it would not recognize any changes made by force of arms. This was as far as the powers were prepared to go. Under the League Covenant they could and should have taken more drastic action. But China seemed far away, and sanctions might prove costly at a time when most of the world was in the throes of depression. So nothing was done. Japan, to have the last word, withdrew from the League of Nations in 1933.

Hitler against Versailles

The moral of the Manchurian story was that if an aggressor acted quickly enough, nobody would dare stop him. This lesson was not lost on Adolf Hitler. In a series of dramatic moves between 1933 and 1936, he freed Germany from the most onerous restrictions of the Peace Treaty. In October 1933 the Germans withdrew from the Disarmament Conference and the League of Nations. In January 1935 the Saar region voted to return to Germany. Two months later Hitler denounced the disarmament clauses of the Versailles Treaty and Germany openly began a program of full-scale rearmament.

In order to forestall any opposition to his unilateral policy, Hitler was careful at every step to stress Germany's peaceful intentions. In January 1934 he signed a nonaggression pact with Poland. This was seen as a sign that the Germans had become reconciled to their eastern frontiers. In the spring of 1935 Hitler quieted Britain's fears of German rearmament by concluding an Anglo-German naval agreement. The British thereby acquiesced in the *Führer's* violation of the Treaty of Versailles and added considerably to France's feeling of insecurity. It is hardly surprising, then, that France should have sought help elsewhere. In May 1935 it concluded an alliance with the Soviet Union. But this merely gave Hitler the pretext he needed for his next major *coup.*

On March 7, 1936, Hitler ordered the German army to march into the demilitarized zone of the Rhineland. It was the *Führer's* most daring move to date. Had he been forced to back down at this crucial point, the future would doubtless have been far different. But again nothing happened. The French were afraid to act without the British. The British government officially criticized Germany's act. But the general feeling in England was that the Germans merely did what any people would have done under the circumstances—namely, to establish mastery over their own territory. The far-reaching implications of Germany's action were overlooked. Should Germany want to move quickly, as it had done in 1914 and was to do again in 1940, there was no longer any protective zone to save the Lowlands from German invasion.

Former British Prime Minister Lloyd George visiting Hitler at Berchtesgaden.

Hitler's Visitors

Lloyd George visited Hitler in September 1936, discussed world affairs, and came away convinced that Hitler was a reasonable man with acceptable aims and no desire whatsoever to plunge Europe into war. Conservatives, Liberals, and Socialists alike sought out the Führer, and were mesmerized by him. Even Arnold Toynbee was reported to have been won over at his interview to a belief in Hitler's genuine desire for peace in Europe "and close friendship with England." George Lansbury, a pacifist, and earlier leader of the Labour Party, was convinced after their personal encounter that Hitler "will *not* go to war unless pushed into it by others." Lord Allen of Hurwood told the *Daily Telegraph* on his return from Germany that "I watched him with the utmost vigilance throughout our lengthy conversation, and I am convinced he genuinely desires peace." Halifax recorded after his own visit to Berchtesgaden: "He struck me as very sincere, and as believing everything he said." But all Hitler did at these meetings was to repeat to each visitor the same dreary monologue about the insults of Versailles, the need for German unity on an ethnic basis, the evils of communism which he as a German could appreciate more than they could, the stubbornness of the Czechs, the pugnacity of the Poles, and the long-suffering innocence of the Germans. . . . But . . . when Lord Allen of Hurwood, with greater courage than most of his fellow-visitors, raised the issue of Jewish persecution, Hitler had nothing to say.

From Martin Gilbert, *The Roots of Appeasement* (London: Weidenfeld and Nicolson, 1966), pp. 164–65.

Ethiopian chiefs in the Italo-Ethiopian war, 1935–36.

Mussolini against Ethiopia

One reason why Hitler was able to get away with his daring move in the Rhineland was that it coincided with a serious international crisis elsewhere. On October 3, 1935, an Italian army had invaded the Kingdom of Ethiopia, or Abyssinia, in northeastern Africa. The isolated and backward region had somehow escaped the scramble for colonies among the European powers before 1914. Once before, in 1896, Italy had tried to invade Ethiopia but had been repulsed. This humiliation was never forgotten. In his desire to increase his nation's power and glory, Mussolini now hoped to join Ethiopia with the existing Italian colonies of Eritrea and Somaliland into a sizable imperium. It was for reasons of prestige, therefore, that the Italian Fascist dictator embarked on his anachronistic venture into colonial imperialism.

The Ethiopian war did not last long. Italy's forces were too powerful for the antiquated forces of Emperor Haile Selassie. On May 9, 1936, Mussolini proclaimed the annexation of Ethiopia to Italy. Meanwhile the League of Nations, for once, had not been idle. After declaring Italy an aggressor, it had instituted a program of economic sanctions. But such a program, to be effective, had to be airtight. With several major powers remaining outside the League, it could not be. Still, it might have been possible to stop the Italians if oil had been included in the list of embargoes. But the fear that a ban on oil might lead to a general war made both France and England hesitate to take such a step. The French, who looked upon Italy as a possible ally against Germany, did not wish to endanger their friendly relations with Mussolini. The British feared that their navy would have to bear the major brunt of a possible conflict, and such a risk seemed "unrealistic" over an issue as insignificant as Ethiopia. Without the support of its two most powerful members, the League was powerless to act.

The results of the Ethiopian war were of the greatest significance for the future. Once again the western powers, instead of supporting collective security, had preferred to buy peace by making concessions at someone else's expense. But such concessions, as the next few years were to show, merely whetted the appetites of the dictators. Prior to this time, relations between Hitler and Mussolini had not been very close. Hitler's designs on Austria worried Mussolini, who was himself interested in the Danube region. But with the conquest of Ethiopia Italy's energies had found an outlet elsewhere, and Germany's friendly attitude during the conflict had further paved the way for closer collaboration. On October 25, 1936, the two powers concluded a formal agreement to coordinate their foreign policies. This "Rome-Berlin Axis" was later joined by Japan.

War in Spain

The fateful significance of the "Rome-Berlin Axis" became evident in connection with the Spanish Civil War. Spain had long been a deeply divided country. Although a republic since 1931, the traditionally promonarchist forces—clergy, army, and aristocracy—still wielded considerable power. The Republican regime had been unable to cope

with the economic consequences of the Great Depression. In contrast to the right-wing opposition, the Republican Left was far from solid. In the elections of 1936 Republicans, Socialists, Syndicalists, and Communists buried their differences long enough to form a "Popular Front," and as a result they won a majority. But this Republican victory merely hastened the inevitable clash between Nationalists and Republicans. In July 1936 Spanish army units in Morocco, led by General Francisco Franco, rebelled against the Republic. The Spanish Civil War had begun.

Had the Spaniards been left alone, the war would hardly have become the major tragedy it turned out to be. But the war was not to remain a purely Spanish affair. Both Hitler and Mussolini were quick to recognize General Franco and to send men and materials to the Nationalists. The Russians in turn gave material and ideological support to the Republican, or Loyalist, side. But the Communists alone were incapable of matching the aid supplied by the Fascists. To assure the survival of the Republicans, the wholehearted cooperation of the democracies was needed.

The democracies were no more willing to risk a general war over Spain than they had been to become involved in a war over Manchuria or Ethiopia. Public opinion in general supported the Republicans, but the governments were more cautious. In September 1936 a Nonintervention Committee of some twenty-seven nations—including Germany, Italy, and the Soviet Union—met in London. But the committee could not prevent German and Italian "volunteers" from

Emblem of the International Brigade, which served in the Republican army in the Spanish Civil War.

Barcelona after bombardment by Franco's forces, July 1936.

fighting on Franco's side. In an effort at neutrality, President Roosevelt invoked the Neutrality Act of 1935, prohibiting the export of arms and munitions to both sides in the conflict. But this move hurt mainly the Loyalists, since Franco continued to receive supplies from Germany and Italy.

The Spanish Civil War lasted for almost three years and caused more than 700,000 deaths. By the time the last Republican forces surrendered in Madrid on March 28, 1939, events in Spain had long been overshadowed by more important developments elsewhere. But Hitler's policy of bloodless expansion in central Europe was doubtless aided by the diversion provided by the slow death of democracy in Spain.

THE ROAD TO WAR

Except for the Civil War in Spain, the international situation at the beginning of 1937 seemed quite hopeful. But this impression was mistaken. The preceding years had been a crucial time of preparation for the new German *Wehrmacht,* when determined outside resistance might still have put a stop to Hitler's plans for aggression. From now on the balance of military power began to turn more and more in Germany's favor. In June 1937 Hitler's Minister of Defense issued the first specific directive to prepare for a future war. Five months later Hitler met with his top advisers to present an outline of his strategy. First Germany would seek control over Austria and Czechoslovakia. Then it would be ready to pursue its major aim of eastward expansion to win the living space that the German people were entitled to.

War in the Far East

While Hitler was making his plans in Europe, open warfare had already broken out in the Far East. In July 1937 a minor incident near Peking touched off an undeclared war between China and Japan that lasted until 1945. By the end of 1938 the Japanese were in control of most of northeastern China as far west as the Yellow River and as far south as the Yangtze and Hangchow. Still farther south, Japan had seized the city of Canton and surrounding territory. In March 1938 the Japanese set up a "Reformed Government of the Republic of China" at Nanking.

The government of Chiang Kai-shek, meanwhile, had taken refuge in the interior province of Szechwan, with its capi-

Japanese troops celebrating the taking of Nanking, 1938.

tal at Chungking. The Chinese armies, while superior in numbers, were woefully short of equipment. To fight the invaders more effectively, Chiang Kai-shek and the Chinese Communists agreed to bury their differences. A "scorched earth" policy and constant guerrilla warfare on the part of the Chinese kept the Japanese from consolidating their gains. But despite the determined resistance of the Chinese, their ultimate survival depended on outside aid.

Chinese protests to the League of Nations brought little more than verbal condemnation of Japanese aggression. The French feared that resistance to Japan might lead to a Japanese attack on the French colony of Indochina. And Britain hoped that by appeasing Japan it might keep its commercial interests in China. The United States, too, was careful at first not to antagonize Japan. Only when it became clear that the "Open Door" policy in China was being threat-

ened did the United States begin to aid the Chinese. Of all the major powers, only the Soviet Union supported the Chinese from the beginning of the war. But the aid that reached China was not sufficient to halt the Japanese advance. Beginning in the spring of 1938, furthermore, attention was diverted from Asia to Europe, where Hitler was embarking on his systematic policy of eastward expansion.

The Austrian Anschluss

Hitler's first victim was the small Republic of Austria. Austria's *Anschluss* (that is, joining-together with Germany) had always been a major Nazi aim. The failure of a Nazi *Putsch* in 1934 did not end the Nazi conspiracy. In January 1938 the Austrian government uncovered evidence of another Nazi plot. In the hope of removing the tension resulting from this latest incident, Austria's chancellor,

Hitler's victory parade through Vienna, Austria, on March 14, 1938.

Kurt von Schuschnigg, accepted Hitler's invitation to come to the *Führer's* retreat in Berchtesgaden in early February. Here he was presented with a set of demands that, if fulfilled, would have made Austria a virtual German protectorate. Refusal to accept, Hitler made clear, would result in a German invasion of Austria.

Faced with these alternatives, Schuschnigg had little choice but to give in. But in March he decided to make one final attempt to save his country by appealing directly to the Austrian people in a plebiscite. Hitler's reaction was swift. Once more threatening invasion, he forced Schuschnigg to call off the plebiscite and to resign. One March 11 an Austrian Nazi, Artur Seyss-Inquart, was made chancellor. On March 12, German troops crossed the Austrian frontier "to

EUROPE BEFORE THE SECOND WORLD WAR   1930–39

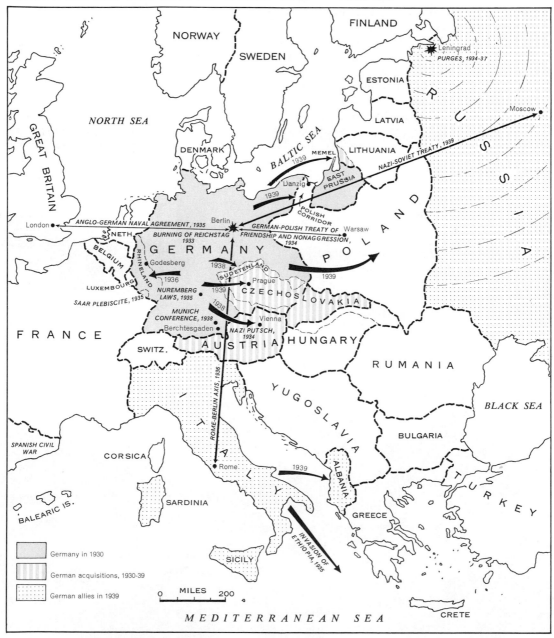

help maintain order." On March 13, Austria was incorporated into the Greater German Reich.

The ultimate success of this latest act of aggression again depended on the attitude of the great powers. As on all earlier occasions, there were loud protests but no action. The French were in the midst of one of their innumerable governmental crises and looked to the British to take the lead. But Britain, while deploring Hitler's methods, saw nothing wrong with an Austro-German *Anschluss*, so long as both peoples wanted it. And Italy, although long a champion of Austrian independence, was by now in the German camp. There was also the hope, of course, that Hitler would be satisfied, now that his dearest wish had been fulfilled. And the *Führer* did his best to confirm that hope by making his usual promises of peaceful intentions. The Soviet Union came forth with suggestions for a collective stand, warning that Czechoslovakia was next on Hitler's list; but the western powers considered these proposals premature.

The Conquest of Czechoslovakia

The pretext for Germany's intervention in Czechoslovakia was provided by the German minority in the Czech border regions. The three million Sudeten Germans, as they were called, had long been a source of trouble to the Czech government, especially since Hitler's rise to power. Beginning in 1936 their leader, Konrad Henlein, had begun to collaborate secretly with the Nazis; and as Germany's power in Europe increased, the demands of the Sudeten Germans became louder. In April 1938, after the fall of Austria, Henlein demanded complete autonomy for the Sudetenland. Nazi propaganda immediately took up this demand. The climax of Germany's campaign against the Czech government of President Eduard Beneš came with Hitler's address to the annual party congress at Nuremberg on September 12, 1938, in which he threatened German intervention on behalf of the Sudeten Germans.

Hitler's threat was no empty boast. The German army had been spending the summer of 1938 in feverish preparation for the invasion of Czechoslovakia. The French and British, meanwhile, had been trying desperately to effect a compromise solution of the Sudeten problem. But the Czechs proved adamant, trusting in their own military strength and the support of their French and Russian allies. When Hitler's speech intensified riots in the Sudetenland, the Czech government proclaimed martial law. War, it seemed, was imminent. It was narrowly averted by the action of Britain's prime minister, Neville Chamberlain, who now initiated a series of last-minute conferences with Hitler that sealed the fate of Czechoslovakia.

Chamberlain on His Trip to Munich

The events of the next 48 hours entailed terrific physical and mental exertions. I was up the night before till after 2 A.M. preparing my speech. Then came the early rising and the scenes at the aerodrome, and the long flight to Munich. The rest of that day, till after 2 o'clock next morning, was one prolonged nightmare, and I have only gradually been able since then to sort out my impressions.

Hitler's appearance and manner when I saw him appeared to show that the storm signals were up, though he gave me the double handshake that he reserves for specially friendly demonstration. Yet these appearances were deceptive. His opening sentences, when we gathered round for our conference, were so moderate and reasonable, that I felt instant relief.

Mussolini's attitude all through was extremely quiet and reserved. He seemed to be cowed by Hitler, but undoubtedly he was most anxious for a peaceful settlement. . . . His manner to me was more than friendly; he listened with the utmost attention to all I said, and expressed the strong hope that I would visit him early in Italy, where I should receive a very warm welcome. . . .

I asked Hitler about 1 in the morning, while we were waiting for the draftsmen, whether he would care to see me for another talk. He jumped at the idea, and asked me to come to his private flat . . . I had a very friendly and pleasant talk. . . . At the end I pulled out the declaration, which I had prepared beforehand, and asked if he would sign it. As the interpreter translated the words into German, Hitler frequently ejaculated "*ja, ja,*" and at the end he said "yes, I will certainly sign it; when shall we do it?" I said "now," and we went at once to the writing-table, and put our signatures to the two copies which I had brought with me.

Letter from Neville Chamberlain to his sisters, October 2, 1938, quoted in Sir Keith Feling, *Neville Chamberlain* (London, 1946), pp. 375–77.

Prime Minister Neville Chamberlain signs the Munich Pact, September 30, 1938.

Sullen Czechs watch the Germans enter Prague, March 15, 1939.

At their first meeting in Berchtesgaden, Hitler seemed to be satisfied with "self-determination" for the Sudeten region. But when Chamberlain returned to Germany a week later for a second meeting, at Godesberg, the *Führer* upped his demands. He now asked for the immediate surrender of the Sudetenland. This the Czechs declared unacceptable. But their protests were ignored at the final meeting in Munich on September 29–30. Hitler and Chamberlain, together with Mussolini and French Premier Édouard Daladier, now agreed on the Godesberg terms. In a separate agreement, Great Britain and Germany promised to renounce war in settling their national differences. "Peace for our time," as Chamberlain hopefully put it, seemed to have been assured.

The first reaction of the world, when the Munich decisions were announced, was one of relief that war had been averted. But it was not long before criticism started. Deprived of its fortifications and most of its heavy industries, which were located in the Sudetenland, Czechoslovakia, the last outpost of democracy in central Europe, was now at Germany's mercy. The Russians, to be sure, had insisted to the end that they would stand by their treaty obligations. But the strength of the Red army was not rated very high, and there was always the fear that the Soviet Union might try to embroil the West in a war with Hitler. The French, in betraying their faithful Czech ally, had assumed a major share of the responsibility for Czechoslovakia's defeat. But how could they have acted differently without the support of Great Britain? And the British, government and people alike, were neither morally nor materially ready for war. Appeasement, ever since Munich, has been an ugly word. But the purchase of peace at the expense of smaller or weaker nations had been going on for some time. The basic cause of the Czech disaster was the failure of the democracies all through the 1930s to understand the true aims of Fascist aggression. Even at Munich these aims were not yet fully understood. It took one more of Hitler's moves to bring home once and for all the futility of appeasement.

On the eve of Munich Hitler had promised that the Sudetenland would be his last territorial claim in Europe. But even before the year was out he issued directives for the final liquidation of Czechoslovakia. On March 15, 1939, German army units crossed the Czech border, and the next day Hitler proclaimed a German protectorate over the Czech regions of Bohemia and Moravia. Slovakia was to become an "independent" German satellite.

This final dismemberment of Czechoslovakia was an important turning point. Up to then, "Pan-Germanism," the desire to unite all German-speaking peoples, had seemed to be the motive of Hitler's expansionist policy. Now suddenly the world recognized his real aim: to gain living space and to subjugate foreign peoples. It was this latest act of Hitler's that brought about a decisive change in the attitude of the western democracies. On March 31, 1939, Great Britain promised the Poles all possible support in resisting any threat to their independence. And in April both England and France gave similar assurances to Rumania and Greece. What the western powers did not know was that on April 3, 1939, a secret directive had been issued to the German army ordering

preparations for war against Poland so that operations could start any time after September 1, 1939.

The Eve of the Second World War

That Hitler should turn against Poland next should have been hardly surprising. Of all the territorial provisions of Versailles, the loss of the Polish corridor and the city of Danzig had been the most resented by Germany.

The world had still not recovered from the dismemberment of Czechoslovakia when the Fascist powers made two more quick moves. On March 21, 1939, Lithuania, in compliance with Hitler's demands, returned to Germany the small territory of Memel; and on April 8, 1939, Mussolini sent his troops to occupy the Kingdom of Albania, which since 1927 had been a virtual Italian protectorate. A month later, Germany and Italy converted their Axis into a full-fledged alliance, the "Pact of Steel."

In late May 1939 Hitler informed his generals that war with Poland was inevitable. The fact that France and Great Britain had promised to protect Poland's independence was denounced by Hitler as an incitement to violence against the German minority in the Polish corridor. On August 22 Hitler held another of his briefing conferences. The *Führer* expressed the hope that France and Britain might decide not to fight. Not that he feared their intervention. The western powers, he said, were completely unprepared. As a final surprise, Hitler then told his generals: "A few weeks from now I shall, on the common German-Russian border, shake hands with Stalin and carry out with him a redistribution of the world."

The Nazi-Soviet Pact

What the *Führer* was referring to was an agreement between Germany and the Soviet Union to which the finishing touches were then being put in Moscow. The role of Russia in a future war, needless to say, was of major importance and had concerned Germany and the western powers for some time. Since April 1939 Russia had been engaged in negotiations with both sides. But France and Britain were unable to overcome their fundamental distrust of the Russians; and they had little faith in the Red army, especially after the recent purges. Still more significant, the western powers were unwilling to concede to Russia the predominance in eastern Europe that Stalin demanded. The Germans, on the other hand, had no hesitation in making concessions in the East if it meant gaining a free hand in the West. The Russo-German talks did not enter their decisive phase until mid-August. From then on events moved swiftly. On August 23 the two powers signed a nonaggression pact. Its most weighty part was a secret protocol that divided eastern and southeastern Europe into respective spheres of Russian and German influence.

The Nazi-Soviet treaty came as a terrible blow to the West. Two powers who, because of their rival ideologies, had heretofore appeared as irreconcilable enemies, now had suddenly buried their differences and established a common front. The advantages of the Russian pact for Germany were obvious: it saved the *Wehrmacht*, once Poland had been disposed of, from having to fight a war on two fronts. Russia's motives in making a deal with Hitler were less clear. According to Stalin, the Soviet Union had long been afraid that the West was trying to turn Nazi aggression against communism. But it has also been argued that Stalin, by supporting Hitler, hoped to embroil Germany in a war with the western powers. Such a conflict might so weaken both sides that Russia would emerge as the decisive factor in the international balance of power.

With the signing of the Nazi-Soviet pact, the stage was set for the outbreak of war. It was still not clear whether the French and British would keep their word and come to Poland's aid. Negotiations for a last-minute compromise continued, and Hitler at one point postponed the start of hostilities to allow the West one more try at appeasement. But the lessons of the last few years had at long last been learned. On September 3, 1939, three days after the German invasion of Poland, England and France declared war on Germany. The Second World War had begun.

Reading of proclamation of war at the Royal Exchange in London.

Suggestions for Further Reading

Note: Asterisk denotes a book available in paperback edition.

General

H. Arendt, *The Origins of Totalitarianism** (1951), and E. Fromm, *Escape from Freedom** (1941), are seminal works on the subject of totalitarianism. C. J. Friedrich and Z. K. Brzezinski, *Totalitarian Dictatorship and Autocracy,* rev. ed. (1965), provides a general theory of the phenomenon. The development of Communist thought from Marx to Stalin is surveyed in R. N. Carew-Hunt, *The Theory and Practice of Communism** (1963), and in B. D. Wolfe, *Marxism: One Hundred Years in the Life of a Doctrine* (1965). Other important books on communism are J. Braunthal, *History of the International,* 2 vols. (1967); R. V. Daniels, *The Nature of Communism** (1962); and M. M. Drachkovitch, ed., *Marxism in the Modern World* (1965). Life under communism is described from personal experience by W. Leonhard, *Child of the Revolution** (1967), and by C. Milosz, *The Captive Mind** (1953). M. Fainsod, *Smolensk under Soviet Rule** (1963), is based on unique Russian sources. G. Orwell, *1984** (1949), presents a perceptive fictionalized account. The Fascist brand of totalitarianism is dealt with historically in F. L. Carsten, *The Rise of Fascism** (1967), and ideologically in E. Nolte, *Three Faces of Fascism** (1966). See also H. Rogger and E. Weber, eds., *The European Right: A Historical Profile** (1965), and S. J. Woolf, ed., *European Fascism** (1968). On life in Nazi Germany, see B. Bielenberg, *The Past Is Myself* (1971), and F. P. Reck-Malleczewen, *Diary of a Man in Despair** (1972).

Communist Russia

The most comprehensive history of the Soviet Union is E. H. Carr, *A History of Soviet Russia* (1950–1969), of which eight volumes have appeared thus far. A good brief history is D. W. Treadgold, *Twentieth Century Russia* (1959). F. B. Randall, *Stalin's Russia: An Historical Reconsideration* (1965), is factual and objective. H. Schwartz, *Russia's Soviet Economy* (1954), is a good introduction. S. Swianiewicz, *Forced Labor and Economic Development: An Enquiry into the Experience of Soviet Industrialization* (1965), is more specialized. M. Fainsod, *How Russia Is Ruled* (1963), discusses the constitution and functioning of Soviet government. L. B. Schapiro, *The Communist Party of the Soviet Union** (1960), is the standard work on the subject. Soviet foreign policy before the Second World War is treated in L. Fischer's two books, *The Soviets in World Affairs** (1951), and *Russia's Road from Peace to War* (1969), as well as in M. Beloff, *The Foreign Policy of Soviet Russia, 1929–1941,* 2 vols. (1947–49). The best and most recent general account is A. Ulam, *Expansion and Coexistence: The History of Soviet Foreign Policy, 1917–1967** (1968). The following are good monographs on various aspects of Soviet history and society: J. Erickson, *The Soviet High Command* (1962); R. Conquest, *The Great Terror: Stalin's Purge of the Thirties* (1968); C. Brandt, *Stalin's Failure in China, 1924–1927* (1958); D. J. Dallin and B. I. Nicolaevsky, *Forced Labor in the Soviet Union* (1947); L. B. Schapiro, *The Origins of the Communist Autocracy** (1955); and L. Kochan, ed., *The Jews in Soviet Russia since 1917* (1970). The best biographies of the Communist leaders are: L. Fischer, *Lenin* (1965); I. Deutscher, *Trotsky,* 3 vols. (1954–65); and by the same author, *Stalin: A Political Biography** (1949).

Fascist Italy

E. Wiskemann, *Fascism in Italy: Its Development and Influence** (1969), is a good brief introduction. The early years of Fascist rule are discussed in A. Rossi, *The Rise of Italian Fascism, 1918–1922* (1938). G. Salvemini, *Under the Axe of Fascism* (1936) and *Prelude to World War II* (1954), are authoritative studies of Italian domestic and foreign policy by a leading anti-Fascist Italian historian. Other good accounts are H. Finer, *Mussolini's Italy** (1935); R. Packard and E. Packard, *Balcony Empire: Italy under Mussolini* (1943); and C. Seton-Watson, *Italy from Liberalism to Fascism* (1967). The structure of Mussolini's government is treated in H. Steiner, *Government in Fascist Italy* (1938), and W. Ebenstein, *Fascist Italy* (1939). On foreign policy, see A. Cassels, *Mussolini's Early Diplomacy* (1970), and E. Wiskemann, *The Rome-Berlin Axis,** 2nd. ed. (1966). Recent biographies of Mussolini are I. Kirkpatrick, *Mussolini: Study of a Demagogue* (1964); and L. Fermi, *Mussolini* (1961). The resistance to Mussolini is dealt with in C. F. Delzell, *Mussolini's Enemies* (1961).

Nazi Germany

The best general work on the subject is K. D. Bracher, *The German Dictatorship: The Origins, Structure, and Effects of National Socialism** (1970). Among the many books dealing with the

roots of nazism, G. L. Mosse, *The Crisis of German Ideology: Intellectual Origins of the Third Reich** (1964); F. Stern, *The Politics of Cultural Despair** (1961); and H. Rauschning, *The Revolution of Nihilism* (1939), are the most revealing. The debate surrounding Hitler's rise is summed up in J. L. Snell, ed., *The Nazi Revolution: Germany's Guilt or Germany's Fate?** (1959). W. L. Shirer, *The Rise and Fall of the Third Reich** (1960), is by a noted journalist. For a briefer and more balanced account, see H. Mau and H. Krausnick, *German History 1933–1945** (1953). The best biography of Hitler is A. Bullock, *Hitler: A Study in Tyranny** (1964). On Hitler's early years, B. F. Smith, *Adolf Hitler: His Family, Childhood and Youth** (1967), sheds much new light. Hitler's aims are stated in A. Hitler, *Mein Kampf** (1939), and more openly in *Hitler's Secret Conversations, 1941–1944* (1953). See also *Hitler's Secret Book** (1961). The early events of Nazi Germany are examined in W. S. Allen, *The Nazi Seizure of Power** (1965).

The domestic affairs of Germany under Hitler are treated in R. Grunberger, *A Social History of the Third Reich* (1971), and its government is discussed in W. Ebenstein, *The Nazi State* (1943). The fateful role of the army in German politics before and during the Hitler years is described in J. W. Wheeler-Bennett, *The Nemesis of Power: The German Army in Politics, 1918–1945** (1953); and in R. J. O'Neill, *The German Army and the Nazi Party* (1966). The best books on the SS are H. Höhne, *The Order of the Death's Head* (1969), and H. Buchheim *et. al., Anatomy of the SS-State* (1968). On the treatment of the Jews, see G. Reitlinger, *The Final Solution** (1953), and R. Hilberg, *The Destruction of the European Jews* (1961). E. Kogon, *The Theory and Practice of Hell** (1958), is the best book on the concentration camps. Other important works on various phases of Nazi rule are: D. Schoenbaum, *Hitler's Social Revolution, 1933–1939** (1967); E. K. Bramsted, *Goebbels and National Socialist Propaganda, 1925–1945* (1965); G. Lewy, *The Catholic Church and Nazi Germany** (1964); B. H. Klein, *Germany's Economic Preparations for War* (1959); B. A. Carroll, *Design for Total War: Arms and Economics in the Third Reich* (1968); and A. Schweitzer, *Big Business in the Third Reich* (1964). J. Fest, *The Face of the Third Reich** (1969) presents vivid portraits of some of Hitler's lieutenants. On the various resistance efforts against Hitler, see T. Prittie, *Germans against Hitler* (1964); H. C. Deutsch, *The Conspiracy Against Hitler* (1968); and G. van Roon, *German Resistance to Hitler* (1971). The final act of the Nazi nightmare is dramatically told in H. R. Trevor-Roper, *The Last Days of Hitler** (1947).

The Road to War   A detailed history of the diplomatic background of the Second World War remains to be written. A. J. P. Taylor, *The Origins of the Second World War** (1961), is stimulating but totally unreliable. G. Weinberg, *The Foreign Policy of Hitler's Germany: Diplomatic Revolution in Europe, 1933–1936* (1970), with a second volume to come, is excellent. Several books discuss Germany's relations with individual countries during the Nazi era: M. Toscano, *The Origins of the Pact of Steel* (1967); E. Wiskemann, *Czechs and Germans* (1938); C. A. Micaud, *The French Right and Nazi Germany, 1933–1939* (1943); J. E. McSherry, *Stalin, Hitler, and Europe* (1968); and E. Presseisen, *Germany and Japan* (1958). Relations between military planning and foreign policy are the subject of E. M. Robertson, *Hitler's Pre-War Policy and Military Plans, 1933–1939* (1963). The following works dealing with British foreign policy in the thirties are all severely critical of appeasement: M. Gilbert, *The Roots of Appeasement** (1966); M. George, *The Hollow Men: An Examination of British Foreign Policy between the Years 1933 and 1939* (1967); and W. R. Rock, *Appeasement on Trial: British Foreign Policy and Its Critics* (1966). Britain's military power and its effects on foreign policy are treated in D. Wood and D. Dempster, *The Narrow Margin* (1961). American diplomacy in the late thirties is analyzed in detail by W. L. Langer and S. E. Gleason, *The Challenge to Isolation, 1937–1940** (1952). On U.S.–German relations, see A. A. Offner, *American Appeasement: United States Foreign Policy and Germany* (1969), and J. V. Compton, *The Swastika and the Eagle: Hitler, the United States, and the Origins of World War II* (1967). The major crises fomented by Hitler are discussed in G. Brook-Shepherd, *The Anschluss* (1963); J. Gehl, *Austria, Germany, and the Anschluss, 1931–1938* (1963); J. W. Wheeler-Bennett, *Munich** (1964); and H. Noguères, *Munich: "Peace for Our Time"* (1965). The best books on the Civil War in Spain are G. Jackson, *The Spanish Republic and the Civil War, 1931–1939* (1965), and H. Thomas, *The Spanish Civil War** (1961). The diplomacy of the Ethiopian War is covered in G. W. Baer, *The Coming of the Italian-Ethiopian War* (1967), and in A. Del Boca, *The Ethiopian War, 1935–1941* (1969). The best brief account of the events preceding the outbreak of the Second World War is C. Thorne, *The Approach of War, 1938–1939** (1967).

33

The Second World War and Its Aftermath, 1939–1950

The Second World War, in its origins and events, was quite different from the First. While the question of responsibility for the First World War has caused much controversy, there can be no doubt that the major responsibility for the Second rests heavily on one country, Germany, and on one man, Adolf Hitler. Still, it might be argued that Hitler would never have been able to go to war if the western Allies had stopped him in time. To that extent England and France, too, may bear some responsibility. As for the Soviet Union, its pact with Hitler made the war well-nigh inevitable.

The war of 1939, far more than the war of 1914, was a world war. Japan had been fighting China intermittently for more than eight years, and before long the conflict was to spread to other parts of Asia and to Africa. The earlier war had been largely a war of position. The Second World War was one of almost constant movement. New weapons, already known but little used in the First World War, were chiefly responsible for the greater speed and mobility of the Second. The airplane in particular revolutionized warfare on land and sea. Its use against civilian targets, furthermore, eradicated all differences between the fighting and the home fronts. The Second World War was a truly total war.

THE AXIS TRIUMPHANT 1939–42

Since he had planned his war at long range, Hitler at first enjoyed all the advantages of the aggressor. He expected the war to be short. Even though England and France had promised to honor their pledges to Poland, he did not believe they would fight.

Blitzkrieg in Poland

Germany's forces crossed the Polish border on September 1, 1939. Everything went according to plan. The Poles were no match for the crack Nazi troops, and the main fighting lasted less than four weeks. During that time the *Wehrmacht* took more than 700,000 prisoners at the cost of only 10,000 German dead. The Germans obviously had lost none of their skill at making war.

The world was stunned by Germany's rapid success. Even the Russians were hardly ready to avail themselves of the spoils that had fallen to them as a result of their recent deal with Hitler. At the end of September 1939 a treaty of partition was signed between the Reich and the Soviet Union. Under its provisions Poland was wiped off the map, Germany taking the western and Russia the eastern half. This operation completed, Germany and Russia announced to the world that there was no longer any reason for Britain and France to continue the war.

War at Sea

This appeal for ending the war was directed primarily at France. The French, as Hitler gauged correctly, were neither enthusiastic nor confident about the war. The French army had dutifully occupied the fortified Maginot Line along France's eastern frontier, but there it sat and waited in the "phony war," as the war in the West came to be called. For their part the British expected a German air attack at any minute. But so long as Hitler thought that his friend Chamberlain might be made to give up the fight, the German air force remained grounded. It was at sea that England felt the first effects of the war. On September 17 the aircraft carrier *Courageous* was torpedoed off the southeastern coast of Ireland, and in mid-October a German submarine sank the battleship *Royal Oak* at its home base of Scapa Flow. It was not until December 1939 that the British scored their first naval victory, against the German battleship *Admiral Graf Spee* off the coast of South America.

The Russo-Finnish War

The next aggressive act on the European continent did not come, as was generally expected, in the West, but in the East. And this time it was the Russians who took the initiative. No sooner had the Soviets shared in the Polish loot than they pressured the small republics

Hitler's Europe: massacred civilians in Russia.

of Estonia, Latvia, and Lithuania to sign "mutual assistance" pacts that allowed the Red army to occupy strategic bases along the Baltic coast and brought these states within the Soviet orbit. The only country to resist this pressure was Finland. So on November 30, 1939, Russia renounced a seven-year nonaggression pact with Finland and crossed the Finnish border at eight points. But this was to be no *Blitzkrieg*. The Finns were finally beaten, in March 1940. In the meantime the Russian armies suffered serious losses and showed themselves woefully unprepared. In protest against Russia's attack on Finland, the League of Nations expelled the Soviet Union from membership, the first major power to be thus censured. But attention was soon diverted away from Finland as the Germans embarked on a second round of aggression against the small nations on their periphery.

Germany Turns North and West

Both Norway and the Low Countries were of great strategic importance to Germany. Possession of Norway would extend Germany's narrow coastline, giving its submarines a wider radius of action. The Low Countries—besides providing a protective glacis for Germany's industrial heart, the Ruhr—would offer the necessary base for operations against France and England. Reports in the fall of 1939 that Britain might occupy Norway made Hitler decide to move. In mid-December he ordered preparations for the northern war. Operations began on April 9, 1940. Simultaneously with their invasion of Norway, the Germans occupied Denmark. The British had been forewarned of the German move against Norway but failed to intercept the German invasion fleet. The main fighting in Norway took only a few days. Some pockets of resistance held out until early June, but by that time the Germans had already turned their attention elsewhere.

The war in the West was launched on May 10, 1940. It was one of the most breathtaking and frightening military performances ever witnessed. As spearheads of tanks and armored vehicles drove relentlessly forward, German par-

achute troops seized bridges and airfields behind the Allied lines, air raids gutted civilian objectives, and dive bombers strafed the endless columns of helpless refugees. It took the Germans less than a week to overrun the Netherlands and little over two weeks to defeat the Belgian, French, and British forces in Belgium. The remains of the Allied armies, more than 300,000 men, were evacuated to England from Dunkirk on the Channel coast. The Allied cause had suffered a resounding defeat.

On the day the Lowlands were invaded, Chamberlain resigned. He was succeeded by Winston Churchill, sixty-five years old and already famous, although his greatest contributions still lay ahead. It was Churchill who inspired the British people to their heroic resistance during the "Battle of Britain."

The Fall of France

There was no one to do for France what Churchill did for England. The man who was pushed into the limelight in the hope that he would unite the French people was Marshal Henri Philippe Pétain. Once before, in 1916, he had been the symbol of his country's resistance in time of national emergency (see p. 702). But in 1940 the old marshal was less concerned with continuing the war than with making peace. France, he felt, had been betrayed by its radical Left and deserted by its British allies. Why not try and save from the wreckage what could be saved by collaborating with Hitler?

As the German armies reached the Channel coast in late May 1940, Hitler was faced with a major decision: Should he invade England, or should he complete the conquest of France? He decided to do the latter, perhaps because he was still hoping to reach a compromise with the British and so did not want to antagonize them unnecessarily. There is no need to go into the melancholy details of the "Fall of France." It was no longer a war, since there was hardly any resistance. When the French were at their lowest and German victory was beyond a doubt, Italian troops invaded southeastern France. Mussolini had stayed out of the war thus far, claiming that he was

Hitler's victory jig, after learning of the fall of France in 1940.

not ready for it. But the collapse of France was too good an opportunity to miss.

The official French surrender to Germany took place on June 21, 1940, at Compiègne. Under the terms of the armistice Germany occupied three-fifths of France, including its entire coast. The French also had to pay occupation costs of 400,000,000 francs per day. There were no final territorial provisions; these were to await a later peace conference. The unoccupied, southern part of France chose as its capital the town of Vichy. Besides Pétain, the leaders of the Vichy government included Pierre Laval and Admiral Jean Darlan. The United States recognized the new regime and used its influence to bolster Vichy efforts to keep the French fleet and overseas possessions out of German hands.

The Battle of Britain

With France out of the war, Great Britain now stood alone. Its most immediate fear was of a German invasion. But Hitler lacked the necessary equipment to launch his "Operation Sea Lion," and besides, he never gave up hope that England would capitulate without fighting to the finish. To break down British resistance, the German *Luftwaffe,* in July 1940, embarked on an all-out air offensive. The Battle of Britain lasted through the rest of the year. Several times the British reached the limits of their reserves in planes and pilots. But they did not give in. Meanwhile, halfhearted preparations for "Operation Sea Lion" continued. But Hitler assumed that a successful invasion of England required complete control of the air, and that the Germans never achieved. In the fall of 1940, invasion plans were postponed and Hitler decided to strike elsewhere.

War in North Africa and the Balkans

An empire as large as that of Britain was vulnerable in many places. The British possession most coveted by Hitler was Gibraltar. To take this strongly fortified gateway to the Mediterranean, however, the *Führer* needed the support of

Prime Minister Winston Churchill inspecting ruins of the House of Commons following bombing by the German *Luftwaffe* in 1940.

A policeman cycles through London to warn of an air raid.

Franco's Spain, which he failed to get. Another important British region was Egypt. The task of ousting the British from there was given to the Italians. In September 1940 an Italian army invaded Egypt from Libya. It was stopped almost immediately by a far smaller British force, which then drove the Italians back into Libya. A major Axis defeat was avoided only by the timely intervention of the German *Afrikakorps* under General Erwin Rommel. By early April 1941 the Axis forces had regained the initiative and were once again on Egyptian soil.

The Italians, meanwhile, had become involved in another venture, this time without even consulting the Germans. In October 1940 Italian troops crossed from Albania into Greece. After some minor gains, they were soon pushed back again into Albania. Once more the Germans had to intervene and thus open another major front. Bulgaria and Hungary were already on the side of the Axis. Yugoslavia was quickly overrun by German, Bulgarian, and Hungarian troops. Greece

German soldier in battle.

was defeated and occupied, and a German airborne invasion took the island of Crete. In the spring of 1941 it seemed that Germany was looking still farther afield, beyond the Balkans, toward the Middle East. But before the *Führer's* schemes went very far, he became occupied with more important objectives in eastern Europe. Combined British and Free French forces were able, therefore, to keep the upper hand in the strategically vital eastern Mediterranean.

There were some other hopeful developments in the spring of 1941, while Britain was still fighting with its back to the wall. The United States was constantly increasing its aid to Great Britain,

and ultimate American involvement in the war appeared a definite possibility. The British navy, meanwhile, won a major victory when it sank the German superbattleship *Bismarck* on May 27. And, most important, there were persistent rumors that relations between Germany and Russia were rapidly deteriorating.

HITLER'S RUSSIAN GAMBLE

Russo-German relations since the outbreak of the Second World War had been far from smooth. Two totalitarian countries, each bent on expansion, could not possibly avoid for long getting in each other's way. To be sure, the two partners maintained a mutually beneficial economic exchange. But on the diplomatic front Russo-German interests were far less complementary. Hitler was disturbed by Russia's expansion along the Baltic, and Stalin was taken aback by Hitler's unexpected successes in the West. More serious still were the differences between Russia and Germany over the Balkans, where no clear line of demarcation had been worked out. Efforts to clarify these and other matters were made in November 1940 at a conference in Berlin. But the attempt failed, partly because of Russia's far-reaching demands for the control of eastern and southeastern Europe, partly because Hitler had already decided to attack the Soviet Union.

The German Invasion of Russia

There were obvious reasons for Hitler's Russian gamble: He wanted *Lebensraum,* and he hated communism. But there was still another reason why he decided to strike at Russia. The stubborn resistance of the British, he felt, was due chiefly to their hope that Germany might ultimately become involved in a war with the Soviet Union. To attack and defeat Russia while it was still weak from the Finnish War, therefore, was the best way of inducing Britain to surrender. The first preparations for the invasion of Russia were made as early as July 1940. The final directives were issued the following

Churchill on the German Invasion of Russia

Hitler is a monster of wickedness, insatiable in his lust for blood and plunder. Not content with having all of Europe under his heel or else terrorized into various forms of abject submission, he must now carry his work of butchery and desolation among the vast multitudes of Russia and Asia. The terrible military machine which we and the rest of the civilized world so foolishly, so supinely, so insensately, allowed the Nazi gangsters to build up, year by year, from almost nothing—the machine cannot stand idle lest it rust, or fall to pieces. It must be in continual motion, grinding up human lives and trampling down the homes and the rights of hundreds of millions of men.

Moreover, it must be fed, not only with human flesh but with oil. So now this bloodthirsty guttersnipe must launch his mechanized armies upon new fields of slaughter, pillage and devastation. Poor as are the Russian peasants, workmen and soldiers, he must steal from them their daily bread. He must devour their harvests. He must rob them of the oil which drives their plows, and thus produce a famine without example in human history, and even the carnage and ruin which his victory, should he gain it—he has not gained it yet—will bring upon the Russian people will itself be only a steppingstone to the attempt to plunge the 400,000,000 or 500,000,000 who live in China and the 350,000,000 who live in India into the bottomless pit of human degradation over which the diabolic emblem of the swastika flaunts itself. . . .

The Nazi regime is indistinguishable from the worst features of Communism. . . . No one has been a more consistent opponent of Communism than I have for the last twenty-five years. I will unsay no words that I have spoken about it. But all this fades away before the spectacle which is now unfolding. The past with its crimes, its follies and its tragedies flashes away.

Speech by Winston Churchill on June 22, 1941. From *The New York Times,* June 23, 1941.

Russian soldiers pursuing remnants of the German Sixth Army in the battle of Stalingrad, 1943.

December. The *Wehrmacht* struck on June 22, 1941.

The German armies at the start were disastrously successful. During the first weeks of fighting, hundreds of thousands of Russian soldiers were killed, wounded, or captured. But the Russians seemed to have inexhaustible manpower. What was surprising was how the Russian people rallied to their country's defense. Stalin emerged as a great national leader, and opposition to his ruthless regime disappeared in the face of foreign aggression. One of Hitler's gravest errors, next to invading Russia in the first place, was not to have posed to the Russian people as a liberator from communist oppression. Instead, the *Führer* ordered Russian prisoners to be herded into vast camps where they died of starvation, or else had them transported to Germany as slave labor.

The Russian war helped close overnight the gap between the East and the West. Great Britain now offered Stalin a military alliance, and the Americans included the Soviets in their program of lend-lease. While the East and West were thus joining forces, the Germans were encountering unforeseen difficulties. Winter came unusually early in 1941, and the German army was not prepared for it. When Germany's commanders wanted to halt their advance, Hitler relieved them and took charge himself. The

Germans suffered terrible hardships, but they continued their advance. In the fall of 1942 Hitler's generals once again urged him to shorten his lines to more defensible proportions. But the *Führer* remained unyielding. Since August, large German forces had been engaged in the siege of Stalingrad on the lower Volga. The battle of Stalingrad has been compared to the battle of Verdun in the First World War. Both were fought with unusual ferocity and both entailed terrific losses. A German victory at Stalingrad would have given Germany control over the rich oil fields of the Caucasus. But instead of ejecting the Russians from Stalingrad, the Germans were caught in the pincers of a Russian counteroffensive and suffered a major defeat by February 1943.

The battle of Stalingrad was not the first Nazi defeat. The western allies were simultaneously advancing and winning in North Africa. But the disaster in Russia was a decisive event. In a gradually mounting offensive, the Russians began to push Hitler's armies back across the plains of eastern Europe. It took almost two more years before the fighting reached German soil. Meanwhile the expansion of Japan in the Far East had also been halted in the winter of 1942–43, and the Japanese were being driven back to their home bases. By the spring of 1943, then, fascist aggression had overextended

The New Order

The following is part of a confidential address given by Heinrich Himmler to his S.S. officers on October 4, 1943.

What happens to a Russian, to a Czech, does not interest me in the slightest. What the nations can offer in the way of good blood of our type we will take, if necessary by kidnaping their children and raising them here with us. Whether nations live in prosperity or starve to death like cattle interests me only in so far as we need them as slaves to our *Kultur*; otherwise it is of no interest to me. Whether 10,000 Russian females fall down from exhaustion while digging an antitank ditch interests me only in so far as the antitank ditch for Germany is finished.

From *Nazi Conspiracy and Aggression* (Washington: U.S. Government Printing Office, 1946), Vol. IV, p. 559.

The "Final Solution"

The first train arrived . . . 45 freightcars with 6,700 people, of which 1,450 were already dead on arrival. . . . A large loudspeaker blares instructions: Undress completely, take off artificial limbs, glasses, etc. Hand in all valuables. Shoes to be tied together (for the clothing collection) . . . Women and girls to the barber, who cuts off their hair in two or three strokes and stuffs it into potato sacks. . . .

Then the line starts moving. . . . At the corner a strapping SS-man announces in a pastoral voice: Nothing will happen to you! Just breathe deeply inside the chambers, that stretches the lungs; this inhalation is necessary against the illnesses and epidemics. When asked what would happen to them, he replies: Well, of course the men will have to work, build houses and roads, but the women won't have to work. If they want to they can help in the household or the kitchen. For a few of these unfortunates a small glimmer of hope which suffices to have them take the few steps to the chambers without resistance—the majority knows what is ahead, the stench tells their fate. . . .

The wooden doors are opened. . . . Inside the chambers, the dead stand closely pressed together, like pillars of stone. . . . Even in death one recognizes the families. They still hold hands, so they have to be torn apart to get the chambers ready for their next occupants. The corpses are thrown out—wet with sweat and urine, covered with excrement, menstrual blood. Children's bodies fly through the air. . . . Two dozen workers use hooks to pry open mouths to look for gold. . . . Others search genitals and anuses for gold, diamonds and valuables. Wirth [an SS-guard] motions to me: Just lift this can of gold teeth, this is only from yesterday and the day before! . . .

From an eyewitness account of mass gassings, in *Vierteljahrshefte für Zeitgeschichte*, Vol. I (1953), pp. 190–91.

itself, and the tide of the war began to turn.

HITLER'S "NEW ORDER"

What was the fate of those areas that for several years suffered under German occupation? There was never any master plan for Hitler's "New Order," since the future depended on the final outcome of the war. Few of the territories under German domination were annexed outright, although the degree to which some of them were being Germanized left no doubt about their ultimate fate. The war had done its share in decreasing the population of eastern Europe. In addition, more than 7 million foreign workers were forced to work in German factories. Into the areas thus vacated, ethnic Germans, mostly from outside the Reich, were sent as pioneers of Hitler's Germanization policy.

But Hitler was not content merely with taking land away from other peoples. The most frightful deed committed in the name of his "New Order" was the willful extermination of from 6 to 8 million people, most of them Jews. Wherever the German armies went, Hitler's private army, the elite SS (*Schutzstaffel*) followed to see that the party's racial policies were carried out. At first there was merely persecution of the Jews, and in this the local populations often participated. But in time more drastic measures were adopted. Hitler's so-called "Final Solution" called for nothing less than the complete extermination of all Jews. This was carried out by means of gas chambers in special extermination camps, such as Auschwitz. There were several such camps, not only for the extermination of Jews but for the "mercy killing" of the incurably ill and insane, and for the liquidation of political prisoners.

These were only the more gruesome acts committed by the Nazis. Additional millions were kept in concentration, slave-labor, and prisoner-of-war camps, where many died more "normal" deaths of starvation. A great many Germans were involved in these crimes; yet after the war almost no one would admit having known of what went on behind the barbed wire of these camps.

AMERICA ENTERS THE WAR

America's involvement in the war was a gradual process. The United States government had followed a policy of strict neutrality during the various acts of German and Italian aggression prior to the Second World War. The question was whether this attitude of aloofness could be maintained in a war among the major European powers. As one country after another fell victim to the Axis powers, America's role in the war became of crucial importance. Axis domination of western Europe and North Africa, once firmly established, would have posed a serious threat to the United States. It was for its self-preservation that America was forced to travel the road from neutrality to belligerency.

Benevolent Neutrality

As early as November 4, 1939, Congress had passed a revised Neutrality Act that lifted the embargo on all implements of war and put all maritime trade on a "cash and carry" basis. This move tended to favor the country with the largest funds and the strongest navy, Great Britain. But Britain's enormous need for material aid made its dollar credits dwindle rapidly. The two governments tried to overcome this difficulty in several ways. One was the "destroyer deal" of 1940, when the United States gave Britain some fifty ships in return for a lease of certain British-held naval bases in the Western Hemisphere. Another way for America to help its future allies was through the Lend-Lease Act of 1941. It gave the President power to provide goods and services to any nation whose defense was considered vital to the United States.

The Lend-Lease Act was an important step away from neutrality. There were other signs that America was getting off the fence. But in August 1941, when Congress was asked to extend the Selective Service Act of the preceding September, which established the draft, the measure was passed only by the slimmest margin. The American people, it seemed, were perfectly willing to go to any limit in helping the antifascist cause so long as they did not become involved in the war themselves. It took the Japanese attack on Pearl Harbor to push the United States across the line from nonintervention to belligerency.

War with Japan

The United States, for some forty years past, had stood in the way of Japan's major aim: to dominate China and extend its power over the trading area of southeastern Asia and the neighboring Pacific. Especially since the start of the Sino-Japanese war in 1937, Washington had been concerned about Japan's violations of the "Open Door" policy in China. To put pressure on the Japanese, the United States, in July 1939, ended its thirty-year-old commercial treaty with Japan and subsequently imposed an embargo on certain strategic goods. By the middle of 1941 the embargo was seriously affecting the Japanese. Tokyo's demand for the cessation of United States restrictions were met with American counterdemands for Japan's withdrawal from China. As far back as January 1941 the Japanese government had begun to prepare for an armed showdown. The final decision to strike was made on December 1.

When the Japanese air force staged its sneak attack against Pearl Harbor, on December 7, 1941, it caught the American forces entirely unprepared. The United States suffered more than 3,000 casualties and heavy material losses, one of the greatest defeats in its history. Yet terrible as the catastrophe of Pearl Harbor was, it had one good effect—it cut short the debate between isolationists and interventionists. As Italy and Germany now declared war on the United States, the American people rallied behind the war effort of their government. With the world's mightiest nation thus fully committed, the outcome of the war looked decidedly more favorable for the British and their Russian allies.

THE DEFEAT OF THE AXIS

In discussing the defeat of the fascist aggressors, it is simpler to deal with each major field of operation separately. But

Pearl Harbor, December 7, 1941.

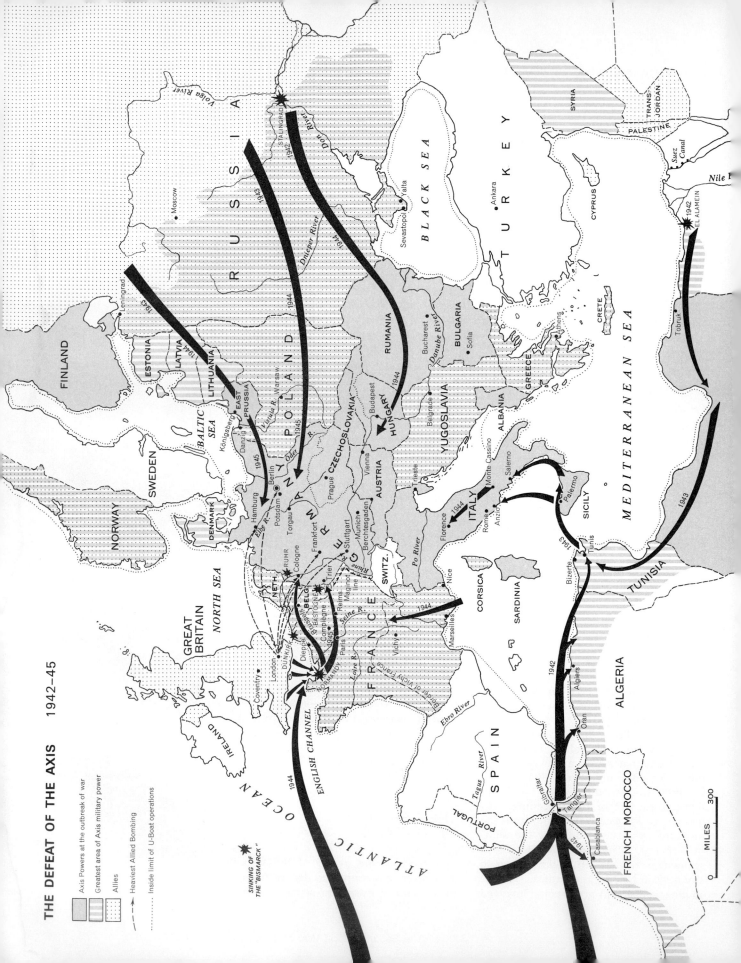

THE DEFEAT OF THE AXIS 1942–45

Axis Powers at the outbreak of war
Greatest area of Axis military power
Allies
Heaviest Allied Bombing
Inside limit of U-Boat operations

SINKING OF
THE "BISMARCK"

ATLANTIC OCEAN

GREAT BRITAIN

IRELAND

London
Coventry

NORTH SEA

ENGLISH CHANNEL

DUNKIRK
Dieppe
NORMANDY
1944

FRANCE

Border of Vichy France

Paris
Reims
Compiègne
Brussels
BELG.
BASTOGNE
NETH.
Cologne
RUHR
Trier
Maginot Line
Stuttgart
Frankfort
Munich
Berchtesgaden
SWITZ.
Vichy
Loire R.
Seine R.
Rhine R.
Rhône R.
Nice
Marseilles

1944

SPAIN

PORTUGAL

Tagus River
Ebro River

Gibraltar
Tangier
Casablanca
1942

FRENCH MOROCCO

ALGERIA

Oran
Algiers
1942

Bizerte
Tunis
1943
TUNISIA

SARDINIA
CORSICA

MEDITERRANEAN SEA

SICILY
Palermo
Salerno
Anzio
Monte Cassino
Rome
Florence
ITALY
1944
Po River
Trieste

Naples

ALBANIA

GREECE
Athens
CRETE

BULGARIA
Sofia
YUGOSLAVIA
Belgrade
Danube River
Bucharest
RUMANIA
1944

HUNGARY
Budapest
AUSTRIA
Vienna
CZECHOSLOVAKIA
Prague

G E R M A N Y

Berlin
Potsdam
Torgau
Hamburg
Elbe R.
Oder R.
1945

DENMARK

SWEDEN

NORWAY

FINLAND

BALTIC SEA

Königsberg
Danzig
1945
EAST PRUSSIA
Vistula R.
Warsaw
P O L A N D

LITHUANIA
1944
LATVIA
ESTONIA
Leningrad
1943

Moscow

R U S S I A

Volga River
STALINGRAD
1942
Don River
1943
Dnieper River
1944

BLACK SEA
Sevastopol
Yalta

T U R K E Y
Ankara

CYPRUS

SYRIA
PALESTINE
TRANS-JORDAN

Suez Canal
Nile R.

EL ALAMEIN
1942

Tobruk

1943

MILES
0   300

it should be kept in mind that the war was being fought on a global scale. The European Allies were worried at first that America's involvement in the Pacific would prevent it from continuing its aid to Europe. The Russians in particular kept up a nagging insistence on the immediate opening of a second front on the Continent. Before such an operation could be thought of, however, large numbers of American troops had to be shipped overseas, and that was possible only after the threat of Germany's submarine fleet had been overcome.

On the eve of the war total Allied merchant tonnage amounted to about 25 million. Of this amount, 21 million tons were lost, mostly to submarine action. The final victory over the submarine menace was due in part to the convoy system, by which naval transports were escorted by warships, and to improved methods of detecting submarines. But the victory at sea could not have been won without the "battle of the shipyards," in which American workers built ships faster than the Germans could sink them. By the middle of 1943 Allied shipping had regained its prewar level and the worst of the danger was past.

The Invasion of North Africa

The first involvement of American ground forces in the war against the Axis took place in North Africa. On November 8, 1942, an Anglo-American invasion force, commanded by General Dwight D. Eisenhower, landed at Casablanca in French Morocco and at various points in Algeria. Allied intervention in North Africa was made easier by the collaboration of the French forces stationed there. The leading French representative in Morocco and Algeria at the time was Admiral Darlan. His cooperation helped keep Allied losses during the landing to a minimum, although the fact that Darlan had in the past been decidedly profascist caused some embarrassment. The admiral was subsequently assassinated by a follower of General de Gaulle. The North African campaign ended on May 13, 1943, with the Allied capture of Tunis and Bizerte. The total losses of the Axis in three years of North African fighting had come close to a million men.

In the meantime, the German people were also feeling the effects of American intervention nearer home. Almost daily, large fleets of United States and British planes penetrated the antiaircraft defenses of the Reich, bombing industrial centers and strategic objectives. The much-advertised *Luftwaffe* of Reichsmarshal Göring, which had earlier failed to bomb the British into submission, now proved equally ineffective in defending German soil.

The Allied Invasion of Italy

Having won North Africa, the Allies next aimed for control of the rest of the Mediterranean. The invasion of Sicily and southern Italy was launched in the summer of 1943. Resistance in Sicily collapsed in mid-August, and on September 2 British and American troops landed on the Italian mainland. The campaign in Italy lasted until the end of the war, slowing down as the emphasis shifted to the northern theater of war. Nevertheless, the war in Italy played a vital part in the final victory, since it helped tie down large German forces that might otherwise have been used on Hitler's two other fronts. But the Italian war also caused one of the first major crises between the Anglo-Saxon powers and their Russian ally.

Stalin had long been annoyed with the West for not opening what he considered a real second front. The invasion of Italy gave new cause for such annoyance. During the Sicilian campaign in July 1943, a number of high officials within the Italian Fascist Party staged a *coup d'etat* and forced Mussolini to resign. The new Italian government under Marshal Pietro Badoglio asked the Allies for an armistice. While this made the subsequent invasion of the mainland much easier, the agreement with Badoglio further aroused the suspicion of Stalin. What he feared was that the West might conclude a separate peace without the Russians.

"Operation Overlord"

The delay in opening a second front in the north was partly due to differences within the western camp on where the

The end of Mussolini. He and his mistress were executed by Italian partisans in Milan, April 29, 1945.

attack against Hitler's "Fortress Europe" should be launched. Winston Churchill favored the Balkans. Not only did he expect fewer losses from striking at the "soft underbelly of Europe"; he wanted to keep the Russians out of that important peninsula. President Roosevelt and his advisers, on the other hand, saw France as the more suitable terrain for a second front, mainly for strategic reasons. The American view prevailed.

The final decision for "Operation Overlord," the code word for the liberation of France, was made at a conference of the "Big Three" at Teheran in December 1943. The supreme command was entrusted to General Eisenhower; the scene of the landing was to be the coast of Normandy; and D-Day was to be June 6, 1944. Since the Germans had expected the invasion nearer Calais, the Allies were able to establish a firm beachhead. Within three weeks more than 2 million men had been landed on the Continent. After three months of fighting, the Allies had driven the Germans out of northwestern France. On August 15 a second amphibious operation landed on the French Mediterranean coast and within

a month made contact with the main invasion forces in the North. In mid-September the first American forces crossed the German frontier. Here they were halted by the fortified German "Siegfried Line."

The German *Wehrmacht*, although on the run, was still far from beaten. During the week before Christmas 1944, Hitler staged his last big offensive of the war. Under cover of fog and snow and in the difficult terrain of the Ardennes, eight German armored divisions drove a deep salient into the Allied lines. This "Battle of the Bulge" proved to be a costly failure for the Germans, but for a brief moment it seemed to threaten the Allied victory in the West.

Germany Invaded from East and West

The Russians, meanwhile, had been pressing slowly but steadily westward. At the end of January 1945 the Red army stood on the Oder River, less than a hundred miles from Berlin. These were terrible months for the Germans, who now felt what it was like to be the victims of invasion. As the fortunes of war turned, sporadic German opposition to Hitler gathered sufficient strength for a final attempt to rid the country of its tyrant. But the plot of July 20, 1944, miscarried, and the *Führer* took horrible vengeance. Thousands of decent men and women, who might have played a leading role in the postwar reconstruction of Germany, were put to death. The rest of the German people were urged on into suicidal resistance, especially since the Allied demand for "unconditional surrender" seemed to leave no alternative.

Early in 1945 the Allies stood poised along the western borders of the Reich, ready for the final phase of the European war. The invasion of the Rhineland was launched on February 8, 1945. From here on events happened with lightning speed. By the end of March the Rhine had been crossed; by the middle of April the Ruhr district had been taken; and on April 25 the first American and Russian patrols met on the Elbe River. On April 30, while the Russians were fighting their

D-Day: the invasion of Normandy, June 6, 1944.

way into the center of Berlin, Adolf Hitler committed suicide. On May 7, 1945, at the headquarters of General Eisenhower at Reims, a German military delegation signed the terms of Germany's unconditional surrender. May 8, 1945, was officially proclaimed V-E Day, victory day in Europe.

THE WAR IN THE PACIFIC

The war against Japan was primarily a naval war in which the United States carried the major burden. Considering America's losses at Pearl Harbor and its heavy commitment of men and material in Europe, the victory in the Pacific was a magnificent achievement. This was particularly true considering the extent of Japanese expansion. A few days after Pearl Harbor, the Japanese overran America's outposts at Guam and Wake Island. Early in 1942, they invaded the Philippines. The Dutch East Indies, the Malay Peninsula, and Burma went next. By May 1942 the whole area east of India and north of Australia, except for the southern part of New Guinea, had fallen into Japanese hands.

American Naval Victories

It was the Japanese attempt to force the Allies out of New Guinea and to gain a base for the invasion of Australia that triggered the first major naval battle between United States and Japanese forces. The battle of the Coral Sea in May 1942 inflicted heavy American losses but it kept the Japanese from their objective. A still more decisive naval battle took place a month later at Midway Island, northwest of Hawaii. The engagement was deliberately sought by the Japanese, who hoped to annihilate the smaller United States fleet and thus open the way to Hawaii. But the Americans anticipated the enemy's move and the battle of Midway brought a resounding Japanese defeat. For the first time America held a slight naval edge in the Pacific. The Japanese achieved some last successes when they occupied Attu and Kiska in the Aleutian Islands. But with the landing of United States marines in the Solomon

The Red Flood

Columns of marching soldiers, dirty, tired, clad in ragged uniforms— tens and hundreds of thousands of columns . . . columns of women and girls in military grey-green uniforms, high boots and tight blouses, with long hair greased with goose-fat . . . children, mainly small boys; the *bezprizorni* from burned-out villages and towns. . . . Behind the first spearheads drive the staff; they drive in German luxury cars . . . cars with their secretaries and secretary-girl friends and secretary companions . . . cars with war-booty, cases of china, kilometres of textile materials, fur coats, carpets, silver. . . . Cars of the the Agitprop Brigade with broadcasting apparatus and theatrical properties . . . lorries belonging to the Political Commissariat, the staffs and motorised units of the NKVD . . . lorries with tons of Russian delicacies, caviar, sturgeon, salami, hectolitres of vodka and Crimean wine. . . . Behind the staffs more marching columns, without a beginning and without an end . . . finally the rearguard; miles and miles of small light cars drawn by low Cossack horses . . . as the Tartars used to drive centuries ago . . . a flood from the Steppes, spreading across Europe. . . .

From J. Stransky, *East Wind over Prague* (London: Hollis and Carter, 1950), pp. 22–25.

Islands in August 1942 Japanese expansion was halted, and soon the tide began to turn.

The Turn of the Tide

In 1942 United States naval supremacy was established in the Pacific; the next year brought the first breaks through the outer perimeter of Japan's defenses. Beginning with the battle of Guadalcanal, one after another of Japan's island outposts were retaken in some of the war's bloodiest fighting. Places most Americans had never heard of—Tarawa, Makin, Eniwetok, Iwo Jima, Okinawa— now suddenly became headlines. Meanwhile, United States submarines were taking a heavy toll of Japanese shipping, and the Japanese islands were put under a blockade. In June 1944 American superfortresses began their first bombing raids on Japan. In October 1944 United States forces under General Douglas MacArthur began their reconquest of the Philippines. And in Burma British imperial forces under Lord Louis Mountbatten, supported by Americans and Chinese, were rounding up the Japanese invaders.

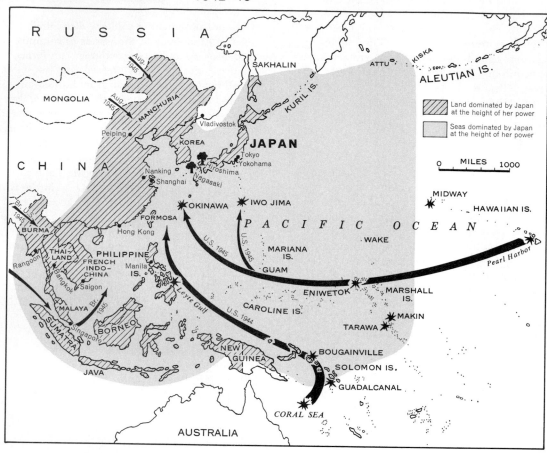

Hiroshima

At about 0815 there was a blinding flash. Some described it as brighter than the sun, others likened it to a magnesium flash. Following the flash there was a blast of heat and wind. The large majority of people within 3000 feet of ground zero were killed immediately. Within a radius of about 7000 feet almost every Japanese house collapsed. Beyond this range and up to 15,000–20,000 feet many of them collapsed and others received serious structural damage. Persons in the open were burned on exposed surfaces, and within 3000–5000 feet many were burned to death while others received severe burns through their clothes. . . . The people appeared stunned by the catastrophe and rushed about as jungle animals suddenly released from a cage. Some few apparently attempted to help others from the wreckage, particularly members of their family or friends. Others assisted those who were unable to walk alone. However, many of the injured were left trapped beneath collapsed buildings as people fled by them in the streets. Pandemonium reigned as the uninjured and slightly injured fled the city in fearful panic.

From "The Effects of Atomic Bombs on Health and Medical Services in Hiroshima and Nagasaki," *The United States Strategic Bombing Survey* (Washington: U.S. Government Printing Office, March 1947), p. 3.

The End of the War

The climax of the war in the Pacific came on October 21–22, 1944, with the battle of Leyte Gulf in the Philippine Sea, one of the biggest naval battles ever fought. Japanese losses were such that their navy, henceforth, was no longer a factor in the war. As Allied successes in Europe mounted, more and more strength could be diverted to the Pacific theater. In the spring of 1945 America's commanders in the Pacific were asked to prepare plans for the invasion of Japan. But while these preparations were still under way, on July 16, 1945, the first atomic bomb was successfully exploded at Los Alamos, New Mexico. The atomic bombing of Hiroshima and Nagasaki on August 6 and 9 led to the surrender of Japan on August 14, 1945, and to the end of the Second World War.

The decision to use this terrible new weapon was not an easy one. Should not efforts be made to lay siege to Japan first? But President Truman and his advisers felt that an early surrender of Japan without invasion was most unlikely. And an invasion of Japan, it was estimated, would cost more than a million Allied casualties and at least again that many Japanese. It was thought preferable, therefore, to bring the war to a quick, though horrible, end: 78,000 people were killed at Hiroshima and 50,000 at Nagasaki. The Atomic Age had begun.

THE SEARCH FOR PEACE

Considering the tremendous political upheaval resulting from the Second World War, it is surprising how little advance thought had been given to the problem of peace. There had been some general pronouncements, especially the Atlantic Charter, which President Roosevelt and Prime Minister Churchill had issued in August 1941. But this idealistic blueprint for the future, which aimed at a world free from want and fear, was drawn up before the harsh realities of the postwar situation were known. Several conferences during the war—between Roosevelt and Churchill at Casablanca and Quebec, and among the two western leaders and Stalin at Teheran—had dealt primarily with immediate military matters and only incidentally with long-range political questions. Only in the final months of the war did the larger issues of the future become the subject of top-level discussions. These took place at two conferences at Yalta and Potsdam, in February and July 1945.

The Yalta Conference

To understand the concessions made at Yalta to the Soviet Union, we must remember that Russia was still an ally of the West and that the expansionist aims of communism were not yet fully understood. Some of Stalin's claims, furthermore, especially in the Baltic, in Poland, and in the Balkans, had already been recognized, at least by implication. And the fact that all these regions were al-

The Yalta Conference. Churchill, Roosevelt, and Stalin sit for a formal picture-taking session with their advisers. Roosevelt clearly shows the strain of their meeting. He was to die two months later, April 12, 1945.

The launching of the UN, as seen by *Punch*.

ready occupied by Red armies gave added strength to Soviet arguments. Most important, finally, was the conviction of western military leaders that Russia's continued contribution to the common war effort was essential to ensure an early victory.

The main issues discussed at Yalta dealt with the future of Germany, Poland, the Far East, and the United Nations. So far as Germany was concerned, the meeting achieved very little. The only firm agreement dealt with the postwar division of the country into four occupation zones, including a French one, administered by an Allied Control Council. The city of Berlin, likewise, was to be divided into separate occupation zones.

A great deal of time at Yalta was spent in trying to determine the future frontiers of Poland and to agree on the composition of its government. On both points the Russians scored a major success. Poland's border was moved westward to the "Curzon Line," where it had been fixed briefly after the First World War. Russia thus received almost 47 percent of Poland's prewar territory. The powers agreed, however, that in return for its losses in the east, Poland should receive compensations in the north and west. The new provisional government of Poland, meanwhile, was to be drawn chiefly from the Soviet-sponsored Committee of National Liberation rather than from the Polish government-in-exile, which the western powers had favored; but to make sure that Poland was ruled

democratically, "free and unfettered elections" were to be held.

The Far Eastern decisions made at Yalta caused little difficulty at the time, although they have come in for a great deal of criticism since. In return for Stalin's promise to participate in the Pacific war, the Soviet Union was granted large concessions at the expense of both China and Japan. Most of these made up for Russia's losses in the Russo-Japanese War of 1904–05 (see p. 642).

The problem that most concerned the American delegation at Yalta was to get Russian and British agreement to final plans for a United Nations organization. Most of the details for such an organization had already been worked out, except for two important points: the extent of the great powers' veto in the Security Council and the number of seats each was to hold in the UN Assembly. Both points were satisfactorily settled, a fact that greatly contributed to the success of the conference in American eyes. There was some hard bargaining at Yalta, but on the whole the atmosphere had been friendly. It remained to be seen whether the powers could carry over their wartime unity of purpose into their postwar search for peace.

The United Nations

The first problem tackled after Yalta was the drafting of a charter for the United Nations. This was done at the San Francisco Conference in the spring of 1945. The main purposes of the United Nations are: to maintain peace; to develop friendly relations among nations; and to help solve economic, social, and cultural problems. Any peace-loving nation may become a member if sponsored by the Security Council and a two-thirds vote of the Assembly, and a state may be expelled for violating the provisions of the charter.

As these provisions suggest, the United Nations owes much to its predecessor, the League of Nations. Like the League, the UN, at least at the start, was entirely dominated by the great powers among its members. The most important agency of the UN is the Security Council, five of whose seats were assigned to the United States, Great Britain, the Soviet

The official symbol of the UN.

Union, France, and Nationalist China. (The latter's place was taken by Communist China in 1972.) Since each of these powers has an absolute veto, the effectiveness of the UN has been seriously hampered. The chief task of the Council is to maintain peace and security. Like the Council of the League of Nations, it can recommend peaceful arbitration or measures short of war, such as economic sanctions. But unlike the League, the Security Council may also take "such actions by air, sea, or land forces as may be necessary to maintain or restore international peace."

The Potsdam Conference

While the San Francisco Conference was still in session, the end of the war in Europe called for another top-level meeting to settle the future of Germany. Russia's unilateral actions in eastern Europe, notably in Rumania and Poland, had already called forth repeated western protests. When the powers assembled at Potsdam in July 1945, therefore, the cordiality that had prevailed at Yalta had given way to coldness. The United States, after President Roosevelt's death in April 1945, was represented by President Harry S. Truman; and Great Britain, after Churchill's defeat at the polls, was represented by Prime Minister Clement Attlee. This left Stalin as the only original member of the Big Three.

The main differences between the East and the West at Potsdam arose over the eastern borders of Germany and over German reparations. As compensation for the territories it had lost to Russia at Yalta, Poland had occupied about one-fifth of Germany, east of the Oder and Neisse rivers. Against Stalin's insistence that these lands become permanently Polish, the western powers at Potsdam won a postponement of any final decision until a later peace conference. As for German reparations, the Soviet Union held on to the high demands it had made at Yalta. But the West got Stalin to agree that Germany was to be left with sufficient resources to support itself and that the country was to be treated "as a single economic unit." Here were several causes for subsequent friction among the victors.

During the closing days of the Potsdam Conference attention shifted to the Far East, where the war with Japan was drawing to a close. The Soviet Union entered the war at the last minute by invading Manchuria. As soon as the fighting had stopped, Russia took possession of the rights and territories it had been promised at Yalta—special rights on the Chinese mainland in Port Arthur and Darien, and annexation of the Kurile Islands and southern Sakhalin from Japan. The United States claimed control over Japan itself. Korea was divided into Russian and American zones. Here was another potential source of conflict.

Peace with the Axis Satellites

With the war finally over, peace negotiations could begin. The peace conference of the twenty-one nations that had fought against the Axis met in Paris in July 1946. Many of its decisions had been made beforehand by the foreign ministers of the great powers. The peace treaties with Italy, Rumania, Hungary, Bulgaria, and Finland were signed in February 1947. Italy, in spite of its Fascist past, was let off remarkably easily. It lost some territory to France, Yugoslavia, and Greece; its colonies were put under the trusteeship of the UN; and Italy had to pay reparations. The settlements with the rest of the powers were similar. Since, with the exception of Finland, these countries were already under Russian domination, the details of the peace terms are not very important. The Soviet Union in each case was the main beneficiary, getting the major share of reparations and extensive territories. Some of these territories—the Baltic states, eastern Poland, and Bessarabia—had formerly belonged to tsarist Russia; but the Baltic states between the wars had been independent and Bessarabia had belonged to Rumania. Stalin's aim, it seemed, was to restore Russia's borders as they had been before the advent of communism.

THE PROBLEM OF GERMANY

The signing of the Paris treaties ended peacemaking for the time being. Treaties

The boundaries shown on this map date from the beginning of World War II.

0   MILES   200

Axis nations after World War II

Lands which changed hands after World War II

had almost 70 million people, and its industrial resources were considerable. There could be little doubt, therefore, that the former Reich would continue to be a vital factor in world affairs. Beginning in 1946, Russia and the western powers tried to reach an agreement on the future of Germany. But it soon became clear that they did not see eye to eye on many crucial points. What each side hoped was to create a united Germany in its own image. And when this proved impossible, the East and West reorganized their respective zones, eventually creating a divided Germany.

The Division of Germany

The first disagreements arose over economic matters. The division of Germany into occupation zones proved a serious obstacle to economic recovery. But western proposals for economic unification were met by Russian counterproposals for political unity first. Since it had been agreed at Potsdam that Germany was to be treated "as a single economic unit," the western powers, in December 1946, merged their zones economically. West Germany's economy was then given considerable American aid. The result was a miraculous turn for the better. By 1950 the industrial output of West Germany had again reached its 1936 level.

While the West was integrating its two-thirds of Germany into the economy of western Europe, the Russians began the thoroughgoing "sovietization" of their eastern zone. In time these diverging policies could not help but lead to partition. At one point, in 1948–49, the Soviet Union tried to force the West out of the former German capital by imposing a blockade on the Allied sectors of Berlin. But a gigantic western airlift of some 300,000 flights foiled Russia's scheme. In May 1949 a West German Parliamentary Council adopted a constitution for the Federal Republic of Germany, with Bonn as capital and with Konrad Adenauer as its first chancellor. In East Germany a Communist-dominated "German Democratic Republic" was founded in October 1949. By 1950 the struggle between East and West over Germany had resulted in the politi-

with Japan and Austria were not signed until several years later, and there is as yet no final settlement with Germany. It was over the issue of Germany that the East and West had their first real falling-out.

Germany, at Potsdam, lost about one-fourth of the territory it had held in 1937, before Hitler embarked on his eastward expansion. But Germany still cal division of the country, each part refusing to recognize the other and claiming to speak for the whole.

THE BEGINNING OF THE COLD WAR

The increasing tension between the western Allies and the Soviet Union grew out of the fundamental difference of their aims. The West envisaged the postwar world largely in prewar terms. The United Nation was to continue the work of the League of Nations, without the latter's shortcomings; and it was hoped that in due time the idealistic principles of the Atlantic Charter would be put into effect. The Soviet Union, on the other hand, endeavored to use the chaos of the postwar world to further its own expansionist and political aims.

The Spread of Communism

The communization of eastern Europe was a gradual process. The region had been "liberated" by the Red army, which had then stayed on. At first some outward show of democracy was maintained, with "popular front" governments and "free" elections. But gradually the non-Communist members were ousted and coalition governments were transformed into "people's democracies." By 1947 this policy was causing deep concern in the West. Poland, Rumania, Yugoslavia, Albania, and Bulgaria all had either Communist or pro-Communist regimes, and the trend in Czechoslovakia and Hungary was in the same direction. The only way to halt this creeping expansion of communism, it was felt, was to meet force with force. The occasion to proclaim such a policy of "containment" came in the spring of 1947, when Russia tried to extend its influence near the entrance to the Black Sea.

The Truman Doctrine and the Marshall Plan

In Greece, a small Communist minority, supported by Communists in neighboring countries, was waging a civil war against the government. The British, after the war, had supplied the Greek monar-

The Berlin airlift, June 1948– May 1949.

chy with aid. But Britain had serious economic problems at home, and it was also supporting Turkey's resistance to Soviet demands for concessions. In the spring of 1947, Great Britain announced that it could no longer give aid to Greece and Turkey. It was at this point that the United States took over. In a message to Congress on March 12, 1947, President Truman called for American support to "free peoples who are resisting attempted subjugation by armed minorities or by outside pressures." Such support, the President added, was to be primarily economic. A comprehensive scheme for American aid to Europe was announced three months later by Secretary of State George C. Marshall. By fighting the economic and social conditions that gave rise to communism, the United States hoped to contain it.

The Cominform and the Molotov Plan

The Truman Doctrine and the Marshall Plan opened a wholly new phase in United States foreign policy. America had broken with its isolationist past and had assumed the leadership of the free world. The significance of this break was not lost on the Soviet Union. Secretary Marshall had included all European nations in his European Recovery Program, but any country in the Russian orbit that tried to participate was prevented from doing so by the Soviets. To tighten its control over eastern Europe, the Soviet Union had already concluded mutual assistance pacts with most of its satellites. In order to coordinate the efforts of European communism, the Russians, in 1947, founded the Communist Information Bureau (Cominform), as successor to the Comintern, which had been dissolved in 1943. In the economic field, finally, the Russians announced their own "Molotov Plan," as counterpart to the Marshall Plan.

The Communist Coup in Czechoslovakia

While East and West were consolidating their positions, the Russians scored another victory in the Cold War. Among the occupied nations of eastern Europe, Czechoslovakia alone had been able to maintain some of its democratic freedoms. But these were gradually undermined by the usual infiltration tactics of native Communists with Russian backing. By early 1948 the country was ripe for a *coup d'état*. In March, Foreign Minister Jan Masaryk, a friend of the West, was killed in a fall from his office window; and in June, President Beneš gave way to Communist leader Klement Gottwald. Except for Finland, all the countries of eastern Europe were now under Communist rule.

The North Atlantic Treaty

The Communist seizure of Czechoslovakia dramatized the need for military as well as economic integration of western resources. Great Britain and France had already concluded a treaty of alliance at Dunkirk in 1947. As an additional safeguard, in 1948 they asked the Benelux countries—Belgium, the Netherlands, and Luxembourg—to join them in the Brussels Treaty. But the nations of western Europe realized that effective resistance to Russia required the help of the United States. There were still isolationists in America who warned against a military alliance, but the majority of Americans agreed with their government that the only language Russia seemed to understand was the language of force. So on April 4, 1949, the United States joined the members of the Brussels Treaty, together with Italy, Portugal, Denmark, Iceland, Norway, and Canada, in the North Atlantic Treaty. These twelve powers were joined later by Greece and Turkey (1951) and by West Germany (1955). The gist of the treaty was contained in Article 5, which stated that "an armed attack against one or more" of its signatories "shall be considered an attack against them all." A North Atlantic Council was set up to direct the formation of the North Atlantic Treaty Organization (NATO).

The Coup d'État in Prague

Letter from President Beneš to the Presidium of the Communist Party:

. . . You know my sincerely democratic creed. I cannot but stay faithful to that creed even at this moment because democracy, according to my belief, is the only reliable and durable basis for a decent and dignified human life.

I insist on parliamentary democracy and parliamentary government as it limits democracy. I state I know very well it is necessary to social and economic content. I built my political work on these principles and cannot—without betraying myself—act otherwise. . . .

Reply by the Presidium of the Communist Party:

The Presidium of the Central Committee of the Communist Party acknowledged your letter dated February 24 and states again that it cannot enter into negotiations with the present leadership of the National Socialist, People's and Slovak Democratic Parties. . . .

Massive people's manifestations during the last few days clearly have shown our working people denounce, with complete unity and with indignation, the policy of these parties and ask the creation of a government in which all honest progressive patriots devoted to the republic and the people are represented. . . .

Being convinced that only such a highly constitutional and parliamentary process can guarantee the peaceful development of the republic and at the same time it corresponds to the ideas of a complete majority of the working people, the Presidium of the Central Committee hopes firmly after careful considerations that you will recognize the correctness of its conclusions and will agree with its proposals.

From H. L. Trefousse, *The Cold War—A Book of Documents* (New York: G. P. Putnam's Sons, 1965), pp. 109–12.

THE UNITED NATIONS IN THE COLD WAR

The growing tension between the East and West was also felt within the United Nations. As long as one of the major powers, through its veto in the Security Council, could prevent joint action, the effectiveness of the UN was limited. Only when international disputes did not involve the interests of a major power could the United Nations make its influence felt. It was thus possible to stop the fighting between Dutch and native forces in Indonesia and between India and Pakistan over Kashmir. In trying to keep Russia from meddling in the affairs of Iran, however, or in calling a halt to the civil war in Greece, United States aid was more important than UN pressure. The United Nations did score one major success before 1950: the founding of the state of Israel. But this was possible only because both the Soviet Union and the United States supported it.

The Founding of Israel

There had already been intermittent clashes between Arabs and Jews in Palestine before the Second World War (see p. 735). When the British after the war found it increasingly difficult to keep peace within their mandate, they decided to withdraw. At this point, in 1948, the UN stepped in, hoping to bring about a peaceful partition of Palestine. The Jews proclaimed the independent state of Israel, which was immediately recognized by the United States and the Soviet Union. But the Arabs, who opposed this solution, resisted. In the ensuing war the Israeli forces proved superior. UN efforts for an armistice finally succeeded in 1949. But peace remained precarious and full-scale war was resumed in 1956.

Other UN Activities

The United Nations had other tasks besides settling international disputes. In some of these economic, social, and cultural activities carried on by special agencies, the UN was highly successful. In December 1948 the General Assembly adopted an ambitious program of technical assistance for underdeveloped areas. The United States made available much of the necessary money and personnel under the Point Four program proclaimed by President Truman in January 1949.

Far more important than these economic and social problems, however, was the need for some regulation of international armaments. And here the United Nations made little headway. The main concern was over the control of atomic weapons. In 1946 America proposed the establishment of an International Atomic Development Authority to which the United States would transfer its atomic knowledge and facilities. The Authority was to be given the right of inspection to prevent the secret manufacture of atomic bombs. Since America still had a monopoly in the atomic field, this proposal was most generous and it was endorsed by an overwhelming majority of the General Assembly. But the Soviet Union vetoed the American proposal, objecting in particular to its provisions for inspection. In July 1949, after three years of fruitless debate, the Atomic Energy Commission adjourned. Two months later, Russia announced the first successful explosion of its own atomic bomb.

Celebrating the partition of Palestine and waving the flag of their new nation, happy Israelis crowd onto an armored British patrol car in Jerusalem.

THE COLD WAR
IN THE FAR EAST

The most momentous changes after 1945 occurred outside Europe. The emancipation of former colonial regions from foreign rule transformed the hitherto passive masses of Asia and Africa into active participants in international affairs. The most important change of the postwar period was the emergence of Red China as a major force in the world's balance of power.

Postwar Japan

Because of its leading role in the occupation of Japan, the United States after the Second World War was more deeply involved in Far Eastern affairs than at any other time in its history. Since there was no rivalry among occupying powers, and since Japan's governmental machinery

was left intact, the transition from war to peace went more smoothly in Japan than in Germany. A democratic constitution, in May 1947, transferred sovereignty from the emperor to the people. The Japanese army and navy had already been dissolved, patriotic organizations were banned, and education was reformed along democratic lines. In the economic sphere, the changes were less drastic. Plans to break up the large industrial and financial combinations of the *zaibatsu*, the great family trusts of Japan, were abandoned when such dismantling was found to interfere with Japan's recovery. Most of the large holdings of absentee landlords, on the other hand, were divided among tenant farmers. Despite these and other reforms, economic revival was slow. Only the war in Korea provided the stimulus for Japan's economic recovery during the 1950s.

THE FAR EAST SINCE THE SECOND WORLD WAR

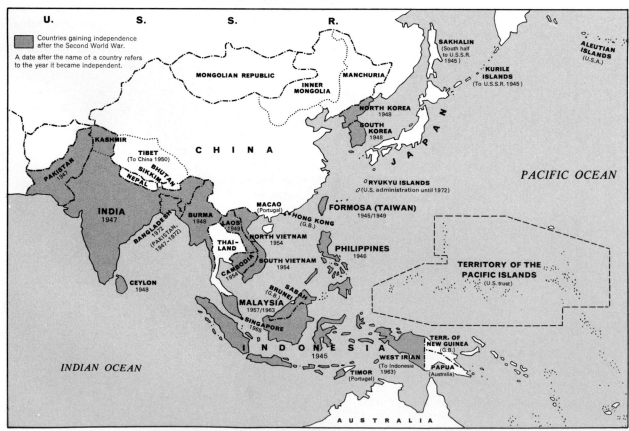

By 1951 the occupation of Japan had accomplished most of its aims and the time had come for a peace settlement. The rift between the United States and Russia, however, made a peace conference impracticable. America therefore assumed the chief responsibility for drafting the treaty. Peace with Japan was signed at San Francisco on September 8, 1951. The treaty was generous, restoring full Japanese sovereignty but permitting the United States to maintain military bases in Japan. America and Japan also concluded a defense agreement that ultimately became an alliance.

Communist Victory in China

While events in Japan were going largely according to American wishes, developments on the Chinese mainland were taking a different turn. The end of the war found most of China still divided between the government forces of Chiang Kai-shek and the Communist armies of Mao Tse-tung. Chiang had the backing of Chinese business and banking interests, while Mao's program of land reform brought him the support of the landless masses. Both sides now began a fight for the regions held until recently by Japan. In this contest the Communists proved more successful. By the end of 1948 most of northern China was in Communist hands.

The United States had given large amounts of financial and military aid to Chiang Kai-shek. But as the Nationalist government failed to introduce much-needed reforms, United States aid was curtailed and finally cut off. In the spring of 1949, Chiang Kai-shek began to withdraw his forces to the island of Formosa. By early 1950 the whole Chinese mainland was in Communist hands. On October 1, 1949, the People's Republic of China was officially proclaimed at Peking, with Mao Tse-tung as president. The Soviet Union immediately recog- nized the new regime whereas the United States continued to recognize the Nationalist government of Chiang Kai-shek.

The East-West Conflict over Korea

The victory of communism in China radically changed the balance of power between East and West. The effects of this change were felt almost immediately, as events in Korea transformed the Cold War in that country into an armed conflict. The Korean peninsula, at the end of the Second World War, had been divided into American and Russian zones of occupation. Just as in Germany, this temporary partition gradually brought about two quite different regimes. In 1948, elections in the United States–occupied southern part of Korea resulted in the founding of the Republic of Korea, with Dr. Syngman Rhee as president. The Russians thereupon sponsored their own Communist-dominated northern People's Democratic Republic, under the presidency of veteran Communist Kim Il Sung.

Late in 1948 the Soviet Union and the United States began to withdraw their troops from North and South Korea. A UN commission remained behind, trying to prevent a possible conflict between the two parts of Korea. Its efforts, however, proved in vain. On June 24, 1950, North Korean forces crossed the thirty-eighth parallel to "liberate" South Korea. Since Russia at the time was boycotting the Security Council, the United Nations was able to act without being hindered by a Soviet veto. When North Korea refused to halt its aggression, the Security Council asked the members of the UN to go to the aid of South Korea. The United States had already decided to intervene and was soon joined by small contingents from other countries. For the first time, the United Nations had gone to war. The Cold War had turned hot.

Suggestions for Further Reading

Note: Asterisk denotes a book available in paperback edition.

General

The most vivid and monumental account of the Second World War is W. S. Churchill, *The Second World War,** 6 vols. (1948–53). An admirably comprehensive treatment is G. Wright, *The Ordeal of Total War, 1939–1945** (1968). C. Wilmot, *The Struggle for Europe** (1952), is brilliant but controversial. Among general military accounts, the following stand out: J. F. C. Fuller, *The Second World War, 1939–45* (1949); P. Young, *World War, 1939–1945* (1966); and B. H. Liddell Hart, *History of the Second World War* (1970). D. Flower and J. Reeves, eds., *The Taste of Courage: The War, 1939–1945* (1966), successfully recaptures the atmosphere of the war at the fronts and at home.

The War: Military and Naval

The most detailed coverage of the major engagements may be found in the multivolume series dealing with America's armed forces in the Second World War: Office of the Chief of Military History, *United States Army in World War II*, 70 vols. (1947–69); S. E. Morison, *History of United States Naval Operations in World War II*, 14 vols. (1947–60); and W. F. Craven and J. L. Cate, *The Army Air Forces in World War II*, 7 vols. (1948–53). Phases of the war not covered in the above are treated in: M. Bloch, *Strange Defeat* (1949), on the fall of France; A. Johnson, *Norway: Her Invasion and Occupation* (1948); M. Cervi, *The Hollow Legions: Mussolini's Blunder in Greece* (1971); A. Clark, *Barbarossa: The Russian-German Conflict, 1941–1945** (1965); and K. Wierzynski, *The Forgotten Battlefield: The Story of Finland* (1944). On the maritime war, J. Creswell, *Sea Warfare, 1939–1945*, rev. ed. (1967); and S. W. Roskill, *The War at Sea, 1939–1945*, 3 vols. (1954–61), are excellent. For some of the war's more dramatic stories, see: R. Grenfell, *The Bismarck Episode* (1949); D. Young, *Rommel: The Desert Fox** (1950); C. V. Woodward, *The Battle for Leyte Gulf** (1947); W. Ansel, *Hitler Confronts England* (1960); C. Ryan, *The Longest Day** (1959), on the Allied invasion of Normandy; and J. Hersey, *Hiroshima** (1946). Most of the war's leading military figures have written their memoirs. Of special interest are D. D. Eisenhower, *Crusade in Europe** (1948); Viscount Montgomery, *Memoirs* (1958); C. de Gaulle, *War Memoirs,** 3 vols. (1960); M. Weygand, *Recalled to Service* (1952); J. Stilwell, *The Stilwell Papers* (1948); and J. Wainwright, *General Wainwright's Story* (1946). For the German side, see H. R. Trevor-Roper, ed., *Blitzkrieg to Defeat: Hitler's War Directives, 1939–1945* (1964); B. H. Liddell Hart, *The German Generals Talk** (1948); H. Guderian, *Panzer Leader* (1952); and E. von Manstein, *Lost Victories* (1958).

The War: Political and Economic

J. L. Snell, *Illusion and Necessity: The Diplomacy of Global War** (1963), is a concise and readable introduction. The gradual involvement of the United States in the war is treated in W. L. Langer and S. E. Gleason, *The Undeclared War, 1940–1941** (1953), and more briefly in R. A. Divine, *The Reluctant Belligerent: American Entry into World War II** (1965). The best account of the diplomatic background of the war with Japan is H. Feis, *The Road to Pearl Harbor** (1950). For highly critical views of Roosevelt's foreign policy, see C. C. Tansill, *Back Door to War* (1952); G. Kolko, *The Politics of War: The World and United States Foreign Policy, 1943–1945* (1968); and B. M. Russett, *No Clear and Present Danger: A Skeptical View of the United States Entry into World War II* (1972). Other aspects of American foreign policy are discussed in H. Feis, *The China Tangle** (1953), and in W. L. Langer, *Our Vichy Gamble** (1947).

R. E. Sherwood, *Roosevelt and Hopkins** (1948), E. L. Stimson, *On Active Service in Peace and War* (1948), R. Murphy, *Diplomat among Warriors** (1964), and W. D. Leahy, *I Was There* (1950), give valuable insights into American policy-making.

The controversial story of the Vichy regime is brilliantly told in R. Paxton, *Vichy France: Old Guard and New Order, 1940–1944* (1973). E. L. Woodward, *British Foreign Policy in the Second World War* (1962), is the standard work on that subject. The relations among the Allies are reviewed in H. Feis, *Churchill, Roosevelt, Stalin** (1957), and in M. Viorst, *Hostile Allies: FDR and Charles de Gaulle* (1965). See also A. W. De Porte, *De Gaulle's Foreign Policy, 1944–1946* (1968). On Russia's foreign policy, see L. Fischer, *The Road to Yalta: Soviet Foreign Relations, 1941–1945* (1972). The Soviet Union's harsh wartime experiences are related in A. Werth, *Russia at War** (1964).

Explanations of Hitler's fateful decision to invade Russia are provided in A. Rossi, *The Russo-German Alliance* (1951), and in G. L. Weinberg, *Germany and the Soviet Union, 1939–1941*

(1954). Hitler's attitude toward the United States is analyzed in A. Frye, *Nazi Germany and the American Hemisphere, 1933–1941* (1967); S. Friedländer, *Prelude to Downfall: Hitler and the United States, 1939–1941* (1967); and J. V. Compton, *The Swastika and the Eagle* (1967). Relations within the Axis are the subject of an excellent study by F. W. Deakin, *The Brutal Friendship: Mussolini, Hitler, and the Fall of Italian Fascism,** 2 vols. (1966). J. M. Meskill, *Hitler and Japan: The Hollow Alliance* (1966), tells a story of failure. See also M. D. Fenyo, *Hitler, Horthy, and Hungary: German-Hungarian Relations, 1941–1944* (1972). Spain's role in the war is the subject of H. Feis, *The Spanish Story: Franco and the Nations at War** (1948), and of C. B. Burdick, *Germany's Military Strategy and Spain in World War II* (1968). On Japan's wartime policy, see F. C. Jones, *Japan's New Order in East Asia: Its Rise and Fall, 1937–1945* (1954).

On the economic aspects of the war, see D. M. Nelson, *Arsenal for Democracy* (1946), and D. L. Gordon and R. Dangerfield, *The Hidden Weapon: The Story of Economic Warfare* (1947). Germany's economic war effort is treated in A. S. Milward, *The German Economy at War* (1965), and in B. A. Carroll, *Design for Total War: Arms and Economics in the Third Reich* (1968).

Hitler's "New Order"

The best general account of Europe under Hitler's rule is still A. Toynbee, ed., *Hitler's Europe* (1954). A. S. Milward, *The New Order and the French Economy* (1971), is an able monograph. A. Dallin, *German Rule in Russia, 1941–1945* (1957), is excellent. The large-scale popular migrations during the war are treated in E. M. Kulischer, *Europe on the Move: War and Population Changes, 1917–1947* (1948). On German use of slave labor, see E. M. Homze, *Foreign Labor in Nazi Germany* (1967). The more horrible aspects of Hitler's tyranny are told in L. Poliakov, *Harvest of Hate* (1954), and G. Reitlinger, *The Final Solution** (1953), which deal with the extermination of the European Jews. On the concentration camps, see R. Hoess, *Commandant of Auschwitz** (1959); B. Naumann, *Auschwitz* (1966); and Lord Russell of Liverpool, *The Scourge of the Swastika: A Short History of Nazi War Crimes** (1954).

The Search for Peace

The plans made during the war for a postwar settlement are discussed in R. Opie *et al.*, *The Search for Peace Settlements* (1951), and more briefly in W. L. Neumann, *Making the Peace, 1941–1945* (1950). Separate phases of the problem are treated in T. A. Wilson, *The First Summit: Roosevelt and Churchill at Placentia Bay, 1941* (1970), which deals with the "Atlantic Charter"; J. L. Snell, *Wartime Origins of the East-West Dilemma over Germany* (1956); and E. F. Penrose, *Economic Planning for the Peace* (1953). See also L. W. Holborn, *War and Peace Aims of the United Nations*, 2 vols. (1948). The conferences at Yalta and Potsdam are described by some of the leading participants: E. R. Stettinius, *Roosevelt and the Russians* (1949); H. S. Truman, *Memoirs, Vol. I, Year of Decisions** (1955); J. F. Byrnes, *Speaking Frankly* (1947); and W. S. Churchill, *Triumph and Tragedy** (1953). The best studies of the two conferences are D. S. Clemens, *Yalta* (1970), and H. Feis, *Between War and Peace: The Potsdam Conference** (1960). On the peace with Japan, see F. S. Dunn, *Peace-Making and the Settlement with Japan* (1963).

The Cold War

The best general account of the early postwar years is H. Feis, *From Trust to Terror: The Onset of the Cold War, 1945–1950* (1970). See also M. F. Herz, *Beginnings of the Cold War* (1966), and J. L. Gaddis, *The United States and the Origins of the Cold War, 1941–1947* (1972). On events in Germany, see A. Grosser, *The Colossus Again: Western Germany from Defeat to Rearmament* (1955); H. Zink, *The United States in Germany, 1944–1955* (1957); L. D. Clay, *Decision in Germany* (1950); and J. P. Nettl, *The Eastern Zone and Soviet Policy in Germany, 1945–1950* (1951). Austria is treated in W. B. Bader, *Austria Between East and West, 1945–1955* (1966). H. Seton-Watson, *The East European Revolution* (1951), treats the victory of communism in that area. The Communist seizure of individual countries is told in S. Mikolajczyk, *The Rape of Poland* (1950); H. Ripka, *Czechoslovakia Enslaved* (1950); and for Hungary in F. Nagy, *The Struggle Behind the Iron Curtain* (1948). Developments in the Far East are analyzed by H. Feis, *The China Tangle** (1953); A. S. Whiting, *China Crosses the Yalu: The Decision to Enter the Korean War* (1960); and H. Feis, *Contest over Japan* (1967). S. E. Ambrose, *The Rise to Globalism: American Foreign Policy since 1938** (1971), is a first-rate survey. For the early years of the United Nations, see C. M. Eichelberger, *UN: The First Ten Years* (1955), and T. Lie, *In the Cause of Peace: Seven Years with the United Nations* (1954). J. Kimche and D. Kimche, *A Clash of Destinies: The Arab-Jewish War and the Founding of the State of Israel* (1960), and E. Berger, *The Covenant and the Sword: Arab-Israeli Relations, 1946–1956* (1965), deal with postwar events in the Middle East.

34 From Cold War to Coexistence

In the past a war like the one in Korea might easily have sparked a third world war. That the conflict remained localized was in large measure due to the deterrent effect of the atomic bomb. With both the United States and Russia accumulating large stockpiles of nuclear weapons, the fear that some incident or accident might upset the precarious "balance of terror" between the East and West became a dominant factor in world affairs. Gradually the perennial crises of the Cold War gave way to a state of watchful coexistence between the Communist and non-Communist worlds.

The years since 1950 have seen other significant changes. In its early phases, the Cold War was primarily a conflict between two superpowers, the United States and the Soviet Union. Europe, which in the past had occupied the center of the stage, seemed to have been relegated to a mere supporting role. More recently, however, the Continent has staged a remarkable comeback. At the same time, the rise of the former colonial and underdeveloped regions, especially China, to independence and influence has injected a wholly new element into the international balance of power. Most present-day international problems are worldwide in their repercussions, involving more than the two superpowers of the Cold War era.

Other, nonpolitical issues today, while not new, have suddenly become far more urgent than they were in the past. Foremost among them is the "population explosion." Demographers estimate that by the end of this century 7 billion people will be alive, almost twice

as many as in 1975. Scientists claim that the development of existing resources, especially atomic energy, could provide ample livelihood for these vast masses. But even in an age of coexistence, much wealth and energy continue to be diverted to nonproductive military uses. It seems that the alternatives faced by mankind today are either to risk, through a nuclear arms race, the possible extermination of all life on earth, or to ensure, through peaceful effort, a good life for all.

THE DECLINE AND RISE OF WESTERN EUROPE

The decline of Europe's role in world affairs had already set in during the First World War, when only the intervention of the United States had enabled the Allies to win. For a brief span between the two wars, a semblance of the old European system of great powers was resurrected. But the Second World War brought the preeminence of Europe definitely to an end.

The postwar problems facing the nations of Europe were alike in many ways. All the major powers of western Europe suffered territorial losses, either in Europe or overseas, and several of them were threatened by communism from without or within. The one concern shared by all countries, big and small alike, was to recover from the economic effects of the war. In trying to cope with these problems, the nations of free Europe were forced to modify somewhat their economic and political nationalism

and to attempt some measure of economic, if not political, union. European recovery was retarded by the fact that the Continent continued to be divided into Communist and non-Communist spheres. But in time the gulf that the Cold War had created between the two halves of Europe grew narrower. As both eastern and western Europe recovered from the war and as relations between the two improved, the reunion of the European continent again appeared possible.

Great Britain: From World Empire to European Power

Great Britain after the Second World War had to cope with two related problems: the need for economic recovery and the loss of most of its empire. In 1945 the British electorate for the first time returned a Labor majority. Under the leadership of Clement Attlee, the government embarked on a program that was denounced as socialist by the Conservatives under Winston Churchill. Most of the enterprises that were nationalized, however—railroads, airlines, utilities, coal mines, and the Bank of England—remained so even after the Conservatives returned to power in 1951. The most far-reaching measures introduced by the Labor government were the various Social Welfare Acts that aimed at equality of opportunity for all citizens.

The tendency of these measures to make British society more egalitarian was enhanced by the drastic program of austerity by which the government hoped to balance the budget and regain Britain's former position in world trade. Under Conservative rule from 1951 to 1964, the country experienced a temporary economic recovery. In 1964, however, dissatisfaction with a weak foreign policy and renewed economic stagnation once more brought a Labor victory. The second Labor cabinet was no more successful in overcoming Britain's economic paralysis than the first had been. When foreign loans, heavy taxation, and reduced government spending failed to

The Brandenburg Gate, once the heart of Berlin, now marks the border between East and West.

improve matters, the government of Prime Minister Harold Wilson in 1967 finally devalued the pound, in the hope of thus solving Britain's perennial trade deficit. But this and other drastic measures failed to improve the country's economic malaise. In 1970 the electorate once again turned against Labor and returned the Conservatives under Edward Heath to power.

One of the causes of Britain's continued depression was the rapid shrinking of its empire after the war. Wherever colonial peoples became restive and demanded independence, British interests were almost always involved. Most of the resulting new states remained within the "Commonwealth of Nations" (as the former "British Commonwealth" was now called). But the ties of this elusive organization grew weaker over the years, partly because of the racial policies pursued by countries like South Africa and Rhodesia. Britain in the past had committed sizable forces to help keep peace in outlying spheres of British interest. Because of economic pressures back home, most of Britain's foreign bases had to be abandoned. Within less than a generation, the once mighty British Empire virtually melted away.

One possible way of improving its position was for Britain to draw closer to the continental nations that had joined forces in the European Economic Community, or Common Market. But the island kingdom was reluctant to do so, for fear that such economic *rapprochement* might conflict with its Commonwealth obligations. It was not until 1963 that Britain applied for membership in the Common Market. At that time it was barred by the veto of France's President de Gaulle, who asserted that the British were not ready to assume the full obligations of membership. Ten years later Britain finally joined the European Economic Community and began to share in that organization's economic prosperity.

France: Search for Lost Grandeur

In France political instability at home and continued colonial wars abroad retarded postwar economic recovery. To make a clear break with the past, the French in 1946 gave themselves a new constitution. But the Fourth Republic was little different from the Third. As old enmities persisted and new ones arose, the traditional bickering among numerous small parties and interest groups again dominated the political scene. The chief beneficiaries of this confusion were the French communists, who until 1958 made up the leading party in the National Assembly. Only in foreign policy did the new republic show some consistency, chiefly as a result of the efforts of

A ''family portrait'' of the leaders of the Commonwealth of Nations who met in Canada for a conference in 1973. Queen Elizabeth is seated in the center and Prince Phillip is seated third from right. Between them is Prime Minister Trudeau of Canada. The other nations represented are (front row) Nigeria, Singapore, Sri Lanka, Tanzania, Barbados, Malta; (second row) Cyprus, Bangladesh, India, Mauritius, Western Samoa, Guyana, Zambia, Ghana, the Bahamas; (third row) Sierra Leone, Lesotho, New Zealand, Britain, Australia, Kenya, Jamaica, Swaziland, Fiji, Uganda, Tonga, Malaysia, Botswana, Gambia, Trinidad and Tobago, Malawi.

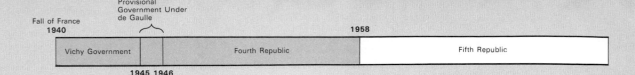

Fall of France
1940

Provisional
Government Under
de Gaulle

1958

| Vichy Government | | Fourth Republic | Fifth Republic |

1945 1946

foreign ministers Georges Bidault and Robert Schuman.

France, like Great Britain, found it difficult at first to regain its economic health. French financial problems were staggering, and their solution required heavy taxation and a stable currency. But reluctant taxpayers, creeping inflation, and incessant strikes counteracted the beneficent effects of American Marshall Plan aid. In 1954 an end came to the war in Indochina, which had caused a steady financial drain back home despite American aid; but at the same time fighting in Algeria gained momentum. It was not until President Charles de Gaulle began to dominate the national scene in the late 1950s that a broad austerity program, combined with careful economic planning, put France back on the road to prosperity.

France, again like Britain, also faced the rapid dissolution of its colonial empire. In 1946 the Fourth Republic tried to maintain some control over its overseas holdings by founding the French Union. This federation, however, was far too centralized to satisfy the more developed territories, and a number of them—Syria, Lebanon, Morocco, and Tunisia—demanded, and were given, their independence. Indochina and Algeria won independence only after drawn-out and costly fighting. In 1958 the French Union was transformed into the French Community, which included France proper, its few remaining overseas possessions, and most of the new African nations that formerly made up French Equatorial and West Africa. The Community was a loose federation whose main significance lay in whatever prestige it held for the former mother country of a once great empire.

Prestige was the main concern of the man who assumed direction of French affairs in 1958. Charles de Gaulle, leader of the Free French forces in the Second World War, had served briefly as provisional president in 1945 but had retired before the domestic confusion that reigned at that time. He was recalled in 1958 at the height of the national crisis caused by the war in Algeria. Under de Gaulle's direction a new constitution was adopted that, in an attempt to ensure greater political stability, vastly increased the power of the president. In December 1958 General de Gaulle was elected first president of the Fifth Republic.

From 1958 until his forced retirement in 1969, the general's towering figure dominated the French scene. De Gaulle's most important achievement was the solution of the Algerian problem. In 1962 an agreement between French and Arab representatives, endorsed by the French electorate, gave Algeria its independence. Elsewhere, in Europe and overseas, de Gaulle's main ambition was to recapture some of France's past "grandeur." To strengthen his country's position in Europe, de Gaulle maintained close ties with West Germany and cemented relations with the communist powers, notably the Soviet Union. To counteract Anglo-Saxon influence, he took France out of NATO, preferring instead to rely on an independent French nuclear striking force, and he barred Britain from membership in the Common Market. Along similar lines, de Gaulle drew closer to Communist China, criticized American involvement in Vietnam, and even encouraged separatist sentiment among French Canadians. Supporters of the French President defended his obstructionist policies as a reassertion not merely of French influence but of European influence as well against the growing encroachment of the United States. His critics, on the other hand, charged that when the general said Europe, he meant France; and when he said France, he meant de Gaulle.

In France itself, moreover, de Gaulle's preoccupation with foreign concerns at the expense of domestic ones gave rise to a wave of discontent, especially among workers and students, that almost led to

Charles de Gaulle, then Prime Minister of France, campaigning in overseas France on behalf of his constitutional proposals in 1958. In December of that year he was elected president.

revolution in 1968. When some of his reform proposals were defeated in a national referendum the following year, de Gaulle resigned and was succeeded by one of his close associates, Georges Pompidou. The new President's major concern was to overcome France's antiquated production methods and to ease its rapid transition into a highly industrialized society. In foreign affairs, Pompidou's readiness to welcome Great Britain into the Common Market was a marked departure from his predecessor's policy.

West Germany: "The Second Republic"

The most spectacular rise from rubble to riches in postwar Europe occurred in West Germany. The partition of the former Reich in 1949 as a result of the Cold War has already been discussed (see p. 788). During the 1950s the western Federal Republic experienced a veritable "economic miracle." In contrast to the nationalization measures adopted by Great Britain and, to a lesser extent, France, Germany followed a more traditional policy of laissez faire. With a favorable balance of trade, a freely convertible currency, and hardly any unemployment, Germany's "free-market economy" aroused the admiration and envy of its neighbors.

Politically, developments in West Germany were remarkably steady, especially compared to the turbulent years after the First World War. The constitution of the Federal Republic was framed to avoid some of the mistakes of the Weimar Republic. The country was fortunate in having as its first chancellor Konrad Adenauer, a conservative opponent of nazism and a sincere friend of the West. The "old man" virtually dominated German politics from 1949 until his retirement in 1963 at age 87. His successor, Ludwig Erhard, was a man of lesser stature. In 1966 the middle-of-the-road Christian Democratic Union (CDU), which hitherto had dominated the government, had to share power with the moderately leftist Social Democratic party (SPD), with Kurt Georg Kiesinger of the CDU as chancellor and Willy

Konrad Adenauer (1876–1967), in 1959.

Brandt of the SPD as foreign minister. The shift toward the Social Democrats continued in 1969, when Willy Brandt became chancellor in a coalition of the SPD with the small liberal Free Democratic party (FDP).

Next to economic development, the two most vital issues before the West German government were reunification and rearmament. To reunite not only East and West Germany but also the region beyond the Oder-Neisse line (occupied by Poland in 1945) was the fervent wish of every German. Repeated proposals of the western powers to achieve German unity through free general elections invariably met with Soviet opposition. Meanwhile the West German Federal Republic refused to recognize the East German Democratic Republic. As time went on, however, and as each section of Germany developed along widely divergent lines, a growing number of Germans became reconciled with the thought that they might not live to see their country reunited. As long as Adenauer was in control, however, any open acquiescence in the partition of Germany was out of the question.

This situation changed with the advent of Willy Brandt. As foreign minister, Brandt had stated his intention of bringing about a *détente* with the communist world, while at the same time maintaining close relations with the West. Once he was chancellor, he proceeded to carry out his design. As first steps he signed treaties with the Soviet Union and Poland in 1970 that called for mutual renunciation of the use of force and establishment of normal relations. The agreement with Poland also included West Germany's recognition of the Oder-Neisse line as the permanent German-Polish frontier. Of equal, if not greater, significance was a treaty in 1972 between East and West Germany that recognized the existence of two sovereign German states and provided for closer collaboration between them. To round out his policy of *rapprochement* with the communist world, the Brandt government also resumed economic relations with a number of East European states and established diplomatic ties with Communist China. Despite much criti-

France and Germany united in the opening of a new waterway on the Moselle River in 1962. Among the dignitaries on board were General de Gaulle, Heinrich Lübke, president of the Federal German Republic, and the Grand Duchess Charlotte of Luxembourg.

to a treaty of friendship in 1963. Collaboration with the Anglo-Saxon powers was close, and Brandt's *Ostpolitik* gave further proof of West Germany's peaceful intentions. In its domestic policy, furthermore, West Germany showed that it had made a clean break with the Nazi past. There were a few incidents of neonazism, and in the late sixties a right-wing group, the National Democratic party, gained some ground in local elections. But the majority of Germans clearly endorsed the moderate and peaceful course of their government. Democracy had taken firm root in West Germany.

Italy: From Poverty to Riches

Italy emerged from the Second World War with its already backward economy in a dismal state. After a slow start, however, the nation staged a remarkable recovery. By 1965 Italy's industrial production had increased fourfold, and the nation's per capita income had doubled. With economic improvement came a period of political stability. The new Italian republic was launched successfully in 1946 under the capable leadership of Alcide de Gasperi and his Christian Democratic party. But with the onset of the Cold War, the government came under increasing attacks from a strong Communist party on the left and a growing neo-Fascist movement on the right. Only when the Christian Democrats, beginning in 1962, started to ally themselves with the moderate Socialists on their left did some measure of political calm return.

Even so, the fact that one out of every four Italians continued to vote Communist showed that all was far from well. While there was prosperity, poverty persisted, especially in the agricultural South. Even in the North real wages did not keep up with the general rise in the economy, and the distribution of income remained uneven. In the late 1960s, economic discontent led to numerous strikes, which, in turn, aggravated an already existing economic crisis. In addition, the center-left coalition broke apart, as Christian Democrats and Socialists differed over the controversial

cism from his political opponents, Brandt's *Ostpolitik* (eastern policy) had the support of the majority of West Germans, as was shown by his clear election victory in 1972.

Brandt's policy also helped to dispel whatever apprehension had arisen over German rearmament. The creation of a West German army caused considerable debate in the 1950s. As the Russians at the time began training a German military force in East Germany, the western powers decided to permit the limited rearmament of West Germany. Under an agreement ratified in 1955, West Germany was to contribute a maximum of 500,000 men to the common defense of the West under NATO. In return, the Federal Republic was granted complete sovereignty in domestic and foreign affairs.

There was some fear, both in Germany and outside, that rearmament would cause a revival of German militarism and nationalism. But such fears proved groundless. Relations with Germany's "traditional enemy" France were better than they had ever been, leading divorce law of 1970 and other issues. Meanwhile, the Communists remained the country's second-largest party and the neo-Fascist Italian Social movement doubled its forces in the elections of 1972. Italy, although more prosperous than ever, clearly had not as yet adjusted to its rapid transition from agriculture to industry.

The Quest for European Unity

Given the similarity of their problems, especially in the economic field, it was only natural that western European nations should try to devise means for common action. The Marshall Plan had shown that lasting recovery could be won only through economic cooperation; and the Brussels Pact, besides calling for a military alliance, had also stressed the need for collaboration in economic, social, and cultural affairs (see p. 790). The first major instance of such collaboration was the Schuman Plan, which established the European Coal and Steel Community (ECSC). In 1952 France, Germany, the Benelux countries, and Italy agreed to merge their resources of coal and steel in a common western European market. By 1957 enough progress had been achieved to make it possible to extend the common market to other goods through the European Economic Community (EEC). In a further attempt at integration, the six members of ECSC and EEC founded the European Atomic Energy Community (Euratom) to promote peaceful atomic research and development.

The European Economic Community was not a closed organization; any country could apply for membership. The admission of Great Britain was delayed until 1973, at which time Ireland and Denmark also joined. Representing more than 256 million people, the EEC constituted the most important and powerful trade area in the world.

Plans for European political union were less successful. Prospects looked bright in 1949 when the Council of Europe was founded at Strasbourg. But it remained a purely consultative body, and the hope for a United States of Europe did not materialize. As Europe recovered economically and as the threat of Soviet expansion subsided, national differences once again came to the fore. The expectation that NATO would in time become more than a purely military alliance likewise proved false. Yet despite these disappointments, the general trend toward European unity was unmistakable. The European powers realized that the only way they could wield any real influence was by joining forces and forgetting the divisive issues of the past.

THE AMERICAS

To the rest of the world the United States in 1945 appeared as a country of unbelievable wealth, untouched by the hardships of war. But to Americans themselves the picture looked quite different. Price controls, wage controls, real or artificially induced shortages of essential goods, incessant waves of strikes, and signs of widespread corruption—these were some of the problems faced by the American people. The

---

Toward a "European Consciousness"?

The adjective "European," which a century ago was understood only by a small minority, and which even in the early twentieth century was accepted perhaps only by the aristocracy, by the high bourgeoisie and by certain intellectuals, today has become an accepted adjective, a designation, a self-ascribed characteristic for the majority of the populations even in Central and Eastern Europe. To many a peasant in the Danube Valley the adjective "European" even twenty or thirty years ago meant either nothing at all or something that was vaguely and suspiciously alien. This is no longer so. Despite Communist political rule and regimentation, life for large masses of people in Warsaw and Belgrade and Budapest and Bucharest has now more in common with life in Berne and Brussels and Paris than it had fifty or one hundred years ago, and this is true of people in Lisbon, Madrid, Palermo, Athens. It is, let me repeat, by no means clear whether the increasing standardization of certain forms of life will, within Europe, lead to a further, and decisive, phase in the development of a European consciousness. That ten thousand Bulgarians watch television or that tens of thousands in Budapest experience their first traffic jam is unimportant. What is important, for our purposes, is to recognize that the collapse of the European state system did not mean the end of European history; that, indeed, we are facing two countervailing historical developments: decline—definite decline—of the European state system on the one hand; rise—vague rise—of a European consciousness on the other.

John Lukacs, *Decline and Rise of Europe* (Garden City, N.Y.: Doubleday, 1965), pp. 169–70.

Democratic administration's attempts to deal with the situation by means of further legislation found little public or congressional support. It seemed that the country was tired of government controls and of a social service state that to most Republicans smacked of socialism.

The Truman Era

President Truman was reelected in 1948 chiefly because of his foreign policy: the Truman Doctrine, the Marshall Plan, the Berlin air lift, the North Atlantic Treaty, and the intervention in Korea. At the time, these measures were applauded by a majority of Americans. Isolationism, of course, did not vanish overnight. But the fact that a Republican administration after 1952 continued substantially the same foreign policy showed that the shift from isolationism was a matter not so much of choice as of necessity.

One aspect of American involvement abroad that was not universally popular was the foreign-aid program. During the first fifteen years after the war, United States economic and military aid amounted to more than $75 billion. Much of it was given in a spirit of genuine helpfulness. But foreign aid was also an important weapon in the Cold War, especially after 1955, when the Soviet Union began stepping up its own foreign-aid program.

In American domestic affairs, one of the major issues at the time was the fear of Communist infiltration. This fear arose shortly after the war, gained momentum as the Communists scored more and more triumphs in Europe and Asia, and reached its climax during the Korean War. Chiefly because of the agitation of Wisconsin's Senator Joseph McCarthy, the American public was led to believe that its government had allowed communists to get into key positions in the State Department and the Army. These largely unfounded accusations created a climate of fear and suspicion and did much to harm the reputations of innocent people.

The reality of the Communist threat abroad, meanwhile, was brought home by events in Korea. As the war there bogged down in a bloody stalemate, critics of the administration demanded an escalation of the war, including the bombing of Communist bases in China. Foremost among these critics was America's commander-in-chief in Korea, General Douglas MacArthur. When efforts to silence him failed, President Truman, in April 1951, relieved the general of his command. The ensuing crisis was the most serious the United States had faced since 1945. Together with a mounting wave of government scandals and continued suspicion of Communist influence in the government, the Korean War was

A unique photograph of the four men who occupied the American presidency between 1945 and 1968—Kennedy, Johnson, Eisenhower, and Truman. The occasion was the funeral of House Speaker Sam Rayburn in 1961.

a major cause of the defeat of the Democrats in the election of 1952.

The Eisenhower Years

The victories of the Republican candidate Dwight D. Eisenhower in 1952 and 1956 were as much personal as partisan. He enhanced his popularity by concluding a Korean armistice in 1953. During his two administrations, bipartisan majorities in Congress collaborated to produce much valuable social legislation. The nation's economy continued to flourish, except in the agricultural sector, where overproduction posed a serious problem. The administration's attempts to reduce price supports and to return to a free market in agricultural products incurred the opposition of farm groups; this opposition was one of the reasons for the overwhelming congressional victory of the Democrats in 1958. Other reasons were the temporary economic recession of that year and the antagonism that the Republican administration had aroused among organized labor.

A major issue that came to the fore during the Eisenhower years was desegregation. In *Brown v. Board of Education of Topeka* (1954), the United States Supreme Court ruled that American blacks had the right to attend the same schools as whites. Desegregation proceeded smoothly in most states, but in the Deep South every possible means was used to prevent it. In 1957–58 President Eisenhower had to send federal troops to enforce desegregation in Little Rock, Arkansas. This was only the beginning of a drawn-out crisis, as blacks began to demand that desegregation be extended to other fields. The resistance of die-hard "white supremacists" to these demands did much to tarnish America's image abroad.

From Kennedy to Johnson

The victory of John F. Kennedy in 1960 injected a fresh and youthful note into American politics. His administration got off to a promising start when Congress approved a series of social service measures chiefly designed to aid the poor. When the President began to tackle the touchy subject of civil rights, however, he lost the support of southern Democrats and his domestic program came to a halt. Some improvement in the status of blacks was made under pressure of nonviolent protests directed by able black leaders. But as police in the South met peaceful demonstrations with violence, the situation became increasingly explosive. Much of President Kennedy's attention was taken up with crises in foreign affairs. In his efforts to stand up to Communist threats in Southeast Asia, Cuba, and Berlin, the President generally found the support that Congress withheld from his domestic program.

President Kennedy was assassinated in Dallas, Texas, on November 22, 1963. A major political crisis was avoided chiefly because of the firm manner in which his successor, Lyndon B. Johnson, took charge. Where Kennedy had labored in vain against congressional opposition, Johnson, a former majority leader in the Senate, was able to achieve some notable successes. By 1964 the new President had gained sufficient popular support to win a landslide victory.

From then on, however, President Johnson found the going more and more difficult. Civil rights had become the key issue in American politics. The Civil Rights Act of 1964 was the most sweeping legislation of its kind ever enacted. But its provisions were still disregarded in many parts of the South. Meanwhile black protests spread to the North, where the demand was for greater equality in employment, housing, and education. Demonstrations that hitherto had been orderly now became increasingly violent as bloody riots swept through major American cities and as advocates of "black power" preached the use of force. To cope with the economic roots of black discontent, the Johnson administration stepped up the antipoverty programs initiated under Kennedy. But while the "war on poverty" called for vast amounts of money, more and more funds were being diverted to another kind of war.

The war in Vietnam, in which the United States had become increasingly involved since 1961, proved the most divisive issue in American politics during

John F. Kennedy (1917–63) brought a vigorous approach to the presidency.

the last two years of the Johnson admin-istration. As "hawks" (advocating victory through war) ranged against "doves" (favoring American withdrawal), many young Americans chose to go to prison or abroad rather than to fight an "unjust" war. The cause of moderation suffered a major loss with the assassination, in June 1968, of Senator Robert F. Kennedy, a leading Democratic contender for the presidency. Racial unrest, meanwhile, had flared up anew after the murder that April of the Reverend Dr. Martin Luther King, Jr., an outstanding figure in the nonviolent civil rights movement. It was a deeply disturbed and divided nation that gave the Republican candidate, Richard M. Nixon, a narrow victory in November 1968.

The Nixon Administrations

The war in Vietnam continued to be the major cause of tension in American politics; more and more people de-manded an end to American involve-ment. The withdrawal of American

American vs. Vietcong: a struggle that lasted almost a decade.

forces beginning in 1972 and the subse-quent start of armistice negotiations were largely responsible for President Nixon's reelection the same year by an over-whelming majority. An uneasy armistice was finally concluded in early 1973. Meanwhile the President had embarked on new ventures elsewhere by paying visits to the Soviet Union and Commu-nist China, thus easing tensions with the Russians and establishing first contacts with the mainland Chinese.

In his domestic affairs, President Nixon had a less fortunate hand. Most problems had already plagued previous administrations; but some of them worsened as time went on. One of these was crime. "Law and order," a key issue in the 1972 elections, was part of a larger question—the rapid decay of American cities into breeding-grounds of crime, often connected with drug addiction. Another growing concern was protection of the environment against pollution by individuals and industries. Unrest among blacks decreased somewhat, as some of their demands were being met. There remained, however, the controversial issue of "bussing" white or black stu-dents outside their school districts to achieve a better racial balance. Many of these problems called for official inter-vention. But such intervention was op-posed by an administration that tried to halt the increasing role of government in the life of the individual.

The country's rising inflation pre-sented the Nixon administration with another major difficulty. Beginning in August 1971, the President imposed wage and price controls, measures never before adopted in time of peace. To im-prove America's growing trade deficit, the dollar was officially devalued by a total of 17 percent in 1972 and 1973. And to curtail government spending at home, President Nixon refused to spend some funds appropriated by Congress for pur-poses he considered wasteful. This action did not endear him to the legislature, and confrontations between the White House and Capitol Hill were frequent. The Nixon administration was also accused of showing less concern than its prede-cessors for minority groups; certainly, its support among blacks was minimal.

A beleaguered President tries to regain the nation's confidence in 1973 in a televised address concerning the events of the Watergate Affair.

Former Vice President Agnew delivers his farewell address to the nation, October 1973.

Far more disquieting than any of these issues, however, was the "Watergate Affair," in which leading members of the President's staff were found to have been involved in illegal acts against the Democratic party during the 1972 campaign. As judicial and Senate hearings uncovered a sordid story of intrigue and attempted cover-up, the question arose whether President Nixon had any part in these events. The President denied any such involvement and appointed a special prosecutor to investigate the matter. At the same time, however, he refused to surrender some key evidence, including tapes of White House conversations. When the special prosecutor refused to support the President's stand, he was fired.

At this point, in October 1973, Congress began seriously to consider impeachment procedures against the President. The situation was complicated by the fact that Vice President Spiro Agnew had recently resigned his position, having been found guilty of income tax evasion. Less than a year after winning almost total victory, the Nixon administration appeared to be on the verge of total defeat.

The United States and Its Neighbors

Since the contest between communism and capitalism was a global one, the maintenance of harmony within the Western Hemisphere was of major concern to every administration after 1945. Relations with America's northern neighbor were, on the whole, cordial. Because of its tremendous economic growth, Canada ranked as one of the world's leading industrial and commercial powers. United States capital played an important part in this expansion, and the resulting American influence caused some resentment among Canadian nationalists. Military relations between the two countries were close, both within NATO and without. Continued membership in the (British) Commonwealth saved Canada from becoming too dependent on its powerful neighbor, although ties with Great Britain grew noticeably weaker.

Relations between the United States and its southern neighbors were far more complicated. The twenty republics of Latin America differed widely in size and significance, and the absence of a strong democratic tradition made many of them prone to authoritarian regimes of the right or left. The most pressing problem of the whole area was its alarming rise in population. Latin America had great economic potentialities, but financial and technical assistance were needed to develop them. The United States was expected to supply this aid. Prior to 1960 little such aid found its way to Latin America. Subsequently, a number of ambitious development schemes were launched, notably the Alliance for Progress, proclaimed by President Kennedy in 1961. But the results of such schemes were disappointing. Under the Nixon administration, a "low profile" policy of aid to Latin America, caused by economic difficulties back home, helped increase ill feelings. The American government, in turn, was annoyed by the large-scale nationalization of United States properties in Latin America and by continuous harassment of United States fishing fleets in the offshore waters of South America.

Besides looking to the United States for help, the nations of Latin America increasingly looked to one another. The Latin American Free Trade Association (LAFTA), set up in 1960, called for the creation of a common market for all of Latin America by 1980; but its progress has been slow. More successful in fostering economic cooperation were various subregional groups, especially the Central American Common Market. Latin America also turned to Europe and the Soviet Union to improve its economic plight.

The United States was concerned with building a united military front against the threat of communism in the Western Hemisphere. In 1947 the Latin American nations and the United States signed the Rio Treaty, which called for mutual assistance in case of war. Subsequent agreements arranged for the exchange of United States arms against strategic raw materials. The most important agency of inter-American cooperation was the Organization of American States (OAS), founded in 1948. It originally included all nations of the Western

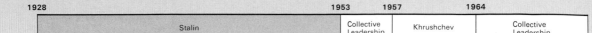

	1928	1953	1957	1964	
	Stalin	Collective Leadership	Khrushchev	Collective Leadership	

Hemisphere except Canada, but Cuba was excluded (though not formally expelled) in 1962. The Charter of the OAS proclaimed the equality of its members and laid down the principle of nonintervention in their external and internal affairs. The OAS proved of great value as a stabilizing influence, especially against Castro's Cuba and against recurrent instances of guerrilla uprisings, urban terrorism, and political kidnappings.

The overthrow of Cuban dictator Fulgencio Batista by Fidel Castro's rebel forces in 1959 at first was hailed in the United States and elsewhere as a victory of democracy. But when Castro's regime revealed itself as an outpost of communism the United States broke off relations with Cuba and then, in 1961, supported an ill-fated invasion attempt by anti-Castro forces. Meanwhile Castro had established close ties with Communist China and the Soviet Union. The latter's attempt, in 1962, to use Cuba as a base for ballistic missiles clearly directed against the United States led to a major showdown between the Soviet Union and the United States in which the Russians had to give way. As time went on, the threat of Castro to the security of the Western Hemisphere subsided and relations between Cuba and some of the leftist Latin American nations, notably Chile, were resumed.

THE COMMUNIST WORLD

For almost two decades after 1945, while the Cold War lasted, the Communist world appeared to be a monolithic bloc dominated by Moscow. It took the rest of the world some time to realize how much this Soviet predominance depended on one man. In retrospect, the death of Joseph Stalin on March 5, 1953, was a major event in world history. It spelled the end of an era, not only for Russian communism but for world communism as well.

Russia under Khrushchev

The main features of the Stalinist era, which reached its high point during the years after 1945, have already been discussed (see p. 749). To repair the staggering damages of the war, two Five-Year Plans called for a new round of industrialization and collectivization. Simultaneously, strictest orthodoxy remained the keynote of Soviet political and cultural life. The slightest deviation from Stalinist-Marxist theory brought imprisonment, slave labor, or death. In a famous speech before the twentieth Party Congress in 1956, Khrushchev charged that Stalin, "a very distrustful man, sickly suspicious," had planned even to liquidate his most intimate political associates.

Stalin's reign of terror came to a sudden end with his death. For the first four years or so, "collective leadership" was instituted. But it was only a matter of time before one of the most determined members of the group, Nikita S. Khrushchev, emerged as the recognized leader of the Soviet Union. As Stalin had done a generation earlier, Khrushchev used his key position as Secretary of the Central Committee of the Communist party to rid himself of his associates. The only novelty was that his rivals were not killed but merely ousted—an example of the "new look" in Soviet policy.

Khrushchev, a career party functionary, never really achieved the absolute power that Stalin had wielded before him. Russia under Stalin had undergone not only an economic but a social revolution. From a nation of illiterate peasants, the Soviet Union had become a nation of educated workers. Although the basic Marxist concept of state ownership of the means of production remained in force, the concept of a

Khrushchev delivers an angry diatribe during a UN debate in 1960.

classless society had been far from realized. Instead, a substantial upper class had grown up: the party elite, the top echelons of the vast political and economic bureaucracy, managerial personnel, technical experts, scientists, and the like. The Soviet Union, in other words, had become a far more complex society than it had been at the start. To run such a nation by regimentation based on terror was no longer possible. Nor was it even desirable, since blind obedience in the long run killed initiative and made for inefficiency.

The most dramatic change in the life of the average Russian came with the retreat from terror after Stalin's death. This did not mean that there were no longer any political prisoners. But it did mean that the number of punishable political crimes became smaller than it had been under Stalin. Henceforth it became possible to criticize certain aspects of the regime without risking execution.

The liberalization of Soviet life was felt in other ways. In factories and on collective farms the strict discipline of the past was relaxed. Consumer goods became more plentiful, and the housing shortage was reduced. Education was broadened to admit more students to secondary schools and universities. With the easing of travel restrictions, the Russian people for the first time came in contact with the outside world. In Russian art and literature, the orthodox emphasis on "socialist realism" gave way to tolerance of some modern trends. Initially, outside observers saw these changes as signs that Russia had abandoned its unbending opposition to the West. But Soviet leaders made no secret of the fact that the "new look" was merely a change in methods and that their aim remained what it had always been: the overthrow of capitalism.

Collective Leadership

The return to virtual one-man rule under Khrushchev was suddenly reversed in October 1964 when the Russian leader was purged by his party's Central Committee and his double role as premier and party secretary was divided between Alexei N. Kosygin and Leonid I. Brezhnev. The main reasons for Khrushchev's dismissal appeared to be domestic, notably his failure to live up to his boastful economic promises, although foreign reversals, such as the Cuban missile crisis, may have played their part. From 1964 on the trend was once again toward collective leadership.

Economic growth in the Soviet Union continued, though at a slower rate than predicted, especially in the agrarian sector. With increased material gain came signs of spiritual unrest. The younger generation in particular, the "grandchildren of the revolution," seemed less and less willing to accept the intellectual restrictions of a totalitarian regime. The reaction of the post-Khrushchev regime to manifestations of dissent was twofold. On the one hand, critical writers like Alexander Solzhenitsyn or Andrei Sinyavsky, advocates of civil liberties like Yosif Brodsky, and various national dissidents in the Ukraine and Lithuania were arrested and in some cases forced to emigrate. But at the same time the government also tried to counter discontent by economic concessions, raising the living standard of the average Soviet citizen. The general tendency, however, was in the direction of repression rather than reform, leading some foreign observers to speak of a return to Stalinism.

Unrest among the Satellites

The effects of the post-Stalin "thaw" were also felt among the satellite nations of eastern Europe. The first defection from the Soviet bloc had occurred as early as 1948, when Marshal Tito of Yugoslavia, preferring "Titoism" to "Stalinism," had struck out on his own. By 1956, Stalin's successors had made peace with Tito and had acknowledged that there were "various roads to socialism." But the satellites were not satisfied with mere promises of greater independence. In the fall of 1956, revolts against Soviet domination broke out first in Poland and later in Hungary. Both countries were motivated by ardent nationalist sentiments. In addition, the Hungarian uprising was strongly anti-Communist. For that reason the Hungarian revolution was brutally suppressed by Russian intervention, while Poland's Communists, under Wladyslaw Gomulka, were given greater autonomy from Russian control.

For the next ten or twelve years, there were no further attempts to resist Russian domination forcefully. The nations of eastern Europe were enjoying far greater freedom of action than they had ever had under Stalin. From mere satellites they were gradually becoming junior partners of the Soviet Union. In 1961 growing tension between Russia and Albania over the latter's continued adherence to Stalinism led to an open break. In 1964 Rumania declared its virtual independence from Soviet influence and, like Yugoslavia before, drew closer to the West. Intermittent unrest in Poland came to a head early in 1968 and brought some easing of restrictions. The most dramatic change, however, occurred in Czechoslovakia, where, as a result of a peaceful revolution in the spring of 1968, the country briefly regained many democratic freedoms. The Soviet Union's armed intervention in Czechoslovakia in August emphasized the threat that these liberalizing tendencies posed to Russia's leadership in the Communist world. It also underlined Russia's determination to meet that threat.

"Socialist Pluralism"

Despite Russia's efforts to maintain its leadership over world communism, the unity that once had prevailed among Communist states and parties had given way to diversity. A Communist world conference in 1968 was attended by only half the world's ruling Communist parties, and even among those present there were wide differences on many key issues. Instead of a monolithic Communist bloc directed from Moscow, there now existed a plurality of socialist states divided into several factions.

The most important split within the Communist camp developed between Moscow and Peking. While Stalin was alive, the potentially powerful People's Republic of China had not contested Russia's claim to leadership. But after 1953 the Chinese gradually began to assert themselves. At first it seemed as though China's influence was to be on the side of moderation. Beginning in 1957, however, and especially after 1963, Peking showed signs of a new, "hard" line. The Sino-Soviet dispute was first and foremost ideological, each side accusing the other of deviating from true "Marxism-Leninism." Following the principles of Mao Tse-tung's "great proletarian cultural revolution," China's radical ideologists preached "liberation" of peoples everywhere through "armed struggle" rather than through peaceful competition, as advocated by Moscow. In time there arose also a number of specific differences: the Soviets withheld the economic aid that the Chinese expected and Moscow refused to share its nuclear know-how with Peking. There were occasional clashes along the Sino-Soviet frontier, especially in 1969; and there was constant rivalry between the two countries for the allegiance of the rest of the world's Communist parties. As the debate between the two contestants became more and more vituperative, Communist China asserted that the center of world revolution and the leadership of world communism had shifted from Moscow to Peking.

THE END OF COLONIALISM IN ASIA

One of the most revolutionary developments since the Second World War was the liberation of virtually all the world's

Hungarians burning Communist books during the uprising in 1956.

former colonial territories. This independence movement had already begun in the years between the two world wars. It was hastened by the weakening of the mother countries in the Second World War and the subsequent rivalry between the free and Communist worlds. Although the various native revolts differed from country to country, they all had one thing in common: intense opposition to any form of colonialism. Some of the new nations took sides in the Cold War, but most of them preferred a "neutralist" stand. The most urgent need for all was economic and technical assistance. At first, most of this aid came from the United States. But in time the Soviet Union, and even Communist China, began to set up foreign aid and compete for the allegiance of these uncommitted regions.

India, Pakistan, and Bangladesh

The first major additions to the community of free nations came with the partition of the subcontinent of India in 1947 into the independent states of India and Pakistan. Although both were republics, they continued as members of the (British) Commonwealth. India was predominantly Hindu and Pakistan mostly Moslem. In the process of separating the two religions, many bloody riots broke out. India and Pakistan also clashed repeatedly over the northern state of Kashmir, to which both laid claim. In addition, there were intermittent border incidents between India and Red China.

The Union of India was by far the more important of the two states. It had a population in 1947 of 550 million, two and one-half times that of America's population in an area one-third the size of the United States. India suffered a tragic loss in 1948, when its political leader, Mohandas K. Gandhi, was assassinated by a religious fanatic. The task of guiding the new nation through its formative years fell to Gandhi's disciple, Jawaharlal Nehru, leader of the ruling Congress party. India's main problems were economic. The only way to support its huge population was through long-range development of the country's abundant natural resources with outside aid. India's dependence on such aid from all sides, together with its closeness to the centers of communism and its recent experience with western imperialism, led to a neutralist stand on most international issues. With Nehru's death in 1964, domestic affairs became less stable, especially under his daughter, Indira Gandhi, who became prime minister in 1966. Yet despite periodic famines and unrest, India's economic achievements were impressive; its national income doubled during the first generation of independence. In its foreign policy, India drew closer to the Soviet Union, as relations with neighboring China remained uneasy. A treaty of friendship with Russia was concluded in 1971.

While India was easily the most successful experiment in democracy on the Asian continent, popular government in Pakistan was slow in taking roots. Like India, Pakistan suffered a serious loss in 1948 when its outstanding leader, Mohammed Ali Jinnah, died. The country's economy was mainly agricultural, and trade with India, its natural market,

Colonial Nationalism

The West, having sown its own national wild oats in the past, is now sometimes inclined to look with a combination of dismay and superior wisdom on the upstart countries which assert an allegedly anachronistic desire to follow the same course. . . . However great the disenchantment of Europe with nationalism, the colonial nationalist is little likely to be persuaded by an argument so easily identifiable with the interest of the West in maintaining some facsimile of its older relationships in a world swiftly sliding out of its grasp. . . . Even if it be conceded that nationalism fails to furnish the foundations for an acceptable world order and has outlived its usefulness for the advanced, thoroughly "nationalized," countries of the West . . . it has by no means exhausted its contribution to the development of the non-Western peoples. Nationalism . . . has a chronology of its own derived not from the calendar but from the stages of the gradually spreading impact of the revolution which originated in Western Europe. . . . One can plausibly argue that in the different but related stages of the cycle in which Asia and Africa are now engaged nationalism intrudes itself not only with an aura of inevitability but also as the bearer of positive goods.

From Rupert Emerson, *From Empire to Nation* (Cambridge, Mass.: Harvard University Press, 1960), p. 379.

Mrs. Indira Gandhi, Prime Minister of India, in 1972.

suffered from political tensions. Economic difficulties in turn led to political instability. When democracy was no longer able to cope with bureaucratic inefficiency and corruption, the head of Pakistan's armed forces, General Ayub Khan, took over and ruled as virtual dictator from 1958 to 1969. Pakistan's foreign policy, at first firmly pro-western, during the 1960s became increasingly neutralist in an effort to attract aid and trade from both sides.

One of Pakistan's major difficulties derived from the fact that it consisted of two parts, separated by a thousand miles of Indian territory. Relations between the two regions were far from smooth; the more numerous and poverty-stricken Bengalis of East Pakistan felt exploited by the affluent and influential Punjabis in West Pakistan. The only bond between the two peoples was their common Moslem religion. Differences between East and West Pakistan came to a head in 1971 when civil war broke out between Bengali and government forces, leading first to the defeat of the Bengalis and then, after intervention by India, to the defeat of West Pakistan. East Pakistan now seceded, taking the name of Bangladesh. In 1972 the new nation signed a treaty of friendship with India and concluded agreements with Soviet Russia for economic aid.

Communist China

The most significant development in Asia after 1950 was the emergence of Communist China as a great power. The People's Republic of China was founded in 1949 (see p. 793). Its government was closely modeled on that of the Soviet Union. As in Russia, all power in China rested with the Communist Party and its leader, Mao Tse-tung. Under the constitution of 1954, the main task of the state was "to bring about, step by step, the socialist industrialization of the country," a goal that was to be achieved in several Five-Year Plans. As was the case in other backward nations, the rapid increase in China's production resulted in some impressive achievements. Symbolic of the country's scientific and technical advances was the detonation of its first

atomic bomb in 1964, followed in record time by a hydrogen bomb in 1967.

In the long run it was only through industrialization that China could solve its most pressing problem of too many people and too little land. With an estimated yearly population growth of more than 16 million, the 1-billion mark would be reached by 1990. Yet the backbone of the Chinese economy was still agriculture, and the government tried by every possible means to boost agricultural production. The second Five-Year Plan of 1958 called for a "great leap forward" in both agriculture and industry. The population was organized in gigantic "people's communes" including as many as 100,000 persons and embracing farms and factories.

But the "great leap" not only failed to reach its goals; it actually brought a decline of production. The cause for this failure was seen in the continued moderation of many leading officials. To purge Chinese communism of these "revisionist" elements, another sweeping revolutionary movement was initiated in the 1960s, the "great proletarian cultural revolution." Spearheaded by younger elements in the party, the "Maoist" revolution repudiated traditional cultural values, emphasized collectivization and austerity, and elevated the figure of China's leader to unprecedented heights of personal adulation. Through indoctrination, brainwashing, and terror China hoped to produce the most regimented society the world had ever seen. At first, these drastic measures aggravated rather than solved China's economic problems. But eventually the discipline and industry of the Chinese people did achieve new high levels of production and make Communist China a major economic power.

In foreign affairs, Red China was deeply anti-American for more than twenty years. The two countries were on opposite sides in the Korean War and in most other conflicts in Asia. Washington's support of the Chinese Nationalists on Taiwan, its alliance with Japan, and its refusal to recognize Peking were major targets for Communist attacks. This situation changed dramatically in 1972 when the United States, having

Celebration of National Day in China, October 2, 1966. The statue of Mao Tse-tung is being carried by the paraders.

abandoned its opposition to Communist China's membership in the United Nations the year before, reciprocated Chinese feelers for normalization of relations. In contrast, relations between China and the Soviet Union, initially very close, became more and more hostile as time went on.

Chinese contacts with the other communist nations of Asia were close and cordial. In its dealings with neutralist Asian countries, China alternated between kindness and threats. There were repeated clashes along the borders of India, Burma, and Nepal, and Tibetan resistance to communization was ruthlessly suppressed in 1959. If Communist China could spread its influence beyond North Korea and North Vietnam, its position within the Communist world would be greatly strengthened and its population pressure relieved. The most promising outlet for Chinese expansion was Southeast Asia, and it was here that the Chinese Communists concentrated their efforts.

Southeast Asia

The region east of India and south of China saw more political changes after the Second World War than any other part of Asia. Prior to 1945 only Thailand (Siam) was fully independent. In the years that followed, the Philippines, Burma, Indonesia, Vietnam, Laos, Cambodia, and Malaysia gained their sovereignty. Southeast Asia was a wealthy region, producing five-sixths of the world's natural rubber, more than half of its tin, and 60 percent of its rice. Like all underdeveloped areas, Southeast Asia was predominantly agricultural; but, except for Indonesia, it did not suffer from overpopulation. Despite its rich natural resources, the living standard of the region was very low. What Southeast Asia needed most was a better-balanced regional economy with more varied commodities and increased industrialization.

With the exception of Thailand, every country of Southeast Asia experienced communist revolts of varying severity. In the case of North Vietnam, Communist conquest was actually successful. Burma, Malaysia, Indonesia, and the Philippines, on the other hand, were able to crush Communist rebellions that flared up in the fifties and sixties. In the countries that formerly made up French Indochina—Laos, Cambodia, and particularly South Vietnam—the threat of communism remained strong, leading to drawn-out civil wars. The menace of communism and the general backwardness of the whole area seriously retarded the growth of democracy and encouraged the emergence of strong-man governments.

Asia and the West

The free world, under American leadership, did its best to contain the spread of communism in Southeast Asia and the Far East by providing massive military and economic aid and by encouraging cooperation among the Asian nations themselves. A start was made in 1950 with the Colombo Plan for Cooperative Development in South and Southeast Asia. In 1961 Malaya, the Philippines, and Thailand formed the Association of Southeast Asia, which ultimately was to become a free trade area. In 1966, another organization, the Asian and Pacific Council, made up of non-Communist countries in the area, called for economic, social, and political cooperation.

In the military field, the United States, Australia, and New Zealand in 1951 signed the ANZUS treaty, a loose military alliance. And the United States, Great Britain, France, Australia, New Zealand, the Philippines, Pakistan, and Thailand in 1954 established the Southeast Asia Treaty Organization (SEATO) for mutual defense against aggression and subversion.* In addition, the United States signed bilateral defense pacts with Taiwan, the Philippines, South Korea, and Japan.

Korea and Japan were the main strongholds of American influence in the Far East. The South Korean army was one of the largest in the world, and the forced resignation of Dr. Syngman Rhee's authoritarian government in 1960 brought the country closer to democracy. American influence in Japan decreased after the signing of the peace treaty in 1951 (see p. 793). The renewal of the United States-Japanese security treaty in 1960 ran into considerable leftist opposition, but its extension in 1970 was accomplished without incident. In the

*Pakistan and France withdrew from SEATO in 1972.

postwar years Japan staged a remarkable economic comeback that made it once again one of the world's leading industrial powers. Much of Japan's trade was with the United States, and this fact, together with the return of the island of Okinawa by the United States in 1972, helped cement the political and military ties between the two nations. As the United States in the 1970s reduced its troops and bases in Japan, the country had to assume responsibility for its own security. A "treaty of peace and friendship" concluded between Japan and Communist China in 1972 did much to ease tension in the Far East.

NATIONALISM IN THE ARAB WORLD

One of the most turbulent scenes of rebellion against western influence after the Second World War was the Arab Middle East, the area bridging Asia and Africa, from Iran in the east to Morocco in the west. Most of the region was extremely backward and desperately poor. But it was also of great strategic importance: it contained about half the world's oil resources, and it was the religious center of hundreds of millions of Arab and non-Arab Moslems living as far away as Southeast Asia. Outwardly, the Arab world was united by its opposition to foreign domination and its hatred of Israel. But below the surface there were many divisive forces, chiefly due to rivalries among Arab leaders.

The Suez Crisis

Before the Second World War the only independent Arab states were Egypt, Saudi Arabia, Yemen, and Iraq. After 1945 all the rest won their freedom. The most vociferous proponent of Arab nationalism was President Gamal Abdel Nasser of Egypt. Following a neutralist course, he accepted large-scale aid from the West and East alike. When the western powers in 1956 withdrew their support for the Aswan Dam, a gigantic power project on the Nile, Nasser retaliated by nationalizing the Suez Canal. The ensuing invasion of Egypt by England,

President Nasser greets fellow Egyptians after having nationalized the Suez Canal, 1956.

France, and Israel might have resulted in a major war had not the United Nations insisted on the withdrawal of foreign troops. Meanwhile Egypt was left in control of the Canal.

To present a united front to the outside world, the Arab nations in 1945 organized the Arab League. Behind this front, however, Arab differences persisted, especially between Egypt on the one hand and Jordan, Lebanon, and Iraq on the other. To meet the threat posed by communist support of Arab nationalism, Great Britain, Turkey, Iran, Iraq, and Pakistan in 1955 signed a mutual assistance treaty, the Baghdad Pact. When Iraq dropped out of the alliance in 1958, a new Central Treaty Organization (CENTO) was formed. It included the United States, which, under the "Eisenhower Doctrine" of 1957, had already promised armed assistance against Communist aggression to any nation in the Middle East that requested it.

Arabs against Israel

The main danger to peace in the Middle East was the intermittent war between the Arabs and Israel. The war started in 1948–49, when Israel's neighbors invaded the newly independent country, only to be beaten and evicted. From here on an uneasy armistice prevailed. The Arabs refused to recognize Israel, and hundreds of thousands of Arab refugees, made homeless by the partition of Palestine, helped keep the conflict alive. Full-scale fighting was briefly resumed during the Suez crisis in 1956, when Israeli forces made a quick dash for the Suez Canal. In 1967, in a furious six-day war, Israel took the Sinai Peninsula and some other territory. Arab attempts to regain these lands led to another bloody war in 1973.

The Israelis vowed to retain their conquests until a final and stable peace could be agreed upon; they believed that they were fighting for the very survival of their nation. Yet the occupation and possible annexation of Arab lands only exacerbated the Arab-Israeli conflict. Beginning in 1972, a rash of bombings, airplane hijackings, and assassinations by Palestinian Arab guerrilla organ-izations and retaliations by Israeli commandos further intensified the crisis. The war in the Middle East, it seemed, never really ended.

Although most of the unrest in the region stemmed from nationalism, its roots lay in the serious domestic problems of the Arab states, in its age-old poverty and illiteracy. Almost everywhere, Arab society was still sharply divided into tiny minorities of extremely wealthy merchants and landowners and huge masses of the poorest peasants. To change this system, a complete social revolution and sweeping reforms were needed. It would also require the aid of the very same foreigners whom Arab nationalists hated.

THE EMERGENCE OF AFRICA

The continent of Africa was the last to be swept by the tide of nationalism. From only four sovereign states in 1950, the number by 1968 had grown to thirty-nine. The only important colonies remaining were those of Portugal. The most recent victories of African nationalism occurred in the most backward part of the continent, south of the Sahara Desert, in areas inhabited by poor, primitive, and illiterate native tribes. The former colonial powers had virtually eradicated tropical diseases, but the resultant population growth had not been matched by a similar increase in food supplies. Most of Africa, therefore, remained underfed. Added to poverty was extreme diversity, with no tradition of political unity and with some 700 different native dialects. The one sentiment common to all Africans was anticolonialism. Just as it did everywhere else in the world, nationalism in Africa demanded immediate independence, whether people were ready for it or not. This rush into freedom caused severe growing pains for most of the new nations.

Crises in the Congo and Nigeria

All African states were founded as democracies. But lack of political experience and tribal disunity soon gave rise

A Ghanian man. His shirt is printed with the portrait of Kwame Nkrumah, Ghana's first president.

Map legend:

Independent nations

A date after the name of an African country refers to the year it became independent.

MILES 0 — 1000

to one-party systems and strong-man rule.

The nation that had more trouble than any other was the Democratic Republic of the Congo. The Belgians had done little to prepare their colony for the independence they were forced to grant it in 1960. As a result, order broke down completely. There were popular riots, mutinies in the army, and threats of secession in some of the Congo's provinces, notably Katanga. The continued presence of Belgian troops further complicated matters.

The first premier of the new republic, Patrice Lumumba, allegedly pro-Communist, was removed in 1960. His subsequent murder made him a martyr to anticolonialists everywhere. United Nations troops were able to maintain a measure of order and to prevent the secession of Katanga. In 1964 the leader of that province, Moise Tshombe, was given the premiership in the hope that he might prove a unifying force. But he was overthrown in 1965 by General Joseph Mobutu, whose pro-Lumumba and anti-Belgian stand made him popular. In spite of continued mutinies in the outlying provinces Mobutu proved to be a stabilizing factor. In 1971, as part of an Africanization campaign, the country was renamed Republic of Zaïre, and the Congo River became the Zaïre River.

Another African country troubled by internal unrest was Nigeria. From the beginning of its independence in 1960, Nigeria was beset by festering disputes among its many tribes, especially between the poor and backward Hausa-Fulanis in the North and the more highly educated and advanced, but less numerous, Ibos in the South. As time went on and tensions mounted, persecution of the Ibos led to some ghastly massacres. In 1967 the coastal Eastern Region, inhabited mostly by Ibos, declared itself independent as the Republic of Biafra. Since the area contained most of Nigeria's richest oil fields and installations, government troops intervened and a civil war was on. The new republic had little chance of survival unless it could obtain outside aid. Yet for the rest of the world to recognize one more African nation might encourage secessions from some of the other new states in which hostile tribal groups were living in uneasy co-existence. By 1970, Biafran independence was extinguished.

Southern Africa: Whites against Blacks

There was one region in Africa where the black quest for political power continued to be suppressed. In the Republic of South Africa, as in Rhodesia and in the Portuguese colonies of Angola and Mozambique, small white minorities controlled their country's political and economic affairs. Increasingly, however, this white power came under attack from black nationalism.

In South Africa, where the white minority constituted only 20 percent of the total population, the government in 1948 introduced a program of strict racial segregation, or *apartheid*. The program provided for complete separation of the races, restricted franchise for nonwhites, forced resettlement of Africans, and separate schools with lower educational standards for black children. The result

Whites versus nonwhites in South Africa.

of this policy was mounting unrest and bloodshed. In 1966 Prime Minister Henrik F. Verwoerd, a leading advocate of *apartheid*, was assassinated. South Africa's racist policies, meanwhile, earned the country the censure of most of the civilized world, including the other members of the Commonwealth. In a show of resentment of such criticism, South Africa withdrew from the Commonwealth in 1961.

In the British dependency of Southern Rhodesia, the ruling white minority amounted to little more than one-twentieth of the total population. When the British government insisted on political equality for the black majority as a condition for granting independence to its former colony, the white regime of Ian Smith in 1965 declared the secession of Rhodesia from the mother country. Subsequent efforts to bring Rhodesia into line through economic sanctions failed, as South Africa and the neighboring Portuguese colony of Mozambique rallied to Rhodesia's support.

To the outside world, Mozambique, together with Angola and Portuguese Guinea, were still "non-self-governing territories," or colonies. In Portuguese eyes, however, they were integral parts of the mother country, overseas provinces whose citizens enjoyed the same rights as those of Portugal. Africans participated in the civil service and married Portuguese, and efforts were made to improve the lot of the poverty-stricken black masses. Yet these efforts were not sufficient to neutralize the appeal of black nationalism, which flared up in bloody rebellions, requiring large-scale intervention by Portuguese troops.

Asian-African Conferences

The political emergence of the non-white peoples was a worldwide movement. While the details of their liberation differed, there were still sufficient similarities to suggest possible collaboration among the many nations that so recently had gained their freedom. As a result, several conferences were held, both among the nations of Asia and Africa and among the nations of Africa alone.

The first Asian-African conference met at Bandung, Indonesia, in 1955. It was attended by delegates from twenty-nine countries, representing about half the world's population. There were few tangible results, but the meeting registered common attitudes on such basic issues as anticolonialism and censure of racial discrimination. The next meeting, at Cairo in 1957, was less successful, largely because it was used by communist nations, including the Soviet Union, to advocate a strongly antiwestern line. The same held true for some of the subsequent meetings. It was only when the Soviet Union was excluded from the proceedings and when the deliberations shifted to economic problems that these meetings became more useful and businesslike.

As time went on and most peoples gained their independence, anticolonialism as a unifying issue lost its importance. Instead, there now were growing differences among the various new nations themselves, as radical and moderate ones clashed. It was due to such differences that the conference scheduled to meet in 1965, on the tenth anniversary of the initial Bandung meeting, was canceled. Meanwhile a series of Afro-Asian Solidarity Conferences had been held, beginning in 1957. Made up of nongovernmental representatives, their rhetoric and resolutions tended to be more radical. The fifth such conference in 1972 was attended by more than 80 delegations.

The Organization of African Unity

In 1958 the nations of Africa founded their own Conference of Independent African States, which held annual meetings thereafter. As more and more African countries became independent, a need for closer cooperation arose, especially in economic matters. In the early 1960s a number of regional groupings developed. The next step was some wider union of all nonwhite Africa. In 1963 an all-African conference at Addis Ababa, Ethiopia, created the Organization of African Unity (OAU) as a permanent instrument for political and economic cooperation and for the common defense of each member's independence.

Progress toward political cooperation was hampered by the large size and great diversity of the continent. In the economic sphere the trend toward regional groupings, such as the East African Community, founded in 1968, was seen as the surest way to overcome Africa's problems. More helpful than economic cooperation among backward countries in Africa and elsewhere, however, was continued aid from the more advanced nations. It was in aiding underdeveloped regions that the free world and the Communist nations found their most fruitful field for competition.

FROM COLD WAR TO COEXISTENCE

The most clearly discernible trend in international relations after 1950 was the gradual shift away from the angry confrontation of East and West in the Cold War to an equally competitive but more peaceful state of coexistence. The Cold War had developed as the result of a gradually mounting crisis; the state of peaceful coexistence came only after a decade of intermittent sparring, in which each side felt out the strength of the other. The avoidance of a major showdown between the East and West was due mainly to the nuclear balance of power that was accomplished during the 1950s.

General MacArthur waves to New York City crowds during a ticker tape parade in his honor after he had returned from Korea in 1951.

The Korean War

The years immediately after 1950 brought to a climax the international tension that had been building up since 1945. In the fall of 1950, United Nations forces fought their way into North Korea, close to the borders of Red China. But when victory seemed almost in sight, the Chinese Communists intervened and drove the UN armies back into South Korea. By the spring of 1951, the front had become stabilized once more along the thirty-eighth parallel, and there it substantially remained during the stalemate that lasted for two years. Armistice negotiations were begun in 1951 but were not completed until 1953. By that time the war had cost America more than 150,000 casualties. The Korean armistice, moreover, merely established an uneasy truce in which North Korean troops continued to face South Korean and American forces across a demilitarized zone.

Escalation in Both Camps

One of the lasting effects of the Korean conflict was a substantial buildup of western military strength. The United States increased its military expenditures fivefold, doubled its armed forces, and extended its network of military bases abroad, and most of America's allies followed suit. It was during the Korean war that NATO perfected its organization and increased its membership by adding Greece and Turkey. At the same time plans were laid for including West Germany in the western alliance. In 1952, furthermore, the United States exploded its first hydrogen bomb, thus regaining the nuclear lead it had held before the Soviet atomic explosion in 1949.

The change from a Democratic to a Republican administration in Washington in 1953 brought to the fore a man who seemed determined to use America's military strength not merely to contain but to challenge communism. Until his death in 1959, the new Secretary of State, John Foster Dulles, was the leading political strategist in the western camp. But his policy of "massive retaliation" and "brinkmanship" did not always have the support of America's friends, nor did it have the desired effect of scaring the Russians into making political concessions.

More decisive than the changing of the guard in Washington were the events touched off by Stalin's death in 1953. While the new Soviet rulers were consolidating their position at home, they adopted a more conciliatory policy abroad. At the same time, however, the Russian government also announced its first successful testing of a hydrogen bomb. And while the West was rallying its forces behind NATO, the Soviets were lining up their eastern satellites behind the Warsaw Pact of 1955.

The Search for Coexistence

The first sign that Russia might be willing to negotiate East-West differences was seen in the Korean armistice, which would have been impossible without Soviet aquiescence. In January 1954 the foreign ministers of the Big Four nations (United States, Britain, France, and Russia) resumed their talks in Berlin after an interval of several years. In April the Geneva Conference on Far Eastern Affairs, with Communist China attending, temporarily divided Vietnam, where the French had recently been defeated by the Vietminh Communist insurgents. Elections for the whole of Vietnam were to be held in 1956, but these never took place.

The culmination of the initial search for coexistence came with the Geneva Summit Conference of 1955. This was the first time since Potsdam ten years earlier that the Big Four heads of state had assembled. On the eve of the meeting, the Russians agreed to an Austrian peace treaty on reasonable terms, another hopeful sign of growing Soviet moderation. Relations at Geneva were cordial, especially between President Eisenhower and Soviet Premier Nikolai Bulganin, though the results of the conference were disappointing. On none of the major issues—German reunification, European security, and disarmament—was there any understanding reached. The only positive achievement was an agreement on cultural exchanges between East and West.

Continuation of the Cold War

While the "spirit of Geneva" appeared to have dissipated some of the suspicions of the Cold War, events in the Middle East soon showed that war to be far from over. The crisis resulting from President Nasser's nationalization of the Suez Canal in the summer of 1956 and the subsequent attack on Egypt by British, French, and Israeli forces has already been discussed (p. 814). The withdrawal of these forces under pressure from the UN and the United States was seen as a victory for Nasser and his backers in the Communist camp. The Soviet Union's reputation as a champion of anticolonialism, however, was immediately tarnished by its brutal intervention against the uprising in Hungary. Both the Suez crisis and the Hungarian revolution might easily have led to a major showdown had it not been for the fear of a nuclear war.

The year 1957 was relatively peaceful. America's proclamation of the Eisenhower Doctrine served notice that the nation was ready to oppose the spread of Soviet influence in the Middle East. In the Soviet Union, meanwhile, Khrushchev emerged as the supreme leader of communism. The most spectacular event of the year, however, was the successful launching of Russia's first earth satellite, Sputnik I, on October 4, 1957. This development proved that the Russians possessed rockets powerful enough to launch a nuclear attack on the United States. The balance of power in the Cold War had suddenly shifted in Russia's favor.

To the Brink of War

For the next five years the initiative in international affairs largely rested with the Soviet Union. The United States launched its first satellite, Explorer I, in January 1958. But the Russians maintained their lead by placing heavier satellites into orbit. Continued Communist attempts to stir up trouble in the Middle East were foiled by American and British landings of troops in Lebanon and Jordan in 1958. Next came a crisis in the Far East, where Chinese Communist attacks on the offshore islands of Quemoy and Matsu were halted only because America stood firmly by its Nationalist Chinese ally. In November 1958 the Soviet Union reopened the German question by once again challenging the western position in Berlin and insisting that the former German capital be made a "free city" within the East German Democratic Republic.

While East-West relations were thus being kept in a state of latent tension, there were feelers from both sides for a second try at summit diplomacy. But the conference finally scheduled for 1960 in Paris never materialized. On the eve of the Paris meeting the Russians downed an American U-2 intelligence plane flying over the Soviet Union. Eisenhower's refusal to make amends for this incident led to Khrushchev's withdrawal from the conference before it started.

There was much concern in the West over the increasingly aggressive Soviet stance in foreign affairs. Aside from trying to scare the United States into making concessions, Russia's policy was also influenced by the growing rift between Moscow and Peking. The beginnings of this rift went back to 1957, when the Chinese Communists began to criticize Khrushchev's policy of de-Stalinization and his proposed strategy of defeating capitalism through peaceful competition rather than revolution or war. In time, outward signs of the Sino-Soviet split began to appear. Russia failed to back the Chinese in their attack on the offshore islands and withdrew its material and technical aid, which was essential to China's industrial development. Much of the conflict between Peking and Moscow was over the allegiance of the underdeveloped and unaligned countries. It was to reassert his claim to leadership over world communism that Khrushchev delivered boastful threats and engaged in bewildering antics in the United Nations Assembly in 1960.

The advent of the Kennedy administration in 1961 at first seemed to bring a slight lessening of East-West tension. The new President was faced by a perplexing array of foreign problems. In April 1961 the ill-fated Bay of Pigs invasion of Cuba—undertaken by anti-Castro refugees with American backing—was quickly suppressed by Castro's

Citizens of West Berlin wave to friends and relatives on the other side of the Berlin Wall.

forces. In South Vietnam, meanwhile, Vietcong guerrillas, supported by Communist North Vietnam, were stepping up their "war of liberation." A similar war was going on between the Communist Pathet Lao and government forces in Laos. The most serious problem Kennedy inherited, however, was the continued Russian demand for western withdrawal from Berlin.

Kennedy and Khrushchev had a brief impromptu meeting at Vienna in June 1961. Khrushchev already had made some cordial gestures toward the President, and the encounter was courteous. But shortly after the Vienna meeting the Russians increased their agitation over Berlin, threatening to sign a peace treaty with the East Germans that would give the latter control over access to West Berlin. Only Kennedy's obvious determination to stand firm and go to war rather than give in made Khrushchev finally back down. To stop the stream of refugees from East Germany into West Berlin, the Communists built the Berlin Wall that henceforth made East Germany a virtual prison. In October 1961 Khrushchev withdrew his ultimatum on Berlin, thus ending the Berlin crisis.

There were other signs that negotiations might replace confrontations in East-West relations. In July 1962 a foreign ministers' conference in Geneva agreed on the formal neutralization of Laos. This, it was hoped, would calm the situation in Southeast Asia. But at the same time the Russians were involved in secret activities in Cuba that soon brought the United States and the Soviet Union to the very brink of war.

The Cuban crisis gained momentum during the summer of 1962 as Washington learned about Russia's stepped-up military support for Castro. In September a Soviet-Cuban security treaty was announced. In October the United States gained proof that the Soviets had supplied Cuba with missiles capable of delivering nuclear warheads and that launching sites were under construction in Cuba. President Kennedy immediately imposed a strict blockade on further arms shipments to Cuba and demanded that all Soviet offensive weapons be withdrawn and all missile bases dismantled. Faced with pressure from the United Nations and American threats of retaliation, Premier Khrushchev backed down, after receiving America's promise not to invade Cuba. The most serious confrontation of the Cold War was over.

On the Brink of War

Sunday, October 28, was a shining autumn day. At nine in the morning Khrushchev's answer began to come in. By the fifth sentence it was clear that he had thrown in his hand. Work would stop on the sites; the arms "which you described as offensive" would be crated and returned to the Soviet Union; negotiations would start at the UN. Then, no doubt to placate Castro, Khrushchev asked the United States to discontinue flights over Cuba. . . . Looking ahead, he said, "We should like to continue the exchange of views on the prohibition of atomic and thermonuclear weapons, general disarmament, and other problems relating to the relaxation of international tension." It was all over, and barely in time. If word had not come that Sunday, if work had continued on the bases, the United States would have had no real choice but to take action against Cuba the next week. No one could discern what lay darkly beyond an air strike or invasion, what measures and countermeasures, actions and reactions, might have driven the hapless world to the ghastly consummation. The President saw more penetratingly into the mists and terrors of the future than anyone else. A few weeks later he said, "If we had invaded Cuba . . . I am sure the Soviets would have acted. They would have to, just as we would have to. I think there are certain compulsions on any major power." . . . When Kennedy received Khrushchev's reply that golden October morning, he showed profound relief. Later he said, "This is the night to go to the theater, like Abraham Lincoln."

From Arthur M. Schlesinger, Jr., *A Thousand Days: John F. Kennedy in the White House* (Boston: Houghton Mifflin, 1965), p. 830.

East-West Détente

The Cuban crisis, surprisingly, ushered in the first genuine *détente* in the East-West conflict. To reduce the risk of accidental war, Washington and Moscow in early 1963 established a "hot line" of direct communication. In early July 1963 the two powers, together with Great Britain, signed a Nuclear Test Ban Treaty outlawing all but underground tests. There were other agreements on minor issues—East-West trade, increased consular service, a Moscow–New York air link. The relaxation of tension, moreover, did not end with Kennedy's death and Khrushchev's fall from power. In the summer of 1967, at the height of the

Middle Eastern crisis, President Johnson and Premier Kosygin held a businesslike conference at Glassboro, New Jersey, which helped lessen the international strain.

The *détente* between Moscow and Washington did not at first resolve any of the major issues of the Cold War. The most serious crisis in the late 1960s was the drawn-out war in Vietnam. In an effort to contain the spread of communism in Southeast Asia, the United States poured several hundred thousand men and billions of dollars into a conflict that was in many ways similar to the war in Korea. Just as in that earlier war, the ultimate threat was Red China. But while at the time of Korea the Soviet Union, in its role as leader of world communism, had been instrumental in helping end the war, such mediation was difficult now that Moscow's leadership was being challenged by Peking.

But even the Vietnam War did not seriously alter the climate of coexistence. One of the more hopeful results of that climate was the Nuclear Non-Proliferation Treaty of 1968, which tried to halt the spread of nuclear weapons. It was not only the fear of nuclear war that made peaceful coexistence appear preferable to warlike confrontation. Another factor working for coexistence was the loosening of ties within the eastern and western camps and the emergence of the uncommitted and underdeveloped nations as a "third force" in world affairs. The dissolution of the formerly monolithic communist bloc has already been noted. Similar changes took place within the western camp. The trend toward "polycentrism," or many-centeredness, was also evident in the United Nations, where the new countries of Asia and Africa increasingly challenged the predominance of the superpowers.

As a result of these various changes and realignments, neither the United States nor Russia could any longer count on unquestioning support from their friends or satellites in every crisis. The days of bipolar, East-West, Communist-capitalist confrontations were over.

The most dramatic moves toward a more pragmatic, nonideological foreign policy came in the 1970s. Most of the

President Nixon and Premier Chou En-lai exchange toasts in Peking in 1972.

important events have already been noted: West Germany's improved relations with Eastern Europe, notably the Soviet Union and Poland; Japan's first contacts with Communist China; President Nixon's historic visits to Moscow and Peking; and the many instances of improved relations between other Communist and non-Communist countries. In 1972, a treaty on Berlin, signed by the four major Second World War allies, including the Soviet Union, removed another perennial source of friction by guaranteeing access to and easing communications within the city. American withdrawal from South Vietnam and the cease-fire agreement in 1973, while not ending the troubles, at least helped to ease the tensions in that part of the world.

But while an improved international climate thus helped solve or at least defuse some explosive issues, others continued and new ones were sure to arise. It remained to be seen whether a "polycentric" world would be as good at preventing a third world war as those two veterans of the Cold War, the United States and Russia, had been. Because although they had been at odds on most issues, their differences had never blinded them to the fact that the only alternative to coexistence was nonexistence. To have learned that lesson was at least one positive result of the Cold War.

Suggestions for Further Reading

Note: Asterisk denotes a book available in paperback edition.

General

The events of the last two decades are put in their wider perspective in G. Lichtheim, *Europe in the Twentieth Century* (1972). One of the best works on the Cold War is L. J. Halle, *The Cold War as History* (1967). A. Fontaine, *History of the Cold War,** 2 vols. (1968–69), by a leading French journalist, is lively and informative. The works by D. F. Fleming, *The Cold War and Its Origins, 1917–1960*, 2 vols. (1961), and by J. Kolko and G. Kolko, *The Limits of Power: The World and United States Foreign Policy, 1945–1954* (1972), are "revisionist," that is, highly critical of American foreign policy. See also P. Seabury, *The Rise and Decline of the Cold War* (1967). H. L. Trefousse, *The Cold War: A Book of Documents** (1965), is excellent. The best book on Soviet foreign policy is A. Ulam, *Expansion and Coexistence: The History of Soviet Foreign Policy, 1917–1967** (1968). The effect of the nuclear revolution on foreign affairs is weighed by H. M. Kissinger, *Nuclear Weapons and Foreign Policy** (1957). Russian thinking on military matters is discussed in H. S. Dinerstein, *War and the Soviet Union* (1962), and in R. L. Garthoff, *Soviet Military Policy: A Historical Analysis* (1962). For the American side, see H. Kahn's controversial *On Thermonuclear War* (1960), and the thoughtful essay by K. E. Knorr, *On the Uses of Military Power in the Nuclear Age* (1966). R. Aron, *The Great Debate: Theories of Nuclear Strategy* (1965), is a judicious synopsis by a noted French political scientist.

The Decline and Rise of Europe

The most reflective book on this theme is J. L. Lukacs, *Decline and Rise of Europe** (1965). W. Laqueur, *Europe Since Hitler** (1970), is admirably comprehensive. On Europe's economic recovery, see C. P. Kindleberger, *Europe's Postwar Growth* (1967), and M. Postan, *An Economic History of Western Europe* (1967). The following are among the many books dealing with individual countries: F. Boyd, *British Politics in Transition** (1964); P. Williams, *Politics in Postwar France* (1965); A. Grosser, *Germany in Our Time* (1971); and N. Kogan, *A Political History of Postwar Italy* (1966). On the quest for European unity and its obstacles, see R. Mayne, *The Community of Europe* (1963); J. Pinder, *Europe Against De Gaulle* (1963); and S. Serfaty, *France, De Gaulle, and Europe* (1967). The perennial "German Problem" is treated in J. L. Richardson, *Germany and the Atlantic Alliance* (1966); F. A. Vali, *The Quest for a United Germany* (1967); and R. McGeehan, *The German Rearmament Question: American Diplomacy and European Defense After World War II* (1971). W. F. Hanrieder, *West German Foreign Policy, 1949–1963* (1967), is a helpful book.

The Americas

The difficulties of postwar adjustment in the United States are portrayed in E. F. Goldman, *The Crucial Decade: America, 1945–1955** (1956). C. Phillips, *The Truman Presidency* (1966), and R. H. Rovere, *Affairs of State: The Eisenhower Years* (1956), deal with the Democratic and Republican periods respectively. On the Kennedy administration, see A. M. Schlesinger, Jr., *A Thousand Days: John F. Kennedy in the White House** (1965); and on Johnson, see E. F. Goldman, *The Tragedy of Lyndon Johnson* (1969). The economic scene is the subject of J. K. Galbraith, *The Affluent Society,** 2nd. ed. (1969), and of W. W. Heller, *New Dimensions of Political Economy* (1966). See also H. H. Landsberg *et. al., Resources in America's Future: Patterns of Requirements and Availabilities, 1960–2000* (1963). The problems of blacks and of poverty are discussed in A. Lewis, *Portrait of a Decade** (1964); I. E. Lomax, *The Negro Revolt** (1963); J. W. Silver, *Mississippi: The Closed Society** (1966); M. Harrington, *The Other America: Poverty in the United States* (1963); and L. Fishman, ed., *Poverty Amid Affluence* (1966).

The growing importance of Canada is pointed out in N. L. Nicolson, *Canada in the American Community** (1963), and in G. M. Craig, *The United States and Canada* (1968). J. Crispo, *International Unionism: A Study in Canadian-American Relations* (1967), deals with the economic impact of the United States on Canada. On Latin America, S. Clissold, *Latin America: New World, Third World* (1972), is a good survey. E. R. Wolf and E. C. Hansen, *The Human Condition in Latin America* (1972), deals with various aspects of Latin American society past and present. D. A. Chalmers, ed., *Changing Latin America: New Interpretations of Its Politics and Society* (1972), is a collection of essays by Latin American specialists. One of the best books on the changes in Cuba is T. Draper, *Castroism: Theory and Practice* (1965). R. P. Fagen, *The Transformation of Political Culture in Cuba* (1969), is a solid and serious book.

The Communist World Many of the books cited for Chapter 32 are also relevant to this later phase of communism. For works on more recent events, see H. Seton-Watson, *From Lenin to Khrushchev** (1960); R. Conquest, *Russia After Khrushchev* (1965); and A. Ulam, *The New Face of Soviet Totalitarianism* (1965). On special phases of Soviet life, see H. Schwartz, *The Soviet Economy since Stalin* (1965); W. W. Kulski, *The Soviet Regime: Communism in Practice** (1963); H. Inkeles and R. A. Bauer, *The Soviet Citizen: Daily Life in a Totalitarian Society* (1959); and P. Reddaway, ed., *Uncensored Russia: Protest and Dissent in the Soviet Union* (1972). There are several general studies of Russia's satellites: Z. K. Brzezinski, *The Soviet Bloc: Unity and Conflict** (1967); J. F. Brown, *The New Eastern Europe* (1967); and S. Fischer-Galati, *Eastern Europe in the Sixties** (1963). On communism in the West, see F. Fetjö, *The French Communist Party and the Crisis of International Communism* (1967), and D. L. M. Blackmer, *Unity in Diversity: Italian Communism and the Communist World* (1968). On the split between the Soviet Union and Red China, J. Gittings, *Survey of the Sino-Soviet Dispute* (1968), and D. W. Treadgold, *Soviet and Chinese Communism: Similarities and Differences* (1967), provide good introductions.

The End of Colonialism R. Strausz-Hupé and W. H. Hazard, *The Idea of Colonialism* (1958), corrects some misconceptions about colonial rule. See also S. C. Easton, *The Twilight of European Colonialism: A Political Analysis* (1960), and R. Emerson, *From Empire to Nation: The Rise to Self-Assertion of Asian and African Peoples** (1962). Changes in the Commonwealth are discussed in Z. Cowen, *The British Commonwealth of Nations in a Changing World* (1965). For the major countries of Asia, old and new, see B. P. Lamb, *India: A World in Transition*, 3rd. ed. (1968); L. Blinkenberg, *India-Pakistan: The History of Unsolved Conflicts* (1972); O. E. Clubb, *Twentieth Century China*, 2nd. ed. (1972); G. C. Allen, *Japan's Economic Recovery* (1958); N. A. Tarling, *A Concise History of Southeast Asia* (1966); and B. Higgins and J. Higgins, *Indonesia: The Crisis of the Millstones* (1963). G. Myrdal, *Asian Drama: An Inquiry into Poverty* (1968), covers important ground. On the Middle East, the following are significant: J. M. Landau, ed., *Man, State and Society in the Contemporary Middle East* (1972); T. C. Bose, *The Superpowers and the Middle East* (1972); and T. Little, *Modern Egypt* (1967). African developments are covered in I. Wallerstein, *Africa: The Politics of Independence* (1962), and the same author's *Africa: The Politics of Unity* (1967). See also D. G. Morrison *et. al.*, *Black Africa: A Comparative Handbook* (1972); R. Emerson and M. Kilson, eds., *The Political Awakening of Africa** (1965); and C. E. Welch, *Dream of Unity: Pan-Africanism and Political Unification* (1966). On continued racial inequality in Africa, see N. Phillips, *The Tragedy of Apartheid* (1960); and R. Gibson, *African Liberation Movements: Contemporary Struggles Against White Minority Rule* (1972). On the attitudes of the two superpowers toward Africa, see R. Emerson, *Africa and United States Policy** (1967), and D. Morison, *The U.S.S.R. and Africa* (1964). B.P. Kiernan, *The United States, Communism, and the Emergent World* (1972), is critical of American policy.

From Cold War to Coexistence Most of the general works mentioned above also cover this subject. The following is a selection of individual studies on the major international crises of the last two decades. Each of these crises was a potential cause for a major war: D. Rees, *Korea: The Limited War* (1964); H. Thomas, *The Suez Affair* (1967); J. Radvány, *Hungary and the Superpowers* (1972); J. E. Smith, *The Defense of Berlin* (1963); C. Young, *Politics in the Congo: Decolonization and Independence* (1965); A. J. Dommen, *Conflict in Laos: The Politics of Neutralisation* (1964); A. Abel, *The Missile Crisis* (1966); W. Laqueur, *The Road to Jerusalem: The Arab-Israeli Conflict, 1967* (1968); and F. FitzGerald, *Fire in the Lake: The Vietnamese and the Americans in Vietnam* (1972). On the more peaceful aspects of international relations, see G. Bluhm, *Détente and Military Relations in Europe* (1967); and J. Laloy, *Western and Eastern Europe* (1967). American foreign policy is the subject of R. Hilsman, *To Move a Nation* (1967), on Kennedy's foreign policy; and P. L. Geyelin, *Lyndon B. Johnson and the World* (1966). Among "futurist" literature, attempting to predict the shape of things to come, H. Kahn and B. Bruce-Briggs, *Things to Come: Thinking about the 70's and 80's* (1972), and T. Geiger, *The Fortunes of the West: The Future of the Atlantic Nations* (1973), are thoughtful contributions.

Epilogue:

The Challenges of Our Time

It seems quite clear in retrospect that the Second World War ushered in a wholly new phase of world history. As yet it is too early to give a name to this new age. Terms like Age of Anxiety, Age of Anarchy, or Age of Uncertainty merely reflect a sense of bewilderment in the face of ceaseless change. Historians realize, of course, that all events, even seemingly sudden ones, have their roots in the past. The "population explosion," the nuclear revolution, world communism, colonial nationalism—they all have their history. But never before have so many crucial developments reached crisis proportions so quickly; never before has a generation been confronted with so many changes and challenges.

THE "POPULATION EXPLOSION"

It is difficult to decide which is the most pressing current problem. The one that has existed longest is the relentless increase of population. When population growth first became obvious, in the eighteenth century, "enlightened" contemporaries saw it as merely another sign of mankind's progress. "Myriads of centuries of still increasing population may pass away," William Godwin wrote in 1793, "and the earth be still found sufficient for the subsistence of its inhabitants." Not long afterward, however, a different voice was heard. "The power of population," Thomas Malthus wrote in 1798, "is indefinitely greater than the power in the earth to produce subsist-

The "population explosion": Coney Island Beach in New York City on a Fourth of July weekend.

ence." Man's fate, Malthus concluded, was not happiness and perfection but misery and decay.

For almost a century and a half Malthus' prognosis appeared overly alarmist. World population expanded as never before; but as the number of people increased, so did their food supply. So long as there were fertile open spaces in moderate climes ready to absorb Europe's surplus millions, and so long as human ingenuity found ways of boosting nature's yield, there was no cause for alarm. All this suddenly changed in this century. Before the Second World War, improvements in medicine and public health in the more highly developed countries had substantially lowered the death rate and prolonged the life span. Since then these advances have spread to the rest of the world. The result has been a dramatic increase in population. While it took a whole century before 1930 to double the world's population from one to two billion, present estimates are that the number of people alive at the end of this century will be close to seven billion. The term "population explosion," coined only a few years ago, has become a household phrase. The possible consequences of this explosion are alarming indeed. Demographers warn that in less than a century there may be "standing room only."

An Age of Abundance

Why does this rising tide of humanity not cause greater general anxiety? One reason is that scientists claim there will always be enough food for everyone. The world will be crowded, they say, but it will not go hungry. An intensively cultivated earth and a more exploited sea will provide man with ample nourishment. Nor will there be any shortage of other necessities. As a matter of fact, life will become easier as technological advancement reduces the need for human labor.

Not only industry but agriculture will become increasingly automated. Deserts will bloom, irrigated by water distilled from the sea, and the oceans will yield their riches of food and raw materials to the inhabitants of manmade islands. The power of our planet to produce subsistence, it seems, is as unlimited as the power of mankind to reproduce itself. The only shortage will be of space.

A Crowded Planet

Despite such optimistic predictions, there have already been severe famines in some parts of the world, notably India and Africa, though these were due more to maldistribution than to shortages in the world's food supply. But the effects of overcrowding have also been felt in other ways. As more and more people congregate in industrial areas and urban centers, many of life's traditional amenities—clean air, pure water, peace and quiet—are rapidly becoming things of the past. The awareness of the threat posed by "pollution" of every kind is of quite recent origin. While governments are trying to save society from suffocating in smog or being buried in refuse, the voracious appetites of growing populations for the luxuries and conveniences of modern technology make any remedial efforts holding actions at best. The only way to stem the rapid decay of man's environment will be to curb the uncontrolled increase of man himself. Modern methods of birth control make large-scale population planning easy, yet very few countries have tried to cope with their population problem. It seems that age-old prejudices and religious scruples work against such a solution.

THE CONQUEST OF OUTER SPACE

Some optimists believe that the conquest of outer space may be the answer to the "population explosion." Man's first probes into extraterrestrial regions are still so recent that they are hardly a subject for the historian. Yet the year 1957, when the first manmade object went into orbit around the earth, may some day

---

"Sardine-Can Existence"

There is . . . [a] much deeper problem involved in living the sardine-can existence that would result if this planet had 10 to 20 billion people. A subtle but extremely important consequence of increased human population density is that diversity between different parts of the world is diminished, and uniformity spreads over everything. The world becomes duller, less exciting, less variable and colorful to the senses. This happens in many ways. The rarer plants and animals will become extinct, and this means less variety to look at and less variety in our diet. Our diet will also become poorer, because we shall have to eat more plant food and less animal food. This is because it takes fewer acres to grow the plant food required to feed a person than it takes to grow animal food, and when the population is 20 billion we shall be very short of acres. Also, as the population grows to 20 billion, it will be progressively more difficult to take a holiday where one can get away from it all. Everywhere one goes there will be teeming multitudes of people. The only holidays available will be the Coney Island or Black Sea type, where the beach is a seething mass of people as far as the eye can see. Different types of places, like tropical rain forests or coral reefs, will be gone. The rain forests will have been cut down for other purposes, and the coral reefs will have been carried home by collectors. There will be nothing rare in the world; everything rare will have been taken home by someone as a prize. Only very common things will be left, and the common things will have become very dull. This process has already become very obvious around wilderness resort areas. In order to sell as many lots as possible in a given tract of land, the first act of many developers in a forested area is to cut down the trees and bulldoze off the topsoil so that although more lots are made available, the area has the appeal of the middle of the Sahara Desert.

Who wants all this? The conclusion seems obvious. It well may be that even if we could find the energy to support 20 billion people on this planet indefinitely, we gradually would come to realize that the life style involved was so unattractive and soul-destroying that we would voluntarily decide to limit births and reduce the population to something in the one to two billion range. Why not decide that before we cover the entire landscape with houses, apartments, hotels, and freeways?

From Kenneth E. F. Watt, "Planning—So There Will Be a Future," in Clifton Fadiman and Jean White, eds., *Ecocide and Thoughts Toward Survival* (New York: Center for the Study of Democratic Institutions, Interbook Inc., 1972), p. 132.

An Apollo 15 astronaut and his lunar rover on the moon in 1973.

take its place alongside that other memorable date, 1492, when Europe discovered a whole new world beyond the horizons of the old. The initial motive behind space exploration was scientific curiosity. But as scientists convinced their governments that the conquest of space was merely a matter of time, individual research turned into government-sponsored space programs.

The conquest of outer space began in earnest when the Soviet Union sent its first Sputnik into orbit on October 4, 1957. The United States launched its first Explorer on January 31, 1958. It was not long before large numbers of manmade satellites were orbiting the earth, the sun, and the moon. The United States held the quantitative and scientific lead in this contest by sending up a greater number of objects and gaining more valuable scientific information from such probes. But the Soviet Union orbited heavier space

vehicles and scored such spectacular firsts as photographing the far side of the moon and launching a space probe to the planet Venus. Russia's greatest feat came on April 12, 1961, when the world's first "cosmonaut," Yuri Gagarin, went into orbit around the earth.

From then on, the United States and the Soviet Union engaged in a spectacular "race for outer space." While bigger and more sophisticated space vehicles were carrying teams of "astronauts" on more extended orbital flights, unmanned satellites made their first landings on the moon and relayed back valuable information. America's greatest triumph came on July 20, 1969, when astronaut Neil A. Armstrong became the first man to set foot on the moon. Subsequent lunar landings in 1971 and 1972 brought back a wealth of scientific information. Meanwhile the United States and the Soviet Union were extending their unmanned space probes to Venus, Mercury, Mars, and Jupiter.

The implications of these extraordinary advances were far-reaching indeed. Within the next hundred years, it is said, voyages to the moon will become commonplace, and luxury hotels will cater to travelers who have come to admire the dramatic scenery. There will be large numbers of satellites orbiting the earth, serving as way-stations to the moon and the planets. Population pressure on earth will ultimately be relieved by giant space ships accommodating more than ten thousand people. To the layman these and other fantastic schemes still would seem to belong in the realm of science fiction. But those who talk about them are among the world's leading scientists.

For the time being, however, the main concern is with developments closer to home, in the space immediately surrounding the earth. It is here that space research may yield important economic and military advantages. Satellites are already being used for communication and reconnaissance. The military potential and danger of satellites are obvious. The nation that controls outer space will control the world. In this connection there have been some encouraging developments. In 1966 the United States and Russia agreed to limit their space exploration to peaceful uses and to ban weapons of mass destruction from outer space. Six years later, the two nations began formulating plans that would lead to joint ventures into outer space, to begin in 1974.

THE NUCLEAR REVOLUTION

The race for outer space had two sides. It spurred the leading contenders on to revolutionary scientific advances; but at the same time it created a potential hazard in international relations. The same potential for good and evil prevailed in another phase of competition, the nuclear race. Here the immediate stakes were higher and the alternatives more fearful. Thanks to atomic energy, twentieth-century man has within his power the final perfection or the total obliteration of his civilization.

The 1952 test of the hydrogen bomb in the Pacific left a depression on the ocean floor a mile in diameter and nearly 200 feet deep.

The Nuclear Arms Race

The nuclear revolution burst upon the world on August 6, 1945, when the first atomic bomb—equivalent to 20,000 tons of TNT—was exploded over the Japanese city of Hiroshima. This was only the beginning. Seven years later, in 1952, the United States exploded the first hydrogen bomb over the Bikini Atoll in the Pacific. Its power was a thousand times greater than that of the first atomic bomb. Even this was not the ultimate. Scientists claim that a country capable of manufacturing megaton bombs, reckoned in millions of tons of TNT, can also produce gigaton bombs, measured in billions of tons. The methods of delivering these frightful weapons, meanwhile, have been perfected to the point that intercontinental ballistic missiles, armed with nuclear warheads and traveling at supersonic speeds, can drop their lethal cargoes on targets thousands of miles away.

For a while after 1945 the United States held an atomic monopoly. But as the Soviet Union developed its own atomic bomb in 1949 and its hydrogen bomb in 1953, America lost its lead. Since then the "nuclear club" has grown to include Britain, France, and Communist China. The atomic race between the United States and Russia has turned into an atomic free-for-all, in which a nuclear attack might be launched from any quarter at any time. The only sure way of avoiding such disaster is through disarmament. But here achievements thus far have been small. A nuclear test ban treaty in 1963 and a non-proliferation treaty in 1968 tried to put limits on the indiscriminate testing and spread of nuclear weapons. But since neither France nor China would sign these treaties, their effectiveness was limited at best. More promising were the Strategic Arms Limitation Talks (SALT) initiated in 1969 between the United States and Russia in Helsinki and Vienna. Their first major achievement was a set of agreements limiting offensive and defensive strategic weapons. These agreements were signed during President Nixon's visit to Moscow in 1972.

Atoms for Peace

With efforts being concentrated on nuclear armaments, much less has been done to develop the peaceful possibilities of the atom. America's Atoms for Peace Program of 1953 was helpful in sponsoring atomic research among friendly nations, and Russia gave similar support to its allies. In 1956 an International Atomic Energy Agency was established at Vienna. The purpose of this body was to aid atomic projects in less developed countries by contributing fissionable materials and nuclear equipment. When it came to implementing this plan, however, Russia and the United States could not agree on the necessary safeguards to make sure that recipients would not use atomic materials for military purposes.

The greatest progress in peaceful atomic development has been in the generation of electric power and the desalinization of seawater. In 1963 the United States and Russia launched a joint nuclear program calling for limited exchange of scientists and scientific information. By 1974, the United States was still leading the rest of the world in nuclear power capacity, far in advance of its nearest contenders—Great Britain, the Soviet Union, West Germany, and Japan.

Competitive Coexistence

The development of nuclear power may well some day determine the outcome of the economic contest between capitalism and communism. In the years after the Second World War, the economic predominance of the United States, and later of West Germany and Japan, was generally recognized. But the communist world has challenged this lead. Communism today claims that it can defeat capitalism without a war, by peaceful economic competition alone. The Soviet Union has boasted repeatedly that in the foreseeable future it will outproduce the United States and that the communist world as a whole will outproduce the free world. While the timing may be too optimistic, the challenge itself, in the opinion of some experts, is not. Russia has greater mineral resources than the United States; it has a well-trained and disciplined labor force; and it can keep abreast of the latest scientific and technological developments.

The economic achievements of communism will be welcomed by anyone concerned with the eradication of poverty the world over. The only danger is that Communist successes will appeal to and sway the world's underdeveloped regions. If communism should provide an answer for their economic problems, these countries might disregard the loss of personal freedom that communism entails, especially since few of them have ever known such freedom.

THE REVOLUTION OF RISING EXPECTATIONS

The population of the underdeveloped countries of Asia, Africa, and Latin America in 1974 was almost three times that of Europe and North America. If present population trends continue, the nonwhite people of the world in the year 2000 will outnumber the whites by almost five to one. Rapid population growth, especially in poor countries, invariably leads to a lower standard of living. Yet the expectation of the masses everywhere is to share in the many benefits that modern technology has to offer.

This revolution of rising expectations, in order to succeed, needs outside help. The major aid to underdeveloped lands thus far has come from the United States. This foreign aid was a heavy burden on the American taxpayer and in time threatened the country's balance of payments. A few nations, notably France and Great Britain, also joined in helping backward areas. Yet the cost of foreign aid is such that it will have to be borne by all advanced nations of the world.

Communist aid programs did not get under way until 1954, when the Soviet Union extended its first credits to underdeveloped countries. Communist China also began to aid some of its neighbors, although it could ill afford to do so. Communist aid was usually given as long-term credits for "trade not aid," a form of assistance preferred by most recipients. Although no nation has yet embraced communism as a result of such aid alone, Communist support has strengthened antiwestern or neutralist tendencies in many countries. To help the poorer nations stand on their own feet and develop a political and economic order suited to their needs is one of the greatest challenges before the world today.

The War on Poverty

The revolution of rising expectations, at first confined to the world's backward regions, in time also made itself felt in the United States. While the government was feeding people in faraway lands, millions of its own citizens went hungry; and while America was helping to improve housing conditions abroad, millions of Americans lived in slums and ghettos. It was primarily among minorities—black, Spanish-, Mexican-, and Indian-Americans—that these economic and social injustices prevailed. In response to the growing militancy of the black community, war was finally declared on poverty. Such a war had to be fought on a broad front—from health and housing to education and employment—in order to ensure a decent living for all. Much of racial prejudice is rooted in economic injustice. To eradicate one will help overcome the other.

Cesar Chavez led a boycott of grapes in 1968 in order to obtain better working conditions for Mexican-American migrant farm workers.

Women's Liberation

The success of militants in helping improve conditions of the black community encouraged other deprived groups to raise their voices against economic and social injustice born of prejudice. The most effective such protest was the women's liberation movement. The agitation for women's rights gained momentum in the early 1970s and won some long-overdue concessions for America's "disadvantaged majority." In the economic sphere, jobs traditionally reserved for men began to be opened to women and the demand of equal pay for equal work was beginning to be heeded. In colleges and universities, there was a trend toward coeducation. In everyday life, the equality of women was symbolized by the growing acceptance of *Ms.* as equivalent to the marital ambiguity of *Mr.* To provide a constitutional basis for women's rights, Congress in 1972 passed an Equal Rights Amendment. But it ran into the refusal of many state legislatures to ratify it.

MAN IN THE NUCLEAR AGE

The major challenges of our time— population explosion, conquest of outer space, nuclear revolution, and revolution of rising expectations—if met imaginatively and courageously, could easily help make the better world that man has dreamed of for so long. So far, however, rather than increase man's happiness, these revolutionary challenges and changes seem to have aggravated his tensions and fears.

Foremost among these fears is the dread of war. Ever since the Second World War statesmen have tried to banish this fear by finding ways of abolishing armaments. They are still trying. Meanwhile, psychologists claim that the ultimate cause of war does not lie in political and ideological rivalries but in man himself, in the human tendency toward aggression. Recent discoveries in the study of human relations seem to hold some cause for hope. According to social scientists, within the next century man will learn more about himself than

Women began to speak out in the women's liberation movement of the seventies.

he has in his whole previous history. He will discover not only the causes and cures of sickness and pain but the causes and cures of hate and aggression. He will at long last learn how to live in peace with his fellow man.

The Biological Revolution

While man is learning more about his inner life and motivations, he is also learning more about his physical being. Biology is making discoveries that may deeply affect and alter human existence. Some of these discoveries—artificial insemination, the transplantation of human organs, and the use of drugs to control moods and feelings—are already being put to use. Other innovations—test-tube babies, the postponement of death, mind control, even the creation of life from inert materials—are still in the experimental stage. In their sum total, the discoveries that biology holds in store amount to a veritable Biological Revolution.

The ethical questions raised by discoveries and practices that so completely change the traditional pattern of human existence are staggering. They have led some biologists to question whether man is ready to tamper with his heredity. But meanwhile the experiments in the laboratories continue.

The Mind Perplexed

An avalanche of unprecedented changes crowded into a span of a single generation has left most people confused and bewildered. In their search for understanding they have turned to a variety of old and new doctrines, none of which seems to provide the inner security they are looking for. The temper of our time is a mixture of anticipation and apprehension, optimism and pessimism, confidence and anxiety.

The philosophy of existentialism well illustrates this blend of hope and despair. Its antecedents go back to the nineteenth century, but its vogue dates from the Second World War. The existentialist maintains that the individual, rather than the abstract concept of humanity, constitutes true reality. He affirms the loneliness of man in a strange and hostile world. Such loneliness, far from leading to desperation, is seen as a challenge, a call to action, since "man's destiny is within himself."

While some people are searching for a new philosophy to fit a new age, others find existing doctrines sufficient to their needs. To the true communist believer, Marxist doctrine still supplies ready-made answers to most problems. He has nothing to fear, his leaders tell him, since history is on his side. There was a time when communism had a large following in the West, especially among intellectuals. But most of these have long since become disillusioned, and new converts to communism in the free world are few. Instead, a modified form of humane socialism has gained ground among the so-called New Left. Its adherents are equally opposed to American capitalism and the bureaucratized communism of the Soviet Union.

Communism's one-time rival, fascism, also has lost most of the following it once had in the West. One of its ingredients, nationalism, is still a potent force, especially in the newly independent nations of Asia and Africa. Where it is used by unscrupulous leaders for selfish ends, nationalism rivals communism as a danger to world peace.

Some of the ground lost by communism and fascism has been reclaimed by religion. There are many reasons for this religious revival, foremost among them the widely felt need for some central belief, some principle of authority, in time of great intellectual and emotional stress. The return to religion has taken many different forms and has involved not only a revival of interest in the traditional faiths of the West but a new interest on the part of many westerners in the religions of the East. A noteworthy trend among western religions in recent years has been the effort of religious leaders to overcome age-old differences and to work toward religious unity.

The Revolt of Youth

These are some of the ways in which men are trying to cope with their feelings of uncertainty and anxiety. There are others. One large segment of society—those in the younger generation—has been particularly shaken by the vicissitudes of a world they had no part in making. During the 1950s, young people everywhere were reproached by their elders for the passivity with which they faced the turmoil of the times. There were some "beatniks" and "angry young men," but they were exceptions in an otherwise "quiet generation."

All this changed during the sixties. As students began to rebel against society, not only in the United States but the world over, the older generation was faced with a new cause for concern in an already deeply troubled world. Most of the unrest was centered in the world's large universities, where huge enrollments, combined with antiquated regulations, tended to dehumanize education. But from the campuses of the "multiversities" the revolt spread to the schools and into the streets. Although the aims of the youthful rebels differed from place to place, they were united in their opposition to what they thought their elders stood for—meaningless discipline, social injustice, and senseless wars. Some of the young expressed their protest by withdrawal rather than action, ignoring traditional manners and mores and becoming "hippies." Others believed that only by attacking the existing "establishment" could they find a way to realize the better world of which they dreamed.

The older generation was put out and perplexed by a movement intent on biting the hand that fed it. Believers in authority hinted at a communist conspiracy and advocated repression. More realistic observers pointed out that the rebels, after all, were only a minority of their generation. But like any spontaneous outbreak of protest in the past, the revolt of the young deserved the serious attention it received from their more thoughtful elders. If ever there was a time for a reassessment of values, this was it.

The revolt of youth ended as suddenly as it had begun. In the early 1970s, the academic climate reverted once again to the placidity of the fifties. Yet the confrontation between the old and the young had not been wholly in vain. The youthful rebels could point to some

Parisian students demonstrating during "the days of May," 1968.

achievements. Not only had their agitation brought about many lasting changes within the universities, but youth's openness to new ideas, its freedom from prejudices, and its advocacy of a less inhibited life-style had jolted the older generation out of many of its traditional habits and attitudes. "Youth culture" had left its imprint on culture as a whole.

In the long-range perspective of human development, the present generation is of course only a mere incident. But in retrospect this age may some day appear as one of the most creative phases of history. Hopefully, it will stand out as an age in which the threat of a nuclear holocaust forced man to learn from his past mistakes; an age in which peaceful competition between rival ideologies brought forth undreamed-of economic progress; and an age in which fruitful debate and cooperation among peoples and races helped create a society in which such progress was shared by all.

Source of Illustrations

626: From Benson J. Lossing's *Pictorial History of the Civil War in the United States of America*
627: *t* United States War Department; *b* Library of Congress
628: Library of Congress
629: Collection of Carl S. Dentzel
630: Union Pacific Railroad Museum Collection
631: The Bettmann Archive
633: Culver Pictures
636: *t* From R. A. Foster's *Pictures for Little Englanders*, 1876, British Museum; *b* Ullstein-Bilderdienst
639: *t* Roger Viollet
b Brown Brothers
640: Library of Congress
641: The Bettmann Archive
642: The Bettmann Archive
643: Board of Missions of the Methodist Church

Chapter 28
646: Jean Villain
648: The Press Association, Ltd.
649: London Transport Executive
650: Brown Brothers
651: *t* Bulloz; *b* Mary Evans Picture Library
652: Trustees of the British Museum
653: Gernsheim Collection, Austin
655: The Granger Collection
656: Bibliothèque Nationale, Paris
657: Roger Viollet
659: The Bettmann Archive
660: Gernsheim Collection, Austin
661: Katherine Young/Archiv für Kunst und Geschichte
663: Sovfoto
664: Sovfoto
665: Culver Pictures
666: Brown Brothers
667: The Bettmann Archive
670: Gernsheim Collection, Austin
671: The Granger Collection

Chapter 29
674: Katherine Young
679: *t* New York Public Library, Picture Collection; *b* Radio Times Hulton
681: *t* Philadelphia Museum, Louis E. Stern Collection; *b* Tate Gallery, London
685: *t* United Press International
686: Historical Pictures Service
688: New York Public Library, Picture Collection
690: The Bettmann Archive
692: The Press Association Ltd.
693: United Press International
694: Radio Times Hulton

Chapter 30
698: United Press International
700: *t* Historical Pictures Service; *b* Imperial War Museum, London
703: Culver Pictures

704: National Archives, Washington, D.C.
705: "L'Illustration," Paris
706: Sovfoto
707: John Freeman
708: Imperial War Museum, London
709: National Archives, Washington, D.C.
710: Radio Times Hulton
713: "L'Illustration," Paris
715: The Bettmann Archive
717: Gernsheim Collection, Austin
718: Wide World Photos
720: *t* The Chase Manhattan Bank Museum of Money of the World; *b* United Press International
721: Radio Times Hulton

Chapter 31
724: New York Public Library, Dance Collection
726: *t* Gernsheim Collection, Austin; *b* Library of Congress
728: Culver Pictures
729: Brown Brothers
730: Radio Times Hulton
731: The Granger Collection
732: Wide World Photos
733: Dr. Erich Salomon
734: United Press International
735: Culver Pictures
736: Topix
737: *t* Earl Leaf, Rapho-Guillumette; *b* Wide World Photos
738: GEC-Marconi Electronics, Ltd.
739: *t* Ford Motor Co.; *m*, *b* ©1973 by National Housewares Manufacturers Assoc. From *The Housewares Story*
740: Clark University
741: Courtesy of Dr. Margaret Mead/ American Museum of Natural History
742: *t* Radio Times Hulton; *b* Brown Brothers
743: Museum of Modern Art, New York

Chapter 32
746: Zeitgeschichtliches Bildarchiv, Munich
748: Lenin Library, Moscow
749: *t* Sovfoto; *b* Radio Times Hulton
750: Sovfoto
751: British Museum/John Freeman
753: Brown Brothers
754: Wide World Photos
757: Library of Congress
758: United Press International
759: Gernsheim Collection, Austin
761: Zeitgeschichtliches Bildarchiv, Munich
762: Frederick Lewis
763: *b* Syndication International/Gernsheim Collection, Austin
764: United Press International
765: Gernsheim Collection, Austin
768: *t* CBS News; *b* Associated Press Photo, London
769: United Press International

Chapter 33
772: Sovfoto
774: Wide World Photos
775: *t* Topix; *b* Associated Press Photo, London
776: American Heritage Publishing Co.
777: Sovfoto
779: National Archives, Washington, D.C.
781: Keystone Press Agency
782: Official United States Coast Guard Photo
785: Imperial War Museum, London
786: Ben Roth Agency
787: United Nations
789: Fenno Jacobs, Black Star
791: Wide World Photos

Chapter 34
797: Axel Grosser
798: United Press International
799: Wide World Photos
800: Keystone Press Agency
801: Pictorial Parade
803: Wide World Photos
804: United Press International
805: United Press International
806: *t* Wide World Photos; *b* Wide World Photos
807: United Nations
809: Erich Lessing, Magnum Photos
811: Wide World Photos
812: Eastfoto
813: Wide World Photos
814: Marilyn Silverstone, Magnum Photos, Inc.
816: Andrew Bailey, Transworld Features Syndicate
818: United Press International
820: Transworld Features Syndicate
821: White House Photograph

Epilogue
824: Ben Ross
827: NASA
828: U.S. Atomic Energy Commission
830: Daniel S. Brody, Editorial Photocolor Archives
831: J. P. Laffont, Sygma
832: Bruno Barbey, Magnum Photos, Inc.

List of Maps

Index

Index

War of the Austrian Succession, 506, 507–08; War of 1866, 607–09
Austria-Hungary, 604, 647, 652, 675; First World War, 694–95, 699–703, 705, 707, 708, 711; in 19th century, 659–61; in 20th-century, 659–61, 689–92 (*see also* Austria; Hungary)
authoritarianism, 747, 759–60, 806
Autobiography (Cellini), 349, 356
Avars, 166, 183
Averroës (ibn-Rushd), 302
Avicenna (ibn-Sina), 302
Avignon, 272
Ayub Khan, Mohammed, 811
Aztec Empire, 400

B
Baalim, 19
Babeuf, "Gracchus," 535
Babur, 326
Babylon, 6, 7, 22
Babylonian Captivity, 22, 272, 344
Babylonian civilization, 5–8, 45 (*see also* Mesopotamia)
Bach, Johann Sebastian, 493
Bacon, Francis, 475–76, 478
Bacon, Roger, 264
Bactria, 54
Badoglio, Pietro, 781
Bagehot, Walter, 648; quoted, 634
Baghdad, 174, 176, 301, 310
Baghdad Pact, 814
Bakunin, Mikhail, 591, 617, 650
balance of power: in 18th century, 497–99; Italian city-states, 347; in 19th century, 538, 540, 542, 595, 612; nuclear, 817, 819; in 16th century, 348 (*see also* Cold War)
Balboa, Vasco de, 399
Baldwin, Count of Flanders, 307
Baldwin, Stanley, 733
Baldwin of Lorraine, 305
Balfour Declaration, 735
Balkan League, 692
Balkan Wars, 692–93
Balkans, 158, 159, 167, 675–78, 689–93; Second World War, 775–76; Slavs in, 161, 166
Balzac, Honoré de, 590, 670
Bancroft, George, 621
Bangladesh, 325, 811
Bank of England, 436, 460
banking: France, 537; growth of, 230–31; Italian, 276, 348, 365 (*see also* economy)
Bannockburn, battle of, 267, 281
Baptists, 385, 455
Barbados, 439
barometer, invention of, 476
baroque style, 449, 450, 451, 480–81
Barras, Paul, 536

Bartòk, Béla, 743
Basham, A. L., quoted, 127
Basil I, Byzantine Emperor, 299
Basil II, Byzantine Emperor, 303
Basle, Council of, 376
Bastille, fall of, 527
Batista, Fulgencio, 807
Bavaria, 156, 181, 187, 195, 432, 463, 507, 508, 565, 714
Bay of Pigs invasion, 819
Bayle, Pierre, 353, 483
Baylen, battle of, 540
Beauharnais, Josephine (*see* Josephine, Empress)
Beauvais Cathedral, 232
Bebel, August, 659
Beccaria, Cesare di, 488
Becker, Carl L., quoted, 488
Becket, Thomas, 237
Belgium, 406, 539, 680, 681, 790, 815; First World War, 695, 700; in 19th century, 546, 557, 559, 575–76, 582, 584; postwar (1919–1939), 718, 719; Second World War, 774
Bell, Alexander Graham, 622
Bellamy, Edward, 632
Belshazzar, 22
Benedict, Ruth, 741; quoted, 12
Benedict XV, Pope, 704
Benedict of Nursia, St., 150–52
Benedictine Rule, 150–51, 219
Benelux countries (*see* Belgium; Luxembourg; Netherlands)
Beneš, Eduard, 728, 767, 790
Bengalis, 811
Bentham, Jeremy, 578–79
Bentinck, Lord William, 634
Beowulf, 200
Berbers, 160, 175
Berchtold, Leopold von, 694
Berlin, 786, 788, 819–21; Congress of, 676; Treaty of, 719
Bernard of Clairvaux, St., 219–20, 221, 223, 224
Bernini, Giovanni, 481
Bernstein, Eduard, 649–50
Berri, Charles, Duke of, 554, 556
Bessarabia, 597, 676, 787
Bethmann Hollweg, Theobald von, 707
Bhagavadgita, 126
Biafra, Republic of, 816
Bibl, Viktor, quoted, 548
Bible: Erasmus and, 376, 377; fundamentalism and, 669; King James, 428; Luther's translation, 380; origins, 668; in 16th century, 376–77; Vulgate, 119; Wiclif and, 279, 280
Bidault, Georges, 799
Bill of Rights, English, 458
birth control, 580, 826

bishops, 106, 108, 149, 153–55, 180, 212, 215–17, 242, 373
Bismarck (German battleship), 776
Bismarck, Otto von, 595, 603, 605–12, 657–59, 675–78
Bizerte, 781
Black Death, 275, 280
Black Hand, 694
Black Sea, 595, 597
Black Stone, 169, 171
Black Thursday, 730
Blacks, in U.S., 628, 629, 804–05
Blanc, Louis, 561
Blanqui, Auguste, 586
Blenheim, battle of, 453
Blitzkreig, 773
Bloody Sunday, 664
Blum, Léon, 734
Boccaccio, Giovanni, 350, 355
Bodin, Jean, 428; quoted, 417, 418
Boer War, 682, 688
Boethius, Anicius Manlius Severinus, 144–46
Bohemia, 229, 291, 361–62, 430, 462, 463, 563, 660, 768
Bokhara, 175
Boleyn, Anne, 385, 386, 408
Bologna, Concordat of, 370, 411
Bolshevik Revolution (*see* Russian Revolution)
Bolsheviks, 663, 705–07, 747–49
Bonaparte, Joseph, 539, 540
Bonaparte, Napoleon (*see* Napoleon I, Emperor)
Bonaventura, St., 250, 264
Boniface, St., 181–82
Boniface VIII, Pope, 270–71
Borgia, Cesare, 363
Borgia, Roderigo (*see* Alexander VI, Pope)
Borodino, battle of, 541
boroughs, 199–200
Bosnia, 660, 677, 690, 691
Bossuet, Jacques Bénigne, quoted, 449
Boston Tea Party, 518
Boulanger, Georges, 655
Bourbon dynasty, 418, 453, 541, 556
Boxer Rebellion, 639, 686
Boyne, Battle of the, 460
Bracton, Henry de, 257
Brahe, Tycho, 477
Brahma, 126, 132
Brahmans, 126, 127, 131, 133, 320, 322
Brandenburg-Prussia, 432, 454, 463–66 (*see also* Prussia)
Brandt, Willy, 800–01
Brave New World (Huxley), 739
Brazil, 407, 439, 632
Breasted, James H., quoted, 9

Charlemagne, 156, 182–87, 192, 301
Charles I, Emperor of Austria, 660, 703, 708
Charles I, King of England, 424, 425–26, 428, 430
Charles I, King of France, 187
Charles II, King of England, 427, 455
Charles II, King of Spain, 452–53
Charles III, King of Spain, 512
Charles IV, Holy Roman Emperor, 361
Charles V, Holy Roman Emperor, 367–68, 370, 379, 381, 386, 402, 405
Charles V, King of France, 288
Charles VI, Holy Roman Emperor, 504
Charles VI, King of France, 285, 366
Charles VII, King of France, 285, 288–89, 366
Charles VIII, King of France, 366
Charles IX, King of France, 411
Charles X, King of France, 557
Charles XII, King of Sweden, 466, 468
Charles Albert, King of Sardinia, 562–63
Charles of Anjou, 261, 366
Charles the Bold, Duke of Burgundy, 366
Charles the Great (*see* Charlemagne)
Charles Martel, 156, 176, 179, 180, 181, 192
Charles of Orléans, 292
Charlotte, Grand Duchess of Luxembourg, 801
Charter Oath, 641
Chartist Movement, 567
Chartist Petition of 1848, 566
Chartres Cathedral, 233
Chaucer, Geoffrey, 266, 282, 292, 293, 355
Chavez, Cesar, 830
Cheap Clothes and Nasty (Kingsley), 590–91
Cheka, 747
Chiang Kai-shek, 737, 738, 765, 793
child labor, 577, 578, 582
Chile, 632, 807
Chilperic I, King of the Franks, 147
Ch'in, 137
Chin dynasty, 334
China, 3, 248, 444, 715; ancient, 123–24, 133–41; Chou dynasty, 134–37; Confucianism, 135–36; exploration, 295, 395; First World War, 711; Han dynasty, 137, 139–41, 330; Manchu dynasty, 636, 638, 640; Ming dynasty, 339; Mongols in, 310–12, 336–38; in 19th century, 614, 621, 636–39; nomad rulers, 140–41; Opium War,

636–37; postwar (1919–1939), 737–38, 760, 764–65, 779; revolution of 1911, 640; science in, 293, 294; Shang dynasty, 134; Sino-Japanese War, 638–39, 642, 688; Sui dynasty, 329; Sung dynasty, 310, 334–36; Taiping Rebellion, 638; T'ang dynasty, 329–34 (*see also* Nationalist China; People's Republic of China)
Chola kingdom, 322
Chou dynasty, 134–37
Chou En-Lai, 821
Christian Democratic Party, Italian, 801
Christian Democratic Union, German, 800
Christian Socialism, 590–91, 652
Christianity, 18, 117, 159; beginnings of, 89–91; in China, 338; doctrine of the Trinity, 108; early organization of, 106; Islam and, 172; in Japan, 341; Mongols and, 311–12; Monophysitism, 164; neoplatonism and, 96; in Roman Empire, 100, 104, 106–09, 112; spread of, 140, 214; Zoroastrianism and, 24 (*see also* names of religions)
Chronicle of Moissac (tr. Bryce), 185
Chu Hsi, 334, 339
Chu Teh, 737
Chuang Tzu, quoted, 136
churches (*see* architecture, Christian; cathedrals)
Churchill, Sir Winston, 774, 782, 785, 787, 797; quoted, 776
Cicero, Marcus Tullius, 71–72, 75, 76, 82, 96, 350, 351, 483
Cid, Le (Corneille), 450
Cimon, 42
Cistercian Order, 219
cities (*see* city-states; towns; urbanization)
City of God, The (St. Augustine), 115, 119
city-states: Greek, 33–35, 46–49; Italian, 346–48; Mesopotamian, 6–8; Philistine, 16; Roman, 88
Civil Constitution of the Clergy, 530
Civil Rights Act of 1964, 804
civil service: in China, 330, 335, 336, 339; in Roman Empire, 87
civil war: American, 627–29; in China, 140, 737, 765; in England, 285, 368, 426; in France, 288, 411–13; in Greece, 789, 791; in India, 133; in Netherlands, 406; in Nigeria, 816; in Pakistan, 811; in Roman Republic, 74; in Russia (15th century), 315; in Spain, 762–64; in U.S.S.R., 748

Civilization of the Renaissance in Italy, The (Burckhardt), 352
Clarendon, Edward Hyde, Earl of, 455, 456
Clarendon Code, 455
Clarissa Harlowe (Richardson), 493
Clark Memorandum, 737
classical economists, 580–81
classicism, 492
Claudius, Roman Emperor, 84–85
Cleisthenes, 38
Clemenceau, Georges, 655, 703, 709, 710
Clement V, Pope, 271, 272
Clement VII, Pope, 278, 363, 385, 386
Cleopatra, Queen of Egypt, 76, 77
clergy, 249; appointment of, 369–70; bourgeoisie and, 230; Charlemagne and, 183, 184, 186; in 16th century, 373–74; taxation of, 243, 254, 261, 262, 270, 369–70 (*see also* bishops)
Clermont, Council of, 217
Cleveland, Grover, 685
Cleves, 464
Clive, Robert, 509
clock, invention of, 295
Clouds, The (Aristophanes), 44
Clovis, King of the Franks, 154–55
Cluny, 214, 219
Cobden-Chevalier treaty, 599
Code (Justinian), 165
Code of Hammurabi, 7
Code Napoléon, 537, 540
coexistence, 796, 817, 818, 821, 829
coinage: invention of, 30; Roman, 118
Colbert, Jean Baptiste, 442, 448
Cold War, 796–97, 803, 810, 817–21; beginnings of, 789–90; in Far East, 792–93; United Nations and, 791
Coligny, Gaspard de, 411, 412
collectivization, 751
Colombia, 686
Colombo Plan for Cooperative Development, 813
Colonial Reformers, 633
colonies: Belgian, 681, 815; British, 439–43, 502, 508–10, 517–19, 633–35, 679–82, 684, 687–88, 737, 798, 816; Dutch, 439–41, 681; French, 439–42, 508, 509, 599–600, 679–81, 684, 736, 798–99; German, 679, 684, 710; Greek, 30; Italian, 681; in North America, 440–43, 502, 508–10, 517–19; Portuguese, 439–40, 443, 816; Russian, 443–44, 683–84; Spanish, 439–40, 555; U.S., 684–86, 737 (*see also* imperialism)
Colosseum, Rome, 92, 94
Columban, St., 155
Columbus, Christopher, 293, 363, 368, 398

Combination Acts, 558, 584
Cominform, 790
Comintern, 714, 719, 747, 749, 790
Commentaries on the Gallic War (Caesar), 74
commerce (*see* trade and commerce)
Commercial Revolution, 501, 571
Committee of General Defense, 534
Committee for General Security, 534
Committee of National Liberation, 786
Committee of Public Safety, 533, 534, 535
Commodus, Roman Emperor, 97–98
Common Market, 798, 799, 802
Commonwealth of Nations (*see* British Commonwealth)
communism, 586, 758, 759; in China (*see* People's Republic of China); in Cuba, 807; postwar (1945–1973), 789, 829, 831; in Russia (*see* Union of Soviet Socialist Republics); in Southeast Asia, 812–13; in U.S., 803 (*see also* Communist Party; Marxism)
Communist China (*see* People's Republic of China)
Communist Information Bureau (*see* Cominform)
Communist League, 586
Communist Manifesto (Marx and Engels), 567–68, 586, 587–88
Communist Party: Chinese, 737; French, 734, 798; German, 726; Italian, 801; Russian, 750, 807–08
Comneni dynasty, 304–05
compass, 395; Chinese, 302; invention of, 334
Compromise of 1850, 626
compurgation, 147
Comte, Auguste, 665, 740
concentration camps, 778
Concert of Europe, 548, 595, 612, 693
Concordat of 1801, 537–38, 655
Condorcet, Marie Jean, Marquis de, 489
Confederate States of America, 627
Confederation of the Rhine, 539
Conference of Ambassadors, 692
Conference of Independent African States, 817
Confessions (Rousseau), 550
Confessions (St. Augustine), 119
Confucianism, 124, 134–36, 331
Confucius, 134–36, 137, 139
Congo, 681, 815
Congregationalists, 385, 455
Congress Party, Indian, 736
Conrad, Joseph, 742
conscription system: French, 533; Russian, 468–69
conservatism, 553

Conservative Party: British, 614, 652, 653, 725, 733, 797; German, 658
Considerations on Representative Government (Mill), 579
Consolation of Philosophy (Boethius), 145
Constance, Council of, 360–61, 362, 376, 379
Constantine, Roman Emperor, 107–09, 154, 181
Constantine XI, Byzantine Emperor, 317
Constantinople, 109, 117, 159, 166, 300, 308; sack of, 306, 307; Turks in, 317; viking attacks on, 190
constitution: American, 487, 520, 624; Athenian, 41; Austrian, 604, 606; English, 427, 486; French, 528–31, 535, 542, 579; German, 566; Italian, 661; Japanese, 641; Polish, 513; Prussian, 604–05; Roman, 58, 355; Russian, 749–50
constitutional monarchy: in England, 422, 454–60; in France, 530–31; in Germany, 566
containment, policy of, 789
Continental System, 539–40, 574
Coolidge, Calvin, 729
Cooper, James Fenimore, 621
Copernicus, Nicolaus, 294, 475, 478
Coral Sea, battle of the, 783
Corbulo, Graeus Domitius, 85
Corcyra, 47
Corfu, 715, 755
Corinth, 30, 47, 64
Corn Laws, 558, 567, 630, 654
Corneille, Pierre, 450, 481, 492
Corporations Act of 1828, 558
Corpus Juris, 165, 166, 224
Corsica, 64
Cortenuova, battle of, 260
Cortes, 369
Cortés, Hernando, 400
Cossacks, 443–44
cotton industry, 573
Council of the Areopagus, 38
Council of Blood, 406
Council of Constance (*see* Constance, Council of)
Council of Five Hundred, 38, 41
Council of People's Commissars, 706
Council of Ten, 348
Counter Reformation (*see* Catholic Reformation)
Courageous, 773
Courçon, Robert de, quoted, 247
Courland, 702
Courtier, The (Castiglione), 354
courts (*see* judicial system)
Craig, Gordon A., quoted, 676
Cranmer, Thomas, 386, 387
Crassus, 71, 72, 74

Crécy, battle of, 282
credit systems, 396
Crete, 3, 11–13, 29, 299, 687, 690, 776
Crimea, 514
Crimean War, 595–98, 601, 612, 616
Crispi, Francesco, 661
Critique of Pure Reason (Kant), 494
Croats, 563, 564, 568, 660
Cro-Magnon man, 4
Crompton, Samuel, 573
Cromwell, Oliver, 426–27
Cromwell, Thomas, 386
Crusades: Albigensian, 244–45, 252; First, 217–19, 305; Fourth, 307–08; influence of, 308–09; Second, 220, 306; Sixth, 256; Third, 306–07
Cuba, 555, 628, 685–86, 807–08, 819–20
Cuban missile crisis, 807, 808, 820
Cunard, Samuel, 575
cuneiform writing, 6
Curaçao, 439
Curie, Marie, 742
Curie, Pierre, 742
currency (*see* coinage; money)
Curzon, Lord, 621
Curzon Line, 748, 786
Cuza, Prince Alexander, 597
Cynics, 53
Cyprus, 299, 404, 676
Cyrillic alphabet, 17
Cyrus, King of Persia, 23
Czechoslovakia, 47, 190, 712, 716; German conquest of, 767–68; postwar (1919–1939), 727–28; postwar (1945–1973), 789, 790, 809
Czechs, 361, 563, 660, 707, 708

D

Dacia, 87
"Daily Telegraph Affair," 658
daimyos, 341
Daladier, Édouard, 734, 768
Dalhousie, James Ramsay, Earl of, 634
Damascus, 174
Danegeld, 201
Danes, in England, 201
Daniel, 22
Dante Alighieri, 220, 264–65, 350
Danton, Georges-Jacques, 532, 534
Darien, 787
Darius, King of Persia, 38, 56
Darlan, Jean, 775, 781
Darnley, Henry Stewart, Lord, 409
Darwin, Charles, 666–67, 669; quoted, 668
Darwinism, 666–69
Das Kapital (Marx), 587, 589
Daudet, Léon, 657
David (Donatello), 356
David, King of Hebrews, 19

da Vinci, Leonardo (*see* Leonardo da Vinci)

Dawes, Charles G., 720

Dawes Plan, 720–21

D-Day, 782

de Gaulle, Charles, 798, 799

De Multro Karoli Comitis Flandriarum (Galbert of Bruges), 191

De rerum natura (Lucretius), 82, 83

De Valera, Eamon, 736

Decameron (Boccaccio), 350

Deccan, 322, 325

Decembrist Revolt, 556

Declaration of Independence, American, 519

Declaration of Indulgence, 455, 457

Declaration of the Rights of Man, 528–29, 530

Decline of the West, The (Spengler), 721, 741

Decretum (Gratian), 225

Defensor pacis (Marsilius of Padua), 279

Dehio, Ludwig, quoted, 658

Deism, 489–90

Delcassé, Théophile, 688, 689

Delhi sultanate, 320, 325, 326

Delian League, 40, 41

democracy, 49, 390, 520, 579, 580, 617, 713, 727, 756; Athenian, 41, 42; British, 653, 725; growth of, 647–48; Indian, 810; theory of, 491–92; U.S., 624; West German, 801

Democracy in America (Tocqueville), 621

Democratic Party, U.S., 626, 629, 631, 733

Democritus, 45

Demosthenes of Athens, 49

Denmark, 466, 539, 568, 790, 802; Schleswig-Holstein question, 606–07; Second World War, 774; Thirty Years' War, 430–31

depression (*see* Great Depression)

Descartes, René, 414, 475, 476, 477, 478, 479, 483, 484, 487

Descent of Man, The (Darwin), 666, 667

Dialogues (Plato), 48

Dias, Bartholomew, 396

Díaz, Porfirio, 632

Dickens, Charles, 590, 670

dictatorships (*see* absolutism; totalitarianism)

Dictatus Papae Gregorii VII (tr. Lewis), 216

Diderot, Denis, 487, 491, 512

Dido and Aeneas (Purcell), 481

Digenis Akritas, epic, 299

Digest, 165

Dingley Tariff Act of 1897, 630

Diocletian, Roman Emperor, 100, 103–04, 107

Directory, French, 535–36

Discourses on Livy (Machiavelli), 354

Disestablishment Act of 1869, 615

Disraeli, Benjamin, 590, 614, 615, 636, 652

Divine Comedy (Dante), 264, 265, 350

divine-right monarchy (*see* absolutism)

"dollar diplomacy," 686, 737

Domesday Book, 213, 235

Dominic, St., 249

Dominican Order, 249–50, 252, 263, 400

Dominican Republic, 686

Domitian, Roman Emperor, 86

Don Quixote (Cervantes), 414

Donatello, 356, 359

Donation of Constantine, 181, 353

Dorians, 16, 29–30

Dover, Treaty of, 456

Drake, Sir Francis, 409

Dravidians, 124, 125

Dred Scott decision (1857), 626

Dreikaiserbund, 675

Dreiser, Theodore, 632, 742

Dreyfus, Alfred, 655–56

Dreyfus case, 655–56, 681

Drusus Senior, 81

Dual Alliance of 1879, 676–77, 678

Dual Monarchy (*see* Austria-Hungary)

Dulles, John Foster, 818

Duma, 647, 664, 705

Dumouriez, Charles François, 533

Dunkirk, 774; Treaty of, 790

Dupleix, Joseph, 509

Durham, John George Lambton, Earl of, 633

Dutch East India Company, 407, 439

Dutch East Indies, 783

Dutch Netherlands (*see* Netherlands)

Dying Gaul of Pergamum, 52

E

Eakins, Thomas, 631

East African Community, 817

East Germany, 788–89, 800, 820

East Pakistan, 811

East Prussia, 701

Easter Rebellion of 1916, 736

Eastern Roman Empire, 114–15, 116, 117, 143, 144, 158–67 (*see also* Byzantine Empire)

Eastern Roumelia, 677, 678

Economic Consequences of the Peace, The (Keynes), 720

Economic Survey (Quesnay), 490

economy: Austrian, 660, 728; Babylonian, 7; Brandenburg-Prussia, 465; Chinese, 140, 811; Egyptian, 9;

English, 285, 460, 501, 653–54, 733, 797–98; European, 205–09, 252, 254, 275–76, 365, 435–39, 499–501, 559; French, 419–20, 448, 501, 523–24, 537, 656, 725–26, 733–34, 799; German, 658, 726–27, 756; Indian, 129, 810; Italian, 661–62, 754, 801; Japanese, 641; Marx on, 587–90; mercantilism, 435, 437–38, 490; Roman, 93–94, 99, 100, 104, 110–12; Russian, 662–63, 808; Spanish, 403–04; U.S., 623, 684–85, 729–32, 805 (*see also* Great Depression; taxation)

Eddington, Sir Arthur, 742

Edessa, 305, 306

Edict of Nantes (*see* Nantes, Edict of)

Edict of Restitution, 431

Edict of Toleration, 108

education, 146, 279; cathedral schools, 224, 225; Charlemagne and, 183; Chinese, 135; democracy and, 647; 18th-century, 550; English, 647; French, 537, 583, 647; German, 647; Humanism and, 351; Italian, 647; liberalism and, 582–83; 19th-century, 551, 582–83; Russian, 617, 647; 12th-century, 223–25; universities, 247–49

Education Act (French), 583

Education Act of 1870 (English), 614, 647

Edward, Prince of Wales (Black Prince), 282

Edward I, King of England, 258, 259, 266–68, 281

Edward II, King of England, 281, 287

Edward III, King of England, 281–82, 287

Edward VI, King of England, 386

Edward VIII, King of England, 733

Edward the Confessor, King of England, 201, 211

Egypt, 3, 45, 64, 317, 536, 736; Alexander the Great in, 50; Arabic conquest of, 173; Assyrian conquest of, 21; British and, 636; emergence of civilization in, 8–9; Fatimid dynasty in, 304; Hellenistic Era, 52; Hyksos invasion of, 11; Mamelukes in, 308, 310; Middle Kingdom, 9, 11; Monophysitism, 164; New Kingdom, 14–16; in 19th century, 556, 679–81; Old Kingdom, 9–11; postwar (1945–1973), 813–14, 819; Second World War, 775

Einstein, Albert, 742

Eisenhower, Dwight D., 781, 782, 804, 818, 819

Eisenhower Doctrine, 814, 819

Elba, Island of, 541

Eleanor of Aquitaine, 235

Elijah, 19
Eliot, T. S., 742
Elisha, 19
Elizabeth, Empress of Russia, 511
Elizabeth I, Queen of England, 387, 406, 408–10, 423–24
Emancipation Bill of 1829, 558
Emancipation Edict, 616, 617
Emancipation Proclamation, 628
Emerson, Rupert, quoted, 810
Ems dispatch, 610
Enabling Act, 757
enclosure movement, 572–73
Encyclopedia (Diderot), 487
Engels, Friedrich, 586, 587, 589, 649; quoted, 578
England: Anglo-Saxon, 115, 116, 152, 199–202; Black Death, 280; Elizabethan, 408–11; feudalism, 195, 201–02; in 15th century, 368; in 14th century, 280–87; Glorious Revolution, 457–62, 470; Hundred Years' War, 281–82, 284–85; mercantilism, 438; Norman conquest, 202, 211–14; Peasants' Rebellion (1381), 280, 283; Puritan Rebellion, 425–26, 461; Restoration, 427–29; Roman Catholic Church in, 152–53; Roman conquest of, 73, 81, 84, 88; in 13th century, 237–38, 256–58, 266–68; towns, 208, 209; in 12th century, 235–37; viking invasions, 188, 190–91; War of the League of Augsburg, 452; War of the Spanish Succession, 453–54; Wars of the Roses, 285, 368 (see also Great Britain)
English Rebellion (see Puritan Rebellion)
Eniwetok, 783
enlightened despotism, 491, 511–17, 536, 538
Enlightenment, 484–92, 537, 538, 545, 550, 551, 553, 571, 578
Entente Cordiale, 689, 695
Epictetus, 96
Epicureans, 53
Epirus, 61, 62, 64
equestrians, Roman, 67, 93
Erasmus, 279, 353, 377, 380, 405; quoted, 376
Eratosthenes, 53
Erhard, Ludwig, 800
Eritrea, 681, 762
Ermak, 443
Escorial, 414
Essay Concerning the Human Understanding (Locke), 484
Essay on the Inequality of the Human Races (Gobineau), 668

Essay on the Principles of Population (Malthus), 580
Estates General, 269, 270, 288, 289, 369, 419, 447, 525–27
Estonia, 774
Ethelred the Ill-Counseled, King of England, 201
Ethics Demonstrated in the Geometrical Manner (Spinoza), 479
Ethiopia, 661, 681, 715, 762
Etruscans, 57, 58, 60, 61
Euclid, 53, 300
Eugene, Prince of Savoy, 453, 463, 464
Eugenius III, Pope, 220
EURATOM, 802
Euripides, 43, 44, 46
Europe, Council of, 802
European Atomic Energy Community (Euratom), 802
European Coal and Steel Community (ECSC), 802
European Economic Community (EEC, see Common Market)
European Recovery Community (ERP, see Marshall Plan)
Evans, Arthur, 11, 12
Evolutionary Socialism (Bernstein), 649
existentialism, 831
expansionism (see imperialism)
exploration: Chinese, 339; circumnavigation of globe, 394, 399; Dutch, 407; English, 409; French, 295; medieval, 295; Portuguese, 396–98, 399; reasons for, 395–96; Russian, 443; Spanish, 398–99 (see also colonies)
Explorer I, 819, 827
Eyck, Hubert van, 293
Eyck, Jan van, 293

F

Fabian Society, 649, 654
factory acts, 582
factory system, 435–36, 573
Far East, 683, 687, 688; Cold War, 792–93 (see also specific country)
farmers (see agriculture; peasants)
Fasci di Combattimento, 753
fascism, 727, 734, 747, 831; Italian, 752–55; Japanese, 759–60 (see also Nazism)
Fashoda crisis, 681, 688
Fatima, 304
Fatimid Caliphate, 304–06
February Revolution, 705
Federal Republic of Germany (see West Germany)
Fenian Brotherhood, 614

Ferdinand I, Emperor of Austria, 564
Ferdinand I, Holy Roman Emperor, 381, 402
Ferdinand II, Holy Roman Emperor, 430, 432, 463
Ferdinand of Aragon, 367, 368, 369, 375
Ferry, Jules, 655
Ferry Laws, 647
Fertile Crescent, 6, 13
feudalism, 201–02, 210, 301, 563, 564; Austrian, 516, 563; English, 195, 201–02; French, 191–95, 209, 238–39; German, 240–41; Japanese, 341, 640, 641
Feuerbach, Ludwig, 665
Ficino, Marsilio, 353
Fielding, Henry, 492
"Fifth Column," 759
"Final Solution," 778
finance (see banking; economy; money; taxation)
Finland, 774, 787
firearms, 282, 326, 335; development of, 294
First Balkan War, 692
First Crusade, 217–19, 305
First Hague Peace Conference, 686
First International, 650
First Memoir on Property (Proudhon), 591
"first treaty settlement," 637
First Triumvirate, 72–74
First World War, 693–95, 698–709
Fitzhugh, George, quoted, 625
Fiume, 710, 711, 716, 755
Five-Year Plans: Chinese, 811; U.S.S.R., 751, 807
Flanders, 207, 209, 238
Flanders, Count of, 194, 209, 214, 268
Flaubert, Gustave, 670
Flavian emperors, 85–86
Fleury, André de, 503
Florence, 346, 347, 348; Cathedral of, 356
Florida, 623
flying shuttle, 573
Fontane, Theodor, 670
Force and Matter (Büchner), 665
foreign aid programs, 810, 817, 830; lend-lease, 777, 779; Marshall Plan, 789, 790, 799, 802, 803
foreign policy: Brandenburg-Prussia, 465; Chinese, 811–12; English, 423, 424, 456, 459, 615; French, 560, 598–600, 798–99; German, 657–58; Italian, 755; Russian, 616; U.S., 555, 621, 624–25, 631, 632, 685–86, 789 (see also Cold War)
Formosa, 337, 639, 642, 793

Hanseatic League, 395
Harding, Warren G., 729
Hargreaves, James, 573
Harold, King of England, 211
Harper's Ferry, 626
Harsha, Rajah, 320, 322
Harun-al-Rashid, 301
Harvey, William, 476; quoted, 477
Hastings, battle of, 211
Haugwitz, Christian von, 508
Hauptmann, Gerhart, 670
Hausa-Fulanis, 816
Hawaii, 631, 685, 686
Hawkins, Sir John, 409
Hay, John, 686
Haydn, Joseph, 493
Haymarket Square riot, 630
Hay-Paunceforte Treaty, 686
Heath, Edward, 798
Hebrews, 16, 17–22, 23
Heckel, Erich, 743
Hegel, Georg Wilhelm Friedrich, 553
Hegira, 170
Heilbroner, Robert L., quoted, 589
Heligoland, 687
Hellenistic Era, 51–54
Heloïse, 223
Hemingway, Ernest, 742
Henlein, Konrad, 767
Henry I, King of England, 235
Henry I, King of Germany, 195, 213–14
Henry II, King of England, 235–37
Henry II, King of France, 411
Henry III, King of England, 256–59, 266, 281
Henry III, King of France, 411
Henry IV, Holy Roman Emperor, 216–17, 278
Henry IV, King of England, 284–85, 287, 366
Henry IV, King of France (of Navarre), 412, 413, 418–19
Henry V, Holy Roman Emperor, 217
Henry V, King of England, 288
Henry VI, Holy Roman Emperor, 242, 243
Henry VI, King of England, 285
Henry VII, King of England, 368
Henry VIII, King of England, 385–86, 387, 408, 423
Henry the Lion, Duke of Saxony and Bavaria, 241
Henry the Navigator, Prince, 396
Heraclitus, 45, 48
Heraclius, Roman Emperor, 166
Herder, Johann Gottfried von, 493–94
heresy, 243–45, 249, 252; Hussite, 361–62 (see also Arianism)
Herod, King of Judea, 80
Herodotus of Halicarnassus, 44–45

Herophilus, 53
Herriot, Edouard, 725
Herzegovina, 676, 677, 690, 691
Herzen, Alexander, 617, 663
Herzl, Theodor, 735
Hesiod, 31
Hetàiria Philikĕ, 555–56
Hideyoshi, Toyotomi, 341
hieroglyphics, 9
Hildebrand, 215 (see also Gregory VII, Pope)
Himmler, Heinrich, quoted, 778
Hincmar, Archbishop, quoted, 148
Hindemith, Paul, 743
Hindenburg, Paul von, 701, 702, 703, 704, 707, 757
Hinduism, 131, 320, 322–26, 328
Hiroshima, 784, 785, 828
historians: Byzantine, 299; Chinese, 331; Greek, 44–45, 47; Italian, 352; medieval, 233; Moslem, 317–18; 19th-century, 551–52; Roman, 66, 82, 95; 20th-century, 741; U.S., 621
Historical and Critical Dictionary (Bayle), 483
History of Civilization (Voltaire), 486
History of the Decline and Fall of the Roman Empire (Gibbon), 492
History of the Franks (Gregory of Tours), 147, 154
History of Jerusalem (Fulcher of Chartres), 218
History of the Peloponnesian War (Thucydides), 42
Hitler, Adolf, 47, 717, 751, 755–59, 761–69, 773–78, 782–83
Hittites, 13, 14–16
Hobbes, Thomas, 428–29, 461, 482
Hobsbawm, E. J., quoted, 571
Hobson, J. A., quoted, 643
Hogarth, William, 493
Hohenstaufen dynasty, 240–42; papal feud, 257, 259–62
Hohenzollerns, 464–66
Holbach, Paul d', 489
Holland (see Netherlands)
Holstein, Friedrich von, 688
Holy Alliance, 548
Holy Roman Empire, 196–97, 240–43, 259–62, 370, 430–33, 435, 462–64, 539, 546
Home Rule Bills, 653
Homer, 18, 27–28, 31, 124
Homer, Winslow, 631
Homestead Act of 1862, 629
Honegger, Arthur, 743
Hong Kong, 637
Honorius, Roman Emperor, 114–15
Hook, Sidney, quoted, 588
Hoover, Herbert, 730, 731
Horace, 82, 83

Horthy, Nicholas, 727
Hosea, 20
Hostiensis, quoted, 244
House of Commons, 287, 423, 425
House of Lords, 258, 287, 423, 426, 654
Hsuan-tsàng, 331
Hudson's Bay Territory, 454
Hugo, Victor, 590
Huguenots, 411–13, 419, 420, 442, 449, 460
Humanism, 352, 353, 357, 474, 482; Christian, 376–77, 380, 405; Italian, 350–51
Humbert I, King of Italy, 661
Hume, David, 493, 494
Hundred Years' War, 275, 281–82, 284–85, 288–89, 366
hundreds, 199–200
Hung Hsiu-ch'üan, 638
Hungary, 190, 291, 312–13, 370, 430, 462, 712, 713, 714, 716, 727; in 18th century, 507, 508; Habsburgs and, 463–64; independence, 708; in 19th century, 559, 563, 564–65, 568, 604; postwar (1919–1939), 755, 759; postwar (1945–1973), 787, 789, 808–09, 819; Second World War, 775; Turks in, 316, 317 (see also Austria-Hungary)
Huns, 112–13, 116, 133, 140, 310, 320, 328
Hunyadi, John, 316
Hus, John, 280, 361, 376, 379
Hussites, 361–62, 384
Hutton, James, 666
Huxley, Aldous, 739
Huxley, Thomas, 666
hydrogen bomb, 818, 828
Hyksos, 9, 11, 14

I

ibn-Khaldun, 317–18
ibn-Rushd, 302
ibn-Sina, 302
Ibos, 816
Ibsen, Henrik, 670
Ice Ages, 4
Iceland, 189, 790
iconoclasm, 180
Iliad (Homer), 32, 49
Illyria, 64, 539, 546
Imitation of Christ (Thomas à Kempis), 292
immigration, to U.S., 622, 629
Imperial Conference of 1926, 735
Imperial Diet, Japanese, 641
Imperial Duties Bill of 1932, 733
Imperial Industrial Code, 652, 659
imperialism: in Africa, 679–82; Athenian, 47; in China, 637–39; decline

imperialism (continued)
of, 734–37; English, 634–36, 679–82, 684; evaluation of, 642–43; French, 538, 540, 679; Italian, 762; Japanese, 737; new, 636, 678–79, 682–84; Russian, 682–84; U.S., 632, 685–86, 736–37 (see also colonies)
Impressionism, 671
Inca Empire, 400
India, 175, 508–10, 511, 791; ancient, 123–33; British in, 328, 439, 518, 614, 634–36, 736; culture, spread of, 322–23; Gupta dynasty, 131–33; independence, 325; Kushan and Andhra dynasty, 131; Mauryan Empire, 128–31; Moguls in, 326–28; Moslem conquest of, 324–26; in 19th century, 621, 684; political weakness of, 323–24; Portuguese in, 397; postwar (1945–1973), 810, 811, 812; under Rajputs, 320, 322
India Act of 1784, 634
India Councils Act of 1861, 635
Indian Mutiny of 1857, 634
Indians: American, 518; in Spanish Empire, 400
Indo-Aryans, 124–27
Indochina, 329, 638, 684, 736, 765, 791, 799
Indo-European languages, 13
Indo-European peoples, 13, 16, 57
Indonesia, 323, 812
indulgences, 373–74, 377–78, 379
Indus Valley, 124, 415
Industrial Revolution, 490, 501, 545, 570, 576; Second, 648–49
industrialization, 617; in Austria, 604; beginnings of, 573–76; in China, 811; in France, 599; in Japan, 640, 641; in Latin America, 632; liberalism and, 577–82; mechanical inventions, 573–74; in Prussia, 604; in Russia, 662, 663, 751; social effects of, 576–78; social reform, 582–83; socialism and, 585–90; Spanish, 403, 404; transportation and, 574–76; in U.S., 622–23, 629–30, 685; working class protest, 583–85 (see also Industrial Revolution)
industry: coal, 573, 574, 576; in 18th century, 499; in 11th century, 207; factory system, 435–36, 573; in 15th and 16th centuries, 364–65; iron, 573, 574, 576, 654, 663; mining, 294, 364, 400; putting-out-system, 435, 571, 574; in 17th century, 435; steel, 654; textile, 207, 285, 435, 573 (see also Industrial Revolution)

Innocent II, Pope, 220
Innocent III, Pope, 243–44, 247, 254, 259, 260, 271, 308, 363
Innocent IV, Pope, 255, 260
Innocent XI, Pope, 464
inquests, Norman, 213, 214
Inquisition, 245, 252, 367, 389, 549, 551
Institutes (Justinian), 165
Institutes of the Christian Religion (Calvin), 382–83, 387
intelligentsia, Russian, 615–16, 617
intendants, 420, 423, 447
intercontinental ballistic missiles, 828
International Atomic Development Authority, 791
International Atomic Energy Agency, 829
International Labor Organization, 716
International Red Cross, 596
international relations (see coexistence; Cold War; foreign policy)
International Workingmen's Association, 650
Interstate Commerce Act, 630, 631
Interstate Commerce Commission, 630
Introduction to Divine and Secular Literature (Cassiodorus), 146
inventions, 294, 476, 571, 573–74
Investiture Conflict, 215–17, 240, 301
Ionia, 30, 31
Iran, 791, 814
Iraq, 735, 813, 814
Ireland, 450, 735–36, 802; in 19th century, 614–15, 652; in 17th century, 460; viking raids, 188
Irish Free State, 736
Irnerius, 224
iron industry, 573, 574, 576, 654, 663
Irving, Washington, 621
Isabella, Queen of England, 281
Isabella of Castile, 367, 368, 369, 375
Isaiah, 20
Islam, 18, 24, 168–72, 174, 175, 312, 318, 325, 328, 404
Israel, 16, 19, 813, 814, 819; Assyrian conquest of, 21; founding of, 791
Istanbul (see Constantinople)
Isthmian Games, 36
Italy, 143, 144, 370, 454, 712; Byzantine influence in, 300; city-states, 346–48, 395; fascism, 752–55; First World War, 700, 702, 704, 707, 709–11; in 14th and 15th centuries, 366; Frankish invasion of, 181; German conquest of, 196; Greek colonies, 30; Hohenstaufens in, 257, 259–62; Lombards in, 155; Napoleonic Wars, 536, 538, 539,

540; 1900–1913, 688, 691–92; in 19th century, 546, 549, 554, 557, 559, 562–63, 568, 574, 576, 597, 598, 601–03, 612, 661–62, 677, 681; Norman conquest of, 210; Ostrogoths in, 116, 144, 155, 160–61; postwar (1919–1939), 715, 716, 718, 721, 729, 752–55, 762, 767, 769; postwar (1945–1973), 787, 790, 801–02; Renaissance, 352–59; Roman Empire and, 60–63, 69–70, 82, 99; Second World War, 773–74, 781; in 13th century, 243, 259–62; towns, 207, 208, 209; in 12th century, 240–42; unification of, 601–03, 612, 675; urban civilization, 348–52
Ivan III, Tsar (the Great), 315
Ivan IV, Tsar (the Dread), 315, 370
Iwo Jima, 783
Iyeyasu, 341
Izvolsky, Alexander, 690

J
Jackson, Andrew, 624
Jacob, 18
Jacobins, 529, 531–35
Jahweh, 18–21, 22, 88
Jamaica, 440
James, William, 740
James I, King of England, 424, 430
James II, King of England, 456–57, 459, 460, 461
Jameson Raid, 682
Jamestown, Virginia, 442
Jansenism, 449, 482
Japan, 130, 333–34, 715, 821, 829; Chinese influence on, 340; First World War, 700, 710, 711; Meiji period, 641; Mongols and, 337; in 19th century, 621, 638–39, 640–42, 688; postwar (1919–1939), 729, 737, 738, 759–60, 764–65; postwar (1945–1973), 792–93, 813; Russo-Japanese War, 642, 683, 686, 688; Second World War, 777, 779, 783–85; Sino-Japanese War, 638–39, 642, 688; Tokugawa shogunate, 341
Jaurès, Jean, 656, 657
Java, 323, 407
"Jazz Age," 730
Jean de Meung, 266
Jefferson, Thomas, 488
Jena, battle of, 539
Jeremiah, 20
Jericho, 18
Jerome, St., 119
Jerome of Prague, 361
Jerusalem, 19, 256, 305–08, 596; First Crusade, 218, 219; sack of, 88

New Deal, 733
New Economic Policy (NEP), 748
New France, 442
New Guinea, 684, 783
New Harmony, Indiana, 586
new imperialism, 636, 678-79, 682-84
New Kingdom (Egypt), 9
New Left, 831
New Mexico, 626
new physics, 742
New Poor Law of 1834, 582
New Rome (see Constantinople)
New Stone Age, 4-5
New Testament, 90-91, 353 (see also Bible)
New Zealand, 633, 813
Newcomen, Thomas, 573
Newfoundland, 454
newspapers: 18th-century, 493; 19th-century, 575
Newton, Isaac, 473, 477, 478-79, 481, 486, 669
Nicaea, Council of, 108
Nicaragua, 686
Nice, 601, 602
Nicholas, Grand Duke, 702
Nicholas I, Tsar, 556, 558, 564, 595, 596, 615-16, 662, 664
Nicholas II, Tsar, 703, 705
Nicholas V, Pope, 362, 363
Nicolson, Harold, quoted, 711
Nicopolis, battle of, 316
Nietzsche, Friedrich, 648, 671, 755
Nigeria, 816
Nightingale, Florence, 596
nihilists, 617
Nile Valley, 5, 8
Nineveh, 22
nirvana, 127
Nixon, Richard M., 805-06, 821, 829
Noailles, Louis Marie, Viscount de, 528
Nobel, Alfred, 648
nobility, 462; bourgeoisie and, 230; French, 448-49, 523-25, 527, 528; Hungarian, 463, 464; Polish, 467; Prussian, 515; Russian, 314, 315, 469, 512-13, 615, 616-17 (see also aristocracy; social classes)
Nogaret, Guillaume de, 270-71
Nonintervention Committee, 763
Normandy, 189, 193, 209, 237, 238, 239, 240, 782
Normandy, Duke of, 194, 209, 214
Normans: England, conquest of, 211-12; Italy, conquest of, 210
Norris, Frank, 630
Norsemen, 394
North Africa, 64, 70, 143, 304, 736; Arab conquest of, 175; Moslem

conquest of, 161; in 19th century, 679; Phoenicians in, 17; Second World War, 775, 777, 781; Vandals in, 160 (see also specific country)
North America: colonization of, 440-43; vikings in, 189, 394 (see also Canada; United States)
North Atlantic Treaty Organization (NATO), 790, 799, 802, 803, 818
North German Confederation, 608
North Korea, 793, 818
North Vietnam, 812, 820
Northmen, 188-90, 211
Northwest Ordinance, 520
Norway, 370, 774, 790
Notebooks (Leonardo da Vinci), 359
Notre Dame, Paris, 233
Nouvelle Héloise (Rousseau), 493
Nova Scotia, 633
Novels (Justinian), 165
Novgorod, Republic of, 315
NSDAP (see Nazism)
Nubia, 14
Nuclear Non-Proliferation Treaty, 821, 829
nuclear power, 829
Nuclear Test Ban Treaty, 820, 829
nuclear weapons, 784-85, 791, 811, 818, 819, 821, 828-29
Nureddin, 306
Nuremberg Laws, 759

O

OAS (see Organization of American States)
Oates, Titus, 456
OAU (see Organization of African Unity)
Octavian, Roman Emperor, 75-77, 78-79 (see also Augustus, Roman Emperor)
October Days, 529
October Manifesto, 664
October Revolution, 706, 747
Octobrists, 664
Odo of Deuil, quoted, 308
Odovacar, King of Italy, 116
Odyssey (Homer), 27-28, 66
Oedipus the King (Sophocles), 44
Of Civil Government: Two Treatises (Locke), 461-62
Okinawa, 783, 813
Old Kingdom (Egypt), 9-11
Old Saxons, 156
Old Stone Age, 4
Old Testament, 18, 52 (see also Bible)
Olney, Richard, 631
Olympic Games, 36
Omar, caliph, 173
Omar Khayyám; 301, 302

Ommiad dynasty, 173-76, 304
On Christian Liberty (Luther), 378
On the Family (Alberti), 353
On the Law of War and Peace (Grotius), 483
On Liberty (Mill), 579
On the Origin of Species by Means of Natural Selection, or the Preservation of Favored Races in the Struggle for Life (Darwin), 666
On the Principles of Political Economy and Taxation (Ricardo), 581
On the Revolutions of the Heavenly Bodies (Copernicus), 475
On the Structure of the Human Body (Vesalius), 475
O'Neill, Eugene, 743
Ontario, 633
"Open Door" policy, 639, 686, 729, 737, 765, 779
open-field system, 572
"Operation Overlord," 782
"Operation Sea Lion," 775
Opium War of 1839, 636-37
Orange Free State, 681
Oration (Pico della Mirandola), 357
Oratory of Divine Love, 388
Oregon Treaty, 625
Oresteia trilogy (Aeschylus), 44
Organization of African Unity (OAU), 817
Organization of American States (OAS), 806-07
Orjonikidze, G. K., 752
Orlando, Vittorio, 709-11
Ortega y Gasset, José, 739
Osborne Judgment, 654
Ossian, 493
ostracism, 41
Ostrogoths, 113, 116, 143, 154, 155, 158, 159, 160-61
Othman, 171
Otto I, Holy Roman Emperor (the Great), 196-97
Otto III, Holy Roman Emperor, 198
Otto IV, Holy Roman Emperor, 243
Otto of Freising, 233
Ottoman Empire, 316-17, 470, 504, 679, 683; Crimean War, 596-97, 616; in 18th century, 514; First World War, 700, 702, 704, 708, 712-13; 1900-1913, 690, 692; in 19th century, 555-56, 595-97, 616, 687-88; revolution (1908), 690; Russo-Turkish War, 676; in 17th century, 463-64
Oudenarde, battle of, 453
Ovid, 83
OVRA, 754
Owen, Robert, 586
Oxford University, 473

physics, 245, 264, 293; Arabic, 301; in Middle Ages, 473, 474; 17th-century, 477–78; 20th-century, 742 (*see also* mathematics; science)

Physics and Politics: Thoughts on the Application of the Principles of Natural Selection and Inheritance to Political Science (Bagehot), 667

picketing, 584

Picasso, Pablo, painting by, 743

Pico della Mirandola, Giovanni, 353, 357, 359

pictographs, 134

Piedmont-Sardinia, 64, 454, 546, 549, 556, 562–63, 596, 601–03

Pietism, 482, 490, 493

Pilate, Pontius, 90

Pillnitz, Declaration of, 532

Pilsudski, Joseph, 727

Pippin II, 156

Pippin III, 179–82, 192

Pirandello, Luigi, 743

Pisa, 207, 229

Pissaro, Camille, 671

Pitt, William, 510, 511

Pitt, William (the Younger), 538

Pius II, Pope, 362

Pius VII, Pope, 537, 549

Pius IX, Pope, 562, 563, 669

Pizarro, Francisco, 400

Place de la Concorde, Paris, 492

plague, 275, 280

Plan XVII, 700

Planck, Max, 742

Plataea, battle at, 39

Plato, 46, 48, 96, 167, 299, 300, 353

Platonic Academy, 353

Platt Amendment, 686

Plautus, 66

plebeians, 58, 59–60

Plehve, Vyacheslav, 662

Plekhanov, Georgi V., 663

Pliny the Younger, 87, 95–96

Plombières agreement, 601, 602, 607

Plutarch, 75, 96

Plymouth, Massachusetts, 442

Pobedonostsev, Constantine, 662

Poe, Edgar Allan, 621

poetry: Byzantine, 299; Chinese, 333; Greek, 31; Latin, 82; medieval, 233–34, 264–65; Roman, 95 (*see also* literature)

Poincaré, Raymond, 694, 717, 725, 726

Poitiers, battle at, 176

Poitou, 239

Poland, 229, 422, 462, 716, 727, 821; in 18th century, 504, 513–14; First World War, 702, 712; in 14th century, 312–13; in 19th century, 546, 558, 559; partitions of, 513–14; postwar (1919–1939), 748, 759, 761,

786, 787; postwar (1945–1973), 789, 808–09; Second World War, 769, 773; in 17th century, 466

Polignac, Prince Auguste Jules de, 557

Politburo, 750

political theory: 18th-century, 490–91; Renaissance, 354; 17th-century, 428 (*see also* Marxism)

pollution, 826

Polo, Marco, 312; quoted, 338

Polybius, 56

polycentrism, 821

Polyptique de l'Abbe Irminon (ed. Guerard), 192

Pomerania, 465

Pompadour, Mme. de, 503, 509

Pompeii, 3, 492

Pompey, 71, 72, 74

Pompidou, Georges, 800

Pontiac, 518

Poor Law, 583

Pope, Alexander, quoted, 485

popes (*see* papacy)

Popish Plot, 456–57

"Popular Front," French, 734

population: growth of, 205, 577, 796; Malthus on, 580–81; Roman, 91; in 20th century, 825–26, 829

Populists, 631, 684

Port Arthur, 639, 787

Portsmouth, Treaty of, 642, 686

Portugal, 328, 339, 367, 432, 759, 790, 814, 816–17; colonization by, 439, 443; in 18th century, 533; exploration by, 295, 396–98; mercantilism, 438; in 19th century, 554, 555

Portuguese Guinea, 816

positivism, 665

Poteidaea, 47

Potsdam Conference, 785, 787, 788

power loom, 573

Pragmatic Sanction of Bourges, 362, 366, 369, 504, 507

pragmatism, 632

prehistoric man, 3–5

Presbyterianism, 383, 424, 426, 455, 460, 461

Prescott, William H., 621

priests (*see* clergy)

Prince, The (Machiavelli), 354, 355

Princip, Gavrilo, 694

Principles of Geology (Lyell), 666

printing: Chinese, 332–33; 15th-century, 364; invention of, 295; movable type, 333

Progress and Poverty (George), 632

Progressive Party: German, 658; U.S., 684

prohibition, 730

protectionism, 630, 654, 661, 721

Protestant Liberalism, 489

Protestant Reformation, 363, 370, 388; in England, 385–87; in Germany, 378–82; radicals in, 384–85; significance of, 389–90; in Switzerland, 382–83

Protestant Union, 429, 430

Protestantism, 387, 390; Louis XIV and, 449–50; science and, 669; Thirty Years' War, 429–33 (*see also* Calvinism; Lutheranism; Methodism; Presbyterianism; Protestant Reformation)

Proudhon, Pierre-Joseph, 591

Proust, Marcel, 742

Provence, 187

Prussia, 229, 454, 462, 546; Crimean War, 596, 598; in 18th century, 499, 504, 506–11, 514–15, 532, 533; Franco-Prussian War, 609–12; mercantilism, 438; Napoleonic Wars, 536, 538–39, 540–41; in 19th century, 549, 559, 565–66, 582, 596, 598, 604–12, 657; in 17th century, 466, 470; War of 1866, 607–09

psychoanalysis, 740

psychology, 740, 743

Ptolemy, astronomer, 96, 396, 474, 478

Ptolemy I, King of Egypt, 51

Puerto Rico, 686

Pugachev, Emelyan, 512

Pullman strike of 1894, 631

Punic Wars, 63–64

Punjabis, 811

Purcell, Henry, 481

Puritan Rebellion, 425–26, 461

Puritanism, 383, 387, 424, 455, 459, 482

putting-out system, 435, 571, 574

pyramids, 9, 10, 15

Pyrenees, Peace of the, 433, 447

Pyrrhus, King of Epirus, 61, 62

Pythagoras, 45

Q

Quadruple Alliance, 548

Quakers, 384, 385, 455

Quebec, 633

Quebec Act of 1774, 519

Quebec Conference, 785

Quemoy, 819

Quesnay, François, 490

Qur'an (*see* Koran)

R

Racconigi Agreement, 691

Rachmaninov, Sergei, 743

racialism, 668, 747

Racine, Jean, 450, 481, 492

Radetzky, Joseph, 563

Radical Protestantism, 384–85

Steele, Richard, 492
Stein, Baron Heinrich vom, 540
Stephen II, Pope, 181
Stettin, 465
Stimson Doctrine, 760
Stinnes, Hugo, 658
Stoicism, 53, 96, 97, 105, 483
Stolypin, Peter, 664
Stone Age, 4–5
"Storm and Stress" movement, 493–94
Strafford, Thomas Wentworth, Earl of, 425, 428
Straits Convention of 1841, 595
Stransky, J., quoted, 783
Strasbourg, 452
Strategic Arms Limitation Talks (SALT), 829
Strauss, David Friedrich, 669
Strauss, Richard, 743
streltsi, 468
Stresemann, Gustav, 717–19
Stuart, House of, 424, 459–61
Study of History, A (Toynbee), 741
submarine warfare, 702, 704, 707, 781
Sudan, 679–81, 687, 688, 736
Sudetenland, 728, 767–68
Suetonius, 95
Suez Canal, 614, 636, 736, 813, 814, 819
"Suffragettes," 647, 648
suffrage, 647; in Austria, 659, 660; in England, 559, 614, 647, 725; in France, 530, 562, 647; in Germany, 647; in Italy, 647, 661; in Japan, 738; in Prussia, 604; in U.S., 621, 624
Suger of St. Denis, Abbot, 220–22, 223
Sui dynasty, 329
Suleiman the Magnificent, 370
Sulla, 70–71, 72
Sullivan, Louis, 631, 743
Sully, Maximilien, 418–19, 448
Sumerians, 6
Summa Contra Gentiles (Thomas Aquinas), 263
Sun King (see Louis XIV, King of France)
Sun Yat-sen, 640, 737
Sung dynasty, 310, 334–36
Supreme Soviet, 749–50
Suttner, Bertha von, 659
Suzdal, 311
Swabia, 195
Sweden, 370; mercantilism, 438; in 17th century, 466, 470; Thirty Years' War, 431–32
Swift, Jonathan, 492
Swinburne, Algernon, 292

Swiss Confederation, 290
Switzerland, 187, 289–90, 432, 538, 546, 647
Sybil (Disraeli), 590
"Syllabus of the Principal Errors of our Times, A" (Pius IX), 669
Sylvester II, Pope, 197–98
Sylvius, Aeneas (see Pius II, Pope)
Symbolism, 671
syndicalism, 591, 662
Synthetic Philosophy (Spencer), 667
Syracuse, 30, 47
Syria, 4, 6, 13, 50, 64, 72, 124, 161, 174, 304, 317, 735, 799; Arabic conquest of, 173; Assyrian conquest of, 21; Monophysitism, 164; Persian Empire, 23

T

Tacitus, Cornelius, 95
Taff Vale decision, 654
Taikwa reforms, 341
Taiping Rebellion, 638
Taiwan, 813
Takahira, Baron Kogoro, 642
Talleyrand, Charles de, 546, 547
Talmud, 89
Tamerlane, 316, 326–28
Tamils, 322
Tanais, 30
T'ang dynasty, 329–34
Tannenberg, battle of, 702
Taoism, 136, 331, 334
Tarawa, 783
Tarentum, 61
Tarik, 175
Tartars, 443
taxation: American colonies, 517; Austrian, 516; Brandenburg-Prussia, 465; of clergy, 242, 254, 261, 262, 270, 369–70; English, 236, 257, 268, 283, 425, 566; French, 268–69, 366, 419, 438, 448, 526, 537; Indian, 325; Roman, 85–86; Russian, 469; in 17th century, 438
Taylor, A. J. P., quoted, 676
technology, 124, 294–95 (see also science)
Teheran Conference, 782, 785
telegraph, 575
telescope, 477, 479
temperance, 621
Tennis Court Oath, 526
Terence, 66
Tertullian, 112
Test Act, 455, 558
Texas, 625
textile industry, 207, 285, 435, 573
Thackeray, William Makepeace, 670

Thailand, 130, 812, 813
Themistocles, 39, 41
Theocritus, 52
Theodora, Empress, 159, 164
Theodore of Tarsus, 153
Theodoric, King of the Ostrogoths, 116, 144, 145
Theodosius, Roman Emperor, 114, 119
Theologia Germanica, 279
theology, 112, 162, 164, 223, 224; in 14th century, 318; Islamic, 172; Roman, 96 (see also religion)
Theory of the Leisure Class, The (Veblen), 632
Thermopylae, pass at, 38–39
Thierry, King of the Franks, 155
Thiers, Adolphe, 610
Third Communist International (see Comintern)
Third Crusade, 306–07
Thirty Years' War, 421, 429–33, 435, 463, 464
Thomas à Kempis, 292
Thomas Aquinas, St. (see Aquinas, St. Thomas)
Thrace, 307
Three Emperors' League: 1872, 675–76; 1881, 677, 678
Three Impostors: Moses, Jesus, and Mohammed, The, 260
Thucydides, 42, 66
Thyssen, August, 658
Tiberius, Roman Emperor, 81, 83, 84
Tibet, 130, 812
Tientsin, Treaties of, 638
Tigris-Euphrates Valley, 5
Timur the Lame (see Tamerlane)
Tirpitz, Alfred von, 691, 692
tithes, 182
Titian, 359
Titus, Roman Emperor, 86, 92
Tocqueville, Alexis de, 621, 647; quoted, 561, 622
Tokugawa shogunate, 341
Toleration Act of 1689, 459
Tolstoy, Leo, 670
Tom Jones (Fielding), 492
Tongking, 323
Torah, 89
Tordesillas, Treaty of, 399
Tories, 457, 458, 502, 558 (see also Conservative Party, British)
Torricelli, Evangelista, 476
totalitarianism, 724, 744, 746–69
Toulouse, Count of, 218
Toulouse Lautrec, Henri de, 670
towns: 11th-century, 207–08; 14th-century, 275–77; gilds, 231; gov-

A 3
B 4
C 5
D 6
E 7
F 8
G 9
H 0
I 1